LATIN VERSE SATIRE

Latin Verse Satire presents a comprehensive variety of texts by the classical Latin satirists and its structure provides students with a rich commentary and a selection of secondary literature. The book will have a broad appeal due to the careful choice of texts and features selections from Ennius, Lucilius, Horace, Persius and Juvenal. The focus on the relation of satire to political and social history makes this book ideal not only for courses on satire but also for those on Roman daily life and gender.

The selection allows students to trace a coherent narrative of the genre's history and to understand its relation to the political and social changes that marked the transition from the Roman republic to the empire. The texts stretch from the genre's earliest manifestations to its final classical flowering in Juvenal. They are accompanied by a detailed introduction that traces the lives and works of the major poets, the evolution of the form, and its relation to Rome's political environment and social mores. The book includes works by Lucilius and Ennius, crucial figures in Roman satire, whose work has never before appeared in a text with appropriate aids and annotations for student translation. Particular attention is paid to the relation between satire and the significant Roman value of *libertas*.

Accessible commentary accompanies the text and focuses on the linguistic difficulties and problems of usage, then relates the individual selection to the author's work as a whole and its historical context, and finally concerns itself with those aspects of metre and style necessary for an appreciation of the poetry. The volume closes with a selection of essays and critical excerpts that both elucidate the genre's most salient features and help understand the history of its modern scholarly reception.

Paul Allen Miller is Professor of Classics and Comparative Literature at the University of South Carolina. He is author of *Lyric Texts and Lyric Consciousness* (Routledge 1994) and edited *Latin Erotic Elegy* (Routledge 2002). He is the editor of *Transactions of the American Philological Association*.

LATIN VERSE SATIRE

An anthology and critical reader

Edited, with an introduction and commentary, by Paul Allen Miller

LONDON AND NEW YORK

To Mom and Dad, with many thanks,
Love,
Allen

First published 2005 by Routledge
2 Park Square, Milton Park, Abingdon, Oxon OX14 4RN

Simultaneously published in the USA and Canada
by Routledge
270 Madison Ave, New York, NY 10016

Routledge is an imprint of the Taylor & Francis Group

Typeset in Garamond by The Running Head Limited, Cambridge
Printed and bound in Great Britain by Antony Rowe Ltd, Chippenham, Wiltshire

British Library Cataloguing in Publication Data
A catalogue record for this book is available from the British Library

Library of Congress Cataloging-in-Publication Data
Latin verse satire: an anthology and critical reader / [edited by] Paul Allen Miller.
p. cm.
Includes bibliographical references.
1. Verse satire, Latin. 2. Verse satire, Latin—History and criticism. I. Miller, Paul Allen, 1959–
PA6134.L38 2005
871'.070801—dc22
2004021780

ISBN 0–415–31715–0 (hardback)
ISBN 0–415–31716–9 (paperback)

CONTENTS

PREFACE AND ACKNOWLEDGMENTS

This text is designed in the first place for students and teachers of advanced undergraduate and MA level classes, but scholars should find it of use as well. The introduction provides a general overview of the genre of Latin verse satire in its historical and literary context. The commentary is designed to aid students in understanding both the language and the poetry, but also contains original observations on the text and its interpretation. Discussion of textual matters and of sources has been limited to those cases where it is necessary for linguistic or artistic intelligibility. The critical anthology at the conclusion of the volume is designed to allow the student both a greater comprehension of the poems themselves and of the history of the debates surrounding them. The essays chosen, while they are all important, have been selected on the basis of their representing certain trends in scholarship on satire rather than on any claim that they are intrinsically better than others that might have been chosen. The emphasis has been on essays that deal with the genre as a whole. Unfortunately, this means that many fine pieces of scholarship have been left out.

Citations have been kept to the bare minimum to aid in accessibility. Those wishing to do further reading should refer to the select bibliography. The texts for the poems are based on OCT editions, except for Ennius where I have used Courtney (1993) and Lucilius where I have used Krenkel (1970). Changes from these texts are acknowledged in the notes.

This book's completion and composition has been greatly aided by the help of my friends, colleagues and students. My friends and colleagues, David H. J. Larmour and Mark Beck, each read and provided invaluable commentary on the introduction, as did my assistant Brittany Powell. My students Priscilla Larkin, Jessica Harvey, and Betsy Williams used an early version of the text in class and were both good humored with its many failings and extraordinarily helpful in pointing them out. My dissertation student and assistant Christel Johnson lent invaluable aid in the initial preparation of the Latin text. To each of you, I owe a special debt of thanks. I also most gratefully acknowledge the Classics Departments at the University of Kansas, Syracuse University, and Hamilton College for allowing me to present the results of my ongoing research to them.

I am also very grateful to Richard Stoneman, my stalwart editor at Routledge who has seen me through three projects and counting. I owe special thanks to my teacher, Barbara Gold, who first taught me Latin satire and directed my MA thesis on Juvenal almost twenty years ago. A debt of gratitude is also owed to my parents, Joe and Mary Miller, who have offered me unwavering support in all my endeavors, to Ann who loves me even when I act like a dork, and to Sam, who is my shining light.

William S. Anderson, "Roman Satirists and Literary Criticism," from *Essays on Roman Satire* © 1982 Princeton University Press, reprinted by permission of Princeton University Press. J. C. Bramble, "The Programmatic Satire and the Method of Persius 1," from *Persius and the Programmatic Satire: A Study in Form and Imagery* © 1974 Cambridge University Press, reprinted by permission of Cambridge University Press. Amy Richlin, "Invective Against Women in Roman Satire," *Arethusa* 17:1 (1984), 67–80 © The Johns Hopkins University Press, reprinted with permission of the Johns Hopkins University Press. Paul Allen Miller, "The Bodily Grotesque in Roman Satire: Images of Sterility," *Arethusa* 31:3 (1998), 257–83 © The Johns Hopkins University Press, reprinted with permission of the Johns Hopkins University Press. Susanna Morton Braund, "The Masks of Satire," from *The Roman Satirists and Their Masks* © 1996 S. Braund, reprinted with permission of S. Braund. Michael Coffey, "The Roman Genre of Satire and Its Beginning," from *Roman Satire* © 1976, reprinted by permission of Gerald Duckworth and Co. Ltd.

Paul Allen Miller
May 19, 2004
Columbia, SC

INTRODUCTION

1. Satire is the quintessential Roman genre. Quintilian says famously, *Satura quidem tota nostra est* ["Satire indeed is wholly ours"] (*Institutiones Oratoris* 10.1.93). This has generally been interpreted to mean that Latin verse satire is without precedent in Greek literature and can therefore be seen as an exclusively Roman invention. Whereas epic, tragedy, comedy, bucolic, lyric, and epigram all have clear Greek models, and their Roman imitators prided themselves on being able to reproduce these forms in the Latin tongue and adapt them to Roman culture, satire, Quintilian argues, is different. He is not alone. Not one of the canonical satirists disagrees. Horace says he is following in the path of Lucilius, and names this work *sermo* and *satura* (1.4, 1.10, and 2.1); Persius cites the precedents of Lucilius and Horace (1); and Juvenal acknowledges Lucilius and Horace while also quoting Persius (1). None of them claims a specific Greek antecedent as founder of the genre and, indeed, one looks in vain for a Greek genre entitled satire.

2. Nonetheless, Quintilian's claim that satire is wholly Roman has a greater significance than the common interpretation admits. What is at stake in this statement may well be more than literary originality, as becomes evident when examining Quintilian's treatment of another genre: erotic elegy, a genre that shares important traits with satire—a first-person speaker, an urban setting, and an often biting and ironic intent. It too has no clear Greek progenitor. It is a commonplace of elegiac criticism that while the elegiac couplet was widely used in Greece and while Callimachus provided a model of the diction, themes, and mythological exempla that characterize Roman elegy, the peculiarly subjective genre that constitutes the Roman form is unique in ancient literature (Miller 2004). Nonetheless, Quintilian makes no analogous claim of exclusivity for the Roman elegists. Nor are the elegists themselves shy about claiming the authority of Callimachus and Mimnermus to authorize their own practices.

3. Clearly, there seems to be more to Quintilian's claim of satire being uniquely Roman than the lack of an unambiguous Greek precedent for the genre. When this great second century CE scholar and rhetorician says "satire

is wholly ours," he points not simply to the fact that *only the Romans* have practiced this particular form of verse, but also to a sense that there is something *peculiarly Roman* about this genre. Satire is wholly Roman. The two central questions facing anyone who studies Latin verse satire, then, are: what is this genre and what makes it uniquely Roman? The first of these is the easiest to answer. The second will occupy us in one way or another for the rest of this introduction and throughout much of the commentary, but in fact the two questions are related.

4. Roman verse satire or *satura* does not denote what contemporary English speakers commonly mean by satire. In the modern world, satire is less a form than an attitude. We speak of satiric novels, plays, poems, and essays. For a Roman of the Classical period, however, *satura* meant something very specific. It was a long poem in hexameter verse that focused on a variety of everyday topics and offered moral, political, and/or aesthetic criticism in a witty or humorous fashion.

5. Normally, *satura* was written in the first person. Certain satires were written in the form of dialogues. Others featured characters besides the satirist as the principal speaker. In spite of these variations, in each book of satires a powerful image of the satirist as speaker emerges, and each has a distinctly different personality. Among critics, this image of the speaker is known as the satirist's persona or mask (Anderson 1982; Braund 1996b). This concept was introduced to combat the all too easy equation of the character of the satirist with that of the poet himself. This distinction is important because not infrequently the character of the satirist is portrayed with as much irony as his ostensible targets.

6. The level of diction is mixed and varies according to the satirist, but in all cases there is a liberal dose of colloquial speech and common, everyday words. This can make satire a difficult genre for the modern reader who needs help with the informal vocabulary that pervades it. It should be remembered that the vocabulary of satire was probably no more difficult for its intended audience than modern slang is for us. The topics, while varied and often seeming to change in mid-poem, reflect the origins of the diction in daily life and feature a healthy emphasis on food, sexuality, the body, and Roman street life.

7. Latin verse satire's cousin, the so-called Menippean satire, was a mixture of prose and verse with a humorous, and sometimes lampooning, intent. While a vague kinship between the genres was recognized, the unmodified term *satura* in the hands of Horace, Quintilian, and the late grammarian Diomedes, clearly referred to what was then perceived as a self-consciously unified literary form: the one practiced by Ennius, Lucilius, Horace, Persius, and Juvenal. This is the form that was in essence wholly Roman.

8. As the description of the genre just outlined makes clear, *satura* had two important qualities in the Roman literary imagination. First, it was a poetry of criticism or "blame," a tradition with deep Greek (*psogos*) and even Indo-

European roots (Nagy 1979). As *satura* grew into a complex, self-reflective literary form, the nature of its criticism often became ambiguous and multi-layered. It found fault and assigned blame as much to itself as others.

9. Satire's second important quality was that it pursued a studied variety of topics (adultery, travelogues, urban poverty, gastronomical excess, and male depilatory practices *inter alia*) both within individual poems and in the genre as a whole. It is not unusual for a *satura* to start off in one direction and end someplace very different, nor is there any one topic that defines the genre in the way love does elegy or war epic. It is a medley. Diomedes describes satire as follows:

> a kind of poetry among the Romans, now composed as invective and for seizing upon the vices of men in the manner of Old Comedy. Lucilius, Horace, and Persius wrote such. But formerly, a kind of poetry that was made up of various poems was called satire. Pacuvius and Ennius wrote such.
>
> (1.445)

The description, however, while useful, is a little too neat. Diomedes is oversimplifying at a distance of more than 400 years, and how much access he had to the complete works of Lucilius, Pacuvius, or Ennius is unclear. Ennius's satires, as the selections included in the present volume make clear, are hardly devoid of blame, nor are the works of the later satirists far removed from the kind of medley attributed to its earliest exemplars. Nonetheless, few would argue with the contention that in Lucilius's poetry blame becomes central to the genre's self-definition. Likewise, Horace was more concerned with the issue of aesthetic unity than his predecessors had been.

10. In spite of its shortcomings, Diomedes's description helps us come to grips with what is central to the genre and hence with what marks it as definitively Roman. If we ask ourselves what a form of discourse would look like whose most salient points were variety and blame, we would be required first to envision the perspective of someone—a voice, a persona, a character, or, at the limit, the satirist himself—for blame can only be assigned from a point of view. Second, that person or persona would present a series of pictures, scenes, or vignettes, loosely connected to one another, each of which frames a vice, a fault, or some aspect of life that is, from the speaker's point of view, in need of reproof if not remediation. This presentation will often take the form of a claim to speak the truth without regard to social niceties, known in Latin as *libertas* or in the Stoic and Cynic philosophy of the period as *parrhesia*. It is this combination of the episodic and discontinuous with the claim to represent unvarnished truth that Gilbert Highet refers to when he portrays the satirist as one who cries "I am a camera, I am a tape recorder" (1962: 3).

11. Of course, one cannot be naively taken in by the satirist's assertion. Satire hardly gives us the unmediated access to social reality that Highet contends.

The satiric voice is artful and formed. It claims to be realist by convention (that's the nature of satire). In the hands of a deft literary artist such as Horace or Juvenal, however, the levels of irony quickly multiply (Anderson 1982). Nonetheless, the essence of Latin verse satire as exemplified by all its extant practitioners is precisely this presentation of a loosely connected series of scenes and characters from the perspective of one who blames, whether with gentle wit or cruel irony.

12. The various proposed etymologies of *satura* reflect this formal essence while inflecting the genre in the direction of a distinctly earthy realism. Although early in the Christian era, the spelling *satyra* arose and led to attempts to derive the genre's name from the hearty vulgarity and grotesque sexuality of the half-man half-goat satyr, and from the comic satyr plays that were performed after the tragic trilogies of classical Athens, this was a specious etymology. *Satura* is a feminine adjective derived from *satur* meaning "stuffed, full" generally with food. Early on it comes to be used as a noun or substantive. Diomedes gives a number of possible meanings. The three most intriguing are: 1) the *lanx satura*, a plate of mixed first fruits; 2) a kind of sausage in which a great variety of foods was ground up; and 3) the name of an omnibus bill in which a variety of different measures was mixed together without regard to their relation to one another. The last meaning is clearly metaphorical and based on the first two: a legal hash. *Satura* is a variety of ingredients blended together. It has clear reference to the world of food and the body, which is appropriate since, as the Russian literary theorist, Mikhail Bakhtin, has demonstrated, the lower bodily stratum, the world of food, digestion, sexuality, and excretion is the realm in which all that is high and idealized is brought low (1968). It is, thus, no accident that grotesque humor plays a central role in satiric invective and that Latin verse satire's themes and images are often derived from the gastronomical, the sexual, and the scatological.

Satura nos est

13. In what sense is this genre—whose self-definition is that of a loosely structured series of vignettes, a hash, or, in Juvenal's terms, a *farrago*, which is articulated from the perspective of an identifiable speaker as a discourse of disproval, and whose very name implies an intrinsic relation to the bodily grotesque—specifically Roman? To answer this question will require us to move from the realm of formal description to that of history and ideology. The key term we must historicize in our formal description is that of the "speaker" or "persona," which I shall hereafter refer to as the "subject of satire." This term is deliberately ambiguous. It refers simultaneously to the voice that says "I" or *ego* in satire, the subject matter of that voice, and the process of subjection that is implied in the formation of the voice. My argument in the next paragraphs is that satire is a genre of aristocratic self-formation. It is intimately connected with the very nature of what it means to

be Roman. As that definition changed over time, so did the aim and subject matter of satire.

14. Early in the second century BCE, Ennius wrote the first work explicitly labelled *satura*. While we have only scattered fragments, they seem, as our discussion has led us to expect, to contain the poet's observations about life in the capital. As Knoche in his classic treatment of the genre contends, "Ennius in his satire produced for the first time in the Latin language a poetic form in which the individual could express himself and describe his own experiences in a very personal way" (1975: 22). Ennius's nephew Pacuvius continued to work in the same vein according to the ancient testimony, although none of his work survives.

15. In the last quarter of the second century, Lucilius took up the genre, giving the form its definitive shape and providing *satura* with a distinctly public function by engaging in political invective. From the fragments we possess, it is unclear how much, if any, inspiration Lucilius drew directly from Ennius's earlier essays in *satura*. With Lucilius, however, satire comes to occupy a prominent position within Roman literary culture. It moves from being a miscellaneous genre of social observation by professional poets who are the dependents of the aristocratic élite and becomes a form of expression by that élite. To return to Knoche's formulation, "Lucilius was the first Roman poet of rank for whom poetry was an expression of personality and not just an amusement" (1975: 34). With Lucilius, *satura* becomes satire.

16. That the genre's initial efflorescence took place at this time, I would contend, is no accident of history. The second century BCE is a period of rapid expansion, in which Roman hegemony was extended across the Mediterranean. It is also a time of cultural revolution that saw the birth of a properly Roman literature and of increased political conflict. Republican Rome was at the height of its power with the end of the Third Punic War. Vast amounts of wealth flooded into the coffers of the leading citizens: the result was increased social inequality and political disruption (Sallust, *Bellum Catilinae* 9–11). These were the circumstances in which Lucilius came to the fore. As Ramage observes, "There was [. . .] a continuing restlessness in politics at Rome during Lucilius's lifetime. The senate maintained its power, but under successful challenge from popular leaders like the Gracchi" (Ramage *et al.* 1974: 27–8).

17. In 133 BCE, Tiberius Gracchus was elected tribune of the people. He passed sweeping land reform that provided small allotments from the *ager publicus* to Rome's landless peasants and urban poor. This public land was leased to private citizens who were supposed to pay a percentage of their harvest to the state in return for its use. Over time, however, the rich magnates who had acquired this land and worked it with slaves came to regard it as theirs by right and ceased paying the fee. Gracchus presented the redistribution of public land as a method of addressing pressing social and political problems. Nonetheless, much of the senatorial class found the proposed redistribution an

infringement of their traditional prerogatives and refused to consider the bill. When Gracchus took the extra-constitutional step of presenting his proposal directly to the people, where it passed easily, his outraged opponents viewed this as an attempt to overthrow the state. After a series of complex and questionable maneuvers on both sides, a gang of senators caught, cornered, and beat to death the tribune and more than one hundred of his followers.

18. As Habinek has argued (1998), the invention of a self-conscious Roman literature was in part a response to the larger set of problems of which Tiberius Gracchus and later his brother, Sempronius, were a symptom. Roman literature, as a cultural practice of the aristocracy that defined, expressed, and constructed the definition of what it meant to be an élite male in Roman society, was neither a spontaneous product of the Latin imagination nor a simple import from Greece. It was a complex set of institutions of which satire was one of its first and most original forms. Certainly there were traditional songs, verse forms, and even farces that pre-dated the second century and can be traced back ultimately to a common Indo-European inheritance (Dumézil 1943). These included ritualized forms of blame poetry such as the obscene Fescinnine verses sung at Roman weddings and the ribald songs with which Roman troops regaled triumphing generals. But the beginning of a self-conscious literary culture is dateable to the appearance of Livius Andronicus in the third century BCE, the first poet in Latin to produce tragedies, comedies, and epic poetry in the Greek manner.

19. Livius Andronicus was a freedman, and he, like Plautus, the comic writer of the next generation, was a producer of entertainments for the Roman people and for the senatorial and equestrian orders whose patronage sustained his work. Ennius himself, the first to write works entitled *saturae*, was an Oscan from the south who only acquired citizenship through the good offices of his aristocratic patron Quintus Nobilior. The first Roman poets, then, were lower-class entertainers who were completely dependent on the patronage of their aristocratic sponsors.

20. Lucilius, however, was a wealthy equestrian. With his generation—that of the elder Cato, Terence (himself a freedman), and the orator G. Laelius Sapiens (consul 140 BCE)—the self-conscious elaboration of an aristocratic literature that seeks to form and enforce codes of conduct, define *Latinitas*, and establish a properly Roman identity comes into being. Roman literature as an institution for the production of cultural legitimation and value is in part a product of this moment of ideological and political challenge to the traditional Roman élite (Albrecht 1997: 1.253). As Habinek observes:

> All aristocracies must devise strategies of recruitment and acculturation [. . .] Whatever the background of the new aristocrats, they must be inculcated into the protocols of aristocratic behavior, and their qualifications as aristocrats must be defended against rival or alternative claimants to authority. At Rome literature participates in

> the "formation" of the aristocracy in both senses of the word, that is by defining, preserving, and transmitting standards of behavior to which the individual aristocrat must aspire and by valorizing aristocratic ideals and aristocratic authority within the broader cultural context.
>
> (1998: 45)

Lucilian satire, therefore, presents one model of the aristocratic speaking subject, even as it dramatizes the subjection of the individual to the norms that make that model possible. Likewise, *satura* through its practice of blame and grotesque degradation stigmatizes deviation from those norms. Humor and invective were long recognized as an effective means of both social power and political subversion in Roman society. For this reason, Julius Caesar—and later Augustus—made efforts to control, even if they could not eliminate, the jokes made by their opponents (Suetonius *Divus Iulius* 56; Corbeill 1996: 3–9).

Satura est nostra libertas

21. Lucilian satire's essential quality was, as Horace notes (1.4), *libertas*. *Libertas* is a complex and contested term to which the mere translation as "freedom" or "liberty" does not do justice. On one level, *libertas* is the quality that defines the *civis Romanus* (Roman citizen) as opposed to the *servus* (slave), *libertinus* (freedman), or any foreigner who does not enjoy citizen's rights (Cicero, *Contra Verrem* 2.1.7). On another level, *libertas* denotes a set of prerogatives that are only able to be exercised fully by the aristocratic élite. The most noted of these rights is freedom of speech. *Libertas* also signifies a fundamental notion of self-determination. This is commonly understood as the ability to be subject to the will of no one else and hence often implies the capacity to enforce one's will upon others. *Libertas* was actualized most concretely by traditional Roman élites through their participation in competitive politics and the governance of the state (Wirszubski 1950: 38; Syme 1960: 155). Thus, Tacitus at the beginning of the *Annales* describes the loss of senatorial freedom under the principate, saying that Augustus

> gradually increased his power and gathered into himself the duties of the senate and the legal magistrates with no one opposing him, since those who were the most warlike had fallen in battle or during the proscriptions. The rest of the nobles were brought along by being offered high office and great wealth, which made them all the more ready for *servitude*, so that becoming enriched under the new state of affairs they preferred the safe world of the present to the dangerous world of the past.
>
> (*Annales* 1.2)

Clearly, Tacitus has a very aristocratic notion of freedom since it can be lost by accepting high office or substantial wealth. This would be a nonsensical description of the loss of *libertas* for the Roman masses since they never had political power in this manner, nor were they likely to be offered wealth and the semblance of personal power in return for their acquiescence to Augustan rule. For the governing classes, however, who had defined their status as free men in terms of their ability to rule others, the acceptance of wealth and titles in return for ceding effective political power to the principate could quite reasonably be portrayed as a form of slavery.

22. Matthew Roller has recently argued that all discussions of *libertas* in Roman ideology have at their root the opposition between freedom and slavery and that, therefore, it is a mistake to argue for different meanings of the term (2001: 213–87). He grants that there may be different metaphorical usages derived from this initial meaning and that those metaphorical usages can be deployed in a variety of different and even opposed contexts, but he contends that the meaning itself does not change and that therefore historians like Wirszubski (1950), Syme (1960), and Ste Croix (1981) are mistaken to see in this term a variety of different significations for different factions and classes. On one level, Roller is right. The opposition between *libertas* and *servitium* is fundamental to all uses of our term. But, on another, his analysis is oversimplified, for it is precisely in the redefinition of *libertas* and the negotiation of its competing meanings that the history of satire can be traced. Moreover, in as much as this term is central to defining what it means to be a *civis Romanus*, then *satura* as the genre that is defined in terms of the changing concept of *libertas* is necessarily a form that is "wholly Roman."

23. The problem is that *libertas* is not in a simple binary relationship with *servitium*, which, as Roller correctly observes, always functions as an antonym to *libertas*. *Libertas* is also simultaneously opposed to *licentia* [licence, excessive liberty] (Wirszubski 1950: 7–8; Ste Croix 1981: 366). *Libertas*, therefore, represents not simply the absence of constraint, but a deliberate balance or an achieved condition. It requires restraint and formation to be achieved in its full sense. Thus, Messalla in Tacitus's *Dialogue of the Orators*, immediately after a discussion of the role demagogic oratory had played in the civil wars, notes that what men call *libertas* with regard to public speaking, i.e., freedom of speech, is in fact often *licentia* and "a goad to an unrestrained populace" (40). It is not possible to understand *libertas* in this context as merely the opposite of *servitium*. Rather, as Cicero makes clear in his speech *On His House*, the *libertas* of the people is dependent on the respect owed to the authority of the senate (130). Here we clearly have two different notions of *libertas*, that of the people, who are guaranteed their freedom and hence restrained from *licentia* through their willing subjection to the senate, and that of the senate or *nobiles* who assert their own *libertas* through a self-restraint that validates their authority over the people. The terms of this opposition, which are only implicit here, become explicit later in the same passage. There, Clodius, the

demagogic tribune of the people, is attacked for his erection of a sacred statue of *Libertas* on the site of Cicero's home. The cult statue was dedicated to celebrate the orator's exile at the urging of the fiery tribune. This sculpture, Cicero notes, would more properly have been erected to *licentia* than to *libertas* because Clodius's freedom represents the opposite of senatorial restraint (131). *Libertas*, then, is not an abstract concept with a single meaning that is merely deployed in different metaphorical contexts. It is the site of a contest about what it means to be a *civis Romanus* and who can claim what rights in relation to whom. Nor is *libertas* commutable. The *libertas* of one group is not equivalent to that of another. The conditions that constitute *libertas* for the people, according to Cicero, would be *servitium* if imposed upon the senate, while if the people or their protectors usurp senatorial prerogatives it is not *libertas* but *licentia*.

24. In other contexts, *libertas* often means "free speech" (Cicero *Pro Cluentio* 118), but it is the free speech of those who have the right to exercise it. In this sense, it is expressly associated with satire as practiced by Lucilius. Satirical *libertas* is the ability to define proper behavior, to exercise one's prerogatives, and to discipline those who either deny one the ability to exercise those prerogatives or violate the norms of conduct. It thus becomes a word in which legal and political rights, artistic license, and aristocratic privilege all come into play. The following passage from a letter to Cicero dated 44 BCE by Trebonius, the conspirator who detained Antony outside the senate on the Ides of March, displays the presence of these different levels of meaning, even as it connects *libertas* directly with satire in the Lucilian mode:

> I heard that there was a certain disturbance, which I certainly hope to be false, so that we might at some point enjoy untroubled freedom [*libertate*]; which I have had very little experience of to this point. Nonetheless, having procured a bit of leisure while we sailed, I put together a little gift for you [. . .]. In these verses if I seem to you rather plain spoken in certain words, the vileness of the person [Marc Antony] whom I am assailing rather freely [*liberius*] will vindicate me. You will also forgive our anger, which is just against men and citizens of this type. Moreover, why should Lucilius be more allowed to take up of this sort of liberty [*libertatis*] than we are, since although his hatred for those he attacked was equal to our own, nonetheless the men he assailed with so much freedom [*libertate*] in his words were certainly no more deserving?
>
> (*Ad Familiares* 12.16)

This letter is a virtual fugue on republican *libertas*. In the first use, the term means freedom from political strife. It refers to the existence of a stable constitutional order and political leadership. The comparative adverb *liberius* refers to the freedom of speech one aristocrat had to assail another in the traditional politics of competitive élites that characterized the Roman republic. The very use of the comparative implies that there were degrees of this freedom and that the possibility of tipping over into *licentia* or at least boorishness had to be guarded against (Corbeill 1996: 16–20, 105–6). The last two uses refer specifically to Lucilius's exercise of this aristocratic freedom of speech in satiric verses directed against the poet's political enemies who are portrayed as no more worthy of public censure than Marc Antony. In such a context, it is difficult indeed to know where one sense of the term leaves off and the next begins. The political, the legal, and the aesthetic are so deeply intertwined that each only gains its full meaning in relation to the other.

25. Nine years later when Horace was preparing to publish his first book of satires he almost certainly had this text or others like it in mind. In 1.4, he begins by contrasting his own practice of satire with that of Lucilius who censured the faults of others freely (*libertate*) in the manner of the Greek Old Comic poets. He then goes on to redefine the practice of satiric censure as a private matter of self-formation learned from his father (himself a *libertinus*), which aims not at public control or political reproof, but private virtue. Near the end of this complex and multileveled poem in which Horace simultaneously lays claim to and distances himself from that same Lucilian tradition that Trebonius invokes, Horace too apologizes if he, like Caesar's assassin, speaks a little too freely (*liberius*, 1.4.103). It would, of course, have been missed by no one in Horace's audience that the satirist too had sided with Brutus and the defenders of republican *libertas* before their defeat at Philippi (Roller 2001: 215).

26. Horace in 1.4 and the following poems is redefining satire for a new era, and consequently redefining freedom itself. He is moving from a political definition of free speech and self-determination toward an Epicurean vision of private virtue (Freudenburg 1993: 72–88). In the process, he is redefining what it means to be a *civis Romanus* for a new era in which the politics of competitive élites has become a dangerous anachronism. Thus in 1.6 where Horace recounts his introduction to Maecenas, Octavian's right-hand man in Rome and his informal minister of culture, the satirist contends that even though his father had been a freedman, he nonetheless lives a less constrained, and hence freer, life than that of a famous (*praeclarus*) senator. The senator is beset by a thousand obligations and forced always to travel in style. The burden of societal expectations weighs upon him constantly. Horace, however, is free to do as he pleases:

> nunc mihi curto
> ire **li**cet mulo vel si **lib**et usque Tarentum
> ....
> hoc ego commo**dius** quam tu, praeclare senator,
> milibus atque aliis vivo. quacumque **lib**ido est,
> incedo . . .

> [I can, if I want, ride a castrated mule all the way to Tarentum . . . In this way, my life is more pleasant than yours and than that of thousands of others. I go wherever I want.]
>
> (1.6.104–12)

And though the word *liberius* is never used here, the import of the passage is clear: Horace enjoys a freedom superior to that of the traditional aristocratic definition, just as he claims in 1.4 and 1.10 that his satire is better and more polished than that of Lucilius. Horatian *libertas* is not that of the senator, the freedom to seek public office and control public affairs. His is the Epicurean freedom to mind his own business, write poetry, and ride his mule where and when he likes. A philosophical vision of subjective or interior freedom has come to qualify, if not replace, the more traditional aristocratic understanding of personal political freedom rooted in power.

27. Lucilius enjoyed the right to expose vice and attack people by name, Horace tells us in 2.1.60–79, because he had the protection of such luminaries as Scipio Aemilianus Africanus and Laelius. Horace implies that he will be protected by Octavian and Maecenas in this new era, but at the same time he never attacks any of Octavian's important political enemies by name. Rather Horace's interlocutor in *Satire* 2.1, Trebatius, reminds the poet that there are laws against *mala carmina* (bad or evil poems), meaning slander and invective. Horace replies that Caesar thinks his poems are "good." The conflation of aesthetic, legal, and political categories is typical, but we should linger a bit over this particular set of rhetorical gestures, for they tell us something about both the limits of republican *libertas* and the nature of its Horatian and Augustan redefinition.

28. *Libertas*, as freedom of speech, never meant that just anybody could say just anything about anyone. There was a law against defamation as early as the Twelve Tables (Pliny the Elder, *Historia Naturalis* 28.4.18) and, until Sulla revised the law in the early first century BCE, it carried with it a capital charge. Yet we know that Lucilius attacked prominent people by name and was not only never brought up on charges but also became the founder of an important poetic genre. Likewise, Catullus accused both Caesar and Pompey of the most outrageous sexual improprieties, but no serious repercussions ensued. What constituted *libertas* and what constituted *licentia* or *convicium* (abuse) depended on the rank of the person speaking, the rank of the person addressed, and their respective political connections. This is not to say that people of the lower classes did not possess a right to free speech (*libertas*). It is to say, however, that in exercising that right they risked retribution, whether of a legal or extralegal sort, if they did not have powerful friends. It is this danger to which Horace humorously alludes in 2.1 (Lafleur 1981).

29. *Libertas* as freedom of speech, then, always existed within a realm constrained by law and political alliance. In the rough and tumble world of

competitive republican politics, *libertas* might well entail the abuse of political opponents and of those who did not share the same image of Roman aristocratic power and self-presentation. Lucilius ranges widely over topics as diverse as adultery, orthography, culinary delights, and petty graft. Satire for him is a tool of social discipline wielded in the perpetual struggle for power and prestige that the Romans defined as the essence of republican *libertas*, in the sense that both Trebonius and Cicero understand it. *Licentia* was in the eye of the beholder and the struggles that ensued as aristocratic competition degenerated into civil war in the first century BCE made this a deadly game indeed. Like Lucilius it was important both to have a high enough social standing to be able make such charges and also to have allies who would back one up. It was also important to make sure they were in a position to do so. By 43 BCE, Trebonius had been killed by the Caesarians' henchman, Dollabella. Brutus and Cassius were not able to protect him in the skirmishes leading up to open warfare. Cicero himself would die later the same year as his reward for attacking Marc Antony in the *Philippics*.

30. Horace presents an allegory of this sad history of *libertas*, *licentia*, and the law in *Epistles* 2.1. In this letter to Augustus, Horace describes how traditional forms of Roman invective grew into communally disruptive forms of *licentia* that masqueraded as *libertas*, until they were finally restrained by law. It is the story of anarchy in the guise of traditional rights and the final, necessary imposition of legal and aesthetic order. The images of the satirist's bloody tooth, of menace going unpunished, and the call to put the care of the community before the individual are all clear, if implicit, references to the civil wars that wracked first-century Rome. The message is unmistakable: this is where republican *libertas* led. Only a more disciplined, classical form—a more restrained *libertas*—could be tolerated:

> The Fescinnine license [*licentia*] . . .
> Poured out rustic blame in alternating verses.
> And free speech [*libertas*] accepted through the years
> Played about amiably. Then a savage joke
> Began to turn into open madness and menace
> Went after respected households with impunity. Those provoked
> Were pained by the bloody tooth. Even those untouched
> Worried about the common condition; so that a law
> And a penalty were brought forth, saying no one should
> Be depicted in bad verse; fearing cudgels they found the limit
> And were led back to the well said and delightful.
>
> (*Epistulae* 2.1.145–55)

As literary history, this is a fanciful reconstruction, but as an allegory of Horace's own satirical practice and his need to redefine *libertas*, it is revealing. Satire in this new era will remain a discourse of aristocratic self-formation, but the nature of the self's freedom must be fundamentally revised and with it the most Roman of genres.

31. By the end of the Augustan regime, there were official book burnings and banishment for the writers of satirical pamphlets; with the accession of Tiberius, impolitic poets were sentenced to death (Syme 1978: 212–20). Traditional republican freedoms were no more respected by the later Julio-Claudian emperors (Wirszubski 1950: 159). As the definition of what it meant to be a free Roman citizen changed, so did the definition of satire. With Persius in the fifties CE, the redefinition of Lucilian satiric *libertas* becomes even more pronounced. Satire loses its vocation as a tool for social control. "Instead, its voice takes an inner turn and patrols the boundaries of a subjectivity in what is represented as a solitary, indeed near solipsistic, performance which is designedly attuned to a reader's reapplication of its upshot to their Self" (Henderson 1993: 13). In the world of Neronian autocracy, satire becomes a technology of the self (Foucault 1986). *Libertas*, as defined in Persius's *Satire* 5, is neither the condition of being a free man as opposed to a slave (5.82), nor the ability to exercise one's social prerogatives, but the attribute of the Stoic sage who stands aloof from the vicissitudes of a world in which meaningful personal action, as traditionally understood by Romans of the governing class, has become all but impossible (Roller 2001: 276–80). This is not the world of Lucilius and Trebonius, nor even that of the late Horace, nor is this their satire either.

32. With Juvenal, at the beginning of the second century CE, the satirist and his *libertas* have been reduced to parody. In Books 1 and 2, the pose of Lucilian *indignatio* is adopted and raised to epic heights but always deflated in a final moment of self-mocking bathos. It is the satire of contradiction. "He purports to describe the world as it really is, but at the same time feels free to indulge in exaggeration and sensationalism as it suits his purpose" (Fredricks in Ramage *et al*. 1974: 166). In *Satire* 1, he will lay bare the vice of the city but only attack the dead. The world of Rome is overrun with cheating foreigners, corrupt and avaricious patrons, adulterous matrons, and poetry recitals in mid-August. Juvenal is always playing a double game, at once invoking traditional values and undermining them. Where Horace evolved a new concept of *libertas* and a new function for satire, Juvenal reduced the virtue itself to mockery (Anderson 1982). Freedom is not the right of every Roman citizen, Umbricius announces in *Satire* 3, but a strictly class-based phenomenon:

> This is the freedom [*libertas*] of the poor man
> Beaten and struck down by fists, he asks and prays
> That he be allowed to go home with a few teeth.
>
> (3.299–301)

The poor man is free to take a beating. But even this moment of ironic bathos is not allowed to stand unchallenged, because Umbricius, while the main speaker in *Satire* 3, is explicitly distanced from the satirist himself. Juvenal, while sympathetic to his friend's complaint, will not join him in fleeing Rome. The satirist is as much satirized as satirizing. In the later books, this element of self-ironizing moralism will come to occupy a larger and larger place in relation to the claims of an uninhibited, but self-confessedly impotent, *indignatio* in Books 1 and 2 (Braund 1988).

33. Satire, then, is the most Roman of genres because it is the form whose subject is *libertas*. Its origin and history are intricately related to the discourses of self-formation that find their origin in Roman literature as a self-conscious institution of aristocratic discipline and legitimation in the second century BCE. The subject of satire is both the form's subject matter and the speaking subject who is empowered to forge this hash of humorous observations, personal reproof, and grotesque degradation. As the history of aristocratic self-formation becomes more problematic in relation to changing political and historical circumstances, satire becomes a more inward and ironic genre. *Satura* is "wholly Roman," then, because its evolution is inseparable from the intertwined political, aesthetic, and legal issues that define what it means to be a *civis Romanus*.

Comedy, iambic, and diatribe

34. None of this, of course, means that the canonical satirists were ignorant of Greek literature or did not make conscious use of it. Horace sees a clear relation between Lucilius and Greek Old Comedy (1.4.1–6). His opinion is echoed by Diomedes the grammarian. On the level of form, the parallel is far-fetched. The Old Comic poets wrote dramas of music and spectacle with costumed choruses (frogs, birds, wasps, etc.); the stories often took place in fantastic environs (the clouds, the underworld, a bizarre Socratic "think shop"); and the poets cared little for the construction of plot or the realistic portrayal of daily life. Old Comedy was part of the Greater Dionysia and cannot be understood outside the democratic and religious institutions that characterized classical Athens. Lucilian satire was a low mimetic genre of social observation and criticism. It was literary—written to be read or declaimed, published in books—not dramatic.

35. Nonetheless Old Comedy was very much part of civic life and directly named and satirized individual Athenian politicians. Aristophanes, the only Old Comic poet from whom a substantial corpus survives, never passes an opportunity to lampoon Cleon. He routinely attacks the tragedian Euripides and may well have contributed, however inadvertently, to Socrates's condemnation with his devastating portait of the philosopher as a corrupt sophist in the *Clouds*. Similarly, Lucilius devoted Book 1 of his satires to a mock counsel of gods called to judge the life of Lentulus Lupus, the former *princeps senatus* (131–130 BCE). Book 2 was given over to the trial of Mucius Scaevola. Lucilius also finds fault with the diction of Accius (28.747) and the verse of Ennius

(9.376–85). Indeed, as the fragments included in the present volume make clear, Lucilius does not hesitate to name important individuals in his poems, nor does he restrict himself to laudatory contexts. But in spite of these acknowledged parallels, Horace and the later grammatical tradition's connection of Lucilius with Old Comedy finds no direct textual support in the works of the master himself.

36. Parallels, however, can also be seen between Lucilius and one of Old Comedy's predecessors, iambic (Coffey 1976: 54). The canonical iambic poets were Archilochus, Hipponax, and Semonides. Iambic in archaic Greece is a ritualized genre of blame poetry that features a number of stock motifs, including suicide by hanging of the named victim. Recent studies have shown that their victims were largely conventional and often had speaking names denoting their poetic function (Nagy 1979; Miller 1994). Nonetheless, the later tradition takes the attacks, which could be both quite direct and earthy, at face value. Archilochus, thus, in the famous Cologne Epode, attempts to seduce the younger daughter of his chief antagonist, Lycambes, while savaging the latter's elder daughter Neoboule:

Know this: let another man have Neoboule
  She becomes overripe
  Her maiden flower has fallen away,
Just as the beauty that was there before.
  For she knows no satisfaction
  And, a frenzied woman,
She has revealed the measure of her youth.
  To hell with her!

The poem closes with an epic periphrasis describing the poet bringing himself to climax without actually penetrating the younger daughter. The result is a poem that not only attacks Neoboule, but effectively savages the reputation of Lycambes and the younger daughter as well. If Lycambes and his family are seen as historical individuals, this is invective of the first order, and iambic was recognized as such in the Roman literary tradition (see Catullus 40).

37. The connection between iambic poetry and satire was openly acknowledged. Apuleius refers to Lucilius in his *Apologia* with the epithet *iambicus*, and Lucilius directly refers to Archilochus (27.732), although it is difficult to deduce much from this one-line fragment. The importance of iambic poetry to satire is also underlined by Horace. In *Satires* 2.3.11–12, Damasippus accuses the poet of wasting space in packing Plato, Menander, Eupolis, and Archilochus to take with him to the Sabine farm since Horace in fact writes so little. This self-deprecating humor is in part a programmatic statement on the nature of Horatian satire. Damasippus, an overzealous Stoic, indicates that Horace's work was a combination of philosophy (Plato), Old Comedy (Eupolis), New

Comedy (Menander), and iambic (Archilochus). This is not far from what Horace himself says in other programmatic passages (1.4 passim, see Piwonka 1978: 64–5), but it is not straightforward either since Horace at this very moment was also working on the *Epodes*, a collection of avowedly iambic poems. Iambic poetry and satire, while recognized as related genres, were considered separate in the Roman tradition. Quintilian treats each form independently.

38. The *Epodes* were in fact directly modeled on Callimachus's *Iambi*, an Alexandrian reworking of the archaic genre (Cameron 1995: 169–70). Yet, it would be a mistake to see this division between the genres as neat or rigid. For at the very moment Horace is composing the *Epodes*, he is also working on Book 2 of the *Satires*. There is in fact a great deal of cross-fertilization. Thus, in *Satires* 2.6.17, he refers to his *saturae* as composed under the sign of his *musa pedestris* or "walking muse." This is a phrase meaning "prosaic." It echoes 1.4's claim that satire is not really poetry but a form of versified prose. Such an interpretation jibes well with the ultimate source of the phrase, Callimachus's description of his *Iambi* as the "walking" or "prosaic pasture of the Muses" (Frg. 112; Cameron 1995: 143–5). Horace, thus, simultaneously recognizes the iambic nature of satire and clearly separates the Roman genre of *satura* from his iambic verse in the Epodes. Nor was he necessarily the first to make this connection between the *musa pedestris* and satire. Piwonka argued that Lucilius may have taken his inspiration as well from Callimachus's *Iambi* (1978). Unfortunately, despite the brilliance of Piwonka's speculations, the evidence from both authors is too fragmentary to allow a definitive conclusion to be reached about the degree of Callimachean influence on Lucilius. Horace, however, certainly sought to portray himself as much more the advocate of Callimachean polish and erudition than his predecessor (1.4.11).

39. Callimachus (third century BCE) was in fact one of the formative influences on classical Roman poetics. Catullus, Horace, Vergil, Tibullus, Propertius, Ovid, Persius, and Juvenal all either quote or allude to him. He was a complex and elusive poet, who was a scholar and librarian at the Museum in Alexandria. His poetry is characterized by learning and studied indirection. Unfortunately, most of his work survives only in fragments. The extant verses, however, are anything but dry and scholarly. They are the clever constructions of a court poet who appears in his poems as an opinionated narrator and polemical poetic theorist. His masterwork, the *Aitia*, opens with a prologue in which the poet defends himself against the charge that he is incapable of producing a single continuous narrative of epic proportions. His witty response is that Apollo had told him to make his sacrifices fat, but to keep his muse slender. The premium is on wit and sophistication: all that is raw and rough-hewn is to be avoided. When Horace in 1.4 charges Lucilius with dictating 200 lines while standing on one leg, he cast him as representing the opposite of Callimachus's small, polished work.

40. The last major influence on satire is Hellenistic diatribe. The world of post-classical Greece and Rome was filled with street-corner philosophers. These Stoic and Cynic preachers harangued their audiences on the importance of following virtue, the vanity of human wishes, and the venality of a life lived as a slave to passion. They used wit, paradox, and an often-coarse sense of humor to drive their points home. Like the authors of *satura*, they presented less a well-reasoned set of philosophical arguments than a series of striking vignettes and *sententiae*.

41. Among the most important of these philosophical preachers was Bion the Borysthenite whose influence Horace acknowledges at *Epistles* 2.2.60. The alleged son of a fishmonger and a prostitute from the Black Sea, Bion arrived in Athens about 315 BCE where he studied philosophy under Academic, Peripatetic, Cyrenaic, and Cynic philosophers. He later went on to be a popular philosopher in his own right, and in his later years occupied a position at the court of Antigonus Gonatas in Macedonia. His influence can be seen most directly in Horace's first three satires, but the influence of diatribe is clear in the hectoring satires of Juvenal and Persius as well as in Lucilius (Duff 1936: 28–33).

Meter and style

42. Ennius's meters vary from iambics to dactylic hexameter and sotadaean. The iambic trimeter is a conversational meter often used in comedy. It allows a great deal of substitution. The basic unit is the iamb, which consists of a short syllable (˘) followed by a long (¯). The rules for determining the quantity of a given syllable can be found in any reference grammar. Iambic trimeter consists of three feet made up of two iambs each. In early usage, substitution of spondees (¯ ¯), anapests (˘˘¯), dactyls (¯˘˘), and tribrachs (˘˘˘) for iambs is possible throughout the line so long as it ends with a true iamb. Fragment 7 thus scans as follows:

˘ – ˘ – | – – – – | – ˘ ˘ ˘ –

mal~~o~~_hercle magno suo convivat sine modo.

[He dines without limit, by Hercules, to his great harm.]

The *u* in *suo* has hardened and is pronounced as a *v* (Gildersleeve and Lodge 1895: §723). Ennius's satiric meters tend to be loose and conversational and take maximum advantage of the licenses offered.

43. The sotadaean meter is based on the ionic foot (¯ ¯ ˘˘). A line has three feet followed by a shortened or catalectic foot that begins with a long (¯) and ends with either a long or a short (ˣ). The final syllable of a Latin verse, however, is always counted as long owing to the pause at the end of the line. Substitution is widely permitted, but the foot rarely begins with a short. The first line of Fragment 18 thus scans:

– – ⏑ ⏑| – – ⏑ ⏑ |– ⏑ – – | – x
nam qui lepide postulat alterum frustrari

[For who cleverly claims to deceive another.]

44. The dactylic hexameter is introduced by Ennius as the meter of his epic on Roman history, the *Annales*. It also appears in two fragments of the satires, but the sample is so small that it is impossible to generalize from it. The basic foot of the hexameter is the dactyl (–⏑⏑) for which a spondee (– –) can be substituted. In classical practice, substitution in the fifth foot is rare. Such lines are known as spondaic and are generally a sign of emphasis in formal epic verse. They were also a common feature of Hellenistic verse and were later popular with the neoteric poets such as Catullus and Calvus of the first century BCE. While it is impossible to know how frequent the spondaic hexameter was in Ennius's satires, it does appear in one of the two fragments that survive:

– – | – x
contemplor
– ⏑ ⏑|– ⏑ ⏑ | – – |– – | – ⏑ ⏑ | – x
inde loci liquidas pilatasqu~~e~~_aetheris oras

[thence I survey the fixed and fluid regions of the heavenly place]

The concentration of alliteration (repetition of the same consonant, especially in initial position) and assonance (repetition of vowel sounds) is typically Ennian.

45. Lucilius's early work (Books 26–30), like that of Ennius, was composed in a variety of meters. Books 26 and 27 feature a meter common in comic dialogue, trochaic septenarius. The basic foot is the trochee (–⏑), for which the spondee (– –), anapest (⏑⏑–), dactyl (–⏑⏑), tribrach (⏑⏑⏑) and proceleusmatic (⏑⏑⏑⏑) may be substituted. A line consists of seven feet, plus an additional syllable at the end of each line. The seventh foot is always a trochee. Thus 26.1.589 scans as follows:

– ⏑ ⏑ | – ⏑ ⏑ | – ⏑ | – ⏑ | – – | – – | – ⏑ | x
nunc itidem populo <placere nol~~o~~>_his cum scriptoribus:

[now in like manner I do not wish to please the masses along with these writers]

Books 28 and 29 also include iambic trimeters.

46. Book 30 is in dactylic hexameters, as are Books 1–21. With this shift to the hexameter, the classical meter of satire is definitively established. In Books 22 through 25, at the end of his career, Lucilius appears to have included ele-

giac distichs, although only one complete couplet survives, and it appears to be a funerary epitaph, a genre conventionally composed in the elegiac meter. Horace, Persius, and Juvenal follow the main tendency in Lucilius's work and compose all their satires, except for Persius's brief prologue, in hexameters.

47. Lucilius's hexameters are frequently end-stopped, that is to say the line forms a complete syntactical unit. Where enjambment occurs (the running over of the syntactical unit from one line to the next) it is seldom pronounced and often coincides with a sense pause. Lucilius also has a large number of elisions, giving his hexameters a harsher feel than those in Horace or Juvenal. Typical is 30.2.1007–8:

> aut c~~um~~_iter est aliqu~~o~~_et causam commenta viai
> aut apud aurific~~em~~,_ad matrem, cognat~~am~~,_ad amicam

> [Or when there is a journey somewhere and she invents a reason for a trip / either to the goldsmith's shop, to her mother, cousin, to her friend]

Note the combination of assonance and alliteration, the frequency of elision, and the repetitive, paratactic syntax. These are all features typical of Lucilian style. Note also the decomposition of the archaic diphthong *ai* (*ae* in classical usage) into its component sounds (*a* + *i*) for purposes of prosody. These are the kind of licenses for which Horace would later censure Lucilius.

48. The Horatian hexameter is at once smoother in its prosody and more likely to feature enjambment. The result is a verse that, while not abandoning the dignity and regularity of the hexameter, carries with it the conversational tone of Lucilius's and Ennius's experiments with iambic and trochaic meters. Horatian style "is plain and unpretentious with a deceptive appearance of simplicity: the structure is loose but not rambling; the language is scrupulously correct" (Rudd 1982: 96). *Satire* 1.4.6–8 is typical in this regard:

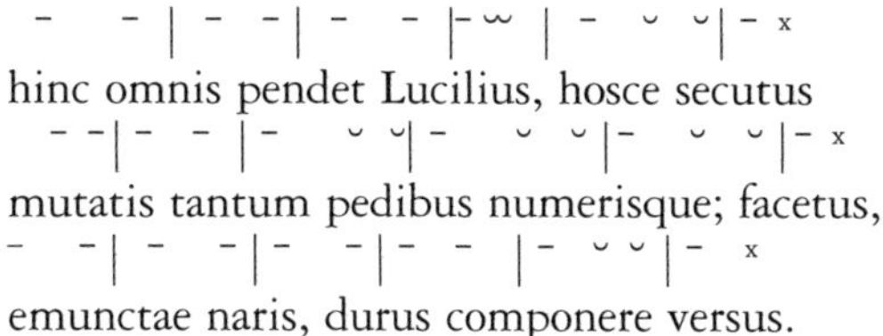

> [All Lucilius derives from here, having followed them / with only feet and meters changed, witty / with a keen nose, harsh in his writing of verse.]

The poet uses simple vocabulary, with a minimum of repetition. Assonance is present, but only slightly more pronounced than what would occur in normal conversation. The line end is only respected when it draws the thought to a natural close. Elision is used sparingly, and the meter is managed to produce specific effects. Observe the predominance of spondees in the final line where the emphasis is on the harshness of Lucilius's versification.

49. Persius's versification is superficially like Horace's. He takes few licenses, and enjambment is frequent, but balanced by end-stopped lines that establish the flow of the verse. Hiatus is avoided. Elision is less frequent than in Lucilius and managed so as not to interrupt the flow of sense. Every line has a main caesura (||) or break that punctuates the sense and avoids prosodic monotony and often a secondary caesura as well (Knoche 1975: 134–5). Yet, where Horace aims for conversational ease, Persius strives for the harsh juxtaposition (*iunctura . . . acri* 5.14) and a boiled down style (*decoctius* 1.125) that jolts readers out of their habitual slumber. A good example can be seen in the following:

> – ˘ ˘ | – ˘ ˘ | – – | – ˘ ˘ | – ˘ ˘ | – x
> auriculas asini || quis non habet? || hoc eg~~o~~_opertum,
> – – | – ˘ ˘ | – – | – – | – ˘ ˘ | – x
> hoc ridere meum, || tam nil, || nulla tibi vendo
> – ˘ ˘ | – – | – – | – – | – ˘ ˘ | – x
> Iliad~~e~~._audaci || quicumqu~~e~~_adflate Cratino
> – – | – ˘ ˘ | – – | – – | – ˘ ˘ | – x
> irat~~um~~_Eupolidem || praegrandi cum sene palles,
> – ˘ ˘ | – – | – ˘ ˘ | – – | – ˘ ˘ | – x
> aspic~~e~~_et haec, || si fort~~e~~_aliquid decoctius audis. (1.121–5)

> [Who does not have ass's ears? I, this secret, / this laugh of mine, so worthless, I would sell for no / Iliad. Whoever you are, inspired by bold Cratinus, / you grow pale in study of angry Eupolis with the great old man, / take a look at these things too, if perchance you listen to something more boiled down.]

The combination of highly wrought verse with a deliberately harsh style ensures that his hexameters achieve the maximum impact. There can be no question but that each word is carefully chosen and consciously placed.

50. The prologue to Persius's book of satires is written in "limping iambics." This meter, invented by Hipponax, recalls both satire's links to Greek iambic and Ennius's and Lucilius's early experiments with iambic meters. The limping iambic is an iambic trimeter whose last foot always ends ˘ – – x. Thus the first line of the prologue scans:

– – ᴗ – | ᴗ – ᴗ– | ᴗ – – x
Nec fonte labra prolui caballino

[I have not rinsed my lips in the nag's spring.]

51. Juvenal's style strives neither for Horace's conversational tone nor Persius's deliberate use of estrangement effects, but for epic and declamatory grandeur. The combination of the high style—rhetorical questions, golden lines, sweeping periods, epic allusions—and satire's low subject matter creates a profound bathos that often results in hilarious laughter and a sense of the world turned upside down. The bathetic effect can be heightened by ending the line with a jarring monosyllable that stops the metrical flow. Juvenal occasionally uses hiatus and a spondaic fifth foot. These are features of epic style. Elision is less frequent than in Horace or Persius (Courtney 1980: 52). Another feature of Juvenal's prosody is his use of the bucolic diaeresis, a strong break at the end of the fourth foot. A good illustration of his stylistic and metrical practice can be found in 1.49–50:

– ᴗ ᴗ | – – | – ᴗ ᴗ | – ᴗ ᴗ | – ᴗ ᴗ | – x
exul ab octava || Marius bibit || et fruitur dis
– – | – – | – – | – – | – ᴗᴗ | – x
iratis, || at tu victrix, || provincia, || ploras.

[Marius drinks from the eighth hour and profits from the gods' / anger, but you the victor, province, weep]

The delay of *iratis* to the second line creates a kind of comic double-take. The first line ends with a jolt in the monosyllabic *dis*, leading the reader to expect that Marius, in spite of being an exile, is enjoying good fortune. The sheer perversity of the situation, however, only becomes clear when we realize that the line rather than being end-stopped is in fact enjambed and that the cause of Marius's good fortune is that he has angered the gods! At the same time, the multiple pauses and the use of alliteration highlights the irony of the fact that it is the victorious province that weeps.

Lives and works

52. It is impossible in the space allowed to give a complete accounting of the texts and contexts surrounding each of our authors. Moreover, in many cases the information we have concerning their lives and personal development is scant, misleading, and highly speculative. Nonetheless, it is important to have a basic conception of the shape of each satirist's work, to the extent it can be defined, and to understand the nature of the circumstances in which the work was produced, in so far as possible.

Ennius

53. Ennius was born in 239 BCE in Rudiae (modern Rugge) in southern Italy. He was a native Oscan, who grew up in a Greek-speaking region under Roman hegemony. He was fluent in all three languages. During his service as a mercenary in an Italian unit serving under Roman command on Sardinia, he met Cato the Elder, who brought him to Rome in 204. Once there, he earned his living as a poet, teacher, and commentator on Greek and Latin texts. Ennius accompanied Marcus Nobilius Fulvior, consul in 189 BCE, on his Aetolian campaign (189–187 BCE) as camp poet. This earned the latter the ire of Cato for introducing such Hellenistic refinements into a Roman military context. Marcus's son Quintus arranged for Ennius to become a citizen in 184 BCE and provided the poet with an allotment of land that relieved him of the necessity of earning a living through teaching. Ennius was also close to Scipio Nasica and wrote a poem lauding Scipio Africanus the elder for his victory over Hannibal at Zama (202 BCE). The poet died in 169 after the production of his *Thyestes*.

54. Ennius's poetic oeuvre was vast and exercised a formative influence on later Latin literature. The *Annales*, an epic poem in hexameters, narrated the history of Rome in eighteen books. Six hundred verses survive in 437 fragments. We have the titles of more than twenty tragedies, two Latin farces (*praetextae*), two Greek style comedies, and a variety of miscellaneous poems including the *Hedyphagetica* or "Fine Dining." The latter is sometimes included among the satires. Regardless of its precise place in the canon, it shows an interest in matters gastronomical that becomes one of the major themes of later satire (Duff 1936: 42; Rudd 1982: 204–5).

55. It is generally thought that Ennius wrote four books of satires, although even here there is some disagreement since some of our fragments are attributed to a sixth book. Only thirty-seven possible lines survive, most quoted by later authors because of grammatical or lexical oddities, and in some cases the attribution to the satires is insecure. It is difficult to date the poems with any accuracy, and it is not known whether they were composed as a group or occasionally over a long period of time. It is also difficult to interpret the fragments with precision, since we often do not know who the speaker is, and it would be a mistake to assume that it was necessarily Ennius. As Quintilian recounts, one poem contained a debate between personified life and death (9.2.36). Likewise Gellius tells of Ennius's use of Aesop's fable of the crested lark. One should be wary, then, of assuming too much about a line or two pulled out of context. Whether it is spoken by the poet or a character in a narrative could change the meaning we assign to it. Nonetheless, from the fragments we possess, it seems evident that the satires provided Ennius with the opportunity to comment upon Roman daily life and to engage in a certain amount of social commentary whether directly or indirectly.

Lucilius

56. Lucilius was born in Suessa Aurunca on the border separating Latium from Campania. Saint Jerome gives his birth date as 148 BCE, but this would make him only fourteen when he served under Scipio Aemilianus Africanus at Numantia in 134. The most plausible solution to this problem is to backdate his birth to 180, when the consuls possessed the same *nomina* as they did in 148. Since Romans indicated years by the names of the consuls, this kind of mistake is relatively common. The dates of 157 and 167 have also been advanced but not won general assent. Lucilius died in 102 BCE at Naples and was granted a public funeral.

57. The first great satirist was born into a wealthy family and was himself a man of means. His brother was a senator and his grandnephew was Pompey the Great. He himself never pursued a political career and remained an equestrian. He had large estates in Apulia, Bruttium, Sardinia, and Sicily. In Rome, he moved in the highest circles and was a close associate of Scipio Aemilianus Africanus and Laelius. His prominence and reputation for learning were such that Clitomachus, the head of the Athenian Academy (127–110 BCE), dedicated a treatise to him.

58. Lucilius wrote no known poetry other than his satires. What we know as Books 26–30 were published first and, by internal references, can be dated to the period between 131 and 124 BCE. A later collection consisting of Books 1–25 was eventually published and became the basis for antiquity's *opera omnia*. Book 1 was first published near 125 BCE, Book 2 after 119, Book 5 no later than 117, and Book 20 circa 107. When Lucilius died in 102 BCE he had published thirty books in less than twenty-nine years, an astounding rate of productivity.

59. Although Ennius had published his satirical miscellanies, and there was a tradition of both ritualized blame poetry and political invective in Rome, there was little real precedent for the satiric genre as Lucilius created it. Spurius Mummius, the brother of Lucius Mummius, sacker of Corinth (146 BCE), had sent home humorous verse epistles to his friends while serving in his brother's camp. These would have been known to Lucilius, since Spurius was a member of Scipio Aemelianus Africanus's circle of friends. Such witty, conversational verse between aristocratic *amici* would have served as a model for Lucilius, who, unlike Mummius, would eventually publish his work. But they hardly account for the genre as a whole.

60. Lucilius twice refers to his poetry as *sermones* (1090, 1091), both times in the context of someone objecting to being subjected to criticism (*maledicendo*). *Sermo* is a term Horace would later use as well. It does not denote ordinary speech, but refined aristocratic conversation that marked its practitioner as a gentleman. It was the badge of *urbanitas* and served both to admit those accomplished at its art into the charmed circle of aristocratic culture and to exclude those who could not compete in the cut and thrust of its witty repartee. For

this reason, Cicero in *De Officiis* (1.133–7) recommends to his son, Marcus, deliberate training in the art of conversation (Ramage in Ramage *et al.* 1974: 31). If we recall our earlier discussion of the role the emergence of Latin literature in the second century BCE played in recruiting and consolidating aristocratic culture in a time of perceived crisis, then the importance of Lucilian *sermo* as a public genre comes into sharper focus (Coffey 1976: 50). It provided a model of what a gentleman (*nobilis*) should strive both to be and to avoid.

61. By examining a series of fragments from Book 30, we can gain a better idea of what the texture of this Lucilian *sermo* might have been. Its witty back and forth can be paralleled to similar interchanges in Horace 1.4, where the latter specifically tries to define his own ideal of satiric *sermo* in relation to that of Lucilius (Krenkel 1970: *ad loc.*). The reconstruction of the passage as a sequence is admittedly speculative, as all such reconstructions must be, but it in no way contravenes the evidence and gives a reasonable facsimile of the way Lucilian satire probably worked:

Interlocutor: Gaudes cum de me ista foris sermonibus differs,
et maledicendo in multis sermonibus differs.

....

Lucilius: summatim tamen experiar rescribere paucis.
Interlocutor: quin totum purges, devellas me atque deuras
Exultesque adites <et> sollicites <, nihil obstat>.
Lucilius: omnes formonsi, fortes tibi, ego inprobus: esto. (1090–5)

[*Interlocutor:* You love it when you spread around those things about me in your satires, and you spread me wide open by attacking me in many satires.

....

Lucilius: Nonetheless, I shall try to respond briefly in a few words.
Interlocutor: Nothing keeps you from cleaning me out altogether, plucking me bare, singeing me, and insulting me, going after and harassing me.
Lucilius: To you everybody is fine and brave, and I'm the reprobate: fine!]

The general drift of the passage is reproduced almost exactly by Persius 1.107–11. Lucilian *sermo* and *libertas* define a certain intellectual and aristocratic style that is inherited, adapted, and problematized by each of its satirical inheritors. It is exemplified both in the censure of others and in the establishment of standards of linguistic and cultural behavior, embodied in the satirist's persona, that serve as models of aristocratic comportment.

Horace

62. Horace was not from aristocratic stock. As he says in *Satires* 1.6, his father was a freedman. Indeed, he insists on his father's humble origins to such a

degree that we may wonder to what extent this is a statement of fact and to what extent an artistic device. Bion too claimed to be the son of a former slave in his diatribes, and Horace's father certainly was better off than the average *libertinus*, if he was able to afford to move to Rome and acquire for his son the finest education available (Freudenburg 1993: 205). Nonetheless, we can be sure that Horace was of relatively humble origins when compared to Lucilius, even if he has exaggerated his youthful poverty for effect.

63. Horace was born in the Apulian town of Venusia in 65 BCE. When he finished his rhetorical instruction in Rome, he went to Athens to study philosophy, the customary capstone of an upper-class Roman education. There he met Brutus, the assassin of Julius Caesar. He apparently impressed Brutus, for when Horace joined the army of the conspirators, he received a commission as a military tribune, a rank that required Horace either to have already attained or to be promoted to the rank of equestrian. After the defeat of the republican cause at Philippi in 42 BCE, Horace returned to Rome where he obtained the position of *scriba quaestorius* (treasury clerk). Such positions were relatively prestigious so Horace's claims that he took up poetry out of poverty (*Epistles* 2.2.50–2) must be taken with a grain of salt. In the early thirties Horace made the acquaintance of Vergil and Varus. They approved of his poetry and in 38 BCE introduced him to Maecenas.

64. Maecenas played a key role in Horace's life and his poetry. *Satires* 1.1, 1.5, 1.6, 1.9, 1.10, 2.3, 2.6, 2.7, 2.8 are all either addressed to, or make prominent mention of, Horace's relation to his patron. Maecenas in some ways defines the first half of the Augustan era. An equestrian from an old Etruscan family, he never sought elective office. He was one of Octavian's earliest supporters and fought with him at Philippi. He became his trusted friend and agent, assuming effective political control of the city when Octavian was away. He also functioned as his chief patron. Maecenas recruited Vergil, Varus, Horace, and, to a certain extent, Propertius to the new regime. He appears to have been neither overbearing nor inattentive as a patron. If one accepts what the poets say at face value—a dangerous thing to do—he encouraged the production of poetry that would reflect well on the emerging principate. Yet, it is clear that he gave those under his protection a great deal of leeway. He neither attempted to micromanage their productions nor to censor work that was frankly critical of the regime such as Propertius 2.7. As a result, some of the finest poetry in the history of the west was produced during the Augustan principate. This was no mere act of disinterested aesthetic patronage, but a shrewd investment in image management. It is largely as result of this poetry that the principate enjoys an image of peace, moderation, and prosperity to this day. That would certainly not have been the case if the only picture we had of Octavian was that of the young triumvir who allowed Marc Antony to slaughter Cicero in the proscriptions or the bloody victor at Perusia (Gold 1986; White 1993).

65. In 35 BCE, shortly after the publication of the first book of satires, Horace received the Sabine farm from Maecenas, a gift that gave the poet personal and

financial independence. The first book of satires is in many ways very different from the work of Lucilius. *Satires* 1.1, 1.2, and 1.3, which borrow heavily from the tradition of diatribe, are the most Lucilian in tone. After 1.3, no living person of note is lampooned, and even in the opening satires there is no real political combat. As Coffey observes, "In the 30s it would have been dangerous, especially for a freedman's son to write political lampoons" (1976: 90–1). What Maecenas and Octavian needed, and what Horace sought in *satura*, was a poetic form in which fundamental Roman values could be redefined for a new era. Horace produced a satire that is both politically and aesthetically disciplined, shorn of the republican excesses that, in the view of Octavian, Maecenas and their circle, had led the republic to collapse in blood and fire.

66. To this end, Horace relies more on paradox and self-deprecating irony than the full frontal assault of traditional invective. In 1.5 he is oblivious to the great political events surrounding him. In 1.9, he subtly pays a compliment to Maecenas while portraying himself as the hapless victim of a tasteless boor. In 2.1, which introduces the second book of satires, published in 30 BCE, Horace presents a new more dialogic style. In this book, he will seldom be the only speaker in the poem, and rarely its central protagonist. In 2.6, he thanks Maecenas for the gift of the Sabine farm, while the rustic Cervius regales Horace's guest with the tale of the city mouse and the country mouse, a fable that gently criticizes the very search for luxury for which Maecenas himself was renowned (Muecke 1997: 228). Finally in 2.8, he contrasts Maecenas's well-tempered urbanity with the pretentious bombast of the would-be gourmet, Nasidienus, through a story recounted by the comic poet, Fundanius.

Persius

67. Aulus Persius Flaccus was born in 34 CE at Volterrae, an Etruscan hill town. He was a wealthy equestrian who never took part in politics and died at the age of twenty-eight of a stomach ailment. He left his mother and sisters a considerable fortune. His father died when he was six, and his life was devoted to poetry, philosophy, and the care of his female relatives. On his death he left his library, which contained over 700 volumes of the Stoic Chrysippus, to his philosophical mentor, Cornutus.

68. In many ways, Persius's satires are the least characteristic of the genre. Published posthumously by the poet, Caesius Bassus, to whom *Satire* 6 is dedicated, Persius's poems make up one slim tome of 664 lines. His satires are the only ones to espouse a position based on the teachings of a single philosophical school, the late Stoa. According to the ancient "Life of Persius," at sixteen the poet entrusted himself to Cornutus, whom he describes in his fifth satire as providing moral and aesthetic guidance. Yet, by far the most unusual characteristic of Persius's satires is his language. Where Lucilius writes in a loose, conversational style, which Horace refines into a sophisticated literary instrument, and where Juvenal offers mock-epic grandeur, Persius eschews the

grand style, writing an idiosyncratic Latin removed from daily conversation. He uses low colloquial terms, forms neologisms, and gives common words a sharp new turn. He creates a demanding style of diction that defies translation and that in large part accounts for why he is so little read today. All the same, Persius could not have seemed as difficult in his day as he does to us. He was immediately popular and rapidly became a school text. Nonetheless, even in antiquity he was recognized as a demanding author. Thus, although Persius's work remained popular throughout the Middle Ages and Renaissance, in part because of its consistent moral message, from ancient times commentators have remarked on his obscurity (Knoche 1975: 132–7).

69. Persius's practice of linguistic invention is part of a deliberate rhetorical strategy. At 5.14, Cornutus admonishes his young charge, *verba togae sequeris iunctura callidus acri* ["You stick to the words of the toga, clever at the sharp juxtaposition"]. This line is at once an explanation and instantiation of Persius's style. If we examine the initial half of the phrase, the most difficult task is to unfold what is meant by "the words of the toga." It appears to refer to a preference for pure Latin diction. The toga, after all, could only be worn by Roman citizens. Hence, "sticking to the words of the toga" would denote a rejection of the common practice in Neronian poetics of using a highly artificial, Greek-influenced vocabulary, for which Persius criticizes his contemporaries in *Satire* 1. In that same first satire, the poet also equates poetic style and personal character, so that the poets who write in this artificial, Greek style are portrayed as morally soft and sexually perverse. Consequently, Persius's refusal of what he deems an overly refined and unnatural Greek poetic diction, in turn, implies the rejection of a decadent lifestyle associated with the Hellenistic east in favor of the rough and ready virtues of the traditional Roman in the mold of Cato. The toga, nonetheless, was not the everyday dress of the soldier or farmer, but the garb worn on formal and official occasions. Associated with it are the qualities of solemnity, seriousness, and the class-consciousness of the ruling strata of Roman society (Persius in *Satires* 3, 4, and 5 shows his low regard for the uneducated masses). We are not talking about common speech but weighty and, by implication, educated speech. The moral gravity of this refined plain speech is portrayed in deliberate contrast to the inflated diction and hollow subject matter dominating contemporary poetic style.

70. The fact that so much can be extracted from this careful placement of two ordinary words in turn serves as an illustration of the second half of the line under examination, "*clever* at the sharp *juxtaposition*." The phrase is a reworking of *Ars Poetica* 47–8 "You will have spoken distinctively, if *clever juxtaposition* will have made a known word new." Persius thus practices a poetic style that is selfconsciously intertextual and possessed of a keen cutting edge. He both imitates Horace and sharpens him. Such a style is appropriate for a corpus whose announced aim is to attack vice and promote virtue. Thus, *Satire* 1 attacks contemporary poetry. *Satire* 2 exposes the foolish and often evil requests people make in prayer. The third satire begins by lampooning the habits of a young

philosophy student (probably Persius) who oversleeps owing to the previous night's debauch and finishes with a sermon on the value of philosophy for diseases of the soul. *Satire* 4 begins with a dialogue in which Socrates admonishes Alcibiades for his vanity and ends with a diatribe on the virtues of self-knowledge. *Satire* 5 begins with Persius's praise of Cornutus, and then defends the Stoic thesis that only the wise man is free, while *Satire* 6 advocates the position that you should enjoy your wealth and not worry about your heirs. In each case, there is a clear target at which Persius's satire is aimed and the "sharp juxtaposition" is his weapon of choice. Moreover, this imagery of the sharp, the keen, and the cutting is a recurring motif found throughout the corpus. One of the most common words in the Satires is *radere*, "to shave or scrape," commonly referring to the healthy abrasive function of philosophy and satire on the human soul (1.85, 1.107, 2.66, 3.50, 3.114, 5.15). In contrast, the poets of whom the satirist disapproves are "soft," "fluid," "effeminate," or "trivial."

71. A good example of Persius's style may be found in the prologue. The poem begins with a rejection of the Greek mythological trappings used to describe poetic inspiration and finishes with the claim that poets only write to feed their bellies. The first line features the phrase *fons caballinus* or "nag's spring," an irreverent translation of the Greek *Hippocrene*, the sacred spring of the muses. By using the vulgar Latin *caballinus*, Persius shows his contempt for those who ape the Greek tradition, even as he demonstrates his knowledge of it. His use of a low level of diction opposes him to his over-refined contemporaries, but his erudition lifts him above the masses. Five lines later, he claims to be a *semipaganus*, a "half rustic." The word itself is a neologism coined specially for the occasion and should not be taken literally: for, even as it proclaims the poet's lack of sophistication, it demonstrates his wit. Persius may be half rustic, but in matters that count (virtue, honesty, philosophical penetration), he far surpasses his rivals.

72. Persius's satires make great demands on the reader. His work cannot be simply browsed, but requires focused, self-critical engagement. His rhetoric forces us to be active participants in the creation of meaning. It scrapes away our illusions of self-mastery and sophistication and forces us to see the world through its sharpened lens.

Juvenal

73. Little is known of Juvenal's life. His name is generally accepted to be Decimus Junius Juvenalis. His birth date is disputed, though it is agreed to fall between 50 and 70 CE. He was probably from a prosperous family since his satires reveal him to have received an excellent rhetorical education as well as formal instruction in philosophy. He never mentions a patron. In *Satire* 3, Umbricius indicates that Aquinum was his hometown. A lost inscription from the same town, a dedication to Ceres, indicates that a Junius Juvenalis held local office. Whether this was the satirist himself or a relative is impossible to

tell. Martial addresses two epigrams and a letter to the satirist (7.24, 7.91, 12.18), which date from the nineties. He refers to Juvenal as eloquent and portrays him as performing the thankless duties of a client, a picture that accords well with the image found in the satires. His satire is marked by the trauma of Domitian's reign (81–96 CE), to which numerous references are made, but he also features monsters from the time of Nero and even Tiberius. After his death, his work was largely neglected until it was rediscovered by Christian writers of the fourth century.

74. Juvenal published five books of satires. Book 1 contained *Satires* 1–5 and was published sometime after 100 CE. Book 2 was wholly devoted to *Satire* 6, "On Women," and it can be dated to some time after 115 CE. His third book contained *Satires* 7–9 and can be dated to the period after Hadrian's accession to the throne in 117. Book 4 consists of *Satires* 10–12. Book 5, which is made up of *Satires* 12–16, can be dated to some time after 127 CE. The last poem is unfinished and so posthumous publication is presumed.

75. The pose of the Juvenalian satirist in the first two books is that of the irate conservative, hostile to all forms of social change. When asked how he is able to write satire adequate to the enormity of the crimes he witnesses, he answers *facit indignatio versum* [anger makes the verse] (1.79). The causes of his indignation are legion but can be grouped under several dominant headings: the breakdown of traditional gender and social roles; the tide of immigrants that threatens to make Romans a minority in their own city; and the neglect of traditional patron–client relations. It is a world turned upside-down, where Roman virtues bring only shame and degradation:

> aude aliud brevibus Gyaris et carcere dignum
> si vis esse aliquid. Probitas laudatur et alget.
>
> [Dare something worthy of exile on Gyara or prison if you want to be something. Goodness is praised and causes pain.]
>
> (1.73–4)

Juvenalian *indignatio* is not the pose of the Stoic sage or self-possessed Epicurean, but of the irate declaimer whose anger renders him incoherent with rage. "It is the impression of incoherence which is of prime importance" (Braund 1988: 9).

76. Juvenal creates this impression of "indignation unbound" through the concentrated deployment of the tools and themes of the rhetorical tradition. Yet, as one recognizes the calculated use of those rhetorical devices, the nature of his *indignatio* as a pose becomes unmistakable. It is not a question of the sincerity of Juvenal's anger, which need be neither doubted nor affirmed, but rather of his inclusion of the angry speaker within the scope of the satire itself. The only thing as ridiculous as the world of matronly gladiators and moralizing perverts in which the subject of satire lives is the satirist himself.

The highly wrought form of the Juvenalian *satura*—its deployment of paradox, aphoristic *sententiae*, hyperbole, and the striking image—ensures that there is always an ironic distance separating the satire from its subject. There is, in fact, something consciously excessive in the satirist's self-presentation.

77. In Books 3–5, this pose alters somewhat. Irony comes to predominate over *indignatio*. The satirist becomes increasingly detached from his subject matter. The change is not total, and the violence of the imagery and invective of *Satire* 9 recalls that of the preceding books. However, the speaker for much of the poem, Naevolus, is clearly separated from the satirist. This is not unprecedented. In *Satire* 3, the speaker is Umbricius. But where Umbricius is a caricature of the stern traditional Roman moralist—i.e., a satirist in the Lucilian mode—Naevolus is a male prostitute. The level of ironic distance between speaker and satirist has clearly widened.

78. In the last two books, this trend toward detachment is only increased. As Conte observes:

> A marked change in tone is observed in the second part of Juvenal's work, that is in the last two books, in which the poet expressly renounces violent *indignatio* and assumes a more detached attitude, which aims at the *apatheia* of the Stoics. In this he is returning to that diatribe tradition of satire from which he has drastically departed [. . .] And yet this façade of impassability cracks open here and there, showing the old fury, and the undying rage sometimes breaks out again.
> (1994: 477)

The subject of Latin verse satire thus comes to an end with the attempt to construct the internal *libertas* of the sage. It is a freedom shielded both from his internal anger and from the external vicissitudes of an authoritarian political universe in which the values of Lucilius no longer have any purchase. The ironic detachment from which that shield is constructed ideally yields to the reader a benign bathos and a melancholy pathos. The construction of this citadel of the self, however, remains a tenuous affair, which the sheer stupidity and viciousness of human desire, both within the satirist and without, constantly threaten to overturn.

Select bibliography

Adams, J. N. 1982. *The Latin Sexual Vocabulary*. Baltimore: Johns Hopkins University Press.

Albrecht, Michael von. 1997. *A History of Roman Literature from Livius Andronicus to Boethius with Special Regard to Its Influence on World Literature*. Two vols. Rev. by Gareth Schmeling and Michael von Albrecht. Trans. by Michael von Albrecht and Gareth Schmeling with the assistance of Ruth R. Caston, Frances and Kevin Newman, and Francis Schwartz. Leiden: Brill.

Anderson, William S. 1982. *Essays on Roman Satire*. Princeton: Princeton University Press.

Anthon, Charles. 1886. *The Works of Horace*. New York: Harper and Brother.

Bakhtin, M. M. 1968. *Rabelais and His World*. Trans. by Hélène Iswolsky. Cambridge, MA: MIT Press.

Berg, Deena. 1996. "The Mystery Gourmet of Horace's Satires 2." *Classical Journal* 91: 141–52.

Bo, Dominicus. 1967. *Auli Persii Flacci Lexicon*. Hildesheim: Olms.

Bowditch, Phebe Lowell. 2001. *Horace and the Gift Economy of Patronage*. Berkeley: University of California Press.

Bramble, J. C. 1974. *Persius and the Programmatic Satire: A Study in Form and Imagery*. Cambridge: Cambridge University Press.

Braund, Susanna. 1988. *Beyond Anger: A Study of Juvenal's Third Book of Satires*. Cambridge: Cambridge University Press.

—— 1992. *Roman Verse Satire. Greece and Rome: New Surveys in the Classics* 23. Oxford: Oxford University Press.

—— 1996a. *Juvenal: Satires 1*. Cambridge: Cambridge University Press.

—— 1996b. *The Roman Satirists and Their Masks*. Bristol: Bristol Classical Press.

Brown, P. Michael. 1993. *Horace: Satires I*. Warminster: Aris and Phillips.

Cameron, Alan. 1995. *Callimachus and His Critics*. Princeton: Princeton University Press.

Casaubon, I. 1605. *Auli Persi Flacci Satyrae*. Paris.

Caston, Ruth Rothaus. 1997. "The Fall of the Curtain (Horace *S*. 2.8)." *Transactions of the American Philological Association* 127: 233–56.

Clausen, W. V. 1956. *A. Persi Flacci Saturarum Liber*. Oxford: Clarendon Press.

—— 1959. *A. Persi Flacci et D. Iuni Iuvenalis: Saturae*. Oxford: Oxford University Press.

Coffey, Michael. 1976. *Roman Satire*. London: Methuen.

Conte, Gian Biagio. 1994. *Latin Literature: A History*. Rev. by Don Fowler and Glenn W. Most. Trans. by Joseph B. Solodow. Baltimore: Johns Hopkins University Press.

Corbeill, Anthony. 1996. *Controlling Laughter: Political Humor in the Late Roman Republic*. Princeton: Princeton University Press.

Courtney, Edward. 1980. *A Commentary on the Satires of Juvenal*. London: Athlone Press.

—— 1984. *The Satires of Juvenal: A Text with Brief Critical Notes*. Rome: Edizioni dell'Ateneo.

—— 1993. *The Fragmentary Latin Poets*. Oxford: Oxford University Press.

Cruquius, Iacobus. 1597. *Q. Horatius Flaccus: cum commentariis veteris et Iacobi Cruquii Messenii, Literarum apud Brugenses Professoris*. Lugdunum Batavorum.

Denyer, Nicholas. 2001. *Plato: Alcibiades*. Cambridge: Cambridge University Press.

Dessen, Cynthia S. 1968. *"Iunctura Callidus Acri": A Study of Persius' Satires*. Urbana: University of Illinois Press.

Dickey, Eleanor. 2002. *Latin Forms of Address: From Plautus to Apuleius*. Oxford: Oxford University Press.

Doering, Fridericus Guil. 1824. *Q. Horati Flacci: Opera Omnia*. Leipzig: Libraria Hahniana.

Dominick, William J. and William T. Wehrle. 1999. *Roman Verse Satire: Lucilius to Juvenal*. Wauconda, IL: Bolchazy-Carducci.

Duff, J. D. 1970. *Juvenal: Satires*. Rev. ed. Cambridge: Cambridge University Press. Original 1904.

Duff, J. Wright. 1936. *Roman Satire: Its Outlook on Social Life*. Berkeley: University of California Press.

Dumézil, Georges. 1943. *Servius et la fortune: Essai sur la fonction sociale de louange et de blâme et sur les éléments indo-européens du cens romain*. Paris: Gallimard.

Edwards, Catherine. 1993. *The Politics of Immorality in Ancient Rome*. Cambridge: Cambridge University Press.

Ferguson, John. 1979. *Juvenal: The Satires*. New York: St Martin's Press.

Fiske, George Converse. 1920. *Lucilius and Horace: A Study in the Classical Theory of Imitation*. Madison: University of Wisconsin Press.

Foucault, Michel. 1986. *The Care of the Self. The History of Sexuality*, vol. 3. Trans. by Robert Hurley. New York: Pantheon.

Freudenburg, Kirk. 1993. *The Walking Muse: Horace on the Theory of Satire*. Princeton: Princeton University Press.

—— 2001. *Satires of Rome: Threatening Poses from Lucilius to Juvenal*. Cambridge: Cambridge University Press.

Friedländer, Ludwig. 1962. *D. Junii Juvenalis: Mit erklärenden Anmerkungen*. Amsterdam: Hakkert. Original 1895.

Gildersleeve, Basil L. 1903. *The Satires of A. Persius Flaccus*. New York: American Book Company.

Gildersleeve, Basil L. and Gonzalez Lodge. 1895. *Gildersleeve's Latin Grammar*. 3rd ed. London: Macmillan.

Gold, Barbara K. 1986. *Literary Patronage in Greece and Rome*. Chapel Hill: University of North Carolina Press.

—— 1998. "'The House I Live in Is Not My Own': Women's Bodies in Juvenal's Satires." *Arethusa* 31: 369–86.

Gowers, Emily. 1993. *The Loaded Table: Representations of Food in Roman Satire*, Oxford: Oxford University Press

Green, Peter. 1974. *Juvenal: The Sixteen Satires*. London: Penguin.

Habinek, Thomas. 1998. *The Politics of Latin Literature: Writing Identity and Empire in Ancient Rome*. Princeton: Princeton University Press.

Harvey, R. A. 1981. *A Commentary on Persius*. Leiden: Brill.

Hart, Samuel. 1896. *Satires of Persius*. Boston: Allyn and Bacon.

Henderson, John. 1993. "Persius' Didactic Satire: The Teacher as Pupil." *Ramus* 20: 123–48.

—— 1999. *Writing Down Rome: Satire, Comedy, and Other Offences in Latin Poetry*. Oxford: Clarendon Press.

Highet, Gilbert. 1961. *Juvenal the Satirist*. Oxford: Oxford University Press.

—— 1962. *The Anatomy of Satire*. Princeton: Princeton University Press.

Hooley, D. M. 1997. *The Knotted Thong: Structures of Mimesis in Persius*. Ann Arbor: University of Michigan Press.

Housman A. E. 1913. "Notes on Persius." *Classical Quarterly* 7: 12–32.

Housman, A. E. 1931. *Iunii Iuvenalis Saturae*. 2nd ed. Cambridge: Cambridge University Press.

Iahn, Otto. 1893. *A Persii Flacci, D. Iunii Iuvenalis, Sulpiciae Saturae*. 3rd ed. Rev. by Franciscus Buecheler. Berlin: Weidmann.

Joshel, Sandra R. 1992. *Work, Identity, and Legal Status at Rome: A Study of the Occupational Inscriptions*. Norman: University of Oklahoma Press.

Kaster, Robert. 1997. "The Shame of the Romans." *Transactions of the American Philological Association* 127: 2–19.

Kiessling, Adolf, and Richard Heinze. 1999. *Q. Horatius Flaccus: Satiren*. Zurich: Weidmann. Original 1921.

Kissel, Walter. 1990. *Aulus Persius Flaccus Satiren*. Heidelberg: Carl Winter Universitätsverlag.

Knoche, Ulrich. 1975. *Roman Satire*. Trans. by Edwin S. Ramage. Bloomington: Indiana University Press.

Köhne, Eckart and Cornelia Ewigleben. 2000. *Gladiators and Caesars: The Power of Spectacle in Ancient Rome*. English version ed. by Ralph Jackson. Berkeley: University of California Press.

Krenkel, Werner. 1970. *Lucilius: Satiren*. Two vols. Leiden: Brill.

Krüger, Gustav. 1911. *Horaz: Satiren*. Leipzig: Teubner.

Jenkinson, J. R. 1980. *Persius: The Satires*. Warminster: Aris and Phillips.

Johnson, Timothy. 2004. *A Symposion of Praise: Horace Returns to Lyric in Odes IV*. Madison: University of Wisconsin Press.

Labriolle, Pierre de and François Villeneuve. 1964.*Juvénal: Satires*. Rev. ed. Paris: Les Belles Lettres.

Lafleur, Richard A. 1981. "Horace and *Onomasti Komidein*: The Law of Satire." *Aufstieg und Niedergang der Römischen Welt*. Vol. 31.4. Ed. Wolfgang Haase. Berlin: De Gruyter: 1790–1826.

Lee, Guy and William Barr. 1987. *The Satires of Persius*. Liverpool: Francis Cairns.

Lejay, Paul. 1966. *Oeuvres d'Horace: Satires*. Hildesheim, Olms. Original Paris, 1911.

Lombardo, Stanley and Diane Rayor, trans. 1988. *Callimachus: Hymns, Epigrams, Select Fragments*. Baltimore: Johns Hopkins University Press.

Martyn, J. R. C. 1979. "Juvenal's Wit." *Grazer Beitrage* 8: 214–38.

Marx, Fredericus. 1963. *C. Lucilii Carminum Reliquiae*. 2 vols. Amsterdam: Hakkert. Original 1904.

Miller, Paul Allen. 1994. *Lyric Texts and Lyric Consciousness: The Birth of a Genre From Archaic Greece to Augustan Rome*. London: Routledge.

—— 1998. "Images of Sterility: The Bodily Grotesque in Roman Satire." *Arethusa* 31: 257–83.

—— 2001. "The Otherness of History in Rabelais' Carnival and Juvenal's Satire or Why Bakhtin Got It Right the First Time." In Peter I. Barta, Paul Allen Miller. Charles Platter and David Shepherd (eds) *Carnivalizing Difference: Bakhtin and the Other*. Routledge: 141–63.

—— 2004. *Subjecting Verses: Latin Love Elegy and the Emergence of the Real*. Princeton: Princeton University Press.

Morris, Edward P. 1968. *Horace: the Satires*. Norman: University of Oklahoma Press. Original 1939.

Muecke, Frances. 1997. *Horace: Satires II*. Warminster: Aris and Phillips.

Nagy, Gregory. 1979. *The Best of the Achaeans: Concepts of the Hero in Archaic Greek Poetry*, Baltimore: Johns Hopkins University Press.

Oliensis, Ellen. 1998. *Horace and the Rhetoric of Authority*. Cambridge: Cambridge University Press.

Parker, Holt N. 1997. "The Teratogenic Grid." In Judith Hallett and Marilyn B. Skinner (eds). *Roman Sexualities*. Princeton: Princeton University Press: 47–65.

Page, D. L. 1975. *Epigrammata Graeca*. Oxford: Oxford University Press.

Pearson, C. H. and Herbert A. Strong. 1892. *Thirteen Satires of Juvenal*. 2nd ed. Oxford: Clarendon Press.

Piwonka, Puelma. 1978. *Lucilius und Kallimachos*. New York: Garland. Original 1949.

Ramage, Edwin S., David L. Sigsbee, and Sigmund C. Fredricks, eds. 1974. *Roman Satirists and their Satire: The Fine Art of Criticism in Ancient Rome*. Park Ridge, NJ: Noyes Press.

Richlin, Amy. 1984. "Invective against Women in Roman Satire." *Arethusa* 17: 67–80.

—— 1986. *Juvenal: Satura VI*. Bryn Mawr: Thomas Library, Bryn Mawr College.

—— 1992. *The Garden of Priapus: Sexuality and Aggression in Roman Humor*. Rev. ed. Oxford: Oxford University Press. Original 1983.

Rolfe, John C. 1962. *Satires and Epistles*. In *Horace: The Complete Works*. Boston: Allyn and Bacon. Original 1935.

Roller, Matthew B. 2001. *Constructing Autocracy: Aristocrats and Emperors in Julio-Claudian Rome*. Princeton: Princeton University Press.

Rudd, Niall. 1982. *The Satires of Horace*. Berkeley: University of California Press. Original 1966.

Rudd, Niall and William Barr. 1991. *Juvenal: The Satires*. Oxford: Oxford University Press.

Spencer, W. G., ed. and trans. 1935. *Celsus: De Medicina*. Cambridge, MA: Harvard University Press.

Ste Croix, G. E. M. de. 1981. *The Class Struggle in the Ancient Greek World: From the Archaic Age to the Arab Conquests*. Ithaca: Cornell University Press.

Syme, Ronald. 1960. *The Roman Revolution*. Oxford: Oxford University Press. Original 1939.

—— 1978. *History in Ovid*. Oxford: Clarendon Press.

Vahlen, Iohannes. 1967. *Ennianae Poesis Reliquae*. Amsterdam: Hakkert. Original 1928.

Walters, Jonathan. 1997. "Invading the Roman Body: Manliness and Impenetrability in Roman Thought." In Judith P. Hallett and Marilyn B. Skinner (eds) *Roman Sexualities*. Princeton: Princeton University Press: 29–43.

Warmington, E. H. 1979. *The Remains of Old Latin*. 2nd ed. 3 vols. Cambridge, MA: Harvard University Press.

White, Peter. 1993. *Promised Verse: Poets in the Society of Augustan Rome*. Cambridge, MA: Harvard University Press.

Wickham, Edward C. 1912. *Q. Horati Flacci Opera*. 2nd ed. rev. by H. W. Garrod. Oxford: Oxford University Press.

Willis, James, 1997. *Iuvenalis Saturae*. Stuttgart: Teubner.

Winkler, Martin M. 1983. *The Persona in Three Satires of Juvenal*. Hildesheim: Olms.

Wiseman, T. P. 1985. *Catullus and His World*. Cambridge: Cambridge University Press.

Wirszubski, C. 1950. *Libertas as a Political Idea at Rome during the Late Republic and Early Principate*. Cambridge: Cambridge University Press.

TEXTS

ENNIUS

7

malo hercle magno suo convivat sine modo.

15

quippe sine cura laetus lautus cum advenis,
infestis malis, expedito bracchio,
alacer celsus, lupino expectans impetu,
mox alterius abligurris cum bona,
quid censes domino esse animi? pro divum fidem,
ill' tristist dum cibum servat, tu ridens voras.

18

nam qui lepide postulat alterum frustrari,
quem frustratur, frustra eum dicit frustra esse;
nam si sese frustrari quem frustra sentit,
qui frustratur is frustrast, si non ille est frustra.

LUCILIUS

26.1.589–94

nunc itidem populo <placere nolo> his cum scriptoribus:
voluimus capere animum illorum – ᵕ – ᵕ –
– ᵕ – ᵕ – ᵕ – <ab indoctissimis>
nec doctissimis <legi me>; Man<ium Manil>ium
Persium<ve> haec legere nolo, Iunium Congum volo

Laelium Decumum volo.

26.1.626–7

– ᵕ – ᵕ – ᵕ – ᵕ ego ubi quem ex praecordiis
ecfero versum ᵕ – ᵕ – ᵕ – ᵕ – ᵕ –

30.2.1007–11

aut cum iter est aliquo et causam commenta viai
aut apud aurificem, ad matrem, cognatam, ad amicam

aut operatum aliquo in celebri cum aequalibus fano

lana, opus omne perit: pallor, triniae omnia caedunt

iuratam se uni, cui sit data deque dicata

30.3.1023–5

multis indu locis sermonibus concelebrarunt

quae quondam populo risu res pectora rumpit

calvus Palantino quidam vir non bonus bello

30.3.1051–2

pulmentaria, ut intubus aut aliquae id genus herba,
et ius maenarum. '–, bene habet se: mictyris haec est'

3.98–118

tu partem laudis caperes, tu gaudia mecum
partisses ˘ ˘ – ˘ ˘ – ˘ ˘ – ˘ ˘ – ˘

– ˘ ˘ – ˘ ˘ – ˘ ˘ – ˘ ˘ – ˘ viamque
degrumabis, uti castris mensor facit olim

– ˘ ˘ – ˘ ˘ bis quina octogena videbis
conmoda te, Capua quinquaginta atque ducenta

– ˘ ˘ – ˘ ˘ – ˘ ˘ – et saepe quod ante
optasti, freta, Messanam, Regina videbis
moenia, tum Liparas, Facelinae templa Dianae

praeterea omne iter est hoc labosum atque lutosum

verum haec ludus ibi, susque omnia deque fuerunt,
susque et deque fuere, inquam, omnia ludus iocusque:
illud opus durum, ut Setinum accessimus finem,
αἰγίλιποι montes, Aetnae omnes, asperi Athones

<Volturnus Capua> longe tria milia passu[u]m

Symmacus praeterea iam tum depostus bubulcus
exspirans animam, pulmonibus aeger, agebat

– ˘ ˘ et spatium curando corpori honestum
sumemus ˘ ˘ – ˘ ˘ – ˘ ˘ – ˘ ˘ – ˘

broncus Novlitanus: dente adverso eminulo hic est
rinoceros velut Aethiopus ˘ ˘ – ˘ ˘ – ˘

7.266–67, 280

rador, subvellor, desquamor, pumicor, ornor,
expolior, pingor ˘ ˘ – ˘ ˘ – ˘ ˘ – ˘

hunc molere, illam autem ut frumentum vannere lumbis

8.302–8

cum poclo bibo eodem, amplector, labra labellis
fictricis conpono, hoc est cum ψωλοκοποῦμαι

tum latus conponit lateri et cum pectore pectus

‾ et cruribus crura diallaxon ⏑ ⏑ – ⏑

– ⏑ ⏑ – ⏑ ⏑ – ⏑ ⏑ – ⏑ ⏑ – ⏑ ⏑ <fusus> 306–306a
intus modo stet rectus, foris subteminis panus

lentet opus ⏑ ⏑ – ⏑ ⏑ – ⏑ ⏑ – ⏑ ⏑ – ⏑

at laeva lacrimas muttoni absterget amica

11.422–4

Quintus Opimius ille, Iugurtini pater huius,
et formosus homo fuit et famosus, utrumque
primo adulescens; posterius dare rectius sese

1342–54

virtus, Albine, est, pretium persolvere verum
quis in versamur, quis vivimus rebus, potesse,
virtus est homini scire id quod quaeque habeat res,
virtus, scire, homini rectum, utile quid sit, honestum,
quae bona, quae mala item, quid inutile, turpe, inhonestum,
virtus, quaerendae finem re scire modumque,
virtus, divitiis pretium persolvere posse,
virtus, id dare quod re ipsa debetur honori,
hostem esse atque inimicum hominum morumque malorum,
contra defensorem hominum morumque bonorum,
hos magni facere, his bene velle, his vivere amicum,
commoda praeterea patriai prima putare,
deinde parentum, tertia iam postremaque nostra.

HORACE

1.2

Ambubaiarum collegia, pharmacopolae,
mendici, mimae, balatrones, hoc genus omne
maestum ac sollicitum est cantoris morte Tigelli.
quippe benignus erat. contra hic, ne prodigus esse
dicatur metuens, inopi dare nolit amico,
frigus quo duramque famem propellere possit.
hunc si perconteris, avi cur atque parentis
praeclaram ingrata stringat malus ingluvie rem,
omnia conductis coemens obsonia nummis,
sordidus atque animi quod parvi nolit haberi,
respondet. laudatur ab his, culpatur ab illis.
Fufidius vappae famam timet ac nebulonis,
dives agris, dives positis in faenore nummis:
quinas hic capiti mercedes exsecat atque
quanto perditior quisque est tanto acrius urget;
nomina sectatur modo sumpta veste virili
sub patribus duris tironum. 'maxime' quis non
'Iuppiter!' exclamat simul atque audivit? 'at in se
pro quaestu sumptum facit hic.' vix credere possis
quam sibi non sit amicus, ita ut pater ille, Terenti
fabula quem miserum gnato vixisse fugato
inducit, non se peius cruciaverit atque hic.
siquis nunc quaerat 'quo res haec pertinet?' illuc:
dum vitant stulti vitia, in contraria currunt.
Maltinus tunicis demissis ambulat; est qui
inguen ad obscenum subductis usque; facetus
pastillos Rufillus olet, Gargonius hircum.
nil medium est. sunt qui nolint tetigisse nisi illas
quarum subsuta talos tegat instita veste;
contra alius nullam nisi olenti in fornice stantem.

quidam notus homo cum exiret fornice, 'macte
virtute esto' inquit sententia dia Catonis,
'nam simul ac venas inflavit taetra libido,
huc iuvenes aequum est descendere, non alienas
permolere uxores.' 'nolim laudarier' inquit
'sic me' mirator cunni Cupiennius albi.
audire est operae pretium, procedere recte
qui moechis non vultis, ut omni parte laborent,
utque illis multo corrupta dolore voluptas
atque haec rara cadat dura inter saepe pericla.
hic se praecipitem tecto dedit; ille flagellis
ad mortem caesus; fugiens hic decidit acrem
praedonum in turbam; dedit hic pro corpore nummos;
hunc perminxerunt calones; quin etiam illud
accidit, ut quidam testis caudamque salacem
demeteret ferro. 'iure' omnes; Galba negabat.
tutior at quanto merx est in classe secunda,
libertinarum dico, Sallustius in quas
non minus insanit quam qui moechatur. at hic si
qua res, qua ratio suaderet, quaque modeste
munifico esse licet, vellet bonus atque benignus
esse, daret quantum satis esset nec sibi damno
dedecorique foret. verum hoc se amplectitur uno,
hoc amat et laudat: 'matronam nullam ego tango.'
ut quondam Marsaeus, amator Originis ille,
qui patrium mimae donat fundumque laremque,
'nil fuerit mi' inquit 'cum uxoribus umquam alienis.'
verum est cum mimis, est cum meretricibus, unde
fama malum gravius quam res trahit. an tibi abunde
personam satis est, non illud quidquid ubique
officit, evitare? bonam deperdere famam,
rem patris oblimare, malum est ubicumque. quid inter
est in matrona, ancilla peccesne togata?
Villius in Fausta Sullae gener, hoc miser uno
nomine deceptus, poenas dedit usque superque
quam satis est, pugnis caesus ferroque petitus,
exclusus fore cum Longarenus foret intus.
huic si mutonis verbis mala tanta videnti
diceret haec animus: 'quid vis tibi? numquid ego a te
magno prognatum deposco consule cunnum
velatumque stola mea cum conferbuit ira?'
quid responderet? 'magno patre nata puella est.'
at quanto meliora monet pugnantiaque istis
dives opis natura suae, tu si modo recte

dispensare velis ac non fugienda petendis
immiscere. tuo vitio rerumne labores
nil referre putas? quare, ne paeniteat te,
desine matronas sectarier, unde laboris
plus haurire mali est quam ex re decerpere fructus.
nec magis huic inter niveos viridisque lapillos—
sit licet hoc, Cerinthe, tuum—tenerum est femur aut crus
rectius, atque etiam melius persaepe togatae est.
adde huc quod mercem sine fucis gestat, aperte
quod venale habet ostendit, nec siquid honesti est,
iactat habetque palam, quaerit quo turpia celet.
regibus hic mos est: ubi equos mercantur opertos
inspiciunt, ne si facies, ut saepe, decora
molli fulta pede est emptorem inducat hiantem,
quod pulcrae clunes, breve quod caput, ardua cervix.
hoc illi recte: ne corporis optima Lyncei
contemplere oculis, Hypsaea caecior illa
quae mala sunt spectes. 'o crus! o bracchia!' verum
depugis, nasuta, brevi latere ac pede longo est.
matronae praeter faciem nil cernere possis,
cetera, ni Catia est, demissa veste tegentis.
si interdicta petes, vallo circumdata—nam te
hoc facit insanum,—multae tibi tum officient res,
custodes, lectica, ciniflones, parasitae,
ad talos stola demissa et circumdata palla,
plurima, quae invideant pure apparere tibi rem.
altera, nil obstat: Cois tibi paene videre est
ut nudam, ne crure malo, ne sit pede turpi;
metiri possis oculo latus. an tibi mavis
insidias fieri pretiumque avellier ante
quam mercem ostendi? 'leporem venator ut alta
in nive sectetur, positum sic tangere nolit'
cantat, et apponit 'meus est amor huic similis; nam
transvolat in medio posita et fugientia captat.'
hiscine versiculis speras tibi posse dolores
atque aestus curasque gravis e pectore pelli?
nonne, cupidinibus statuat natura modum quem,
quid latura sibi quid sit dolitura negatum,
quaerere plus prodest et inane abscindere soldo?
num tibi cum fauces urit sitis, aurea quaeris
pocula? num esuriens fastidis omnia praeter
pavonem rhombumque? tument tibi cum inguina, num si
ancilla aut verna est praesto puer, impetus in quem
continuo fiat, malis tentigine rumpi?

non ego: namque parabilem amo venerem facilemque.
illam 'post paulo: sed pluris: si exierit vir'
Gallis, hanc Philodemus ait sibi quae neque magno
stet pretio neque cunctetur cum est iussa venire.
candida rectaque sit; munda hactenus ut neque longa
nec magis alba velit quam dat natura videri.
haec ubi supposuit dextro corpus mihi laevum
Ilia et Egeria est: do nomen quodlibet illi,
nec vereor ne dum futuo vir rure recurrat,
ianua frangatur, latret canis, undique magno
pulsa domus strepitu resonet, vae pallida lecto
desiliat mulier, miseram se conscia clamet,
cruribus haec metuat, doti deprensa, egomet mi.
discincta tunica fugiendum est ac pede nudo,
ne nummi pereant aut puga aut denique fama.
deprendi miserum est; Fabio vel iudice vincam.

1.4

Eupolis atque Cratinus Aristophanesque poetae,
atque alii, quorum comoedia prisca virorum est,
si quis erat dignus describi quod malus ac fur,
quod moechus foret aut sicarius aut alioqui
famosus, multa cum libertate notabant.
hinc omnis pendet Lucilius, hosce secutus
mutatis tantum pedibus numerisque; facetus,
emunctae naris, durus componere versus:
nam fuit hoc vitiosus: in hora saepe ducentos,
ut magnum, versus dictabat stans pede in uno:
cum flueret lutulentus, erat quod tollere velles:
garrulus atque piger scribendi ferre laborem,
scribendi recte: nam ut multum, nil moror. ecce
Crispinus minimo me provocat: 'accipe, si vis,
accipe iam tabulas; detur nobis locus, hora,
custodes; videamus uter plus scribere possit.'
di bene fecerunt inopis me quodque pusilli
finxerunt animi, raro et perpauca loquentis:
at tu conclusas hircinis follibus auras,
usque laborantis dum ferrum molliat ignis,
ut mavis imitare. beatus Fannius ultro
delatis capsis et imagine, cum mea nemo
scripta legat, vulgo recitare timentis ob hanc rem,
quod sunt quos genus hoc minime iuvat, utpote pluris
culpari dignos. quemvis media elige turba:

aut ob avaritiam aut misera ambitione laborat:
hic nuptarum insanit amoribus, hic puerorum;
hunc capit argenti splendor; stupet Albius aere;
hic mutat merces surgente a sole ad eum quo
vespertina tepet regio, quin per mala praeceps
fertur uti pulvis collectus turbine, ne quid
summa deperdat metuens aut ampliet ut rem:
omnes hi metuunt versus, odere poetas.
'faenum habet in cornu; longe fuge: dummodo risum
excutiat sibi, hic non cuiquam parcet amico;
et quodcumque semel chartis illeverit, omnis
gestiet a furno redeuntis scire lacuque,
et pueros et anus.' agedum, pauca accipe contra.
primum ego me illorum dederim quibus esse poetas
excerpam numero: neque enim concludere versum
dixeris esse satis; neque si qui scribat uti nos
sermoni propiora, putes hunc esse poetam,
ingenium cui sit, cui mens divinior atque os
magna sonaturum, des nominis huius honorem.
idcirco quidam comoedia necne poema
esset quaesivere, quod acer spiritus ac vis
nec verbis nec rebus inest, nisi quod pede certo
differt sermoni, sermo merus. 'at pater ardens
saevit, quod meretrice nepos insanus amica
filius uxorem grandi cum dote recuset,
ebrius et, magnum quod dedecus, ambulet ante
noctem cum facibus.' numquid Pomponius istis
audiret leviora, pater si viveret? ergo
non satis est puris versum perscribere verbis,
quem si dissolvas, quivis stomachetur eodem
quo personatus pacto pater. his, ego quae nunc,
olim quae scripsit Lucilius, eripias si
tempora certa modosque, et quod prius ordine verbum est
posterius facias, praeponens ultima primis,
non, ut si solvas 'postquam Discordia taetra
Belli ferratos postis portasque refregit,'
invenias etiam disiecti membra poetae.
hactenus haec: alias iustum sit necne poema,
nunc illud tantum quaeram, meritone tibi sit
suspectum genus hoc scribendi. Sulcius acer
ambulat et Caprius, rauci male cumque libellis,
magnus uterque timor latronibus; at bene si quis
et vivat puris manibus contemnat utrumque.
ut sis tu similis Caeli Birrique latronum,

non ego sim Capri neque Sulci; cur metuas me?
nulla taberna meos habeat neque pila libellos,
quis manus insudet vulgi Hermogenisque Tigelli.
nec recito cuiquam nisi amicis, idque coactus,
non ubivis coramve quibuslibet. in medio qui
scripta foro recitent sunt multi quique lavantes:
suave locus voci resonat conclusus. inanis
hoc iuvat, haud illud quaerentis, num sine sensu,
tempore num faciant alieno. 'laedere gaudes'
inquit, 'et hoc studio pravus facis.' unde petitum
hoc in me iacis? est auctor quis denique eorum
vixi cum quibus? absentem qui rodit amicum,
qui non defendit alio culpante, solutos
qui captat risus hominum famamque dicacis,
fingere qui non visa potest, conmissa tacere
qui nequit, hic niger est, hunc tu, Romane, caveto.
saepe tribus lectis videas cenare quaternos,
e quibus unus amet quavis aspergere cunctos
praeter eum qui praebet aquam; post hunc quoque potus,
condita cum verax aperit praecordia Liber.
hic tibi comis et urbanus liberque videtur,
infesto nigris. ego si risi quod ineptus
pastillos Rufillus olet, Gorgonius hircum,
lividus et mordax videor tibi? mentio si quae
de Capitolini furtis iniecta Petilli
te coram fuerit, defendas ut tuus est mos:
'me Capitolinus convictore usus amicoque
a puero est, causaque mea permulta rogatus
fecit, et incolumis laetor quod vivit in urbe;
sed tamen admiror, quo pacto iudicium illud
fugerit.' hic nigrae sucus lolliginis, haec est
aerugo mera: quod vitium procul afore chartis
atque animo, prius ut, si quid promittere de me
possum aliud vere, promitto. liberius si
dixero quid, si forte iocosius, hoc mihi iuris
cum venia dabis: insuevit pater optimus hoc me,
ut fugerem exemplis vitiorum quaeque notando.
cum me hortaretur, parce, frugaliter, atque
viverem uti contentus eo quod mi ipse parasset,
'nonne vides Albi ut male vivat filius, utque
Baius inops? magnum documentum ne patriam rem
perdere quis velit': a turpi meretricis amore
cum deterreret, 'Scetani dissimilis sis':
ne sequerer moechas concessa cum venere uti

possem, 'deprensi non bella est fama Treboni'
aiebat: 'sapiens, vitatu quidque petitu
sit melius, causas reddet tibi: mi satis est si
traditum ab antiquis morem servare tuamque,
dum custodis eges, vitam famamque tueri
incolumem possum; simul ac duraverit aetas
membra animumque tuum, nabis sine cortice.' sic me
formabat puerum dictis; et sive iubebat
ut facerem quid, 'habes auctorem quo facias hoc';
unum ex iudicibus selectis obiciebat;
sive vetabat, 'an hoc inhonestum et inutile factu
necne sit addubites, flagret rumore malo cum
hic atque ille?' avidos vicinum funus ut aegros
exanimat mortisque metu sibi parcere cogit,
sic teneros animos aliena opprobria saepe
absterrent vitiis. ex hoc ego sanus ab illis,
perniciem quaecumque ferunt, mediocribus et quis
ignoscas vitiis teneor. fortassis et istinc
largiter abstulerit longa aetas, liber amicus,
consilium proprium: neque enim, cum lectulus aut me
porticus excepit, desum mihi: 'rectius hoc est:
hoc faciens vivam melius: sic dulcis amicis
occurram: hoc quidam non belle; numquid ego illi
imprudens olim faciam simile?' haec ego mecum
compressis agito labris; ubi quid datur oti
illudo chartis. hoc est mediocribus illis
ex vitiis unum; cui si concedere nolis,
multa poetarum veniat manus auxilio quae
sit mihi (nam multo plures sumus), ac veluti te
Iudaei cogemus in hanc concedere turbam.

1.5

Egressum magna me accepit Aricia Roma
hospitio modico: rhetor comes Heliodorus,
Graecorum longe doctissimus; inde Forum Appi,
differtum nautis, cauponibus atque malignis.
hoc iter ignavi divisimus, altius ac nos
praecinctis unum: minus est gravis Appia tardis.
hic ego propter aquam, quod erat deterrima, ventri
indico bellum, cenantis haud animo aequo
exspectans comites. iam nox inducere terris
umbras et caelo diffundere signa parabat.
tum pueri nautis, pueris convicia nautae

ingerere. 'huc appelle!' 'trecentos inseris: ohe
iam satis est!' dum aes exigitur, dum mula ligatur,
tota abit hora. mali culices ranaeque palustres
avertunt somnos, absentem ut cantat amicam
multa prolutus vappa nauta atque viator
certatim: tandem fessus dormire viator
incipit, ac missae pastum retinacula mulae
nauta piger saxo religat stertitque supinus.
iamque dies aderat, nil cum procedere lintrem
sentimus, donec cerebrosus prosilit unus
ac mulae nautaeque caput lumbosque saligno
fuste dolat. quarta vix demum exponimur hora.
ora manusque tua lavimus, Feronia, lympha.
milia tum pransi tria repimus atque subimus
impositum saxis late candentibus Anxur.
huc venturus erat Maecenas optimus atque
Cocceius, missi magnis de rebus uterque
legati, aversos soliti componere amicos.
hic oculis ego nigra meis collyria lippus
illinere. interea Maecenas advenit atque
Cocceius Capitoque simul Fonteius, ad unguem
factus homo, Antoni non ut magis alter amicus.
Fundos Aufidio Lusco praetore libenter
linquimus, insani ridentes praemia scribae:
praetextam et latum clavum prunaeque vatillum.
in Mamurrarum lassi deinde urbe manemus,
Murena praebente domum, Capitone culinam.
postera lux oritur multo gratissima; namque
Plotius et Varius Sinuessae Vergiliusque
occurrunt, animae qualis neque candidiores
terra tulit neque quis me sit devinctior alter.
o qui complexus et gaudia quanta fuerunt!
nil ego contulerim iucundo sanus amico.
proxima Campano ponti quae villula, tectum
praebuit, et parochi quae debent ligna salemque.
hinc muli Capuae clitellas tempore ponunt.
lusum it Maecenas, dormitum ego Vergiliusque;
namque pila lippis inimicum et ludere crudis.
hinc nos Coccei recipit plenissima villa,
quae super est Caudi cauponas. nunc mihi paucis
Sarmenti scurrae pugnam Messique Cicerri,
Musa, velim memores, et quo patre natus uterque
contulerit litis. Messi clarum genus Osci;
Sarmenti domina exstat: ab his maioribus orti

ad pugnam venere. prior Sarmentus: 'equi te
esse feri similem dico.' ridemus, et ipse
Messius 'accipio,' caput et movet. 'o, tua cornu
ni foret exsecto frons,' inquit, 'quid faceres, cum
sic mutilus minitaris?' at illi foeda cicatrix
saetosam laevi frontem turpaverat oris.
Campanum in morbum, in faciem permulta iocatus,
pastorem saltaret uti Cyclopa rogabat:
nil illi larva aut tragicis opus esse cothurnis.
multa Cicirrus ad haec: donasset iamne catenam
ex voto Laribus, quaerebat; scriba quod esset,
nilo deterius dominae ius esse. rogabat
denique cur umquam fugisset, cui satis una
farris libra foret, gracili sic tamque pusillo.
prorsus iucunde cenam producimus illam.
tendimus hinc recta Beneventum; ubi sedulus hospes
paene macros arsit dum turdos versat in igni:
nam vaga per veterem dilapso flamma culinam
Vulcano summum properabat lambere tectum.
convivas avidos cenam servosque timentis
tum rapere, atque omnis restinguere velle videres.
incipit ex illo montis Apulia notos
ostentare mihi, quos torret Atabulus et quos
numquam erepsemus, nisi nos vicina Trivici
villa recepisset lacrimoso non sine fumo,
udos cum foliis ramos urente camino.
hic ego mendacem stultissimus usque puellam
ad mediam noctem exspecto: somnus tamen aufert
intentum Veneri; tum inmundo somnia visu
nocturnam vestem maculant ventremque supinum.
quattuor hinc rapimur viginti et milia raedis,
mansuri oppidulo quod versu dicere non est,
signis perfacile est: venit vilissima rerum
hic aqua; sed panis longe pulcherrimus, ultra
callidus ut soleat umeris portare viator;
nam Canusi lapidosus, aquae non ditior urna
qui locus a forti Diomede est conditus olim.
flentibus hinc Varius discedit maestus amicis.
inde Rubos fessi pervenimus, utpote longum
carpentes iter et factum corruptius imbri.
postera tempestas melior, via peior adusque
Bari moenia piscosi; dein Gnatia Lymphis
iratis exstructa dedit risusque iocosque,
dum flamma sine tura liquescere limine sacro

persuadere cupit. credat Iudaeus Apella,
non ego: namque deos didici securum agere aevum,
nec, siquid miri faciat natura, deos id
tristis ex alto caeli demittere tecto.
Brundisium longae finis chartaeque viaeque est.

1.6

Non quia, Maecenas, Lydorum quidquid Etruscos
incoluit finis, nemo generosior est te,
nec quod avus tibi maternus fuit atque paternus
olim qui magnis legionibus imperitarent,
ut plerique solent, naso suspendis adunco
ignotos, ut me libertino patre natum.
cum referre negas quali sit quisque parente
natus, dum ingenuus, persuades hoc tibi vere:
ante potestatem Tulli atque ignobile regnum
multos saepe viros nullis maioribus ortos
et vixisse probos, amplis et honoribus auctos;
contra Laevinum, Valeri genus unde superbus
Tarquinius regno pulsus fugit, unius assis
non umquam pretio pluris licuisse, notante
iudice quo nosti populo, qui stultus honores
saepe dat indignis et famae servit ineptus,
qui stupet in titulis et imaginibus. quid oportet
nos facere a vulgo longe longeque remotos?
namque esto populus Laevino mallet honorem
quam Decio mandare novo, censorque moveret
Appius, ingenuo si non essem patre natu;,
vel merito, quoniam in propria non pelle quiessem.
sed fulgente trahit constrictos Gloria curru
non minus ignotos generosis. quo tibi, Tilli,
sumere depositum clavum fierique tribuno?
invidia accrevit, privato quae minor esset.
nam ut quisque insanus nigris medium impediit crus
pellibus et latum demisit pectore clavum,
audit continuo 'quis homo hic est? quo patre natus?'
ut siqui aegrotet quo morbo Barrus, haberi
et cupiat formosus, eat quacumque puellis
iniciat curam quaerendi singula, quali
sit facie, sura, quali pede, dente, capillo:
sic qui promittit civis, urbem sibi curae,
imperium fore et Italiam, delubra deorum,
quo patre sit natus, num ignota matre inhonestus,

omnis mortalis curare et quaerere cogit.
'tune Syri, Damae, aut Dionysi filius, audes
deicere de saxo civis aut tradere Cadmo?'
'at Novius collega gradu post me sedet uno;
namque est ille, pater quod erat meus.' 'hoc tibi Paulus
et Messalla videris? at hic, si plaustra ducenta
concurrantque foro tria funera magna sonabit
cornua quod vincatque tubas; saltem tenet hoc nos.'
nunc ad me redeo libertino patre natum,
quem rodunt omnes libertino patre natum,
nunc quia sim tibi, Maecenas, convictor; at olim
quod mihi pareret legio Romana tribuno.
dissimile hoc illi est; quia non, ut forsit honorem
iure mihi invideat quivis, ita te quoque amicum,
praesertim cautum dignos adsumere, prava
ambitione procul. felicem dicere non hoc
me possim, casu quod te sortitus amicum;
nulla etenim mihi te fors obtulit: optimus olim
Vergilius, post hunc Varius, dixere quid essem.
ut veni coram, singultim pauca locutus,
infans namque pudor prohibebat plura profari,
non ego me claro natum patre, non ego circum
me Satureiano vectari rura caballo,
sed quod eram narro. respondes, ut tuus est mos,
pauca: abeo; et revocas nono post mense iubesque
esse in amicorum numero. magnum hoc ego duco
quod placui tibi, qui turpi secernis honestum,
non patre praeclaro, sed vita et pectore puro.
atqui si vitiis mediocribus ac mea paucis
mendosa est natura alioqui recta, velut si
egregio inspersos reprehendas corpore naevos;
si neque avaritiam neque sordis nec mala lustra
obiciet vere quisquam mihi, purus et insons
(ut me collaudem) si et vivo carus amicis;
causa fuit pater his, qui macro pauper agello
noluit in Flavi ludum me mittere, magni
quo pueri magnis e centurionibus orti,
laevo suspensi loculos tabulamque lacerto,
ibant octonos referentes Idibus aeris:
sed puerum est ausus Romam portare, docendum
artis quas doceat quivis eques atque senator
semet prognatos. vestem servosque sequentis,
in magno ut populo, si qui vidisset, avita
ex re praeberi sumptus mihi crederet illos.

ipse mihi custos incorruptissimus omnes
circum doctores aderat. quid multa? pudicum,
qui primus virtutis honos, servavit ab omni
non solum facto, verum opprobrio quoque turpi;
nec timuit sibi ne vitio quis verteret olim
si praeco parvas aut, ut fuit ipse, coactor
mercedes sequerer; neque ego essem questus: at hoc nunc
laus illi debetur et a me gratia maior.
nil me paeniteat sanum patris huius, eoque
non, ut magna dolo factum negat esse suo pars,
quod non ingenuos habeat clarosque parentes,
sic me defendam. longe mea discrepat istis
et vox et ratio: nam si natura iuberet
a certis annis aevum remeare peractum
atque alios legere ad fastum quoscumque parentis,
optaret sibi quisque, meis contentus honestos
fascibus et sellis nollem mihi sumere, demens
iudicio vulgi, sanus fortasse tuo, quod
nollem onus haud umquam solitus portare molestum.
nam mihi continuo maior quaerenda foret res,
atque salutandi plures, ducendus et unus
et comes alter uti ne solus rusve peregreve
exirem; plures calones atque caballi
pascendi, ducenda petorrita. nunc mihi curto
ire licet mulo vel si libet usque Tarentum,
mantica cui lumbos onere ulceret atque eques armos:
obiciet nemo sordis mihi quas tibi, Tilli,
cum Tiburte via praetorem quinque sequuntur
te pueri lasanum portantes oenophorumque.
hoc ego commodius quam tu, praeclare senator,
milibus atque aliis vivo. quacumque libido est,
incedo solus; percontor quanti holus ac far;
fallacem Circum vespertinumque pererro
saepe Forum; adsisto divinis; inde domum me
ad porri et ciceris refero laganique catinum;
cena ministratur pueris tribus, et lapis albus
pocula cum cyatho duo sustinet; adstat echinus
vilis, cum patera gutus, Campana supellex.
deinde eo dormitum, non sollicitus, mihi quod cras
surgendum sit mane, obeundus Marsya, qui se
vultum ferre negat Noviorum posse minoris.
ad quartam iaceo; post hanc vagor, aut ego lecto
aut scripto quod me tacitum iuvet, unguor olivo,
non quo fraudatis inmundus Natta lucernis.

ast ubi me fessum sol acrior ire lavatum
admonuit, fugio Campum lusumque trigonem.
pransus non avide, quantum interpellet inani
ventre diem durare, domesticus otior. haec est
vita solutorum misera ambitione gravique;
his me consolor victurum suavius ac si
quaestor avus pater atque meus patruusque fuisset.

1.9

Ibam forte via Sacra, sicut meus est mos,
nescio quid meditans nugarum, totus in illis.
accurrit quidam notus mihi nomine tantum,
arreptaque manu, 'quid agis, dulcissime rerum?'
'suaviter, ut nunc est,' inquam 'et cupio omnia quae vis.'
cum adsectaretur, 'num quid vis?' occupo. at ille
'noris nos' inquit; 'docti sumus.' hic ego 'pluris
hoc' inquam 'mihi eris.' misere discedere quaerens,
ire modo ocius, interdum consistere in aurem
dicere nescio quid puero, cum sudor ad imos
manaret talos. 'o te, Bolane, cerebri
felicem!' aiebam tacitus, cum quidlibet ille
garriret, vicos, urbem laudaret. ut illi
nil respondebam, 'misere cupis' inquit 'abire;
iamdudum video: sed nil agis; usque tenebo;
persequar hinc quo nunc iter est tibi.' 'nil opus est te
circumagi: quendam volo visere non tibi notum:
trans Tiberim longe cubat is, prope Caesaris hortos.'
'nil habeo quod agam et non sum piger: usque sequar te.'
demitto auriculas, ut iniquae mentis asellus,
cum gravius dorso subiit onus. incipit ille:
'si bene me novi non Viscum pluris amicum,
non Varium facies: nam quis me scribere pluris
aut citius possit versus? quis membra movere
mollius? invideat quod et Hermogenes ego canto.'
interpellandi locus hic erat: 'est tibi mater,
cognati, quis te salvo est opus?' 'haud mihi quisquam:
omnis composui.' 'felices! nunc ego resto.
confice; namque instat fatum mihi triste, Sabella
quod puero cecinit divina mota anus urna:
hunc neque dira venena nec hosticus auferet ensis,
nec laterum dolor aut tussis, nec tarda podagra;
garrulus hunc quando consumet cumque: loquaces,
si sapiat, vitet, simul atque adoleverit aetas.'

ventum erat ad Vestae, quarta iam parte diei
praeterita, et casu tum respondere vadato
debebat; quod ni fecisset, perdere litem.
'si me amas' inquit 'paulum hic ades.' 'inteream si
aut valeo stare aut novi civilia iura;
et propero quo scis.' 'dubius sum quid faciam' inquit,
'tene relinquam an rem.' 'me, sodes.' 'non faciam' ille,
et praecedere coepit. ego, ut contendere durum est
cum victore, sequor. 'Maecenas quomodo tecum?'
hinc repetit. paucorum hominum et mentis bene sanae.
'nemo dexterius fortuna est usus. haberes
magnum adiutorem, posset qui ferre secundas,
hunc hominem velles si tradere: dispeream, ni
summosses omnis.' 'non isto vivimus illic
quo tu rere modo; domus hac nec purior ulla est
nec magis his aliena malis; nil mi officit' inquam
'ditior hic aut est quia doctior; est locus uni
cuique suus.' 'magnum narras, vix credibile.' 'atqui
sic habet.' 'accendis quare cupiam magis illi
proximus esse.' 'velis tantummodo, quae tua virtus,
expugnabis; et est qui vinci possit, eoque
difficilis aditus primos habet.' 'haud mihi deero:
muneribus servos corrumpam; non, hodie si
exclusus fuero, desistam; tempora quaeram;
occurram in triviis; deducam. nil sine magno
vita labore dedit mortalibus.' haec dum agit, ecce
Fuscus Aristius occurrit, mihi carus et illum
qui pulchre nosset. consistimus. 'unde venis? et
quo tendis?' rogat et respondet. vellere coepi,
et pressare manu lentissima bracchia, nutans,
distorquens oculos, ut me eriperet. male salsus
ridens dissimulare: meum iecur urere bilis.
'certe nescio quid secreto velle loqui te
aiebas mecum.' 'memini bene, sed meliore
tempore dicam: hodie tricesima sabbata: vin tu
curtis Iudaeis oppedere?' 'nulla mihi' inquam
'religio est.' 'at mi: sum paulo infirmior, unus
multorum: ignosces: alias loquar.' huncine solem
tam nigrum surrexe mihi! fugit improbus ac me
sub cultro linquit. casu venit obvius illi
adversarius et 'quo tu turpissime?' magna
inclamat voce, et 'licet antestari?' ego vero
oppono auriculam. rapit in ius: clamor utrimque:
undique concursus. sic me servavit Apollo.

1.10

{Lucili, quam sis mendosus, teste Catone
defensore tuo, pervincam, qui male factos
emendare parat versus; hoc lenius ille,
quo melior vir et est longe subtilior illo,
qui multum puer et loris et funibus udis
exoratus, ut esset opem qui ferre poetis
antiquis posset contra fastidia nostra,
grammaticorum equitum doctissimus. ut redeam illuc:}
Nempe incomposito dixi pede currere versus
Lucili. quis tam Lucili fautor inepte est
ut non hoc fateatur? at idem, quod sale multo
urbem defricuit, charta laudatur eadem.
nec tamen hoc tribuens dederim quoque cetera: nam sic
et Laberi mimos ut pulchra poemata mirer.
ergo non satis est risu diducere rictum
auditoris: et est quaedam tamen hic quoque virtus:
est brevitate opus, ut currat sententia, neu se
impediat verbis lassas onerantibus auris;
et sermone opus est modo tristi, saepe iocoso,
defendente vicem modo rhetoris atque poetae,
interdum urbani, parcentis viribus atque
extenuantis eas consulto. ridiculum acri
fortius et melius magnas plerumque secat res.
illi scripta quibus comoedia prisca viris est
hoc stabant, hoc sunt imitandi: quos neque pulcher
Hermogenes umquam legit, neque simius iste
nil praeter Calvum et doctus cantare Catullum.
'at magnum fecit quod verbis Graeca Latinis
miscuit.' o seri studiorum quine putetis
difficile et mirum, Rhodio quod Pitholeonti
contigit? 'at sermo lingua concinnus utraque
suavior, ut Chio nota si commixta Falerni est.'
cum versus facias, te ipsum percontor, an et cum
dura tibi peragenda rei sit causa Petilli?
scilicet oblitus patriaeque patrisque Latini
cum Pedius causas exsudet Publicola atque
Corvinus, patriis intermiscere petita
verba foris malis, Canusini more bilinguis?
atque ego cum Graecos facerem, natus mare citra,
versiculos, vetuit me tali voce Quirinus,
post mediam noctem visus cum somnia vera,
'in silvam non ligna feras insanius ac si

magnas Graecorum malis implere catervas.'
turgidus Alpinus iugulat dum Memnona dumque
defingit Rheni luteum caput, haec ego ludo,
quae neque in aede sonent certantia iudice Tarpa,
nec redeant iterum atque iterum spectanda theatris.
arguta meretrice potes Davoque Chremeta
eludente senem comis garrire libellos
unus vivorum, Fundani; Pollio regum
facta canit pede ter percusso; forte epos acer
ut nemo Varius ducit; molle atque facetum
Vergilio adnuerunt gaudentes rure Camenae:
hoc erat, experto frustra Varrone Atacino
atque quibusdam aliis, melius quod scribere possem,
inventore minor; neque ego illi detrahere ausim
haerentem capiti cum multa laude coronam.
at dixi fluere hunc lutulentum, saepe ferentem
plura quidem tollenda relinquendis. age, quaeso,
tu nihil in magno doctus reprehendis Homero?
nil comis tragici mutat Lucilius Acci?
non ridet versus Enni gravitate minores,
cum de se loquitur non ut maiore reprensis?
quid vetat et nosmet Lucili scripta legentis
quaerere, num illius, num rerum dura negarit
versiculos natura magis factos et euntis
mollius, ac si quis pedibus quid claudere senis,
hoc tantum contentus, amet scripsisse ducentos
ante cibum versus, totidem cenatus, Etrusci
quale fuit Cassi rapido ferventius amni
ingenium, capsis quem fama est esse librisque
ambustum propriis? fuerit Lucilius, inquam,
comis et urbanus, fuerit limatior idem
quam rudis, et Graecis intacti carminis auctor,
quamque poetarum seniorum turba: sed ille,
si foret hoc nostrum fato dilatus in aevum,
detereret sibi multa, recideret omne quod ultra
perfectum traheretur, et in versu faciendo
saepe caput scaberet vivos et roderet unguis.
saepe stilum vertas, iterum quae digna legi sint
scripturus, neque te ut miretur turba labores,
contentus paucis lectoribus. an tua demens
vilibus in ludis dictari carmina malis?
non ego: nam satis est equitem mihi plaudere, ut audax
contemptis aliis explosa Arbuscula dixit.
men moveat cimex Pantilius, aut cruciet quod

vellicet absentem Demetrius, aut quod ineptus
Fannius Hermogenis laedat conviva Tigelli?
Plotius et Varius, Maecenas Vergiliusque,
Valgius, et probet haec Octavius, optimus atque
Fuscus, et haec utinam Viscorum laudet uterque!
ambitione relegata te dicere possum,
Pollio, te, Messalla, tuo cum fratre, simulque
vos, Bibule et Servi, simul his te, candide Furni,
compluris alios, doctos ego quos et amicos
prudens praetereo; quibus haec, sint qualiacumque,
arridere velim, doliturus, si placeant spe
deterius nostra. Demetri, teque, Tigelli,
discipularum inter iubeo plorare cathedras.
i, puer, atque meo citus haec subscribe libello.

2.1

Sunt quibus in satira videar nimis acer et ultra
legem tendere opus; sine nervis altera quidquid
composui pars esse putat, similisque meorum
mille die versus deduci posse. Trebati,
quid faciam praescribe. 'quiescas.' ne faciam, inquis,
omnino versus? 'aio.' peream male si non
optimum erat: verum nequeo dormire. 'ter uncti
transnanto Tiberim somno quibus est opus alto,
irriguumque mero sub noctem corpus habento.
aut si tantus amor scribendi te rapit, aude
Caesaris invicti res dicere, multa laborum
praemia laturus.' cupidum, pater optime, vires
deficiunt: neque enim quivis horrentia pilis
agmina nec fracta pereuntis cuspide Gallos
aut labentis equo describit vulnera Parthi.
'attamen et iustum poteras et scribere fortem,
Scipiadam ut sapiens Lucilius.' haud mihi deero
cum res ipsa feret: nisi dextro tempore, Flacci
verba per attentam non ibunt Caesaris aurem,
cui male si palpere recalcitrat undique tutus.
'quanto rectius hoc quam tristi laedere versu
Pantolabum scurram Nomentanumque nepotem,
cum sibi quisque timet, quamquam est intactus, et odit!'
quid faciam? saltat Milonius, ut semel icto
accessit fervor capiti numerusque lucernis;
Castor gaudet equis, ovo prognatus eodem
pugnis; quot capitum vivunt, totidem studiorum

milia: me pedibus delectat claudere verba
Lucili ritu, nostrum melioris utroque.
ille velut fidis arcana sodalibus olim
credebat libris, neque si male cesserat usquam
decurrens alio, neque si bene; quo fit ut omnis
votiva pateat veluti descripta tabella
vita senis. sequor hunc, Lucanus an Appulus anceps:
nam Venusinus arat finem sub utrumque colonus,
missus ad hoc, pulsis, vetus est ut fama, Sabellis,
quo ne per vacuum Romano incurreret hostis,
sive quod Apula gens seu quod Lucania bellum
incuteret violenta. sed hic stilus haud petet ultro
quemquam animantem et me veluti custodiet ensis
vagina tectus; quem cur destringere coner
tutus ab infestis latronibus? o pater et rex
Iuppiter, ut pereat positum robigine telum,
nec quisquam noceat cupido mihi pacis! at ille
qui me commorit (melius non tangere, clamo),
flebit et insignis tota cantabitur urbe.
Cervius iratus leges minitatur et urnam,
Canidia Albuci quibus est inimica venenum,
grande malum Turius, siquid se iudice certes.
ut quo quisque valet suspectos terreat, utque
imperet hoc natura potens, sic collige mecum:
dente lupus, cornu taurus petit: unde nisi intus
monstratum? Scaevae vivacem crede nepoti
matrem: nil faciet sceleris pia dextera: mirum,
ut neque calce lupus quemquam neque dente petit bos:
sed mala tollet anum vitiato melle cicuta.
ne longum faciam: seu me tranquilla senectus
exspectat seu Mors atris circumvolat alis,
dives, inops, Romae seu fors ita iusserit exsul,
quisquis erit vitae scribam color. 'o puer, ut sis
vitalis metuo, et maiorum ne quis amicus
frigore te feriat.' quid, cum est Lucilius ausus
primus in hunc operis componere carmina morem,
detrahere et pellem, nitidus qua quisque per ora
cederet, introrsum turpis, num Laelius aut qui
duxit ab oppressa meritum Carthagine nomen
ingenio offensi aut laeso doluere Metello
famosisque Lupo cooperto versibus? atqui
primores populi arripuit populumque tributim,
scilicet uni aequus virtuti atque eius amicis.
quin ubi se a vulgo et scaena in secreta remorant

virtus Scipiadae et mitis sapientia Laeli,
nugari cum illo et discincti ludere donec
decoqueretur holus soliti. quidquid sum ego, quamvis
infra Lucili censum ingeniumque, tamen me
cum magnis vixisse invita fatebitur usque
invidia, et fragili quaerens illidere dentem
offendet solido; nisi quid tu, docte Trebati,
dissentis. 'equidem nihil hinc diffindere possum;
sed tamen ut monitus caveas, ne forte negoti
incutiat tibi quid sanctarum inscitia legum:
si mala condiderit in quem quis carmina, ius est
iudiciumque.' esto, si quis mala; sed bona si quis
iudice condiderit laudatus Caesare? si quis
opprobriis dignum latraverit, integer ipse?
'solventur risu tabulae, tu missus abibis.'

2.6

Hoc erat in votis: modus agri non ita magnus,
hortus ubi et tecto vicinus iugis aquae fons
et paulum silvae super his foret. auctius atque
di melius fecere. bene est. nil amplius oro,
Maia nate, nisi ut propria haec mihi munera faxis.
si neque maiorem feci ratione mala rem
nec sum facturus vitio culpave minorem,
si veneror stultus nihil horum 'o si angulus ille
proximus accedat qui nunc denormat agellum!
o si urnam argenti fors quae mihi monstret, ut illi,
thesauro invento qui mercennarius agrum
illum ipsum mercatus aravit, dives amico
Hercule!' si quod adest gratum iuvat, hac prece te oro:
pingue pecus domino facias et cetera praeter
ingenium, utque soles custos mihi maximus adsis.
ergo ubi me in montis et in arcem ex urbe removi,
quid prius illustrem satiris musaque pedestri?
nec mala me ambitio perdit nec plumbeus Auster
autumnusque gravis, Libitinae quaestus acerbae.
Matutine pater, seu 'Iane' libentius audis,
unde homines operum primos vitaeque labores
instituunt, sic dis placitum, tu carminis esto
principium. Romae sponsorem me rapis: 'eia,
ne prior officio quisquam respondeat, urge.'
sive Aquilo radit terras seu bruma nivalem
interiore diem gyro trahit, ire necesse est.

postmodo quod mi obsit clare certumque locuto,
luctandum in turba et facienda iniuria tardis.
'quid vis, insane,' et 'quas res agis?' improbus urget
iratis precibus; 'tu pulses omne quod obstat,
ad Maecenatem memori si mente recurras?'
hoc iuvat et melli est, non mentiar. at simul atras
ventum est Esquilias aliena negotia centum
per caput et circa saliunt latus. 'ante secundam
Roscius orabat sibi adesses ad Puteal cras.'
'de re communi scribae magna atque nova te
orabant hodie meminisses, Quinte, reverti.'
'imprimat his, cura, Maecenas signa tabellis.'
dixeris, 'experiar': 'si vis, potes,' addit et instat.
septimus octavo propior iam fugerit annus
ex quo Maecenas me coepit habere suorum
in numero, dumtaxat ad hoc, quem tollere raeda
vellet iter faciens et cui concredere nugas
hoc genus, 'hora quota est?' 'Thraex est Gallina Syro par?'
'matutina parum cautos iam frigora mordent':
et quae rimosa bene deponuntur in aure.
per totum hoc tempus subiectior in diem et horam
invidiae noster. ludos spectaverat una,
luserat in campo: 'Fortunae filius!' omnes.
frigidus a Rostris manat per compita rumor:
quicumque obvius est me consulit: 'o bone, nam te
scire, deos quoniam propius contingis, oportet,
numquid de Dacis audisti?' nil equidem. 'ut tu
semper eris derisor!' at omnes di exagitent me
si quicquam. 'quid, militibus promissa Triquetra
praedia Caesar an est Itala tellure daturus?'
iurantem me scire nihil mirantur ut unum
scilicet egregii mortalem altique silenti.
perditur haec inter misero lux non sine votis:
o rus, quando ego te aspiciam? quandoque licebit
nunc veterum libris, nunc somno et inertibus horis
ducere sollicitae iucunda oblivia vitae?
o quando faba Pythagorae cognata simulque
uncta satis pingui ponentur holuscula lardo?
o noctes cenaeque deum! quibus ipse meique
ante Larem proprium vescor vernasque procaces
pasco libatis dapibus. prout cuique libido est
siccat inaequalis calices conviva, solutus
legibus insanis, seu quis capit acria fortis
pocula seu modicis uvescit laetius. ergo

sermo oritur, non de villis domibusve alienis,
nec male necne Lepos saltet; sed quod magis ad nos
pertinet et nescire malum est agitamus: utrumne
divitiis homines an sint virtute beati;
quidve ad amicitias, usus rectumne, trahat nos;
et quae sit natura boni summumque quid eius.
Cervius haec inter vicinus garrit anilis
ex re fabellas. si quis nam laudat Arelli
sollicitas ignarus opes, sic incipit: 'olim
rusticus urbanum murem mus paupere fertur
accepisse cavo, veterem vetus hospes amicum,
asper et attentus quaesitis, ut tamen artum
solveret hospitiis animum. quid multa? neque ille
sepositi ciceris nec longae invidit avenae,
aridum et ore ferens acinum semesaque lardi
frusta dedit, cupiens varia fastidia cena
vincere tangentis male singula dente superbo;
cum pater ipse domus palea porrectus in horna
esset ador loliumque, dapis meliora relinquens.
tandem urbanus ad hunc "quid te iuvat" inquit, "amice,
praerupti nemoris patientem vivere dorso?
vis tu homines urbemque feris praeponere silvis?
carpe viam, mihi crede, comes; terrestria quando
mortalis animas vivunt sortita, neque ulla est
aut magno aut parvo leti fuga: quo, bone, circa,
dum licet, in rebus iucundis vive beatus;
vive memor, quam sis aevi brevis." haec ubi dicta
agrestem pepulere, domo levis exsilit; inde
ambo propositum peragunt iter, urbis aventes
moenia nocturni subrepere. iamque tenebat
nox medium caeli spatium, cum ponit uterque
in locuplete domo vestigia, rubro ubi cocco
tincta super lectos canderet vestis eburnos,
multaque de magna superessent fercula cena,
quae procul exstructis inerant hesterna canistris.
ergo ubi purpurea porrectum in veste locavit
agrestem, veluti succinctus cursitat hospes
continuatque dapes nec non verniliter ipsis
fungitur officiis, praelambens omne quod adfert.
ille cubans gaudet mutata sorte bonisque
rebus agit laetum convivam, cum subito ingens
valvarum strepitus lectis excussit utrumque.
currere per totum pavidi conclave, magisque
exanimes trepidare, simul domus alta Molossis

personuit canibus. tum rusticus: "haud mihi vita
est opus hac" ait et "valeas: me silva cavusque
tutus ab insidiis tenui solabitur ervo."'

2.8

Ut Nasidieni iuvit te cena beati?
nam mihi quaerenti convivam dictus here illic
de medio potare die. 'sic ut mihi numquam
in vita fuerit melius.' da, si grave non est,
quae prima iratum ventrem placaverit esca.
'in primis Lucanus aper; leni fuit Austro
captus, ut aiebat cenae pater; acria circum
rapula, lactucae, radices, qualia lassum
pervellunt stomachum, siser, allec, faecula Coa.
his ubi sublatis puer alte cinctus acernam
gausape purpureo mensam pertersit, et alter
sublegit quodcumque iaceret inutile quodque
posset cenantis offendere; ut Attica virgo
cum sacris Cereris procedit fuscus Hydaspes
Caecuba vina ferens, Alcon Chium maris expers.
hic erus: "Albanum, Maecenas, sive Falernum
te magis appositis delectat, habemus utrumque."'
divitias miseras! sed quis cenantibus una,
Fundani, pulchre fuerit tibi, nosse laboro.
'summus ego et prope me Viscus Thurinus et infra,
si memini, Varius; cum Servilio Balatrone
Vibidius, quos Maecenas adduxerat umbras.
Nomentanus erat super ipsum, Porcius infra
ridiculus totas simul absorbere placentas;
Nomentanus ad hoc, qui siquid forte lateret
indice monstraret digito: nam cetera turba,
nos, inquam, cenamus avis, conchylia, piscis,
longe dissimilem noto celantia sucum;
ut vel continuo patuit cum passeris atque
ingustata mihi porrexerat ilia rhombi.
post hoc me docuit melimela rubere minorem
ad lunam delecta: quid hoc intersit ab ipso
audieris melius. tum Vibidius Balatroni:
"nos nisi damnose bibimus moriemur inulti,"
et calices poscit maiores. vertere pallor
tum parochi faciem nil sic metuentis ut acris
potores, vel quod male dicunt liberius vel
fervida quod subtile exsurdant vina palatum.

invertunt Allifanis vinaria tota
Vibidius Balatroque, secutis omnibus; imi
convivae lecti nihilum nocuere lagoenis.
adfertur squillas inter murena natantis
in patina porrecta. sub hoc erus: "haec gravida" inquit
"capta est, deterior post partum carne futura.
his mixtum ius est: oleo quod prima Venafri
pressit cella; garo de sucis piscis Hiberi;
vino quinquenni, verum citra mare nato,
dum coquitur (cocto Chium sic convenit, ut non
hoc magis ullum aliud); pipere albo, non sine aceto
quod Methymnaeam vitio mutaverit uvam.
erucas viridis, inulas ego primus amaras
monstravi incoquere, illutos Curtillus echinos,
ut melius muria quod testa marina remittat."
interea suspensa gravis aulaea ruinas
in patinam fecere, trahentia pulveris atri
quantum non Aquilo Campanis excitat agris.
nos maius veriti, postquam nihil esse pericli
sensimus, erigimur. Rufus posito capite, ut si
filius immaturus obisset, flere. quis esset
finis ni sapiens sic Nomentanus amicum
tolleret "heu, Fortuna, quis est crudelior in nos
te deus? ut semper gaudes illudere rebus
humanis!" Varius mappa compescere risum
vix poterat. Balatro suspendens omnia naso
"haec est condicio vivendi" aiebat, "eoque
responsura tuo numquam est par fama labori.
tene, ut ego accipiar laute, torquerier omni
sollicitudine districtum, ne panis adustus,
ne male conditum ius apponatur, ut omnes
praecincti recte pueri comptique ministrent!
adde hos praeterea casus, aulaea ruant si,
ut modo; si patinam pede lapsus frangat agaso.
sed convivatoris uti ducis ingenium res
adversae nudare solent, celare secundae."
Nasidienus ad haec "tibi di quaecumque preceris
commoda dent! ita vir bonus es convivaque comis":
et soleas poscit. tum in lecto quoque videres
stridere secreta divisos aure susurros.'
'nullos his mallem ludos spectasse; sed illa
redde age quae deinceps risisti.' 'Vibidius dum
quaerit de pueris num sit quoque fracta lagoena,
quod sibi poscenti non dantur pocula, dumque

ridetur fictis rerum, Balatrone secundo,
Nasidiene, redis mutatae frontis, ut arte
emendaturus fortunam: deinde secuti
mazonomo pueri magno discerpta ferentes
membra gruis sparsi sale multo, non sine farre,
pinguibus et ficis pastum iecur anseris albae,
et leporum avulsos, ut multo suavius, armos,
quam si cum lumbis quis edit; tum pectore adusto
vidimus et merulas poni et sine clune palumbes,
suavis res, si non causas narraret earum et
naturas dominus; quem nos sic fugimus ulti,
ut nihil omnino gustaremus, velut illis
Canidia adflasset peior serpentibus Afris.'

PERSIUS

Prologus

Nec fonte labra prolui caballino
nec in bicipiti somniasse Parnaso
memini, ut repente sic poeta prodirem.
Heliconidasque pallidamque Pirenen
illis remitto quorum imagines lambunt
hederae sequaces; ipse semipaganus
ad sacra vatum carmen adfero nostrum.
quis expedivit psittaco suum 'chaere'
picamque docuit nostra verba conari?
magister artis ingenique largitor
venter, negatas artifex sequi voces.
quod si dolosi spes refulserit nummi,
corvos poetas et poetridas picas
cantare credas Pegaseium nectar.

Satura 1

O curas hominum! o quantum est in rebus inane!
'quis leget haec?' min tu istud ais? nemo hercule. 'nemo?'
vel duo vel nemo. 'turpe et miserabile.' quare?
ne mihi Polydamas et Troiades Labeonem
praetulerint? nugae. non, si quid turbida Roma
elevet, accedas examenve inprobum in illa
castiges trutina nec te quaesiveris extra.
nam Romae quis non—a, si fas dicere—sed fas
tum, cum ad canitiem et nostrum istud vivere triste
aspexi, ac nucibus facimus quaecumque relictis,
cum sapimus patruos. tunc tunc—ignoscite (nolo,
quid faciam?) sed sum petulanti splene—cachinno.
  scribimus inclusi, numeros ille, hic pede liber,

grande aliquid quod pulmo animae praelargus anhelet.
scilicet haec populo pexusque togaque recenti
et natalicia tandem cum sardonyche albus
sede leges celsa, liquido cum plasmate guttur
mobile conlueris, patranti fractus ocello.
tunc neque more probo videas nec voce serena
ingentis trepidare Titos, cum carmina lumbum
intrant et tremulo scalpuntur ubi intima versu.
tun, vetule, auriculis alienis colligis escas,
articulis quibus et dicas cute perditus 'ohe'?
'quo didicisse, nisi hoc fermentum et quae semel intus
innata est rupto iecore exierit caprificus?'
en pallor seniumque! o mores, usque adeone
scire tuum nihil est nisi te scire hoc sciat alter?
'at pulchrum est digito monstrari et dicier "hic est."
ten cirratorum centum dictata fuisse
pro nihilo pendes?' ecce inter pocula quaerunt
Romulidae saturi quid dia poemata narrent.
hic aliquis, cui circum umeros hyacinthina laena est,
rancidulum quiddam balba de nare locutus
Phyllidas, Hypsipylas, vatum et plorabile siquid,
eliquat ac tenero subplantat verba palato.
adsensere viri: nunc non cinis ille poetae
felix? non levior cippus nunc inprimit ossa?
laudant convivae: nunc non e manibus illis,
nunc non e tumulo fortunataque favilla
nascentur violae? 'rides' ait 'et nimis uncis
naribus indulges. an erit qui velle recuset
os populi meruisse et cedro digna locutus
linquere nec scombros metuentia carmina nec tus?'
  quisquis es, o modo quem ex adverso dicere feci,
non ego cum scribo, si forte quid aptius exit,
quando haec rara avis est, si quid tamen aptius exit,
laudari metuam; neque enim mihi cornea fibra est.
sed recti finemque extremumque esse recuso
'euge' tuum et 'belle.' nam 'belle' hoc excute totum:
quid non intus habet? non hic est Ilias Atti
ebria veratro? non siqua elegidia crudi
dictarunt proceres? non quidquid denique lectis
scribitur in citreis? calidum scis ponere sumen,
scis comitem horridulum trita donare lacerna,
et 'verum' inquis 'amo, verum mihi dicite de me.'
qui pote? vis dicam? nugaris, cum tibi, calve,
pinguis aqualiculus propenso sesquipede extet.

o Iane, a tergo quem nulla ciconia pinsit
nec manus auriculas imitari mobilis albas
nec linguae quantum sitiat canis Apula tantae.
vos, o patricius sanguis, quos vivere fas est
occipiti caeco, posticae occurrite sannae.
'quis populi sermo est? quis enim nisi carmina molli
nunc demum numero fluere, ut per leve severos
effundat iunctura unguis? scit tendere versum
non secus ac si oculo rubricam derigat uno.
sive opus in mores, in luxum, in prandia regum
dicere, res grandes nostro dat Musa poetae.'
ecce modo heroas sensus adferre docemus
nugari solitos Graece, nec ponere lucum
artifices nec rus saturum laudare, ubi corbes
et focus et porci et fumosa Palilia feno,
unde Remus sulcoque terens dentalia, Quinti,
cum trepida ante boves dictatorem induit uxor
et tua aratra domum lictor tulit—euge poeta!
est nunc Brisaei quem venosus liber Acci,
sunt quos Pacuviusque et verrucosa moretur
Antiopa aerumnis cor luctificabile fulta?
hos pueris monitus patres infundere lippos
cum videas, quaerisne unde haec sartago loquendi
venerit in linguas, unde istud dedecus in quo
trossulus exultat tibi per subsellia levis?
nilne pudet capiti non posse pericula cano
pellere quin tepidum hoc optes audire 'decenter'?
'fur es' ait Pedio. Pedius quid? crimina rasis
librat in antithetis, doctas posuisse figuras
laudatur: 'bellum hoc.' hoc bellum? an, Romule, ceves?
men moveat? quippe, et, cantet si naufragus, assem
protulerim? cantas, cum fracta te in trabe pictum
ex umero portes? verum nec nocte paratum
plorabit qui me volet incurvasse querella.
'sed numeris decor est et iunctura addita crudis.
cludere sic versum didicit "Berecyntius Attis"
et "qui caeruleum dirimebat Nerea delphin,"
sic "costam longo subduximus Appennino."
"Arma virum", nonne hoc spumosum et cortice pingui
ut ramale vetus vegrandi subere coctum?'
quidnam igitur tenerum et laxa cervice legendum?
'torva Mimalloneis inplerunt cornua bombis,
et raptum vitulo caput ablatura superbo
Bassaris et lyncem Maenas flexura corymbis

Euhion ingeminat, reparabilis adsonat echo.'
haec fierent si testiculi vena ulla paterni
viveret in nobis? summa delumbe saliva
hoc natat in labris et in udo est Maenas et Attis
nec pluteum caedit nec demorsos sapit unguis.
'sed quid opus teneras mordaci radere vero
auriculas? vide sis ne maiorum tibi forte
limina frigescant: sonat hic de nare canina
littera.' per me equidem sint omnia protinus alba;
nil moror. euge omnes, omnes bene, mirae eritis res.
hoc iuvat? 'hic' inquis 'veto quisquam faxit oletum.'
pinge duos anguis: 'pueri, sacer est locus, extra
meiite.' discedo. secuit Lucilius urbem,
te Lupe, te Muci, et genuinum fregit in illis.
omne vafer vitium ridenti Flaccus amico
tangit et admissus circum praecordia ludit,
callidus excusso populum suspendere naso.
me muttire nefas? nec clam? nec cum scrobe? nusquam?
hic tamen infodiam. vidi, vidi ipse, libelle:
auriculas asini quis non habet? hoc ego opertum,
hoc ridere meum, tam nil, nulla tibi vendo
Iliade. audaci quicumque adflate Cratino
iratum Eupolidem praegrandi cum sene palles,
aspice et haec, si forte aliquid decoctius audis.
inde vaporata lector mihi ferveat aure,
non hic qui in crepidas Graiorum ludere gestit
sordidus et lusco qui possit dicere 'lusce,'
sese aliquem credens Italo quod honore supinus
fregerit heminas Arreti aedilis iniquas,
nec qui abaco numeros et secto in pulvere metas
scit risisse vafer, multum gaudere paratus
si cynico barbam petulans nonaria vellat.
his mane edictum, post prandia Callirhoen do.

3

Nempe haec adsidue. iam clarum mane fenestras
intrat et angustas extendit lumine rimas.
stertimus, indomitum quod despumare Falernum
sufficiat, quinta dum linea tangitur umbra.
'en quid agis? siccas insana canicula messes
iam dudum coquit et patula pecus omne sub ulmo est'
unus ait comitum. 'verumne? itan? ocius adsit
huc aliquis. nemon?' turgescit vitrea bilis—

'findor'—ut Arcadiae pecuaria rudere credas.
iam liber et positis bicolor membrana capillis
inque manus chartae nodosaque venit harundo.
tum querimur crassus calamo quod pendeat umor.
nigra sed infusa vanescit sepia lympha,
dilutas querimur geminet quod fistula guttas.
'o miser inque dies ultra miser, hucine rerum
venimus? a, cur non potius teneroque columbo
et similis regum pueris pappare minutum
poscis et iratus mammae lallare recusas?'
'an tali studeam calamo?' 'cui verba? quid istas
succinis ambages? tibi luditur. effluis amens,
contemnere. sonat vitium percussa, maligne
respondet viridi non cocta fidelia limo.
udum et molle lutum es, nunc nunc properandus et acri
fingendus sine fine rota. sed rure paterno
est tibi far modicum, purum et sine labe salinum
(quid metuas?) cultrixque foci secura patella.
hoc satis? an deceat pulmonem rumpere ventis
stemmate quod Tusco ramum millesime ducis
†censoremve tuum vel quod trabeate salutas?†
ad populum phaleras! ego te intus et in cute novi.
non pudet ad morem discincti vivere Nattae.
sed stupet hic vitio et fibris increvit opimum
pingue, caret culpa, nescit quid perdat, et alto
demersus summa rursus non bullit in unda.
'magne pater divum, saevos punire tyrannos
haut alia ratione velis, cum dira libido
moverit ingenium ferventi tincta veneno:
virtutem videant intabescantque relicta.
anne magis Siculi gemuerunt aera iuvenci
et magis auratis pendens laquearibus ensis
purpureas subter cervices terruit, "imus,
imus praecipites" quam si sibi dicat et intus
palleat infelix quod proxima nesciat uxor?
'saepe oculos, memini, tangebam parvus olivo,
grandia si nollem morituri verba Catonis
discere non sano multum laudanda magistro,
quae pater adductis sudans audiret amicis.
iure; etenim id summum, quid dexter senio ferret,
scire erat in voto, damnosa canicula quantum
raderet, angustae collo non fallier orcae,
neu quis callidior buxum torquere flagello.
haut tibi inexpertum curvos deprendere mores

quaeque docet sapiens bracatis inlita Medis
porticus, insomnis quibus et detonsa iuventus
invigilat siliquis et grandi pasta polenta;
et tibi quae Samios diduxit littera ramos
surgentem dextro monstravit limite callem.
stertis adhuc laxumque caput conpage soluta
oscitat hesternum dissutis undique malis.
est aliquid quo tendis et in quod derigis arcum?
an passim sequeris corvos testaque lutoque,
securus quo pes ferat, atque ex tempore vivis?
  'elleborum frustra, cum iam cutis aegra tumebit,
poscentis videas; venienti occurrite morbo,
et quid opus Cratero magnos promittere montis?
discite et, o miseri, causas cognoscite rerum:
quid sumus et quidnam victuri gignimur, ordo
quis datus, aut metae qua mollis flexus et unde,
quis modus argento, quid fas optare, quid asper
utile nummus habet, patriae carisque propinquis
quantum elargiri deceat, quem te deus esse
iussit et humana qua parte locatus es in re.
disce nec invideas quod multa fidelia putet
in locuplete penu, defensis pinguibus Umbris,
et piper et pernae, Marsi monumenta clientis,
maenaque quod prima nondum defecerit orca.
  'hic aliquis de gente hircosa centurionum
dicat: "quod sapio satis est mihi. non ego curo
esse quod Arcesilas aerumnosique Solones
obstipo capite et figentes lumine terram,
murmura cum secum et rabiosa silentia rodunt
atque exporrecto trutinantur verba labello,
aegroti veteris meditantes somnia, gigni
de nihilo nihilum, in nihilum nil posse reverti.
hoc est quod palles? cur quis non prandeat hoc est?"
his populus ridet, multumque torosa iuventus
ingeminat tremulos naso crispante cachinnos.
  "inspice, nescio quid trepidat mihi pectus et aegris
faucibus exsuperat grauis halitus, inspice sodes"
qui dicit medico, iussus requiescere, postquam
tertia conpositas vidit nox currere venas,
de maiore domo modice sitiente lagoena
lenia loturo sibi Surrentina rogabit.
"heus bone, tu palles." "nihil est." "videas tamen istuc,
quidquid id est. surgit tacite tibi lutea pellis."
"at tu deterius palles; ne sis mihi tutor.

iam pridem hunc sepeli; tu restas." "perge, tacebo."
turgidus hic epulis atque albo ventre lavatur,
gutture sulpureas lente exhalante mefites.
sed tremor inter vina subit calidumque trientem
excutit e manibus, dentes crepuere retecti,
uncta cadunt laxis tunc pulmentaria labris.
hinc tuba, candelae, tandemque beatulus alto
conpositus lecto crassisque lutatus amomis
in portam rigidas calces extendit. at illum
hesterni capite induto subiere Quirites.'
'tange, miser, venas et pone in pectore dextram;
nil calet hic. summosque pedes attinge manusque;
non frigent.' 'visa est si forte pecunia, siue
candida vicini subrisit molle puella,
cor tibi rite salit? positum est algente catino
durum holus et populi cribro decussa farina:
temptemus fauces; tenero latet ulcus in ore
putre quod haut deceat plebeia radere beta.
alges, cum excussit membris timor albus aristas;
nunc face supposita fervescit sanguis et ira
scintillant oculi, dicisque facisque quod ipse
non sani esse hominis non sanus iuret Orestes.'

4

'Rem populi tractas? (barbatum haec crede magistrum
dicere, sorbitio tollit quem dira cicutae)
'quo fretus? dic hoc, magni pupille Pericli.
scilicet ingenium et rerum prudentia velox
ante pilos venit, dicenda tacendave calles.
ergo ubi commota fervet plebecula bile,
fert animus calidae fecisse silentia turbae
maiestate manus. quid deinde loquere? "Quirites,
hoc puta non iustum est, illud male, rectius illud."
scis etenim iustum gemina suspendere lance
ancipitis librae, rectum discernis ubi inter
curva subit vel cum fallit pede regula varo,
et potis es nigrum vitio praefigere theta.
quin tu igitur summa nequiquam pelle decorus
ante diem blando caudam iactare popello
desinis, Anticyras melior sorbere meracas?
quae tibi summa boni est? uncta vixisse patella
semper et adsiduo curata cuticula sole?
expecta, haut aliud respondeat haec anus. i nunc,

"Dinomaches ego sum" suffla, "sum candidus." esto,
dum ne deterius sapiat pannucia Baucis,
cum bene discincto cantaverit ocima vernae.
  'ut nemo in sese temptat descendere, nemo,
sed praecedenti spectatur mantica tergo!
quaesieris "nostin Vettidi praedia?" "cuius?"
"dives arat Curibus quantum non miluus errat."
"hunc ais, hunc dis iratis genioque sinistro,
qui, quandoque iugum pertusa ad compita figit,
seriolae veterem metuens deradere limum
ingemit 'hoc bene sit' tunicatum cum sale mordens
cepe et farratam pueris plaudentibus ollam
pannosam faecem morientis sorbet aceti?"
at si unctus cesses et figas in cute solem,
est prope te ignotus cubito qui tangat et acre
despuat: "hi mores! penemque arcanaque lumbi
runcantem populo marcentis pandere vulvas.
tum, cum maxillis balanatum gausape pectas,
inguinibus quare detonsus gurgulio extat?
quinque palaestritae licet haec plantaria vellant
elixasque nates labefactent forcipe adunca,
non tamen ista filix ullo mansuescit aratro."
  'caedimus inque vicem praebemus crura sagittis.
vivitur hoc pacto, sic novimus. ilia subter
caecum vulnus habes, sed lato balteus auro
praetegit. ut mavis, da verba et decipe nervos,
si potes.' 'egregium cum me vicinia dicat,
non credam?' 'viso si palles, inprobe, nummo,
si facis in penem quidquid tibi venit, amarum
si puteal multa cautus vibice flagellas,
nequiquam populo bibulas donaveris aures.
respue quod non es; tollat sua munera cerdo.
tecum habita: noris quam sit tibi curta supellex.'

JUVENAL

1

Semper ego auditor tantum? numquamne reponam
vexatus totiens rauci Theseide Cordi?
inpune ergo mihi recitaverit ille togatas,
hic elegos? inpune diem consumpserit ingens
Telephus aut summi plena iam margine libri
scriptus et in tergo necdum finitus Orestes?
nota magis nulli domus est sua quam mihi lucus
Martis et Aeoliis vicinum rupibus antrum
Vulcani; quid agant venti, quas torqueat umbras
Aeacus, unde alius furtivae devehat aurum
pelliculae, quantas iaculetur Monychus ornos,
Frontonis platani convolsaque marmora clamant
semper et adsiduo ruptae lectore columnae.
expectes eadem a summo minimoque poeta.
et nos ergo manum ferulae subduximus, et nos
consilium dedimus Sullae, 'privatus ut altum
dormiret.' stulta est clementia, cum tot ubique
vatibus occurras, periturae parcere chartae.
cur tamen hoc potius libeat decurrere campo,
per quem magnus equos Auruncae flexit alumnus,
si vacat ac placidi rationem admittitis, edam.
   cum tener uxorem ducat spado, Mevia Tuscum
figat aprum et nuda teneat venabula mamma,
patricios omnis opibus cum provocet unus
quo tondente gravis iuveni mihi barba sonabat,
cum pars Niliacae plebis, cum verna Canopi
Crispinus Tyrias umero revocante lacernas
ventilet aestivum digitis sudantibus aurum
nec sufferre queat maioris pondera gemmae,
difficile est saturam non scribere. nam quis iniquae

tam patiens urbis, tam ferreus, ut teneat se,
causidici nova cum veniat lectica Mathonis
plena ipso, post hunc magni delator amici
et cito rapturus de nobilitate comesa
quod superest, quem Massa timet, quem munere palpat
Carus et a trepido Thymele summissa Latino;
cum te summoveant qui testamenta merentur
noctibus, in caelum quos evehit optima summi
nunc via processus, vetulae vesica beatae?
unciolam Proculeius habet, sed Gillo deuncem,
partes quisque suas ad mensuram inguinis heres.
accipiat sane mercedem sanguinis et sic
palleat ut nudis pressit qui calcibus anguem
aut Lugudunensem rhetor dicturus ad aram.
quid referam quanta siccum iecur ardeat ira,
cum populum gregibus comitum premit hic spoliator
pupilli prostantis et hic damnatus inani
iudicio? quid enim salvis infamia nummis?
exul ab octava Marius bibit et fruitur dis
iratis, at tu victrix, provincia, ploras.
haec ego non credam Venusina digna lucerna?
haec ego non agitem? sed quid magis? Heracleas
aut Diomedeas aut mugitum labyrinthi
et mare percussum puero fabrumque volantem,
cum leno accipiat moechi bona, si capiendi
ius nullum uxori, doctus spectare lacunar,
doctus et ad calicem vigilanti stertere naso;
cum fas esse putet curam sperare cohortis
qui bona donavit praesepibus et caret omni
maiorum censu, dum pervolat axe citato
Flaminiam puer Automedon? nam lora tenebat
ipse, lacernatae cum se iactaret amicae.
nonne libet medio ceras inplere capaces
quadrivio, cum iam sexta cervice feratur
hinc atque inde patens ac nuda paene cathedra
et multum referens de Maecenate supino
signator falsi, qui se lautum atque beatum
exiguis tabulis et gemma fecerit uda?
occurrit matrona potens, quae molle Calenum
porrectura viro miscet sitiente rubetam
instituitque rudes melior Lucusta propinquas
per famam et populum nigros efferre maritos.
aude aliquid brevibus Gyaris et carcere dignum,
si vis esse aliquid. probitas laudatur et alget;

criminibus debent hortos, praetoria, mensas,
argentum vetus et stantem extra pocula caprum.
quem patitur dormire nurus corruptor avarae,
quem sponsae turpes et praetextatus adulter?
si natura negat, facit indignatio versum
qualemcumque potest, quales ego vel Cluvienus.
  ex quo Deucalion nimbis tollentibus aequor
navigio montem ascendit sortesque poposcit
paulatimque anima calverunt mollia saxa
et maribus nudas ostendit Pyrrha puellas,
quidquid agunt homines, votum, timor, ira, voluptas,
gaudia, discursus, nostri farrago libelli est.
et quando uberior vitiorum copia? quando
maior avaritiae patuit sinus? alea quando
hos animos? neque enim loculis comitantibus itur
ad casum tabulae, posita sed luditur arca.
proelia quanta illic dispensatore videbis
armigero! simplexne furor sestertia centum
perdere et horrenti tunicam non reddere servo?
quis totidem erexit villas, quis fercula septem
secreto cenavit avus? nunc sportula primo
limine parva sedet turbae rapienda togatae.
ille tamen faciem prius inspicit et trepidat ne
suppositus venias ac falso nomine poscas:
agnitus accipies. iubet a praecone vocari
ipsos Troiugenas, nam vexant limen et ipsi
nobiscum. 'da praetori, da deinde tribuno.'
sed libertinus prior est. 'prior' inquit 'ego adsum.
cur timeam dubitemve locum defendere, quamvis
natus ad Euphraten, molles quod in aure fenestrae
arguerint, licet ipse negem? sed quinque tabernae
quadringenta parant. quid confert purpura maior
optandum, si Laurenti custodit in agro
conductas Corvinus ovis, ego possideo plus
Pallante et Licinis?' expectent ergo tribuni,
vincant divitiae, sacro ne cedat honori
nuper in hanc urbem pedibus qui venerat albis,
quandoquidem inter nos sanctissima divitiarum
maiestas, etsi funesta Pecunia templo
nondum habitat, nullas nummorum ereximus aras,
ut colitur Pax atque Fides, Victoria, Virtus
quaeque salutato crepitat Concordia nido.
sed cum summus honor finito conputet anno,
sportula quid referat, quantum rationibus addat,

quid facient comites quibus hinc toga, calceus hinc est
et panis fumusque domi? densissima centum
quadrantes lectica petit, sequiturque maritum
languida vel praegnas et circumducitur uxor.
hic petit absenti nota iam callidus arte
ostendens vacuam et clausam pro coniuge sellam.
'Galla mea est' inquit, 'citius dimitte. moraris?
profer, Galla, caput. noli vexare, quiescet.'
  ipse dies pulchro distinguitur ordine rerum:
sportula, deinde forum iurisque peritus Apollo
atque triumphales, inter quas ausus habere
nescio quis titulos Aegyptius atque Arabarches,
cuius ad effigiem non tantum meiere fas est.
vestibulis abeunt veteres lassique clientes
votaque deponunt, quamquam longissima cenae
spes homini; caulis miseris atque ignis emendus.
optima silvarum interea pelagique vorabit
rex horum vacuisque toris tantum ipse iacebit.
nam de tot pulchris et latis orbibus et tam
antiquis una comedunt patrimonia mensa.
nullus iam parasitus erit. sed quis ferat istas
luxuriae sordes? quanta est gula quae sibi totos
ponit apros, animal propter convivia natum!
poena tamen praesens, cum tu deponis amictus
turgidus et crudum pavonem in balnea portas.
hinc subitae mortes atque intestata senectus.
it nova nec tristis per cunctas fabula cenas;
ducitur iratis plaudendum funus amicis.
  nil erit ulterius quod nostris moribus addat
posteritas, eadem facient cupientque minores,
omne in praecipiti vitium stetit. utere velis,
totos pande sinus. dices hic forsitan 'unde
ingenium par materiae? unde illa priorum
scribendi quodcumque animo flagrante liberet
simplicitas? "cuius non audeo dicere nomen?
quid refert dictis ignoscat Mucius an non?"
pone Tigillinum, taeda lucebis in illa
qua stantes ardent qui fixo gutture fumant,
et latum media sulcum deducis harena.'
qui dedit ergo tribus patruis aconita, vehatur
pensilibus plumis atque illinc despiciat nos?
'cum veniet contra, digito compesce labellum:
accusator erit qui verbum dixerit "hic est."
securus licet Aenean Rutulumque ferocem

committas, nulli gravis est percussus Achilles
aut multum quaesitus Hylas urnamque secutus:
ense velut stricto quotiens Lucilius ardens
infremuit, rubet auditor cui frigida mens est
criminibus, tacita sudant praecordia culpa.
inde ira et lacrimae. tecum prius ergo voluta
haec animo ante tubas: galeatum sero duelli
paenitet.' experiar quid concedatur in illos
quorum Flaminia tegitur cinis atque Latina.

3

Quamvis digressu veteris confusus amici
laudo tamen, vacuis quod sedem figere Cumis
destinet atque unum civem donare Sibyllae.
ianua Baiarum est et gratum litus amoeni
secessus. ego vel Prochytam praepono Suburae;
nam quid tam miserum, tam solum vidimus, ut non
deterius credas horrere incendia, lapsus
tectorum adsiduos ac mille pericula saevae
urbis et Augusto recitantes mense poetas?
sed dum tota domus raeda componitur una,
substitit ad veteres arcus madidamque Capenam.
hic, ubi nocturnae Numa constituebat amicae
(nunc sacri fontis nemus et delubra locantur
Iudaeis, quorum cophinus fenumque supellex;
omnis enim populo mercedem pendere iussa est
arbor et eiectis mendicat silva Camenis),
in vallem Egeriae descendimus et speluncas
dissimiles veris. quanto praesentius esset
numen aquis, viridi si margine cluderet undas
herba nec ingenuum violarent marmora tofum.
  hic tunc Vmbricius 'quando artibus' inquit 'honestis
nullus in urbe locus, nulla emolumenta laborum,
res hodie minor est here quam fuit atque eadem cras
deteret exiguis aliquid, proponimus illuc
ire, fatigatas ubi Daedalus exuit alas,
dum nova canities, dum prima et recta senectus,
dum superest Lachesi quod torqueat et pedibus me
porto meis nullo dextram subeunte bacillo.
cedamus patria. vivant Artorius istic
et Catulus, maneant qui nigrum in candida vertunt,
quis facile est aedem conducere, flumina, portus,
siccandam eluviem, portandum ad busta cadaver,

et praebere caput domina venale sub hasta.
quondam hi cornicines et municipalis harenae
perpetui comites notaeque per oppida buccae
munera nunc edunt et, verso pollice vulgus
cum iubet, occidunt populariter; inde reversi
conducunt foricas, et cur non omnia? cum sint
quales ex humili magna ad fastigia rerum
extollit quotiens voluit Fortuna iocari.
quid Romae faciam? mentiri nescio; librum,
si malus est, nequeo laudare et poscere; motus
astrorum ignoro; funus promittere patris
nec volo nec possum; ranarum viscera numquam
inspexi; ferre ad nuptam quae mittit adulter,
quae mandat, norunt alii; me nemo ministro
fur erit, atque ideo nulli comes exeo tamquam
mancus et extinctae corpus non utile dextrae.
quis nunc diligitur nisi conscius et cui fervens
aestuat occultis animus semperque tacendis?
nil tibi se debere putat, nil conferet umquam,
participem qui te secreti fecit honesti.
carus erit Verri qui Verrem tempore quo vult
accusare potest. tanti tibi non sit opaci
omnis harena Tagi quodque in mare volvitur aurum,
ut somno careas ponendaque praemia sumas
tristis et a magno semper timearis amico.
quae nunc divitibus gens acceptissima nostris
et quos praecipve fugiam, properabo fateri,
nec pudor obstabit. non possum ferre, Quirites,
Graecam urbem. quamvis quota portio faecis Achaei?
iam pridem Syrus in Tiberim defluxit Orontes
et linguam et mores et cum tibicine chordas
obliquas nec non gentilia tympana secum
vexit et ad circum iussas prostare puellas.
ite, quibus grata est picta lupa barbara mitra.
rusticus ille tuus sumit trechedipna, Quirine,
et ceromatico fert niceteria collo.
hic alta Sicyone, ast hic Amydone relicta,
hic Andro, ille Samo, hic Trallibus aut Alabandis,
Esquilias dictumque petunt a vimine collem,
viscera magnarum domuum dominique futuri.
ingenium velox, audacia perdita, sermo
promptus et Isaeo torrentior. ede quid illum
esse putes. quemvis hominem secum attulit ad nos:
grammaticus, rhetor, geometres, pictor, aliptes,

augur, schoenobates, medicus, magus, omnia novit
Graeculus esuriens: in caelum iusseris ibit.
in summa non Maurus erat neque Sarmata nec Thrax
qui sumpsit pinnas, mediis sed natus Athenis.
horum ego non fugiam conchylia? me prior ille
signabit fultusque toro meliore recumbet,
advectus Romam quo pruna et cottana vento?
usque adeo nihil est quod nostra infantia caelum
hausit Aventini baca nutrita Sabina?
quid quod adulandi gens prudentissima laudat
sermonem indocti, faciem deformis amici,
et longum invalidi collum cervicibus aequat
Herculis Antaeum procul a tellure tenentis,
miratur vocem angustam, qua deterius nec
ille sonat quo mordetur gallina marito?
haec eadem licet et nobis laudare, sed illis
creditur. an melior cum Thaida sustinet aut cum
uxorem comoedus agit vel Dorida nullo
cultam palliolo? mulier nempe ipsa videtur,
non persona, loqui: vacua et plana omnia dicas
infra ventriculum et tenui distantia rima.
nec tamen Antiochus nec erit mirabilis illic
aut Stratocles aut cum molli Demetrius Haemo:
natio comoeda est. rides, maiore cachinno
concutitur; flet, si lacrimas conspexit amici,
nec dolet; igniculum brumae si tempore poscas,
accipit endromidem; si dixeris "aestuo," sudat.
non sumus ergo pares: melior, qui semper et omni
nocte dieque potest aliena sumere vultum
a facie, iactare manus laudare paratus,
si bene ructavit, si rectum minxit amicus,
si trulla inverso crepitum dedit aurea fundo.
praeterea sanctum nihil †aut† ab inguine tutum,
non matrona laris, non filia virgo, nec ipse
sponsus levis adhuc, non filius ante pudicus.
horum si nihil est, aviam resupinat amici.
[scire volunt secreta domus atque inde timeri.]
et quoniam coepit Graecorum mentio, transi
gymnasia atque audi facinus maioris abollae.
Stoicus occidit Baream delator amicum
discipulumque senex ripa nutritus in illa
ad quam Gorgonei delapsa est pinna caballi.
non est Romano cuiquam locus hic, ubi regnat
Protogenes aliquis vel Diphilus aut Hermarchus,

qui gentis vitio numquam partitur amicum,
solus habet. nam cum facilem stillavit in aurem
exiguum de naturae patriaeque veneno,
limine summoveor, perierunt tempora longi
servitii; nusquam minor est iactura clientis.
  quod porro officium, ne nobis blandiar, aut quod
pauperis hic meritum, si curet nocte togatus
currere, cum praetor lictorem inpellat et ire
praecipitem iubeat dudum vigilantibus orbis,
ne prior Albinam et Modiam collega salutet?
divitis hic servo cludit latus ingenuorum
filius; alter enim quantum in legione tribuni
accipiunt donat Calvinae vel Catienae,
ut semel aut iterum super illam palpitet; at tu,
cum tibi vestiti facies scorti placet, haeres
et dubitas alta Chionen deducere sella.
da testem Romae tam sanctum quam fuit hospes
numinis Idaei, procedat vel Numa vel qui
servavit trepidam flagranti ex aede Minervam:
protinus ad censum, de moribus ultima fiet
quaestio. "quot pascit servos? quot possidet agri
iugera? quam multa magnaque paropside cenat?"
quantum quisque sua nummorum servat in arca,
tantum habet et fidei. iures licet et Samothracum
et nostrorum aras, contemnere fulmina pauper
creditur atque deos dis ignoscentibus ipsis.
quid quod materiam praebet causasque iocorum
omnibus hic idem, si foeda et scissa lacerna,
si toga sordidula est et rupta calceus alter
pelle patet, vel si consuto volnere crassum
atque recens linum ostendit non una cicatrix?
nil habet infelix paupertas durius in se
quam quod ridiculos homines facit. "exeat" inquit,
"si pudor est, et de pulvino surgat equestri,
cuius res legi non sufficit, et sedeant hic
lenonum pueri quocumque ex fornice nati,
hic plaudat nitidus praeconis filius inter
pinnirapi cultos iuvenes iuvenesque lanistae."
sic libitum vano, qui nos distinxit, Othoni.
quis gener hic placuit censu minor atque puellae
sarcinulis inpar? quis pauper scribitur heres?
quando in consilio est aedilibus? agmine facto
debuerant olim tenues migrasse Quirites.
haut facile emergunt quorum virtutibus obstat

res angusta domi, sed Romae durior illis
conatus: magno hospitium miserabile, magno
servorum ventres, et frugi cenula magno.
fictilibus cenare pudet, quod turpe negabis
translatus subito ad Marsos mensamque Sabellam
contentusque illic Veneto duroque cucullo.
pars magna Italiae est, si verum admittimus, in qua
nemo togam sumit nisi mortuus. ipsa dierum
festorum herboso colitur si quando theatro
maiestas tandemque redit ad pulpita notum
exodium, cum personae pallentis hiatum
in gremio matris formidat rusticus infans,
aequales habitus illic similesque videbis
orchestram et populum; clari velamen honoris
sufficiunt tunicae summis aedilibus albae.
hic ultra vires habitus nitor, hic aliquid plus
quam satis est interdum aliena sumitur arca.
commune id vitium est: hic vivimus ambitiosa
paupertate omnes. quid te moror? omnia Romae
cum pretio. quid das, ut Cossum aliquando salutes,
ut te respiciat clauso Veiiento labello?
ille metit barbam, crinem hic deponit amati;
plena domus libis venalibus: accipe et istud
fermentum tibi habe. praestare tributa clientes
cogimur et cultis augere peculia servis.
  quis timet aut timuit gelida Praeneste ruinam
aut positis nemorosa inter iuga Volsiniis aut
simplicibus Gabiis aut proni Tiburis arce?
nos urbem colimus tenui tibicine fultam
magna parte sui; nam sic labentibus obstat
vilicus et, veteris rimae cum texit hiatum,
securos pendente iubet dormire ruina.
vivendum est illic, ubi nulla incendia, nulli
nocte metus. iam poscit aquam, iam frivola transfert
Ucalegon, tabulata tibi iam tertia fumant:
tu nescis; nam si gradibus trepidatur ab imis,
ultimus ardebit quem tegula sola tuetur
a pluvia, molles ubi reddunt ova columbae.
lectus erat Cordo Procula minor, urceoli sex
ornamentum abaci, nec non et parvulus infra
cantharus et recubans sub eodem marmore Chiron,
iamque vetus Graecos servabat cista libellos
et divina opici rodebant carmina mures.
nil habuit Cordus, quis enim negat? et tamen illud

perdidit infelix totum nihil. ultimus autem
aerumnae cumulus, quod nudum et frusta rogantem
nemo cibo, nemo hospitio tectoque iuvabit.
si magna Asturici cecidit domus, horrida mater,
pullati proceres, differt vadimonia praetor.
tum gemimus casus urbis, tunc odimus ignem.
ardet adhuc, et iam accurrit qui marmora donet,
conferat inpensas; hic nuda et candida signa,
hic aliquid praeclarum Euphranoris et Polycliti,
haec Asianorum vetera ornamenta deorum,
hic libros dabit et forulos mediamque Minervam,
hic modium argenti. meliora ac plura reponit
Persicus orborum lautissimus et merito iam
suspectus tamquam ipse suas incenderit aedes.
si potes avelli circensibus, optima Sorae
aut Fabrateriae domus aut Frusinone paratur
quanti nunc tenebras unum conducis in annum.
hortulus hic puteusque brevis nec reste movendus
in tenuis plantas facili diffunditur haustu.
vive bidentis amans et culti vilicus horti
unde epulum possis centum dare Pythagoreis.
est aliquid, quocumque loco, quocumque recessu,
unius sese dominum fecisse lacertae.
  plurimus hic aeger moritur vigilando (sed ipsum
languorem peperit cibus inperfectus et haerens
ardenti stomacho); nam quae meritoria somnum
admittunt? magnis opibus dormitur in urbe.
inde caput morbi. raedarum transitus arto
vicorum in flexu et stantis convicia mandrae
eripient somnum Druso vitulisque marinis.
si vocat officium, turba cedente vehetur
dives et ingenti curret super ora Liburna
atque obiter leget aut scribet vel dormiet intus;
namque facit somnum clausa lectica fenestra.
ante tamen veniet: nobis properantibus obstat
unda prior, magno populus premit agmine lumbos
qui sequitur; ferit hic cubito, ferit assere duro
alter, at hic tignum capiti incutit, ille metretam.
pinguia crura luto, planta mox undique magna
calcor, et in digito clavus mihi militis haeret.
nonne vides quanto celebretur sportula fumo?
centum convivae, sequitur sua quemque culina.
Corbulo vix ferret tot vasa ingentia, tot res
inpositas capiti, quas recto vertice portat

servulus infelix et cursu ventilat ignem.
scinduntur tunicae sartae modo, longa coruscat
serraco veniente abies, atque altera pinum
plaustra vehunt; nutant alte populoque minantur.
nam si procubuit qui saxa Ligustica portat
axis et eversum fudit super agmina montem,
quid superest de corporibus? quis membra, quis ossa
invenit? obtritum volgi perit omne cadaver
more animae. domus interea secura patellas
iam lavat et bucca foculum excitat et sonat unctis
striglibus et pleno componit lintea guto.
haec inter pueros varie properantur, at ille
iam sedet in ripa taetrumque novicius horret
porthmea nec sperat caenosi gurgitis alnum
infelix nec habet quem porrigat ore trientem.
  respice nunc alia ac diversa pericula noctis:
quod spatium tectis sublimibus unde cerebrum
testa ferit, quotiens rimosa et curta fenestris
vasa cadant, quanto percussum pondere signent
et laedant silicem. possis ignavus haberi
et subiti casus inprouidus, ad cenam si
intestatus eas: adeo tot fata, quot illa
nocte patent vigiles te praetereunte fenestrae.
ergo optes votumque feras miserabile tecum,
ut sint contentae patulas defundere pelves.
ebrius ac petulans, qui nullum forte cecidit,
dat poenas, noctem patitur lugentis amicum
Pelidae, cubat in faciem, mox deinde supinus:
[ergo non aliter poterit dormire; quibusdam]
somnum rixa facit. sed quamvis inprobus annis
atque mero fervens cavet hunc quem coccina laena
vitari iubet et comitum longissimus ordo,
multum praeterea flammarum et aenea lampas.
me, quem luna solet deducere vel breve lumen
candelae, cuius dispenso et tempero filum,
contemnit. miserae cognosce prohemia rixae,
si rixa est, ubi tu pulsas, ego vapulo tantum.
stat contra starique iubet. parere necesse est;
nam quid agas, cum te furiosus cogat et idem
fortior? "unde venis" exclamat, "cuius aceto,
cuius conche tumes? quis tecum sectile porrum
sutor et elixi vervecis labra comedit?
nil mihi respondes? aut dic aut accipe calcem.
ede ubi consistas: in qua te quaero proseucha?"

dicere si temptes aliquid tacitusve recedas,
tantumdem est: feriunt pariter, vadimonia deinde
irati faciunt. libertas pauperis haec est:
pulsatus rogat et pugnis concisus adorat
ut liceat paucis cum dentibus inde reverti.
nec tamen haec tantum metuas; nam qui spoliet te
non derit clausis domibus postquam omnis ubique
fixa catenatae siluit compago tabernae.
interdum et ferro subitus grassator agit rem:
armato quotiens tutae custode tenentur
et Pomptina palus et Gallinaria pinus,
sic inde huc omnes tamquam ad vivaria currunt.
qua fornace graves, qua non incude catenae?
maximus in vinclis ferri modus, ut timeas ne
vomer deficiat, ne marra et sarcula desint.
felices proavorum atavos, felicia dicas
saecula quae quondam sub regibus atque tribunis
viderunt uno contentam carcere Romam.
  his alias poteram et pluris subnectere causas,
sed iumenta vocant et sol inclinat. eundum est;
nam mihi commota iamdudum mulio virga
adnuit. ergo vale nostri memor, et quotiens te
Roma tuo refici properantem reddet Aquino,
me quoque ad Helvinam Cererem vestramque Dianam
converte a Cumis. saturarum ego, ni pudet illas,
auditor gelidos veniam caligatus in agros.'

6

Credo Pudicitiam Saturno rege moratam
in terris visamque diu, cum frigida parvas
praeberet spelunca domos ignemque laremque
et pecus et dominos communi clauderet umbra,
silvestrem montana torum cum sterneret uxor
frondibus et culmo vicinarumque ferarum
pellibus, haut similis tibi, Cynthia, nec tibi, cuius
turbavit nitidos extinctus passer ocellos,
sed potanda ferens infantibus ubera magnis
et saepe horridior glandem ructante marito.
quippe aliter tunc orbe novo caeloque recenti
vivebant homines, qui rupto robore nati
compositive luto nullos habuere parentes.
multa Pudicitiae veteris vestigia forsan
aut aliqua exstiterint et sub Iove, sed Iove nondum

barbato, nondum Graecis iurare paratis
per caput alterius, cum furem nemo timeret
caulibus ac pomis et aperto viveret horto.
paulatim deinde ad superos Astraea recessit
hac comite, atque duae pariter fugere sorores.
anticum et vetus est alienum, Postume, lectum
concutere atque sacri genium contemnere fulcri.
omne aliud crimen mox ferrea protulit aetas:
viderunt primos argentea saecula moechos.
conventum tamen et pactum et sponsalia nostra
tempestate paras iamque a tonsore magistro
pecteris et digito pignus fortasse dedisti?
certe sanus eras. uxorem, Postume, ducis?
dic qua Tisiphone, quibus exagitere colubris.
ferre potes dominam salvis tot restibus ullam,
cum pateant altae caligantesque fenestrae,
cum tibi vicinum se praebeat Aemilius pons?
aut si de multis nullus placet exitus, illud
nonne putas melius, quod tecum pusio dormit?
pusio, qui noctu non litigat, exigit a te
nulla iacens illic munuscula, nec queritur quod
et lateri parcas nec quantum iussit anheles.
  sed placet Ursidio lex Iulia: tollere dulcem
cogitat heredem, cariturus turture magno
mullorumque iubis et captatore macello.
quid fieri non posse putes, si iungitur ulla
Ursidio? si moechorum notissimus olim
stulta maritali iam porrigit ora capistro,
quem totiens texit perituri cista Latini?
quid quod et antiquis uxor de moribus illi
quaeritur? o medici, nimiam pertundite venam.
delicias hominis! Tarpeium limen adora
pronus et auratam Iunoni caede iuvencam,
si tibi contigerit capitis matrona pudici.
paucae adeo Cereris vittas contingere dignae,
quarum non timeat pater oscula. necte coronam
postibus et densos per limina tende corymbos.
unus Hiberinae vir sufficit? ocius illud
extorquebis, ut haec oculo contenta sit uno.
magna tamen fama est cuiusdam rure paterno
viventis. vivat Gabiis ut vixit in agro,
vivat Fidenis, et agello cedo paterno.
quis tamen adfirmat nil actum in montibus aut in
speluncis? adeo senuerunt Iuppiter et Mars?

porticibusne tibi monstratur femina voto
digna tuo? cuneis an habent spectacula totis
quod securus ames quodque inde excerpere possis?
chironomon Ledam molli saltante Bathyllo
Tuccia vesicae non imperat, Apula gannit,
sicut in amplexu, subito et miserabile longum.
attendit Thymele: Thymele tunc rustica discit.
ast aliae, quotiens aulaea recondita cessant,
et vacuo clusoque sonant fora sola theatro,
atque a plebeis longe Megalesia, tristes
personam thyrsumque tenent et subligar Acci.
Urbicus exodio risum movet Atellanae
gestibus Autonoes, hunc diligit Aelia pauper.
solvitur his magno comoedi fibula, sunt quae
Chrysogonum cantare vetent, Hispulla tragoedo
gaudet: an expectas ut Quintilianus ametur?
accipis uxorem de qua citharoedus Echion
aut Glaphyrus fiat pater Ambrosiusque choraules.
longa per angustos figamus pulpita vicos,
ornentur postes et grandi ianua lauro,
ut testudineo tibi, Lentule, conopeo
nobilis Euryalum murmillonem exprimat infans.
nupta senatori comitata est Eppia ludum
ad Pharon et Nilum famosaque moenia Lagi,
prodigia et mores urbis damnante Canopo.
inmemor illa domus et coniugis atque sororis
nil patriae indulsit, plorantisque improba natos
(utque magis stupeas) ludos Paridemque reliquit.
sed quamquam in magnis opibus plumaque paterna
et segmentatis dormisset parvula cunis,
contempsit pelagus; famam contempserat olim,
cuius apud molles minima est iactura cathedras.
Tyrrhenos igitur fluctus lateque sonantem
pertulit Ionium constanti pectore, quamvis
mutandum totiens esset mare. iusta pericli
si ratio est et honesta, timent pavidoque gelantur
pectore nec tremulis possunt insistere plantis:
fortem animum praestant rebus quas turpiter audent.
si iubeat coniunx, durum est conscendere navem,
tunc sentina gravis, tunc summus vertitur aer:
quae moechum sequitur, stomacho valet. illa maritum
convomit, haec inter nautas et prandet et errat
per puppem et duros gaudet tractare rudentis.
qua tamen exarsit forma, qua capta iuventa

Eppia? quid vidit propter quod ludia dici
sustinuit? nam Sergiolus iam radere guttur
coeperat et secto requiem sperare lacerto;
praeterea multa in facie deformia, sicut
attritus galea mediisque in naribus ingens
gibbus et acre malum semper stillantis ocelli.
sed gladiator erat. facit hoc illos Hyacinthos;
hoc pueris patriaeque, hoc praetulit illa sorori
atque viro. ferrum est quod amant. hic Sergius idem
accepta rude coepisset Veiiento videri.
  quid privata domus, quid fecerit Eppia, curas?
respice rivales divorum, Claudius audi
quae tulerit. dormire virum cum senserat uxor,
sumere nocturnos meretrix Augusta cucullos
ausa Palatino et tegetem praeferre cubili
linquebat comite ancilla non amplius una.
sed nigrum flavo crinem abscondente galero
intravit calidum veteri centone lupanar
et cellam vacuam atque suam; tunc nuda papillis
prostitit auratis titulum mentita Lyciscae
ostenditque tuum, generose Britannice, ventrem.
excepit blanda intrantis atque aera poposcit.
continueque iacens cunctorum absorbuit ictus.
mox lenone suas iam dimittente puellas
tristis abit, et quod potuit tamen ultima cellam
clausit, adhuc ardens rigidae tentigine volvae,
et lassata viris necdum satiata recessit,
obscurisque genis turpis fumoque lucernae
foeda lupanaris tulit ad pulvinar odorem.
hippomanes carmenque loquar coctumque venenum
privignoque datum? faciunt graviora coactae
imperio sexus minimumque libidine peccant.
  'optima sed quare Caesennia teste marito?'
bis quingena dedit. tanti vocat ille pudicam,
nec pharetris Veneris macer est aut lampade fervet:
inde faces ardent, veniunt a dote sagittae.
libertas emitur. coram licet innuat atque
rescribat: vidua est, locuples quae nupsit avaro.
  'cur desiderio Bibulae Sertorius ardet?'
si verum excutias, facies non uxor amatur.
tres rugae subeant et se cutis arida laxet,
fiant obscuri dentes oculique minores,
'collige sarcinulas' dicet libertus 'et exi.
iam gravis es nobis et saepe emungeris. exi

ocius et propera. sicco venit altera naso.'
interea calet et regnat poscitque maritum
pastores et ovem Canusinam ulmosque Falernas—
quantulum in hoc!—pueros omnes, ergastula tota,
quodque domi non est, sed habet vicinus, ematur.
mense quidem brumae, cum iam mercator Iason
clausus et armatis obstat casa candida nautis,
grandia tolluntur crystallina, maxima rursus
murrina, deinde adamas notissimus et Beronices
in digito factus pretiosior. hunc dedit olim
barbarus incestae gestare Agrippa sorori,
observant ubi festa mero pede sabbata reges
et vetus indulget senibus clementia porcis.
'nullane de tantis gregibus tibi digna videtur?'
sit formonsa, decens, dives, fecunda, vetustos
porticibus disponat avos, intactior omni
crinibus effusis bellum dirimente Sabina,
rara avis in terris nigroque simillima cycno,
quis feret uxorem cui constant omnia? malo,
malo Venustinam quam te, Cornelia, mater
Gracchorum, si cum magnis virtutibus adfers
grande supercilium et numeras in dote triumphos.
tolle tuum, precor, Hannibalem victumque Syphacem
in castris et cum tota Carthagine migra.
'parce, precor, Paean, et tu, dea, pone sagittas;
nil pueri faciunt, ipsam configite matrem'
Amphion clamat, sed Paean contrahit arcum.
extulit ergo greges natorum ipsumque parentem,
dum sibi nobilior Latonae gente videtur
atque eadem scrofa Niobe fecundior alba.
quae tanti gravitas, quae forma, ut se tibi semper
inputet? huius enim rari summique voluptas
nulla boni; quotiens animo corrupta superbo
plus aloes quam mellis habet. quis deditus autem
usque adeo est, ut non illam quam laudibus effert
horreat inque diem septenis oderit horis?
....

unde haec monstra tamen vel quo de fonte requiris?
praestabat castas humilis fortuna Latinas
quondam, nec vitiis contingi parva sinebant
tecta labor somnique breves et vellere Tusco
vexatae duraeque manus ac proximus urbi
Hannibal et stantes Collina turre mariti.
nunc patimur longae pacis mala, saevior armis

luxuria incubuit victumque ulciscitur orbem.
nullum crimen abest facinusque libidinis ex quo
paupertas Romana perit. hinc fluxit ad istos
et Sybaris colles, hinc et Rhodos et Miletos
atque coronatum et petulans madidumque Tarentum.
prima peregrinos obscena pecunia mores
intulit, et turpi fregerunt saecula luxu
divitiae molles. quid enim venus ebria curat?
inguinis et capitis quae sint discrimina nescit
grandia quae mediis iam noctibus ostrea mordet,
cum perfusa mero spumant unguenta Falerno,
cum bibitur concha, cum iam vertigine tectum
ambulat et geminis exsurgit mensa lucernis.
i nunc et dubita qua sorbeat aera sanna
Tullia, quid dicat notae collactea Maurae
Maura, Pudicitiae veterem cum praeterit aram.
noctibus hic ponunt lecticas, micturiunt hic
effigiemque deae longis siphonibus implent
inque vices equitant ac Luna teste moventur,
inde domos abeunt: tu calcas luce reversa
coniugis urinam magnos visurus amicos.
nota bonae secreta deae, cum tibia lumbos
incitat et cornu pariter vinoque feruntur
attonitae crinemque rotant ululantque Priapi
maenades. o quantus tunc illis mentibus ardor
concubitus, quae vox saltante libidine, quantus
ille meri veteris per crura madentia torrens!
lenonum ancillas posita Saufeia corona
provocat et tollit pendentis praemia coxae,
ipsa Medullinae fluctum crisantis adorat:
palma inter dominas, virtus natalibus aequa.
nil ibi per ludum simulabitur, omnia fient
ad verum, quibus incendi iam frigidus aevo
Laomedontiades et Nestoris hirnea possit.
tunc prurigo morae inpatiens, tum femina simplex,
ac pariter toto repetitus clamor ab antro
'iam fas est, admitte viros.' dormitat adulter,
illa iubet sumpto iuvenem properare cucullo;
si nihil est, servis incurritur; abstuleris spem
servorum, venit et conductus aquarius; hic si
quaeritur et desunt homines, mora nulla per ipsam
quo minus inposito clunem summittat asello.
atque utinam ritus veteres et publica saltem
his intacta malis agerentur sacra; sed omnes

noverunt Mauri atque Indi quae psaltria penem
maiorem quam sunt duo Caesaris Anticatones
illuc, testiculi sibi conscius unde fugit mus,
intulerit, ubi velari pictura iubetur
quaecumque alterius sexus imitata figuras.
et quis tunc hominum contemptor numinis, aut quis
simpuvium ridere Numae nigrumque catinum
et Vaticano fragiles de monte patellas
ausus erat? sed nunc ad quas non Clodius aras?

....

sunt quas eunuchi inbelles ac mollia semper
oscula delectent et desperatio barbae
et quod abortivo non est opus. illa voluptas
summa tamen, quom iam calida matura iuventa
inguina traduntur medicis, iam pectine nigro.
ergo expectatos ac iussos crescere primum
testiculos, postquam coeperunt esse bilibres,
tonsoris tantum damno rapit Heliodorus.
conspicuus longe cunctisque notabilis intrat
balnea nec dubie custodem vitis et horti
provocat a domina factus spado. dormiat ille
cum domina, sed tu iam durum, Postume, iamque
tondendum eunucho Bromium committere noli.

....

sed cantet potius quam totam pervolet urbem
audax et coetus possit quae ferre virorum
cumque paludatis ducibus praesente marito
ipsa loqui recta facie siccisque mamillis.
haec eadem novit quid toto fiat in orbe,
quid Seres, quid Thraces agant, secreta novercae
et pueri, quis amet, quis diripiatur adulter;
dicet quis viduam praegnatem fecerit et quo
mense, quibus verbis concumbat quaeque, modis quot.
instantem regi Armenio Parthoque cometen
prima videt, famam rumoresque illa recentis
excipit ad portas, quosdam facit; isse Niphaten
in populos magnoque illic cuncta arva teneri
diluvio, nutare urbes, subsidere terras,
quocumque in trivio, cuicumque est obvia, narrat.
nec tamen id vitium magis intolerabile quam quod
vicinos humiles rapere et concidere loris
experrecta solet. nam si latratibus alti
rumpuntur somni, 'fustes huc ocius' inquit
'adferte' atque illis dominum iubet ante feriri,

deinde canem. gravis occursu, taeterrima vultu
balnea nocte subit, conchas et castra moveri
nocte iubet, magno gaudet sudare tumultu,
cum lassata gravi ceciderunt bracchia massa,
callidus et cristae digitos inpressit aliptes
ac summum dominae femur exclamare coegit.
convivae miseri interea somnoque fameque
urguentur. tandem illa venit rubicundula, totum
oenophorum sitiens, plena quod tenditur urna
admotum pedibus, de quo sextarius alter
ducitur ante cibum rabidam facturus orexim,
dum redit et loto terram ferit intestino.
marmoribus rivi properant, aurata Falernum
pelvis olet; nam sic, tamquam alta in dolia longus
deciderit serpens, bibit et vomit. ergo maritus
nauseat atque oculis bilem substringit opertis.
illa tamen gravior, quae cum discumbere coepit
laudat Vergilium, periturae ignoscit Elissae,
committit vates et comparat, inde Maronem
atque alia parte in trutina suspendit Homerum.
cedunt grammatici, vincuntur rhetores, omnis
turba tacet, nec causidicus nec praeco loquetur,
altera nec mulier. verborum tanta cadit vis,
tot pariter pelves ac tintinnabula dicas
pulsari. iam nemo tubas, nemo aera fatiget:
una laboranti poterit succurrere Lunae.
inponit finem sapiens et rebus honestis;
nam quae docta nimis cupit et facunda videri
crure tenus medio tunicas succingere debet,
caedere Silvano porcum, quadrante lavari.
non habeat matrona, tibi quae iuncta recumbit,
dicendi genus, aut curvum sermone rotato
torqueat enthymema, nec historias sciat omnes,
sed quaedam ex libris et non intellegat. odi
hanc ego quae repetit volvitque Palaemonis artem
servata semper lege et ratione loquendi
ignotosque mihi tenet antiquaria versus
nec curanda viris. opicae castiget amicae
verba: soloecismum liceat fecisse marito.

....

est pretium curae penitus cognoscere toto
quid faciant agitentque die. si nocte maritus
aversus iacuit, periit libraria, ponunt
cosmetae tunicas, tarde venisse Liburnus

dicitur et poenas alieni pendere somni
cogitur, hic frangit ferulas, rubet ille flagello,
hic scutica; sunt quae tortoribus annua praestent.
verberat atque obiter faciem linit, audit amicas
aut latum pictae vestis considerat aurum
et caedit, longi relegit transversa diurni
et caedit, donec lassis caedentibus 'exi'
intonet horrendum iam cognitione peracta.
praefectura domus Sicula non mitior aula.
nam si constituit solitoque decentius optat
ornari et properat iamque expectatur in hortis
aut apud Isiacae potius sacraria lenae,
disponit crinem laceratis ipsa capillis
nuda umeros Psecas infelix nudisque mamillis.
'altior hic quare cincinnus?' taurea punit
continuo flexi crimen facinusque capilli.
quid Psecas admisit? quaenam est hic culpa puellae,
si tibi displicuit nasus tuus? altera laevum
extendit pectitque comas et volvit in orbem.
est in consilio materna admotaque lanis
emerita quae cessat acu; sententia prima
huius erit, post hanc aetate atque arte minores
censebunt, tamquam famae discrimen agatur
aut animae: tanta est quaerendi cura decoris.
tot premit ordinibus, tot adhuc conpagibus altum
aedificat caput: Andromachen a fronte videbis,
post minor est, credas aliam. cedo si breve parvi
sortita est lateris spatium breviorque videtur
virgine Pygmaea nullis adiuta cothurnis
et levis erecta consurgit ad oscula planta.

....

hic magicos adfert cantus, hic Thessala vendit
philtra, quibus valeat mentem vexare mariti
et solea pulsare natis. quod desipis, inde est;
inde animi caligo et magna oblivio rerum
quas modo gessisti. tamen hoc tolerabile, si non
et furere incipias ut avunculus ille Neronis,
cui totam tremuli frontem Caesonia pulli
infudit. quae non faciet quod principis uxor?
ardebant cuncta et fracta conpage ruebant
non aliter quam si fecisset Iuno maritum
insanum. minus ergo nocens erit Agrippinae
boletus, siquidem unius praecordia pressit
ille senis tremulumque caput descendere iussit

in caelum et longa manantia labra saliva.
haec poscit ferrum atque ignes, haec potio torquet,
haec lacerat mixtos equitum cum sanguine patres.
tanti partus equae, tanti una venefica constat.
  oderunt natos de paelice; nemo repugnet,
nemo vetet, iam iam privignum occidere fas est.
vos ego, pupilli, moneo, quibus amplior est res,
custodite animas et nulli credite mensae:
livida materno fervent adipata veneno.
mordeat ante aliquis quidquid porrexerit illa,
quae peperit, timidus praegustet pocula papas.
fingimus haec altum satura sumente coturnum
scilicet, et finem egressi legemque priorum
grande Sophocleo carmen bacchamur hiatu,
montibus ignotum Rutulis caeloque Latino?
nos utinam vani. sed clamat Pontia 'feci,
confiteor, puerisque meis aconita paravi,
quae deprensa patent; facinus tamen ipsa peregi.'
tune duos una, saevissima vipera, cena?
tune duos? 'septem, si septem forte fuissent.'
credamus tragicis quidquid de Colchide torva
dicitur et Procne; nil contra conor. et illae
grandia monstra suis audebant temporibus, sed
non propter nummos. minor admiratio summis
debetur monstris, quotiens facit ira nocentes
hunc sexum et rabie iecur incendente feruntur
praecipites, ut saxa iugis abrupta, quibus mons
subtrahitur clivoque latus pendente recedit.
illam ego non tulerim quae conputat et scelus ingens
sana facit. spectant subeuntem fata mariti
Alcestim et, similis si permutatio detur,
morte viri cupiant animam servare catellae.
occurrent multae tibi Belides atque Eriphylae
mane, Clytemestram nullus non vicus habebit.
hoc tantum refert, quod Tyndaris illa bipennem
insulsam et fatuam dextra laevaque tenebat;
at nunc res agitur tenui pulmone rubetae,
sed tamen et ferro, si praegustarit Atrides
Pontica ter victi cautus medicamina regis.

9

Scire velim quare totiens mihi, Naevole, tristis
occurras fronte obducta ceu Marsya victus.

quid tibi cum vultu, qualem deprensus habebat
Ravola dum Rhodopes uda terit inguina barba?
(nos colaphum incutimus lambenti crustula servo.)
non erit hac facie miserabilior Crepereius
Pollio, qui triplicem usuram praestare paratus
circumit et fatuos non invenit. unde repente
tot rugae? certe modico contentus agebas
vernam equitem, conviva ioco mordente facetus
et salibus vehemens intra pomeria natis.
omnia nunc contra, vultus gravis, horrida siccae
silva comae, nullus tota nitor in cute, qualem
Bruttia praestabat calidi tibi fascia visci,
sed fruticante pilo neglecta et squalida crura.
quid macies aegri veteris, quem tempore longo
torret quarta dies olimque domestica febris?
deprendas animi tormenta latentis in aegro
corpore, deprendas et gaudia; sumit utrumque
inde habitum facies. igitur flexisse videris
propositum et vitae contrarius ire priori.
nuper enim, ut repeto, fanum Isidis et Ganymedem
Pacis et advectae secreta Palatia matris
et Cererem (nam quo non prostat femina templo?)
notior Aufidio moechus celebrare solebas,
quodque taces, ipsos etiam inclinare maritos.
'utile et hoc multis vitae genus, at mihi nullum
inde operae pretium. pingues aliquando lacernas,
munimenta togae, duri crassique coloris
et male percussas textoris pectine Galli
accipimus, tenue argentum venaeque secundae.
fata regunt homines, fatum est et partibus illis
quas sinus abscondit. nam si tibi sidera cessant,
nil faciet longi mensura incognita nervi,
quamvis te nudum spumanti Virro labello
viderit et blandae adsidue densaeque tabellae
sollicitent, αὐτὸς γὰρ ἐφέλκεται ἄνδρα κίναιδος.
quod tamen ulterius monstrum quam mollis avarus?
"haec tribui, deinde illa dedi, mox plura tulisti."
computat et cevet. ponatur calculus, adsint
cum tabula pueri; numera sestertia quinque
omnibus in rebus, numerentur deinde labores.
an facile et pronum est agere intra viscera penem
legitimum atque illic hesternae occurrere cenae?
servus erit minus ille miser qui foderit agrum
quam dominum. sed tu sane tenerum et puerum te

et pulchrum et dignum cyatho caeloque putabas.
(vos humili adseculae, vos indulgebitis umquam
cultori, iam nec morbo donare parati?)
en cui tu viridem umbellam, cui sucina mittas
grandia, natalis quotiens redit aut madidum ver
incipit et strata positus longaque cathedra
munera femineis tractat secreta kalendis.
dic, passer, cui tot montis, tot praedia servas
Apula, tot milvos intra tua pascua lassas?
te Trifolinus ager fecundis vitibus implet
suspectumque iugum Cumis et Gaurus inanis
(nam quis plura linit victuro dolia musto?);
quantum erat exhausti lumbos donare clientis
iugeribus paucis? Melius nunc rusticus infans
cum matre et casulis et conlusore catello
cymbala pulsantis legatum fiet amici?
"improbus es cum poscis" ait. sed pensio clamat
"posce," sed appellat puer unicus ut Polyphemi
lata acies per quam sollers evasit Ulixes.
alter emendus erit, namque hic non sufficit, ambo
pascendi. quid agam bruma spirante? quid, oro,
quid dicam scapulis puerorum aquilone Decembri
et pedibus? "durate atque expectate cicadas"?
verum, ut dissimules, ut mittas cetera, quanto
metiris pretio quod, ni tibi deditus essem
devotusque cliens, uxor tua virgo maneret?
scis certe quibus ista modis, quam saepe rogaris
et quae pollicitus. fugientem saepe puellam
amplexu rapui; tabulas quoque ruperat et iam
migrabat; tota vix hoc ego nocte redemi
te plorante foris. testis mihi lectulus et tu,
ad quem pervenit lecti sonus et dominae vox.
instabile ac dirimi coeptum et iam paene solutum
coniugium in multis domibus servavit adulter.
quo te circumagas? quae prima aut ultima ponas?
nullum ergo meritum est, ingrate ac perfide, nullum
quod tibi filiolus vel filia nascitur ex me?
tollis enim et libris actorum spargere gaudes
argumenta viri. foribus suspende coronas:
iam pater es, dedimus quod famae opponere possis.
iura parentis habes, propter me scriberis heres,
legatum omne capis nec non et dulce caducum.
commoda praeterea iungentur multa caducis,
si numerum, si tres implevero.' iusta doloris,

Naevole, causa tui; contra tamen ille quid adfert?
  'neglegit atque alium bipedem sibi quaerit asellum.
haec soli commissa tibi celare memento
et tacitus nostras intra te fige querellas;
nam res mortifera est inimicus pumice levis.
qui modo secretum commiserat, ardet et odit,
tamquam prodiderim quidquid scio. sumere ferrum,
fuste aperire caput, candelam adponere valvis
non dubitat. nec contemnas aut despicias quod
his opibus numquam cara est annona veneni.
ergo occulta teges ut curia Martis Athenis.'
  o Corydon, Corydon, secretum divitis ullum
esse putas? servi ut taceant, iumenta loquentur
et canis et postes et marmora. claude fenestras,
vela tegant rimas, iunge ostia, tollite lumen,
e medio fac eant omnes, prope nemo recumbat;
quod tamen ad cantum galli facit ille secundi
proximus ante diem caupo sciet, audiet et quae
finxerunt pariter libarius, archimagiri,
carptores. quod enim dubitant componere crimen
in dominos, quotiens rumoribus ulciscuntur
baltea? nec derit qui te per compita quaerat
nolentem et miseram vinosus inebriet aurem.
illos ergo roges quidquid paulo ante petebas
a nobis, taceant illi. sed prodere malunt
arcanum quam subrepti potare Falerni
pro populo faciens quantum Saufeia bibebat.
vivendum recte, cum propter plurima tunc est
idcirco ut possis linguam contemnere servi.
[praecipve causis, ut linguas mancipiorum
contemnas; nam lingua mali pars pessima servi.
deterior tamen hic qui liber non erit illis
quorum animas et farre suo custodit et aere.]
  'utile consilium modo, sed commune, dedisti.
nunc mihi quid suades post damnum temporis et spes
deceptas? festinat enim decurrere velox
flosculus angustae miseraeque brevissima vitae
portio; dum bibimus, dum serta, unguenta, puellas
poscimus, obrepit non intellecta senectus.'
  ne trepida, numquam pathicus tibi derit amicus
stantibus et salvis his collibus; undique ad illos
convenient et carpentis et navibus omnes
qui digito scalpunt uno caput. altera maior
spes superest, tu tantum erucis inprime dentem.

'haec exempla para felicibus; at mea Clotho
et Lachesis gaudent, si pascitur inguine venter.
o parvi nostrique Lares, quos ture minuto
aut farre et tenui soleo exorare corona,
quando ego figam aliquid quo sit mihi tuta senectus
a tegete et baculo? viginti milia fenus
pigneribus positis, argenti vascula puri,
sed quae Fabricius censor notet, et duo fortes
de grege Moesorum, qui me cervice locatum
securum iubeant clamoso insistere circo;
sit mihi praeterea curvus caelator, et alter
qui multas facies pingit cito; sufficiunt haec.
quando ego pauper ero? votum miserabile, nec spes
his saltem; nam cum pro me Fortuna vocatur,
adfixit ceras illa de nave petitas
quae Siculos cantus effugit remige surdo.'

10

Omnibus in terris, quae sunt a Gadibus usque
Auroram et Gangen, pauci dinoscere possunt
vera bona atque illis multum diversa, remota
erroris nebula. quid enim ratione timemus
aut cupimus? quid tam dextro pede concipis ut te
conatus non paeniteat votique peracti?
evertere domos totas optantibus ipsis
di faciles. nocitura toga, nocitura petuntur
militia; torrens dicendi copia multis
et sua mortifera est facundia; viribus ille
confisus periit admirandisque lacertis;
sed pluris nimia congesta pecunia cura
strangulat et cuncta exuperans patrimonia census
quanto delphinis ballaena Britannica maior.
temporibus diris igitur iussuque Neronis
Longinum et magnos Senecae praedivitis hortos
clausit et egregias Lateranorum obsidet aedes
tota cohors: rarus venit in cenacula miles.
pauca licet portes argenti vascula puri
nocte iter ingressus, gladium contumque timebis
et mota ad lunam trepidabis harundinis umbra:
cantabit vacuus coram latrone viator.
prima fere vota et cunctis notissima templis
divitiae, crescant ut opes, ut maxima toto
nostra sit arca foro. sed nulla aconita bibuntur

fictilibus; tunc illa time cum pocula sumes
gemmata et lato Setinum ardebit in auro.
iamne igitur laudas quod de sapientibus alter
ridebat, quotiens a limine moverat unum
protuleratque pedem, flebat contrarius auctor?
sed facilis cuivis rigidi censura cachinni:
mirandum est unde ille oculis suffecerit umor.
perpetuo risu pulmonem agitare solebat
Democritus, quamquam non essent urbibus illis
praetextae, trabeae, fasces, lectica, tribunal.
quid si vidisset praetorem curribus altis
extantem et medii sublimem pulvere circi
in tunica Iovis et pictae Sarrana ferentem
ex umeris aulaea togae magnaeque coronae
tantum orbem, quanto cervix non sufficit ulla?
quippe tenet sudans hanc publicus et, sibi consul
ne placeat, curru servus portatur eodem.
da nunc et volucrem, sceptro quae surgit eburno,
illinc cornicines, hinc praecedentia longi
agminis officia et niveos ad frena Quirites,
defossa in loculos quos sportula fecit amicos.
tum quoque materiam risus invenit ad omnis
occursus hominum, cuius prudentia monstrat
summos posse viros et magna exempla daturos
vervecum in patria crassoque sub aere nasci.
ridebat curas nec non et gaudia volgi,
interdum et lacrimas, cum Fortunae ipse minaci
mandaret laqueum mediumque ostenderet unguem.
  ergo supervacua aut quae perniciosa petuntur?
propter quae fas est genua incerare deorum?
  quosdam praecipitat subiecta potentia magnae
invidiae, mergit longa atque insignis honorum
pagina. descendunt statuae restemque secuntur,
ipsas deinde rotas bigarum inpacta securis
caedit et inmeritis franguntur crura caballis.
iam strident ignes, iam follibus atque caminis
ardet adoratum populo caput et crepat ingens
Seianus, deinde ex facie toto orbe secunda
fiunt urceoli, pelves, sartago, matellae.
pone domi laurus, duc in Capitolia magnum
cretatumque bovem: Seianus ducitur unco
spectandus, gaudent omnes. 'quae labra, quis illi
vultus erat! numquam, si quid mihi credis, amavi
hunc hominem. sed quo cecidit sub crimine? quisnam

delator quibus indicibus, quo teste probavit?'
'nil horum; verbosa et grandis epistula venit
a Capreis.' 'bene habet, nil plus interrogo.' sed quid
turba Remi? sequitur fortunam, ut semper, et odit
damnatos. idem populus, si Nortia Tusco
favisset, si oppressa foret secura senectus
principis, hac ipsa Seianum diceret hora
Augustum. iam pridem, ex quo suffragia nulli
vendimus, effudit curas; nam qui dabat olim
imperium, fasces, legiones, omnia, nunc se
continet atque duas tantum res anxius optat,
panem et circenses. 'perituros audio multos.'
'nil dubium, magna est fornacula.' 'pallidulus mi
Bruttidius meus ad Martis fuit obvius aram;
quam timeo, victus ne poenas exigat Aiax
ut male defensus. curramus praecipites et,
dum iacet in ripa, calcemus Caesaris hostem.
sed videant servi, ne quis neget et pavidum in ius
cervice obstricta dominum trahat.' hi sermones
tunc de Seiano, secreta haec murmura volgi.
visne salutari sicut Seianus, habere
tantundem atque illi summas donare curules,
illum exercitibus praeponere, tutor haberi
principis angusta Caprearum in rupe sedentis
cum grege Chaldaeo? vis certe pila, cohortis,
egregios equites et castra domestica; quidni
haec cupias? et qui nolunt occidere quemquam
posse volunt. sed quae praeclara et prospera tanti,
ut rebus laetis par sit mensura malorum?
huius qui trahitur praetextam sumere mavis
an Fidenarum Gabiorumque esse potestas
et de mensura ius dicere, vasa minora
frangere pannosus vacuis aedilis Ulubris?
ergo quid optandum foret ignorasse fateris
Seianum; nam qui nimios optabat honores
et nimias poscebat opes, numerosa parabat
excelsae turris tabulata, unde altior esset
casus et inpulsae praeceps inmane ruinae.
quid Crassos, quid Pompeios evertit et illum,
ad sua qui domitos deduxit flagra Quirites?
summus nempe locus nulla non arte petitus
magnaque numinibus vota exaudita malignis.
ad generum Cereris sine caede ac vulnere pauci
descendunt reges et sicca morte tyranni.

eloquium ac famam Demosthenis aut Ciceronis
incipit optare et totis quinquatribus optat
quisquis adhuc uno parcam colit asse Minervam,
quem sequitur custos angustae vernula capsae.
eloquio sed uterque perit orator, utrumque
largus et exundans leto dedit ingenii fons.
ingenio manus est et cervix caesa, nec umquam
sanguine causidici maduerunt rostra pusilli.
'o fortunatam natam me consule Romam:'
Antoni gladios potuit contemnere si sic
omnia dixisset. ridenda poemata malo
quam te, conspicuae divina Philippica famae,
volveris a prima quae proxima. saevus et illum
exitus eripuit, quem mirabantur Athenae
torrentem et pleni moderantem frena theatri.
dis ille adversis genitus fatoque sinistro,
quem pater ardentis massae fuligine lippus
a carbone et forcipibus gladiosque paranti
incude et luteo Volcano ad rhetora misit.
bellorum exuviae, truncis adfixa tropaeis
lorica et fracta de casside buccula pendens
et curtum temone iugum victaeque triremis
aplustre et summo tristis captivos in arcu
humanis maiora bonis creduntur. ad hoc se
Romanus Graiusque et barbarus induperator
erexit, causas discriminis atque laboris
inde habuit: tanto maior famae sitis est quam
virtutis. quis enim virtutem amplectitur ipsam,
praemia si tollas? patriam tamen obruit olim
gloria paucorum et laudis titulique cupido
haesuri saxis cinerum custodibus, ad quae
discutienda valent sterilis mala robora fici,
quandoquidem data sunt ipsis quoque fata sepulcris.
expende Hannibalem: quot libras in duce summo
invenies? hic est quem non capit Africa Mauro
percussa oceano Niloque admota tepenti
rursus ad Aethiopum populos aliosque elephantos.
additur imperiis Hispania, Pyrenaeum
transilit. opposuit natura Alpemque nivemque:
diducit scopulos et montem rumpit aceto.
iam tenet Italiam, tamen ultra pergere tendit.
'acti' inquit 'nihil est, nisi Poeno milite portas
frangimus et media vexillum pono Subura.'
o qualis facies et quali digna tabella,

cum Gaetula ducem portaret belva luscum!
exitus ergo quis est? o gloria! vincitur idem
nempe et in exilium praeceps fugit atque ibi magnus
mirandusque cliens sedet ad praetoria regis,
donec Bithyno libeat vigilare tyranno.
finem animae, quae res humanas miscuit olim,
non gladii, non saxa dabunt nec tela, sed ille
Cannarum vindex et tanti sanguinis ultor
anulus. i, demens, et saevas curre per Alpes
ut pueris placeas et declamatio fias.
unus Pellaeo iuveni non sufficit orbis,
aestuat infelix angusto limite mundi
ut Gyarae clausus scopulis parvaque Seripho;
cum tamen a figulis munitam intraverit urbem,
sarcophago contentus erit. mors sola fatetur
quantula sint hominum corpuscula. creditur olim
velificatus Athos et quidquid Graecia mendax
audet in historia, constratum classibus isdem
suppositumque rotis solidum mare; credimus altos
defecisse amnes epotaque flumina Medo
prandente et madidis cantat quae Sostratus alis.
ille tamen qualis rediit Salamine relicta,
in Corum atque Eurum solitus saevire flagellis
barbarus Aeolio numquam hoc in carcere passos,
ipsum conpedibus qui vinxerat Ennosigaeum
(mitius id sane, quod non et stigmate dignum
credidit. huic quisquam vellet servire deorum?)—
sed qualis rediit? nempe una nave, cruentis
fluctibus ac tarda per densa cadavera prora.
has totiens optata exegit gloria poenas.
'da spatium vitae, multos da, Iuppiter, annos.'
hoc recto voltu, solum hoc et pallidus optas.
sed quam continuis et quantis longa senectus
plena malis! deformem et taetrum ante omnia vultum
dissimilemque sui, deformem pro cute pellem
pendentisque genas et talis aspice rugas
quales, umbriferos ubi pandit Thabraca saltus,
in vetula scalpit iam mater simia bucca.
plurima sunt iuvenum discrimina, pulchrior ille
hoc atque †ille† alio, multum hic robustior illo:
una senum facies, cum voce trementia membra
et iam leve caput madidique infantia nasi;
frangendus misero gingiva panis inermi.
usque adeo gravis uxori natisque sibique,

ut captatori moveat fastidia Cosso.
non eadem vini atque cibi torpente palato
gaudia; nam coitus iam longa oblivio, vel si
coneris, iacet exiguus cum ramice nervus
et, quamvis tota palpetur nocte, iacebit.
anne aliquid sperare potest haec inguinis aegri
canities? quid quod merito suspecta libido est
quae venerem adfectat sine viribus? aspice partis
nunc damnum alterius. nam quae cantante voluptas,
sit licet eximius, citharoedo sive Seleuco
et quibus aurata mos est fulgere lacerna?
quid refert, magni sedeat qua parte theatri
qui vix cornicines exaudiet atque tubarum
concentus? clamore opus est ut sentiat auris
quem dicat venisse puer, quot nuntiet horas.
praeterea minimus gelido iam in corpore sanguis
febre calet sola, circumsilit agmine facto
morborum omne genus, quorum si nomina quaeras,
promptius expediam quot amaverit Oppia moechos,
quot Themison aegros autumno occiderit uno,
quot Basilus socios, quot circumscripserit Hirrus
pupillos, quot longa viros exorbeat uno
Maura die, quot discipulos inclinet Hamillus;
percurram citius quot villas possideat nunc
quo tondente gravis iuveni mihi barba sonabat.
ille umero, hic lumbis, hic coxa debilis; ambos
perdidit ille oculos et luscis invidet; huius
pallida labra cibum accipiunt digitis alienis,
ipse ad conspectum cenae diducere rictum
suetus hiat tantum ceu pullus hirundinis, ad quem
ore volat pleno mater ieiuna. sed omni
membrorum damno maior dementia, quae nec
nomina servorum nec vultum agnoscit amici
cum quo praeterita cenavit nocte, nec illos
quos genuit, quos eduxit. nam codice saevo
heredes vetat esse suos, bona tota feruntur
ad Phialen; tantum artificis valet halitus oris,
quod steterat multis in carcere fornicis annis.
ut vigeant sensus animi, ducenda tamen sunt
funera natorum, rogus aspiciendus amatae
coniugis et fratris plenaeque sororibus urnae.
haec data poena diu viventibus, ut renovata
semper clade domus multis in luctibus inque

perpetuo maerore et nigra veste senescant.
rex Pylius, magno si quicquam credis Homero,
exemplum vitae fuit a cornice secundae.
felix nimirum, qui tot per saecula mortem
distulit atque suos iam dextra conputat annos,
quique novum totiens mustum bibit. oro parumper
attendas quantum de legibus ipse queratur
fatorum et nimio de stamine, cum videt acris
Antilochi barbam ardentem, cum quaerit ab omni,
quisquis adest, socio, cur haec in tempora duret,
quod facinus dignum tam longo admiserit aevo.
haec eadem Peleus, raptum cum luget Achillem,
atque alius, cui fas Ithacum lugere natantem.
incolumi Troia Priamus venisset ad umbras
Assaraci magnis sollemnibus Hectore funus
portante ac reliquis fratrum cervicibus inter
Iliadum lacrimas, ut primos edere planctus
Cassandra inciperet scissaque Polyxena palla,
si foret extinctus diverso tempore, quo non
coeperat audaces Paris aedificare carinas.
longa dies igitur quid contulit? omnia vidit
eversa et flammis Asiam ferroque cadentem.
tunc miles tremulus posita tulit arma tiara
et ruit ante aram summi Iovis ut vetulus bos,
qui domini cultris tenue et miserabile collum
praebet ab ingrato iam fastiditus aratro.
exitus ille utcumque hominis, sed torva canino
latravit rictu quae post hunc vixerat uxor.
festino ad nostros et regem transeo Ponti
et Croesum, quem vox iusti facunda Solonis
respicere ad longae iussit spatia ultima vitae.
exilium et carcer Minturnarumque paludes
et mendicatus victa Carthagine panis
hinc causas habuere; quid illo cive tulisset
natura in terris, quid Roma beatius umquam,
si circumducto captivorum agmine et omni
bellorum pompa animam exhalasset opimam,
cum de Teutonico vellet descendere curru?
provida Pompeio dederat Campania febres
optandas, sed multae urbes et publica vota
vicerunt; igitur Fortuna ipsius et urbis
servatum victo caput abstulit. hoc cruciatu
Lentulus, hac poena caruit ceciditque Cethegus

integer et iacuit Catilina cadavere toto.
formam optat modico pueris, maiore puellis
murmure, cum Veneris fanum videt, anxia mater
usque ad delicias votorum. 'cur tamen' inquit
'corripias? pulchra gaudet Latona Diana.'
sed vetat optari faciem Lucretia qualem
ipsa habuit, cuperet Rutilae Verginia gibbum
accipere atque suam Rutilae dare. filius autem
corporis egregii miseros trepidosque parentes
semper habet: rara est adeo concordia formae
atque pudicitiae. sanctos licet horrida mores
tradiderit domus ac veteres imitata Sabinos,
praeterea castum ingenium voltumque modesto
sanguine ferventem tribuat natura benigna
larga manu (quid enim puero conferre potest plus
custode et cura natura potentior omni?),
non licet esse viro; nam prodiga corruptoris
improbitas ipsos audet temptare parentes:
tanta in muneribus fiducia. nullus ephebum
deformem saeva castravit in arce tyrannus,
nec praetextatum rapuit Nero loripedem nec
strumosum atque utero pariter gibboque tumentem.
i nunc et iuvenis specie laetare tui, quem
maiora expectant discrimina. fiet adulter
publicus et poenas metuet quascumque mariti
irati debet, nec erit felicior astro
Martis, ut in laqueos numquam incidat. exigit autem
interdum ille dolor plus quam lex ulla dolori
concessit: necat hic ferro, secat ille cruentis
verberibus, quosdam moechos et mugilis intrat.
sed tuus Endymion dilectae fiet adulter
matronae. mox cum dederit Servilia nummos
fiet et illius quam non amat, exuet omnem
corporis ornatum; quid enim ulla negaverit udis
inguinibus, sive est haec Oppia sive Catulla?
deterior totos habet illic femina mores.
'sed casto quid forma nocet?' quid profuit immo
Hippolyto grave propositum, quid Bellerophonti?
erubuit nempe haec ceu fastidita repulsa,
nec Stheneboea minus quam Cressa excanduit, et se
concussere ambae. mulier saevissima tunc est
cum stimulos odio pudor admovet. elige quidnam
suadendum esse putes cui nubere Caesaris uxor
destinat. optimus hic et formonsissimus idem

gentis patriciae rapitur miser extinguendus
Messalinae oculis; dudum sedet illa parato
flammeolo Tyriusque palam genialis in hortis
sternitur et ritu decies centena dabuntur
antiquo, veniet cum signatoribus auspex.
haec tu secreta et paucis commissa putabas?
non nisi legitime volt nubere. quid placeat dic.
ni parere velis, pereundum erit ante lucernas;
si scelus admittas, dabitur mora parvula, dum res
nota urbi et populo contingat principis aurem.
dedecus ille domus sciet ultimus. interea tu
obsequere imperio, si tanti vita dierum
paucorum. quidquid levius meliusque putaris,
praebenda est gladio pulchra haec et candida cervix.

nil ergo optabunt homines? si consilium vis,
permittes ipsis expendere numinibus quid
conveniat nobis rebusque sit utile nostris;
nam pro iucundis aptissima quaeque dabunt di.
carior est illis homo quam sibi. nos animorum
inpulsu et caeca magnaque cupidine ducti
coniugium petimus partumque uxoris, at illis
notum qui pueri qualisque futura sit uxor.
ut tamen et poscas aliquid voveasque sacellis
exta et candiduli divina tomacula porci,
orandum est ut sit mens sana in corpore sano.
fortem posce animum mortis terrore carentem,
qui spatium vitae extremum inter munera ponat
naturae, qui ferre queat quoscumque labores,
nesciat irasci, cupiat nihil et potiores
Herculis aerumnas credat saevosque labores
et venere et cenis et pluma Sardanapalli.
monstro quod ipse tibi possis dare; semita certe
tranquillae per virtutem patet unica vitae.
nullum numen habes, si sit prudentia: nos te,
nos facimus, Fortuna, deam caeloque locamus.

COMMENTARY

ENNIUS

Frg. 7

The theme of culinary excess (**sine modo**) had been part of satire from its very beginning and may well be part of its name [12, 54].* It is reflected later in Lucilius, Horace's second book, Persius, and Juvenal. The satiric pose seems to be intrinsically linked to gastronomic and sexual excess. The grotesque figures prominently in its Greek forebears, iambic poetry and Old Comedy [34–7], as well as in the related genre of Mennippean satire [7]. Meter: iambic trimeter [42].

Convivat < *convivo, –are*: "to dine, to have a banquet" = deponent in later Latin.

Frg. 15

This is the longest fragment we have from Ennius's satires. It shows satire's socially regulative function. It is a sharp picture of a hungry wolf. The text is cited in the scholia to Terence's *Phormio*, which probably indicates that the character is to be understood as a comic parasite. Note the paratactic syntax throughout, with very little sustained subordination. Meter: iambic trimeter [42].

Lautus < *lavo, –are, lavi, lautum*: wash, bathe.

Infestis malis: a military metaphor: "with cheeks arrayed," ablative of attendant circumstances.

Malis < *mala, –ae*: cheek, jaw.

Expedito = "at the ready."

Alacer = "quick."

Celsus = "proud, haughty."

Expectans < *exspecto, –are*: "to long for or await." This usage takes the ablative.

*Bold numbers (e.g., [1]) in brackets refer to paragraphs in the introduction where a more expanded discussion of the topic can be found.

Abligurris < *abligurrio*, *–ire*, *–ivi*, *–itum*: "to lick away, consume."

Quid censes domino esse animi?: "What do you estimate your host thinks?" *Dominus* may well imply more a relation of subservience than simply "host." The parasite is often a social climber or freedman in comedy.

Pro divum fidem = accusative of exclamation with the interjection **pro**.

Ill' tristist = archaic contraction for *ille tristis est*, which will not scan. The host is saddened as he watches the food he has put back devoured (**voras**).

Frg. 18

The word play and alliteration in this fragment are typically Ennian, while the homely morality would be at home in even the latest exemplars of the genre. The poet here rings all the possible changes on the verb *frustror*, "to deceive" and the related indeclinable adjective *frustra* (here with short final syllable). *Frustra* on its own means "in vain, without success," but *frustra esse* means "to be in error." The result of the word play is a confusion that mirrors that of the deceptions described. Meter: sotadean [43].

Postulat = "claims."

Quem refers back to **alterum**.

Eum refers back to **qui**. **Is** also refers back to **qui**.

Ille refers back to **quem**.

LUCILIUS

Frg. 26.1.589–93

This passage anticipates similar programmatic statements from Horace, particularly 1.10.76–90. Lucilius announces his intended audience to be neither the pedant nor the rube, but the sophisticated man of taste. These lines come from the beginning of Lucilius's first published collection [58] and would constitute the poet's introduction to his work. Meter: trochaic septenarius [45].

589–90. Lucilius does not aim to please the crowd, but neither is he interested only in the approval of professional writers. It should be noted that most professional writers from this period would have been of lower-class origins [19]. One of the striking things about Lucilius is he is the first upper-class Roman we hear speaking *in propria persona* [20].

Itidem = "in like manner."

Populo = "the masses."

591–3. We must assume *volo* or a similar verb in the lacuna.

Manium Manilium: consul in 149. He was a respected jurist. **Persium** = C. Persius, a learned orator, who was active in the time of the Gracchi [17–18].

Iunium Congum = Marcus Iunius Congus, at the time of the writing of this satire, was a twenty-five-year-old man of good birth and education; he would later go on to write a historical work and possibly one on law before his death in 54 BCE. Lucilius thus does not seek out the audience of the established, but that of good men from good families on whom his satirical wit can exercise its formative powers.

594. This last line is quoted by Cicero at *De Oratore* 2.25. Crassus explains that **Laelius Decumus**, was a good, not uneducated man, but nothing compared to **Persius**. At *De Finibus* 1.3.7, Cicero recalls the passage and explains that he too would have liked to appeal to Persius, but even more to Scipio and Rutilius. Scipio, of course, was Lucilius's patron and anything but uncultured. Rutilius was consul in 105 BCE and served under Scipio at Numantia in 133 with Lucilius. There are quite possibly political undercurrents in the fragment that elude us.

Frg. 26.1.626–7

These lines also appear to form part of the opening programmatic poem. Lucilius adopts the stance, made famous by Juvenal, of the satirist as one who speaks directly from the heart (**ex praecordiis**). Meter: trochaic septenarius [45].

Frg. 30.2.1007–11

These lines form part of larger poem on the temptations open to a lonely wife when her husband has left on a journey. The use of an additive list is typically Lucilian. On the one hand, this type of paratactic rhetoric represents the stylistic looseness Horace would later criticize [47]. On the other, the open, freewheeling style was part of the appeal. The tone is that of the relaxed raconteur [60–1]. The fragment also provides insight into the satirical depiction of daily life and into the double standards that characterized Roman gender relations.

1007–8. Reasons for leaving the house.
Commenta < *comminiscor*, *comminisci*, *commentum*: "to contrive, invent."
Viai = archaic *viae*.
Aurificem < *aurifex*, *–ficis*: "goldsmith."

1009. Operatum = supine with implied verb of motion from *operor*, *–ari*: "to work, to be busy," often as here "to be engaged in worship through the bringing of sacrifice." This might well involve a feast.
Fano < *fanum*: "temple."

1010. Lana: the archetypically virtuous wife in Rome spent her days spinning for her family or supervising the slaves occupied with such chores, hence the famous tombstone inscription for a dutiful wife "*lanam fecit*."
Pallor here = "moldiness, unsightliness."
Triniae < *trinea*, *ae*: "a gnawing moth or worm."

1011. Iuratam se uni: "having sworn one herself to one man alone." Lucilius alludes to the ideal of the *univira*, a woman who had only known one man. Such ideals of fidelity were not equally binding on Roman men. See **Horace** 1.2.
Deque dicata = tmesis, the splitting apart of a compound word, for *dedicataque*.

Frg. 30.3.1023–5

A certain "Baldy" did not perform well in the Palantine War. This fragment is a good example of satire's socially regulatory function in disciplining deviance through ridicule. It represents the mainstream of republican *libertas* [21–4] and can be profitably compared with much of Catullus's iambic poetry [28, 37].

1023. Indu = archaic form of *in*.

Concelebrarunt < *concelebro, –are*: "to spread a rumor or report about."

1024. There appears to be a missing line, but the sequence of thought is still intelligible. Take **quae** as adjectival with **res**.

1025. Calvus = "baldy," but the adjective may also be a cognomen. The pun may be part of the joke, but the **Calvus** in question has not been identified.

Palantino . . . bello: the Palantine campaign was led by Marcus Aemilius Lepidus in 137 against Palencia in Spain.

Frg. 30.3.1051–2

This passage shows satire's focus on matters culinary [6, 12]. If Krenkel (1970) is correct in seeing this fragment as part of the same poem as the previous one (hardly a sure thing), then excessive attention to concerns of the table might be one reason for "Baldy's" poor performance in the Palantine war. Compare **Horace 2.8.**

Pulmentaria < *pulmentarium, –i*: "a relish or anything eaten with bread."

Intubus = "endive."

Aliquae = *aliqua*, neuter plural.

Ius = "sauce," not law.

Maenarum < *maena, –ae*: a kind of small salted fish eaten by the poor.

Bene habet se: "that's well and good."

Mictyris = "piss."

Frg. 3.98–118

These lines form a coherent sequence of fragments drawn from Book 3's treatment of Lucilius's journey to Sicily, the model for Horace's *Satire* 1.5. Lucilius starts from Rome and passes through Capua before continuing on to his estates [57]. Together, they serve as a fine example of Lucilius's leisurely narrative style and relaxed, playful diction.

98–9. This first fragment is from the book's opening where Lucilius addresses his companion and tells him that he will share in the glory won by Book 3.

Partisses = *partivisses* < *partio, –ire*: "to share out, distribute." The subjunctives are potential.

100–1. Lucilius describes the way distance was measured using a surveyor's iron rod or *gruma*. This is probably addressed to his travelling companion as he prepares to accompany him. The *gruma* also marked the center of a military camp where the rod was planted to divide it in quarters.

Degrumabis < *degrumo, –are*: "to measure out."

102–3. Lucilius continues discussing his proposed route with his companion. They chart a course from Capua to an unknown town fourteen miles north of Vibo on the *via Popilia*, built in 132 BCE. The same town would be 170 miles from Acerronia by road. Marx (1963) in his edition theorizes that Lucilius and his companions are discussing the relative merits of land and sea travel. Note the playful listing of the numbers. It represents an oral, paratactic style that delights in improvisatory play.

Bis = "twice."

Quina < *quini, –ae, –a*: "five."

Octogena < *octogeni, –ae, –a*: "eighty."

Commoda here = "whole." Understand *milia passum*.

104–6. Lucilius tells of the sites his interlocutor will see in Sicily.

Optasti = *optavisti.*

Freta = "the straits of Sicily." Poetic plural.

Messanam = modern Messina.

Regina . . . moenia = "the walls of Regium," modern Reggio di Calabria. This is an example of the rhetorical figure *hysteron proteron*, or the placing of what comes after before. Coming down the coast one would come to Reggio, then the straits, then Messina. The arrangement of the words may owe as much to the demands of meter, however, as to a desire for rhetorical variation.

Liparas < *Liparae, arum*: the Aeolian islands, north of Sicily.

Facelinae templa Dianae: a temple of Diana (Artemis) located in Mylae (modern Milazzo) on the cape of Artemesium. The plural is poetic. *Facelina* is an adjective related to *fasces*, referring to a bundle of rods that were an attribute of Taurian Diana. Her cult statue was said to have been smuggled into Italy by Orestes and Iphigenia when they made their escape from the Tauric Chersonese (the modern Crimea). There is also a river Facelinus in the area of the temple.

107. labosum = an adjective that appears to have been coined by Lucilius from *labor, labi, lapsus* meaning "slippery."

108–11. This passage features the colloquialisms and repetition for which Horace would later criticize Lucilius. In the past, there has been a tendency to take Horace at his word and see Lucilius as less refined. What is really at stake, however, is two very different aesthetic sensibilities. Lucilius exhibits the easy playfulness of the self-confident aristocrat [20, 59–61]. Horace's polished perfection betrays an anxiety not only of influence, but also of social and personal instability. Lucilius in this fragment describes the approach to Aricia on the *via Appia* from Rome en route to Setia (modern Sezza), **Setinum . . . finem**.

Susque . . . deque is cited by Gellius and others as an idiom meaning "indifferent." Lucilius here plays on the literal meaning of "up and down." Aricia was at the base of the Alban hills. **Susque** < *subsque.*

Αἰγίλιποι = "deserted even by goats," i.e. "extremely high." The direct use of Greek is a stylistic feature of Lucilius not found in later satirists. This affectation, as we know from Cicero's letters, was part of casual speech among the educated. The humor comes from terming every foothill a Mount Aetna or Athos.

112. Becker's emendation, cited by Krenkel (1970), is reasonable. The river **Volturnus** crosses the *Via Appia* three miles from Capua in Casilinum.

113–14. This passage is variously interpreted. Marx (1963) reads it as the cause of Lucilius's trip and puts it early. He takes **depostus** in the strong sense of "having died." He somewhat naively pictures Lucilius going to Sicily to see his dying oxherd. This seems unlikely. Krenkel agrees on the sense of **depostus**, but notes that, since Porphyrion in his scholia on Horace *Satires* 1.5 says Lucilius stopped at Capua, Symmachus's illness could have provided the reason for the stop. Without more context, it is impossible to judge definitively. It should be noted, however, that **depostus** < *depositus*, past participle of *depono*, *deponere*, need not necessarily mean "died," but can mean simply "collapsed." The image of an out-of-breath old oxherd (**bubulcus**) collapsing and forcing Lucilius to pause in his journey is more in keeping with the playful tone of the other fragments and the description of the hills in **lines 108–11**. The fact that **expirans animam** can mean equally "giving up the ghost" and "losing his breath" would add to the humor. *Agere animam* often means "to be in the death throes," but its basic meaning is "to drive out the breath" and hence "the animating spirit."

115–16. **Sumere** = "take." As Krenkel (1970) observes, this most likely refers to a stop to care for Symmachus in Capua.

117–18. There were two gladiatorial schools in Capua. This passage is generally thought to introduce a mock battle between two gladiators similar to that found in Horace, *Satires* 1.5.51–70. **Broncus** = "bucktoothed."

Eminulo < *eminulus*, *–a*, *–um*: diminutive of *eminens*, "standing out." The diminutive is ironic.

Frgs. 7.266–67, 280

Lucilius details in comic fullness the toilette and skills of the courtesan [6, 12]. The text is a precedent for Horace ***Satires*** 1.2 and Ovid's *Ars Amatoria*.

266–7. **Subvellor** = "I am plucked down below." **Desquamor** = "I am scaled." **Pumicor** = "I am rubbed with pumice." **Ornor** = "I am adorned." **Expolior** = "I am polished." **Pingor** = "I am painted."

280. **Molere** = "to grind as in flour," a common sexual metaphor. See **Horace**

1.2.35. **Vannere** = "to winnow." Note the continuity of the culinary metaphor with the sexual referent.

Frg. 8.302–8

This fragment is another representative of satire's frank portrayal of sexuality. It shows the precedent Lucilius set for Catullus [2, 6, 12] and the elegists as well as other satirists.

302–3. **poclo** = *poculo* < *poculum, –i*: "drinking cup."

Fictricis = genitive of *fictrix*: "schemer, contriver." **Ψωλοκοποῦμαι** = a graphic sexual expression for having an erection in which the foreskin is drawn back. The explicit nature of the phrase may be one of the reasons for Lucilius's use of Greek. Horace would later criticize his habit of mixing Greek and Latin in **1.10.20–35.**

305. Porphyrion cites this passage as a gloss on Horace **1.2.125. Diallaxon** = a transliteration of the Greek διάλλαξων: "about to cross or intertwine."

306. A vivid sexual image taken from the world of wool-work. **Fusus**: "spindle," here = phallus. **Foris subteminis panus**: "Outside, the threads woven together (**subteminis** < *subtemen*) are wound round the bobbin (**panus**)."

307. **Opus** is a common sexual euphemism (Adams 1982). **Lentet** < *lento, –are*: "to bend, to ply like an oar."

308. **laeva**: understand *manu*. **Muttoni** < *muto, mutonis*: rare poetic term for "penis," see Horace **1.2.68. Absterget** < *abstergeo, –tergere, –tersi, –tersum*: "to dry by wiping."

Frg. 11.422–4

This poem is a good example of early satire's ability to lampoon prominent people by name [27–8, 35]. **Quintus Opimius ille, Iugurtini pater huius**: Quintus Opimius was consul in 154 BCE. His son Lucius was consul in 121. He was bribed by Jugurtha in 116 and condemned in 110 before being sent into exile. The point of the lines seems to be that while the father grew out of early bad habits, the son did not.

Famosus = *infamosus*. Note the alliteration: **formosus . . . fuit . . . famosus.**

Frg. 1342–54

This is the longest continuous fragment we have from Lucilius. We do not know the book from which it is derived. It provides a rough and ready definition of one Roman ideology's most central terms, **virtus**. **Virtus** is difficult to translate. Derived from *vir*, its fundamental meaning is "manliness." From there, it often means martial courage, as one of the fundamental virtues of manliness. Lastly, it means "virtue," i.e. the appropriate behavior for a *vir* or free man (slaves were *pueri* and by definition could not possess *virtus*). What follows is not a philosophical examination, but a list of examples.

1342–3. The basic structure is *virtus est potesse persolvere pretium verum*. **Potesse** = *posse*. **Quis** in both cases = *quibus*. **Albinus** cannot be securely identified. In this first definition, **virtus** is defined not only as paying one's debts, both fiscal and moral, but also as having the ability to do so. It should be recalled that to be a member of the equestrian or senatorial order, those whom Cicero refers to as the *boni* or "good men," it was necessary to have a certain *census* or "net worth." There was, then, in traditional Roman ideology very little differentiation between the external markers of virtue and its internal manifestations. This lack of differentiation is the basis of Horace's attempt to redefine terms such as *libertas*, *nobilitas*, and *ingenuitas* in 1.4.

Res here and throughout the fragment means both "a business transaction" and "a situation or affair."

1344–6. In this section, **virtus** is defined as knowledge. **Virtus** thus is knowledge of how to size up a situation and of what it is proper to do and not to do.

1347. **Virtus** is to know moderation in seeking.

1348. This line essentially repeats the first two. It represents the stylistic laxity that drove Horace to distraction in 1.4 and 1.10. **Divitiis** adds the idea of paying from one's own store, of being self-sufficient.

1349. **Honos** means both "honor" and "office," maintaining the parallel between abstract virtue and social hierarchy, or the internal and external dimensions of **virtus**.

1350–1. One of the standard maxims of Greek practical ethics, submitted to a painful dissection by Plato at the beginning of the *Republic*: "to be a friend to a friend and an enemy to an enemy."

1352. **Hos magni facere**: "to hold in high esteem." **Magni** is genitive of value.

1353–4. These last sentences are standard Stoic sentiments repeated almost verbatim by Cicero at *De Officiis* 1.17.58.

HORACE

1.2

Satire 1.2 is a diatribe [40–1, 66] often entitled either "Moderation in All Things" or "On Adultery." This duality reflects not only the shifting focus of Horace's rant, but also a certain asymmetry between the putative message of the satire and the eccentric position it constructs for its audience. The majority of the satire consists of a series of vignettes that narrate (on the denotative level) an oscillation between what Freud would call the pleasure and the reality principles—between the desire for pleasure and the attempt, in the name of pleasure, to avoid pain. After the first twenty-four lines, this elusive search for moderation narrows to the realm of sexuality, in general, and to adultery in particular.

The basic structure of an alternation between extremes is repeated throughout the satire. No real hope for moderation exists, since people in pursuit of the pleasure principle inevitably overcorrect in their encounter with the reality principle: **vitant stulti vitia, in contraria currunt** (24). A set of alternatives is presented, but always with a moment of excess, a moment of obscene enjoyment that cannot be folded back into the simple logic of alternating contraries and an ideal middle point. **Nil medium est**. Maltinus wears his tunic too low, his opposite number too high. What "sticks out" is precisely the **inguen obscenum** (26). The search for moderation leads us to images of **albi cunni** (36), anal rape (44), talking penises (68–72), as well as an admonition to rape a slave boy or girl whenever a raging erection threatens (116–18). In each case, the denotative lesson contains a surplus of sadistic enjoyment for the audience that affirms its separation from the overt limits marked out by the narrative and invites it to take pleasure in that very distance. The audience is not so much to be convinced by Horace's street-corner preacher as it is invited to laugh both at the target of his lampoons and his own excessive nature.

1. **Ambubaiarum** < *ambubaia, –ae*: "Syrian flute girl." A comically grotesque word with which to begin the satire. Flute girls were synonymous with promiscuity. Horace anticipates the sexual theme of the second part of the satire. The juxtaposition of this word with **collegia**, a formal term used of priests and poets, is designed to provoke hilarity.

Pharmacopolae < *pharmacopola, –ae*: "a seller of drugs, a quack." The bracketing of the good Latin word **collegia** by the Syriac derived **ambubaiarum** and this Greek term, plunges us into the world of immigrants, freed slaves, cheap entertainers, sex workers and mountebanks that was both Tigellius's home and satire's frequent setting. Compare the openings of **Juvenal 1** and **3.**

2. **Balatrones** < *balatro, –onis*: "jester." A word found only twice more in classical literature, both times in Horace. Compare *Satire* 2.8.21.

3–6. **Tigelli** = Hermogenes Tigellius, the subject of the opening of *Satire* 1.3 as well. There he is portrayed as a man who always goes to extremes. Here he is the immoderate patron of flute girls and jesters, in contrast to the man (**contra hic**) who is stingy to his *amicus*, lest he be called a spendthrift, **prodigus**. The proper model is the man of means who controls his desires while being generous to the deserving in the manner of Maecenas.

There is a submerged literary polemic pursued in these lines. Tigellius was a musician known to Caesar, Cicero, Cleopatra, and Octavian, who, according to the scholiast, Porphyrion, had criticized Horace's metrics and was an advocate of the neoteric poet Calvus. Tigellius is also the subject of satire in the more specifically literary *sermones* 1.4 and 1.10. His lifestyle as lampooned here also serves as a metaphor for his lack of restraint in poetics.

Some distinguish two Tigellii, a father and son or a master and freedman: the earlier one whose death is recounted here and the later critic of 1.4 and 1.10. This distinction, according to many commentators, helps to clarify the chronology of composition, since the coarse tone of 1.2 is often taken to mark it as an early effort. External evidence for two separate Tigellii is lacking (Freudenburg 1993).

Frigus, *–oris*: neuter noun.

7. **Hunc**: Most argue that this person cannot be the same stingy person described above (**hic**), in spite of the potential confusion caused by applying the same pronoun to both.

8–9. **Stringat** < *stringo, –are*: "to strip" as the leaves from a tree.

Ingluvie < *ingluvies, –ei*: "maw" used of animals, metonymy for "gluttony, greed." Note the low provenance of the imagery.

Coemens < *coemo, –emere*: "to buy in large quantities."

Obsonia < *obsonium, –i*: "a dish eaten with bread and wine." The Greek term from which it is derived ὀψώνιον) can also mean "salary" or "payment." Greed is dehumanizing. The spendthrift is transformed into a wild animal that swallows up vast quantities of money and comestibles.

Conductis . . . nummis = "hired" and hence "borrowed" money as Porphyrion confirms.

10. Here begins the response to Horace's indirect question in **lines** 7–9. **Quod** is postponed.

Parvi . . . animi: genitive of description. The opposite of being magnanimous.

12. **Fufidius**: unknown. **Vappa** and **nebulo** both denote a lack of substance. There is a deliberate ambiguity between the moral and material meanings of these terms.

13. **Positis in faenore nummis**: "money loaned at interest." Horace shifts into the colloquial language of business.

14. **Quinas hic capiti mercedes exsecat**: "He deducts 5% of the principle." The regular rate of interest was 1% per month. Fufidius charges the usurious rate of 5% and takes his first payment out of the principle of the loan, effectively loaning his client only 95% of the principle while charging him the full amount of interest.

15. **Perditior**: "in arrears."

16. **Nomina**: "debts" from the names written on the promissory notes. *Sector* is frequentative of *sequor*.

Veste virili = *toga virilis*, assumed by the age of sixteen.

17. **Tironum** < *tiro, –onis*: "a beginner." Young men on tight allowances would be easy prey for the unscrupulous loan shark.

17–19. The entire quotation should be taken together. By breaking it up across three lines, Horace produces an excited, exclamatory tone.

19. **Pro quaestu**: "in proportion to his income."

20–2. "You would scarcely believe how this man lived, worse than Menedemus in Terence's *Heautontimorumenos*," who lived like a poor man in the midst of great riches in mourning for a son he had chased away (**gnato . . . . fugato**) because he fell in love with a poor woman's daughter. Fufidius and Tigellius are mirror images of excess. Freudenburg (1993) see this passage as a subtle acknowledgement of the comic nature of Horace's speaker. Compare 1.4.45–52.

Inducit . . . vixisse = "represents to have lived."

23–4. This end-stopped couplet sums up the first part of the satire: "foolish people fall into excess to avoid vice." The last part of the satire focuses on sexual excess and adultery.

25–7. Maltinus, Rufillus, and Gargonius are unknown. *Malta*, however, Rudd (1982: 143) notes, is a word found in Lucilius meaning "effeminate fop."

25. The alternation between extremes extends even to fashion. **Tunicis demissis** = "with garments trailing." Flowing tunics were a sign of effeminacy. See Cicero, *In Catilinam* 2.17–23.
Est qui = "there is another."

26. **Subductis**: understand *tunicis*.

27. **Pastillos** < *pastillus, –i*: an ancient breath mint.

28–9. The ultimate violation of the principle of moderation is represented by those who only lust after women wearing the **instita**, a flounce sewn on around the edge (**subsuta**) of the *stola*. This is the dress of the respectable *matrona*.

30. **Fornice** < *fornix, –icis*: an arch or arcade where cheap prostitutes hawked their wares and hence metonymy for a brothel.

31–5. The mixture of high and low registers is part of the humor. Cato the elder (234–149 BCE) was known as an advocate of stern traditional morality. While serving as *censor*, he had a senator expelled for embracing his wife in the daylight.
Notus implies an individual of some stature in the community.
Macte < *mactus, –a, –um*: "honored," in the vocative an expression of congratulations. The use with *virtus* was conventional, but the association of *virtus* (derived from *vir*) with virility adds to the fun.
Esto: third person future imperative.
Dia < *dius, –a, –um*: "godlike, inspired."
Permolere: the image of "grinding" is at once graphic and good humoredly rustic.

36. **Cunni . . . albi**: "white cunt," metonymy for a woman dressed in white and hence a *matrona*. Prostitutes wore dark togas. The graphic image, however, drives the point of the exercise home. The obscenity is deliberate and direct.
Cupiennius: a speaking name derived from the participle *cupiens*. Note the alliteration with **cunni**. Porphyrion suggests a reference to C. Cupiennius Libo, a friend of Octavian, which does not eliminate the pun.

37–40. A parody of Ennius's *Annales* frag. 465 (Vahlen 1967): *Audire est operae pretium procedere recte / qui rem Romanam Latiumque augescere vultis* ["The cost of proceeding in the proper manner is for all of you who wish the Roman commonwealth and Latium to prosper to listen."] The mixture of the high epic register with low comic material produces a humorous effect, while recapitulating on a formal level the convergence of extremes that is the burden of the poem's opening argument.

Moechis = dative.

41–6. Adulterers must always fear the revenge of wronged husbands. This passage contains a catalog of the dangers. **Praedonum** < *praedo, –onis*: robbers.

Hunc perminxerunt calones: a commonly described form of revenge for adultery is to have your servants rape the offender. Within the Roman sexual system, the humiliation would be double: the adulterous man is penetrated like a woman and subjected by his social inferiors (Parker 1997).

Demeteret < *demeto, –ere*: cut off. **Cauda** is slang for penis. **Testis** = accusative plural.

Galba = a jurist dissenting from the common opinion that adulterers receive these punishments justly (**iure**). It is unknown whether the name refers to a real person. Horace is parodying legal discourse.

47–9. Freed women (*libertinae*) constitute the second class after the respectable wives of citizens.

Sallustius is thought by most commentators to be the nephew of the historian, but some object on the ground that the same person has a very complimentary ode addressed to him (2.2). As Catullus's poetry demonstrates, however, obscene raillery hardly precludes personal affection. On the other hand, as Rudd (1982) points out, it may well be the historian himself.

Non minus insanit: even in permitted vices, excess is possible.

49–53. But if fortune (**res**) and reason (**ratio**) persuaded, he would wish to be known as good and generous, paying not so much as would do harm to himself or be unbecoming (**dedecori**). On **benignus**, see **line 4.**

53–4. **Verum hoc se amplectitur uno** = "but he prides himself on this one thing alone." Even in his moderation, Sallustius tips over into ridiculous excess.

55–7. **Marsaeus** is unknown, but **Originis** was an actress of Cicero's time. Actresses were all *libertinae.*

Fundumque laremque: he would give away the very material and religious symbols that constituted his family's claim to Roman identity. The *Lares* are primitive gods whose origins are shrouded in mystery. The *Lar familiaris* was a household guard of the hearth.

58–9. The suggestion that his **fama** brought forth a graver/heavier **malum** than did his reduced fortune (**res**) presents an oxymoronic conflation of the material and the spiritual. The lighter his fortune, the lower his reputation sinks.

59–61. The earlier pairing of **res** and **fama** is here paralleled in the fool's desire to avoid the role (**persona**) of *moechus* (understood), as opposed to steering clear of all harm that lies in his way (**officit**).

Evitare: predicate of **satis est**. Its direct object is **personam**. The hyperbaton, i.e. the disturbance of normal word order, is harsh but highlights the contrast in meaning between **evitare** and **officit**. Again, the notion of trying to avoid one vice by embracing another (**line 24**) is the unifying theme of the poem.

62. **Malum est ubicumque**: this is the strict corollary of **nil medium est** (**line 28**). It is not only that no one exhibits the *aurea mediocritas*, but also that the mean seems not to exist.

62–3. **Quid inter est . . . peccesne** = "what is the difference between whether you trespass."

In: a graphic sexual image.

Togata: prostitutes wore the toga, symbolizing their transgression of the proper sexual role. **Ancilla** implies that the woman in question was not free.

64–7. **Villius in Fausta**: understand **peccavit**. This was a famous scandal in Cicero's time. Fausta was the wife of Milo and daughter of Sulla, the dictator. **Gener** here is ironic.

Hoc . . . uno nomine = "by this alone, her name."

Exclusus fore: recalls the elegiac figure of the *exclusus amator*.

Longarenus is otherwise unknown. He is apparently one of Fausta's other lovers.

68–71. **Mutonis**: see **Lucilius 8.308**. The comic scene is the lustful man addressed by his own penis, who reminds his owner that the needs of the body are easily satisfied.

Verbis: ablative of means. The sexual organs normally have other means of address.

Numquid: interrogatory particle.

Conferbuit < *confervesco, –ere, –ferbui*: "to grow hot, to begin to boil."

72. The *muto*'s owner can only respond with an assertion of the woman's status, showing that he, not the organ in question, is the one prey to irrational desire.

73–6. Hyperbaton makes this sentence difficult. The subject of **monet** is **natura** modified by **dives opis . . . suae**. The direct objects are the neuter substantives **meliora** and **pugnantia**. **Istis** = dative with **pugnantia**. **Pugnantia** here means, "opposed." Epicurean doctrine taught that nature itself was the source of true wealth, not money or political prominence. In context, however, the sense is that nature provides ample opportunities for relieving one's lust.

Dispensare: the poet returns to the theme of adultery's expense. The term has both a material and a moral sense. It also means to "weigh out" and hence "evaluate."

Fugienda petendis immiscere = "to mix up those things which are to be fled with those that are to be sought."

76–7. **Tuo vitio rerumne labores nil referre putas?** = "Do you think it does not matter whether your travails are from your own fault or that of circumstances?" The shift from the ablative to the genitive makes the sentence more difficult. The street-corner philosopher in his diatribe appeals to the listener's free will. The problem is whether the satire offers a position of rational moderation or if excess is our fate, **nil medium est**. Horace leaves this question open, by both appealing to judgment and demonstrating that the very powers of rationality to which we hearken often lead us to excess: **vitant stulti vita, in contraria currunt**.

77–9. **Sectarier** = archaic infinitive of *sector*, *–ari*, frequentative of *sequor*.

Laboris and **fructus** are both partitive genitives.

Haurire = "to derive."

80–2. **Huic** refers to the *matrona*. **Magis** modifies **tenerum**.

Niveos viridisque lapillos = "green and white pebbles," hence "pearls and emeralds." Horace deliberately uses plain language to demystify the attraction of the jewels.

Sit licet hoc . . . tuum: as we would say in colloquial American English, "although this may be your thing." See Krüger (1911). Cerinthus is unknown.

83–5. **Sine fucis** = "without dyes" and hence "without disguise."

Venalis, –e: "to be sold."

Nec goes with **quaerit**. **Honesti** here refers to physical charms. The idea that prostitutes, because they are involved in a cash transaction, are more forthcoming about their blemishes is disingenuous at best. One need only think of the *meretrices* in comedy. If anything, they have a more compelling reason to mask defects.

86–9. The choice of a lover is compared to the purchase of a good horse. The image of choosing lovers wearing bags on their heads is highly amusing.

Opertos < *operio*, *–ire*, *–vi*, *–tum*: "to cover."

Ne is taken with **inducat**, a negative result clause.

Fulta . . . est < *fulcio*, *–ire*, *fulsi*, *fultum*: to prop up support.

Hiantem < *hio*, *–are*: "to stand open; to desire with open mouth."

Clunes < *clunis*, *–is*: the buttocks. If one picks a lover without regard for the head, neck, face, or buttocks, what part remains to be considered, except the sexual organs themselves? One could not be further from lyric and elegiac sentimentality.

90–2. **Hoc illi recte** = "in this they act rightly."
Ne . . . contemplere: jussive subjunctive from *contemplor, –ari*. **Lynceus** was a member of the Argonauts famed for his eyesight. **Hypsaea** is unknown.

93. **Depugis**, *–is*: "without buttocks."
Nasuta < *nasutus, –a, –um*: "having a large nose."

94–5. *Matronae* were covered to the ankles by their long *stolae*. Porphyrion lists Catia as a notorious adulteress who liked to show off her legs.

96–100. The list of woes for the adulterer recounted here are essentially those described by the elegiac love poets in their intrigues.
Vallo < *vallum, –i*: "a palisade or rampart."
Lectica, –ae: the litter.
Ciniflones < *ciniflo, –onis*: an attendant who curled the hair with hot irons.
Invideant = "begrudge."

101–3. Coan silks were favored by wealthy courtesans for their elegance and transparency. They had advantages for the potential client as well.

103–5. **Avellier** = archaic passive infinitive < *avello, –vellere*: "to tear away, take away with violence."
Mercem < *merx, mercis*: "merchandise." Note the frankly commercial vocabulary.

105–8. The interlocutor replies: but the thrill is in the chase. The passage is a paraphrase of Callimachus epigram 1 (Page 1975) [39].

109–10. Elegiac verse presents itself as the antidote to love. Horace says, "don't believe it." The followers of Callimachus will suffer even so [2].
Hiscine < *hicine, haecine, hocine*: an emphatic form of *hic, haec, hoc*.
Aestus < *aestus, –us*: "anxiety."

111–13. Read *nonne plus prodest quaerere modum quem natura statuat cupidinibus . . . et abscindere inane soldo*. In Epicurean doctrine, an empty desire (**inane**) would be one without a limit (Cicero, *De Finibus* 1.45).
Latura and **dolitura** modify **natura**.
Abscindere = "to divide, separate."
Soldo is syncopated for *solido* < *solidus, –a, –um*.

114–16. **Fastidis** < *fastidio, –ire*: "to turn up one's nose at."
Pavonem < *pavo, pavonis*: "peacock."
Rhombum < *rhombus, –i*: "turbot."

117. **Verna** refers to a house-born slave.
Impetus: note the violence of the language. This is a rape, not a seduction.

118. **Malis** = present subjunctive of *malo*. **Tentigine** < *tentigo, –inis*: from *tendo*, a graphic image of an erection.

119. **Parabilem** < *parabilis, –e*: from *paro*, "easy to procure."

120–2. The quotation marks denote what **illam**, the *matrona*, says: "Come back later, but with more money, if my husband will have left." Philodemus, the Epicurean philosopher says that she (**illam**) is fit only for the eunuch priests (**Gallis**) of the Great Mother goddess Cybele. He prefers the girl (**hanc**) who is cheap and comes when she is called. The text in which Philodemus said this is lost.
Cunctetur < *cunctor, –ari*: "to delay, linger."

123–4. Let her be comely and natural. **Hactenus** = "only in so far as."

125–6. When she slips her body under mine, she's as beautiful as **Ilia** and **Egeria**. **Ilia** was the first Vestal virgin. She became mother of Romulus and Remus when raped by Mars. **Egeria**, a nymph, was the consort of Numa Pompilius.

127–31. **Futuo**: a low word for intercourse.
Conscia = the *matrona*'s accomplice.
Cruribus: the slave fears having her shins broken, *crurifragium* (see Plautus, *Poenulus* 882).
Deprensa doti: an adulteress would forfeit her dowry and, if her birth family refused to accept her back in their home, would be left without the means to support herself. The sudden shift in referents for the various feminine nominatives in this sentence reflects the confusion of the moment.
Egomet mi: understand *metuam*.

132–3. **Fugiendum est**: passive periphrastic.
Puga: see *depuga*, **line 93**. The poet fears anal rape, see **line 44**. Adulterers were liable to have radishes and mullets inserted in their rectums. See Catullus 15.

134. **Fabius** appears to be a Stoic referred to in *Satire* 1. Stoic doctrine was that no harm could befall the wise man, but even Fabius would be forced to

grant Horace's case. Porphyrion asserts that the philosopher was himself caught in *flagrante delicto*.

1.4

Where 1.2 represented satire in the old republican style, owing much to Lucilius, the traditions of Roman invective [9–11, 18, 20, 27, 30, 59], and the Greek traditions of iambic poetry [36–8] and street-corner philosophy [40–1], Poem 1.4 represents a departure. Horace both explicitly embraces Lucilius and takes his distance from his great forebear. His new satire will be urbane and polished in the manner of Callimachus [38–9] and come closer to the comedy of manners we associate with Menander than to the tradition of personal attack associated with the Old Comedy of Aristophanes [37]. Horatian satire is no longer the discourse of a self-defining and self-policing oligarchic élite that we find in Lucilius and much other republican literature, in which humor is a political weapon [13–20].

It represents a vision of refined speech and social intercourse that underwrites an as yet undefined, but ultimately very different political vision, which will become the principate and then the empire. It is a discourse of self-criticism as much as social discipline [60–6]. Horace claims to have learned this from the example of his freedman father who was constantly pointing out examples of virtue and vice to him. "As a grown man, the son dutifully internalizes his satiric father, becoming his own ever present moral instructor" (Oliensis 1998: 25). Horace ultimately seeks to redefine not only satire, but also the nature of poetry itself.

The scenes with his father, Freudenburg (1993) and others have shown, derive directly from Terence's *Adelphi*, an example of the refined new comedy that Horace likens his satire to, as opposed to the Old Comic roots of Lucilian satire. This is not to say that Horace's father never did any of the things attributed to him. Rather it is to note that the personal, the political, and the generic are so presented in this poem as to form a seamless whole.

1–5. **Eupolis** and **Cratinus** were practitioners of Athenian Old Comedy.

Sicarius = "assassin."

Libertas was the watchword of the tradition of aristocratic free speech in Rome. Horace seeks to redefine this concept in the context of emerging autocracy [21–30].

Notabant: *notare* was a technical term for the black mark placed by a *censor* next to a Roman senator's name to reprove an illicit lifestyle.

6–8. **Lucilius** is at once associated with some of history's greatest literary figures and firmly relegated to the past. **Hosce** < *hice*, *haece*, *hoce*: a strengthened form of *hic*. On the style of these lines, see the introduction [48].

Tantum = adverbial: "only."

Emunctae naris = "with a clean nose," an odd phrase that does not have the same meaning as the English idiom. The general sense seems to be that Lucilius was able to sniff out vice. We might translate "with a keen nose." The construction is a genitive of description.

Componere = epexigetical infinitive. Horace faults Lucilius's versification as crude.

9–13. Lucilius is pictured as composing in a haphazard fashion, improvising on one foot. The lack of metrical control, however, implies a lack of self-control and potential excess. Thus **vitiosus**, while here referring to verse composition (**hoc**), commonly has a moral sense.

Ut magnum: "as if this were a good thing."

Lutulentus = "muddily." Compare Callimachus's *Hymn to Apollo* (lines 108–12) where he advocates the slender style of composition: "The river Euphrates has a powerful current / but the water is muddy and filled with refuse. / The Cult of bees brings water to Deo / but their slender libations are unsullied and pure, / the trickling dew from a holy spring's height" (Lombardo and Rayor 1988) [39].

Piger = "lazy."

Nam ut multum = "as for quantity."

Nil moror: an idiom. "I don't give it a moment's notice."

13–16. For Horace, as an adherent of the Callimachean cult of craft, the ability to write quickly is no virtue [39].

Crispinus: a Stoic and poetaster. He challenges Horace to a poetic duel.

Minimo: understand *digito*. As the scholiast Porphyrion (third century CE) explains, the phrase is proverbial and refers to a gesture made with the little finger that signifies there is more force in the little finger than in the whole body of the person challenged (*provocat*). As Kiessling and Heinze note (1999), it is strange that the scholiast's explanation should have been so commonly rejected in favor of a gloss that assumes the word *pignore* instead. Porphyrion, while unreliable on historical questions, is much closer to Horace's Latin.

Custodes = "referees."

17–18. Hyperbaton makes these lines difficult. Read: *Di bene fecerunt quod me inopis pusillique animi finxerunt*—a good example of Horace's self-directed irony. **Di bene fecerunt** is a colloquialism meaning, "thank the gods."

Loquentis: agrees with **animi** and takes **perpauca** as its direct object. There is a lack of parallelism between the adverbial **raro** and the substantive **perpauca**.

19–21. Crispinus is a windbag. **Hircinis** < *hircinus, –a, –um*: "made of goat skins."

Follibus < *follis, –is*: "bellows."
Imitare: imperative of *imitor, –ari*.

21–5. This passage is much vexed. The scholiasts give a variety of different possible interpretations. The gist seems to be a contrast between the happy (**beatus**), and thus presumably popular, **Fannius**, and Horace, whom no one reads because the genre of satire is one that finds fault (**culpari**). **Fannius**: is an otherwise unknown poet mentioned again in **1.10.80**. The problem centers on what is meant by **delatis**.

Ultro = "voluntarily, gratuitously."

Delatis < *defero, deferre, detuli, delatum*: "to bring out," and hence "offer." The question is who is doing the offering and for what purpose. The most economical explanation is that Fannius's works are widely sold and his bust (**imagine**) commonly displayed. But theses abound about what precisely Horace intends for us to understand.

Capsis < *capsa, –ae*: "book case."

Timentis agrees with the genitive implicit in **mea**.

Genus = "genre."

Utpote = "since, inasmuch as."

25–33. Vice is rampant. All have cause to fear the satirist.

Nuptarum . . . puerorum: the gender of the object of desire was not a moral question of great moment in the ancient world. But love itself was often seen as a sickness (**insanit**) that overpowered reason and self-control.

Argenti . . . aere: silver plate and bronze statues were both popular collector's items in Rome.

Stupet = "is crazed for."

Mutat merces = "trades his wares."

Surgente a sole ad eum [supply **solem**] **quo / vespertina tepet regio**: this passage contains an elegant ambiguity. The greedy merchant plies his trade from dawn to dusk and from east to west.

Quin: the scholiast tells us to assume *etiam*. Translate "indeed."

Metuens introduces fear clauses governed by **ne** and **ut** respectively.

Summa < *summa, –ae*: "total."

Odere = perfect.

34–8. The satirist's potential victim voices his fears.

Faenum habet in cornu: bulls' horns were wrapped in straw to keep them from harming their handlers.

Excutiat: concessive subjunctive. Often translated to "raise a laugh" [**risum**], the image in Latin is more violent. The root *quatio* means to "shake or strike." Compare *percutio*. I have adopted an alternative reading of line 35.

Illeverit< *inlino, –linere, –levi, –litum*: "to smear or daub" and hence "to scribble on."

Omnis . . . redeuntis: accusative plural.
Gestiet < *gestio, –ire*: "will desire eagerly."
Furno . . . lacuque: communal ovens and fountains used by the poor.
Pueros = "slaves."

38–44. Horace launches his defense. He is not a poet, but a mere prosaic versifier. This seeming modesty establishes strict criteria for the title of poet that neither Lucilius nor Horace's detractors could meet. Satire is redefined as purified *sermo*, a form of metrically heightened conversational speech [60–1]. The term poetry is reserved for the higher genres of lyric, epic, and tragedy.

Dederim, **excerpam**, and **dixeris** are potential subjunctives. Horace is making a hypothetical argument, not asserting fact. Note the elision between **me** and **illorum** in which he metrically includes himself in the number of those (**illorum . . . numero**) called poets even as he grants the possibility of excluding himself. See **1.10.48**. This ambiguity prepares us for the close of the satire. It also shows Horace subtly redefining what it means to be a poet.

40. **Concludere versum** = "to produce a verse." Verse is conceived of as the bounding of language within metrical feet.

43–4. **Ingenium** = "natural talent." **Mens divinior** = "an inspired mind." **Os magna sonaturum** = a grand style suited to a noble matter.

45–8. Returning to the comparison of satire with comedy that opened 1.4, Horace argues that comedy itself should not be considered poetry, citing the debates of scholars. Implicit in the examples Horace supplies in the next passage is an analogy between Horatian *sermo* and the New Comedy associated with Menander and his Roman followers, Plautus and particularly Terence. Lucilius is identified with the rough and ready vigor of Old Comedy [9, 25, 34–5], with its frequent use of personal invective, and Horace with the more polished and restrained works of its successor.

45–6. The normal prose order would be; *quidam quaesivere (utrum) comoedia esset poema necne*. The concision and hyperbaton undermine the argument that this poem is nothing but metrical prose.

48. **Sermo merus** = literally "unadulterated speech" and hence prose. But **merus** also implies "pure." **Merus** is most often used of wine that has not been mixed with water. Horatian satire is a heady and concentrated form of speech, nothing watered down. It is sophisticated conversation raised to the level of art [60]. Thus Horace's argument that he is not writing poetry must be taken with a grain of salt (Freudenburg 1993).

49–52. Horace's interlocutor replies that comedy does not lack **spiritus** and

vis because in the stock plot of New Comedy the **pater ardens** ("angry father") always **saevit** ("rages") and the **insanus filius** ("crazed son") is always **ebrius** ("drunk"). This was not the sort of "inspiration" and "power" Horace had in mind. He was alluding to that of the lyric, epic, or tragic poet.

Nepos = "a spendthrift, prodigal."

Dedecus = "shame," neuter noun.

51–2. The son leads a drunken torch-lit procession to his mistress's door where he would serenade her and if need be break the door down. **Ante noctem**: to walk about with torches in the daylight was proverbial for folly.

52–3. Horace's point is that comedy, like satire, merely represents the prosaic events of normal life, not the great heroes of myth and legend found in epic and tragedy. **Pomponius**, otherwise unknown, would hear words no less harsh (**istis . . . leviora**), if his father **viveret** ("were alive," either in the sense of "still alive" or in the sense of "not being a fiction" like the **pater ardens** of comedy). **Pomponius** = the proverbial spendthrift heir.

Numquid = interrogative particle.

54–6. Horace summarizes his argument on satire's prosaic nature.

Puris . . . verbis: compare **sermo merus** in 48.

Dissolvas: i.e., if you rearranged the word order so the line no longer scanned as verse.

Stomachetur = "would rage."

Personatus . . . pater = "would wear the comic mask of the father." Note the poetic hyperbaton.

Pacto: an idiomatic use of *pactum*, meaning "way" or "manner."

57–62. This is a long period whose syntactical complexity both heightens the diction and illustrates Horace's point about word order in his and Lucilius's satires.

His = neuter, dative after **eripias**, functioning as the antecedent to both **quae nunc** and **quae olim**.

Tempora certa modosque = "regular rhythms and meters."

Verbum is modified by both **prius** and **posterius**.

Non goes with **invenias** in 62.

Ut = "as."

Si solvas: compare **si dissolvas** in 55.

60–1. The quoted passage is from Ennius's *Annales*. In addition to the elevated subject matter and the personification of **Discordia** and **Bellum**, note the pronounced use of alliteration characteristic of Ennius's epic diction [44]: *postquam . . . postis portasque*. Lest we be completely taken in by Horace's refusal of the name poet, we should note that *poetae* in the following line continues the alliterative pattern, even as *prius . . . posterius . . . praeponens primis* anticipates it. The boundary between the poetic and prosaic is thus more difficult to determine than the literal content of the sentence would lead one to believe. **Sermo merus** is a heightened, purified language and not the mere versification of the colloquial.

62. The image of the poet ripped apart recalls Orpheus, even as the transfer of epithet involved in having **disiecti** modify **poetae** rather than **membra** exemplifies the poetic diction Horace disclaims. The **membra** of the poet are a metaphor for the verse that is pulled apart as the word order is regularized and the meter "dissolved."

63–5. "But this kind of genre parsing is beside the point. The real question is: are the accusations made against satire justified?" Note that *satura* is never used by Horace in this discussion of the genre, thus adding an extra degree of distance between his work and Lucilius's, even as he acknowledges that he has taken up **genus hoc scribendi**.

Hactenus haec = "that's the way things are." Horace sums up the current state of the discussion.

Alias = the adverb, "at another time."

65–8. **Sulcius** and **Caprius** were the names of two professional informers (*delatores*). While, as Horace indicates, such men were looked down upon (**contemnat**) in the republic and early principate, they became a major source of terror and corruption in the imperial period.

Libellis = "notebooks."

69–70. I am no *delator*. **Ut** = concessive.

Latronum = genitive plural in apposition to **Caeli Birrique**. **Similis** takes the genitive. Caelius and Birrus are otherwise unknown.

71–2. Nor are my books widely sold. Horace takes a fastidious pride in his own lack of popularity. It is the mark of adherence to Callimachean principles of composition, which stress labor, erudition, and brevity of composition. Lucilius, of course, was very popular and, as portrayed by Horace, very un-Callimachean [39]. See **lines 6–13**.

Pila = a pillar in an arcade where booksellers hung their wares.

Quis = *quibus*, dative with **insudet**.

Hermogenisque Tigelli: see 1.2.3–6.

73–4. Horace recites his poetry only to close friends, and only when forced (**idque coactus**). Clearly, we must not take such a statement at face value. Horace, however, is neither the aristocratic scourge of vice on the model of Lucilius, nor a lower-class informer out for a quick buck, but the practitioner of a refined and modest art for a small circle of worthy friends. Such a profession of poetic faith is at odds with his earlier claim not to be a poet at all. Horace is redefining satire as a subtle art of purified daily speech that provides delight and instruction to friends, not a force of public discipline as in the case of Lucilius nor a heroic work in the manner of epic, tragedy, and the higher forms of lyric.

75–6. "Many recite their works in public places like the Forum or the baths." The image of the vaulted ceilings of the baths echoing with these poets' voices offers an elegant metaphor for empty bombast.

76–8. **Inanis** and **quaerentis** are accusative plural.
Num = "whether."
Tempore . . . alieno = "at the wrong time."

79–80. The interlocutor returns: the satirist gains a perverse (**pravus**) pleasure from his work.
Studio = "with zeal."

79–80. **Petitum** = substantive participle from *peto, –ere*, meaning "attack."

80–1. **Quis** = *aliquis* "someone."

81–5. Beware the slanderous friend. Horace turns the standard accusation against the satirist back on his accuser.
Rodit < *rodo, –ere, rosi, rosum*: "to gnaw" and hence "to eat away at" or "disparage." The metaphor is vivid.
Solutos = both "relaxed"—the image is of men at leisure in conversation—and "unrestrained, licentious," i.e., not bound by the rules of decorum. The scene is the banquet described below.
Dicacis = genitive singular of *dicax*: "witty."
Non visa = "things never witnessed."
Commissa tacere = "to keep secret."
Niger: the scholiast glosses this as *maledicus, malignus, et lividus, sive obscurus et latens* ["slanderous, mean-spirited, and envious or secretive and hiding"].
Hunc tu, Romane, caveto: Kiessling and Heinze (1999) note the resemblance between the formal and archaic quality of this clause and the pronouncement of a prophecy, citing parallel passages in Vergil and Livy. **Caveto** = future imperative.

86–9. The scene switches to a banquet. The Roman table was surrounded on three sides by couches (*lecti*) on each of which normally three diners reclined. This banquet is marked as excessive, though not unusual (**saepe**), by the inclusion of a fourth diner on each couch. See Gellius 13.11.12. The **unus** is the *scurra*, a hanger-on to his aristocratic host, who would amuse the party as jester and buffoon. The emphasis on number (**tribus, quaternos, unus**) leads the reader to believe that the *scurra* is the **unus** in excess. In the strict hierarchy of a Roman party he would normally recline in the final position (*imus*) on the last couch (*imus*), with the host. He marks the transgression of decorum that Horatian satire refuses. Implicit is a denial that Horace occupies the position of *scurra* in Maecenas's household [64], a barb aimed at Horace's relatively low social status [62–3]. Such a charge could never have been made against Lucilius.

Aspergere = "to sprinkle," and hence "to speak ill of indiscriminately." The image anticipates the next line's periphrasis for the host.

Eum qui praebet aquam: this was the host, who offered both hot water for washing before the meal and cool water for mixing with the wine during and after it. The host was therefore also in a position to regulate the amount of wine consumed.

Post . . . potus: after the *scurra* has drunk, even the host (**hunc**) becomes the target of abuse.

Liber = Bacchus, metonymy for wine.

90–1. This seems witty and urbane (**urbanus**) to you. Note the pun between *liber* ("worthy of a free Roman citizen") and **Liber**, a name for Bacchus, the god who makes you free with your tongue.

Infesto nigris: **infesto** agrees with **tibi**, Horace's interlocutor: a foe to all who slander others. *Infestus* = "hostile." On **nigris**, see **niger, line 85.**

91–100. "You chastise me because I twit Rufillus and Gargonius for their foolishness, while you bring up far more serious charges against your friend Petillius Capitolinus and then laugh them off." See **line 82** on defending absent friends. The satirist's foe is a hypocrite. **Line 92** is a direct quotation of 1.2.27.

De Capitolini furtis . . . Petilli: Petillius was *quaestor* in 43 BCE. Coins have been found with his name on them. He was charged with theft and later acquitted despite strong evidence to the contrary.

Iniecta < *inicio, –icere, –ieci iectum*, in agreement with **mentio**. The image is of a topic tossed in at random in casual conversation.

Te coram = "in your presence."

Convictore usus amicoque = "has been my host and treated me as a friend."

Usus < *utor, uti, usum. Utor* takes the ablative.

Pacto: see **line 56.**

100–3. Nigrae . . . lolliginis < *lolligo, lolliginis*, f.: a cuttle-fish or squid. Note the repeated use of the adjective **niger**. Cf. **85** and **91.**

Aerugo mera = "pure copper rust." This substance was thought to be a poison if ingested. Hence, "this is unadulterated poison." Contrast this with Horace's **sermo merus line 48.**

Vitium = the subject of **afore** in indirect discourse, governed by **promitto**.

103–15. If I speak freely, it is from the example of my father who was accustomed to point out examples of virtue and vice to me. **Liberius** should be taken in both its literal and social senses. If I speak more freely, in the manner of one who is *liber*, it is because of my father who is *libertus*. The idea on one level is perfectly transparent, but, in terms of Roman social hierarchy, it presents a paradox.

104. **Hoc mihi iuris . . . dabis** = "you will grant me this privilege." **Iuris** = partitive genitive.

105. **Insuevit** < *insuesco, –ere, insuevi, insuetum* = "to accustom." It can take a double accusative.

Pater optimus: Horace consistently speaks with great affection for his father. His status as a freedman is not made clear till **1.6.45. Optimus** is also a common way of referring to a member of the traditional aristocracy. Hence the political conflicts between the *optimates* and the *populares*. Horace is deliberately conflating ethical with social and political categories.

106. **Notando** recalls **line 5**. Horace's father was thus a kind of poor man's Lucilius.

107–8. The prose order would be *uti parce atque frugaliter viverem contentus eo.*

Parasset = a syncopated pluperfect subjunctive, *paravisset*, "prepared, set aside."

109–10. **Albius, Baius** and the other people mentioned throughout this section are almost certainly fictional.

Ut = "how."

Magnum documentum: understand *est*. The neuter refers to the general situation described in the previous sentence.

Patriam rem = "inheritance."

111–14. These lines review the subject matter of 1.2. **Concessa . . . venere** = the sexual favors of readily available slaves and prostitutes, not expensive *meretrices*.

115–29. Horace's father, unlike the *delator* or the man who will not defend his absent friend, seeks neither material nor social benefit from his observations, but simply teaches virtue in the traditional Roman fashion. This is the homely office Horace marks as his own, even as he claims a level of refinement and exclusivity to his *sermo* that was not the domain of Lucilian *satura*. Where Lucilius's satire served as a form of social control of and for the ruling élite, Horace's work offers a technology of the self in the service of private virtue.

Sapiens = the educated man or *sophos* in Greek. Horace's father's wisdom was homespun.

Vitatu and **petitu** = supines.

116. **Traditum ab antiquis morem**: the return to the *mos maiorum* was a central part of the Augustan political program.

117–18. **Tuamque** modifies **vitam famamque**.

120. **Nabis sine cortice** = "you will swim without a float," a vivid proverbial image. **Nabis** = *natabis*.

122. **Quid** = *aliquid*.

Auctorem = "exemplar."

123. The metaphor comes from jury selection by the praetor. These would be equestrians, men of substance and good social standing but not the political class. Its wider implications should not be lost: those on whom Horace is to model his behavior are also his judges. This formulation nicely captures the duality of ethical practice in daily life. We judge ourselves by how we appear in the eyes of those we also judge.

124. **An** introduces the main question: **addubites**.

Factu = supine.

Cum = "when"

Flagret < *flagro, –are*: "to blaze, to suffer."

126. **Avidos** = "gluttons."

Funus = neuter.

Ut = "as."

127. **Exanimat** = "to take the breath away, stun."

Sibi parcere = "to take care of themselves."

129–38. Thanks to my father's teaching I am only afflicted by moderate vices that anyone would forgive. His habit of observation and drawing instruction from the behavior of others stays with me. These reflections form the basis of my satire. **Hoc** = neuter ablative referring to the whole experience.

Illis modifies **vitiis** and serves as the antecedent for **quaecumque**.

130. **Quis** = **quibus**.

131. **Fortassis** = *fortasse*.
Istinc = **ab istis mediocribus vitiis**.

132–3. **Largiter** = "much, abundantly."
Longa aetas, liber amicus, consilium proprium = "long age, a frank friend, [or] my own reflection." The suppression of the conjunction is an example of the rhetorical figure of asyndeton. What follows is Horace's **consilium proprium**.

133–4. **Neque . . . desum mihi** = "I am not unaware of my behavior." Horace practices the kind of attention to virtue that Socrates recommends in the *Apology*. This "care for the self" would become an important motif in imperial philosophy.
Lectulus = a little couch, often used for reading or study.
Porticus = the colonnades through which one strolled. As Pseudo-Acron observes, the sense is "whether sitting or standing I am always thinking about virtue."

135–7. **Sic dulcis amicis occurram** = "Acting in this fashion I would be a pleasure to my friends."
Quidam = "so and so." The subject of an understood *fecit*.
Numquid anticipates a negative answer.
Olim = "one day."

138. **Oti** = contracted form of *otii* < *otium*. This is the common form of the genitive for nouns in *–ius* or *–ium* during the republican period (before 31 BCE).

139. **Illudo** = "to play around with." The idea of poetry as a *lusus* can be traced to the neoteric poets and is common in Catullus.

139–43. If you will not forgive my dabblings in verse, may the whole great troop of poets come to my aid. Note that the satire begins with **poetae** (**line** 1) and ends with **poetarum** (141). In the first instance, Horace denies that he is the same kind of poet as Lucilius, whom he associates with the harsh invective of Old Comedy. In the middle of the poem, he denies that he is a poet at all, but associates his work with that of New Comedy. By the end, poetry has been redefined and Horace not only includes himself among the poets (**plures sumus**), but also imagines them coming to his aid.

140. **Concedere** = "pardon."

141–2. **Auxilio quae sit mihi** = double dative construction.

143. **Iudaei cogemus in hanc concedere turbam**: this line refers to the large number of Jews living in Rome at the end of the first century and their efforts to proselytize. Thus, Pseudo-Acron glosses **cogemus** as *cogemus te poetam fieri* "we shall force you to become a poet."

1.5

This poem works on three levels simultaneously. First, it is an object lesson in Horace's rewriting of satire as defined by Lucilius. It fulfils the poetic program outlined in 1.4. Where Lucilius takes the whole of his Book 3 to narrate his trip to Sicily in his typical leisurely, and unconstrained style, Horace polishes off the journey to Brundisium in a mere 104 lines. This will be Callimachean satire [39].

Second, 1.5 forms the bridge between 1.4 and 1.6. In 1.4, Horace introduces his new satiric program and hints at the reasons why the broad Old Comic style of Lucilius was no longer practicable in Rome, and certainly not by someone of Horace's status [65]. In 1.6, we are told the story of Horace's introduction to Maecenas [64]. In 1.4, we find out that Horace learned to write satire from his father's habit of pointing out models of behavior to be imitated and those to be shunned. In 1.6, we learn that the virtues Horace's father taught earned the poet his entrance into Maecenas's inner circle. In 1.5, Horace goes on a journey with Maecenas and his retinue to Brundisium. The purpose is only vaguely insinuated in the satire. It is in part this very discretion that earned Horace his position at Maecenas's side. In 1.5, then, we have not Old Comic political invective, but a New Comic satire of personal foibles and comic situations.

Third, 1.5's political subtext reveals a fundamentally changed social and historical situation from that of Lucilius's. This requires a new type of satire: polished and discreet. In 38 BCE, Maecenas was sent to Athens to arrange a meeting between Antony and Octavian. That meeting took place in 37 BCE in Tarentum. It successfully mended fences between the two triumvirs for the next six years. The dramatic date of the satire is either 38 BCE, when Maecenas left for Athens from Brundisium, or 37, in which case Horace's party is supposed to have stopped at Brundisium while Maecenas continued on to Tarentum to meet with Octavian and Antony. The period between the assassination of Julius Caesar (44 BCE) and the battle of Actium (31 BCE) was one of instability and civil war. During this last great paroxysm of political bloodshed, the republic and the aristocratic order to which Lucilius and his patrons belonged disappeared.

1.5 suggests, but never describes, the brave new world of violence and political intrigue in which Horatian satire came to be. In the final analysis, this poem, with its placement between 1.4 and 1.6 reveals that the political, the stylistic, and the personal cannot be disentangled in these texts. Each of these elements—metonymically represented by Maecenas, the switch from an Old to a New Comic and Callimachean style, and Horace's father—conditions and is conditioned by all the others. Poem 1.5, in its very anodyne recounting of a trip among friends, articulates the space in which these seemingly disparate elements come together.

1–6. Horace's initial route directly recalls Lucilius's. He departs from Rome and takes the *via Appia* south to Aricia (modern La Riccia). From there, he goes to **Forum Appi** (Foro Appio) where he will proceed by barge on a canal that led to the grove of Feronia. Like Lucilius, he begins with a traveling companion (**comes**), the Greek orator, **Heliodorus**. The first verse is almost a golden line. This kind of delicate attention to the aesthetics of word order are alien to the spirit of Lucilian improvisation.

Differtum < *differtus, –a, –um*: "crammed, stuffed, crowded," modifies **Forum**.

Nautis = the boatmen who navigated the canal and the Pomptine marshes southeast of Rome.

Cauponibus < *caupo, –onis*: "innkeeper."

Divisimus: they took two days to make this portion of the journey.

Altius . . . praecinctis = literally "those who have gird themselves more highly," i.e., "those prepared to move more swiftly." The phrase was sufficiently elliptical to require a gloss in the scholia.

Ac = "than."

Minus . . . gravis = *facilius*, an example of the rhetorical figure of litotes.

7–9. Due to the bad water, Horace declares war (**indico bellum**) on his stomach. Note the mock epic style. **Cenantis**: the final syllable is long.

9–10. A lovely poetic image in the midst of a most prosaic context. It continues the mock epic tone but contains a hint of the sublime. **Diffundere** = "sprinkle."

11–12. The mood is broken with a quick return to comic realism as slaves (**pueri**) and sailors curse each other when the travelers prepare to embark.

Nautis = dative.

Convicia < *convicium*: "shout, clamor, abuse, insult."

Ingerere = historical infinitive, "heap upon."

12–13. Examples of their exchanges. **Huc appelle** = "land it over here," i.e., the barge.

Trecentos: understand *homines*.

Mula = the barge's means of conveyance.

14–19. Meanwhile the noise and flies ensure the weary traveler gets no rest.

Culices < *culex, culicis*: "gnat."

Ranae < *rana*: frog.

Prolutus < *proluo, –ere, –i, –tum*: "to wash" and hence "to soak."

Vappa: here taken in its literal sense, "sour wine." Compare 1.2.12.

Nauta atque viator certatim: the drunken boatman and the driver of the mule engage in a singing contest. This is a realistic send up of the pastoral trope of singing shepherds. **Viator** here = the mule driver, as Pseudo-Acron notes. Otherwise the following lines make little sense.

Pastum < *pasco, –ere, pavi, pastum*: "to graze," supine of goal of motion with **missae**.

Retinacula = "the traces."

Stertit < *sterto, –ere*: "to snore."

20–3. The travelers awake to find the boat stopped as the mule grazes and the boatmen sleep.

Lintrem < *linter, –tris*: "skiff or small boat," the subject of **procedere** in indirect discourse governed by **sentimus**.

Cerebrosus < *cerebrosus, –a, –um*: "hot headed."

Saligno < *salignus, –a, –um*: "willow."

Fuste < *fustis, –is*: "stick, cudgel."

Dolat = "work over," literally "to hew with an axe."

23–6. The travelers awake, eat, and continue on to **Anxur** (modern Terracina) atop limestone cliffs (**saxis . . . candentibus**).

Quarta . . . hora: the fourth hour after sunrise.

Exponimur < *expono, –ere, –posui, positum*: "to put out, disembark."

Feronia: an Italic goddess often identified with Juno whose temple was near **Anxur**.

Repimus < *repo, –ere, repsi, reptum*: "to creep or crawl." The verb gives a vivid image of the travelers clambering up the hill on all fours. Compare **Lucilius 108–11.**

27–31. Only here is mention made of the political purpose of the trip. Horace treats it almost as an afterthought. He is not a part of, let alone a commentator on, the momentous events of the day. Rather, in a moment of ironic bathos, he juxtaposes the mission of **Maecenas** and **Cocceius** to reconcile Antony and Octavian (**aversos . . . componere amicos**) with his own petty ocular discomforts.

Cocceius = L. Cocceius Nerva, consul in 39 BCE. He was a mutual friend of Octavian and Antony and was sent to moderate the negotiations.

Soliti: this was not the first time. Maecenas and Cocceius had been sent on a similar mission in 40 BCE when they negotiated the treaty of Brundisium.

Collyria = "salve."

Lippus = "having conjunctivitis." Oliensis (1998: 26–30) suggests that Horace's "eye trouble" may represent a willful blindness to the political stakes involved in this trip. He is the soul of discretion.

Illinere = "to smear," historical infinitive.

31–3. While Horace attends to his eyes, the delegates for the conference gather.

Capitoque . . . Fonteius = C. Fonteius Capito, consul in 33 BCE, a partisan of Antony.

Ad ungem factus = literally "made for the thumbnail." Porphyrion tells us that this colloquial expression for elegance and urbanity comes from checking the joints in marble work by running your thumbnail over them to look for gaps. Note the humorous contrast between **Capito**'s elegance and the blear-eyed Horace, his eyelids smeared with black salve.

Antoni non ut magis alter amicus = *Antoni amicus ut non alter {sit} magis.*

34–6. The delegation is greeted by the mayor of Fundi decked out in all his official finery. The understated nature of Horace's party, which, though on a mission of great moment for the state, proceeds with the air of friends going on holiday, contrasts with the self-importance of the provincial official. Note the compressed narrative style. **Linquimus** pictures the party's departure without ever having described its arrival.

Aufidio Lusco praetore = "in the praetorship of Aufidius Luscus." The joke here is double. *Praetor* is an exalted title to give a small town mayor and the manner of Horace's expression recalls the way of recording dates in Rome. Years were not numbered. Instead, a person was born or died, for example, in the consulship of Caesar and Bibulus, *Caesare et Bibulo consule* [56]

Libenter = "gladly."

Insani . . . scribae = Aufidius. He had formerly been a scribe, like Horace. As 1.6 makes clear, however, Horace understood the limits of his status. Aufidius plays the buffoon.

Praemia = "insignia of office."

Praetextam = *toga praetexta*, the toga with a purple border worn by magistrates.

Latum clavum = the broad purple stripe down the front of the tunic that was normally reserved for those of the senatorial order. Aufidius's puffery is particularly out of place since Maecenas himself only wore the narrow stripe of the equestrian.

Prunaeque vatillum = "a small shovel of coals" for burning incense.

37–8. From there they make their way to Formiae, home of the *gens Mamurrae*, immortalized in Catullus's invective against one its members, Julius Caesar's *praefectus fabrum*, to whom he gave the sobriquet, *Mentula*.

Murena = L. Licenius Terentius Varro Murena, brother of Maecenas's wife, Terentia.

Capitone: understand *praebente*.

Culinam < *culina*: "kitchen," often metonymy for "food."

39–42. They are joined by other members of Maecenas's circle.

Plotius et Varius: M. Plotius Tucca and L. Varius Rufus were Vergil's literary executors. Varius was an esteemed epic poet and tragedian in his own right.

Sinuessae is the locative of *Sinuessa*, a Roman colony in Latium, near the coast.

Animae is in apposition to the names in the previous line. **Qualis** is nominative plural. "Souls such as neither has the earth brought forth, nor may any other be dearer than me to these."

Quis = *quibus*, dative.

Me: ablative of comparison.

Sit: optative subjunctive.

Devinctior: comparative of *devinctus*, past participle of *devincio*, *–ire*, *–vinxi*, *–vinctum*: "to bind, attach."

44. **Contulerim**: potential subjunctive of *conferro*: "to compare." Note the implicit contrast between the personal friendships Horace values and the political *amicitia* between Antony and Octavia (**aversos . . . amicos, line 29**). *Amicitia* in this period is a much-contested term. Traditionally, it refers at least as much to political alliances based on reciprocal *benefacta* as to personal relationships. The poets of the previous generation had increasingly used it for ties of purely personal affection (Miller 2004: chapter 1). Horace plays on the two senses of the term in this satire as he also redefines *satura* along the lines outlined in **1.4.**

45–6. Next they stayed at public accommodations set up for travelling officials (**villula**). The antecedent of **quae** is **villula**. *Est* should be understood.

Parochi = the officials charged with supplying the basic necessities (**ligna salemque**) for those traveling.

47. **Capuae** = locative. Capua was a mere thirteen miles from where they started the day.

Clitellas < *clitellae*, *–arum*: "a pack-saddle."

Tempore = "in good time."

48–9. **Lusum** and **dormitum** are both supines.

Pila = ablative of means, "with a ball."

Crudis = "those with indigestion," i.e., Vergil. On **lippis**, see **line 30.**

50–1. The next stop was Cocceius's villa. **Cauponas**: see **line 4.**

Caudi = the Samnite town of Caudium.

51–4. Horace pauses for a mock epic invocation of the muse prior to recounting the contest between two lower-class *scurrae* (see **1.4.86–9**). The passage is based on a similar scene from Lucilius's journey to Sicily (**lines 117–18**). The contest is the longest episode in *Satire* **1.5** (**lines 51–70**). Sarmentus is described at some length in the scholia on Juvenal 5 and mentioned in Quintilian. He was a freedman who had become a *scriba*. Messius Cicirrus (Messius "the fighting cock") is otherwise unknown. The cognomen is Oscan and may indicate he was part of the local talent. Sarmentus was with Maecenas's party.

Paucis: assume *verbis*.

Quo patre natus: a parody of epic genealogies.

Contulerit litis = "joined the conflict." On **contulerit**, see **line 44.**

54–6. The mock epic vain continues. **Osci**: the Oscans were seen as particularly uncouth. **Clarum** is ironic.

Domina = "slave mistress."

Exstat = "still living."

Ab his: note that the 'h' cannot be counted to make a double consonant and hence make the preceding vowel long by position.

56–61. Horace treats us to what passes for witty repartee at a provincial table. The humor is double. The mock epic frame is comically inappropriate and we are clearly invited to laugh at the two clowns as much as with them. Horace and Maecenas's party remain graciously aloof from these proceedings, even as the satirist allows us to witness them. There is always a protective distance between Horace and the buffoons, one made all the more necessary by the fact that Horace, like Sarmentus, was a *scriba* of ultimately servile origins. Moreover, his status as a poet in the great man's retinue would have appeared to many traditionalists little different from that of other entertainers. Horace must carve out a place for himself that is neither that of Lucilius nor that of Sarmentus. *Satires* 1.4, 1.5, and 1.6 dramatize the difficulty and necessity of this negotiation.

Equi . . . feri = "a unicorn." See Lucilius's **rinoceros (line 118)**.

Messius accepts the sobriquet and plays the part, shaking his head in a threatening fashion. The joke, however, is on him since the scar (**cicatrix**) which gave rise to the comparison shows the Oscan to have already lost his horn (**cornu . . . exsecto**).

Cum = "since."

Saetosam < *saetosus, –a, –um*: "bristly."

62–4. Sarmentus, then, asks **Messius** to perform the Cyclops's shepherd's dance, presumably a rustic affair based on the myth of Polyphemus's clumsy attempts to woo the sea nymph Galatea, recounted in Theocritus. We have artistic renditions of Cupid inspiring Polyphemus to song.

Campanum morbum: an unidentified disease that scarred the face.

Larva aut tragicis . . . cothurnis = "a mask or tragic buskins," the traditional garb of tragic actors. They are ablatives with **opus esse**, an idiom expressing necessity. **Messius** needs no costume. The irony of comparing him to a tragic actor should not be lost. **Messius**'s performance is clearly comic. Indeed, this broad burlesque would most properly have been performed in the satyr plays that rounded off each tragic trilogy. It is perhaps indicative of the typical content of these plays that the sole surviving exemplar is Euripides's *Polyphemus*.

65–70. **Messius** responds with his own raillery on Sarmentus's servile origins. **Sarmentus** is asked if he had dedicated his chains (**catenam**) to the household gods (**Laribus**) of his mistress.

Multa Cicirrus: understand *dixit*.

Scriba . . . esse: understand *dicebat* implied by the two verbs of asking (**quaerebat** and **rogabat**) governing the surrounding clauses. **Sarmentus** may now be a scribe, but his mistress's legal claim to him is no less strong (**nilo deterius**). **Messius** implies that **Sarmentus** was not a freed man but a runaway.

Farris < *far*, *farris*: "spelt," a coarse grain. The implication is that the minimum slave-ration, as prescribed by the Twelve Tables, of one pound of grain a day, should have been more than enough for one of such small stature. Cato moreover—never one given to expansive generosity—recommended four to five pounds of bread a day for his field slaves, depending on the season. **Sarmentus**, however, can be safely assumed not to have fallen into this category, given his educational level.

Prorsus = "in this manner."

Producimus = "we drew out," historical present. Note how the use of the present tense not only makes the scene more vivid, but also effectively "draws it out" to the present moment of our reading.

71–4. The next day the party sets off for **Beneventum** (modern Benevento). There the overzealous host nearly burns the house down. In trying to make his guests "well-come," (*bene venti*) he almost makes them "ill-come," which is what the original name of the town (*Maleventum*) would have meant in Latin. The name, in fact, was based on the transliteration of a Greek word that had no sinister connotations, but it was later changed for obvious reasons. Horace, then, engineers a subtle pun for those in the know.

Arsit < *ardeo*, *–ere*, *arsi*, *arsum*: "to burn," intransitive. **Paene** goes with **arsit**. The disruption of normal word order is given various interpretations, none of them persuasive. Kiessling and Heinze (1999) allege it reflects the hunger of the guests, Morris (1968) says it reveals the confusion of the host.

Turdos < *turdus*, *–i*: "thrush."

Vulcano is metonymy for *igne*. Note the mock epic alliteration with **vaga** and **veterem**.

75–6. Hungry guests and panicked slaves struggle to save their dinner and put out the fire.

77–81. From here the mountains of Horace's native **Apulia** come into view. The description of the rigors of climbing the hills recalls Lucilius **lines 108–11.**

Montis = accusative plural.

Atabulus = the Apulian term for the sirocco. As Horace approaches his home, he briefly lapses into the native patois.

Erepsemus = syncopated form of *erepsissemus* < *erepo, –ere, erepsi*: "to creep up."

Camino < *caminus, –i*: "forge, fireplace."

82–5. Horace waits for a young girl who has promised him her favors. When she does not appear, his sleep is disturbed by a wet dream. The passage is the sole description of a nocturnal emission in ancient literature, outside of a technical philosophical or medical context. This passage is an example of that gentle, if somewhat grotesque, self-mockery that is the trademark of Horatian satire. Horace's little comedy is kept at a safe distance from Maecenas. By marginalizing his own misadventures, while subtly juxtaposing the small trials of private life with the unnamed anxieties of the public man, Horace carefully leaves the structures of power and their ruling ideology firmly in place.

Intentum: understand *me*. There is sexual pun. The literal meaning of *intendo* is "to stretch or extend."

Visu < *visus, –us*: "sight, vision."

86–92. Horace then continues onto a city impossible to name in verse for metrical reasons. It can be recognized by its horrible water and wonderful bread. The town, according to the scholiasts, is Aequus Tuticus, but all modern commentators note this would be a geographical impossibility and favor the region near Ausculum.

Raedis < *raeda, –ae*: "a four-wheeled carriage."

Quod versu dicere non est: Porphyrion lists a parallel for this passage in Lucilius's sixth book of satires. Understand *pote.*

Venit < *veneo, –ivi, –itum*: "is sold." Here they sell that which everywhere else is free (**vilissima**).

Canusi = Canusium, a town in Apulia. Understand *panis est.*

Lapidosus = "gritty."

Aquae non ditior urna: "not richer by one urn of water." **Aquae** = genitive of material. **Urna** = ablative of degree of difference. The comparison is relative to the unnamed town in the previous lines. Note the compression and acceleration of the narrative.

93. The mock epic tone of Varius's departure goes well with the invocation of Diomedes in the previous line.

94–5. Rubos = *Rubi*, the modern Ruvo.

Utpote = "since," explaining **fessi**.

96–100. The narrative passes quickly through a series of uneventful stops.

Piscosi < *piscosus, –a, –um*: "abounding in fish."

Gnatia = Egnatia.

Lymphis iratis exstructa = "built on angry springs." The water was either scarce or bad.

Cupit: the subject is **Gnatia**. The complement is **persuadere**, on which **liquescere** depends in indirect discourse. The subject of **liquescere** is **tura**. **Sine** is postpositive with **flamma**. Pliny in his *Historia Naturalis* 2.107.240 recounts that visitors were shown the miracle of an altar on which the wood took fire of itself. This mountebank show was the cause of the party's **risusque iocosque**.

100–3. "Let the superstitious believe in such. I rest secure in the knowledge that the gods live in distant serenity, unconcerned with human affairs." Horace here identifies with the Epicurean belief that the gods inhabit a separate realm and do not intervene in our affairs.

Iudaeus Apella: the Jewish population in Rome at this time was substantial. They were considered superstitious. Pseudo-Acron records a possible pun on circumcision in **Apella**—a common name among freedmen—taking it as a privative form of *pellis* or "skin." See **1.9.70.**

Tristis: accusative plural. Wonders are not signs the gods are angry, but facts of nature.

104. Chartaeque viaeque: the end of the road is also the end of the page and hence the end of the story. The abrupt conclusion pointedly does not tell us the result of Maecenas's mission.

1.6

At the midway point in the first book of *sermones*, Horace rededicates his work to Maecenas [64]. He recounts his initial introduction to the great patron and explains how his father played the role of satirist in his youth, pointing out examples of virtue and vice [62–3]. Thus Horace ties together the personal, political, generic, and stylistic themes already explored in 1.4 and 1.5, while explicitly renouncing ambitions for personal political power.

In the process, Horace seeks to move *nobilitas*, *ingenuitas*, and *libertas* away from their traditional Roman definitions as external public virtues in favor of a new vision of them as internal ethical values. These new internal ethical values, in turn, are often derived from Hellenistic popular philosophy. Thus, in response to a question from King Antigonos about his family and city of origin, Bion the Borysthenite the main exponent of the diatribe form [40–1], replied, "examine me for myself" (Diogenes Laertius 4.46), thus declaring the irrelevance of inherited status, wealth, or prestige. This was a position that would have been inimical to the traditional Roman aristocracy with which Lucilius was identified [20–31]. Fiske (1920: 316–18) has argued that **1.6** is extensively indebted to Bion.

Of course, no overly strict dichotomy should be established between the public and private. These new definitions of traditional Roman virtues only become operational to the extent that they were recognized by others. The proof of Horace's personal *ingenuitas* was its public recognition by Maecenas. The emerging Augustan regime had not substituted the private for the public, but had sought to replace the public recognition of externally determined virtues such as aristocratic birth, wealth, and competition for political and military honors, with the public promotion of internally determined ethical values such as modesty, honor, and fidelity. This program would become increasingly important as the regime hardened its grip on power and controlled access to both elective office and traditional military honors such as the triumph. In effect, the traditional realms of achievement—the *cursus honorum* and military excellence—would cease to exist for most upper-class Romans. Accordingly, the definitions of what it would mean for a *civis Romanus* to practice *virtus* would have to change as well. It was Maecenas's recognition of Horace's ability to practice (and through his poetry to promote) these new forms of virtue and self-definition that made him a worthy patron. It was Horace's ability to practice the satiric genre, in accord with the aesthetic and ideological norms required for such a shift, that definitively differentiated his work from that of Lucilius.

1–6. "Not because some of the Lydians possessed Etruscan land is no one nobler than you." **Quidquid**: we might more logically expect *quisquis*. The construction has a colloquial feel (Rolfe 1962).

Lydorum: the Etruscans were commonly supposed to be of Lydian descent. Maecenas was said to be descended from Etruscan nobility. Thus **generosior** in **line 2**, which comes from the same root as *genus* and *genero*, must be taken first in its literal sense of "well-born" and only upon rereading as "noble in character." Of course, within traditional aristocratic ideology, the two meanings were not separable.

Finis = accusative plural.

Imperitarent = frequentative of *impero*. There is no evidence that any of Maecenas's ancestors held high military command in Rome. The reference, then, would be to his legendary Etruscan forebears.

Naso suspendis adunco = "turn up your nose at," a colloquial expression.

Ignotos = *ignobiles*. *Nobilis* derives from *notabilis* and at base means a person who is "known," hence someone who is "prominent," or as we would say in colloquial English, "someone who is somebody."

Libertino patre natum: little is known about Horace's father. He appears to have been a man of some education and wealth since he was able to send his son to the best teachers in Rome. The circumstances under which he became a slave and later a freedman are unknown. This phrase, which is repeated throughout the satire both verbatim (**lines 45, 46**) and with slight variation (**lines 29, 36, 58**), is a direct translation of Bion (Freudenburg 1993: 205).

7–17. Rome itself is founded on the revolt of the ignoble against the tyranny of the Tarquins. Even the people can sometimes see through the external signs of inherited nobility.

Referre < *refert, referre, retulit*: "to matter, to make a difference." From *res* + *fert*.

Dum ingenuus = "so long as he is freeborn." This attempt to redefine *ingenuitas* retained strict limits. A slave by definition could not be *generosus*. In effect, this redefinition of terms was less an exercise in philosophy—as in Stoicism where only the wise man is truly free—than the elaboration of a social ideology that sought to reconstruct what it meant to be a Roman citizen after the fall of the republic.

Persuades hoc tibi vere: The commentaries all elide the force of the reflexive construction. It is not simply that Maecenas rightly believes this (**hoc**) to be true, but that he correctly convinces himself that this is true. The construction implies that Maecenas is engaged in an active effort to overcome his own lingering aristocratic biases. The fact that Maecenas never sought senatorial rank and that his family had never been prominent in Rome, whatever the nobility of his Etruscan ancestors, cannot help but give the clause an ironic cast.

9. **Ante potestatem Tulli atque ignobile regnum**: Servius Tullius, sixth king of Rome, was said to have been the son of a captured Latin slave and of an unknown father, raised in the household of Tarquinius Priscus.

11. **Honoribus** = "elected offices."

12. **Contra** = adverb, "on the other hand."

Laevinum: this individual is otherwise unknown, which may well be part of the point.

Valeri genus = "descendant of Valerius." M. Valerius Poplicola helped Brutus expel Tarquinius Superbus and was one of the consuls for the first year of the republic.

Unde = *a quo*.

13. **Unius assis** = genitive of value.

14. **Licuisse** < *liceo, –ere, –ui, –itum*: "to be sold for, to be valued at."

Notante iudice quo nosti populo = a lengthy and complex ablative absolute, "even with that judge whom you know, the people, rating him (i.e., Laevinus)." **Notante** < *noto, –are*: see 1.4.5. The people here act as *censor* by refusing to elect Laevinus to office. **Nosti** is a syncopated form for *novisti*. **Quo** is attracted into the ablative from the accusative.

15–16. **Stultus . . . ineptus**: note that the *populus* is derided, even if on occasion it can differentiate personal worth from social class or inherited excellence. This is not a call for democracy, but for the cultivation of an intellectual and spiritual élite that would supplant the traditional aristocracy and its competition for social, political, and military honors.

17. **Imaginibus** refers to the masks of dead consular ancestors kept in the *atria* of aristocratic households.

17–18. "What then should those of us who are far, far from the madding crowd do?" As the rest of the poem reveals, Horace was, in the opinion of many in the political class, not as far removed from the *vulgus* as this line would lead us to believe. There is a nice ambiguity in **a**, depending on whether we take it as introducing an ablative of separation or an ablative of agent.

19–22. "Even if the **populus** or the **censor** should reject me because of my birth, it would be a matter of no consequence since I have no desire for office." **Esto** = third person imperative, "let it be the case."

Decio = P. Decius Mus, a man of obscure birth who, as consul in 340 BCE, defeated the Latins at Veseris by performing a *devotio*. The *devotio* was a ritual in which a Roman general vowed his own life to the gods of the underworld in return for the lives of his enemies. Decius offered his prayer and rode directly into the enemy lines, thereby becoming an archetype of patriotism. He was the first member of his family to reach consular rank and hence was referred to as a *novus homo*.

Moveret: understand *me*.

Appius = Appius Claudius Pulcher, brother of the demagogue Clodius, who served as **censor** in 50 BCE. He purged the rolls of the senate, expelling all sons of freedmen.

Ingenuo: note that this is the fourth use of a word built on the stem *gen–* in this satire's opening lines.

Vel merito = "and rightly too."

In propria non pelle quiessem: proverbial expression for being happy with one's position in life. The French still refer to someone who is *bien dans sa peau*. Horace would deserve to be kicked out because he would have shown that he was not happy with his status. Romans frowned on social climbers.

Horace, however, has climbed a great deal. At the same time, he wants to call for both an aristocracy of the spirit and a conservative maintenance of traditional social hierarchies. This could only be achieved by an autocracy that remained sensitive to the social niceties of traditional Roman life, which is what the Augustan regime offered.

23–4. "We can all be slaves to Glory." The image is that of a triumphal procession with **Gloria**'s captives led behind the general's chariot. The triumph would normally be the pinnacle of a Roman noble's military career. **Gloria** is a positive value in traditional Roman ideology. Cicero in the *Pro Sestio* defines *dignitas*, *laus*, and **gloria** as the characteristics of a life that eschews *otium*. In the *De Officiis*, those who do not pursue **gloria** are suspected of effeminacy.

Ignotos generosis: compare **lines** 2 and 6. **Generosis** is ablative of comparison.

24–5. "Why has Tillius once again entered the lists?" Understand *profuit*. The scholiasts suggest that Tillius had been expelled from the senate and was recalled after the death of Julius Caesar.

Clavum: see 1.5.34–6.

Tribuno = dative, in agreement with **tibi**. As the following lines make clear, the reference is to becoming tribune of the people.

26. **Gloria** only produces **invidia**.

27–9. "As soon as (**ut**), one assumes senatorial garb, everybody asks who your father is." **Nigris . . . pellibus**: Senators wore shoes strapped on by black leather thongs. On **pellibus**, see **pelle, line 22**. Horace would not be comfortable in the senatorial shoe. The irony of **impediit** for binding on the shoe should not be lost. In strapping on the senatorial shoe, Tillius has lost the ability to move about freely. In assuming the highest social rank Rome has to offer, Tillius has given up the very *libertas* that separates the free man from the slave.

Demisit pectore = "has hung from the chest."

Patre natus: this is the third time a line has ended with this phrase or its close relative **patre natum (line** 6). See also **line** 21, the line before **in propria non pelle quiessem**. We are clearly intended to note the parallels between the two passages. **Patre natum** appears twice more as a line-ending, **lines** 45 and 46.

30–7. "The would-be politician is like the would-be lover. He must be willing to suffer every indignity and be inspected from head to foot. The politician, like the lover, is little better than the slave on the block." Horace here plays with inverting the elegiac motifs of *servitium amoris* and *militia amoris*. Instead of Ovid's later, "every lover is a soldier," we get instead "every politician is a lover." Horace is presumably working from Gallus's poetry and the Hellenistic precedents for the work of the later elegists who only became prominent in the twenties.

Barrus cannot be securely identified, but the scholiasts name him as someone accused of committing an illicit sexual act (*stuprum*) with the Vestal virgin Aemilia. He would thus be one who seeks to seduce the unseduceable. Understand *aegrotat* with **Barrus**.

Haberi = "to be considered."

Iniciat curam: "he would arouse curiosity."

Sura = "calf."

Civis = accusative plural.

Urbem, imperium, Italiam, delubra are each in turn the subject of **fore** in indirect discourse. **Delubra** = "shrines." These represent the would-be politician's campaign promises.

Patre sit natus: another variation on the theme.

Omnis mortalis = accusative plural.

Cogit is slyly ironic.

38–9. There follow examples of the kind of slurs on the candidate's family background that Tillius could expect. **Syrus, Dama**, and **Dionysus** are slave names indicating foreign birth. **Syrus** = "the Syrian." **Dionysus** is a Greek name.

Saxo = the Tarpeian rock from which traitors were hurled to their death by order of the tribune of the people. The point of the slur is to pretend outrage at the prospect that foreign-born slaves could condemn Roman citizens (**civis**) to death.

Cadmo: another Greek and hence servile name. The scholiast tells us he was an executioner at the time.

40–1. Tillius makes his reply: the man elected with him to the tribunate is of lower lineage than he. **Novius** = a speaking name, meaning *novus homo*.

Gradu post me sedet uno: equestrians sat behind senators in the theater according to the law of Otho, passed in 67 BCE. Once Tillius had reassumed the *latus clavus*, he was entitled to sit with the senatorial order. Yet **Novius** is a freedman, just as Tillius's father was. Tillius's point is that he is from higher stock than his colleague, but in fact both have climbed above their station. The period of the civil wars was a time of great social instability [29–30]. Many of lower-class and obscure origins were promoted to fill the ranks of an aristocracy decimated by decades of self-slaughter. Such newly created aristocrats were clearly beholden to the generals or autocrats who created them and they were subject to the resentments, as well as recriminations, of others.

41–4. Tillius's interlocutor replies with cutting irony: "do you therefore fancy yourself an aristocrat when Novius's only virtue is an exceptionally loud voice?" an allusion to the bluster associated with office of tribune of the people, a post that had attracted reformers, revolutionaries, and demagogues, from the Gracchi to Clodius [16–18, 23].

Hoc = "on this account."

Paulus et Messalla = the names (*cognomina*) of two of the oldest and most distinguished patrician families.

Hic = **Novius**.

Plaustra = the noise of the wagons in Rome was proverbial. See **Juvenal 3**.

Tria funera: Roman aristocratic funerals were noisy affairs accompanied by horns and trumpets. They wound their way to the Forum where a formal *laudatio* was given. The intersection of two hundred plebian wagons and three aristocratic funerals in the city's legal and political center is an apt emblem of the conflicts to which this satire is devoted.

Magna goes with both **funera** and **cornua**.

The subject of **sonabit** = **Nonius**. The verb is more often used for inanimate objects than the human voice. This is not articulate speech but noise comparable to the wagons and horns.

Quod = "to the extent that."

Saltem tenet hoc nos: "at all events this holds our attention." The clear implication is that Tillius lacks even that virtue. He is not only lowborn but also possessed of no distinguishing characteristics.

45–8. Back to our main topic. People envy me because I am Maecenas's friend. The repeated **libertino patre natum** gives the effect of a mocking chant and recalls the opening of the satire (**line** 6).

Nunc ad me redeo: Horace affects a Lucilian casualness of construction.

Rodunt: a vivid image of slander's effect.

Nunc quia . . . Maecenas recalls **non quia, Maecenas** (**line** 1)

Convictor = "dinner guest," metonymy for friend.

Quod mihi pareret legio Romana tribuno: Horace was a military tribune under Brutus and Cassius at Philippi [63]. One had to be of at least equestrian rank to hold the office. Horace, thus, had already begun to advance into the ranks of the aristocracy at the time of Caesar's assassination. The whole line recalls **qui magnis legionibus imperitarent** (**line** 4).

49–52. "But I am no longer possessed of ambition for honors and office." **Hoc** refers back to the previous clause beginning with **quia**, while **illi** refers back to that beginning with **quod**.

Ut = "as."

Forsit = "perhaps."

Honorem = "office" as in the *cursus honorum*.

Amicum is in apposition to **te**. **Invideat** is assumed here again.

Cautum modifies **te**, subject of **adsumere**.

Dignos: the word is highly charged. It normally referred to an individual's social status and the privileges that went with it. Caesar crossed the Rubicon to defend his *dignitas*. But, as Horace points out, Maecenas's circle of worthies is not made up of those who claim their social prerogatives, but of those who are "far from depraved ambition." *Dignitas*—the value whose defense led to the final collapse of the republic and eventually to Horace finding himself a military tribune at Philippi—has been redefined to signify the opposite of its traditional meaning.

52–5. "It was not mere chance (**fors**) that brought me to you but Vergil and Varius." We are immediately brought back to the world of Horace's friends on the journey to Brundisium (1.5). There we see the same cast of characters relaxing, obsessed with the small cares of daily life, and even enjoying a game of ball, as events of great political moment loom in the background. Here we flash back to how they all became associates. **Hoc** anticipates the clause introduced by **quod**.

56–60. "When first introduced, I showed due modesty and simply recounted who I was." **Singultim** = "stammeringly."

Pudor prohibebat plura profari: note the alliterative stutter. **Pudor** was a positive value. It represented the internalized sense of shame a proper Roman citizen possessed. The best account is in Kaster (1997).

Satureiano . . . caballo = "a Tarentine nag." The area around Tarentum was renowned for its vast and pleasant estates. *Caballus*, however, was the vulgar term for *equus*. The mixture of high and low registers in diction and social status reveal the pretentiousness of any such claim on Horace's part.

60–2. Maecenas responds but briefly. After nine months Horace is officially invited to join his circle.

62–4. I consider this a great thing, since you judge me by my life not birth. **Non patre praeclaro** directly recalls **line 58, claro natum patre**, which in turn calls to mind the earlier cited examples of lines ending in **patre natum** and **natus**.

65–78. "In fact, my father was the cause of my advancement! But, not in the usual fashion. He taught me to shun vice and embrace virtue." We are reminded of the picture of Horace's father in 1.4.103–43 using examples drawn from daily life to teach his son. It was from this habit, Horace tells us, that he took up the practice of writing satire. The phrase **vitiis mediocribus** is an echo of 1.4.139–40. Thus, Horace ties together his birth, his practice of satire, and his pursuit of virtue. 1.4, 1.5, and 1.6 constitute a comprehensive meditation on the theory, practice, and social context of satire at the dawn of the Augustan age.

Naevos = "moles."

68. Lustra = "bogs" and thus "brothels." It often functioned as metonymy for debauchery.

71. **Macro . . . agello** = "a meager little plot." *Agellus* is the diminutive of *ager*. Horace's father's poverty should not be taken too literally. He had sufficient resources to procure a first-rate education for his son and enough slaves to be able to leave his fields in their charge while he saw to the education of his son. This would not have been an opportunity open to the average Roman peasant or subsistence farmer. Horace's father's poverty is relative to that of the senators and equestrians with whose sons the poet went to school.

72. **Flavi ludum** = "the school of Flavius," Flavius was a *grammaticus* in Venusia.

Magni . . . magnis: the repetition underlines the bitter sarcasm. Veterans had been given land grants in Venusia and constituted the local aristocracy.

73. **Orti** = "sprung from." Note Horace's avoidance of the colorless word.

74. **Loculos tabulamque** = "satchel and writing tablet," the latter was made of wood and covered with wax into which the letters were incised.

75. **Octonos . . . aeris** = eight coppers. Teachers, then as now, were poorly paid.
Idibus: bills were paid on the Kalends and the Ides.

76. **Est ausus**: Horace's father has already stepped beyond his station in seeking to educate his son at Rome in the same fashion as the child of a **senator** or an **eques**.

78–80. Horace's father spared no expense so that the boy would appear to come from aristocratic stock. **In magno ut populo**: the exact translation of this passage is disputed, although the general sense is clear. The most natural Latin would be "as in a great mass of people." This would indicate first what is customary in the crowded city of Rome, as opposed to provincial Venusia. Second, it would pick up on **magni . . . magnis** in **lines** 72–3. The *magnus populus* would be those who are truly great, as opposed to the pretensions of the rural magnates.

Avita . . . re = "ancestral fortune."

81–2. **Custos**: Roman boys were accompanied by a guardian who was a trusted family slave. He was charged with the boy's moral and physical wellbeing. Horace's father here plays the servile part, but this serves as a marker of his concern with virtue. His nobility is manifested in his willingness to play an ignoble part.

82–8. "He watched for my reputation nor gave a thought to his." Horace's father, on a quiet bourgeois level, is the model of Roman self-sacrifice in the name of *pietas* ("duty to family, state, and the gods"), which on the heroic level was represented by characters like Aeneas and Horatius at the bridge. **Pudicum**: *pudor* often refers to sexual modesty and purity. Tales of predatory pederasts seeking positions as tutors of handsome boys are a staple of Roman comic literature.

Turpi refers both to **facto** and to **opprobrio**.

Vitio . . . verteret = an idiom, "should reproach him." The essence of the charge is that Horace's father is reaching beyond his station for a boy who is bound to follow in his footsteps as an auctioneer (**praeco**) or collector of debts (**coactor**). People who worked for wages were looked down upon as not fully free. They sold their time and abilities in the same way as a slave's whole person was sold. In traditional Roman terms, only those who lived off the incomes of their estates or large-scale mercantile ventures were truly free.

Neque ego essem questus: a contrary to fact use of the pluperfect potential subjunctive.

89–92. I am as proud of my father as if I had been born of aristocratic parents.

Paeniteat < *paeniteo, –ere*: "to cause regret or sorrow," usually used in the impersonal with an accusative of person affected and genitive of reference.

Eoque non . . . sic me defendam = "and I would not defend myself in this fashion."

Dolo is a technical legal usage that, as the scholiasts tell us, is equivalent to *vitio* or *culpa*. i.e., most defend themselves from the charge of base birth by responding that it is not their fault.

92–9. "Given the choice, I would have the same parents again." **A certis annis** = " from a certain age."

Remeare = "to live again."

Ad fastum = " for the sake of pride."

Honestos = "those who have been honored," as in the *cursus honorum*.

Fascibus: the *fasces* were the symbols of office of consuls, praetors, curule aediles, and quaestors, as was the *sella curulis*.

Tuo: Porphyrion says this is addressed to Maecenas. Understand **iudicio** again. Maecenas, while possessing great power and influence, never held formal office and remained an equestrian.

99. Nollem . . . molestum: Horace redefines *libertas* as freedom from the burden of office. This was the opposite of *libertas* as understood by the traditional Roman aristocracy, who defined freedom as the power to rule oneself and others.

100–4. Political life means not controlling one's destiny, but being subject to the conventions and expectations of others. This is an argument for Epicurean quietism [26].

Maior quaerenda foret res: the pursuit of wealth and power is never ending and never satisfied. This is certainly good advice to the disenfranchised political grandees of the late republic just prior to the dawn of the principate. But it applies equally well to Octavian as he neared a final showdown with Antony at Actium.

Salutandi plures: Horace refers to the morning *salutatio*, a daily ritual in which clients went to their patrons' houses at the crack of dawn to greet them and sometimes accompany them to the Forum. An aspiring young politician would have a very demanding schedule of morning rounds among the rich and powerful. A successful politician could expect an all but endless stream of well-wishers and favor-seekers.

Peregre = an adverb, "to a foreign country, abroad."

Calones atque caballi: the pretender to power must maintain a vast retinue of retainers and livestock. On **caballus**, see **line 59.** On **calones**, see **1.2.42.**

Pertorrita = "four-wheeled Gallic carriages."

104–9. "Now I am free to go where I please, how I please." **Curto . . . mulo**: a gelded mule is not only a humble means of transport, but also a metaphor for Horace's own estate.

Usque Tarentum: recall that in **1.5** this was where Maecenas and Cocceius were to meet up with Antony, but Horace and his satire are cut short in Brundisium.

Mantica = "saddle bags."

Armos = "shoulders." The image of the mule weighed down by Horace and his baggage is comic.

Sordis = accusative plural, "meanness." Roman officials were expected to travel in a style befitting their rank. The fact that Tillius's train consists of only five slaves (**pueri**) is taken as evidence of his humble origins.

Tiburte < *Tiburs, –burtis*: "pertaining to the village of Tibur" (modern Tivoli).

Lasanum . . . oenophorumque = "chamber pot and wine cask." As Kiessling and Heinze (1999) note, these are things that would normally be packed away in a wagon. But poor Tillius's meager entourage is forced to parade his personal items through the street. A number of commentators attempt to translate **lasanum** as "cook pot," but the gloss of the scholiast is clear. See also Petronius 41.9. The argument for a greater parallelism between the cooking utensil and the wine cask, in addition to suffering from a lack of evidence and being transparently based on prudishness, fails to recognize the frequent identification of food and excrement in the comic and grotesque tradition (Bakhtin 1968, Miller 1998). Besides, the parallelism remains in the literal translation, as a comic chiasmus links the result of consumption with its precondition.

110–18. "My life is better than that of a famous senator." This passage concludes with one of the classic genre scenes of Roman literature: Horace at his humble table. The picture of his daily routine represents more an Epicurean ideal than reality. The poet as we know from other poems had social and political obligations to Maecenas and Augustus. He also certainly devoted more time to writing and study than pictured here [26].

Libido est = *libet*,

Percontor = "I inquire."

Quanti = genitive of price.

Holus = "vegetables."

Far = "spelt."

Fallacem Circum: the Circus Maximus was a favorite gathering place for hucksters and mountebanks. The scholiast notes that the circus was also deceptive in itself since the outcomes of the races, on which substantial sums were bet, was uncertain.

Vespertinumque: in the evening, when the day's business was done, the Forum became a popular gathering spot. For Horace, the *forum matinale* of legal and political business is to be avoided.

Divinis: He listens to the fortune-tellers. Horace's life is that of the sophisticated *flâneur*.

115. **Ad porri et ciceris . . . et laganique catinum**: "for a dish of fritters, chickpeas, and leeks." Horace returns home for a simple vegetarian meal, yet that simplicity is deceptive. The last two words are Greek. This is a cultivated simplicity.

116. **Pueris tribus**: a modest, but hardly poverty stricken service.

Lapis albus: "a plain white marble table" as Porphyrion explains

117. **Cyatho** < *cyathus, –i*: "ladle," another Greek term.

Echinus: another Greek term. The scholiasts offer a variety of guesses about the nature and material of this utensil. The literal meaning of the word is "sea urchin." Many assume it is a salt cellar.

118. **Gutus** = "a narrow-necked jug."

Campana supellex = "Campanian crockery," i.e. everyday earthenware.

119–21. "My sleep is untroubled by thoughts of the next day's obligations." Horace defines freedom as *otium* and *inertia*, "leisure" and "idleness." See Tibullus 1.1. **Dormitum** = supine with verb of motion.

Mane = "crack of dawn."

Marsya < *Marsyas*: Greek third-declension noun, the name of a satyr flayed by Apollo after challenging the god to a musical contest. He was remarkable for his ugliness. A statue of him stood in the Forum near the *rostra*, and other such statues are found in similar contexts in other cities. He appears to stand for presumption punished and was pictured with one hand raised. Horace's joke is that not even Marsyas can bear the ugly face of the younger Novius (**Noviorum . . . minoris**) and so holds up his hand to stop him from entering the Forum. The combined image of the busy *patronus* rushing off to the Forum and Novius's homely mug (**vultum**) creates a moment of comic bathos.

122–4. "When you are up about your business, greeting clients and head off to court, I'm still in bed." **Quartam**: see **1.5.23–6.**

Lecto . . . scripto = frequentative verbs, as Porphyrion notes.

Unguor olivo = "I am rubbed down with oil" preparatory to a ball game.

Quo: the antecedent is **olivo. Natta** is otherwise unknown. He is rubbed down with oil destined for his lamps (**lucernis**). This would be of a lower grade than that normally used for personal care. Horace's life is modest, but far from rustic or mean. The humorous image of **Natta** smearing himself with oil stolen (**fraudatis**) from his own (or others') lamps should be noted.

125–6. "After some light exercise, it's off to the baths." **Lavatum**: supine with verb of motion.

Trigonem < *trigo, –onis*: a ball game with players at the apexes of a triangle. Small round balls were thrown and caught, much like a game of catch with a baseball, only without gloves.

127–8. Then, after a light lunch, I laze around the house. **Interpellet** < *interpello, –are*: "to prevent," subjunctive with **quantum** in a clause of purpose. Understand *me* as the subject of **durare**.

Domesticus otior is a humorous periphrasis. **Otior** is a verb formed from *otium* and only found once before in a humorous context in Cicero. The scholiast labels it a Horatian coinage. **Domesticus** is here used to mean *domi*.

128–30. I would not trade my life for all the honors the republic and illustrious ancestors have to offer. **Misera ambitione gravique**: compare **prava ambitione, lines 51–2.** Note the initial ambiguity of **misera**. Because of the elision between it and **ambitione** the quantity of the final syllable is impossible to determine. The reader only realizes that it must be ablative and modify **ambitione**, rather than nominative and modify **vita**, at **gravique**. Of course, to the typical Roman aristocrat, motivated by the pursuit of wealth and office, Horace's life is **misera**. But from Horace's perspective, the shoe is on the other foot.

Victurum < *vivo, –ere, vixi, victus.*

1.9

Horace is bothered by a social climber envious of his access to Maecenas. Many think the pest in question is Propertius. The identification is most uncertain. It is based on the facts that the pest uses clearly identified neoteric vocabulary, identified with that of the elegists [2], and that Propertius was finishing his first book at this time, on the strength of which he was offered admission into Maecenas's charmed circle [64].

The main problem with the identification, however, is not that it is false. In fact, there is no way of knowing who the pest was or if an actual person lies behind the comic portraiture. What is demonstrably true, however, is that any attempt to reduce this poem to the level of the clever anecdote is a vast oversimplification. Beyond its manifest status as an exercise in character drawing, 1.9 works on at least four other interconnected levels.

First, it begins and ends with direct imitations of Lucilius. In the last instance, Horace imitates in Latin a line from Homer Lucilius had cited in the original Greek. Horace criticizes Lucilius for this mixing of languages in 1.10.20–1. Thus, 1.9 continues the practice of stylistic imitation and simultaneous criticism of Horace's generic predecessor seen in 1.4 and 1.5.

Second, as Anderson (1982: 84–102) has shown, the satire is shot through with military vocabulary. Maecenas is portrayed as a city to be besieged by Horace's overeager companion. Horace himself, in the line he imitates from Lucilius, is portrayed as Hector at the end of the *Iliad*, saved by Apollo, god of poets. The mock epic language both deflates the poetaster's pretensions and humorously portrays Horace as unable to fend off the assault of his determined foe.

Third, poem 1.9 functions in an analogous structural fashion to 1.5 earlier in the collection. Where 1.5 presented itself as a straightforward anecdotal account of a journey, 1.9 presents itself as a straightforward anecdotal account of a personal encounter. Where 1.5 was an imitation and correction of Lucilius, which was sandwiched between a more direct discussion of Lucilius's style and an evocation of Maecenas and his coterie, 1.9 is an imitation and correction of Lucilius that immediately precedes a direct discussion of Lucilius in the context of a poem on Horace's relationship to Maecenas and his coterie. Lastly, where 1.5 portrayed itself as a purely personal poem, while actually being a work of no small political import, 1.9's day in the life of Horace reveals much about how the inner workings of Maecenas's circle were meant to be perceived by the world at large.

Fourth, poem 1.9 is indirectly a poem about Maecenas and the new model of a post-republican aristocracy he and those gathered around Augustus were striving—even if only subconsciously—to create. As Rudd put it so well:

> Maecenas and his friends knew very well that this was their poem. Not only were they the object of the pest's endeavours, but without

> them the whole episode would have been inconceivable. As they listened to Horace's account of the fellow's efforts to ingratiate himself their amusement must have been spiced with a dash of self-congratulation. Secure in their own eminence they could smile on the antics of the social climber.
>
> (1982: 82–3)

Of course, as we know from 1.6, the real social climber was none other than Horace himself.

1–5. "I happened to be going down the Sacred Way completely absorbed in my own thoughts, when I was accosted by a man I barely knew." **Ibam forte**: *ibat forte* begins two lines in Lucilius (1159 and 16.535). Most think the echo deliberate.

Via Sacra: one of the main roads in central Rome. It was lined with temples.

Nugarum: a common neoteric euphemism for light poetic verse. See Catullus 1. As Timothy Johnson notes (2004: chapter 1), the pest's greeting, **dulcissime rerum**, and Horace's response, **suaviter**, are equally Catullan. Horace's additional **ut nunc est** could be read one of two ways: "as things are now," i.e. I'm doing fine for the moment, but if you keep bugging me it could change; or "as is said now," i.e. I can speak this same poetic lingo too, if I choose. These are clearly two poets marking off their ideological and aesthetic territories.

6–13. "When he followed, I tried to give him the brush off." **Occupo** = "I break in," but also "I attack," an example of the military vocabulary found throughout the poem.

Noris = syncopated form of *noveris*, perfect subjunctive used in a hortatory sense. "You should have made our acquaintance."

Docti = "learned," a common adjective of approbation for poets. Note the poetic plural.

Pluris = genitive of value. **Hoc** = ablative of cause. Note the curtness of Horace's reply.

Sudor: the image of the warrior drenched in sweat is common in epic.

'o te, Bolane, cerebri felicem': although Bolanus has not been identified, the scholiasts and commentators are in agreement that he was one who did not suffer fools gladly and would have used more direct means of shedding himself of the pest. **Cerebri felicem** = accusative of exclamation. Bolanus is happy in his temper. It may not be coincidental that **Bolane** recalls *Bellona*, the Roman goddess of war.

13–16. The pest understands very well the meaning of Horace's behavior but has no intention of letting him go. **Persequar**: the image of pursuit is appropriate to a battle scene.

16–18. "No really, I'm going to visit a sick friend on the far side of town." **Cubat** = "has taken to his bed."

Caesaris hortos: gardens donated to the city by Julius Caesar. They lay on the far side of the Tiber.

19. "I'm not doing anything and I don't mind strenuous exercise."

20–1. Demitto auriculas: there is a pun here on Horace's cognomen, Flaccus, meaning "floppy eared."

21–5. In a deliciously ironic passage that sums up Horace's criticisms of his predecessors and contemporaries, the pest claims that Horace will rate him a better friend than Viscus and Varius because he embodies the common literary vices and thinks them virtues. **Si bene me novi**: it is of course the boor's almost total lack of self-knowledge that makes him so obnoxious.

Viscum = a fellow poet in Maecenas's circle. See **1.10.83.**

Pluris: genitive of value.

Varium: see 1.5.40 and 1.6.55.

Nam quis me scribere pluris / aut citius possit versus: compare 1.4.9–21.

Membra movere / mollius = "to dance more lasciviously/gracefully." *Mollis*, while a term of poetic praise in neoteric and elegiac circles, carried with it connotations of effeminacy. Dancing, in general, was a suspect art in Roman morality.

Hermogenes: see 1.2.1 and 1.10.18, 80, 90.

26–8. Horace squeezes a word in. "Don't you have relatives for whose sake you need to stay healthy?" The tone is threatening. Does the pest invite Nemesis by his bragging? Might he become ill if he accompanies Horace to visit his fictional sick friend? Might Horace clobber him if he doesn't shut up? All are possibilities. But the pest brushes off the implicit threat and answers in a completely literal manner.

Quis = *quibus*.

Omnis composui = "I've laid them all to rest."

28–34. This is an aside addressed to the audience rather than the pest. The epic parody of the oracular pronouncement is to be noted and forms part of the epic and martial subtext that runs throughout the poem. **Felices**: "lucky them!" referring to the pest's dead relatives.

Instat fatum me triste: Anderson (1982: 94) notes that this passage directly recalls Hector's statement at *Iliad* 22.303 before he turns and faces Achilles in his final battle. Recall that the present poem concludes with a parody of Lucilius's quotation from *Iliad* 20.443, where Hector is initially saved by Apollo from the raging Achilles. Horace, thus, takes over Lucilius's use of Homer, naturalizes it into Latin rather than quoting the Greek, and at the same time converts the Homeric subtext into a consistent organizing principle for the satire as a whole. The consistent application of the heroic paradigm to such a banal context only increases the bathos in which the piece as a whole is bathed.

Sabella . . . anus: a humorous reference to rustic divining practices, a Sabine wise woman.

Divina mota . . . urna: ablative absolute. The urn contained slips of papers with prophecies written upon them. After a question was asked, the urn would be shaken until one fell out.

Hunc: the young Horace. Note that the list of possible deaths begins with the bizarre and the heroic and moves swiftly to the banal.

Laterum dolor = "pleurisy."

Quando . . . cumque = tmesis, the splitting apart of a compound word, for *quandocumque*: "some time or other." Tmesis is a common figure in epic verse.

Simul atque = "as soon as."

35–7. The pest must decide whether to appear in court or follow Horace, in which case he will lose his suit.

Ventum erat: impersonal pluperfect passive of the intransitive verb. This construction allows Horace to avoid including the pest in the first person plural.

Ad Vestae: understand *aedem*. The Vestal shrine was located in the Forum near the law courts.

Quarta . . . parte = *quarta hora*, see **1.5.23** and **1.6.122.**

Respondere: a technical term meaning to appear in court.

Vadato: impersonal ablative absolute construction, "for which he had given a bond." The pest is involved in a civil suit. If he fails to appear, he will forfeit to the other party the bond posted.

Perdere litem: understand *debebat* again.

38. Si me amas: a formulaic phrase meaning, "please." Here it ironically retains its literal meaning. Horace does not love him.

38–40. Horace quickly tries to excuse himself. **Inteream**: a colloquialism equivalent to "I'll be damned." Again it regains some of its literal force in this context, see **confice, line 29.**

Valeo stare: it was customary to stand in the praetor's court. Horace's excuse that he would not be able to stand up through the proceedings is completely inconsistent with his professed need to continue on his long walk to visit his friend on the other side of the Tiber. Desperate times call for desperate measures.

40–3. The pest hesitates a moment and resolves to forfeit his bond and keep hold of Horace.

Sodes = "if you please."

Sequor: note that it is now Horace who follows the pest. He has become his captive. Observe the martial vocabulary, **contendere** and **victore**.

43–8. Horace, however, is a mere hostage. The pest really aims to conquer Maecenas himself.

There is great disagreement on how to distribute these lines. The scholiasts assign **paucorum hominum et mentis bene sanae** to Horace in response to the pest. The German editors have generally followed suit (Doering 1824; Krüger 1911; Kiessling and Heinze 1999), whereas most anglophone editors have assigned the whole passage to the pest (Anthon 1886; Wickham 1912; Rolfe 1962; Morris 1968; Brown 1993). The reasons for ignoring the ancient testimony, however, are purely subjective and not grounds for overturning the received tradition.

Maecenas quomodo tecum: "how's Maecenas treating you?" The tone is colloquial.

Hinc repetit: "he returns to his original point," i.e., this is what he's been after all along.

Paucorum hominum et mentis bene sanae: genitives of quality. What would a man of sound mind and who does not have a broad circle of friends do with someone like the pest?

Nemo dexterius fortuna est usus: the referent of the comparison is ambiguous: Maecenas or Horace? Arguably, both had made good use of fortune. Maecenas, although an equestrian, had risen to be Octavian's political second-in-command. Horace, although *libertino patre natus*, had risen to be in the coterie of poets who received patronage from Octavian's first minister.

Posset qui ferre secundas: understand *partes*. The reference is to actors who play supporting roles in a drama. The pest understands the poets' relation to Maecenas as part of an elaborate charade in which the players jockey for position and favor. He wants to make clear to Horace that he is not trying to steal the limelight, but willing to play a bit part.

Hunc hominem: i.e., the pest. This circumlocution is common in comedy. It amounts to "yours truly."

Tradere = "introduce."

Dispeream ni / summosses omnis: "I'll be damned if you wouldn't have cleared the field [had I been there to aid you]." **Dispeream** is the equivalent of **intereaam** at **line 38. Summosses** = a syncopated form of *summovisses*.

48–52. Horace replies, "it's not like that at all." As Oliensis astutely observes, "what matters here is less the truth-value than the pragmatic value of Horace's idealizing description of Maecenas's circle. The encounter gives Horace the chance to act the part of a faithful friend—a man who knows both how to keep his mouth shut and when to open it" (1998: 39).

Nil mi officit = "it does not stand in my way."

Est locus uni cuique suus: "each one's place is his own." Horace's idealizing picture does not in any way imply a complete breakdown in social hierarchy or a democracy of the spirit. While internal values are recognized, everyone knows his place. This is not a place for vulgar social climbers. Horace is involved in a very delicate ideological balancing act.

52–60. The pest refuses to believe that Maecenas's circle is not characterized by jockeying for power and position. He even proposes to bribe the slaves to ease access to the great man. **Accendis** = "you inflame."

Proximus: the superlative here is a kind of Freudian slip. The pest in fact does have his eye on supplanting Horace.

54–6. Horace here transfers the martial language that had earlier been used to describe his relation with the pest onto Maecenas, who now becomes a citadel to be stormed.

Velis tantummodo, quae tua virtus, / expugnabis: Horace ironically suggests that the pest need only wish it (**velis tantummodo**), and his boldness (**virtus**) is such that he will take Maecenas by storm (**expugnabis**). There is a deliberate play on two different senses of **virtus**: martial courage and moral virtue. The dissociation of these two senses from one another is part of the same ideological process that is involved in the redefinition of *libertas* and *ingenuitas* in poems **1.4** and **1.6.** Here martial **virtus** is humorously redefined as tactless boldness. Maecenas, however, values **virtus** in the moral sense for those who form part of his coterie.

Vinci: another example of martial language.

Eoque: *eo* = the old dative form of *is* used in the adverbial sense of "to this point, there."

Primos aditus: more martial language.

56. The pest typically confuses the literal with the figurative sense of Horace's words. If Maecenas is difficult to approach (**aditus**), then he will bribe the slaves who block the way.

60–2. Help arrives! **Fuscus Aristius** = Aristius Fuscus, a fellow poet. See **1.10.83.** He is also the recipient of *Odes* 1.22 and *Epistles* 1.10. The inversion is for metrical reasons.

Illum / . . . pulchre nosset: "Knew him pretty well."

62–74. But **Aristius** leaves Horace high and dry.

62–3. **'Unde venis et quo tendis?'**: a standard greeting.

Rogat et respondet = "we ask each other."

63–5. **Vellere**: understand *togam*, i.e. "I began to tug on his sleeve."

Pressare = "to squeeze," some manuscripts have *prensare* "to grab," but that seems too unsubtle for the context.

Lentissima = "unresponsive."

65–6. **Male salsus / ridens dissimulare**: a condensed colloquial phrase. See Anthon's "With cruel pleasantry he laughed and pretended not to understand me" (1886).

Meum iecur urere bilis: the liver (**iecur**) was regarded as the seat of the emotions. **Urere** = historical infinitive. **Bilis** = nominative.

68–70. **Tricesima sabbata** = "the thirtieth sabbath." The meaning of this phrase is much debated. Clearly, Aristius is alleging a flimsy pretext for abandoning Horace to his plight. The holiday is likely fictitious.

Curtis = "circumcised." See also **1.4.142–3** and **1.5.100.**

Oppedere < *ob pedere*: literally "to fart at" and hence "insult."

70–1. **Religio** = "religious scruples."

71–2. "**At mi . . . alias loquar**": the transparently false nature of Aristius's claim only makes it all the more infuriating.

72–4. **Surrexe** = *surrexisse* < *surgo, –ere, surrexi, surrectum*: "to rise," explanatory infinitive with **solem** as the subject.

Cultro < *culter, –tri*: "knife." Horace is like a sacrificial animal.

74–8. Horace is saved by the pest's legal opponent who hauls him off to court. **Licet antestari** = "May I call you as a witness?" The plaintiff in a case, according to the Twelve Tables, has the right to seize someone who has refused a summons after appealing to a witness. The witness signals his assent by allowing the plaintiff to touch his ear. The ear was considered the seat of memory.

Sic me servavit: this is a translation of Lucilius's τὸν δ'ἐξήρπαξεν 'Απόλλον (6.238), which is a direct quote from *Iliad* 2.443. Horace changes the passage in several significant ways. First, he translates it into Latin. Second, he switches the pronoun to the first person. Third, Apollo saves him as the god of poets, where he saves Hector as protector of Troy. Fourth, where Hector is saved by being pulled from the scene of battle, Apollo saves Horace by having the pest, his Achilles, hauled off to court. Each one of these changes is both appropriate to Horace's poetic context and shows close attention to the original text. He thus demonstrates the "proper" way to use a Greek subtext in a Roman poem. He eschews slavish imitation in favor of holistic integration.

1.10

In this poem, Horace returns to the topic of his debt to Lucilius and delineates the intended audience for his work: Maecenas and the poets who surround him. He thus draws together the social, political, generic and stylistic threads that have run through the collection. Where 1.2 exemplified satire in its form as diatribe, a form of discourse derived from Hellenistic popular philosophy, but in this case owing much to Lucilius's example, it also undercut that form through the very excessive nature of the speaker. 1.4 introduces the topic of the poet's differences with Lucilius and the relation of satire to poetry in general. 1.5 introduces us to Maecenas, while treating a topic already dealt with by Lucilius in the new refined mode of *sermo merus* Horace proposes. In 1.6, we see Horace's introduction to Maecenas, and the question of Horace's low social status is directly broached. In 1.9, the same stylistic problems broached in 1.4, and the social and political questions of 1.6, are dramatized in his encounter with the pest.

Poem 1.10 returns to each of these topics. It applauds Lucilius's diatribes against vice while criticizing his versification. It examines the nature of poetry and what is proper to its respective genres, while answering the poet's presumed critics. Lastly, it defines his audience as a small circle of *literati* under the patronage of Octavian's chief political advisor. Horace, thus, establishes a centralization of poetic authority and implicitly redefines the nature of *libertas*, *virtus*, and of what it means to be a *poeta* in this new *res publica*.

[1–8.] These lines are generally thought to be spurious and thus bracketed. They are not commented upon by the scholiasts, are missing from a number of manuscripts, and contain stylistic infelicities. Nonetheless, they are normally printed because they appear to contain accurate and useful information about Lucilius's text and those who supported him.

Mendosus = "full of faults."

Catone = P. Valerius Cato, the famous scholar and poet who was apparently preparing an edition of Lucilius and proposing emendations to some of the master's verses. What Cato viewed as faults in transmission, the writer of these lines views as faults in composition (**male factos / . . . versus**). Cato was an important influence on poets like Catullus and Gallus who first established the principles of Callimacheanism as the guiding light of Roman poetry.

Pervincam < *pervinco*: in this context, "I will clearly prove."

2. **Qui**: antecedent = **Catone**.

3. **Hoc**: ablative of comparison. The identity of this other critic is unknown.

Ille = Cato.

4. **Illo**: refers back to **quo** and ultimately **hoc**. The switch in pronouns is clumsy.

5. **Qui**: antecedent = **illo.**

Loris et funibus udis = "whips and wet ropes." The latter critic had his principles beaten into him at school when he was a boy (**puer**).

6. **Exoratus** = "prevailed upon."

Opem is the direct object of **ferre.**

8. **Doctissimus** is in apposition to **qui (line 5).**

1–4. "Lucilius wrote rough verse, but he also lampooned vice in the city." **Fautor** = "partisan, promoter," probably originally *favitor*.

Sale multo / urbem defricuit = "scrubbed down the city with much wit." The literal meaning of *sal* as "salt" is also important here. Lucilius's wit was a harsh, if salutary, abrasive.

5–6. "The one does not preclude the other. If that were true, I would have to admire Laberius as a poet." Decimus Laberius (105–43 BCE) raised the early mimes from the level of common farce to a literary form. They do not, however, seem to have reached the level of refinement that Horace posits as the *sine qua non* of true poetry. It may not be coincidental that Laberius was a foe of Julius Caesar, the uncle of Octavian.

7–14. "Humor while a virtue does not make a poem. A certain level of technical perfection is required so the thought flows and does not tire the ears." Note that this definition of poetry differs substantially from that offered at **1.4.40–8.** But see our discussion of how Horace there undercuts the definition he proffers in ways that point toward the reformulation found here.

Risu diducere rictum = "to pull open the mouth in a toothy grin."

Defendente < *defendo, –ere, defensi, defensum*: here in the relatively unusual sense of "to play a part." See *Ars Poetica* 193–94.

Urbani: *urbanitas* is the quality of wit and sophistication much prized by Roman aristocratic society of the later republic in general and the neoteric poets in particular. Its opposite is *rusticitas*. See **1.4.90.**

Parcentis viribus atque / extenuantis eas consulto = "of one sparing his forces and holding them back in reserve." Lucilius appears not to have practiced the virtue of understatement.

14–19. This is the real lesson of the Old Comic poets, *varietas* and humor, not a misplaced *libertas*. Compare **1.4.1–5. Ridiculum acri fortius**: a famous tag. **Acri** = ablative of comparison.

Secat = "cuts" and hence "decides."

Hoc = ablative.

Stabant = "succeeded," as the scholiasts note.

Hermogenes: see **1.2.1, 1.9.5,** and **1.10.80, 90.**

Simius iste: the identity of the "ape" is unsure, but Porphyrion identifies him with the Demetrius of **line 90**, based on his looks.

Calvum = C. Licinius Calvus, a noted poet and orator associated with Catullus and the neoterics. Horace here is less criticizing Calvus and Catullus per se than **Hermogenes** and the ape's single-minded devotion to them. These men are portrayed as presumed advocates of Lucilius and yet they have never read the Old Comic poets, or at least they have not read them correctly [34–5].

Doctus: here the primary meaning is "having been trained," but it is also ironic. How can those who have not truly read the Old Comic poets claim to be **doctus** concerning satire?

20–30. Horace here debates with an interlocutor the value of Lucilius's use of direct Greek quotations. See **1.9.**

Seri studiorum = "slow learners." Porphyrion notes that Horace is translating the Greek *opsimatheis*, thus beating his putative critics at their own game.

Quine: "who really?"

Pitholeonti: an unidentified poet who apparently mixed Latin and Greek, sometimes thought to be the poet Pitholaus mentioned by Suetonius for his lampoons against Caesar. This would at least account for why a Greek poet would be mixing Latin into his poems, certainly not a common practice.

Contigit < *contingo*, *–tingere*, *–tigi*, *–tactum*: "to happen, befall," when used intransitively with the dative. Note the impersonal usage. This was not something Lucilius or Pitholeon achieved, but something that happened to them.

Concinnus = "well put together, harmonious."

Suavior: neoteric vocabulary appropriate to a follower of Calvus and Catullus. See **1.9.1–5.**

Nota: the label on the Falernian. **Chio** < *Chius*, *–a*, *–um*: Chian. Falernian was a dry native Italian wine. Chian was a sweeter Greek import.

25. Cum versus facias . . . an et cum: "when you versify . . . also when?" Horace's point is that no one would gratuitously mix in Greek with Latin when trying to win a difficult court case (**dura . . . causa**). The goal there is to communicate clearly. Should clarity not be a goal of poetry as well? Yet another meaning of *sermo merus*.

26. Tibi peragenda . . . sit: passive periphrastic with dative of agent.

Petilli: see 1.4.94.

27. Oblitus modifies the subject of **malis**.

Patris Latini = father Latinus, ancestor of the Latin-speaking people. The OCT prints *patris, Latine,* which is also attested.

28. Pedius . . . Publicola: the scholiasts identify this advocate as the brother of M. Valerius Messalla **Corvinus**. This contradicts the testimony of Dio (10.1.7.24), but confirms that of Pliny (*Historia Naturalis* 35.21). It also fits nicely with **line 85** below. Messalla was a soldier, statesman, orator, and patron of the arts. His most famous protégé, Tibullus, wrote an exceptionally pure Latin. It is only natural then that he and his brother should be pictured sweating (**exsudet**) over their forensic speeches (**causas**).

29. **Petita / verba** = "foreign words."

30. **Canusini . . . bilinguis**: Canusium was a region that spoke both Greek and Oscan. The scholiasts note that both Ennius [53] and Lucilius had referred to the inhabitants as **bilinguis**.

31–5. This is a very elaborate intertextual figure. In his great epic poem, the *Annales*, Ennius, the first Roman to write in a genre he termed *satura*, began with a dream in which Homer in the company of the Muses crowned him his successor (Vahlen 1967: 1–6). Ennius's scene is based on passages from Hesiod and Callimachus [39]. The proem to the *Theogony* features Hesiod's initiation by the Muses into hexameter didactic poetry, which positions him as a challenger to the tradition of Homeric epic. The "Prologue" to Callimachus's *Aetia* is a response to the poet's critics who charge him with never having created a large continuous narrative in the style of Homeric epic. He responds with the story of how Apollo appeared to him in his youth and admonished him, "fatten your animal for sacrifice poet, / but keep your muse slender" (Lombardo and Rayor 1988: lines 25–6). This passage is immediately followed by a dream in which the Muses appear to a young Callimachus, a passage that makes direct reference to Hesiod's initiation by the Muses. For more on these passages, see Cameron (1995: 127–32, 361 n. 89).

Both Hesiod and, *a fortiori*, Callimachus deal with the difficulties of being a belated poet, following in the wake of an esteemed but problematic predecessor, Homer, and his often obtuse advocates. This, of course, is precisely the position in which Horace finds himself in relation to Lucilius and, to a lesser extent, Ennius. Horace, it will be recalled, had already alluded to Callimachus's advocacy of the slender style in his earlier criticism of Lucilius's verbosity (1.4.11). Likewise, when Ennius had sought to appropriate Homeric prestige for Roman literature by casting himself as the bard's reincarnation, he did so in terms that recalled Hesiod's and Callimachus's respective poetic initiations. Horace in the present passage, which deals not with the question of epic but with the use of Greek words in Latin poetry, has Romulus (**Quirinus**) appear to him in his dream (**somnia vera**) and forbid (**vetuit**) the use of anything but Latin. Horace, thus, shows a completely mastery of the Greek tradition and its self-conscious Roman successors. He also successfully integrates that knowledge into a thoroughly Roman context. He thus trumps both Lucilius and Ennius, being simultaneously more Greek and more Roman.

Graecos . . . versiculos: presumably a product of the poet's student days in Athens.

Quirinus / . . . visus: compare Ennius line 6 *visus Homerus*.

In silvam non ligna feras = carrying coals to Newcastle, i.e., Greek poetry does not need us to enrich it.

Ac si = "than if."

Catervas < *caterva, –ae*: "ranks."

36–9. Horace now turns to his own work in contrast to that of his contemporaries. Unlike them, he does not seek the applause of the professional poets or of the crowd.

Alpinus = M. Furius Bibaculus who wrote an epic *Aethiopis* in which Memnon is slain by Achilles. Furius murders (**iugulat**) him a second time. He also wrote a poem on Gaul that probably contained the description of the headwaters of the Rhine (**Rheni luteum caput**). On the Callimachean significance of "muddy rivers," see **1.4.11** [39]. Even this, **Alpinus** misshapes (**defingit**). Horace quotes from the poem on Gaul at 2.5.41.

Ludo: see **illudo, 1.4.139.**

Quae neque . . . sonent . . . nec redeant: relative clauses of characteristic, hence subjunctive.

Aede: identified by Porphyrion as the temple of the Muses where poetic recitations and competitions (**certantia**) were held.

Tarpa = Spurius Maecius Tarpa, picked by Pompey to choose plays for his new theater in 55 BCE. He was head of the *collegia poetarum* or poets' guild.

40–9. Horace now runs through the various genres practiced by contemporaries whom he admires.

40–3. Fundanius is able to rattle off (**garrire**) charming scrolls (**comis . . . libellos**) in which the accused *meretrix* and the slave Davus escape old Chremes. These are standard characters in New Comedy. See **1.4.48–52.** Fundanius describes the banquet in **2.8**, but is otherwise unknown. The emphasis on **libellos**, Brown notes (1993), may indicate that these were plays to be read rather than to be performed like those in **line 39. Chremeta** = Greek accusative of Chremes.

43–4. C. Assinius **Pollio** was a multi-talented orator, general, historian, and literary critic. He is here celebrated as a writer of tragedy through reference to its typical meter for dialogue, iambic trimeter (**pede ter percusso**). Vergil dedicated *Eclogue* 4 and Horace *Odes* 2.1 to Pollio.

43–4. **Varius**, see **1.5.40** and **1.6.55.** He was considered the supreme practitioner of epic before Vergil wrote the *Aeneid*. Unfortunately, his work is lost.

44–5. The reference here is to Vergil's *Eclogues*. The *Georgics* are just in the early stages of composition and the *Aeneid* will not be begun until 29 BCE.

Camenae is the traditional Latin term for the Muses, as opposed to the Greek *Musae*. See the discussion of mixing Latin and Greek above.

46–9. "This was what I could do." **Hoc** = *saturam*. Varro of Atax, not to be confused with the great antiquarian scholar of the same name, had attempted (**experto** in an ablative absolute construction) to write satire without success. This later Varro was born in Gaul and was an unsuccessful practitioner of a variety of genres. The unnamed other satirists (**quibusdam aliis**) are not even worthy of mention by name. Horace could best (**melius**) these latter-day Lucilians, but not the founder of the genre himself (**inventore**). Horace's role was that of refining and perfecting this sort of writing, not creating it as Lucilius had. Note the elision between **ego** and **illi** so that Horace and Lucilius become one. See 1.4.39.

Ausim = old perfect subjunctive of *audeo, –ere*, expressing potential in a hypothetical situation.

50–5. "Yes, I criticized Lucilius. Is that not what each generation does to its predecessors? Did not Lucilius do the same?" **At dixi** recalls **nempe dixi** in **line 1.**

Fluere . . . relinquendis: see 1.4.11–12 and **line 37** of this poem.

Doctus: the criticism of Homer had been the province of the "learned" since his first Alexandrian editors in the third century. Lucilius too had admitted that at times the great bard nodded (9.383–5 Krenkel). The neoteric sympathies of Horace's apparent detractors should have already familiarized them with this practice. Thus they must either accept it or renounce their title to being *docti*.

Accius was considered, with Pacuvius and Ennius, one of Rome's greatest tragedians. He was active in the second century. There is ample testimony in Porphyrion, Gellius, and Lucilius's own fragments of his criticism of all three writers of tragedy.

Cum = concessive.

Reprensis = ablative of comparison from *reprendo, –prendere, –prendi, –prensum*: "to hold back, check, restrain, blame." A shortened form of *reprehendo*.

56–64. "What forbids us from asking the same questions of Lucilius?" Note the elaborate period and highly rhetorical nature of Horace's question as he moves to the climax of his argument. **Legentis** = accusative plural.

Num illius, num rerum dura . . . natura: "whether his own harsh nature and that of the times . . .?" **Rerum** also refers to his themes, which were drawn from his aristocratic social milieu. The conjoining of the personal with the historical argument is particularly powerful here. Not only are Lucilius's failings as an artist being critiqued but there is a realization that the times have fundamentally changed. Artistic techniques have been perfected and, implicitly, what once constituted *libertas* now appears as irresponsibility [26–30].

Factos = *perfectos*.

Euntis mollius: "more metrically smooth." *Mollis*, however, is a term of stylistic approbation used by the neoterics and their followers, the elegists. Horace turns his critics' vocabulary against them. It is also semantically the opposite of *durus*. **Euntis** = accusative plural.

Ac = *quam* in a comparison.

Hoc = ablative. It is a gloss on **pedibus quid claudere senis**: "to close something in six feet." See 1.4.40. Both depend on **contentus**.

Scripsisse ducentos / ante cibum versus: see 1.4.9.

Quale fuit Cassi . . . ingenium = "such was the talent of Cassius." The implied *talis* clause is unexpressed. Cassius the Etruscan is unidentified, unless we accept the suggestions of the scholiast that he was the Cassius of Parma mentioned in *Epistles* 1.4.3. That, however, is unlikely since the latter Cassius appears to be still alive and admired by Horace.

Rapido ferventius amni: we return to Callimachean river imagery [39]. See 1.4.11–12 and **lines** 37 and 50 of this poem.

Quem = accusative because subject of **esse**. The antecedent is **Cassi**. The normal prose would be *cuius fama est eum ambustum esse*. Cassius wrote so much that his books and their cases (**capsis . . . librisque . . . propriis**) were used as his pyre. See the somewhat obscure joke about the prolific Fannius and his bookcases at 1.4.21–2.

64–71. Horace sums up the case for and against Lucilius. On **urbanus**, see 1.4.90 and **line** 13 of this poem.

Limatior = "more refined," literally "more filed down." The file is a metaphor for poetic revision at *Ars Poetica* 291.

Quam rudis . . . quamque poetarum seniorum turba: note the parallel construction.

Graecis intacti carminis auctor: on the lack of precise Greek precedents for Roman verse satire, see introduction [1]. As Porphyrion observes, *Hoc ideo dixit, quia nulli Graecorum hexametris versibus hoc genus operis scripserunt*. It is for this reason that Lucilius is termed satire's *inventor* in **line** 48. The parallels with Greek Old Comedy, cited at the opening or 1.4, are only partial. Not only are the differences metrical, but also the forms of representation are radically different [9, 34–5]. Moreover, as Horace argues in **lines** 14–19, the true value of Old Comedy for satire is commonly misunderstood, thus qualifying the statement at the beginning of 1.4.

This line is much debated. Most readers do not place a comma after **rudis** and identify this person with the **auctor**. This has led to implausible speculations that either Ennius is referred to, which would exclude him from the next line where he clearly belongs, or a generic author of Saturnian verse. This latter solution ignores the testimony of the scholiasts, renders **et** otiose, and forces us to posit a generic type nowhere else mentioned in the poem. Still others see that **auctor** must refer to Lucilius but are then forced into a variety of improbable solutions to explain the relation to **rudis**, lest the force of the comparison, **limatior idem quam rudis**, be blunted. All in all the easiest solution and the one that does the least violence to the text while preserving the ancient *testimonia* is to separate **rudis** from **auctor**. See Doering (1824), Anthon (1886), Krüger (1911), Morris (1968), Brown (1993), Kiessling and Heinze (1999).

Hoc nostrum . . . in aevum = "into this time of ours."

Detereret < *detero, –terere, –trivi, –tritum*: "to rub down, away." See **limatior, line 65.**

Vivos = "to the quick," predicative with **roderet**.

72–5. In short, Lucilius, were you alive today you would be a lot more like me. Note the shift to direct address in the second person. **Stilum vertas** = "turn over the stylus" used to write on wax tablets so that the offending word could be excised.

Neque te ut miretur turba labores: such labor is not undertaken for the applause of the crowd but for the discernment of the few.

Contentus: compare **line 60.**

Vilibus in ludis dictari: schoolmasters would dictate poems to students who would write them on their tablets and memorize them. The irony is that Horace became a school text, displacing Lucilius, so that Horace survives *in toto* while Lucilius comes down to us only in fragments.

76–91. This passage clearly echoes Lucilius **26.1.589–93.** Like Lucilius, Horace seeks a select audience, and, like Lucilius's audience, Horace's includes the political élite. The emphasis on fellow poets who share his emphasis on formal perfection, however, is uniquely Horatian. See Brown (1993).

76–7. Arbuscula was a mime actress in the time of Cicero. **Equitem** is generally thought to refer to the seating section of the theater where the knights sat. Hence Arbuscula, after being hissed (**explosa**) off the stage by the crowd, says she only wants to appeal to the better elements, just as Horace claims that he too only wants to appeal to the cultured. **Equitem**, however, could be a true singular, rather than synecdoche, and refer to **Arbuscula**'s lover, in which case **equitem** for Horace would refer to Maecenas, who was well-known for his refusal of senatorial honors.

78–80. "What do I care if the usual lot of fools criticize me?" **Men** (*me* + *ne*) is the object of all three verbs.

Cimex = "bug."

Pantillius: the name is attested but also can be derived from the Greek *pan tillein*, "to pick at everything." It may well be both a real and a speaking name, or at least a recognizable nickname.

Quod vellicet absentem Demetrius is the subject of **cruciet** as is the correlative clause beginning **aut quod ineptus**. **Demetrius** is associated with

Hermogenes Tigellius in **line 90** below. The scholiast identifies him with the **simius** of **line 18** above. **Vellicet** < *vellico, –are*: "to pick at, to criticize." On **Fannius**: see 1.4.21. **Conviva, ae** = "table companion," a masculine noun. On Hermogenes, see 1.2.1–3, 1.9.25 and **lines 18** and **90** of the present poem.

81–3. Horace seeks the approval first of those who introduced him to **Maecenas** and accompanied him on the journey to Brundisium: **Plotius** (1.5.40), **Varius** (1.5.40, 1.6.55, and **lines** 43–4), and Vergil (1.5.40, 1.6.55, and **lines** 44–5). And then of those in their immediate circle: C. **Valgius** Rufus, the elegist; **Octavius** Musa, the historian; Aristius **Fuscus**, the poet who refused to rescue Horace from the pest (1.9.61); **Viscorum**, unknown except for the mention of one of them in 1.9.22.

84–90. Outside the immediate circle around Maecenas, these are the people I wish to please: **Pollio** (**lines** 42–3), **Messalla** and his brother (**lines** 27–30), **Bibulus** (respected republican and Antonian politician, a fellow student of Horace in Athens), **Servius** (poet and son of the jurist and consul Servius Sulpicius Rufus, who married Messalla's sister Valeria), and **Furnius** (identity uncertain; Pseudo-Acron lists him as a historian of renown, possibly the consul of 17 BCE). All of these are not only skilled writers, but politically important individuals. Horace is dropping too many names for his initial proviso, **ambitione relegata**, to be taken at face value. Nonetheless, see 1.6.51–2, 128–30 on the significance of this and like formulas in the political context of the times.

Quibus haec . . . arridere velim: the poems here are personified as "smiling upon" the readers. Note the transfer of epithet. Normally you would wish the readers to smile upon the poems. A nice poetic turn of phrase.

Sint qualiacumque: a trope of poetic modesty often found in dedications. See Catullus 1.8–9: *quare habe tibi quidquid hoc libelli / qualecumque*.

90–2. "I bid (**iubeo**) you Demetrius and you Tigellius to go wail (**plorare**) amid the seats of your lady students (**discipularum**)." A parting shot; Horace's critics are pictured as the servants of ladies, while he seeks the approval of the newly emergent post-republican male aristocracy in Rome. As Juvenal makes clear, men who provide instructions for ladies are generally suspected of providing other services as well. Horace implicitly reduces his critics to gigolos.

93. The last poem is complete. "Away boy, and add it to the others in the book."

2.1

The opening satire of Horace's second book is cast in the form of a dialogue [66] with the noted jurist, C. Trebatius Testa, about whom we are well informed in Cicero's letters (*Ad Familiares* 7.5–22). The dialogue works on two incommensurate levels, the legal and the poetic. The result is a series of puns, double meanings, and comic misunderstandings. Trebatius plays the serious, well-intentioned traditional Roman. He is literal-minded and prudent in his discussion of the "law of satire," by which he intends the practice of writing defamatory verse [28]. He recommends that Horace keep silent or write encomiastic verse for Caesar. Horace, however, understands everything aesthetically. For him the "law of satire" is the set of generic expectations that define the form. He cites the precedent of Lucilius and responds to the charge of writing defamatory (*mala*) poetry that his verse is good (*bona*) [27].

Structurally, 2.1 is a transitional poem. It looks forward to the rest of Book 2, introducing it with an ironic meditation on the nature of the genre and its relation to the political realities of the emerging Augustan state, and the changed nature of his situation versus that of Lucilius. This poem also signals the new level of artistic polish to be found in this second book: the irony is sophisticated, the humor self-deprecating and indirect, the satirist supremely confident in his own powers and the social position he has won from his patrons [64–5]. At the same time, this poem deliberately revisits many of the themes found in 1.10, directly addressing the poet's relation to Lucilius, even as Horace adopts a new-found generosity toward his predecessor. He also returns once more to the question of whether satiric *libertas* means naming one's opponents [27–8, 35].

1–5. "Trebatius some think I go too far in writing satire, others think I don't go far enough. What am I to do?" **Satira**: the first extant use of the term.

Legem: Horace speaks in *Ars Poetica* (135) of the *lex operis* or "set of generic expectations" that limit what the writer of a given form can do and what will be accepted by his audience. Trebatius understands Horace's question as pertaining to civil not poetic law.

Sine nervis = "without strength, impotent." For the sexual meaning, see Catullus 67.27–8.

Mille die versus: turning Horace's charge against Lucilius back on himself (see 1.4.40, 1.10.60–1).

5–6. Trebatius's one-word response parodies the laconic style of Roman legal discourse.

6–7. "I have to write; I've got insomnia." **Peream male** = "I'll be damned."

7–9. "Those who need sleep should swim the Tiber thrice and soak themselves in wine." **Uncti**: athletes oiled their skin in the ancient world.

Transnanto = third person plural imperative, also known as the "legal imperative" (Muecke 1997): "let them swim across." Cicero records that Trebatius was fond of swimming (*Ad Familiares* 7.10).

Irriguumque mero . . . corpus = "and the body soaked with unmixed wine." Cicero also records that Trebatius enjoyed his wine (*Ad Familiares* 7.22).

Sub noctem = "near nightfall."

10–12. "If you have to write though, why not tell of Caesar's accomplishments?" **Laturus** modifies the subject of **aude**: if Horace dares to undertake the task, he will be rewarded.

12–15. "The spirit is willing, Trebatius, but the flesh is weak." Horace uses here the rhetorical device known as the *recusatio*, a common form in Augustan poetics in which a poet alleges his inability to write one kind of verse, normally epic, and indicates his preference for staying with a less strenuous form such as satire or elegy. *Recusationes* are an expected part of the Callimachean poet's arsenal [39]. As Horace's descriptions of the dying Gauls and the wounded Parthian demonstrate, he is perfectly capable of writing epic. The Gauls and Parthians were conspicuous enemies of the Romans on the eastern and western edges of the empire. **Cupidum**: understand *me*.

Pater optime: "The respectful tone of the refusal is perhaps humorously exaggerated" (Muecke 1997).

Quivis = "just anyone."

Horrentia pilis / agmina: this line recalls Ennius *Annales* 285 and 393. Servius (11.61), the ancient commentator on Vergil, observes that these very constructions are derided by Lucilius (1211), and cites Horace in **1.10.54** on Lucilius's criticism of Ennius. Thus Horace's *recusatio* alludes simultaneously to the archaic epic tradition and its satiric critique (Freudenburg 2001: 87–9), while picking up the thread of his argument from the previous book.

16–17. "But Lucilius praised Scipio." **Scipiadam** = an epic patronymic for the unmetrical *Scipionem*.

17–20. "I'll be ready when the time comes, but Caesar is a temperamental beast." The image of a Caesar as a horse kicking with his rear hooves (**recalcitrat**) is at once humorous and a warning to those outside the inner circle to be careful in how they approach the great man.

Attentam = "pricked up," like the ear of a temperamental stallion, in contrast to old floppy ears (**Flacci**). Horace plays the ass to Caesar's horse.

Palpere < *palpor, –ari*: "to stroke" and hence "to flatter."

Tutus = following Porphyrion, *inaccesibilis*, and hence "protected."

21–3. "Well, you'd be better off spending your time at this than lacerating Pantolabus and Nomentanus." **Line 22** is quoted from 1.8.11. Pantolabus is a fictional name meaning, "Grab all." **Nomentanus** appears also at 1.1.102 and 2.3.175, 224. He is the type of the prodigal. The ancient commentators identify **Pantolabus** as a nickname for a Mallius Verna and Nomentanus as a certain Cassius Nomentanus, but neither is attested outside of Horace and the scholia. **Scurram**: see 1.4.86–9.

Nepotem = "spendthrift."

24–9. "Everyone has his vice. Mine is writing in the manner of Lucilius." Note that Horace defends his practice by engaging in the very satire of individuals by name that he claims (apparently with reason) not to be able to stop. **Saltat** = "dances."

Milonius is otherwise unknown, so even as Horace pretends to satirize people by name he uses either fictional straw men or those of obscure status.

Icto . . . capiti: a euphemism for drunkenness.

Numerusque lucernis: he's seeing double.

Ovo prognatus eodem: Castor and Pollux, in some versions of the myth, were born from the same egg, like Helen and Clytemnestra, as a result of Leda's encounter with Jupiter in the form of a swan. Castor loved horses, Pollux boxing.

Capitum, as often, = *hominum*: partitive genitive.

Pedibus . . . claudere verba = "to versify." Compare **1.10.59.**

Ritu = "manner."

Melioris modifies **Lucili** and **utroque** is ablative of comparison.

30–4. "Lucilius confided all his deepest secrets to his books." **Cesserat** = impersonal: "it had turned out."

Alio: than his books.

Quo = "on account of which."

Votiva . . . tabella: a thank offering in the form of a picture dedicated to a deity whose aid has rescued one from impending doom. The picture depicted the disaster from which the offerant had been saved. Such paintings can still be seen at Catholic shrines in Europe and Latin America.

34–9. "I follow his lead, because we Venusians are of warlike stock." **Anceps** = "uncertain": it modifies the subject of **sequor**. Horace's hometown of Venusia was on the border between Lucania and Apulia. Horace here claims descent from the warlike opponents of the Romans who were driven out of Venusia at the end of the Third Samnite war in 291 BCE (**pulsis . . . Sabellis**). The captives were enslaved like his father, although in his case this must have happened much later, perhaps during the Social War (91–87 BCE). Roman colonists (**colonus**) resettled the city along with a garrison to guard a strategic road from the predations of the local inhabitants. See Kiessling and Heinze (1999) on this passage as well as Muecke (1997). The joke is that Horace owes his predilection for satire to this breeding.

Quo ne = *ut non*: a difficult, unparalleled construction.

39–42. "But I only fight in self-defense." **Stilus** = "pen," but its point makes an apt analogy to the **ensis** ("sword").

Quem: the antecedent = **ensis.**

Tutus: Horace, Augustus (**line 20**), will lash out at all perceived threats.

Latronibus < *latro*, *latronis*: "brigand."

42–4. "Let my sword rust in its scabbard."

44–6. "But he who disturbs me, will be on the lips of everyone in the city." Infamy is the standard threat of the iambist. See Catullus 40.5 [36]. **Commorit** = a syncopated form for *commoverit.*

47–8. "In a world of such corruption, I can't go out unarmed." None of the people Horace names are of real consequence and were most likely fictitious or generic when not long dead. His satire is Lucilian in *name* only. **Cervius** = an informer who cannot be securely identified. See **2.6.77.** The sixteenth-century scholar Cruquius, who had access to manuscripts and commentaries since lost, claims him to be the accuser of Gnaeus Calvinus, consul in 55, on a false charge of being an assassin (Kiessling and Heinze 1999). **Urnam** = the voting urn used by jurors.

Canidia is portrayed as a poisoner and witch in Horace (*Satires* 1.8, 2.8 and *Epodes* 5 and 7). She corresponds to no known historical personage.

Albucius = unknown. Porphyrion says he poisoned his wife.

Grande malum Turius = "a heavy penalty." Understand *minitatur.* **Turius** appears to be a corrupt judge of the Ciceronian period.

Se iudice = ablative absolute.

50–3. "Each fights with his own weapon." **Ut** = "as"

Quo = "with that which."

Suspectos = *inimicos.*

Collige = "infer."

Nisi intus monstratum = *nisi hoc monstraretur natura.*

53–6. "Lefty does not attack with his right hand, anymore than the bulls kicks or the cow bites." **Scaeva** = unknown. The cognomen *Scaevola* was common in Rome, but the joke on **dextra** ("right hand") is obviously a prime motivation for choosing it.

Vivacem = "long lived," and hence depriving the prodigal Scaeva of the possibility of gaining his inheritance.

Mirum = ironic.

Calce < *calx*, *–cis*: "heel," and hence a "kick." See **recalcitrat, line 20.**

Mala modifies an implied *scaeva.*

Cicuta = ablative: "hemlock."

57–60. "In short, no matter my fate, I'll call them like I see them." The claim to mimetic realism is common in satire [10–11]. **Quisquis** modifies **color**: "complexion."

60–2. "Boy, you are taking your life in your hands and courting the anger of the great" [27–8].

62–8. "Lucilius, who founded this mode of writing, dared to attack Lupus and Metellus, and Scipio and Laelius were unperturbed" On L. Cornelius Lentulus **Lupus**, consul 156, censor 147, *princeps senatus* 131–24 BCE, see introduction [35]. **Metellus** = Q. Caecilius Metellus Macedonicus, consul 143 BCE, a political enemy of Scipio Aemilianus Africanus, whom Lucilius apparently attacked [56–9]. **Detrahere et pellem** = to expose what lies beneath external appearances, possibly a reference to the fable of the ass in the lion's skin. The construction depends on **ausus est**.

Qua: antecedent = **pellem**.

Cederet = "would go."

Laelius: see introduction [20, 27, 57].

Qui duxit . . . Carthagine nomen: an elaborate periphrasis for the unmetrical Scipio. In 146 BCE, he captured and destroyed Carthage, thus bringing to an end the Third Punic War. His adoptive grandfather, Scipio Africanus the elder, had defeated Hannibal [53].

Cooperto < *cooperio*, *–ire*, *–ui*, *–tum*: "to cover entirely, to overwhelm."

69–70. "He made no discrimination of rank and was fair to virtue alone and its friends." See **Lucilius 1342–54.** *Arripio* is a technical legal term: "to arraign."

Tributim = "tribe by tribe." The tribe was a political unit of republican Rome.

71–4. "Yet, when they withdrew from public, Scipio, Laelius, and Lucilius would let their hair down while their simple fare stewed." **Virtus Scipiadae** = epic periphrasis. Scipio was publicly associated with **virtus**, erecting a temple to its personification in 134 BCE. It is a complex value term in Latin referring to what is expected of an aristocratic man (*vir*): manliness, bravery, good conduct. Hence, Scipio would have been the *amicus* of **virtus (line** 70). In Latin *amicus* is often a polite synonym for *patronus*.

Sapientia: Laelius's cognomen was *Sapiens*. The puns on the **sapientia** of Laelius and the **virtus** of Scipio open an ironic gap between the literal meaning of Lucilius being fair to virtue and its friends alone and a figurative meaning in which he would be a partisan of his friends and receive their protection. See Freudenburg (2001: 102). Horace will claim just such protection from Caesar and Maecenas below.

Nugari = "kid around."

Discincti = "no longer wearing the formal toga" and hence "relaxed."

74–9. "And although I may not be Lucilius's social or artistic equal, I too have lived with the great, which should blunt envy's bite." **Censum** = "fortune" as determined by the census that qualified one for admission into the ranks of the senatorial and equestrian élite. Horace too was an equestrian, but Lucilius was quite wealthy [57, 62–3].

Invita = "unwillingly," i.e., "in spite of itself."

Fragili . . . solido = neuter substantives.

Illidere = *in* + *laedo*: "to strike against."

Dissentis = legal vocabulary.

79–83. "I cannot disagree, but nonetheless I warn you, there is a law against defamatory verses (**mala . . . carmina** [27–8])." **Negoti . . . quid** = "some trouble."

Condiderit = "undertaken, created."

Ius est iudiciumque = "there is law and the courts" as a remedy.

83–5. "But what if someone has created good poetry praised by Caesar?" **Latraverit** = "barked."

86. "The indictments will be dissolved in laughter." The general sense is clear, but the exact reference of **tabulae** is much debated.

2.6

In this poem, the poet thanks Maecenas for the gift of the Sabine farm and tells the fable of the city mouse and the country mouse [64–6]. Fable was a traditional part of both Greek diatribe and iambic poetry. It is found in Ennius and Lucilius as well [36–8, 40–1, 55].

As Bowditch has demonstrated (2001: 142–54), the poem is more than a simple thank-you note. It is a complex negotiation of the obligations the poet incurs as a result of this gift and the potential financial and personal independence it grants him. Horace's personal *libertas*, ratified by the acquisition of this modest estate, is in fact a function of his relation to Maecenas and of Maecenas's to Caesar. Moreover, just as Horace's father had lost his estate in the civil war, so this estate too was more than likely acquired in the proscriptions. The poem is not unaware of these facts. The granting of land to Caesar's veterans in Sicily is also directly alluded to in **lines 55–6**. In the case of Horace and the veterans, the land granted would have originally been another's. The hand that giveth taketh away.

For Horace, the Sabine farm becomes a symbol of personal freedom. It is a pastoral retreat from the pressures of the city. It is also a symbolic affirmation of his social status as a landowner and equestrian. It represents the very *libertas* that separates him from his father, the *libertinus*, and the very social mobility that aroused the jealousy and suspicion portrayed in 1.6. Yet Horace's *libertas* is dependent upon the goodwill of another and the unstated question is what must Horace do, if anything, to make sure that this gift remains his own (**propria, line 5**). The new internal *libertas* Horace had sought to define in 1.4 and 1.6 is ultimately tied to external instances of power to which he is necessarily subjected [25–6].

The Sabine farm is also a symbol of the poet's own modest Callimachean ambitions. He seeks no large poetic estate. He is, as he declares at 1.6. 51–2, *prava ambitione procul* [free of improper ambition]. His will be the modest work of the **musa pedestris (line 17)** [38–9], not the epic and encomiastic bluster recommended by Trebatius in 2.1.

Nonetheless, as the closing tale of the city mouse and the country mouse demonstrates, the temptations of the city are ever alluring. But the modest mouse easily falls victim to the larger, more dangerous figures that populate the city. It is better to stay on one's country estate and cultivate the modest joys of the "walking muse" and a *libertas* that one can hope to make truly one's own.

This poem reveals the personal, the political, and the aesthetic to be deeply interrelated, not only discursively but also existentially. The poet's freedom rests on the very forces that could destroy it. Yet it is no less real for its precarious nature. Likewise, Horace's gratitude to Maecenas is as genuine as is his desire not to have his sense of obligation transformed into dependence. Lastly, while his prosaic muse is modest in relation to claims of epic grandeur, its polish is hard-won and its simplicity every bit as deceptive as the bucolic freedom that reigns over the Sabine farm.

1–15. The poem opens with a prayer of thanks to Mercury, god of exchange, for the gift of the Sabine farm.

1–3. "My prayers have been answered." **Non ita** = "not so very," a self-consciously modest locution.

Iugis < *iugis, –e*: "joined together," hence "continuous, perpetual."

3–4. "The gods have done more than I asked." As **lines 51–2** make clear, on a cynical reading the gods are Octavian, Maecenas, and their circle.

4–5. "Son of Maia I wish nothing more, except that you make these gifts mine forever." **Maia nate** = Mercury. The connection between Mercury as god of exchange and Horace's relation to Maecenas and Octavian is not hard to find. Horace needed the Sabine farm because he had fought on the wrong side at Philippi. It was his poetry that saved him from the consequences of this act, and he received the farm because of his poetry. As Bowditch observes (2001: 153), **Maia [g]nate** recalls *Maecenas*, ablative *Maecenate*. On the relation between Maecenas, Mercury, and Octavian/Augustus, see Miller (1994: chapter 8).

Faxis = archaic perfect subjunctive. Archaicisms are common in prayers and curses.

6–15. "If my prayers do not display the venality or stupidity of most men, grant that my cattle be fat, but not my talent." The moral, religious, and political message is converted into a declaration of adherence to Callimachean poetics [39]. **Rem** = "fortune."

Angulus . . . proximus = "neighboring corner."

Denormat = "makes crooked."

10–13. Horace here alludes to a fable recounted in full by Porphyrion. A farmer, who worked a plot for hire, prayed to Hercules to reveal to him a hidden treasure. Hercules took the man to Mercury who revealed to him the treasure. The man then bought the plot and continued to work it as before. Whereupon Mercury pronounced that no amount of money would make the man happy, since he continued to do exactly the same as he did before he found the treasure. Horace does not include the moral, but clearly we are supposed to recall it and perhaps ask if Horace will be any happier if his prayer is answered. How will his life be different? **Urnam argenti**: on the ill consequences of finding a pot of money, see Plautus's *Aulularia*.

Mercennarius = "a man for hire." **Mercatus** < *mercor*, *–ari*: "to buy." Note the prominence of words beginning in *merc-* in the context of this story and Horace's prayer to Mercury.

13–15. Summarizing the previous condition. **Iuvat**: understand *me*.

16–17. "When I head for my mountain retreat what should I celebrate before my farm?" **Prius**: understand *quam agro*.

Satiris musaque pedestri continues the self-conscious allusions to Callimachus [38].

18–19. The farm is a poetic retreat from the pressures of life in Rome. **Ambitio**: see introductory note.

The hot winds of the sirocco (**Auster**) were especially oppressive in autumn and thought to bear disease.

Quaestus < *quaestus*, *–us*: "profit, gain, advantage." **Libitina** was the goddess of burial.

20–3. His introduction complete, Horace now prepares to recount a typical day. This section opens with an invocation of morning in the style of a prayer. This marks a new beginning in the poem, while recalling the earlier prayers offered to Mercury. **Matutinus** is not elsewhere attested and may well be humorous (Kiessling and Heinze 1999). The poem ends with after-dinner conversation thus marking the conclusion of the day that begins here.

'Iane' libentius audis: Janus, in his capacity as god of new beginnings, was another name for the spirit of the morning. Roman prayers routinely tried to include all possible names under which a deity could be invoked both to avoid offense and to bind the god contractually by removing any excuse for claiming it had not been addressed. The proper name of the deity has a quasi-magical power in many religions.

Unde = *a quo*.

Operum . . . vitaeque = "of their individual projects and whole life" (Kiessling and Heinze 1999).

Esto = second person future imperative.

Principium = "beginning."

23–39. The daily grind in Rome. This passage recalls many scenes from **1.9**.

23–4. The subject of **rapis** is Janus.

Sponsorem: "In an action before the *praetor* both parties needed *sponsores*, who promised to cover the costs should their principal default in any way" (Muecke 1997).

Eia = "come on."

Urge = "hurry."

25–6. Neither rain, nor sleet, nor snow will keep Horace from his appointed rounds. **Aquilo** = the north wind.

Interiore diem gyro trahit = "pulls the day into a tighter circle": a reference to the contraction of the day in winter.

27–8. A very compressed sentence recapping the scene before the praetor and its aftermath. In two lines we are asked to picture Horace being admonished in court to speak up, his misgivings, and his subsequent hurrying through the crowd to make his next appointment.

Quod mi obsit = "which may be harmful to me," i.e., if Horace's friend defaults on his obligation: potential subjunctive.

Locuto modifies **mi**. Its object is **clare certumque** taken as a substantive that serves as an antecedent to **quod**. **Clare certumque** is an example of **hendiadys**, the rhetorical figure for referring to a single thing through two coordinated terms. **Mi** must essentially be taken three times: once with **obsit**, once with **locuto**, and as the dative of agent with **luctandum** and **facienda**. *Est* must be assumed with the two gerundives.

29–31. Horace incurs the wrath of his fellow citizens as he jostles them in his haste to get to Maecenas's house. The picture is at once a fine example of Horace's self-deprecating irony, a declaration of his allegiance to Maecenas, and a subtle attempt through comic relief to maintain his independence from the great man. **Improbus** = "rogue"; like many modern drivers, Horace impugns the character of the man whom he has upset with his own rude behavior.

32. "I can't lie, when I am impugned for my relation to you it's a cause for joy."

32–4. "But, as soon as I arrive at the Esquiline, a hundred tasks for other people jump about me on all sides." Everyone wants to catch Horace's ear on the way to the morning *salutatio* with Maecenas. The *salutatio* was an obligation of all Roman *clientes* to their patrons. Compare 1.6.101, where Horace claims to be exempt from this onerous task and defines this as part of what gives him a *libertas* superior to that of the aspiring senator [26]. Horace's success, which he owes to Maecenas, has compromised the very *libertas* that the Sabine farm symbolizes.

Ventum est = impersonal passive: the construction removes Horace from any role as active agent.

Atras . . . Esquilas: Maecenas's house and famous gardens were located on the site of a former cemetery on the Esquiline hill.

34–5. **Secundam**: understand *horam*: see 1.6.122. **Puteal** = a place in the Forum where lightning had struck and which was considered sacred. It was near the praetor's court.

36–7. Horace as a former *scriba quaestorius* [63] was still a member of the guild. **Quinte**: to refer to someone by *praenomen* alone is a sign of great familiarity often used when trying to insinuate yourself in someone's good graces (Dickey 2002: 63–7).

38. **Imprimat** < *imprimo, –ere, –pressi, –pressum*: "to press on," jussive subjunctive.

Cura = imperative.

Signa = "seal" or "signet ring," probably poetic plural. The use of your seal on a document was the ancient equivalent of a signature. It is probable from other information in the satire that its composition can be dated to the end of 31 BCE or the beginning of 30. At this time, immediately after the defeat of Antony and Cleopatra at Actium, Maecenas was in charge of the city and provided with a copy of Octavian's seal [64].

39. **Dixeris** = future perfect with conditional force: Horace addresses himself in the second person. Note that this line, a *tour de force*, has six verbs.

40–58. Horace describes his relationship with Maecenas: how other people often misconstrue it, and how it has evolved since first portrayed in 1.6. Horace has become a trusted friend, *cliens*, and confidant whose discretion extends to a denial of all knowledge of the governmental affairs in which Maecenas is directly involved. It is hardly conceivable that Horace knew nothing of these matters. Compare **1.5** where Horace seems almost completely oblivious of the immense political import of Maecenas's mission.

40–6. It's been seven years since Maecenas invited me to join his circle so that I could ride in his coach and engage in small talk. **Dumtaxat ad hoc** = "only to this extent."

Raeda: see **1.5.86.**

Quem = "as someone."

Thraex = "the Thracian": a kind of gladiator who wore two tall greaves and a broad-brimmed helmet with a tall crest. He carried a small rectangular shield and a curved short sword (Köhne and Ewigleben 2000: 51–7).

Gallina = "Hen," a nickname.

Syro = a slave name: "Syrian." Thracians were normally matched against *murmillones*, who carried swords and shields like those of a Roman infantryman and wore a brimmed helmet and a short greave on the left leg (Köhne and Ewigleben 2000: 48–51).

Rimosa . . . in aure = "an ear full of holes" and hence "indiscreet." Before we take this self-description too seriously, it should be remembered that Augustus later invited Horace to be his personal secretary and help him with his correspondence, an honor the poet declined (Suetonius, *Vita Horatii*).

47–8. per totum hoc tempus = the last seven years. **Noster** = colloquial for "our friend": here used of Horace himself. **In diem et horam** = "every day and every hour."

48–58. "If they see us relaxing together, they instantly assume that I have access to state secrets." **Una**: understand *cum te*, referring to Maecenas.

Omnes: understand *clamant*.

50. Note the artistic construction of the line. The words **frigidus** and **rumor**, here portraying a maleficent liquid (*humor*), are at opposite ends of the line, while the verb **manat** is in the middle. The structure enacts the slow drizzle of chilly gossip as it starts in the Forum (**a Rostris**) and spreads through the crossroads (**per compita**). The *Rostra* was the speaking platform in the Forum. It was fashioned from the prows of captured enemy ships.

52. Deos = slang for the upper reaches of society.

53. Dacis = "the Dacians": a Balkan tribe north of the Danube that had sided with Antony. An invasion was feared. War was declared against them in 30 BCE.

54. **Derisor** = "joker," a rare word.
Di exagitent = "may the gods come after me," a common oath.

55. **Quicquam**: assume *audivi*.

55–6. "Is Caesar about to give the booty promised to the soldiers in Sicily or Italy?" The reference is to land grants promised to veterans. The land was seized from defeated enemies and political opponents. This is how Horace lost his family estate during the civil wars and more than likely the source of the land for the Sabine farm. It was a matter of great importance for all concerned to know where these seizures would be occurring. **Triquetra** = "Triangle Land," hence "Sicily."

57–8. There is a double irony in these lines. The primary level says "they wonder at my extraordinary silence when in fact I know nothing." The secondary level says to those in the know "see the extent to which my discretion extends."

59–76. The scene shifts to life on the Sabine farm.

59–60. Return to the main motif: "As the day passes, I long for my country retreat."

60–2. "When will I be able to lose myself in study of the ancients and lazy sleep?"

63–4. **Faba Pythagorae cognata**: Pythagoras is supposed to have forbidden the eating of meat and beans. Vegetarianism was due to the Pythagorean doctrine of the transmigration of souls. Horace here assumes that the stricture against beans is for the same reason. Hence beans would be the relatives of Pythagoras, according to Horace's joke. The ancient sources do not agree on whether the stricture against eating beans was truly Pythagorean or apocryphal.
Ponentur = "served."

64. The humble fare of greens cooked with bacon, typical of southern cuisine in the United States, is described in a golden line. The ironic distance between simplicity and aesthetic refinement should give the reader pause before taking this picture too literally.

65–7. "What wonderful dinners my friends (**mei**) and I (**ipse**) eat there with my talkative slaves": an idealized picture of rural contentment. **Libatis dapibus** = "after making a traditional offering from our feast." As Muecke notes, however, "the expression *libatis dapibus* is ambiguous and some commentators take as 'after we had tasted the feast'" (1997).

Vescor = "I feed on."

67–70. "Everyone drinks to his own taste." **Prout** = "just as."

Legibus insanis: at formal drinking parties the *magister bibendi* prescribed what would be drunk and at what strength. In the relaxed atmosphere of Horace's bucolic paradise, there are no such formalities.

Uvescit = "to become wet," hence "to drink."

70–6. "The dinner conversation is not idle gossip and envious chatter, but concerns the basic questions of life." **Sermo** also = the title Horace gives to his satires in 1.4. His work is ideally a refined version of the free and elegant conversation of men addressing the fundamental issues of life in a charming, civilized fashion [60–1].

Agitamus = "discuss."

Trahat = "leads."

Summumque quid eius = "what is its highest form": the question of the *summum bonum* was a common one in ancient philosophy.

77–117. It is in the context of one such dinner that Cervius, Horace's country neighbor, tells the tale of the city mouse and the country mouse. This is a tale of two banquets told within the frame of an idealized country dinner.

We may well ask ourselves: if the rustic Cervius qualifies as the country mouse, does that make Horace the city mouse? The story and its application are not as simple as they first appear. "As the fable develops, it becomes clear that [. . .] leisure and exertion have been switched. For the city mouse can hardly be said to wear himself out, and his friend in the country certainly does not pass his time 'in sleep and idle hours'. It might therefore be argued that this tale of mice and men is less firmly integrated into the structure of the poem than is sometimes assumed" (Rudd 1982: 252).

77–8. **Inter** = postpositive. **Garrit**: see 1.9.40–3.

Anilis . . . fabellas = "old wives' tales."

78–9. Morris (1968) cites Greenough's apposite note, "after all human nature was too much for them, and they did talk 'de villis domibusve alienis.'" **Sollicitas ignarus** = "ignorant of the trouble they bring."

79–83. **Olim** = "once upon a time." **Asper et attentus quaesitis** = concessive: "though frugal and watchful over that which he had attained."

Solveret indicates an opening of the **artum . . . animum**.

83–9. The country mouse's generosity is in vain. **Sepositi** < *sepono, –ponere, –posui, –positum*: "to set aside."

Ciceris < *cicer, –eris*: "chickpea."

Invidit = "begrudge."
Avenae < *avena, –ae*: "oat."
Acinum = "grape."
Semesa < *semesus, –a, –um*: "half-eaten."
Tangentis male singula = "barely touching a thing."
Palea = "chaff."
Horna < *hornus, –a, –um*: "this year's."
Esset < *edo, esse, edi, esum*: "to eat."
Ador = "spelt."
Lolium = "a wild grass."

90–7. "Finally, the city mouse said, why do you cleave to rustic poverty? Come to the city and see how the other half lives." **Praerupti nemoris . . . dorso**: "on the crag of a steep wood."
Carpe viam = "take to the road."
Quando = "since."
Mortalis animas = direct object of **sortita**. The city mouse assumes the pose of Epicurean philosopher.
Quo . . . circa = tmesis for *quocirca*: "wherefore."
Bone: note the patronizing tone.

97–100. They head for the city. **Agrestem** < *agrestis, –is*: "countryman, rustic."
Pepulere < *pello, pellere, pepuli, pulsum*: "strike."
Aventes < *aveo, –ere*: "to long for, desire."
Subrepere = "to crawl up from below."

100–5. They arrive at a rich palace. **Rubro . . . cocco** = "scarlet dye."
Fercula = "platters."
Exstructis < *exstruo, –struere, –struxi, –structum*: "to pile up."
Hesterna = "the evening before's."
Canistris < *canistra, –orum*: "baskets."

106–9. Having settled his rustic friend on a purple coverlet, the city mouse scurries to serve him in style. **Succinctus** = one whose clothes are tucked up in the girdle for work like a slave.
Verniliter = like a *verna* or "house-born slave."
Praelambens = "first licking," and hence "tasting."

110–12. At first, the country mouse greatly enjoys his changed fortune. **Agit laetum convivam** = "he plays the happy dinner guest."
Valvarum < *valvae, –arum*: "folding doors."

113–15. **Currere** and **trepidare** = historical infinitives.

Conclave, *–is* = "room, hall."
Molossis . . . canibus: Molossian hounds were kept as watch-dogs.

115–17. The country mouse bids his urban confrere farewell. The safety of his humble hearth and fare suit him fine. **Ervo** < *ervum*, *–i*: "bitter vetch."

2.8

Poem 2.8 presents the dinner party as a metaphor for social decorum [66]. The gastronomic has been a theme throughout Book 2. In 2.6, much is made of the conflicting culinary philosophies of the city mouse and the country mouse. Likewise, the story of 2.6 is told in the context of a simple country meal of boiled greens, the same meal Lucilius is described as sharing with Scipio and Laelius at 2.1.74. Poem 2.2 features a disquisition on the virtues of modest country cuisine by Ofellus, who is often read as model for the country mouse in 2.6, while 2.4 features a long discourse by a gourmand, which has been read as a model for both the city mouse and Nasidienus in 2.8 (Berg 1996; Caston 1997).

2.8, moreover, is a poem about a failed dinner party. It is the story of an opportunity for conviviality (*convivium*, literally "living together") that is missed. The results are comic and Nasidienus is clearly the butt of the joke. The end result is that he is excluded from Maecenas's circle. He lacks the requisite *urbanitas*, the easy-going elegance and charm that marked the cultural élite. His culinary extravagances—pregnant lamprey (*murena*) and boar (*aper*) captured only in the south wind—strive to impress but only revolt (Braund 1992: 24–5).

Yet, Horace is rarely straightforward. Two mitigating circumstances need to be kept in mind when reading this satire. First, Horace is not present at the dinner and thus keeps his distance from the behavior of all parties. He does not necessarily endorse the behavior of Vibidius, Balatro, or even Maecenas. Second, the entire story is retold by the comic poet, Fundanius (1.10.40–2), and hence the slapstick and overdrawn narrative reflect his preferred genre as much as they do external reality.

A number of Lucilian precedents have been alleged for this satire, and certainly culinary concerns played a substantial role in his satires (see, for example, 30.3.1051–2). Yet for the most part these passages deal with poor food, lousy furniture, and regrettable female companionship. There is no precise parallel to the *Cena Nasidieni*'s combination of pretentious refinement and vulgarity. Ennius likewise featured at least one comic banquet in his *saturae* (frgs. 7 and 15), but here the emphasis is on the greedy parasite not the overbearing host (Coffey 1976: 51; Rudd 1982: 214). Poem 2.8 thus draws on a number of precedents from Book 2 and satire as a whole, but ultimately presents an original creation.

1–5. Horace meets the comic poet Fundanius and asks him to give an account of a recent dinner chez Nasidienus. Nasidienus has not been identified and is generally thought to represent a type rather than a specific individual.

1–3. Beati = "rich," but also "happy." The first is true, but the second is not.

Mihi quaerenti convivam: Horace was himself inviting Fundanius to a dinner that would presumably have more resembled the humble fare in **2.6** than the ostentation described below.

De medio . . . die: normal Roman dinner parties began in the ninth hour, around three o'clock. This was to be more elaborate and by implication excessive.

Potare: nor was it a sober affair in any sense of the word.

3–4. Fundanius's sarcasm sets the tone from the beginning.

5. Esca = "delicacies, *mignardises*."

6–17. Fundanius describes the first courses. **Pater cenae**: an ironic honorific.

Rapula = "baby turnips."

Lactucae = "lettuces."

Radices = "radishes."

Pervellunt = "goad, stimulate."

Siser = a plant with a pungent edible root, generally identified with the skirret, but some argue for the parsnip.

Allec = "fish-pickle," actually the brine in which salted fish had been kept.

Faecula Coa = "dried lees of Coan wine."

10–15. Ubi introduces **pertersit** and **sublegit**. **Pertersit** < *pertergeo, –ere, –tersi, –tersum*: "wipe."

Cinctus alte see **succinctus 2.6.107.**

Gausape < *gausape, –is*: a long napped woolen cloth, a towel. This clause is a virtual quotation of Lucilius 570.

Ut Attica virgo / cum sacris Cereris: a slave who brings in the wine with ridiculous solemnity is compared to a maiden in an Athenian religious procession. The Eleusinian mysteries for Demeter (Roman **Ceres**) featured a *kanephoros* who carried sacred symbols (**sacris**) in a basket balanced on her head.

Hydaspes = a slave from India. His name indicates his origin from the region near the river of the same name. Having such an exotic slave would be a mark of luxury.

Caecuba = one of the most valued Italian wines.

Alcon: a slave with a Greek name brings in the Greek wine.

Maris expers: Chian wine was often mixed with a bit of seawater. Nasidienus's vintage needs no such adulteration.

16–17. Nasidienus tries to impress his guests by offering two other vintages in addition to those served with such pomp. It is only here that we find out that Maecenas was present [64]. He remains carefully distanced from the ensuing buffoonery. **Albanum . . . Falernum**: two fine Italian wines.

Appositis = ablative of comparison. Understand *vinis*.

18–41. Now that Maecenas's presence has been revealed, Horace inquires into the identity of the other guests. Fundanius complies and describes the seating arrangements.

18–19. Divitias miseras: a wonderfully ambiguous phrase. Does it refer to Nasidienus, whose riches bring him no real pleasure and contentment, hence he is *miser*, or to the guests, in whom the excessive nature of the display inspires disgust not wonder?

Quis = *quibus*.

Pulchre fuerit tibi = "you enjoyed yourself?"

20–4. The guests at a Roman dinner party reclined on couches (*lecti*) that surrounded the table on three sides. The fourth side was left open for serving. See 1.4.86–9. The diagram illustrates the arrangement of the guests.

medius lectus

Maecenas	Vibidius	Servilius Balatro

imus lectus

Nomentanus
Nasidienus Rufus
Porcius

summus lectus

Varius
Viscus
Fundanius

The position at the left end of each couch, facing the table, was called the **summus**. **Infra** and **super** refer to this designation. The most distinguished guests were placed on the *medius lectus*. **Maecenas** occupies the place of honor, known as the *locus consularis*. It would normally be immediately next to the position of the host on the *imus lectus*, but **Nasidienus** has put **Nomentanus** next to Maecenas so that he can instruct him concerning the food. This is a faux pas and reveals the host's lack of tact. The *summus lectus* is occupied by men of letters from Maecenas's circle.

Viscus Thurinus: one of the brothers mentioned at 1.10.83.

Varius: see 1.5.40 and 1.10.44.

Cum Servilio Balatrone Vibidius: these were Maecenas's **umbrae** (additional guests brought by those who were actually invited). From their names and behaviors, we gather that these were Maecenas's *scurrae* or lower-class wits expected to entertain the guests (1.4.86–9). **Balatro** means "jester" (1.2.2) and is a fictional name that complements the implications of **Servilius**. **Vibidius** is unknown.

Nomentanus is sometimes distinguished from the spendthrift mentioned at 2.1.22, but there seems no compelling reason to do so. He, like **Porcius**, is a *scurra* of Nasidienus. Porcius ("Piggy") is another speaking name.

Ipsum = colloquial for *dominum*.

Totas simul = "all at once."

Placentas < *placenta, –ae*: "cake."

25–6. **Lateret** < *lateo, –ere*: "to lie hidden, to escape the notice."

26–30. The uninitiated (**cetera turba**) required Nomentanus's instruction because of the unusual nature (**longe dissimilem noto celantia sucum**) of the dishes. This passage is difficult and its exact translation is disputed, although the general sense is clear.

Conchylia = "shell-fish."

Ut vel continuo patuit cum = "as for example became evident at once when."

Passeris < *passer, –eris*: a flat fish like a flounder.

Ilia is used only here of fish. Some translate "loins" (Muecke 1997), others "roe" (Morris 1968). Inasmuch as the usage is unusual, we can presume so is the dish (it has not been tasted "**ingustata**"). I follow Rolfe (1962) and translate "entrails."

Rhombi < *rhombus, –i*: "turbot."

31–3. Nomentanus passes on more esoteric knowledge. **Melimela** = "honey apples," a quick-ripening variety with a sweet taste. Apples would not have normally been served until dessert. Nomentanus is just showing off the extent of his epicurean training, as the second clause makes clear.

Minorem = "waning."

32. Hoc refers to the entirety of the previous clause.

Ipso = Nomentano.

33–5. "We'll die unavenged unless we drink heavily!" The language is a parody of epic.

35–8. Nasidienus turns pale, fearing either bad behavior or palates dulled from drink. **Parochi** = "our caterer," compare **1.5.46.** The term is contemptuous.

39–41. Allifanis < *Allifana, –orum*: large drink vessels in the style of those from the town of Allifae.

Vinaria = "jugs."

Lagoenis < *lagoena, –ae*: "a large earthenware jar with a narrow neck and handles."

42–53. The climax of the dinner is the serving of a pregnant (**gravida**) lamprey eel. *Murenae* were widely believed in the ancient world to mate with vipers (Athenaeus 7.312e; Pliny the Elder *Historia Naturalis* 9.23; Cruquius 1597; Lejay 1966). Thus Nasidienus's *pièce de résistance* was not simply grotesque but, to a Roman audience, potentially dangerous. It is served in *trompe l'oeil* fashion swimming in pepper sauce surrounded by shrimp (**squillas**). **Erus** = Nasidienus.

Carne = ablative of specification.

45–50. The recipe for the sauce (**ius**). **Prima Venafri pressit cella** = an elaborate periphrasis for "Virgin olive oil from Venafrum." Venafrum was famed for the quality of its olives.

Garo < *garum, –i*: Romans loved this sauce made from liquid strained from boiled fish entrails, salted then fermented. Numerous recipes have been found. Pliny (*Historia Naturalis* 31.93–4) confirms the best comes from Spanish mackerel.

Citra mare nato = another elaborate periphrasis for "domestic."

Dum coquitur: the wine is added during the actual cooking. Chian is added to a sauce that is already cooked (**cocto**).

Aceto < *acetum, –i*: "vinegar."

Methymnaeam . . . uvam = "the Methymnaean grape cluster," i.e. Lesbian wine, considered among the finest.

Vitio mutaverit = another elaborate periphrasis, this time for "fermented."

51–3. Nasidienus details his own specific culinary innovation. **Erucas** = "arugula," a variety of pungent salad greens.

Inulas = "elecampane," a hardy perennial.

Incoquere = "to cook into [the sauce]."

Curtillus = another gastronome who showed how to cook unwashed sea urchins (**illutos . . . echinos**) in the sauce. Nasidienus cites a fellow researcher in the culinary arts to demonstrate his scholarly *bona fides*.

Muria = "brine," that is to say the commercial product, not that naturally emitted by the sea urchins' unwashed shells.

Testa = "the shell" of the sea urchin.

54–6. Disaster strikes! The fall of the tapestries (**aulaea**) is a turning point in the satire introduced with epic language and mock grandeur. It destroys the platter (**patinam**) on which the lamprey was served. Note the epic simile introduced by **quantum non**.

57–9. While the guests in Maecenas's circle react sensibly when it becomes clear that the danger has passed, Nasidienus weeps as if he has lost a son. **Flere** = historical infinitive, giving the passage a mock epic coloring.

59–63. Nomentanus, in an effort to comfort Nasidienus, launches into a threnody bemoaning Fortune's blows. **Sapiens** = ironic.

Illudere = "to make sport of."

63. **Mappa** = a napkin.

64–74. **Balatro** joins the fun and offers an ironic speech of encouragement that the boorish Nasidienus accepts at face value. It begins with a series of quasiphilosophic observations on the human condition and then applies them to the details of a dinner party, thereby revealing the essential triviality of the matter at hand. **Suspendens omnia naso** = "mocking all things." Compare 1.6.5. There is also a pun on Nasidienus's name.

Eoque = "and on that account."

67–70. **Tene . . . torquerier** = an exclamatory question. Translate "to think that you are tortured" (Gildersleeve and Lodge 1895: §534). **Torquerier** = archaic deponent infinitive.

Laute = "finely, elegantly."

Male conditum = "badly prepared."

Praecincti: see **line 10** and **2.6.107.**

72. **Agaso** = "stable boy."

73–4. "Adverse circumstances allow a general to prove his mettle!"

75–6. The ever-obtuse Nasidienus detects not a bit of sarcasm.

77–8. The general consults with his staff. **Divisos** = "first on one side then the other." Note the prominent "s" sounds that imitate the sound of the whispering.

79–80. The return of Horace marks the end of the middle section of the dialogue and the start of the conclusion.

80–5. Nasidienus rallies his troops and returns for a final onslaught. **Ridetur** = impersonal.

"**Fictis rerum** is a Graecism for *fictis rebus*. The guests laugh at the avarice and folly of Nasidienus but pretend to have their mirth excited by other causes" (Anthon 1886).

Nasidiene, redis: the use of apostrophe, or direct address of a character or abstraction, is reminiscent of epic style.

85–93. He is followed by a new set of culinary extravagances. **Mazonomo** < *mazonomus, –i*: "a large dish."

Gruis < *grus, –uis*: "crane."

Pastum iecur = *foie gras*.

Avulsos < *avello, –ere, –vulsi, –vulsum*: "tear away, separate."

Edit = archaic present subjunctive.

Merulas < *merula, –ae*: "blackbird."

Palumbes < *palumbes, –is*: "ring dove."

Suavis res, si non causas narraret earum et / naturas dominus: this line sums up the whole problem with Nasidienus, it is less the food per se, although it is certainly extravagant by the standards of **2.6**, than his and Nomentanus's insistent discourse about it.

93–5. The guests are revenged (**ulti**) by fleeing before tasting a bite. **Canidia** is often mentioned as a poisoner. See *Satires* 1.8 and *Epodes* 5 and 17.

PERSIUS

Prologus

This is Persius's classic statement of satire's low vocation in anti-Callimachean terms [39]. On the one hand, the poem makes a great show of rejecting traditional literary tropes. On the other, there is hardly an element in it that cannot be derived directly from the earlier tradition. This is not incompetence but programmatic paradox. Persius deploys the whole tradition of Greco-Roman poetry in general, and satire in particular, to push, strain, and twist its devices to reveal the world of the unexpressed or even the inexpressible, beyond the banalities of contemporary Roman poetry [68]. This is part and parcel of his program of deliberate Stoic estrangement [69–70]. The choliambic meter recalls both the iambic tradition to which satire owes a direct debt [36–8, 49, 70] and Ennius and Lucilius's use of iambic meters at the genre's birth [42, 45].

The poem falls neatly into two parts. **Lines 1–7** present Persius's rejection of traditional stories of poetic inspiration and initiation. They are spoken in the first person. **Lines 8–14** are written in the third person and indict the shallow, materialistic motivations of Persius's contemporaries.

1–7. On the dream of poetic initiation in Hesiod, Callimachus, Ennius, and its parody in Horace, see **1.10.31–5.**

Fonte . . . caballino = a literal translation of the Greek Hippocrene (ἵππου κρήνη), the spring of inspiration on Mount Parnassus, home of the Muses, opened by the foot of Pegasus. *Caballus* is a low word for horse, see Horace 1.6.59, 103.

Bicipiti = "twin-peaked."

Memini: the emphasis on personal memory is comic, as if the poet could have forgotten such an experience. He lampoons here a convention that by this point had become a dreary device in the poet's repertoire.

Repente = "suddenly." Poetry is the product of a facile declaration of inspiration, not hard work and revision.

Heliconidasque = "the daughters of Helicon," a mountain in Boeotia sacred to Apollo and the Muses.

Pirenen = Pirene, the name of a spring near Corinth where Bellerophon caught Pegasus. As several commentators note, students and poets are often referred to in the ancient sources as *pallidus*. **Pallidamque Pirenen**: would thus represent a transfer of epithet from effect to cause.

Lambunt: a vivid metaphor for the snaking of the ivy tendrils (**hederae**) around the busts (**imagines**). Its grotesque quality is designed to inspire revulsion. It anticipates Persius's use of images of oral gratification (both sexual and gustatory) later in the corpus. Ivy was a traditional symbol of Bacchus and of Dionysian inspiration. Poetic busts in libraries were frequently garlanded with ivy (Lee and Barr 1987).

Semipaganus = "half a bumpkin," the learned compound ironically undercuts the claim. Persius's satire is his own (**ipse, nostrum**), not the product of specious inspiration and slavish adherence to convention, nor, as the second half of the poem makes clear, of material reward. See Freudenburg (2001: 146).

Vatum < *vatis, –is*: the traditional Roman term for an inspired bard, as opposed to the Greek derived *poeta*. The word was a favorite of Horace's and the Augustan poets in general.

8–14. "Anyone who has ever tried to teach a parrot or a magpie to speak knows that the secret is to appeal to the belly. Poets are no different." **Expedivit** < *expedio, –ire, –ivi, –tum*: the exact force of the verb here and of its distinction from **docuit** in the next line is unclear. It is probably best to follow Bo (1967) and translate "brings it about easily," from the notion of removing an obstacle. Gildersleeve (1903) has a nice discussion of the notion of the Greek parrot (**psittaco** < *psittacus*) as being a better mimic than the native Italian magpie (**picamque**). This tallies well with Juvenal's depiction of hungry Greeks in Rome as able to transform themselves into whatever is needed (**3.73–80**) and presumably represents a standard stereotype.

'Chaere': Greek for "*vale.*"

Artifex sequi = *artifex sequendi*.

Dolosi < *dolosus, –a, –um*: "crafty, deceitful, alluring."

Corvos: crows are, of course, not noted for the beauty of their song.

Poetridas < *poetris, –idos*: "poetess," a rare word and rare bird in Latin.

Pegaseium nectar = the sweet song of the Hippocrene. The absurdity of the mixed metaphor (a horse producing nectar?), however, quickly undercuts the elevation of the image.

1

Satire 1 is Persius's programmatic poem outlining satire's role in a corrupt society. Persius engages in a dialogue with an imaginary interlocutor that recalls Horace's with Trebatius in **2.1** [**27–8**]. He begins by decrying the state of things in Rome and the interlocutor immediately tries to exercise some restraint on the satire's savage attack. He asks "**quis leget haec?**" ("Who will read these?") (**line** 2). The question is two edged. On the one hand, it asks: given the current state of literary taste, who would want to read something like this? On the other, it implies that the satirist should exercise caution. You never know who might read these, and such scathing criticism could be dangerous.

Like Horace, Persius says he can't help himself, but, unlike Horace, he does not have powerful friends upon whom he can rely. Rather he will dig a hole into which he can whisper his broadsides (**line 119**), though even that is not safe. Like Horace, Persius too will claim the precedent of Lucilius (**lines** 114–15), but unlike Horace, Persius's attacks truly are savage. He mixes sexual, gastronomic, and grotesque bodily imagery in an unsettling melange that is designed to undermine the reader's smug satisfaction.

This poem is an exercise in Stoic self-observation and self-criticism as much as an attack on external vice [31, 67–9]. Every reader is forced to turn inward and ask whether they too wear asses' ears, can they discern hard from soft, true from false, virtue from vice, real poetry from meretricious verse. Thus, as John Henderson observes,

> The poems of Persius reproduce in the mimetic form an absolutism in despite of civic power-relations as seen from the perspective of the Roman élite: their turn away from "Politics" toward policing the individual acts a scene of mastery, the fantasy ideology of an absolute control of Self as the boundary and teleology of human freedom.
>
> (1993: 27)

1. The satirist clears his throat and begins. The scholiast claims the first line is a quotation from Lucilius. There is no confirmation and several commentators have noted parallels to Lucretius 2.14 and other passages from *De Rerum Natura*. Many, therefore, suspect a conflation between two similar names on the part of the scholiast. The parallels with the Lucretian subtext are indisputable. If Lucilius lurks behind the great Epicurean poet as well, in the very first line we would have a fusion of this collection's twin concerns, satire and philosophy. Although, as Kissel (1990) remarks, it seems odd that a committed Stoic would begin with a line from an Epicurean poet. At minimum, Persius's opening *cri de coeur* comes trailing clouds of intellectual glory. There are parallel texts that can be cited for almost every line of this poem. It is beyond the scope of this commentary to examine all of them. The best discussions are Hooley (1997) and Bramble (1974).

2–3. The interlocutor immediately breaks in. A short dialogue ensues. **Min** = *mihi* + *ne*.

Hercule = "By Hercules," a common interjection.

Nemo: compare Horace 1.4.22–3.

3–5. "I don't care if they prefer the worst doggerel to my verse. It's trivial." **Polydamas** = a character in the *Iliad* who on several occasions gives Hector advice that he ignores at his peril. In one of the climactic scenes of the poem (22.99–101), Hector decides he must fight Achilles because he cannot face the chiding he would receive from **Polydamas** who had advised that all retreat within the safety of the city walls (18.254).

Troiades: "the daughters of Troy." The shift to the feminine after the heroic reference is deflating. In addition to speaking of Rome's, and satire's in particular, misogynistic tendencies (see **Juvenal 6**), the term lampoons the pretensions of the Roman patriciate to Trojan ancestry.

Labeonem: identified by the scholiast as Attius Labeo, the author of a very poor translation of the *Iliad*.

Nugae = a common self-deprecatory word for neoteric verse. See Horace 1.9.2. Does Persius refer to public opinion or his own poetry?

5–7. "Rome counts this as lightweight, you do not need to correct the scale."

Non stands for *ne* and is taken with **accedas**.

Elevet < *elevo, –are*: either "to elevate," as in Labeo, or metaphorically "to make light of," as in Persius. The introduction of the metaphor of the scale (**trutina**) in the next clause makes the latter the dominant sense, in spite of the scholiast's gloss to the contrary. Nonetheless, the real sense is that we should be above whatever the crowd praises or blames and so both senses are operative.

Examen = "the tongue of the scale."

Nec te quaesiveris extra: Stoic self-reliance is the rule. **Te** may be either the direct object of the verb, the object of the postpositive **extra**, or both.

8–11. "For who at Rome does not . . .? If it can be said." We have to wait till **line 121** for the question to be completed, but we are given a strong hint at **line 59.** The exact sense of the next lines is debated. They are exceedingly dense. On one level, Persius says "why can't I say what I mean to say (**sed fas tum**), since (**cum**) we're all adults (**ad canitiem**) and should know better?" On another, the burden of the satire is that Rome is filled with anything but serious old gray-beards of proverbial wisdom and *gravitas*, and that all those adopting such a stance (witness **Polydamas, line** 4 or the **Titos** of **line 20**), are in fact morally and aesthetically bankrupt. "Our old age is not that of a wise uncle, but of a worn-out reprobate" (Bramble 1974: 71). Most of the complications in these lines unfold in the tension between these poles.

Ad canitiem et nostrum istud vivere triste / aspexi = "I have seen that we live with white hair and that this life of ours is harsh." The question is why has our hair turned white and for what reason is our life "harsh." As subsequent lines make clear, it is not because of primeval poverty or the self-imposed discipline of a wise maturity. *Canities* can refer to premature old age, as all the commentators remind us. But as Bo notes (1967), we should not dismiss the scholiast's suggestion that Persius believes it is **fas** to say that all Rome has asses' ears (**line 121**) because he has looked to (**aspexi**) the sober seriousness of the old poets, in relation to whom the present age represents such a marked decline (and hence premature *canities*).

Nucibus . . . relictis: in the traditional obscene Fescinnine verses that accompany the Roman marriage ceremony, the bridegroom is called upon to leave behind the childish delights of his slave-boy, sexual playmate and the boy is commanded to "give nuts." This is a sign of putting aside childish things and assuming manhood proper. See Catullus 61.124–9.

Sapimus patruos: this clause has two related senses. *Patrui*, paternal uncles, were figures of proverbial austerity and moral rectitude. **Sapimus patruos** here means first: "we taste or smell of austere old uncles." This meaning derives from the basic sense of *sapio* + the accusative, to "taste of something." The second meaning is a metaphorical intransitive use, derived from the transitive use just discussed. Here **patruos** must be taken as an accusative of respect: "we are wise like our austere old uncles." The etymological relation between *sapio* and *sapientia* becomes paramount here.

11–12. "Forgive, what else can I do but laugh?" i.e., in the face of such absurdity, I must write satire. **Nolo** = "I can't help myself."

Quid faciam: compare Horace 2.1.24.

Splene: Pliny tells us the spleen is the seat of laughter.

Cachinno = "to guffaw, to cackle."

13–43. This section portrays the perversion of literary taste in Rome.

13–14. Grandiloquence is the rule in verse (**numeros**) and prose (**pede liber**).

Inclusi: "shut away in our studies."

Pulmo . . . praelargus = "a preternaturally large lung." The grotesque transformation of the breath of poetic recitation into a giant lung reduces the literary product to little more than phlegm that needs to be expelled in the guise of art to be savored.

Anhelet < *anhelo, –are*: "to puff, pant, roar."

15–25. We go directly to a scene of poetic recitation envisioned as a species of sexual penetration. The penetrating party here is ironically a degraded and effeminized poetry that lacks the rough solidity that Persius and Roman ideology prizes. This kind of poetry is traditionally embodied within the Roman universe of genres by the soft verse of elegy, which stands in opposition to masculine satire. The penetrated party is Rome's cultural élite attending a recitation.

The shifting images that characterize this scene offer a tour of the Roman satirical grotesque in all its sexual and alimentary dimensions. There is the dandified poet whose pallor (**albus**) is a sign of excessive sexual passion (Bramble 1974: 72–5). The emphasis on the throat (**guttur**), its moisture, and rippling quality (**liquido cum plasmate . . . mobile**), puts the reader in mind of the reciter's affected speech and prepares the audience for the combined images of perversion and *gourmandise* (**escas**) yet to come. The throat is not only the site of poetic articulation and potential gluttony but also of the passive sexuality implicit in the poet's demeanor. This reading is strengthened by the description of the poet as both effeminate (**fractus**) and possessed of an "orgasmic" eye (**patranti . . . ocello**), whose quivering adds yet another level of fluidity that threatens to undermine the dry, solid virtues of the masculinist, Roman norm (Bramble 1974: 76–7; Lee and Barr 1987; see **Horace 1.5.84**). The poetry itself becomes the instrument by which the audience's loins are probed (**carmina lumbum / intrant**), unmanning even the most burly of old-time Romans (**ingentis . . . Titos**), as they are metonymically penetrated by the poet's throat (i.e., his quavering organ of poetic articulation). This creates a bizarre image of oral/genital, or oral/anal, contact in which both parties are passive—since the action moves from one open orifice to the other—an impossible sexual monstrosity in Roman ideology (Bramble 1974: 78–9; Lee and Barr 1987; Parker 1997). This last image is metamorphosed into an evocation of poetry as a kind of food for the ears in which the image of penetration is transformed into one of passive consumption, but with the emphasis once again on the use of an inappropriate orifice. On **line 22**'s **auriculis** as pun on *auri-culis*, see Bramble (1974: 95).

The final image of fermentation and sterility that we see in the wild fig (**caprificus**), which by definition bears no fruit, bursting forth from the frustrated poet's guts (**rupto iecore exierit**), sums up the sterile perversity of the poetic exercise. At the same time, the phallic thrust of the fig tree from the poet's liver (*iecur*), the seat of passion, implies a destructive and empty eroticism. "The connotations of the *caprificus* must be derived from the *membrum virile*" (Bramble 1974: 90–3; although Adams 1982: 113–24 notes that the *ficus* itself generally represents the site of anal penetration).

16–18. **Natalicia . . . sardonyche** = a birthday ring of sardonyx.

Plasmate < *plasma*, *–tis*: the term is debated. Some see it as a gargle, but Quintilian makes clear it is a warbling to warm up the voice that he considers effeminate (1.8.2).

Fractus = "broken," and hence "powerless" or "impotent." Quintilian, in a passage on corrupting music, uses **fractus** as a gloss on the adjective *effeminatus* (1.10.31). See Bramble (1974: 76–7).

19–21. **Scalpuntur** < *scalpo*, *scalpere*, *scalpsi*, *scalptum*: "to scrape, scratch, tickle."

22–3. **Tun** = *tu* + *ne*. **Vetule** = diminutive of *vetus*: "my little old man" or "old boy." Diminutives are often effeminizing. The allusion to age recalls *ad canitiem* in **line 9**.

Quibus: the antecedent = **escas**.

Articulis . . . et . . . cute perditus: "gone with the gout and dropsy," as a result of over-indulgence in food and drink. Bramble (1974: 146–8) offers an alternative reading of **cute perditus**, meaning "with ruined prepuce" as a result of presumed sexual excess. The possibility of both readings should be maintained since the use of the word **escas** has already introduced a conflation between the sexual and the gustatory in describing the reciter's effeminizing excesses.

Dicas . . . "ohe": "you would say, 'enough!'" The reprobate can dish it out but he can't take it anymore, worn out as he is with vice.

24–5. These lines may be attributed either to the reciter or to Persius's initial interlocutor who reappears at **line 28.** These are not clearly delineated voices and on one level of reading, this poem is an internal dialogue. Indeed, Persius in **line** 44 admits the interlocutor to be a generic fiction.

Didicisse < *disco, discere, didici*: "to learn."

Caprificus: the wild fig was proverbial for its power to sprout in rocks, cliffs, and cracks of buildings.

26–43. This section deals in a less concentrated way with the uses and abuses of poetic fame in contemporary Rome.

26–7. **Pallor** = another common sign of sexual excess, but also of poetic study. On **senium**, see **canitiem (line 9)** and **vetule (line 22)**.

Scire tuum = nominative use of the infinitive with **est**, versus **te scire hoc** where the infinitive is the object of **sciat** in indirect discourse.

28–30. **Dicier** = archaic form of *diceri*.

Ten = *te* + *ne*.

Cirratorum < *cirratum, –i*: "the curly-haired," i.e., schoolboys. This clause is a direct echo of Horace 1.10.74–5.

Pendes: the metaphor of weighing recalls **lines 6–7.**

30–1. **Ecce inter pocula . . .**: "What a fine state we've reached! The well-stuffed (**saturi**) sons of Romulus discuss divine poems when they're in their cups." The pun on *satura* should not be missed.

Dia poemata = the subject of **narrent**.

32–5: Here every lisper is crowned a poet. **Hic aliquis** = subject of **eliquat** < *eliquo, –are*: "to flow smoothly."

Hyacinthina laena = "a hyacinth-colored cloak"; the obvious affectation should be noted.

Balba de nare: "with a nasal lisp." Contrast Lucilius's **emunctae naris** at Horace 1.4.8. See also **lines 40–1** and **118.** Lisping in Ovid and Martial is associated with effeminacy.

Phyllidas: Phyllis, fearing that Demophon had deserted her, hanged herself and was changed into an almond tree. **Hypsipylas**: Jason abandoned Hypsipyle of Lemnos after she bore him two children. Both myths represent common sentimental topics in elegy and Hellenistic poetry. The nouns are generic plurals: "Phyllises" and "Hypsipyles."

Tenero subplantat verba palato: a deliberate swallowing of the articulation to affect a smoother style of reading.

36–40. The vanity of insubstantial poetic fame is brought home by this sarcastic Stoic *memento mori*. **Adsensere** = perfect.

Cippus = "gravestone."

Manibus < *manes, –ium*: "shades, remains."

Violae = "violets," as in our phrase "pushing up daisies."

40–3. The interlocutor returns. "Laugh if you like, but you seek poetic immortality as well." **Uncis naribus**: compare Horace 1.6.1–6 on Maecenas, **non . . . naso suspendis adunco ignotos**. See also **lines 33** and **118.**

Os meruisse populi = "to have earned the people's praise."

Cedro digna . . . carmina: the image of poems worthy of being preserved in cedar oil comes from Horace's *Ars Poetica* 330–2. As Hooley observes (1997: 44), Persius's putting this quotation into the interlocutor's mouth denotes a state of corruption of taste wherein Horace's classicism is no longer a sufficient antidote to the prevailing decadence. Something more astringent is needed. It is supplied in the next line **nec scombros metuentia carmina nec tus**: the image of poems becoming wrappers for mackerels (**scombros**) is from Catullus 95. The conflation of Horatian *sermo merus* with rough Catullan wit forms a nice synecdoche for Persius's stylistic program. **Tus** = "incense"

44–62. "I do not fear fame, but that's not why I write. I respect sound judgment not cheap applause."

44–7. **Quem ex adverso dicere feci**: a wonderful send-up of the fiction of the interlocutor.

Fibra = "heart."

48–51. **Recti** = substantive.

'**Euge**' = Greek for "well done." '**Belle**' = its Latin synonym. These were common ejaculations during poetic readings.

Excute: "shake out," like a cloth.

Ilias Atti: see **lines 4–5.**

Veratro < *veratrum, –i*: "white hellebore," a purgative, sometimes taken as a cure for madness. Here, the pairing with **ebria** emphasizes the drug's primary effect: the production of vomit and stool.

51–4. "Don't dyspeptic nobles (**crudi . . . proceres**) dictate little elegies (**elegdia**) [as a cure]? Is anything not written on [luxurious] couches of citron wood (**lectis . . . citreis**)?" **Crudus** when used of food refers to that which is not digested and thus continues the imagery implicit in *veratrum*. Poetry is depicted as the pastime of the vulgar rich who are applauded by their poor clients who offer their praise in return for none-too-expensive handouts. Compare Horace, *Ars Poetica* 422–5 and the image of Lucilius dictating 200 lines before and after dinner at **Satires 1.10.60–1**.

Ponere = "to serve."

Sumen = "sow's udder," considered a delicacy.

Horridulum: the diminutive adds pathos to the image of the poor client shivering in anticipation of a worn-out cloak (**trita . . . lacerna**). The sadism of the *patronus* here is worthy of Juvenal. **Donare** = "to present" someone (accusative) with something (ablative).

Amo = "please," more frequently *amabo*.

56–7. The poor client may not be able to speak the truth, but Persius can. **Qui pote**: understand *est verum dicere*.

Nugaris < *nugor*, *–ari*: "to babble." See **line 5**.

Aqualiculus = "a water vessel," used metaphorically for the "belly."

Sesquipede = "a foot and a half."

58–62. Janus alone has no one mocking him from behind. Janus was the Roman god of passages and transitions; he was always portrayed as facing both forward and backward simultaneously. There is no verb in this sentence. Assume something like *es felix*.

Ciconia < *ciconia*, *–ae*: "stork," a derisive hand gesture in which the fingers and thumb are used to imitate the opening and closing of the bill.

Pinsit < *pinso*, *–ere*, *–i*, *pinsum* or *pistum*: "to pound," hence "mock," to be understood with all three gestures.

Auriculas . . . albas: "asses' ears," in anticipation of **line 121**, made by holding both hands next to the head and waving them. The scholiast informs us that they are white by synecdoche for their interiors.

Imitari mobilis = "quick to imitate."

Canis Apula: Apulia was proverbial for its heat and dryness.

Vos, o patricius sanguis . . .: a recollection and parody of Horace's call on his fellow Romans to reject shoddy poetic craftsmanship, *vos, o Pompilius sanguis . . .* (*Ars Poetica* 291–4). See Hooley (1997: 48–9).

Occipiti < *occiput*, *–itis*: "back of the head," *ob/caput*.

Sannae = "grimace," dative with **occurite**.

63–90. But has our poetry not achieved the very smoothness and polish which Horace himself demanded?

63–8. The interlocutor resumes. **Quis populi sermo est?** "What do the people say?"

Ut per leve severos / effundat iunctura unguis = "so that the joint passes lightly beneath the strictest thumbnail." See Horace 1.5.32, but more importantly *Ars Poetica* 292–4, *carmen reprehendite quod . . . praesectum decies non castigavit ad unguem* ["blame the poem which the well-cut nail has not corrected ten times"]. The image comes from a sculptor testing the joins between separate pieces of stone. Persius distances himself from the strict Horatian position by putting this formula in the mouth of the interlocutor. It also recalls another passage from the *Ars* in which Horace calls for renewing everyday speech (**populi sermo**?) through the use of the ***callida . . . iunctura*** ["the clever joining" or "juxtaposition"]. Persius sharpens this formula in 5.14, *verba togae sequeris* ***iunctura*** *callidus acri* ["you follow words of the toga, clever at the harsh juxtaposition"]. Thus, Persius proposes the necessity of renewing a Roman poetry that has become effeminately smooth with a deliberate program of harsh, masculine abrasion. This, however, is anything but a call for a return to pre-Horatian standards of self-conscious composition, rather it is a call for their Stoic radicalization.

Secus = "otherwise."

Ac = "than."

Rubricam derigat: another of Persius's homely metaphors, this one taken from carpentry. It refers to the use of a red chalk line (**rubricam**) to sight a straight line.

Opus: assume *est*.

In = "against." The poet can even be a moralist if need be. The irony of the interlocutor's trying to dissuade Persius from satire while extolling contemporary poetry's power to rail against vice should be savored.

Res grandes = is it the Muse that supplies rich subject matter or the times? The divorce between the two is the nub of the problem.

69–75. Satire's tendency toward xenophobia, a pronounced characteristic in Juvenal, becomes manifest here. Persius replies to the interlocutor that our poets do nothing but present heroes accustomed to babble in Greek (**heroas . . . nugari solitos Graece**), and neglect traditional Roman topics.

Heroas sensus: **heroas** here is used as an adjective modifying **sensus** ["sentiments"], most commentaries note. In fact, the figure is more complex. The element of personification remains very strong in the image of these "heroic sentiments" babbling in Greek. It might be better to see **sensus** as the adjective, hence, rather than fully drawn characters, our poets learn to bring forth (**adferre docemus**) mere ideas of heroes.

Ponere lucum: "to describe a sacred grove."

Ubi: understand *sint*.

Corbes < *corbis, –is*: "wicker basket used for the harvest."

Palilia: also known as the Parilia, a festival celebrated in honor of Pales, a primitive pastoral divinity, on April 21, the foundation day of Rome. It was a day of purification, on which farmers used a special powder (*suffimen*) prepared by the Vestals to ensure their family's and their livestock's continuing fertility. The holiday featured milk offerings to Pales and the ritual leaping over of burning piles of straw (**feno**) by drunken peasants.

Unde = "on what account." **Remus** appears in place of Romulus for metrical convenience.

Sulco < *sulcus, –i*: "furrow."

Dentalia < *dentalia, –ium*: "the beam over which the plough-share was fitted" (Lee and Barr 1987).

Quinti: vocative for L. Quinctius Cincinnatus, the legendary Roman general who was called from his plough to serve as dictator (**dictatorem**). His wife is pictured clothing him (**induit**) in the robe of office. The adverbial **ante boves** is a comic touch that shows even Persius cannot take these tales of homely Roman virtue too seriously.

Euge poeta!: after its earlier usage, this ejaculation cannot be read without irony. The traditional poet, for all his virtue, cannot avoid the slide into bathos. This prepares us for the next section's attack on archaicisms in poetry of the period.

76–82. In contrast, to those who pursued the over-refined diction of neo-Callimacheanism [39], there were the deliberate archaicists who sought to impose the literary standards of the second and third centuries BCE on those of the first century CE. They may be less offensive to Persius than the decadents, but they are no more successful. In the end, they too represent the triumph of style over substance, as opposed to Persius whose rigorous pursuit of style bodies forth a new substance of radical self-examination and critique.

76–8: The basic structure is: *est nunc quem {moretur} liber Brisaei Acci, sunt quos {moretur} Pacuvius et moretur Antiope?* **Quem** = *aliquem*. **Quos** = *aliquos*.

Brisaei . . . Acci = Lucius Accius, second century BCE tragedian, here called Brisaeus from a cult title of Dionysus. He wrote a *Bacchae*.

Venosus = "varicose-veined." Lee and Barr (1987) point out a pun on *vinosus* ["boozy"] after **Brisaei**.

Pacuvius = Marcus Pacuvius, second and third century BCE tragedian and satirist [9, 14], a nephew of Ennius and friend of Accius, his *Antiope* (**Antiopa**) was singled out for criticism by Lucilius. Antiope was the mother of Amphion and Zethus, enslaved and mistreated by Dirce. **Verrucosa** = "warty," referring both to Antiope's sad condition and Pacuvius's diction.

78. As Lee and Barr note (1987), the diction of this line is "a piece of archaicising grotesquerie." **Aerumnis** < *aerumna, –ae*: "labor." **Luctificabile** < *luctificabilis, –e*: "grief-causing." **Fulta** < *fulcio, –ire, fulsi, fultum*: "to prop up, support."

79–82. And since you see blear-eyed fathers (**patres . . . lippos**) pouring this mumbling nonsense into their sons, "where do you think this mess comes from?"

Monitus < *monitus, –us*: "warning, counsel," but particularly "signs and omens of the gods." The old men babble the kind of sententious nonsense found in Accius and Pacuvius to their sons, hence encouraging the archaic style.

Sartago = "frying pan." See Bramble (1974: 122), "Two basic motifs recur [in the satire], concrete form now embodying metaphoric analogy: the association of literature with food and effeminacy. Poetic diction is a hash cooked up in a frying pan."

Dedecus = *de* + *decus*, neuter noun.

Trossulus = an originally honorary term for the *equites*, stemming from their capture of an Etruscan town by the same name without the aid of the infantry. It later, however, came to signify aristocratic dandyism and effeminacy. Compare **Titos (line 20)** and **Romulidae (line 31)**.

Subsellia < *subsellium, –i*: "bench," as in the recitation hall. Although, given the focus on forensic pleading in the next section, the reference may be to the law courts as well.

Levis: as in modern slang, "a little light in the loafers."

83–91. "Is it not shameful to be so caught up in the pursuit of style that you are unable to defend a gray head from danger?" Forensic eloquence was one of the few realms of advancement for young men that had not been curtailed by the empire. On **cano**, see **canitiem, line 9.**

Decenter is relatively mild applause.

Quin . . . optes = "without your wishing": after a verb of hindering, **quin** is often translated "without." See Gildersleeve and Lodge (1895: §556).

Ait: subject = implied *aliquis*.

Pedius: This is a complicated figure embodying both a rare contemporary allusion and a borrowing from Horace. On the one hand, Tacitus mentions a Pedius Blaesus, condemned by Nero for temple robbery, who responded to the charges by writing a verse apologia. Bramble's argument that no reference could be intended since the condemnation happened only two years before Persius's death hardly seems cogent (1994: 125 n.2), especially given that the satires appeared in a posthumous collection. On the other hand, Horace at **1.10.28** mentions a Pedius Publicola as an orator of great power and pure Latinity. This can hardly be the person referred to in this passage, but that does not mean the intertextual resonance is not functional. Rather, it underlines the difference between the Pedii of today and those of yesteryear. Moreover, the Horatian influence on this first satire, as has already been noted, is vast. There are at least twenty-two allusions to the *Ars Poetica* alone (Hooley 1997: 30–1). Thus, the presence of such an intertextual reminiscence would be the rule.

Crimina rasis / librat in antithetis: **Pedius** spends less time responding to the charges (**crimina**) than in crafting them into finely balanced rhetorical antitheses. For a careful reading of Persius's prosody in these lines, see Anderson (1982: 187–8).

Doctas posuisse figuras / laudatur: worse yet, he's praised for this.

Bellum: compare **line 49.**

Romule: compare **Titos (line 20)**, **Romulidae (line 31)**, and **trossulus (line 82)**, all names for traditional Romans and their associated virtues, now effeminized.

Ceves < *ceveo*, *cevi*: "to shake the hips, to shimmy."

Cantet si naufragus: refers to the practice of shipwrecked sailors begging, often with pictures illustrating their plight (**fracta te in trabe pictum**). A song and dance in this context would obviously be inappropriate; in the same way **Pedius**'s elaborate rhetorical antitheses in the face of serious charges (**crimina**), are out of season.

Nocte paratum: **paratum** is neuter substantive from *paro* and the object of **plorabit**, "to wail over": "He who wishes to have bent (**incurvasse**) me with his plaint, will not wail over something gotten up the night before (**nocte paratum**)."

92–106. Contemporary poetry versus Vergil. The interlocutor returns. **Iunctura** here implies "harmonious joining," whereas **crudis** implies "the raw, undigested." Compare **lines 51** and **65.**

Cludere . . . versum: see **Horace 1.4.40.**

"Berecyntius Attis": a poem on Attis's dedication to the Great Mother Goddess, Cybele. With its tales of orgiastic rites and self-castration, this was a favorite neoteric and Hellenistic topic. See Catullus 63. Berecyntus is a mountain in Phrygia.

94–5. The two specimen lines that follow are technically perfect. There is no elision, no false quantities. They flow smoothly and fluently, with alliteration and internal rhyme. The same is true of **lines 99–102.** That of course is the problem. These lines are all liquid smoothness devoid of ethical content or of a salutary roughness that could rouse the reader's critical thought. We can presume the two lines are meant to be quotations from the "Attis." The spondaic ending of **line 95 (subduximus Appennino)** [43, 50] was common in Hellenistic poetry and the neoterics, but also in those striving for epic grandeur.

Dirimebat < *dirimo*, *–imere*, *–emi*, *–emptum*: "to split, separate."

Nerea: Greek accusative of Nereus, god of the sea, here used metonymically for the sea itself.

Delphin: nominative, masculine singular.

96. **"Arma virum"**: the opening words of the *Aeneid*. They would have served as the title. The Augustan masterpiece seems crude to the ear of the interlocu-

tor. That it might possess virtues besides lilting versification is beyond his ken. Note the two elisions in the line.

Spumosom = "swollen."

Cortice pingui . . . coctum = "dried with fat cork." **Coctum** < *coquo coquere coxi coctum*: "to cook, bake."

Ramale = diminutive of *ramus*.

Vegrandi < *vegrandis, –e*: "small."

Subere < *suber, –eris*: "cork tree."

98. Understand **est**. *Tener* is a common term of neoteric praise. **Laxa cervice** is a puzzling phrase, but probably meant to recall **guttur mobile (lines 17–18)**.

99–102. Whether these lines are an actual quotation or a pastiche on the part of Persius, they manage to include almost every neoteric affectation possible in the space of four lines of "sound and fury signifying nothing": the golden line (**line 99**), internal rhyme, end rhyme, bucolic diaeresis [51], and the borrowing of Greek common and proper nouns. Not one of these stylistic devices is objectionable in itself and all can be found in Vergil, Horace, their predecessors, and contemporaries. It is their degree of unrestrained concentration combined with the inanity of the subject matter that raises hackles. The scholiast attributes the lines to Nero without offering any proof. The scene described is a Bacchic *sparagmos*. The lines are spoken by the interlocutor in response to Persius's question in **line 98.**

Torva < *torvus, –a, –um*: "grim, savage."

Mimalloneis < *Mimalloneus, –a, –um*: Greek proper adjective, "Bacchant." The scholiast tells us Bacchus was called Mimallo.

Inplerunt: understand Bacchae as subject.

Bombis < *bombus, –i* < Greek βόμβος: "a loud noise," onomatopoetic.

Bassaris: feminine, nominative. See Lee and Barr (1987), "From Bassareus, a surname of Dionysus . . . used in reference to his wearing the pelt of a fox βασσάρα."

Lyncem: the lynx was sacred to Bacchus.

Corymbis < *corymbus, –i*: "a bunch of ivy berries," sacred to Bacchus.

Euhion: another name for Bacchus.

Reparabilis: here in the unusual active sense, "restoring." The adjective is otiose and chosen more for sound than sense.

103–6. "If we had half the balls our fathers had, would this tripe survive?" **Delumbe** < *delumbis, –e*: "without loins, impotent, castrated." See **lumbum (line 20)**.

Udo < *udus, –a, –um*: "wet," used as a substantive.

Maenas et Attis stand both for the poems themselves and in the next line are synecdoche for the their authors.

Pluteum < *pluteus*, *–i*: the backboard of a reading couch that served as a desk. The true poet pounds the desk and chews his nails (**demorsos sapit unguis**). See **Horace 1.10.70.**

107–34. The interlocutor concedes that perhaps all is not perfect, but why does Persius need to offend people by writing satire? The poet makes his defense of the genre.

107–10. **Opus**: assume *est*.

Sis = *si vis*: "if you please."

Maiorum = "the great." Satire and truth are dangerous because they offend. Effeminacy and stylistic decadence are the corollaries of ethical and political cowardice in the face of tyranny and philistinism.

Canina littera: the letter "r," for its perceived snarling sound. Persius should take the hint.

110–12. "By all means then, I'll say everything is just dandy (**alba**)." Persius feigns concession.

112–14. "I forbid anyone to commit any offense." **Faxit** = an archaic subjunctive of *facio*, adding an air of legal solemnity.

Oletum = "human excrement."

Duos anguis: a sign of religious dedication. Such signs were painted as warnings to boys not to relieve themselves in sacred precincts. Shopkeepers often used them for the same purpose. Persius portrays the satirist as a mischievous boy who stands outside society and pisses on his supposed betters.

Meiite < *meio*, *meiere*: "to urinate."

114–15. On Lucilius, compare **Horace 1.10.3** and **2.1.69**, and **Juvenal 1.154. Lupe**: See **Horace 2.1.62–8. Muci** = Q. Mucius Scaevola Augur, praetor 120 BCE, later governor of Asia. His prosecution for extortion by T. Albucius in 118 formed the subject of Lucilius's second book of satires [35]. These men are precisely the kind of high-profile political figures that Horace, Persius, and Juvenal were no longer able to satirize by name.

Genuinum < *genuinus*, *–i*: "molar."

116–18. **Vafer . . . Flaccus** = "sly Flaccus," a nice formula for Horace's more indirect style.

Excusso populum suspendere naso: a nice image of Horatian contempt for the crowd, best exemplified in *Odes* 3.1.1, *odi profanum vulgus*. Persius combines images from Horace **1.4.8** on Lucilius and from **1.6.5** on Maecenas to produce this passage. Compare also **lines 33** and **40–1. Excusso** < *excutio*, *–cutere*, *excussi*, *excussum*: "shake out," in this context "blow."

119–21. The poem reaches its climax. The question interrupted in **line 8** can finally be posed. Ovid tells, in *Metamorphoses* 11.172–93, how Midas after judging Apollo's music inferior to Pan's was cursed with ass's ears. He hid them under a turban, but his barber knew. Unable to resist telling someone, the slave dug a hole in the forest and uttered the secret there. Later, reeds grew over the spot and whispered to all who passed by. Persius, however, will confide his secret to his *libellus*. On Lucilius's confiding to his books, see **Horace 2.1.30–3. Muttire** = "to mutter."

Scrobe < *scrobis, –is*: "a ditch, a grave." Compare **Juvenal** 1.170–1.

Infodiam < *infodio, –fodere, –fodi, –fossum*: "to dig in, bury."

Auriculas asini: see **line 59.**

Quis non: according the *vita Persii* attached to the manuscripts this originally read *Midas rex* and was removed by Cornutus [68–8] who felt a reference to Nero might be too readily perceived. There is no confirmation of this story and it is much disputed. The text as it reads now works better structurally in terms of completing the interrupted question at **line 8** than the alternative. Moreover, the reference to Midas is still sufficiently clear that Nero could have taken offense had he so chosen. Hence, the vulgate text appears sound.

121–5. On the style of these lines, see the introduction [49].

121–3. **Opertum** < *operio, –perire, –perui, –pertum*: "to cover, bury," hence the participle is used as a substantive meaning "a secret place" or "a secret."

Ridere = substantive use of the infinitive.

Nulla . . . Iliade = ablative of price. Is this Homer or Labeo's *Iliad* (**lines** 4–5)?

123–5. On *Cratinus* and *Eupolis*, the writers of Old Comedy [34–5], see **Horace** 1.4.1–5. Persius, like Lucilius (26.1.589–93) and Horace (1.4.73, 1.10.76–90), only seeks a certain restricted audience.

Audaci quicumque adflate Cratino = "whoever you are who is inspired by bold Cratinus." This predicative use of a vocative participle (**adflate**) with a second person verb is repeated at 3.28–9. It is not common.

Praegrandi cum sene = periphrasis for Aristophanes, the third member of the Old Comedy triumvirate.

Palles = "grow pale [with study]."

Haec: understand *carmina*.

Decoctius = "more boiled down" and hence, "stronger, more concentrated."

126–34. Persius rejects the coarse humor of the vulgar crowd. See Horace 1.4.39. **Vaporata . . . aure** = a "steamed," and hence well-cleaned ear. Contrast **line 121**, but compare also **lines 107–8.**

In . . . ludere = "to mock." The construction does not normally require the preposition, and is best viewed as tmesis for *illudere*.

Crepidas < *crepida, –ae*: " Greek sandals." Roman manhood was in many ways a very brittle construct. The slightest deviation from the norms of dress, comportment, and body language were enough to prompt mockery and insinuations of effeminacy (Corbeill 1996: chapter 4).

Lusco < *luscus, –a, –um*: "one-eyed."

Qui possit = relative clause of characteristic.

Sese aliquem credens: understand *esse*.

Supinus: the adjective is much debated. Some take it as referring to the aedile's general attitude and hence translate "lazy." Others see a reference to the provincial official's head thrown back in an attitude of disdain. There seems no adequate way to judge. Parallels for the second meaning are relatively hard to come by, although in some ways it seems more natural to the context.

Italo . . . honore = "provincial office."

Fregerit heminas . . . iniquas: one of the jobs of the aedile was to vouch for the accuracy of weights and measures in the marketplace. The false were broken. **Heminas** < *hemina, –ae*: roughly a pint.

Arreti = Arretium (modern Arezzo).

Secto in pulvere metas: refers to the drawing of geometric figures in the sand, a practice that goes back to Pythagoras. **Metas** < *meta, –ae*: here in the technical sense, "cone."

Scit risisse vafer: clearly ironic. The buffoon thinks it clever to know how to have laughed at the mathematician.

Nonaria: this word is a *hapax legomenon*, i.e. a word that only appears once in ancient literature. Its meaning is thus obscure. The scholiast, however, glosses it: "**nonaria** is a name for a *meretrix*, because among our elders they were not allowed to ply their trade before the ninth hour (*nona hora*), lest the young men miss their military training in the morning." The vulgar man laughs when the **nonaria** plucks the beard of the Cynic philosopher.

His = "for these sorts of men."

Edictum = "praetor's edict," daily posting of legal notices.

Callirhoen: the reference again is much debated. Some take this as the title of a mythological poem on a heroine of the same name, such as those lampooned at the satire's opening. Others see it as the name of courtesan. It's not clear that for Persius there is much difference.

Do: note the abrupt ending.

3

The scholiast tells us that this is a poem based on a satire from Lucilius's fourth book. A young student with a hangover is urged by his *comes* to live by Stoic virtue. As Housman (1913) recognized at the beginning of the twentieth century, there is more than a passing resemblance between the student and Persius. But who, then, is the *comes* who voices Stoic sentiments not much different from Persius's own? And how are we to understand the voice of the narrator who cannot be fully equated with either of the other two, but at times seems to identify with the student, through the use of the first person plural (**lines 3** and **12**)? Different commentators have proposed different solutions. Some see all the voices as Persius's and ask us to picture a complex internal monologue. Others seek to assign one to Persius and the others to other dramatic characters and narratological functions (Dessen 1968: 48–9; Harvey 1981: 78; Lee and Barr 1987: 100–1; Kissel 1990: 367–73).

On one level, the problem is insoluble: for fundamentally all the voices are those of the satirist; and yet he asks us to picture a dialogue. That dialogue, however, has no clearly demarcated speakers. As Hooley has recognized (1997), the poem owes an extensive debt to Horace 2.3. In that poem, Horace is the object of a diatribe by the Stoic Damasippus. Damasippus is portrayed as a wild-eyed fanatic, but not a few of his darts hit home before Horace chases him from the stage. Nonetheless, where Horace's poem has no narrator but proceeds solely through dialogue, and where Damasippus and Horace are always clearly distinguished, **Persius 3** presents a deliberate muddle. Indeed, the commentators and editors vary not only in how they identify the voices that inhabit the poem, but also with regard to which voices they assign which lines. One must therefore conclude either that Persius was an incompetent poet whose mess only an ingenious commentator could untangle or that the confusion of voices serves a larger purpose.

The real question is how do these formal and intertextual complexities advance the poem's main argument? The key issue with regard to content is: to what extent has the student actually internalized the Stoic precepts to which he has been exposed (**lines 25–62**)? The answer would appear to be "very little." The poem ends with the interlocutor's claim that he is not sick. The philosophical *comes* replies that the latter (presumably the student of the poem's beginning) "says and does what even insane Orestes would have recognized as mad" (**lines 117–18**). In short, the patient does not recognize his own illness. At the same time, the poem presents us with an intertextual labyrinth in which extensive borrowings from Horace are matched by what the scholiast claims are equally important borrowings from Lucilius (the exact contents of which are lost to us). The question on the formal level is then: to what extent has Persius made these borrowings his own? In short, the poem's relation to its generic predecessors recapitulates the basic philosophical problem its central argument poses. Moreover, the confusion over to whom the various voices of the poem are to be attributed is itself a perfect embodiment of the very problematic process of internalizing Stoic precepts or poetic models and making them one's own. At what point does shallow, rote imitation become an authentic creative act whether of an ethical or an aesthetic nature? When does the truth become our own as opposed to a superficial appurtenance? At the deepest level, what does it mean to have a voice of one's own, to fashion a self, and hence finally to awake from our drunken slumber? These are the questions that Persius's radical satire makes us pose.

1–2. The narrative voice sets the scene. It is morning and the sun is fully risen (**clarum mane**). **Nempe haec adsidue**: The satire presents a typical, not a unique, scene.

Rimas < *rima*, *–ae*: "cracks, fissures." The windows are shuttered.

3–4. The shift to the first person plural introduces the confusion of voices discussed in the introductory note. **Quod** refers to the time expression in **quinta dum linea tangitur umbra**, an image taken from the sundial. The dissolute youth has slept long enough to "skim off"—i.e., "sober up from"—(**despumare**) the strong Falernian wine. **Stertimus** < *sterto*, *–ere*: "to snore."

5–6. The *comes* speaks. "Do you sleep while midsummer scorches the flocks and fields?" **Insana canicula**: the rising of the dog star, *Canis Maior*, in late July begins the dog-days of summer. It is a period of proverbial ill health when those who can leave Rome for cooler climes.

Patula < *patulus*, *–a*, *–um*: "spreading."

7–8. The student wakes with a start and calls for a servant (**aliquis**), but receives no response. **Itan** and **nemon** = *itane* and *nemone*.

8–9. Our pupil's frustration shows him to be anything but a model of Stoic self-possession. **Bilis**: bile was considered an index of anger in ancient medicine.

Rudere = "bray." Arcadia was known for its donkeys.

10–11. Writing materials are brought so the day's work can begin. **Membrana** = "parchment," in this case referring to a portfolio made of treated sheepskin (hence **positis . . . capillis**) used to hold loose rough drafts (**chartae**). Though such parchments were smoothed with pumice, they were never the same shade on both sides (**bicolor**) and were on occasion dyed. The **liber** is the text our student is to study. He is either preparing a commentary for personal use or a *hypomnemata*, a notebook of quotations used for recollection and meditation.

Harundo = "a reed," used as a pen.

12–14. "Even with all these preparations, we are still not able to settle down to the task at hand. There is always an excuse." **Calamo** = the **harundo** above. **Umor** = ink.

Sepia = "cuttle fish" and hence its "ink."

Fistula = another term for "pen."

15–16. We switch back from the narrator to the *comes*, but the continued use of the first person plural deliberately clouds the issue of who is speaking to whom and to what extent these represent separate voices. **O miser inque dies ultra miser** = mock epic grief. The student has lost all sense of proportion.

16–18. "Why don't you like a spoiled pet or child demand tender food and a lullaby, then refuse them from the nurse?" This is a difficult passage filled with subliterary words. The gist, however, is clear: our young charge is acting like a brat, calling for his pen and paper, then refusing to use them. **Columbo** = "dove," which the scholiast tells us was a common pet name for children. Think "sweetie pie."

Pappare = infinitive used as a substantive: "to eat liquid or mashed food," from the word babies used to call for their food *pap{p}a*; the phonetic similarity with *papilla*, "nipple," should be observed. **Minutum**, "chopped into tiny pieces," modifies the infinitive.

Lallare = another substantive from the habit of nurses singing "lalla, lalla" to soothe an infant that will not go to sleep.

Mammae = "breast" and hence by metonymy "nurse," but the literal meaning is still functional: our charge acts as if he is barely weaned from the teat.

19–118. After a weak retort from the student, the *comes* launches into a lengthy diatribe that in the opinion of some editors continues till the end of the satire. Others see external voices interrupting. These cruxes (**lines 44–51, 76–118**) will be discussed as they occur.

19–20. "Who are you trying to fool?" **Cui verba**: understand *das*.

Succinis < *succino, –ere*: "a low continuous accompaniment or whine."

Ambages = "evasions."

Tibi luditur: "you've placed your bets." See **Juvenal 1.90**.

20–2. "You are only making a fool of yourself; stop it. The ill-fired pot doesn't ring true." **Contemnere** = second person future passive, "you will be held in contempt."

Fidelia = "an earthenware pot," but observe the pun on *fides*.

23–4. "You are nothing but unformed wet mud. Hurry off to the potter's wheel." Note the metaphor of the achieved Stoic self as an artifact or product of craft [31]. The authentic self is not a given to be discovered, but the product of artisanal, if not artistic, endeavor. **Sine fine**: the labor of self-fashioning is endless.

24–9. The *comes* anticipates the student's response: he cannot be characterized as *vitiosus* because he is of aristocratic heritage and possessed of Etruscan estates. Persius here pursues Horace's program in 1.4 of redefining traditional aristocratic virtues and republican *libertas* for an imperial age [25–6, 30–1]. In the case of Persius, however, the old verities are not simply in need of refashioning but have become a shoddy dodge.

Far modicum = "modest spelt," metonymy for a decent yearly grain harvest from the student's ancestral estates. The claim is simultaneously one of modesty and élite status. "I do not want too much and I have more than enough, thank you very much." Spelt and the ancestral salt cellar (**salinium**) are images of simplicity and old Roman *frugalitas*, as the scholiast notes, even as they are also here claims to landed estates and distinguished lineage. See **Horace 1.6.110–18** and *Odes* 2.16.13–14. The student thinks he has all his bases covered, but he confuses the outward signs of virtue with their inner reality.

Patella = a small plate used for making offerings to the *Lar familiaris*, the guardian of the hearth. Understand *est*.

Hoc satis?: the referent for **hoc** is ambiguous. If it refers to the student's ancestral estate, then it asks if he is content with his lot or does he long for more. If it refers to the statement, then it asks if this will be the only objection the student will make.

Stemmate quod Tusco ramum = the image of a family tree tracing the student's roots back to the Etruscan nobility. It is perhaps no coincidence that Persius himself is of Etruscan descent. *Stemma* refers to a "garland" hung around an ancestral image and hence to a group of those images formed into a genealogical chart. Each branch of the family tree was a *ramus* or *virga*.

Millesime = vocative: " a thousand times removed."

29. This line has been vexed by several difficulties, none of which has been solved to the satisfaction of most commentators. First, there is the seemingly redundant, **–ve . . . vel**. It has been suggested that they refer to two separate alternatives, "you are puffed with pride either because you greet your *censor* or because you wear the *trabea*." Syntactically, this makes good sense, but both alternatives refer to the same institution: the annual *transvectio* in which the knights paraded before the *censor* wearing the short *trabea* instead of the more usual tunic. Some solve this problem of seeming tautology by referring to the adjective **tuum** and deducing that the alternative is: either you are proud because you are a knight or because your (**tuum**) relative is the *censor*. But this is hardly credible since at this period the emperor held the office of censor. The advocates of this interpretation are then forced to make the subsidiary assumption that Persius is referring to municipal knights in a provincial city not the capital. In that case, the hypothesis that the student will respond to the charges of the *comes* by invoking his **stemma** would lose much of its point. Moreover, we have no evidence that the *transvectio* took place outside of Rome (Harvey 1981). Nor does **tuum** necessarily imply any closer relationship than that of the *censor* to the knights under his review. The textual tradition provides little help. Casaubon (1605) conjectured *censoremne* for **censoremve** and Clausen (1956) claims to have found it in *nonnulli libri*, but there is no manuscript support for this reading, though many find it tempting. There is some manuscript support for *censoremque*, but what this would mean is far from clear. Kissel's argument that, *–que* here functions as an inten-

sifier rather than a conjunction is unconvincing (1990). I have, therefore, marked the text with daggers, though its gist seems clear.

30. "You're not fooling anyone!" **Phaleras** < *phalerae, –arum*: "brass ornaments worn by the horses of the *equites*." Again there is a double meaning. On the one hand, the poet continues the image of the *transvectio*. On the other, he dismisses these insignia as baubles, mere ornaments, for the people (**ad populum**). The *comes* knows the student **intus** and out (**in cute**). He looks for a *nobilitas* that springs from deeper sources.

31. **Discincti . . . Nattae**: Natta is not known. A person by the same name is mentioned at Horace 1.6.124 as a miser of unclean hygienic practices. See Seneca's description of Maecenas in *Epistles* 114.4–6, where he says that the great man's loose attire betrayed his effeminacy.

32–4. "But he does not know better and drowns deep in his own ignorance."

Fibris increvit opimum / pingue = "he has piled rich fat round his heart," a complex image. Natta through his very acquisitiveness has coarsened his heart and rendered himself even more insensitive to his own depravity. On **fibris**: see 1.47.

Bullit < *bullio, –ire*: "to bubble up."

35–8. "Father of the gods, may you offer no greater punishment for even the worst tyrants than to see virtue and turn away from it." **Velis** = hortatory subjunctive.

Intabescant = "may they melt [in tears]."

39–43. "Or does the bull of Phalaris and the sword of Damocles strike more terror in the heart than the knowledge that one is plunging into vice?" Phalaris was tyrant of Agrigentum in the sixth century BCE. Perillus was said to have constructed for him an ingeniously crafted bronze bull such that when his enemies were roasted alive in it the bull bellowed with their screams. Perillus was the first victim.

Dionysus II of Syracuse (fourth century BCE) forced the courtier Damocles to sit under a sword suspended by a single hair after the latter had suggested that the life of a tyrant was carefree. **Auratis . . . laquearibus**: gilded ceilings are a regular symbol of luxury and excess.

Purpureas . . . cervices: purple was the color of monarchs.

Quod = "dependent on the notion of fear contained in **palleat**" (Gildersleeve 1903).

44–51. "I too used to dodge my studies as well, but I was just a boy." Most editions give these lines to the *comes*, but some (e.g., Jenkinson 1980; Dominick and Wehrle 1999) divide them between the student and the *comes*.

The question is wholly interpretive. Those who give **lines** 44–7 to the student, see a dawning recognition of his own flawed nature as he recalls his deeply ingrained bad habits. The rest understand these lines as a rhetorical ploy on the part of the *comes* whereby he first identifies with his charge and then demonstrates how he has grown beyond such slovenliness. The question of which reading is correct may be the wrong one since the distinction between externalized recollection and internalized virtue is precisely what is at stake in this satire's sustained confusion of voices (Hooley 1997: chapter 5). In that case, the exemplum of a student forced to memorize a speech by the Stoic hero, Cato Uticensis, is particularly apt. Cato, after the defeat of the republican cause at the battle of Thapsus (46 BCE) committed suicide. The younger Seneca at Epistles 24.6–7 preserves his last words, known as *ad contemnendam mortem*. He notes that the declamation of this short speech was a common exercise in schools.

Olivo: oil was a common ingredient in ointments for the eye. The *comes* was not truly ill, but trying to avoid having to declaim Cato's speech in a display staged by his teacher for his father and his father's friends.

Non sano: presumably because the *magister* would praise such a ridiculous exercise, or perhaps he was ill from having to listen to it.

Sudans: the father is overcome with nerves.

48–51. "At that time I prayed for nothing but luck at dicing and tops." **Dexter senio**: three sixes was the best throw in *tesserae*. The worst throw, three ones, was the **canicula**.

Angustae collo non fallier orcae: the reference is to a game played by trying to throw small objects like nuts into the narrow neck of a jar (**orcae**). **Fallier** = archaic form of *falleri*, used in parallel with **scire**.

Buxum = "a top," made of box wood.

52–7. "But you are now no child unschooled in the ways of the porch." **Haut tibi inexpertum** = "it is not an unheard-of thing to you."

Curvos = "twisted."

Sapiens . . . inlita . . . porticus: Zeno, the founder of Stoicism, used to teach at the *Stoa Poikile* ("Painted Porch") in Athens. It was adorned with a fresco depicting the defeat of the "trousered Persians" (**bracatis . . . Medis**) at the battle of Marathon. **Inlita** < *inlino*, *–ere*, *–levi*, *–litum*: "to daub, smear," and hence "paint."

Quibus is neuter and refers back to **quaeque**.

Detonsa: Roman Stoics traditionally wore their hair cropped close as a sign of their *virtus*.

Pasta < *pasco*, *–ere*, *pavi*, *pastum*: "to feed on" + the ablative. The simple hearty diet was a sign of virtue. Compare the diet of the country mouse in Horace 2.6. **Siliquis** < *siliqua*, *–ae*: a traditional porridge of beans, peas, and lentils. **Polenta** was an analogous Greek porridge made from barley. It is the ancient ancestor of the modern Italian specialty made from ground corn. **Grandi** is ironic.

56–7. "The Greek letter γ or, more precisely, an earlier form of it Ⴗ is meant Or. 1.3.7 explains how Pythagoras used it as a symbol for the choice between the good life and the bad that confronts the young. The earliest years of life are represented by the shank, the easy path of vice by the gently inclining left arm, the difficult path of virtue by the steep right arm" (Lee and Barr 1987). **Samios**: Pythagoras was from Samos.

Littera is the antecedent of **quae** and the subject of **monstravit**.

Diduxit < *diduco*, *–ducere*, *–duxi*, *–ductum*: "to draw apart."

Callem < *callis*, *–is*: "a narrow track." *Callis* and *limes* are oddly tautological.

58–62. The *comes* sees his sermon has not had the desired effect. **Conpage** < *conpages*, *–is*: "joint, seam, connection."

Oscitat hesternum = "yawns off yesterday."

Dissutis undique malis = "with cheeks having come unsewn in all directions," a striking image of slack-jawed stupor.

60. "Do you have an aim?"

61–2. "Or are you on a wild goose chase?" **Testaque lutoque** = "with pottery shards and mud," difficult weapons with which to try to bring down crows (**corvos**).

Ex tempore = "for the moment."

63–5. Some assume a change of addressee at this point. Certainly, at **line 64** the *comes*, if that is whom we are still to imagine speaking these lines, changes from using the second person singular (**videas**) to the plural (**occurite**) in mid sentence, but it is less than assured that the student has left the scene or whence this mysterious audience has arrived. All attempts to imagine a consistent, unambiguous dramatic context for this surreal dialogue are doomed to fail. **Elleborum** = "black hellebore," used in the treatment of dropsy.

Poscentis = accusative plural.

Videas = "you should consider."

Cratero: an eminent physician mentioned by Cicero and Horace (*Satires* 2.3.161).

Magnos . . . montis: understand *auri*. The phrase is proverbial for vast expense.

66–72. Through learning the Stoic definitions of the nature of things (**causas rerum**) we in turn come to understand our own natures and hence our duties and responsibilities. In this way, our suffering (**miseri**) will cease if we take philosophy as our physic.

Victuri = "future participle of purpose" (Gildersleeve 1903).

Metae qua mollis flexus et unde: a metaphor taken from chariot racing. The skilled driver must know how to make the turns. Hence, the winners in life's race must know where the posts (**metae**) are and from where (**unde**) they should begin their turns, if they are not to overturn their cars and be trampled.

69–72. Compare **Lucilius 1342–54.**

73–6. "If you learn this lesson, then you won't envy the lot of those advocates who focus on material possessions." The shift back to the singular returns the focus to the student. Note the emphasis on containers of rotting foodstuffs. The person innocent of philosophy may be wealthy on the outside, but putrefying within. **Putet** < *puteo, –ere*: "to stink."

Fidelia: compare **line 22.**

Penu < *penus, –us*: "provisions."

Defensis pinguibus Umbris = ablative absolute, "when fat Umbrians have been defended." Patrons were expected to defend their clients for free, but in return for their services they would generally receive gifts in kind on their birthdays or the Saturnalia. Umbrians were proverbially prosperous.

Piper = "pepper."

Pernae = "hams."

Marsi monumenta clientis: it is unclear whether this phrase is in apposition to **et piper et pernae** or it refers to an additional set of gifts. Juvenal 3.169 shows that the Marsians were proverbial for their simplicity. Likewise, hams and pepper were not rare and expensive gifts. In that case, however, what precisely did the fat Umbrians provide? **Multa fidelia** is oddly vague compared with the specificity of **et piper et pernae**. Nonetheless, the lack of a coordinating conjunction before **Marsi monumenta clientis** tips the balance toward apposition.

Maena: Pliny (*Historia Naturalis* 9.16) tells us, and the scholia confirm, a kind of chopped fish preserved in jars of brine.

Prima . . . orca: the wealthy advocate has not yet finished his first jar.

77–87. The *comes* introduces an objection from a hypothetical centurion (**dicat** is potential subjunctive). This device is used both to inject humor into the portrait of the philosopher and, ultimately, to discredit the typical objections of the crowd to the life of philosophical study. **Hircosa** = "goat-like," hence smelly (see Catullus 69), but also crude and animalistic.

Quod sapio satis est mihi: "I may not know much about art, but I know what I like."

Quod Arcesilas aerumnosique Solones: understand *sunt*. **Arcesilas** was founder of the second Academy (third century BCE), which taught the impossibility of absolute knowledge. **Solon** was the great seventh-century

BCE Athenian lawgiver and one of the seven sages. The plural is generalizing and contemptuous, "those Solons." **Aerumnosi** = "toiling."

Obstipo < *obstipus, –a, –um*: "bowed down."

Trutinantur < *trutinor, –ari*: "to weigh."

Labello = contemptuous diminutive of *labrum*.

Aegroti veteris . . . somnia: philosophical ideas were often portrayed as the fantasies of the old and sick (Kissel 1990).

Gigni / de nihilo nihilum, in nihilum nil posse reverti = a parody of Epicurean dogma offered as an indictment of Stoicism by the ignorant centurion.

Quis = *aliquis*.

86. The switch from the potential subjunctive (**dicat**) to the indicative (**ridet**) makes the scene more vivid and prepares for the dialogue that follows. **Torosa** = "muscular."

87. Crispante < *crispo, –are*: "to curl," as in "to turn up one's nose."

88–106. The *comes* introduces a dialogue within the dialogue in the form of a parable about a man who believes himself to have recovered from illness and is no longer willing to follow doctor's orders. The result is death. The metaphor of physical for moral health was common in ancient philosophy. The multiplicity of perspectives introduced here is typical of the satire as a whole and anticipates the return of the student in **107**.

88–93. Our little scene begins with the patient asking for help and being ordered to rest. This interchange parallels the student's initial exposure to the principles of Stoic moral hygiene as an antidote to the suffering that comes from the common life in this world. But like the student, the patient, once he begins to feel better, ignores his physician's advice. **Faucibus** < *faux, faucis*: "gullet."

Sodes is a colloquial compound (*si* + *audes*) used to soften the imperative.

Tertia . . . nox: certain mosquito-borne illnesses have recurring fevers. The patient thinks he has the sort that returns after only two days, but in fact he has a quartan fever, which recurs after three.

Conpositas . . . venas = "a normal pulse."

De maiore domo = *de patroni domo*.

Modice sitiente lagoena = "from a moderately thirsty jar." Compare **Horace 2.8.41**.

Lenia . . . Surrentina: the wine of Sorrento was light and recommended, Pliny the Elder assures us, for convalescents (*Historia Naturalis* 23.35).

Loturo < *lavo, –are, –vi, –lotum*: "to bathe." He will take the wine to drink in the bath.

94–7. A brief exchange takes place on the way to the baths. **Lutea pellis** = a "sallow hide."

Ne sis mihi tutor = hortatory subjunctive. A **tutor** is a legal guardian.

Hunc = his actual **tutor**.

Perge, tacebo = "never mind, I'll shut up."

98–106. On death in the baths, compare **Juvenal 1.140–6.**

98–9. A vivid picture of ill-health and self-indulgence. **Albo ventre**: compare **lutea pellis**.

Mefites < *mefitis, –is*: the vapor arising from a sulphur spring.

100–2. A shockingly realistic description of seizure and death. **Inter vina** = "in the midst of drinking his wine."

Calidumque trientem: a *triens* is a cup holding one third of a *sextarius* (roughly a pint). It was warm owing to the Roman habit of mixing hot water with their wine, often for medicinal purposes.

Pulmentaria: see Lucilius 30.3.1051.

103–5. The funeral follows. **Tuba**: see **Horace 1.6.44. Candelae**: a normal part of the funeral, a wax or tallow candle.

Beatulus = "the man himself, bless his heart."

Crassis lutatus amomis: "Every word is contemptuous: 'bedaubed with lots of coarse ointments'" (Gildersleeve 1903).

In portam rigidas calces extendit: prior to the funeral and subsequent cremation the corpse was laid on a couch in the *atrium* with its heels pointed toward the door.

105–6. It was a common practice for Romans to free many of their slaves upon death. These new freedmen would then follow the bier wearing their caps of freedom. Observe the way the final sentence unfolds, "but that man, a group who only yesterday placed [the cap of freedom] on their heads followed close upon, now Roman citizens."

107–18. "The adversary [student] convicts himself most eloquently, however, when he comments on the imaginary scene between a patient and his doctor: unable to perceive the close relationship between spiritual and physical illness, he assumes that he is healthy because he has no chills or fever, and he turns a deaf ear to his friend's warnings" (Dessen 1968: 52).

109–11. "But at the first sight of money or a pretty girl your heart skips a beat." **Molle** = adverbial.

Rite = "regularly."

111–14. "And your throat is too tender for common food." **Catino** < *catinus, –i*: "a deep dish or bowl."

Algente < *algeo, –ere, alsi*: "to be cold."

Holus: see **Horace 2.1.74**.

Populi cribro: " with the common sieve," i.e., coarsely ground.

Ulcus . . . putre = "a rotting ulcer."

Beta = "beet." The irony is that while the beet may be *plebeia*, it is proverbially soft. On the importance of **radere**, see introduction [70].

115–18. "Besides, you chill when struck by fear, and are often fevered with anger." **Aristas** = "goose bumps."

117–18. See introductory note. Orestes went mad when pursued by the Furies after slaying Clytemnestra.

4

This poem, ostensibly on Alcibiades, investigates the complex relations that governed the conjunction of sexual practices, self-cultivation, and political power in Neronian society [70]. It is universally agreed that the first twenty-two lines of the poem are based on the (pseudo-?) Platonic *Alcibiades I*. In this dialogue, and in a series of lost dialogues that follow the same essential scenario (Dessen 1968: 97–105), Socrates challenges Alcibiades's presumption that he is equipped to lead the Athenian people. He demonstrates to the young man that, in as much as he knows neither the good, nor the just, nor himself, he—in spite of his noble ancestry, aristocratic upbringing, and good looks—is not truly qualified to advise the *dêmos*. The dialogue concludes with Alcibiades begging Socrates to instruct him on how to acquire the self-knowledge demanded by the Delphic inscription, *gnôthi seauton* (know yourself), and on how to care for himself (*epimeleia heautou*) so that he might know virtue and thus be of use to the *polis*.

Alcibiades's conversion, however, rests on shaky ground. Socrates ends the dialogue with the warning, "I would wish that you accomplish this. Yet I shudder, not because I mistrust anything in your nature, but when I see the power of the city, I fear it will overcome you and me." The reference to the power of the city is at once an allusion to Socrates's later condemnation by the Athenian court for corrupting the youth, a proceeding in which the debauched Alcibiades served as exhibit A, and to Alcibiades's seduction by the adoration of the crowd. For Socrates, it is clear that the blandishments of the people are more to be feared than their condemnation.

Seduction is one of the major themes of the *Alcibiades I*. Socrates, in fact, introduces himself as Alcibiades's suitor. He has been waiting in the wings until Alcibiades's youth had begun to fade and the crowd of potential lovers the handsome lad attracted had left. Socrates, however, loves not Alcibiades's passing beauty but the inner nobility he could possess if he were to care for himself properly (103–106B).

The conclusion of *Satire* 4 echoes Socrates's final words, but the satire ends on a more acerbic note than the *Alcibiades I*. The young man's interlocutor admonishes him: **respue quod non es; tollat sua munera cerdo. / tecum habita: noris quam sit tibi curta supellex** ["Spit out what you are not; let the common man take back his gifts. / Live with yourself: you will know how paltry is your furnishing"]. Like Socrates in the *Alcibiades I*, the interlocutor fears that Alcibiades will fail to know and care for himself and that he will be seduced by the blandishments of the crowd. The expression of Persius's Socrates may be less ironic and more caustic than that of the Greek original—as befits the satiric genre—but the parallels are nonetheless striking.

They are, moreover, crucial to an understanding of the structure and significance of the poem: for, while the relation between the *Alcibiades I* and the first twenty-two lines is universally conceded, there is considerable controversy about the relation of this opening passage, and its Greek source, to the rest of the poem. The problem is that the middle section of the poem (**lines 24–50**) consists of two vignettes that many contend have no precise parallel in the Platonic text (Hooley 1997: 124–5). Dessen, however, sees these vignettes as simply a set of examples designed to emphasize the dominant philosophical message of the importance of self-knowledge and of care of the self (1968: 61–2). Once we realize, however, that the final lines of *Satire* 4 recall the final lines of the dialogue, just as the opening lines recall the themes of the dialogue as whole, it becomes difficult not to see the entirety of the poem as taking place under the sign of its Platonic predecessor.

In fact, however, the examples chosen by Persius not only recall the dominant themes of the dialogue but they have precise analogues in the *Alcibiades I*. The miser Vettidius (**lines 25–32**), who pathologically cares only for the accumulation of his own possessions, represents an acid caricature of the Platonic *khrêmatistês* ("business man," but literally "one who is occupied with his *khrêma* or things/possessions"). The *khrêmatistês* does not care for himself or for the things that truly are his own (i.e., his body), but only for the accumulation of the things of his things (i.e., doubly external possessions). He, like Vettidius, is completely without self-knowledge (131A–C).

In *Satire* 4, the example of Vettidius leads directly to the image of Alcibiades sunning himself in an obscene pose, with a shaven crotch, like a male prostitute. In the Platonic text, the next example after the *khrêmatistês* is that of Alcibiades himself as *eromenos* or "pederastic beloved." Again, the emphasis in the dialogue is on a failure to love what is essential and a tendency to concentrate on externals to the detriment of an authentic care of the self that would lead to the love of wisdom (*philosophia*). Yet, these sentiments are hardly foreign to the more grotesquely eroticized Alcibiades presented by Persius. Thus, Socrates in the Greek text says, "Likewise, if someone had become the lover of the body of Alcibiades, he would not be the lover of Alcibiades, but of one of the things of Alcibiades" (131C6–8). Similarly at 132A Alcibiades is described as the *dêmerastês*, the "darling" of the people. His relation to the Athenian public is portrayed as an essentially pederastic one. Alcibiades proposes to prostitute himself. Socrates, however, hopes to lure him to his own corner.

The two vignettes in Persius certainly elaborate these examples of the man concerned with wealth alone and of the seduced and seducing Alcibiades at greater length and in more detail than is found in the *Alcibiades I*. In particular, the detailed and grotesque erotic imagery of **lines 33–41** is without parallel. Moreover, the extensive elaboration of these images stands in for a set piece in the dialogue where Socrates gives a long speech demonstrating that, though Alcibiades may be proud of his aristocratic heritage and vast wealth, they were laughable compared to those of the kings of Sparta and Persia. These monarchs were the traditional foes of Athens, and thus the two adversaries about whom Alcibiades would presume to advise the Athenian body politic (121A–124B5). As such, they also represent the world of democratic Athens, the ultimate background to the dialogue's epistemological and ethical investigations.

Thus the essential frame of the *Alcibiades I* is the young man's political ambitions and his role in the city, while that of Persius 4 is personal vice. It is only natural then that those aspects dealing with sexuality's relation to personal probity are highlighted in this satire. The foregrounding of the sexual represents less a deviation from the framework supplied by the *Alcibiades I* than its reinterpretation for the conditions found in the mid-first century CE.

The structural problem of the relation between the two halves of the satire as well as the intertextual question of the relation of the *Alcibiades I* to the poem as a whole are thus really one and the same. What we see in fact is not a shift in focus away from the *Alcibiades* in the last half of the satire, but a shift from the political concerns that are central to the dialogue in its Athenian setting to a focus on the private morality that characterize Stoic meditations on the meaning of *libertas* in the age of Neronian autocracy [31]. The central problem of the satire is in fact the necessity of the descent into the self. It is precisely the withdrawal from the all too public world rather than the question of who is fit to lead it that is at the core of this poem. **Ut nemo in sese temptat descendere, nemo, / sed praecedenti spectatur mantica tergo**! ["how no one tries to make the journey deep inside himself, no one, but each sees the sack [of vice] on the next person's back!"] (**lines 23–4**). Likewise, the oft-cited shift from a predominantly Greek scene in **lines 1–22** to a predominantly Roman scene in **lines 23–52** merely underlines the process of reinterpretation that the Greek text undergoes as it is naturalized in its Roman imperial setting (*pace* Kissel 1990: 496). Although even this is oversimplified, as demonstrated by **line 8**'s invocation of the **Quirites** (Roman citizens) in the supposedly Greek portion of the poem. The presence of both Greek and Roman elements is a common device in Horace (see, *inter alia*, *Odes* 1.9).

1–3. Socrates approaches Alcibiades and asks on what basis he would presume to handle the affairs of the people. **Crede** = an imperative from the narrator directed at the reader.

Sorbitio = "draught."

Cicutae = "of hemlock."

Fretus = "relying on."

Pupille Pericli: Alcibiades and his brother were the wards of the Athenian statesman, Pericles.

4–5. "You show amazing wisdom for a barely pubescent (**ante pilos**) youth." Socratic irony is well in evidence. **Calles** = "know by experience."

6–8. "When the crowd roils, what will you say to it when a momentary calm settles?" **Plebecula**: the diminutive is contemptuous.

Bile: see **3.8–9.**

Fert animus . . . fecisse silentia = "the spirit bids you to have brought forth silence," ironic epic periphrasis.

Calidae: "hot with anger."

8–9. "Will you say 'citizens of Rome (**Quirites**), don't think the former is just, the latter bad, but prefer the latter instead'?" One of Socrates's points throughout the *Alcibiades I* is that his beloved should not presume to advise the Athenian assembly when he does not himself know what is just and unjust. The conflation of Greek and Roman settings and institutions is found throughout the satire. See introductory note.

10–13. "You know how to weigh right and wrong," heavily ironic. **Lance** < *lanx*, *lancis*: "platter, pan," as in *lanx satura* [12], but here referring to the pan of a scale.

Ancipitis < *anceps*, *ancipitis*: "two-sided."

Rectum discernis ubi inter / curva subit vel cum fallit pede regula varo: a complex metaphor derived from carpentry. **Rectum** here, as in **line 9**, means primarily "right," but Persius also plays upon the literal meaning, "straight." Thus **inter curva** denotes the difficulty of discovering the "straight path" in a world of curves, while the **regula** refers to a carpenter's *norma*, a square made up of two feet (**pede**) placed at right angles. In short, though sometimes our rule is not true to what needs to be measured and squared, Alcibiades's powers of ethical perception are so keen that he can discover the straight even when forced to use a crooked rule. The reference is to situations in which one's normal ethical canon is not fitted to the task at hand.

Nigrum vitio praefigere theta = "to place the black mark of death before a man's name for vice." The practice refers to a judge placing a θ before a man's name. θ stands for θάνατος. It is unclear whether this was a Roman practice at the time this satire was written—though it certainly later came to be—or whether this is a bit of Athenian local color.

14–16. The irony of Socrates's previous compliments becomes clear as he shifts to direct abuse. "Why don't you stop prancing before the people and take a good stiff draught of hellebore instead?" **Summa . . . pelle decorus** = "handsome on the surface of your skin." Alcibiades is *decorus* only in a superficial sense.

Ante diem: in the *Alcibiades I* he is not quite twenty years old and not yet eligible to address the assembly, but already making grand political plans (105A7–B7).

Blando . . . popello: the seduction of political power. **Popello** is a contemptuous diminutive for *populus*.

Iactare caudam: the scholiast sees a reference to a dog wagging his tail. This is possible, in which case it refers to Alcibiades's fawning for the people's affection. However, given the later graphic sexual vocabulary of the satire and the fact that **caudam** can mean *penem*, there is also a reference to a lewd dance. Translate "to shake your tail."

Anticyras < *Anticyra, –ae*: a town in Phocis famous for its hellebore, a purgative used for madness and dropsy (see **1.51** and **3.63**).

Sorbere: see **sorbitio, line 2.**

Meracas < *meracus, –a, –um*: "pure, unadulterated," compare *merus*.

17–18. "Do you think the highest good is to laze about and eat dainties?" **Summa** is a substantive with **vixisse** and **cuticula** (another contemptuous diminutive) in apposition.

Uncta . . . patella = "a sumptuous dish" (Harvey 1981).

19. "This old woman would reply no differently": Persius asks us to imagine a Socratic street scene.

19–22. "Brag about your lineage and good looks all you like. **Baucis**, the herb seller, knows as much as you do." **"Dinomaches ego sum"** = "I am the son of Dinomache," Alcibiades's mother. As most commentaries observe, she was an Alcmaeonid, and it was from her that Alcibiades inherited his connection to the traditional Athenian aristocracy and Pericles. Yet the construction is unusual and, as Kissel rightly notes (1990), alludes directly to a passage in the *Alcibiades I* where Socrates pictures the amused reaction of Amestris, the mother of the Great King of Persia, to the news that Alcibiades proposes to compare himself to her son (123C5–7). As Denyer notes (2001: 187–8), the use of the matronymic is very rare in Greek. In poetry, it refers either to the sons of the gods or to children without fathers. Hence, the formulation, which Persius has Socrates ironically cast as a vaunt, subtly calls into question Alcibiades's legitimacy.

Pannucia = "shriveled."

Ocima = "basil," considered an aphrodisiac by the Elder Pliny (*Historia Naturalis* 20.48), hence the slave to whom **Baucis** hawks her wares is **bene discincto** (see **3.31**).

23–41. Many commentators assume a change of speakers here, since these lines do not follow the *Alcibiades I* as closely as the initial twenty-two. There are a number of objections to this. First, as discussed in the introductory note, the two vignettes found in this section do in fact parallel a sequence in the *Alcibiades I*, likewise the end of the poem directly recalls the end of the dialogue. Second, the figure of the sunbather in the second vignette (**lines 33–41**) has been anticipated in **line 18** and so must refer to Alcibiades. Jenkinson (1980) as well as Dominick and Wehrle (1999) solve this problem, by attributing **lines 23–32** to Alcibiades. But, as Hooley (1997: 126–7) observes, it is difficult to imagine that Alcibiades would be assigned the summary statement, **ut nemo in sese temptat descendere, nemo, / sed praecedenti spectatur mantica tergo**, which in many ways stands for the whole satire. If any character should utter this pronouncement it should be Socrates. Indeed, the whole burden of Socrates's demonstration both in **lines 1–22** and throughout the *Alcibiades I*, is to indict Alcibiades's lack of self-knowledge. Third, the use of the second person singular to introduce both vignettes (**quaesieris, cesses**) naturally lead the reader to expect a continuation of the dialogic situation introduced in the first line. It is better then to follow Dessen (1968: 58–70) and Harvey (1981) and assume that the Socratic figure continues as the main speaker.

23–4. in sese . . . descendere: note the image of profound interiority. The Delphic oracle's commandment to "know yourself" makes no such assumption about the mystery of our inner nature or the need to delve "deep" inside.

Praecedenti . . . mantica tergo: an allusion to the Aesopic fable in which the gods assigned men two packs, one worn on the front with the faults of others and the other on the back with our own.

25. Quaesieris: potential subjunctive. The speaker introduces an imaginary dialogue to sketch his caricature of Vettidius.

Nostin = *nostine.*

Vettidi = otherwise unknown.

26. Curibus = locative of *Cures*, a Sabine town with a reputation for frugality.

Quantum non = *plus quam.*

Miluus = "the kite," proverbially long of flight.

27–32. "Do you mean that miser who dines worse than his slaves?" Vettidius so values his **praedia** that his life has become wretched.

28. An obscure reference to the Compitalia, a holiday honoring the gods of the crossroads (*compita*). The scholiast takes **compita**, here, as a reference not to the crossroads but to the shines found there. **Pertusa**, he says, refers to the fact that these shrines were open on all four sides.

More problematic is what **iugum . . . ad compita figit** means. It should refer to affixing the yokes to the shrines themselves. The scholiast argues that this indicates a dedication of broken yokes, but there is nothing in the Latin to support that reading nor any evidence that such breakages were regular occurrences. Many assume that the reference is to hanging up the yoke as a sign of rest for the holiday, but then why Vettidius would affix it (i.e., with a nail) **ad compita** is difficult to explain. Kissel points to a satiric purpose: the miser fears thieves (1990). While clever, such a reading is difficult to prove. In the end, we must side with Harvey, "P.'s words are still some way from being understood" (1981).

29–32. The miser fears to give his slaves their festive rations while he dines on inferior food. **Seriolae** = diminutive of *seria*: a large jar. The diminutive is appropriate for a miser. Slaves were normally given extra wine on holidays. The fact that Vettidius must scrape off the **veterem . . . limum** tells us that it has been some time since he last dipped into his supply.

"Hoc bene sit": a common formula in toasts, here used as a blessing for the perilous enterprise of this modest feast. Note the agonized tone of **ingemit**.

Cepe = "an onion." **Tunicatum** = "with the skin on."

Pueris plaudentibus = ablative absolute. The slaves applaud their **farratam . . . ollam**: a porridge made from spelt. This was plain fare, but a holiday luxury chez Vettidius.

Pannosam faecem morientis . . . aceti: "The wine was not very good which could be called 'the ragged dregs of dying vinegar'" (Hart 1896: 58).

33–41. Here the young Alcibiades, whose political aspirations have been deflated by Socrates's biting irony at the beginning of this satire, is pictured as sunning himself naked when a stranger suddenly compares the youth's efforts at depilation to those of a man unsuccessfully weeding his garden. The use of the verb *figo* for the rays of the sun introduces a veiled image of penetration.

35. **Hi mores** recalls Cicero's *O tempora, o mores!* at the beginning of the first Catilinarian, a reminiscence reinforced by Alcibiades's political ambitions. **Penemque** illustrates how far a satire of Alcibiades in the age of Nero was removed from the moral condemnation of Catiline in the time of Cicero. The young, dissolute aristocrat is no longer threatening to overturn the republic, but has become emperor in the person of Nero.

36. The interlocutor accuses Alcibiades of displaying his depilated private parts to the general public. The verb *pando*, is used in the same context in Catullus 6, where the poet demands that Flavius display his *latera ecfututa*. *Pando* is not widely used and is found nowhere else in Latin literature in an explicitly sexual context. Thus Persius's usage is striking and the sentence

penemque arcana lumbi / . . . marcentis *pandere* vulvas can be read as an allusion to its lone literary predecessor. **Marcentis . . . vulvas** = "shriveled hollows." The use of *vulva* for masculine anatomy is unparalleled. The scholiast assumes it refers to the anus, but remarks on the unusual usage. The plural is likewise difficult to explain except as a poeticism inapt for this plain speaking context and metrically unnecessary. Nonetheless, the theme of effeminacy is a constant throughout Persius and this image merely takes it to its logical conclusion.

A second Catullan allusion can be seen in 41. The plough that the interlocutor claims will not be able to tame the brush that grows round Alcibiades's anus (**non . . . ullo mansuescit *aratro***) recalls Catullus's evocation of Lesbia at the end of poem 11. There, her voracious, phallic sexuality is compared to the traditionally masculine image of the plough, and Catullus himself is portrayed as the effeminized flower that is her victim ("flos . . . tactus *aratro* est"). In both Persius and Catullus the central point of the image is the inversion of expected gender relations; neither Catullus nor Alcibiades should be ploughed. But whereas the image in Catullus is pathetic, since he is portrayed as the victim of Lesbia's brutality, in Persius, Alcibiades is merely perverse. Yet, his cinaedic desires will remain unfulfilled. Depilate as he might, no plough will penetrate that bracken.

The Catullan and Ciceronian allusions in this passage provide an implicit republican context for this description of Alcibiades. The tissue of republican literary allusions that Persius deploys here shows that on every level Alcibiades is an absurd and degraded figure. He not only lacks the stature of a statesman such as Cicero, he does not even have that of a villain like Catiline. These references to the literary past, therefore, create a subtle counterpoint that reinforces the condemnation of Alcibiades.

36–41. A series of agricultural metaphors runs throughout the passage. Beginning with **runcantem** ("weeding"), continuing with **gurgulio** ("worm," also spelled *curculio*), **plantaria** ("seedlings" or "hair"), **labefactent** ("loosen as with a plough," see Vergil, *Georgics* 1.264) and finishing with **filix** ("hedge") and **aratro** ("plough"), Alcibiades's groin is consistently allegorized as a field of weeds. Compare also *Georgics* 1.238–41. Yet this profusion of vegetative growth gives no hint of a harvest to be enjoyed. The closest the reader comes to a feast is the boiling (**elixas**) of Alcibiades's buttocks, preparatory to the failed attempt at depilation. For more on this topic, see Harvey (1981), Kissel (1990), and Hooley (1997: 149–50).

37. **Maxillis** < *maxilla, –ae*: "jaw."

Balanatum = "anointed with balsam," hence "perfumed."

Gausape = "fleece," and hence "beard," but compare Horace 2.8.11.

39. **Palaestritae** = "trainers."

40. **Nates** = "buttocks."
Forcipe adunca = "hooked tweezers."

42–52. The satire ends with a lamentation at the universal lack of self-knowledge, even among those who would point out the faults of others (including the satirist). We can take neither the compliments nor the derision of others at face value, but must descend within ourselves.

42–3. Even as we engage the enemy in close combat (**caedimus**), we leave ourselves open to an attack by distant archers.

43–5. Each of us bears an inner wound that we try to shield with a protective belt (**balto**). The reference is to a gladiator who tries to hide his injury from an opponent.

45–6. **Decipe nervos / si potes**: you can hide your wound, but not escape its pain. Literally, "deceive your strength, if you can."

46–7. Alcibiades finally responds. "Why should I not believe it when the neighborhood calls me exceptional?"

47–50. "If you have not practiced virtue, then you lend the people your thirsty ears to no purpose." **Viso si palles . . . nummo**: compare 3.109.
In penem ironically substituted for *in mentem*. Compare 3.110.
Amarum / si puteal multa cautus vibice flagellas: this passage has long been much disputed. The standard interpretation, which almost every commentator admits is inadequate, has been that **puteal** refers to the *Puteal Libonis*, the place in the Forum where the money-changers gathered, and that this passage therefore refers to whipping-up interest rates or to some other fashion of making money. Yet, this interpretation involves a needless allegorical reading and is an unnecessary repetition of the point made in 47. The most basic meaning of **puteal** is the rim around a well or other hole in the ground. Kissel (1990) has seen correctly that a more straightforward interpretation, and one more consonant with the structure of the poem as whole, can be obtained by recognizing here a reference to Alcibiades's desire for homoerotic anal penetration (see **lines** 35–41). Translate: "if you slyly beat the fruitless hole with many a blow."

51–2. See introductory note. **Cerdo** = "the common man." This last couplet echoes the end of *Satire* 3 (**lines** 107–11), where the young student protests to the doctor of philosophy that he is not ill, but the *comes* responds, "just wait till you see a beautiful woman or a pile of money."

JUVENAL

1

How can anyone not write satire today? Juvenal in his opening programmatic satire explains why, unlike Lucilius (line **165**) he will only attack the dead (**lines** 170–1). The burden of the poem is that vice has so overrun Rome that Juvenal can no longer remain silent. Each vice is lovingly sketched in its own individual vignette. One scene's relation to the next is sometimes tangential, but the power of the individual images and their accompanying *sententiae* obscures the relative lack of narrative and argumentative development [10–13, 39, 75]. The effect is cumulative. "Every new figure he sees rouses him to fresh fury, for every new figure typifies a different kind of outrage on moral feeling" (Highet 1961: 50).

The basic thesis is that the traditional Roman virtues of *fides* and *virtus* cannot exist in a city such as that described in the first catalog of vices (**lines** 22–80) (Anderson 1982: 197–254). The root of this moral rot is two-fold [75]. In the first instance, it is the result of an influx of foreigners, mostly but not exclusively from the Greek east. Rome is no longer Roman in either values or bloodline. This is a theme that will be dealt with at some length in *Satire* 3. Yet, lest we oversimplify, as the opening of *Satire* 6 makes clear, the Romans themselves were never all that Roman. Or at least the good old days were not quite as good as they sometimes seem. So here in poem 1, we see Pyrrha portrayed as a procuress before the waters of the flood that was supposed to have wiped out human iniquity were even dry (**line** 84).

The second cause of moral decline is related to the first: social mobility. As Rome has become a more and more cosmopolitan city, the specter of the wealthy foreign freedman came to haunt the imagination of the city's disenfranchised. One need only think of Trimalchio's feast in the *Satyricon* to conjure the *libertinus* bogeyman in all his seeming vulgarity. Native Romans were in competition with freedmen and foreigners for the generosity of the wealthy. At the same time, in the absence of republican political institutions, the wealthy had less and less need of the services of the poorer classes either as voters in elections or to demonstrate their potential political power (**lines**

127–46). The material basis for relations between patron and client, which traditionally had bound the upper orders to their less fortunate confreres, had begun to erode with the establishment of imperial government. The result, as Juvenal depicts it, is a commodification of traditional power relations: *clientes* were seen less as *amici* and more as expenses (**lines** 97–101).

The fact is that the traditional class structure of an inherited senatorial élite, supported by wealthy equestrian gentry, had come under greater and greater strain during the first two centuries of imperial rule. Social mobility represented the antithesis of this old order (see **Horace** 1.4), and the wealthy foreign interloper crystallized the worst fears of the aristocracy and those who depended on it. At the same time, this image was in many ways a false one. The empire itself had destroyed the economic and social basis of the republican aristocracy, not freed slaves of foreign birth. The few wealthy freedmen who actually did emerge were symptoms, not the cause, of this disenfranchisement of the traditional élite.

The reality of this disenfranchisement is depicted in the opening section of the satire (**lines** 1–21), which forms a pendant to the final section's discussion of Juvenal's reasons for lampooning only the dead (**lines** 147–71). The satirist asks how can he remain silent any longer. Will he always be a listener and never reply (**semper ego auditor tantum? numquamne reponam**)? In part, this opening section is recapitulation of **Persius** 1. Juvenal is surrounded by bad poets. How can he stand to listen to this rot any more? Satire is the only response to a world of corrupted literary, and hence moral, standards. Yet, as Freudenburg has pointed out (2001: 234–9), this pose of breaking a long silence is a standard trope in the period after the death of Domitian [73]. Analogous statements can be found in Pliny and Tacitus. Silence had been externally imposed. Now the poet or orator can speak. However, as Freudenburg observes, this rush to utter the truth is suspect. Tacitus and Pliny were more closely implicated in the previous regime than either would care to admit, and the desire to proclaim the virtues of a new *libertas* was, if not crudely self-interested, at least designed not to offend Trajan and Hadrian.

Juvenal's famous **indignatio** (**line** 79) at once acknowledges the liberalization that has occurred under Trajan and yet reflects a strategic decision to indict only the vices of the recent past. Things are not always what they seem. In fact, the satire may be read as an indictment of this very rush to speak a truth that can only be articulated once it is no longer consequential. To that extent, this opening programmatic poem is also a satire of the moralist's claim to *parrhesia* or to speaking the unvarnished truth [10]. It is a satire of satire [32]. Or in the poet's own ambiguous words: **difficile est saturam non scribere** (**line** 30).

1–21. Must I always be a spectator and never a participant?

1–2. Ego auditor: understand *ero*.

Reponam = " reply."

Rauci < *raucus*, *–a*, *–um*: "hoarse" from continual recitation.

Theseide Cordi = an epic poem on Theseus by Cordus, presumably the same man of letters mentioned at 3.203.

3–6. Note the rhetorical devices Juvenal uses to produce a sense of continuity: the repetition of **inpune** in two different metrical positions and the chiastic arrangement of the heroes' names, **Telephus** and **Orestes**.

Ille = another poet, this time a dramatist as indicated by **togatas**, comedies in Roman dress, as opposed to adaptations of Greek plays such as those found in Plautus and Terence.

Hic = a third poet who composed elegies (**elegos**), an erotic genre whose most notable authors were Propertius, Tibullus, and Ovid, though it was still practiced in Juvenal's day.

Telephus = son of Hercules and Auge, wounded by the spear of Achilles but healed by its rust. A tragedy by this name was written by Euripides and the topic was presumably popular among his latter-day imitators. **Telephus** was himself **ingens**, but the clear intimation from the next line is that so were the tragedies written about him.

Orestes = son and avenger of Agamemnon. A tragedy with this title was also written by Euripides. **Summi plena iam margine libri** = ablative absolute: "with the margin of the end of the book already full." **In tergo**: this ***Orestes*** is so over-inflated it not only fills up the white space on one side of a scroll, but it can't even be finished on the back. Note the enjambment between **lines 5** and 6, as one line spills over to the next just as a single scroll could not contain the **Orestes**.

7–9. "I know better the standard pieces of mythological geography than anyone knows their own home!" While much of the mythology mentioned in the following lines is standard epic fare, many of the items have special reference to the *Argonautica*. It has been generally assumed that the target is Valerius Flaccus whose version of the story had recently been published. Courtney (1980) however disagrees. **Lucus Martis** = the grove in Colchis where the Golden Fleece was kept.

Aeoliis vicinum rupibus antrum / Vulcani: a group of seven volcanic islands north of Sicily where Aeolus, king of the winds in the *Odyssey*, was thought to live. Vulcan was said to have his forge on one of these. Flaccus, however, locates it on Lemnos.

9–13. Each of these indirect questions depends on **clamant**.

Quid agant venti: an epic topos.

Aeacus = one of the judges of the underworld with Minos and Rhadamanthys.

Alius: a contemptuous reference to Jason.

Pelliculae = diminutive of *pellis*: "hide," for the fleece.

Monychus = a centaur involved in the battle with the Lapiths, a common theme of Greek art. See the frieze on the Parthenon. According to Flaccus it was painted on the *Argo*.

Frontonis: a wealthy patron who lends his house and gardens for poetic recitations; perhaps the same Fronto addressed by Martial (1.55).

Convolsaque marmora: a vivid hyperbole.

Semper recalls the opening of the poem.

Ruptae . . . columnae: the peeling voices of inanity shatter the house's columns.

14. One of Juvenal's most common rhetorical strategies is the simultaneous assertion and undermining of hierarchical relations. The *summus* and *minimus poeta* ultimately produce the same thing. Note: this is not the same as saying there is no difference between them, but rather that the difference is irrelevant, and yet nonetheless needs to be asserted. One is *summus* and the other *minimus*. The result is a topsy-turvy world in which judgment is demanded—who is the best? who is the worst?—yet impossible. Compare **lines 147–9. Expectes** = hortatory subjunctive.

15–18. "We've had the same rhetorical training as the rest of them. Why should we alone be silent?" **Ferulae** < *ferula, –ae*: "cane," the proverbial rod that Roman schoolmasters feared if you spared, you would spoil the child.

Consilium dedimus Sullae: an example of a popular *suasoria*. *Suasoriae* were common exercises in Roman rhetorical training. The student was generally assigned to give advice to a prominent historical figure. L. Cornelius Sulla's decision to retire after having achieved supreme power as dictator was a common topic. Sulla (138–78 BCE) was a reactionary politician whose proscriptions set a brutal precedent later to be followed by Antony and Octavian.

Vatibus < *vates vatis*: originally "prophet" or "soothsayer," with the Augustan poets it became associated with "the inspired poet." Here, it is clearly sarcastic.

Periturae parcere chartae is in apposition to **clementia**. Rome is crawling with poets. The paper will perish anyway. **Clementia** was a virtue claimed by imperial power since the time of Julius Caesar. The image of sparing those about to die would have conjured up more sinister images than that of bad poets wasting papyrus. Note the contemptuous alliteration and assonance.

19–21. "Nonetheless, I'll tell you why I wish to practice the genre of Lucilius." The poet rounds off the proem and prepares for the satire proper. **Cur tamen** introduces an indirect question dependent on **edam**.

Magnus . . . Auruncae . . . alumnus = Lucilius [56] who came from Suessa Aurunca in Campania.

Vacat = impersonal construction: "if there is leisure."

22–80. The poet immediately launches into a vivid catalog of vice, the violence of which is all the more unexpected given the casual courtesy of the three preceding lines.

22–30. This opening period sets out a list of conditions introduced by **cum** (**lines 22, 24, and 26**), all leading to the climactic conclusion, **difficile est saturam non scribere**, which means not only that in the face of such outrage how can one not write satire, but also that under such conditions no matter what one writes it becomes satire. This is an age of irony. Compare **Persius** 1.11–12.

Ducat < *duco, ducere, duxi, ductum*: "to lead," the common verb for a man marrying a woman, since he "leads" her to his house.

Spado = "eunuch."

Mevia fights in the arena dressed as an Amazon (**nuda . . . mamma**). She is taking part in the *venatio* or beast hunt. The name is a common one in Latin and appears to designate a woman of good family, though she cannot be positively identified. Fighting in the arena was considered a sign of degradation for a free Roman. It was doubly so for a woman. There are however recorded instances from the reigns of Nero and Domitian. Note the chiastic relation between the eunuch husband who is not a man and the gladiator woman who acts the part of one.

Venabula < *venabulum, –i*: "hunting spear."

24–9. A second pair is introduced. **Patricios omnis**: the patricians were the traditional aristocracy of birth in Rome. Their numbers were vastly depleted by the end of the first century BCE. The point here is that wealth (**opibus**) challenges (**provocet**) birth.

25. Quo tondente: ablative of attendant circumstances. **Tondente** < *tondeo, –ere, totundi, tonsum*: "to shave, shear clip." The barber in question is thought to be one Cinnamus who, apparently owing to a bequest from his mistress, became an *eques*. Barbering was a low profession, generally practiced by slaves. **Gravis** has been variously explained without any consensus having been achieved. It can be attached either to **barba** or taken adverbially with **sonabat**. The epic grandeur of the line belies its trivial subject matter. The line is a parody of *Eclogues* 1.28, *candidior postquam tondenti barba cadebat*. See Braund (1996a), "Here the happy world of Virgil's Tityrus is contrasted with the corrupt world the speaker sees surrounding him. Parody of pastoral is found again on a larger scale in Satire 3."

26–9. The two hemistiches (half lines) are in apposition to one another. Both refer to **Crispinus** (v. 27) who, as a foreign-born freedman who has achieved great wealth, epitomizes Juvenal's fears. He came to Rome as a seller of fish. He later rose to the rank of knight and was appointed to Domitian's privy council. He plays a prominent part in *Satire 4*. **Verna** = "house-born slave," as opposed to one purchased on the block. **Canopi**: Canopus was an Egyptian town near Alexandria.

Tyrias . . . lacernas = "Tyrian purple mantle": Tyrian purple was made from crushed shellfish. It was very expensive.

Revocante = "hitching up."

Ventilet < *ventilo, –are*: "to fan, wave in the air, brandish."

Aestivum . . . aurum: as the scholiast notes, Crispinus is so rich he has winter and summer rings. Equestrians wore plain gold rings as a sign of their rank.

Maioris pondera gemmae: either his summer wear is quite heavy or Crispinus is quite dissipated.

30–9. Who is so hardened to this parade of iniquity that he can hold himself in check? **Ferreus**: i.e., as unyielding as "iron."

Ut teneat se = "that he would control himself." Note the harsh rhythmic effect of ending the hexameter with a monosyllable [51].

Causidici > *causidicus, -i*: "advocate" (*causa/dico*). This is not a laudatory term such as *orator*. It implies a gun for hire.

Mathonis: a lawyer under Domitian. By poem 7 he is bankrupt, presumably as a result of his excess.

Plena ipso: a **lectica** normally accommodated two but Matho is so corpulent that he fills the litter himself. Note how the elision enacts his spilling over its bounds.

Magni delator amici: *amicus* was often a euphemism for patron. This character enriched himself by informing on his aristocratic (*magnus*) patron. Under Tiberius it was enacted that informers received a quarter of the property of anyone they caused to be convicted of treason.

Comesa < *comedo, –esse, –edi, –esum*: "to devour," a vivid image of the informer feeding on the corpse of the fallen *nobilis*.

Massa = Baebius Massa, a notorious informer under Domitian as is Mettius **Carus**. Our *delator* is a *delator delatorum*.

Palpat = "strokes."

A trepido Thymele summissa Latino: understand *ad quem*. "Latinus was Domitian's favorite actor, possibly a member of his court, and Thymele was Latinus's leading lady" (Freudenburg 2001: 214). **Summissa** is best understood first in its most literal sense as the perfect participle of *sub* + *mitto*: she was "put under" both the informer and his authority.

37–9. **Testamenta** = "bequests." Legacy hunters are a common theme of imperial literature. **Summoveant** also has the technical sense of excluding someone from a legacy.

Merentur noctibus: "earn at night," deponent.

Processus = "advancement," genitive.

Vesica = "bladder," used as metonymy for the female sexual organ. It is in apposition to **via**.

40–1. **Proculeius** and **Gillo** are gigolos servicing wealthy widows and compensated proportionally to their equipment (**ad mensuram inguinis**). **Unciolam** = one twelfth. **Deuncem** = eleven twelfths. Roman fractions were done according to a duodecimal system.

42–3. **Sanguinis** here = "semen," which according to Aristotelian medical theory was highly refined blood. Note the assonance with **inguinis**, which occupies the same metrical sedes in the previous line, and with **anguem** in the sixth foot in the next. The two monosyllabic words ending 42 are extraordinarily harsh.

Palleat: sexual excess and loss of blood were thought to produce pallor, but also fear. See **Persius 1.26.** These men approached their work with the same apprehension they would have in stepping on a snake (**anguem**). The simile is found in Homer (*Iliad* 3.33–5) and Vergil (*Aeneid* 2.329–80). The incongruity of the present context with the simile's heroic past is part of the fun.

44. Caligula, in the winter of 39–40 CE, held a contest in oratory at Lyons (Lugdunum). According to Suetonius, winners were rewarded but losers faced flogging or a dunking in the Rhone, or were forced to lick away their offending words.

45–8. "What should I say when one (**hic**) and another (**hic**) criminal roam free?" **Iecur**: see Horace **1.9.66** and **Persius 1.25.**

Populum . . . premit: "he crowds the people," but also he "importunes, oppresses." In one way or another, as we say, he is "putting the squeeze" on the people.

Gregibus comitum: ablative of means. This would be the entourage of *clientes* that traditionally followed a great man around and served as a visual marker of his political and social status. These markers now belong to a criminal who should represent the opposite of a great Roman *patronus*.

Spoliator = "despoiler" both fiscally and sexually.

Pupilli < *pupillus*: an orphan placed under another's guardianship.

Prostantis < *prosto*, *–are*, *–stiti*: he has been so despoiled that he is forced to prostitute himself.

Infamia: a technical legal term for the loss of civil rights.

49–50. **Marius** Priscus was prosecuted by Tacitus and Pliny in 100 CE for financial misappropriations during his proconsulship in Africa. He was sentenced to banishment (*relegatio*), which did not involve a loss of property rights. **Exul** here is used in the general, not the technical legal sense, as is often the case in Ovid's exilic poetry. The **victrix provincia** evidently was unable to secure full restitution, since **Marius** enjoys the life of luxury. **Ab octava** = from the eighth hour after sunrise, about 2 pm. Normally dinner parties and drinking began at the ninth hour. On the style of these lines, see the introduction [51].

Fruitur dis iratis: deliberately oxymoronic.

51. **Venusina . . . lucerna**: Horace was from Venusia (2.1.34–5).

52–61. "How can I not attack (**agitem**) these things? When husbands are pimping their own wives should I write mythological epics?"

Magis = "rather."

Heracleas and **Diomedeas** = nouns formed by analogy with *Odyssea*, i.e., epics on Heracles and Diomedes. Note the spondaic fifth foot in **Heracleas**, giving the line a heavy epic feeling [51].

Mugitum labyrinthi = "the mooing of the labyrinth," a bathetic deflation after the high epic tone just established. Pasiphaë, queen of Crete, conceived a lust for the bull of Minos. The product of their union was the Minotaur.

54. Daedalus (**fabrum**) designed both the hollow cow that allowed Pasiphaë to consummate her lust and the labyrinth that imprisoned her monstrous offspring. When he sought to escape the island he fashioned wings of wax and feathers for himself and his son (**puero**). The latter, however, flew too close to the sun, causing the wax to melt, and fell into the sea (**mare**). Notice how the topics of epic discourse get more perverse as Juvenal gets closer to resuming his portrait of contemporary vice.

Accipiat . . . si capiendi: this is technical legal vocabulary. As Courtney (1980) summarizes Ulpian on this point, "*capere* is used of legal heirs . . . *accipere* of the provisional possession of a *heres fiduciarius* who accepts a legacy as a *fideicommissum* to be passed on to someone else." According to the *lex Voconia* (169 BCE), women of questionable morals were disallowed from receiving inheritances. This husband, however, in effect acts as his wife's pimp (**leno**) by ignoring her lovemaking with another so as to receive an inheritance that he will share with her, since she cannot receive it directly. Such acts of *lenocinium* had been explicitly outlawed by the *lex Julia de adulteriis* of Augustus.

Ius nullum: understand *sit*.

56–7. **Doctus**: "The ironic *doctus* demonstrates how Juvenal examines the Roman scene and hints at the cause of its degradation. As one of his crucial methods throughout this section, he indicates the total overthrow of Roman *virtus* by transferring terms of moral approval to the description of immorality" (Anderson 1982: 201).

Lacunar = "a paneled ceiling."

Stertere = "to snore."

58–61. **Puer** is the subject for **putet**. He hopes to command a cohort of auxiliaries (**curam . . . cohortis**) even as he dissipates the family fortune (**omni maiorum censu**) by spending all his money (**bona**) on horses. The army was a normal way of social advancement, but to accede to the *praefectura cohortis sociorum* required that one possess the equestrian census of 400,000 sesterces.

Praesepibus < *praesepes*, *–is*: " stalls," generally of stables, but can refer to brothels as well.

Flaminiam = *via Flaminia*, the main road north from Rome.

Automedon = the charioteer of Achilles, clearly ironic.

61–2. The **puer** is a character right out of New Comedy, spending the family fortune on horses to impress a woman of low virtue.

Lacernatae: i.e. dressed in a *lacerna* (**line** 27) and hence like a man. This would either be a sign of moral turpitude or indicate that she is a prostitute.

Se iactaret = "he was boasting."

63–8. "In such a world, is it not pleasing to stand on the street corner and fill up notebooks with images of vice?" **Ceras** = "wax tablets," on which poets wrote their first drafts.

Quadrivio < *quadrivium*, *–i*: "an intersection of four streets."

Sexta cervice: the **signator falsi** is borne (**feratur**) on a litter (**cathedra**) carried by six slaves, a sign of opulence.

Iam = "already," soon he will have more slaves. The largest litters were carried by eight.

Patens ac nuda paene cathedra: he does not travel with the curtains closed, but openly flaunts his luxury and shows no shame for the means through which he attained it. The **cathedra** was a woman's chair.

Multum = adverbial. **Maecenate**: Maecenas was known for his effeminacy and luxury. Naturally, this is not mentioned by Horace.

Signator falsi = "the signatory of a forged document," often a will, as can be seen from parallel usages (e.g., Juvenal 8.142).

Gemma . . . uda: the signet ring was wetted to prevent the wax from adhering.

69–72. "Now upper class matrons poison their husbands." **Molle Calenum**: a light wine from Cales. This is the direct object of **porrectura**.

Rubetam < *rubeta*, *–ae*: the bramble frog, whose liver was deemed poisonous.

Instituit: she not only practices the dark art, she instructs her less knowledgeable relatives (**rudes . . . propinquas**).

Melior Lucusta = "a superior Lucusta," Nero's preferred poisoner.

Per famam et populum = "in the face of scandal and before the eyes of the people" (Duff 1970): a zeugma or nonparallel usage of the same construction. **Per populum** refers to the practice of funerals passing through the Forum on the way to burial sites outside the city walls.

Nigros: from the effects of the poison.

73–6. "Propriety is praised and punished." **Brevibus Gyaris** = Gyara, a small island with poor water in the Aegean. It was used for deportations. **Carcere dignum**: prison was not a common means of punishment in Rome. Jail cells were used as holding areas before execution.

Aliquid: the repetition adds a bitter ironic quality.

Praetoria = "mansions, palaces."

Mensas = a common luxury item, much attacked in the literature of the period. The most expensive were made from a single slab of citrus wood.

Vetus, *–eris*: an adjective in one termination, modifying **argentum**: silver plate worked by an old master.

Stantem extra pocula caprum: a goat stands in high relief from the cup.

77–8. **Nurus** = genitive singular, "daughter-in-law."

Sponsae = "fiancées."

Praetextatus = "wearing the *toga praetexta*." This was worn before the *toga virilis*, which was normally donned between the ages of fourteen and sixteen. See **Horace 1.2.16.** This is one precocious adulterer!

79–80. "If talent is lacking, *indignatio* will write my verse," Juvenal's most famous line. **Cluvienus** is otherwise unknown.

81–126. Juvenal begins a second programmatic survey of vice. This second part concentrates on money and degraded social relations, especially between *patronus* and *cliens*.

81–6. "Whatever men have done or desired since the time of the flood. This is my subject." **Ex quo**: understand *tempore*.

Nimbis tollentibus aequor = ablative absolute. "With rain-clouds raising the water (level)" (Braund 1996a).

Poposcit < *posco, –ere, poposci*: "to ask, request."

Saxa: **Deucalion** and his wife, **Pyrrha**, were told that they could regenerate the human race after the flood by tossing the bones of their mother over their shoulder. They correctly surmised that the reference was to Mother Earth whose bones were stones. **Mollia** describes the stones as they come to life.

Maribus nudas . . . puellas: Pyrrha plays the procuress. The rot goes deep. This is a recurrent theme in Juvenal. The present is fallen and decadent. The past was just as bad if not worse. The rhetoric allows for no real development, either narrative or moral, since there is no standard to which we can appeal.

Farrago = "a mash of grain fed to cattle." Juvenal here is clearly playing on the traditional explanations of the origins of the word *satura* [12–13].

87–90. "When was there ever a better time to write satire?" **Sinus** = the fold in the toga used as a pocket.

Alea = "dice," understand *sumpsit* or a similar verb.

Loculis comitantibus = "accompanying small money boxes," as opposed to the **arca** of the following line.

Itur = impersonal passive, "there is no going." This is not small-time gambling for pleasure.

Casum < *casus, –us*: "chance," but also the literal throw of the dice, derived from *cado*.

Tabulae = "the gaming table."

Posita . . . arca = ablative absolute: "with the treasure chest put down / staked."

Luditur = "the game is played."

91–3. An epic description of the battles surrounding the gaming table. **Dispensatore** = the slave in charge of the **arca**.

Simplexne furor = "is it just madness?"

Sestertia centum = 100,000 sesterces, one quarter of the equestrian census.

Horrenti = "shivering."

Reddere = "to give as his due." Cato, no great humanitarian, says a slave should receive a new shirt and blanket every two years. The flip side of excess is neglect of one's social duties.

94–6. The same people who build extravagant pleasure palaces and eat seven-course meals neglect the most basic care of their *clientes*. Compare **lines 75–6.**

Quis: take with **avus**, a man of times past.

Fercula = "courses." The normal number was three.

Secreto = "by himself." This was not a dinner party, but pure personal indulgence.

Sportula = originally a little basket of food left for one's poorer clients, later money to buy food. Far from sharing his table with his dependents, the rich man sets their **parva . . . sportula** out on the **primo limine**. The **sportula** is the topic of **lines 95–126**, the most developed set of scenes in the poem.

Turbae . . . togatae: dative of agent. These are Roman citizens.

97–9. "Even so, he worries lest he spend an extra penny." **Suppositus** = "added fraudulently."

Agnitus < *agnosco, –noscere, –novi, –nitum*: "to recognize."

99–101. Even the patricians are reduced to waiting in line at his door. **Troiugenas** = those claiming birth from the Trojans who accompanied Aeneas.

Praecone < *praeco, –conis*: "herald, auctioneer." See Horace 1.6.86.

102–9. But the foreign freedman (**libertinus**) claims pride of place since he is richer than the noble-born Romans. **Euphraten** = the Euphrates, the great river of Mesopotamia, modern Iraq.

Molles . . . fenestrae = "effeminate piercings."

Arguerint = "would prove," potential subjunctive.

Licet = "even though."

105–6. Quinque tabernae = "five shops." This **libertinus** represents the kind of aggressive petty-bourgeois social climber that Cicero seeks to defend the traditional aristocracy against when he argues that only agriculture and large-scale mercantile ventures are fit sources of income for a *bonus*, a member of the senatorial or equestrian élite.

Quadringenta = 400,000 sesterces, the equestrian census.

106–9. Quid confert . . . optandum: "why does one wish for?" literally "what wished for thing does the **purpura maior** bring?" **Purpura maior** = the broad purple stripe on the tunic that indicates membership in the senatorial order.

Laurenti = Laurentum, a town in Latium Pliny describes as good for grazing sheep.

Conductas . . . ovis = "hired sheep." **Corvinus** has been reduced to sharecropping. **Corvinus** = M. Valerius Messalla Corvinus, scion of the family of the great Messalla who is cited as a model of eloquence by Horace (1.10.29, 85). Consul in 58 CE, he lived in such reduced circumstances that Nero granted him a pension.

Pallante = Pallas, an immensely wealth freedman of Claudius, who certainly outstripped our friend by a good margin. **Licinis** = people like Licinus, a Gaul captured by Julius Caesar. He served him as *dispensator* and was emancipated in his will. He was later *procurator* of Gaul (16–15 BCE) where he amassed an immense fortune.

109–16. Wealth conquers all. Money is god. **Expectent, vincant**, and **cedat** = jussive subjunctives. **Honori**: see Horace 1.6.11.

Pedibus . . . albis: foreign slaves put up for sale had their feet marked with chalk.

Sanctissima divitiarum / maiestas: understand *est*. Note the elevated diction.

Pecunia, in fact, was a minor goddess but did not have a temple.

115. These are traditional abstract virtues that were personified as gods and possessed temples. This is almost certainly a parody of Horace's "Carmen

Saeculare" 57–60, *iam* ***Fides*** *et* ***Pax*** *et Honos Pudorque / priscus et neglecta redire* ***Virtus*** */ audet, apparetque beata pleno / Copia cornu* (Martyn 1979: 225).

116. According to the scholiast, storks nested in the temple of **Concordia** at the entrance to the Capitoline. When a passerby would utter a traditional prayer of salutation, the storks would seem to answer by clattering (**crepitat**) with their bills.

117–20. "How are those who just scrape by supposed to survive when even the consul (**summus honor**) counts on the **sportula**?"

Rationibus = "accounts."

Fumus = "firewood."

120–2. "Even those who can afford litters come for the mere pittance that is offered." **Densissima . . . lectica** = "a vast crowd of litters," poetic singular for plural.

Centum quadrantes: a *quadrantis* is a small copper coin worth one fourth of an *as*. An *as* is worth one fourth of a sesterce. The sum here is twenty-five *asses*, the traditional amount for the *sportula*.

123–6. "One fine fellow even used an empty sedan chair (**sellam**), with the curtains drawn (**clausam**) to claim a double portion for an absent wife (**coniuge**)."

Nota iam . . . arte = "a well known trick."

127–46. Like Horace in **1.6.111–31**, Juvenal runs through a typical day, but his is a constant rush of unremunerated labor that ends with the satisfaction of the greedy *patronus*' untimely death (line 144). We are far from Horace's **vita solutorum misera ambitione** (1.6.129), but we are equally far from the life of republican commitment pictured in Lucilius.

127–31. First are the *salutatio* and the morning's legal business. **Distinguitur** = is divided.

Sportula: here conflated with the *salutatio*, on which see **Horace 1.6.101.**

Iurisque peritus Apollo: referring to the statue of Apollo in the Forum Augusti, the legal center of Rome.

Triumphales: understand *statuas*, which is also the assumed antecedent of **quas**. The Forum Augusti was decorated with statues of famous generals lining the colonnade of the temple of Mars Ultor.

Nescio quis . . . Aegyptius atque Arabarches: **Arabarches** (also *Alabarches*) = a customs official who collected taxes in Egypt and Judea. The person referred to is generally agreed to be Tiberius Julius Alexander, an apostate Jew who became a Roman *eques* and later prefect of Egypt. His father had held the post of **Arabarches**.

Non tantum meiere: understand *sed etiam cacare*.

Fas est implies divine sanction, whereas pissing on the statue of the emperor was a treasonous offense.

132–4. We fast forward to the ninth hour and time for dinner at the great man's house. Work normally ended at the seventh hour and the eighth was spent in exercise (Martial 4.8). The discontinuity between these lines and those that immediately precede them has been felt to be severe, and some posit a lacuna after **line 131. Abeunt**: they give up on their desires (**vota**) of receiving an actual dinner invitation.

Caulis < *caulis, –is* m.: "cabbage,"

Miseris = dative of agent with **emendus** (*est*).

135–6. **Rex horum**: an ironic appellation for the greedy *patronus* who dines on delicacies by himself. **Rex** is never a complimentary term in Latin.

137–8. "Although they are well equipped to feed many, they dine from a single table." **Pulchris et latis orbibus** = "beautiful and broad round tables," made from a single horizontal cut from the tree trunk. These were objects of great expense. See **line 75.**

Comedunt: the switch from the singular to the plural indicates that it is the class of *patroni* in general who are being indicted.

Patrimonia: not only are they ungenerous but they are prodigal, literally consuming their family fortunes in private orgies of gluttony.

139. **Parasitus** = *cliens.*

139–40. **Luxuriae sordes**: a wonderful oxymoron.

140–1. **Gula**: note the grotesque reduction of the glutton to his gullet.

142–3. Juvenal turns to direct address. "Your penalty awaits you in the bath." **Crudum pavonem** = "undigested peacock," a luxury dish.

144. See **Persius 3.98–106** on strokes triggered by gluttons taking hot baths.

145–6. The *patronus* becomes nothing more than a **nova fabula** that circulates among the other dinners going on throughout the city, as his death is applauded by his erstwhile friends (**plaudendum . . . amicis**).

147–71. The final section returns to the explicitly programmatic and generic concerns of the first part. Here Juvenal makes his famous vow to satirize only the dead.

147–9. One of the most striking images in Juvenal. The thesis of this passage is: "We have reached the high point which is also our low point. The future holds no turning back. Everything will always be the same." The very rhetorical structure of the passage imitates its semantic content. The enjambment of the first and second lines gives the impression of vice literally spilling over from one line into the next. "The limit has been reached and surpassed; the young will do and desire the same." Normal vertical relations of value have become conflated. The **minores** ("the lesser ones" or "the younger ones") are to be no less than their "betters," the **maiores**, who are also their "elders." The phrase **eadem facient** likewise recalls the beginning of the poem where Juvenal had warned **expectes eadem a summo minimoque poeta (line 14)**. In short, one of the founding paradoxes of this poem is Juvenal's thesis that "everything has become the same, only worse."

Ferguson (1979) explains the logic of the image as follows:

> *omne in praecipiti vitium stetit*: a vivid visual picture of a gang of vices standing on a high peak with a steep drop in front of them, but what does J mean to convey by it? (a) We should not lose altogether the idea that vice has "peaked"; it is implicit in the picture. Future generations cannot go higher . . . (b) But *in praecipiti* stresses the point that it has nowhere to go but down. This in turn links two ideas: (i) that vice leads to disaster . . . (ii) that it is there for the satirist to push it over the precipice. The picture is not quite a single one.

The point that the picture is not single is well made. "In reaching the highest we have topped the lowest. There is no place to go but down." Yet, this is not the sole reversal. For, if the satirist does push vice over the precipice, do we then reach the moral high ground by crashing to bottom, or just the abyss? Standards of measure and comparison are turned against one another (compare 3.6–9, and **lines 22–3**). Logical development is thus impossible; the only avenue open for expansion is the accumulation of examples, which is typical of Juvenal's style.

149–50. "Open wide the sails!" i.e., don't hold back. **Sinus** here = "the belly of the sail."

150–7. Juvenal introduces the mandatory interlocutor in programmatic satires found in **Horace 2.1** and **Persius 1**. As in both of those cases, the interlocutor warns the satirist of the dangers of his chosen genre. **Illa** modifies **simplicitas**. Juvenal here invites a double reading. On the one hand, the writers of old possessed a certain uncomplicated sincerity. On the other hand, he warns us that his satire is anything but simple.

Priorum = predecessors in the genre. That they simply wrote whatever pleased them is clearly not true in the case of either Horace or Persius. That is how Horace portrays Lucilius, but he does so for his own purposes.

153–4: **"cuius . . . non"**: while clearly meant to be read as a quotation from Lucilius, this sentence must be a paraphrase, since the shortening of the final *o* in **audeo** is a feature of post-Augustan poetry.

Mucius: see **Persius 1.114**.

155–7. "Put **Tigillinus** in your verse and you'll end up one of Nero's party torches." **Tigillinus** = C. Ofonius Tigillinus: Nero's prefect of the praetorian guard, a notoriously bloodthirsty sexual monster. Otho forced him to commit suicide in 69 CE. On the juxtaposition of Tigillinus with Lucilius, see Freudenburg (2001: 244).

Taeda = the *tunica molesta* or "robe of pain." Nero and Tigillinus both had the habit of dipping those who incurred their displeasure, especially Christians, in pitch and other flammable materials and then using them as torches.

Sulcum deducis harena: i.e., when you body is taken down and dragged through the sand. The manuscripts are divided between *deducit* and *deducis*, just as they are divided between *lucebit* and *lucebis*. If *deducit* is kept, a lacuna after 156 must be posited as Housman noted (1931). It is more economical to assume the same error in both locations.

Fixo gutture = "pinned by the throat."

158–9. "Should poisoners therefore get off scot-free?"

Aconita = "aconite," a deadly poison, reputedly undetectable in wine.

Pensilibus plumis = "on suspended feather pillows," i.e. in a well-padded litter. Note the contemptuous alliteration of liquids, plosives, and sibilants.

160–70. Once more, the interlocutor reminds Juvenal that discretion is the better part of valor.

Cum veniet contra = "when you run into him."

Compesce < *compesco, –pescere, –pescui*: "to hold in, restrain."

161. **"Hic est"**: It is enough to simply point someone out to be labeled an accuser. See **Persius 1.28.**

162–4. You can write epic in peace. Compare **Persius 1** and **Horace 2.1**, as well as the opening panel of the present satire. **Committas**: "you can pit x against y." Imaginary battles are the safest.

Hylas: Hercules's pederastic beloved in the *Argonautica*. He was stolen by water nymphs when sent for water (**secutus urnam**). Hercules left the Argonauts to search for him and did not return to them. The story is treated at length in Propertius 1.20 and mentioned as a topic for treatment by Gallus in *Eclogues* 6.43–4.

165–6. On Lucilius, compare **Horace 2.1.39–41** for the same image and **Persius 1.114** for a cognate idea. **Infremuit** < *infremo, –ere, –ui*: "to growl."

167. **Sudant praecordia**: a striking image. Their chests begin to sweat.

168–70. Think it over before you enter battle. **Voluta** < *voluto, –are*: "to tumble about, turn over, consider."
Tubas = "battle trumpets."
Galeatum < *galeo, –are*: "to cover with a helmet."
Duelli = archaic for *belli*, giving a mock epic tone.

170–1. In that case, let's see what the dead will allow. **Flaminia** and **Latina**: understand *via*. The *via* Latina ran south, as the *via* Flaminia ran north. All the main roads leading from Rome were lined with tombs.

3

Umbricius is leaving Rome for Cumae, Aeneas's initial landing spot in Italy. Rome is no longer a fit place for a Roman. It is overrun by Greeks, just as Troy was when Aeneas fled. Besides, the streets are unsafe, and living in the tenements leads to an early death (Freudenburg 2001: 267).

This satire is the model for Samuel Johnson's "London." In many ways, it is Juvenal's most stinging, and certainly his most complete, indictment of contemporary Rome. It is also one of the most rhetorically ambiguous poems in the corpus. Juvenal deliberately separates himself from the speaker, and he does not join **Umbricius** in his decision to leave Rome.

Umbricius, whose name is derived from *umbra*, meaning "shade" or "shadow," is a parody of the figure of the satirist, a shadow of Juvenal himself. He represents a set of traditional Roman values that is out of place in the imperial metropolis. As such, he serves as both an indictment of that metropolis and a candid admission of the satirist's own anachronism. There is something more than a little quaint and contradictory about his old-fashioned moral outrage expressed in rhetorically crafted hexameters and declaimed in the grand style. *Umbra* was also used of the hangers-on to great men, those who "shadowed them." Umbricius thus represents the archetypical displaced *cliens* of the Roman imperial metropolis. Lastly, *umbra* refers to the soul of a dead man, his shade. **Umbricius** is both someone who is already dead to Rome and someone who is moving from the scene of life (Rome) to a kind of rural netherworld. Cumae is where Aeneas made his entrance into the underworld.

We might say that **Umbricius**, then, represents the ghost of satire past [32, 75–6]. He is a figure who no longer has a place in contemporary Rome, except as the unwelcome hanger-on of great men. We are a long way from Lucilius! Still there is no going back to a mythical Golden Age, as Juvenal admits in his own decision to stay in Rome. Thus, beneath the simplicity of Umbricius's moral outrage lies a much more sophisticated and ambiguous appreciation of the second-century CE Rome, one not that far removed from

Ovid's famous quip in the *Ars* (2.277–8), *Aurea sunt vere nunc saeculae*: *plurimus auro / venit honos* ["This truly is the Golden Age: most honor comes from gold"]. The satirist both condemns, and founds his identity on, the venality that surrounds him. It is the source of his *indignatio* and of his and the reader's enjoyment.

1–3. "Although I am saddened by the departure of my old friend from Rome, I praise his decision." **Cumis** = locative of Cumae, the place where Aeneas and his Trojans first made landfall in Italy. It is also the site to which Daedalus fled when escaping Crete and the location of one of the entrances to the underworld. Ironically, Daedalus represents precisely the kind of versatile Greek that Umbricius seeks to flee by leaving Rome. Cumae was the oldest Greek colony in Italy. At this time, it had become somewhat depopulated, but hardly abandoned (Braund 1996a).

Sybillae = the Sybil, a wise woman and prophet who escorted Aeneas on his journey to the shades below (*Aeneid* 6).

4–5. Umbricius has found the proverbial *locus amoenus* of pastoral—the opposite of Rome's urban bustle—on the doorstep (**ianua**) of Rome's poshest resort, Baiae, proverbial for sexual license (see Propertius 1.11). Is this the simple life or an urbane caricature?

Secessus = genitive of description.

5–9. "I'd prefer a desert island to the Subura." Note the way the enumeration of the dangers of life in the city moves from the concrete, material, and real (**incendia, lapsus tectorum**) to the abstract and ridiculous (**Augusto recitantes mense poetas**). This kind of deliberate anticlimax is one of Juvenal's favorite rhetorical strategies.

Prochytam = Prochyta (modern Procida), a barren island off the coast of Baiae.

Subura = a street leading from the Forum to the Esquiline gate. It was notorious as Rome's red-light district.

Incendia: compare **lines 197–222.** Fire was a constant danger amid Rome's tightly packed tenements (*insulae*), as were collapses (**lapsus**: see **lines** 190–6). On poetry recitations (**recitantes . . . poetas**), see 1.1.1–14.

10–11. As Umbricius's household goods are packed into a cart, he pauses. **Raeda** = "a four-wheeled coach." See **Horace 1.5.86.**

Veteres arcus madidamque Capenam = the arches of the *aqua Marcia*, which ran above the *porta Capena*, one of the southern gates leading to the *via Appia*. It was the first aqueduct to make extensive use of arches. **Arcus** = accusative plural.

12–18. Here we descend into the valley where **Numa** once met Egeria, and where now Jewish beggars live. The descent from past mythic greatness and nostalgic fantasies of ethnic purity to present poverty and xenophobia is emblematic of Umbricius's perception of Rome as a whole.

Numa = the legendary second king of Rome, to whom is attributed the basic structure of Roman civic religion. In some traditions he is portrayed as an early adherent of Pythagoras, in others he receives instruction from the water nymph Egeria who was worshipped with Diana at Aricia, one of the oldest shrines in Latium. As one of the *Camenae*, she would have been identified with the Roman equivalent of the Greek Muses. Juvenal, in a typical ironic, deflating move, portrays Egeria as Numa's *amica* or "girlfriend," thereby granting little credence to Rome's fantasies of divine foundation even as he uses their borrowed grandeur as a foil to present decadence. This is a sophisticated satire that consistently devours its own assumptions, without ever retracting its assertions.

Nemus = "sacred wood." **Delubra** < *delubrum, –i*: "shrine, temple." The reference is to a shrine to the *Camenae* located neat the *porta Capena*.

Locantur < *loco, –are*: "to place, set; to lease, invest."

Iudaeis: with the fall of Jerusalem in 70 CE, Rome's Jewish population increased substantially. Many would have been refugees and beggars. Their refusal to participate in Roman civic religion was met with fear and mistrust. Ancient religion was by and large syncretistic rather than exclusive. This made monotheism appear to be a rejection of communal values.

Quorum cophinus fenumque supellex = "whose possessions are a hamper and hay." The reference is obscure, but is thought to refer to a box designed to keep food warm on the Sabbath when cooking was prohibited, though, others citing Martial, see it as a reference to eggs being sold (3.47.14). They would be packed in straw for protection.

15–16. These lines are quite difficult, although the gist seems clear. The whole wood has now been ordered to pay rent to the people (as the Jews do to the central treasury for the use of the wood) and has consequently been reduced to beggary. **Mendicat silva** = a bold personification. **Eiectis . . . Camenis** = ablative absolute.

17–18. Speluncas dissimiles veris: artificial grottoes had replaced the formerly pristine setting of Numa's nocturnal encounters.

18–20. The artificiality of the now marble-lined shrine is lamented. **Tofum** < *tofus, –i*: "tufa." Does the fact that the **numen** of the waters is not **praesentius** indicate to us that the speech delivered by **Umbricius**, which takes up the rest of the satire, is lacking the inspiration of the **Camenae**?

21–8. Umbricius begins: "in a city where there is no place for honest skills, we propose to flee to where **Daedalus** once rested his tired wings." The absurdity of Umbricius's elevated diction and his use of epic periphrasis is to be savored at the opening of a speech that purports to lament the loss of traditional Roman simplicity.

Artibus . . . honestis: the term is an oxymoron, since the man who is truly *honestus*, "noble, honorable," practices no *ars*, "trade, technical skill, profession," in the strict sense. It is the descendant of **Daedalus**, the **esuriens Graeculus**, who is the practitioner of a thousand skills or *technai*. See **lines 75–8.**

Eadem modifies **res**, which is the subject of **est**, **fuit**, and **deteret**. **Deteret** < *detero, –terere, –trivi, –tritum*: "rub away." The object is **aliquid**. **Exiguis** = ablative of separation. "My means today are less than they were yesterday and tomorrow they rub away something from what little is left." The final clause is oddly reflexive but not unprecedented. See Courtney's discussion (1980).

Nova canities = only an apparent oxymoron, "the first dusting of grey hair."

Lachesi = the Fate who spins (**torqueat**) the wool that is the thread of a man's life.

Bacillo < *bacillum, –i*: "a small staff."

29–33. "Only those who can turn black into white can live in Rome. There's no place for an honest man." **Artorius . . . et Catulus** are unknown. They are, however, traditional Roman aristocratic names but are here portrayed as practicing trades. As Cato and Cicero agree, such occupations are inherently dishonest and hence not to be practiced by a Roman aristocrat, who is to live off his rents or, as in the case of Juvenal and Umbricius, depend on patronage [75].

Aedem conducere, flumina, portus, / siccandam eluviem: then as now public works contracts were assumed to be opportunities for graft.

Portandum ad busta cadaver: being an undertaker was a servile occupation, unfit for a free man let alone an *honestus*.

Hasta = "spear." Auctions were held "under the spear" as a sign of the transfer of *dominium*, the practice was a relic of sales of the spoils of war. **Artorius, Catulus**, and the like are metaphorically selling themselves into slavery, but the possibility of a literal sale is not foreclosed. Another example of Juvenal punctuating a rhetorical series with an ironic climax.

34–8. While the once respectable sell themselves into virtual slavery, the former companions of gladiators now give lavish games and are the toast of the town. **Cornicines** < *cornicen, –cinis*: "horn player," a player of music that accompanied gladiatorial displays.

Comites: these horn players traveled with the troop of gladiators. They are not only the companions of the lowest of the low, but also provincials to boot.

Buccae: their cheeks are puffed out from blowing the trumpets.

Munera: the technical term for gladiatorial games, which were conceived as a gift to the *populus*, originally associated with aristocratic funeral games.

Verso pollice: the crowd would signal the fate of a fallen gladiator by either pressing their thumbs down (*premere pollicem*) to save his life or by turning them up (*vertere pollicem*) to condemn him. The exact nature of the gestures denoted by these phrases is debated, but not their significance.

Populariter = "by the will of the people."

Conducunt foricas et cur non omnia = "they lease the public toilets and why not everything else." These men hold the concession on the pay toilets and collect the revenues. In short, in spite of their spectacular ascent, they still take on the lowest jobs. Why should there be any limits?

38–40. Read: **cum sint quales [quos] ex humili magna ad fastigia rerum extollit . . . Fortuna. Fastigia** < *fastigium*, *–i*: "the top of a gable or pediment, the summit."

Iocari = deponent.

41–8. What is an honest man like me to do at Rome?

Motus = accusative plural. I am no astrologer who can promise the early death of a father to an expectant heir.

Ranarum < *rana*, *–ae*: "frog," either a form of divination or the harvesting of poison or both. See **1.70**.

Quae mittit = the presents the adulterer sends.

46–8. The context shifts to corruption in provincial administration, which will be the central topic of the next ten lines. **Comes exeo**: a technical term for accompanying a governor to his province. **Me . . . ministro** = "with me as his servant."

Mancus < *mancus*, *–a*, *–um*: "maimed, infirm, crippled."

Extinctae . . . dextrae = genitive of quality modifying **corpus non utile**.

49–50. No one is picked for such missions unless he is a willing accomplice.

51–2. Honest confidences bring one nothing.

53–4. If you want to be dear to the corrupt, you need to be able to blackmail them. **Verres** was a corrupt governor famously prosecuted by Cicero.

54–7. All the gold of the Tagus should not be worth your loss of piece of mind in blackmailing your patron (**magno . . . amico**). **Tagus** = a river in Spain and Portugal famed for its gold. **Tanti** = genitive of value. **Opaci** = "shady" as Martial 1.49.15–16 attests.

Ponenda = "which will have to be given up," because of either subsequent betrayal or death. The gerundive also has the force of obligation. Another level of meaning, then, would be "which should be given up." These are not mutually exclusive translations.

58–125. This section deals primarily with Rome being overrun by Greeks and those from the Greek east. There is no longer room for a Roman in Rome.

58–61. **Quirites** = Roman citizens, a traditional term ironically juxtaposed with **Graecam urbem**. *Urbs*, as often, = Rome.

Quamvis quota portio faecis Achaei? = "And yet, what part of the dregs is actually Achaean?" Umbricius's point is that he is talking less about mainland Greeks, the descendant of Homer's Achaeans, than about the assorted flotsam of the Greek-speaking east that flooded into Rome.

62–5. "We are overrun with a flood of Orientals!" **Orontes** = the main river in Syria.

Chordas obliquas = the sambuca, a type of harp.

Gentilia tympana: small drums used in the worship of Cybele, the Phrygian Great Mother goddess. They are native (**gentilia**) to the east. She was worshipped by castrated priests (*Galli*).

Circum = Circus Maximus, a common place for prostitutes (**prostare**) to be found.

66. **Barbara lupa** = "foreign prostitute." *Lupa* was a common slang term. **Mitra** = "turban."

67–8. "Romulus, even your native stock dons strange garments." **Trechedipna** = a Greek compound meaning "run to dinner." It seems to denote a kind of shoe, but is used in this sense only here. In Greek, the term regularly refers to parasites who cadge free dinners. It is clearly pejorative. Note the way in which traditional Latin terms are interwoven with rare Greek words in these lines to reproduce on the linguistic level what Umbricius claims is occurring on the social level.

Quirine = Romulus in his divinized form.

Ceromatico < *ceromaticus, –a, –um*: "rubbed with *ceroma*." *Ceroma* was a compound of wax, dirt, and oil used by Greek athletes in the *palaestra*, where they wrestled in the nude. Romans traditionally looked down on the practice.

Niceteria = "prizes given for athletic victories," another Greek term.

69–72. They flock from round the world to the Esquiline and Viminal hills. **Sicyon** = a town in the Peloponnese. **Amydon** = a town in Macedonia. **Andros** and **Samos** = islands in the Aegean. **Tralles** and **Alabanda** = towns of Asia Minor.

Esquilias = the "Esquiline hill." The Esquiline is elsewhere in Juvenal portrayed "as a pleasant place (11.51) where rich patrons live (5.77–8)" (Braund 1996a).

A vimine collem = periphrasis for the unmetrical *Viminalis*: "the Viminal hill." *Vimen* = "willow." The *Viminalis* was the site of a number of grand houses.

Viscera = "heart and soul" (Courtney 1980), generally taken as predicate nominative with **dominique futuri**. It may also be a direct object of **petunt**, in which case **dominique futuri** would be genitive singular. In the first reading, the Greeks come to occupy pride of place in the houses of the great, thereby displacing the Roman *clientes*, and eventually coming to inherit the house, fortune, and social position of their former masters. In the second reading, they are portrayed as parasites who attack the vitals of the great houses (compare Catullus 77) and worm their way into the heart of the house's future heir. The two readings, while grammatically mutually exclusive, are ideologically complementary. The grammar is ambiguous, and the ambiguity is poetically productive.

73–4. Understand *est huic*. **Audacia perdita** = "criminal daring."

Isaeo = Isaeus, an Assyrian rhetorician who came to Rome in 97 CE, noted by Pliny for the fullness of his delivery.

74–8. "Just say what you want him to be. The hungry Greek can be anything." Versatility is not a positive value in ancient societies that placed a premium on the preservation of traditional roles. See Plato's insistence in the *Republic* that each person only play one role in his ideal *polis*.

Aliptes = "masseur."

Schoenobates = "tight-rope walker."

Graeculus: the diminutive is pejorative.

Iusseris: understand *si*.

79–80. "It was not a Moor, a Sarmatian, or a Thracian who learned to fly, but a native Athenian!" The reference is to Daedalus. **In summa** = "in sum."

81. Conchylia = neuter plural, referring to clothes dyed purple with a compound made from conch shells. They were considered exotic signs of luxury, just like the word itself.

81–3. "Will that one brought by the same wind as the imported groceries be better received in the houses of the wealthy than I?" **Signabit** = "will affix his seal." Witnesses to wills and contracts affixed their seals in order of social importance.

Toro meliore: the seating order at Roman dinner parties was strictly hierarchical. See **Horace 1.4.86–91** and **2.8.**

Pruna et cottana = "plums and figs," neuter nouns. Understand *advecta sunt*.

84–5. "Is it worth nothing that my childhood was nourished by the Sabine olive?" **Hausit caelum** = "drank in the air."

Aventini = the Aventine, the most southerly of Rome's seven hills.

Baca . . . Sabina: the Sabines were proverbial for their rough simplicity.

86–93. "The Greekling is the consummate flatterer." **Quid quod** = "what of the fact that?"

Adulandi gens prudentissima = "a people with a genius for flattery." The construction *prudens* + genitive gerund is attested in Tacitus (*Annales* 3.69).

Longum invalidi collum cervicibus aequat / Herculis: "Hercules is the bull-necked type, short and thick" (Courtney 1980).

Antaeus was a giant and son of Earth. He was defeated by Hercules who would not let him touch his mother's body, the source of his strength.

90–1. This final comparison is awkward and difficult. As usual in Juvenal, the last item in a series is a rhetorical anticlimax. The flatterer favorably compares his patron's thin voice (**vocem angustam**) to that of a cock who bites the hen (**gallina**) in the course of mating (Courtney 1980). **Gallina**, however, recalls *Gallus*, the term for the castrated priests of Cybele. Hence, Martial (13.64.1–2) makes a similar pun, *succumbit sterili frustra gallina marito. / hunc matris Cybeles esse decebat avem*. **Marito** in Juvenal is attracted into the relative clause, when logically it goes with **ille**.

93–7. "The Greek is a flexible actor who can play all the women's parts." While it is true that men played female parts in the ancient theater and that most actors were foreign-born, there is a clear sexual innuendo in these lines as well. There were three main female parts in New Comedy: *meretrix* (Thais); *uxor*; and *ancilla* or maid (Doris).

Palliolo < *palliolum* diminutive of *pallium*: "cloak." The image works on two levels. On the one hand, the *pallium* was an outer garment that was frequently discarded when there was work to be done. On the other, the Greek actor is so good (or so effeminate) he can play a woman even without his/her clothes on, as the next lines make clear.

Tenui distantia rima = "parted by a thin crack."

98–100. "This is not a trick mastered by a few well-known names. It's a nation of actors." **Antiochus**, **Stratocles**, **Demetrius**, and **Haemus** are all the names of famous actors from the period.

100–3. "He can display whatever thought or emotion is needed. He can even sweat (**sudat**) on command." **Cachinno** < *cachinnus*, *–i*: "giggle."

Nec dolet: "it's all an act."

Endromidem < *endromis*, *–idis*: a rough cloak worn after exercise, the equivalent of a sweatshirt.

104–8. "We can't compete with people who are able to throw up their hands in praise every time their protector has burped loudly or peed in a straight line."

Trulla = "drinking cup." The sound comes from polishing off the last drops as it's tipped up (**inverso . . . fundo**). Other explanations have been advanced, but none carry much conviction. When in doubt, the most literal reading is to be preferred.

109–11. "Nothing holy is safe from the randy Greek's crotch." The exact reading of the line is in dispute. Most manuscripts have *aut* after **nihil**, which is metrically impossible. The general sense is clear. Willis's (1997) **illi et** gives good sense and makes paleographic sense.

Inguine: see **Horace 1.2.26.**

Laris: the *Lar* stands as metonymy for the *domus*.

Sponsus = "betrothed, bridegroom." It is less the fact that the Greek seduces both men and women that offends than that he violates the sacred boundaries of the *domus*. See **Horace 1.2.116–19.**

Levis = "smooth, effeminate, beardless."

112. "If he can't get these, he'll bend his own patron's grandmother over."

113. This line is universally believed by recent editors to be an interpolation, even though it is attested in all manuscripts. It appears to be a gloss on the motivation behind the Greek's sexual conquests by an unimaginative scholiast who combined **lines** 52 and 57 (Ferguson 1979; Courtney 1980; Braund 1996a; Willis 1997: xxi–xxii).

114–15. "And while I'm on the subject of Greek vice!" **Transi** and **audi** = imperatives.

Gymnasia: we'll pass over the scandalous things that happen in the place where the Greeks exercise in the nude.

Abollae < *abolla, –ae*: a heavy woolen cloak favored by certain Greek Cynic and Stoic philosophers, although worn by other people as well. The phrase presents something of a conundrum. One of the scholiasts cites it as proverbial, but it is not repeated elsewhere. The real question is whether **maioris abollae** is genitive of possession or value. The answer in this case is both. The crime is both that of a philosopher who is more important (**maioris**) than the mid-level fops we have been discussing so far—taking **abolla** as metonymy for the person wearing it—and of greater weight.

116–18. "A Stoic informer (**delator**), nourished on the shores of the river Cydnus, killed his patron Barea." **Ad quam Gorgonei delapsa est pinna caballi**: represents a complex figure. The reference in the first place is to P. Egnatius Celer from Berytus who, according to Tacitus (*Annales* 16.21–33), was called as a witness against his patron and pupil (**discipulum**) Barea Soranus. Egnatius appears to have been educated in Tarsus, a major center of philosophical study. Tarsus, on the banks of the river Cydnus, "was supposed to owe its name to [a] ταρσός (feather or hoof) of Pegasus which fell there" (Duff 1970). Pegasus was born from the blood of the Gorgon Medusa when Perseus beheaded her.

The same line is also a gloss on Persius **Prologue** 1, *Nec fonte labra prolui caballino*, in which the satirist claims not to have the Greek learning that characterizes Egnatius and that Umbricius here disclaims. The Hippocrene too was said to have been created by the hoof of Pegasus.

119–22. "There is no place for a Roman here where the Greek reigns supreme." **Protogenes**, **Diphilus** and **Hermarchus** are generic names as **aliquis** indicates.

Partitur = deponent.

Gentis vitio = "on account of the national vice," greed?

122–5. "He fills the great man's ear with slander and all other clients are shown the door." **Facilem**: "note how the indictment of the plausible Greek includes an indictment of the gullible Roman aristocrat" (Ferguson 1979).

Exiguum + **de** + ablative, instead of the more usual **exiguum** + partitive genitive.

Nusquam minor: understand *quam Romae.*

Iactura = "a throwing away, disposal."

126–89. In Rome today, the poor man has no chance. Money talks and character counts for nothing. The satiric target in this sections shifts from foreign to domestic menaces. Poverty is demeaning and the rich no longer meet their obligations to the poor. With the collapse of the republican political system, patronage was no longer central to aristocratic success, but became a burden. What had once been a complex personal, political, and social relationship between unequal partners, had become a financial liability to the wealthy.

126–30. "Furthermore, what can the duty or merit of the poor man be here, if he always comes running lest his fellow client, the praetor, beat him to the morning *salutatio?*" Rome has become a rat race. **Porro** = "furthermore."

Ne nobis blandiar = "lest I flatter us [Romans]" in comparison to the Greeks just discussed.

Curet nocte togatus / currere = "takes the trouble to run before dawn, already dressed in his toga." Roman citizens were expected to wear the toga to the morning *salutatio.*

Cum = "since."

Lictorem: lictors carrying the fasces accompanied official magistrates. It was their job to clear the way. Here the praetor uses his official entourage to go legacy hunting and to best the dutiful client in seeking the patronage of a wealthy childless magnate.

Dudum vigilantibus = "long since awake."

Orbis < *orbus, –a, –um*: "childless."

130. This line is replete with ironies. First, **Albina** and **Modia** are otherwise unknown, childless women. Women were not normally the objects of the morning *salutatio*, but these are wealthy widows. It is impossible to tell the gender of **orbis** until you reach these names. The natural assumption from context, however, is that it would be masculine until these proper names are reached. Second, **collega** is a technical term used for a fellow office-holder, but here may be taken to mean a fellow *cliens* or *captator* ("legacy hunter"). However, Umbricius and the praetor are anything but colleagues. The whole point of this passage is the image of the rich and powerful beating the poor and honorable in the race for patronage. Yet to what extent does the poor man deserve the **meritum** accrued from his **officium**, if he is not attending a great man but cruising the wealthy widows in search of a bequest? There is more than a touch of sexual innuendo. Alternatively, **collega** may refer to the other praetor, in which case Umbricius and his lot have even less of a chance.

131–6. "Here, rank, birth, and character subordinate themselves to money." This is the world upside-down. On the one hand, people subject themselves to slaves for money. On the other, huge sums are spent on high-class mistresses (**Horace 1.2.28–30**). This leaves little for the needy client.

Cludit latus = a military term that originally meant to cover the flank. This would normally be on the left-hand or shield side, so that right hand might work freely with the sword. It became a phrase meaning "to accompany respectfully." The irony here is that it is not the great man himself who is escorted but his slave. Thus, the freeborn son of freeborn parents (*ingenuorum filius*) subordinates himself to a slave (**servo**).

Alter = "the other of two," hence the slave.

Quantum in legione tribuni: tribunes were well paid, though we do not have exact figures for the period. Money that in the past would have gone to benefit the community by paying a military tribune is now going to the sexual indulgences of slaves.

Calvinae vel Catienae = aristocratic names. A Junia Calvina was condemned for incest with her brother under Claudius (Tacitus, *Annales* 12.4.8).

Illam palpitet: a degrading image that serves to deflate the aristocratic aura created by the upper-class names in the previous line.

134–6. Meanwhile, you and I can hardly afford the services of a common streetwalker. **Vestiti . . . scorti**: not the lowest class of hooker who was displayed naked on the street. *Scortum* nonetheless is a harsh word. Juvenal does not here refer to a refined *meretrix*.

Chionen: a Greek accusative meaning "Snow-White." As Martial attests, it was a common name for prostitutes.

Sella = a type of couch associated with brothels as early as Plautus. The verb **deducere** leads us to believe it was used for display purposes, not the act itself.

137–46. "The poor man's testimony is not even accepted in court, though he be as honest as Numa himself." **Hospes numinis Idaei** = Publius Cornelius Scipio Nasica. In the second Punic War, the Sybilline books said Rome would be saved if the Great Mother goddess, Cybele, were brought from Mount Ida in Phrygia to Rome. Scipio was chosen as her escort owing to his reputation for outstanding purity.

Numa: see **line 12.**

Qui / servavit trepidam flagranti ex aede Minervam = Lucius Caecilius Metellus who as *Pontifex Maximus* in 241 BCE rescued the Palladium from the burning temple of Vesta. He lost his sight in the attempt.

Censum = "net worth."

Paropside < *paropsis, –idis*: "a dish."

Iures = subjunctive from *iuro, –are*: "to swear."

Licet = "although."

Samothracum < *Samothraces*: "the inhabitants of Samothrace," home of a mystery cult second in fame only to that at Eleusis in this period.

Dis ignoscentibus ipsis = "with the gods themselves forgiving" because, as Courtney (1980) observes, the **pauper** "perjures himself through necessity, not wickedness."

147–51. The poor man's attire is the source of callous laughter. **Quid quod** = "what of the fact that?"

Hic idem = the pauper.

Toga sordidula: togas were difficult to keep spotlessly white in Rome's muddy streets and having them cleaned was expensive.

Calceus = "shoe."

Consuto volnere = ablative absolute: "when the wound has been sewn up." In the first instance, this refers to the hole in the shoe, but it also refers to a deeper wound to the poor man's dignity.

Crassum / atque recens linum = "a sloppy new set of stitches." **Recens** is an adjective in one termination.

Non una cicatrix = "more than one scar."

152–3. One of Juvenal's most brilliant and penetrating epigrams.

153–8. People born of equestrian stock who have fallen on hard times are displaced in the theater by the sons of whores and pimps. **Inquit** = "someone says."

De pulvino . . . equestro: i.e., from the seats reserved for the equestrian order in the theater.

Res legi non sufficit: equestrians were required to have a census worth 400,000 sesterces.

Fornice: see **Horace 1.2.30.**

Pinnirapi = "feather snatcher," a Juvenalian coinage for the gladiator fighting the Samnite who wore a plumed helmet. **Iuvenes** here = *filios*. **Cultos** is ironic, inasmuch as gladiators were generally thought to represent the dregs of society.

Lanistae = "a trainer of gladiators."

159. In 67 BCE, L. Roscius Otho passed the *lex Roscia theatralis* that reserved the first fourteen rows behind the senators for the equestrians. It was revived by Domitian. **Vano** here = "foolish, empty-headed."

160–2. "Three indignant questions highlighting the pre-eminence of wealth and the neglect of the 'poor' in their exclusion from the conventional ways of increasing one's property (marriage, inheritance and patronage) in Rome (*hic*)" (Braund 1996a).

Gener = predicative: "as a son-in-law."

Sarcinulis = diminutive of *sarcina*: "luggage," i.e., the wealth the girl brings to the household. The periphrasis and diminutive indicate an informal usage.

Consilio = the aedile's group of advisors and assessors who aided him in his duties as superintendent of weights and measures, traffic regulations, water supply, and public order.

162–3. The poor citizens of Rome should have left long ago. **Agmine facto** = *en masse*: an allusion to the secessions of the plebs in the fifth century BCE and the proposal to move the city to Veii after the Gauls's sack of Rome circa 387 BCE.

Tenues = "poor."

164–7. Umbricius here parodies Aristotle in the *Nicomachean Ethics* on the difficulty of the poor man exercising virtue due to lack of means. **Emergunt** < *emergo, –mergere, –mersi, –mersum*: "to cause to rise up, to rise, to come to the top."

Domi = locative.

Conatus, *–us*: "the attempt."

Magno = ablative of cost. Note the insistent repetition.

Hospitium = "hospitality," and by metonymy "guest quarters, a room."

Servorum: note that Umbricius and Juvenal are members of the genteel poor, not the urban proletariat. They still have slaves, if only a few. Compare **Horace 1.6.116.**

Frugi is an indeclinable adjective, meaning "frugal," modifying **cenula** (< *cena*). The diminutive indicates that this is not a lavish affair.

168–70. "Although you will make a show of homely virtue, it is embarrassing to eat off simple crockery." A Roman gentleman needed to keep up appearances if he was not to lose face. **Fictilibus** < *fictilis, –is*: "earthenware."

Negabis: note the use of the indicative. This is not a conditional construction. Juvenal or Umbricius's imaginary interlocutor is thus actually **translatus**, which must mean he is "transported" in his mind, i.e., he imagines himself in the midst of, and thus makes a show of, traditional Italic simplicity.

Marsos: the Marsi were a rustic tribe that served as an archetype of antediluvian simplicity.

Sabellam = Sabine, another type of primitive frugality.

Contentusque . . . Veneto duroque cucullo: the scholiast remarks that Veneto refers either to the fact that this hood (**cucullo**), which would not be worn in the city, comes from the northern province of Venetia or to its dark blue color. As Friedländer observes (1962), a thriving wool production was found throughout Cisalpine Gaul. Several commentators note that dark blue cloaks were the conventional dress of poor men in comedy. **Duro** indicates that the fabric was coarse.

171–2. In most of Italy, "the toga is only worn for your funeral."

172–9. Umbricius calls forth a scene of pastoral simplicity in which peasants celebrate a festival with homespun theatricals in an atmosphere of equality and innocence. **Herboso . . . theatro** = a simple stage set up in a field.

Si quando = " if ever," sometimes written as one word.

Pulpita = "platform, stage."

Exodium = "a farce," probably of the native Italian, Atellan type, despite the Greek term. Compare **6.71. Notum** indicates that the same piece was played each year. Sophisticated city dwellers demanded more variety.

Personae pallentis hiatum = "the gaping mouth of the whitened mask." Actors in all Roman drama, except mime, wore masks.

Habitus < *habitus, –us*: "condition, style."

Orchestram = the semicircular space between the stage and the audience. Originally the dancing floor for the chorus, in Roman times it became the place where the senatorial order sat.

Clari velamen honoris = "as the garb of glorious office." The irony of *clarus* indicates that Umbricius's idealized rural magistrates do not take themselves more seriously than their office admits. Compare **Horace 1.5.34.**

Tunicae as opposed to *togae*.

180–3. In Rome, however, people go into debt just for their clothes. **Vires** = "means."

Nitor = "splendor."

Arca = "cash box."

Ambitiosa paupertate: a wonderful oxymoron.

183–5. At Rome everything has its price. **Cossum** = a noble whose slaves one apparently had to bribe just to be admitted to the morning *salutatio*. A man by the same name was consul in 60 CE.

Veiiento = nominative, a noble named at 4,133. A bribe is necessary to get him to look at you, without even speaking (**clauso . . . labello**).

186–9. **Ille . . . hic**: there is controversy over whether these pronouns refer to the slaves one has to bribe in **lines 183–5** (Ferguson 1979) or their noble owners (Friedländer 1962; Braund 1996a). Parallelism with the previous lines as well as sense favors the latter solution.

Metit barbam: understand **amati**. Cossus of course did not trim his favorite's beard but arranged for its ceremonial first clipping. This was a traditional celebration for Roman boys. The extension to house slaves is a clear perversion of what would have been normal practice in the time of Cato.

Crinem: wealthy Roman households often kept good-looking slave boys who served at table. Their hair was kept long. When they reached manhood, it was cut with some ceremony.

Libis < *libum*, *–i*: "a birthday cake offered to the gods."

Venalibus < *venalis*, *–e*: "on sale, to be sold." No expense was spared, and clients were expected to pay for cakes and participate in ceremonies in which their own status as inferior to that of their *patronus*'s slaves was ratified.

Accipe et istud fermentum tibi habe: "take the money and keep the cake for your self," the client's angry words. **Fermentum** = literally "yeast" and, by metonymy, that in which it is used.

Peculia: the savings accumulated by many slaves and sometimes used to purchase their own freedom. Such nest-eggs were not legally recognized, but the practice was common.

190–231. City dwellers have to live in constant fear of collapsing buildings and fire. Yet, even in disaster, the poor man is treated worse than the rich. The country costs less and you can grow your own vegetables.

190–2. **Praeneste** (modern Palestrina) a town outside Rome, perched high on a hillside, hence **gelida**.

Ruinam = "the collapse of a building."

Volsiniis < *Volsinii*: a town in Etruria, 130 kilometers northwest of Rome.

Gabiis < *Gabii*: a town twelve miles east of Rome.

Proni Tiburis arce = "on the citadel of downward-facing Tivoli."

193–6. Rome is a city of towering buildings supported by the thinnest of pillars. **Tibicine** < *tibicen*, *–inis*: " a flute, pillar, or prop."

Vilicus = the "landlord's agent," i.e., the superintendent.

Rimae < *rima, –ae*: "crack, fissure."

Securos . . . iubet dormire: a more ironic phrase would be hard to imagine. **Securos** = "without a care."

Pendente . . . ruina = "with a collapse hanging over our heads."

197. **illic**: i.e., outside Rome.

198–202. Fire was a constant danger in Rome's crowded tenements. This is a very rich passage. The first thing to note is the spatial contrast evoked by **imus** and **ultimus**, and the corresponding inversion of fortunes they represent. This inversion of expected hierarchies is a common rhetorical strategy in Juvenal. Yet, it is a legitimate question to ask whether this detail should be read as topographically significant, or as a piece of simple realism since, as Ferguson observes, the poor were regularly housed at the top of Roman tenements (1979). Juvenal however, uses this detail for purposes that exceed simple mimesis. Consider the passage's final line: **molles ubi reddunt ova columbae**. Note the marked contrast between the delicacy of the phrase **molles columbae** and the projected interlocutor's fate. Observe also how the predominance of vowels and liquids in line 202, echoing the cooing of the doves, underlines this contrast, particularly when compared with the harshness of **Ucalegon, tabulata tibi iam tertia fumant** (Ferguson 1979). Moreover, as *Odyssey* 12.62–5 reveals, doves were created by Zeus, and carry him ambrosia. Thus, the poor man, who by virtue of being at the bottom of the income ladder lives at the top of the tenement, ironically enjoys the company of the very companions of the gods. By the same token, when fire comes, he has the furthest to fall. The total image, then, includes an implicit final scene of our poor wretch jumping from the tenement's top floor as the flames approach, while the doves ascend to heaven.

Poscit aquam = "shouts fire."

Frivola = "meager furnishings."

Ucalegon: the name indicates epic parody. At *Aeneid* 2.311, during the sack of Troy, we find the same name surrounded by the same vocabulary of fire and *ruina*. *iam Deiphobi dedit ampla* ***ruinam*** */* ***Vulcano*** *superante domus; iam proximus* ***ardet*** */* ***Ucalegon***. **Ucalegon** first appears in *Iliad* 3.148 where it is the name of one of Priam's counselors. It is derived from the Greek οὐκ ἀλέγειν, meaning "not to care." In Homer's context, it would be an aristocratic name denoting ease. In Vergil's, it would be primarily a Homeric citation, though the meaning of the name would provide an added pathos. In Juvenal, the name serves both to point the contrast between Rome's past epic grandeur and its contemporary squalor and to provide, through its original meaning, an example of Juvenalian irony.

Tabulata . . . tertia = "the third story." The unnamed interlocutor addressed in **tibi** lives higher still and so is unaware (**tu nescis**) of the danger below him (οὐκ ἀλέγειν).

Trepidatur = "the alarm is raised," impersonal passive.

Tegula = "roof tile."

203–7. The poor man loses all his meager belongings. Compare **Horace 1.6.114–18. Cordo**: presumably the poet of **1.2.** Martial mentions a poor Cordus in 3.15.

Procula = ablative of comparison with **minor**: although unknown, one imagines a preternaturally petit paramour.

Urceoli = diminutive < *urceus*, *–i*: "jug or pitcher," in apposition to **ornamentum**. Compare **10.64.**

Abaci = a table-top, generally made of marble (**marmore**), often used for the display of silver. Cordus, however, can only afford diminutive crockery.

Parvulus . . . cantharus = "a tiny tankard," a deliberate oxymoron. A **cantharus** is normally a drinking cup of some size.

Chiron: a statue of the recumbent centaur formed the support of the table.

Vetus: an adjective in one termination.

Cista = a wicker hamper for keeping clothes. Cordus cannot afford a proper *capsa* or bookshelf.

Opici = a Greek version of *Osci* or "Oscan," used pejoratively of Romans as uncultured barbarians. Thus Courtney (1980) observes, "the juxtaposition of *divina opici* . . . is particularly pointed, as if the mice would have had more respect for the *divina carmina* if they had known Greek."

208–9. **Cordus** lost the little bit of nothing he had.

209–11. Nobody, however will help him when he is naked and begging. Understand *est* in the main clause.

212–13. When the rich man's home collapses, it is all very different. **Asturici . . . domus**: *Asturicus* is the name of a previous owner. He is otherwise unknown, but the name suggests a noble with a military connection to the province of Asturia in Spain. The current owner's name is **Persicus (line 221).**

Horrida = "disheveled," a sign of mourning. Understand *est.*

Pullati = "dressed in black." On **proceres**, see **Persius 1.51.** Understand *sunt.*

Differt vadimonia praetor = "the praetor postpones court proceedings," i.e., for an official day of mourning.

215–20. People come running to offer gifts of great expense to replace what has been lost while the fire still burns (**adhuc**).

Marmora is one of the **inpensas** or "things bought" for reconstruction.

Nuda et candida signa = hendiadys or the rhetorical figure of saying "one thing through two": "beautiful nude statues." Note the ironic contrast with **nudum** in **line 210.**

Euphranoris et Polycliti: noted artists of the fourth and fifth centuries BCE.

218–20. The manuscript is much disputed here. Courtney (1980), Braund (1996), Willis (1997) and all accept Housman's proposed emendation of *aera* for **haec**. The main argument seems to be that "the feminine **haec** is surprising" (Courtney 1980). As Friedländer (1962) had pointed out, however, this is precisely what makes it typically Juvenalian.

Asianorum vetera ornamenta deorum = works of art looted from temples in Asia Minor.

Forulos < *forulus*, *–i*: " a tiered book case."

Mediam = "to stand in the middle."

Minervam = goddess of wisdom and learning.

Modium < *modius*, *–i*: "a peck." There was so much money that it was measured rather than counted.

220–2. **Persicus** made out so well he is now suspected of having set fire to his own house. A Persicus who was consul in 34 CE might be a relative. **Orborum**: Persicus is childless, which is why he is the object of such lavish generosity.

223–5. "If you could tear yourself away (**avelli**) from the distractions of the city, you would find how much cheaper it is to live in the country." **Sora**, **Fabrateria** and **Frusino** were all small towns in Latium.

Tenebras < *tenebrae*, *–arum*: "darkness" and hence "a dark place or room," but it also means "death," which is what a dark room in a tenement will procure for you on both the literal and the metaphorical levels.

Conducis < *conduco*, *–ere*, *–duxi*, *–ductum*: "to rent."

226–9. An idealized image of farming life whose atmosphere owes much to Tibullus. **Puteus** = "a well." **Reste** < *restis*, *–is*: "a rope." **Movendus**: modifies **puteus**; the well is so shallow there is no need for a rope. **Diffunditur**: subject = **puteus** standing by metonymy for its contents.

Facili . . . haustu presents a mild paradox. Compare Tibullus 1.1.7–8, *ipse seram* ***teneras*** *maturo tempore vites / rusticus et* ***facili*** *grandia poma manu*. **Amans** recalls that the Tibullan *rusticus* is also a lover. **Haustu** < *haustus*, *–us*: "a drawing of water."

Bidentis < *bidens*, *–dentis*: a type of hoe. See Tibullus 1.1.29, *nec tamen interdum pudeat tenuisse* ***bidentem***.

Vilicus = "bailiff, manager."

Pythagoreis: the Pythagoreans were vegetarians and hence with a well-watered garden you could easily offer them a hundred banquets (**epulum . . . centum**).

230–1. "It is something to say that you are the owner of even just one lizard (**unius . . . laceratae**)." Samuel Johnson famously interpreted this to mean the amount of land on which one could find a lizard. Lizards being very common in Italy, this would be small indeed. At the same time, there is a clear deflation of Umbricius's claims in the image of asserting one's mastery over a lizard.

232–314. Juvenal takes us through an expanded version of his recounting of a typical day at **1.127–34** (compare **Horace 1.6.111–31**) from one sleepless night to the next evening's mugging. Besides the sheer expansion, there are two major innovations in this example of the satiric topos: 1) the emphasis on the contrasting conditions of rich and poor, thus continuing the theme of the previous section; and 2) the vivid description of the dangers of life on the streets in Rome.

232–6. The poor man who is ill perishes from want of sleep in Rome. **Aeger** = substantive.

Peperit < *pario, –ere, peperi, partum*: "to bring forth, bear, produce."

Inperfectus is universally glossed as "undigested," even as it is admitted that the usage is rare. Only one parallel can be cited: Celsus 4.23.1. It does not, however, refer to a failure to digest one's food so that it remains in the stomach (**haerens ardenti stomacho**), but to food that has passed through the bowel before the process of digestion is complete as a consequence of advanced dysentery. The parallel is not exact. More precisely, the problem is that it is not undigested food that makes you sick, as the commentators suggest, but the sickness that causes you not to digest your food. That the poor would eat bad food that would make them sick is not only a reasonable assumption, but it is also the only interpretation that fits with the structure of the passage, which depends on a contrast between rich and poor. Therefore, it should be the **cibus** itself that is bad and the cause of the illness (see Spencer 1935 in his note on Celsus 4.22.1). **Inperfectus**, thus, should be translated as "defective." Labriolle and Villeneuve (1964) recognize the problem when they add to the standard translation ("insuffisament digérée") that the food not only remains in the stomach undigested but "y fermente" ["ferments there"], thus acknowledging the need for a gloss to explain the causal relation between **cibus inperfectus** and **aeger**.

Meritoria = "lodgings let out for rent, often in another home" (*Digest* 7.1.13.8).

Dormitur = impersonal passive.

Caput morbi: a striking phrase.

236–8. "The noise of the traffic and livestock moving through the narrow lanes of the neighborhood at night will raise even the soundest sleeper." Wheeled traffic was banned in Rome during the day, except for wagons carrying construction materials, thus allowing business to be transacted in a relatively unobstructed manner. The nights were consequently quite noisy. **Raedarum**: see **Horace 1.5.86.**

Stantis convicia mandrae: *mandra* is a Greek term referring to animal pens. **Convicia** means "insults or reproaches." So this passage has been understood three different ways: 1) the noise coming from the animals whose way is blocked by traffic in the street (**mandrae** = subjective genitive); 2) the cursing coming from the herdsmen presumed to accompany them (**mandrae** = subjective genitive); 3) the cursing coming from the neighbors at the lowing beasts who disturb their rest (**mandrae** = objective genitive). While the first two have generally been favored, there is no reason not to assume that Juvenal was a sufficiently competent poet to have allowed for all three.

Druso = the emperor Claudius, famed for his ability to sleep through entire law cases.

Vitulisque marinis = "seals." The Elder Pliny says no animal sleeps more deeply (*Historia Naturalis* 9.15).

239–42. "The rich man, however, passes through the traffic easily and sleeps even on the run." **Ingenti . . . Liburna** = a large warship in the fashion of those used by the Liburni, a people from the Eastern Adriatic. The conceit of the wealthy man's litter sailing over a sea of upturned faces (**ora**) is striking and original.

Obiter = "in passing."

243–6. "The wave (**unda**) he sails over blocks our passage" **Ante tamen veniet** = he will beat us even in his sleep.

Cubito < *cubitus, –i*: "elbow."

Assere < *asser, –eris*: "a pole for a litter."

Tignum = "a beam of wood."

Metretam < *metreta, –ae*: "a small barrel."

247–8. I am covered with filth and constantly trod upon (**calcor**). **Pinguia crura lutro**: understand *sunt*.

Planta . . . magna: a humorous evocation of the many feet treading upon poor Umbricius.

Digito = "toe."

Clavus = "nail," here synecdoche for the soldier's (**militis**) hobnail boots.

249–53. Umbricius describes an outdoor party or picnic held in the street. This was more than likely a food distribution by a guild or *collegium*. **Sportula** here does not refer to a gift of food or money from a patron to a client, as it does elsewhere in Juvenal, but to the actual basket in which the food was given and from which the institution gets its name. **Sportula** is thus metonymy for "picnic."

Culina = "a portable stove."

Corbulo = Cn. Domitius Corbulo, a general under Claudius and Nero, known for his size.

Quas recto vertice portat / servulus infelix et cursu ventilat ignem: a hilarious and pathetic picture of the diminutive slave, head piled high, fanning the flame that warms his master's picnic dinner as he runs behind him.

254–61. The streets are crowded and dangerous with wagons hauling marble and lumber. The juxtaposition of the freshly mended tunics (**tunicae sartae modo**) with the massive wagons is particularly effective. **Coruscat** = "shakes."

Serraco < *serracum, –i*: a wagon used for hauling heavy goods.

Abies = "fir."

Nutant = "sway."

257–61. "In the event of an accident, you'd be crushed beyond recognition." **Axis** = the antecedent of **qui** and subject of **procubuit**: "an axle," and hence by metonymy a "wagon."

Saxa Ligustica = marble from Luna in Etruria, formerly part of Liguria: the best quality Italian marble.

Obtritum = "crushed."

More animae: just as the soul slips from the body at the time of death, so the body of the poor man slips away without notice.

261–3. "Meanwhile at home, all goes forward in anticipation of the master's bath and dinner." A scene of great pathos. **Patellas** = "plates."

Striglibus = syncope for *strigilibus* < *strigilis -is*: "a scraper used in the bath." The slaves prepare the bath to be taken before dinner.

Guto < *gut{t}us, –i*: "a small, narrow-necked jar" to be filled (**pleno**) with oil. An oil massage preceded the bath.

264–5. "But he shivers on the shore of the Styx." **Novicius**: "a new slave." "We have just seen his old slaves. He, recently free, is now the slave of death" (Ferguson 1979).

Porthmea = Greek masculine accusative: "ferryman."

Caenosi < *caenosus, –a, –um*: "muddy."

Alnum < *alnus, –i*: "the alder tree": metonymy for Charon's boat and the wood from which it was made.

Quem = aliquem qui.

Trientem < *triens -entis*: "the third part of an *as*," a small coin. Traditionally a coin was placed in the mouth of the dead to pay their passage to the underworld.

268–72. "Think of the other perils of the night!" **Quod spatium tectis sublimibus** = "what a height there is to the lofty roofs" (Braund 1996a).

Testa = "tile."
Rimosa < *rimosus, –a, –um*: "cracked."
Silicem < *silex, silicis*: "pavement."

272–5. The ways of death are legion; only a fool (**ignavus**) goes to dinner with his will unmade (**intestatus**). **Vigiles**: "The windows seems to be watching for him to pass" (Ferguson 1979).

276–7. "You hope and pray that they are content to pour out the contents of their open basins (**patulas . . . pelves**)." Better garbage and excrement on your head than the basin itself.

278–82. If you survive the falling crockery, the mugger waits in ambush. **Qui nullum forte cecidit**: a true psychopath, the thug is agitated because he has not yet killed anyone that night.

Noctem patitur lugentis amicum / Pelidae: the comparison of the thug's discomfort at not having killed anyone to Achilles's grief for the death of Patroclus is almost absurdly ironic. **Pelidae** = "of the son of Peleus," i.e., Achilles.

281. I have deleted this patently spurious line following Ferguson (1979), Courtney (1980) and Braund (1996a).

282. **Somnum rixa facit** = "a brawl makes for a good night's sleep."

282–5. Although young (**inprobus annis**) and (**mero fervens**) drunk, the mugger has the good sense to avoid the rich man and his sizeable retinue. **Coccina laena** = "scarlet cloak," a sign of wealth.

Lampas = Greek, nominative feminine singular: "lamp, torch."

286–9. "I, however, am fair game." **Filum** = "wick."
Prohaemia = an elevated Greek word: "prelude."
Vapulo = "I am beaten."

290–2. You have no choice but to submit to the humiliation. **Stari** = Impersonal passive: "to halt."

292–6. "Whose cheap wine have you been drinking? Whose peasant cuisine have you been eating? What synagogue do you frequent?" the thug demands. **Aceto** < *acetum, –i*: "sour wine or vinegar."
Conche < *conchis, –is*: "a type of bean."
Sectile porrum = "green leeks," cut before they grow to a head.
Sutor = "cobbler," an icon of the lower classes.
Elixi vervecis labra = literally "the lips of a boiled castrated ram." It is

metonymy for boiled sheep's head. But the literal meaning ensures the reader's repugnance. *Vervex* was also a slang term for "blockhead." The thug manages to slip in an implicit insult against the victim and his host. The ram's impotence mirrors the victim's.

Calcem < *calx, –cis*: "heel" and hence "kick."

Proseucha = "synagogue," a Greek term.

297–9. "Whether you speak or remain silent, you still take a beating." **Vadimonia . . . faciunt** = "make the victim post a bond that he will appear in court," i.e., the thug charges the victim with assault.

299–301. A bitter epigram. **Libertas** [21–32] was the property of the upper classes during the republic. Nonetheless a concept of basic legal rights was part of what it meant to be *civis Romanus*. Now it means the freedom to ask that you return (**reverti**) home with a few of your teeth (**paucis . . . dentibus**).

302–4. After the muggers come the burglars. **Qui te spoliet** = relative clause of characteristic: "the kind of man who would loot you bare."

304 is a golden line of the ABCAB variety, with interlaced participles flanking the verb on one side and nouns on the other. The high-flown rhetoric contrasts markedly with the content.

Compago = the shutters that closed street-front stores in Rome. They were locked with a chain and were quite noisy. The burglars come out only once the shutters fall silent.

305–8. "The bandits have all come to Rome, after they've been chased from the swamps and the forests." **Grassator** = "robber."

Palus Pomptina = the Pomptine marshes southeast of Rome, a desolate refuge for bandits and criminals.

Gallinaria pinus = the Gallinarian pine forest near Cumae, a known assembly point for pirates.

Vivaria = "game preserves." The brigands, chased from the countryside, once they reach Rome are like the proverbial fox in the chicken coop.

309–11. We risk having to forge so many manacles that we shall run short of ploughs and hoes. "How is it that heavy chains are not in the forge (**fornace**), how not on the anvil (**incude**)?"

Marra = "a mattock."

Sarcula = "hoes."

312–14. "Happy was Rome when it was satisfied with a single jail." Prison was not a common punishment in Rome. Incarceration's main use was as a way-station on the road to execution.

Proavorum atavos = "the great-great-great-grandfathers of the great-grandfathers," i.e. remote ancestors. **Atavos** and **saecula** are accusatives of exclamation.

Regibus = the seven kings of early Rome.

Tribunis = the period from 445–367 BCE when military tribunes with consular power were appointed on occasion.

315–22. "I could go on and on, but it's getting late. I'll come to listen to your satires the next time you retreat to the countryside." Umbricius departs. **Iumenta** = the pack animals pulling his cart, not an allusion to pastoral as some suggest.

Mulio = "mule driver," the final *o* is short.

Aquino: Aquinum is generally taken to be Juvenal's birthplace [73].

Helvinam Cererem: Ceres was the goddess of grain. This phrase probably refers to a temple built by the Helvii, a prominent family from the area. A local inscription (*CIL* x 5382) refers to a dedication to Ceres by a Juvenal [73].

Converte = imperative < *converto, –ere, –i, –versum*: here, "invite."

Saturarum: Umbricius here portrays himself as the ideal **auditor** of Juvenal's satires. The whole of *Satire* 3 thus becomes a self-reflexive (and hence ironic) project in which the ideal image of satire's audience, as projected by the genre, becomes the speaker.

Caligatus = "wearing hobnail boots" of the kind worn by soldiers and (as Courtney 1980 shows) rustics.

6

These excerpts present the highlights (or lowlights) of Juvenal's book-length satire on women. *Satire* 6 is without doubt one of the most misogynistic poems ever produced. It is also one of the funniest. The poem presents a distinct challenge to the modern reader: how do we reconcile our enjoyment with the frequently offensive content?

We cannot simply say: "It's a joke, Juvenal didn't mean it." Roman humor is rife with misogyny (Richlin 1984 and 1992). Fear and hatred of women are deeply rooted in Roman culture, as they were in most of the ancient Mediterranean. It is no accident that the basic meaning of *virtus* is "manhood" and only secondarily "courage" and "virtue." Juvenal 6, therefore, merely makes us deal in a more concentrated manner with an aspect of the culture that is present in every artifact we possess from the ancient world.

Yet Roman misogyny and this poem are not simple matters. Both are complex structures that perform multiple and sometimes competing functions within the culture. Thus, as Barbara Gold has observed, *Satire* 6 is at least as much about deviant men as it is about women (1998: 382):

> This *Satire* [. . .] is usually entitled "Against Women," "The Legend of Bad Women," "Roman Wives," "The Ways of Women," or the like. True, many different types of women are pilloried in this diatribe, but there are as many men who act/dress/look/think/like women here and elsewhere in Juvenal's *Satires*. Moreover, when women themselves are described, it is in the language of, by analogy, or in relation to men. The satirist's primary fascination seems to be with men who act like women (or, at least, who do not act like men) or women who appropriate and imitate normatively male behavior; he has a special horror of disintegrating gender codes and holes in the net of the system.

Likewise, as Peter Green notes (1974: 25), the satire is also at least as much about the breaching of class boundaries as it is about gender. It is less the fact that women might be unfaithful than that they might be so with members of the lower classes that is particularly offensive to the satirist. Misogyny turns out to be a complex term that encodes a variety of social and behavioral expectations not just concerning women, but equally (in fact more so) men. What we see in *Satire* 6, on one level, is *satura* functioning as a tool of social discipline in much the same ways as it does in Lucilius [20, 29, 75].

Yet, the poem itself is no simple exemplar of an ideological truism, it is also an elaborately staged rant. While one cannot discount its misogynistic venom, neither can one take its statements at face value. They are characterized throughout by hyperbole, self-canceling propositions and rhetorical anticlimaxes. The speaker of this poem is not the voice of reason. He is an extremist who frequently undercuts his own arguments [76]. This is part of the humor.

The poem thus begins with an evocation of the Golden Age when **Pudicitia** still walked the earth. The most memorable scene of this little homily, however, is not a lost world of female virtue, but the image of the primitive acorn-belching husbands who ruled the roost. By the same token, one must take none too seriously the satirist's claim to his friend Postumus that since marriage is unthinkable there are only two alternatives: pederasty or suicide (**lines 30–7**). The very extremity of the position can hardly have been intended to convince the average Roman of its veracity, but rather to draw attention to its artistic and rhetorical construction: the more outrageous the claim, the greater the skill of the writer who presents it in a plausible manner.

1–20. "In the Golden Age when Saturn ruled, **Pudicitia** ('Chastity') still walked the earth and women were poor but faithful to their unkempt, acorn-belching husbands. All that changed when Jupiter began to rule." Juvenal's Golden Age is a harsh primitive time, not one of spontaneous plenty such as that found in Tibullus. On the myth of the five ages (Gold, Silver, Bronze, Heroic, and Iron) see Hesiod's *Works and Days* 109–201. In the Augustan period, the return to the Golden Age was widely evoked, as it was later in Neronian poetry (see Calpurnius Siculus 1.42–5). But as Winkler notes (1983: 30), for Juvenal "this precise satiric vignette of earliest human society with its picture of horribly unattractive, uncouth people shows that the old traditional view of life in the Golden Age no longer carries any value for Rome's modern times." In sum, the Golden Age was not a time before the fall, nor a time when justice prevailed. It was, instead, a time when people were too poor and too miserable to have the energy or opportunity to pursue vice. Adultery is reserved for those sophisticated enough to enjoy it, a Cynthia or a Lesbia; the **montana uxor** is not so much an image of virtue as one of disgust and repugnance.

1–10. The elaborate opening period announces that this will be satire in the grand style.

Montana . . . uxor: Juvenal's faithful woman is a grotesque hag living in a cave with her husband and livestock.

Sterneret < *sterno, –ere, stravi, stratum*: "stretch out."

Culmo < *culmus, –i*: "straw."

Cynthia is the name of Propertius's elegiac beloved. She is portrayed as beautiful, sophisticated, and unfaithful.

Tibi, cuius / turbavit nitidos extinctus passer ocellos = Lesbia, the beloved of Catullus, generally thought to be the Clodia Metelli that Cicero caricatured in the *Pro Caelio*. The allusion is to Catullus 3 on the death of Lesbia's sparrow (**passer**).

Ructante < *ructo, –are, –vi, –atum*: "to belch."

11–13. Juvenal gives two myths for the origins of humans: they were either born from oaks (**robore nati**) or made by Prometheus out of clay (**luto**).

14–18. Juvenal concedes that there might have been traces (**vestigia**) of **Pudicitia**'s former presence in the salad days of Jupiter's reign. **Aut aliqua** qualifies **multa . . . vestigia**.

Graecis iurare paratis / per caput alterius: Romans traditionally swore on their lives or on something dear to them, and hence called down the wrath of the gods if they failed keep their oath. The perfidious Greeks, however, Juvenal says, swear by the head of someone else. See 3.58–125.

Caulibus = "cabbages": indirect object like **pomis**. The vegetarian diet hints at the simplicity of the Golden Age.

Aperto . . . horto: i.e., without a wall.

19–20. **Astraea** = a daughter of Zeus and the personification of justice. She was said to be the last of the immortals to leave the earth. She became the constellation Virgo.

Hac = Pudicitia.

21–37. The focus now shifts to the satirist's friend, Postumus, whose contemplation of marriage ostensibly occasions the satire.

21–2. Postumus is otherwise unknown. **Vetus**, an adjective in one termination = neuter substantive like **anticum**.

Concutere = "to shake or rattle," and hence implicitly to commit adultery.

Fulcri < *fulcrum, –i*: "headboard."

23–4. "Before the Iron Age brought forth any other crime, the Silver saw adultery."

25–7. "Knowing this are you still preparing to get married?" **Sponsalia** = the contract of betrothal.

Nostra modifies **tempestate**.

Pignus here = "engagement ring."

29. "What sort of demon has driven you to this?" **Tisiphone** = one of the three Furies. They had snakes (**colubris**) for hair.

30–2. "Can you bear a wife when suicide is a perfectly reasonable alternative?" **Restibus** < *restis, –is*: "rope."

Caligantes = "dizzying."

Aemilius pons = the main bridge over the Tiber.

33–4. "Why not try pederasty?" **Pusio** = "little boy."

35–7. "It's really so much easier." Note, however, that pederastic poetry such as Tibullus 1.4 complains that boys make the very demands that Juvenal here denies. The irony would not have gone unnoticed.

Lateri < *latus, lateris*: "flank," i.e. "groin."

Anheles < *anhelo, –are*: "to pant."

38–59. "Ursidius was famed for his adulteries, but now he wants heirs and a chaste wife." There is disagreement among the commentators on whether he is to be identified with Postumus. The use of the second person in **line 42** indicates, however, that the person addressed is not Ursidius and hence the latter should not be identified with Postumus.

38–40. Lex Iulia = *lex Iulia de maritandis ordinibus* (18 BCE). It provided legal and financial incentives for marriage and the production of heirs.

Turture < *turtur, –ris*; "turtle dove," a delicacy.

Iubis < *iuba, –ae*: "mane," or in this case, the "beard" of a mullet (*mullus*), another delicacy.

Captatore = "legacy hunter," the person who would have been providing these treats before an heir came into the picture. It is in apposition to **macello** < *macellus, –i*: "market." The legacy hunters have served Ursidius as a veritable delicatessen. See **1.37–9.**

41–4. "If Ursidius, the most notorious of adulterers, gets married, what will happen next?" **Maritali . . . capistro** = "the marital halter," the image is that of a horse extending its neck to assume the harness.

Texit < *tego, –ere, texi, tectum*: "to cover, hide."

Cista = "chest." *Latinus* was an actor in adultery mimes who often portrayed a character who hid in a chest to avoid being caught (see **1.36**).

45–6. "Call the doctors, he's gone mad. He seeks a girl of old-fashioned virtue." **Pertundite venam**: Juvenal orders the doctors to bleed him.

47–9. "You will need the help of the gods to find such a girl!" **Delicias hominis**: accusative of exclamation.

Tarpeium limen = The Capitoline temple of Jupiter, Juno, and Minerva. The legend of the Vestal, Tarpeia, who broke her vow of chastity for love of the Sabine Tatius, comes to mind in this context (see Propertius 4.4).

Auratam . . . iuvencam = a heifer with beaten gold wrapped round its horns, an extraordinary sacrifice.

Iunoni: goddess of marriage.

Capitis . . . pudici: "could be a periphrasis for *pudica*, 'chaste' but the following lines (50–1) turn this into a joke about the *os impurum* (mouth contaminated by oral intercourse): a whole group of these jokes revolved around the idea that people who engage in oral intercourse (a) have bad breath and (b) contaminate all they touch [. . .]. The Romans customarily greeted each other with a kiss" (Richlin 1986).

50–1. The reference in the first line is a bit obscure. The **vittas** are ribbons worn either by the celebrants (Richlin 1986) or placed on the cult statue (Courtney 1980) in a celebration of the fertility goddess Ceres. In either case, abstention from sexual relations was required for participation in the rites. Understand *sunt*.

51–2. Customary decorations for a marriage ceremony. **Corymbos** = clusters of flowers or ivy berries.

53–4. The ideal Roman woman was only married once (*univira*), although in the late republic and early empire among the upper classes this was an ideal more realized in the breach than in the observance. **Hiberina** is otherwise unknown.

55–9. "Country girls have a great reputation for chastity, but who knows what goes on in those hills and caves." **Gabiis** and **Fidenis** = locatives, small towns outside Rome.

Agello = diminutive of *ager*, "little farm."

Iuppiter et Mars: famed for their rapes of wandering maidens. The shift to the mythological is more bathetic than sublime. The two monosyllables draw the line up short.

60–113. "Women today are obsessed with lower-class and disreputable characters: actors, mimes, and gladiators." Respectable Roman citizens did not appear on stage and most gladiators were slaves. **Lines 60–77** concern the theater, 78–113 the arena.

60–1. **Porticibus** = the covered walkways that Ovid recommends in the *Ars Amatoria* as good places to pick up girls.

61–2. **Cuneis** < *cuneus*, *–i*: "a seating section in the theater," another hunting ground recommended by Ovid.

Quod . . . quodque: note the contemptuous neuter.

63–5. "The dancers and mimes cause female spectators to wet themselves and squeal with orgasmic delight." **Chironomon** < *chironomos*, *–i*: "mime," a Greek term in apposition to **Ledam**.

Molli = "effeminate, lascivious."

Tuccia and **Apula** = otherwise unknown.

Vesicae = "bladder."

Gannit < *gannio*, *–ire*: "to yelp or squeal."

65. This line is often bracketed, but there is no compelling reason. The transmission is all but unanimous. Some late manuscripts print *subitum* in place of **subito**, making the syntax more parallel, but this is hardly necessary and a scribe is more likely to "correct" **subito** to *subitum* than the other way around. Two texts omit **et**, which is metrically plausible, but again hardly necessary. Translate, "just as in an embrace, suddenly and at wretched length."

66. **Thymele** was an actress in adultery mimes. Even she can learn a thing or two watching Bathyllus. See 1.36. **Rustica** = feminine nominative.

67–70. "Others, who prefer more highbrow fare, sadly fondle Accius's dramatic paraphernalia between theatrical seasons." Juvenal contrasts the tragic theater, with the more titillating mime described in the previous lines.

Aulaea = "curtains," of a theater. On the Roman stage, the curtain came down at the beginning of the performance and went up at the end.

Recondita = "out of sight again."

Sonant fora sola: serious theatrical performances were held as part of the games on holidays. During this period, the legal business of the Forum shut down. In between the games—here the Plebeian (November 4–17) and the Megalesian in honor of the Magna Mater (April 4–10)—only the law courts provided entertainment.

Personam = "theatrical mask," from *personare*.

Thyrsum = symbol of Bacchus, god of theatrical performances. It was a suitably phallic rod with a pine-cone on the end.

Subligar = "loin cloth," part of the tragic actor's uniform. Note the Juvenalian rhetorical anticlimax. We move from the dramatic mask, to the divine sponsor, to women fondling underwear.

Acci = an otherwise unknown actor.

71–2. "Aelia loves Urbicus in the Atellan farces." **Urbicus** = an otherwise unknown actor.

Exodio < *exodium, –i*: a comic piece performed after a serious dramatic work, such as the tragedies alluded to in **lines 67–70.** Atellan farces were native Italian works, as opposed to comedies based in the Greek tradition [18]. **Atellanae** is genitive of definition with **exodio.**

Autonoes = Greek genitive singular of Autonoe: she was the mother of Actaeon.

73–5. Having dealt with tragedy and the farces that followed, we turn our attention to comedy proper. Note the rhetorical structuring of the entire passage: Juvenal gives us a tour of Roman theatrical genres in the guise of describing feminine perversity. **His** = "for these women" referring to **sunt quae.**

Magno = ablative of price.

Fibula = "a penis-sheath with a pin running through the foreskin" (Richlin 1986), worn by athletes and actors to prevent sexual emission, which was thought to weaken performance.

Chrysogonum = apparently a Greek singer. The name, however, means "Golden Gonad."

Hispulla = unidentified, but several women of this name were in the circle of the younger Pliny.

Quintilianus = the famous professor of rhetoric and representative of serious culture as opposed to popular theatrical glitz. At age fifty, he married a young woman who died at nineteen after giving birth to two children. One could have hardly blamed her if she had found actors of interest. Quintilian would have appreciated the methodical way in which Juvenal covered the theatrical genres.

76–7. Wrapping up this section on theatrical entertainments, the satirist asks "Do you want a wife who would make a father of so many musicians?" All the names are Greek. **Citharoedus** = someone who played the *cithara* or lyre.

Choraules = one who accompanied the chorus on the flute.

78–81. We switch from theatrical to gladiatorial spectacles. Continuity is provided by the theme of respectable women making fathers of those of low repute. We are invited to picture preparations for an upper-class wedding whose ironic purpose (**ut . . . exprimat**) is to allow the baby born of the union to show its resemblance to a well-known gladiator. **Longa . . . pulpita** are thought to refer to viewing stands erected along the route of the wedding procession, but such stands are only mentioned here.

Testudineo . . . conopeo = "a tortoise-shell cradle with a mosquito net," an object of great value. The exoticism is highlighted by the spondaic fifth foot [44].

Lentule = an aristocratic cognomen.

Nobilis . . . infans: i.e., descended from a consular family.

Euryalum = an epic name, as in the *Aeneid*'s story of Nisus and Euryalus. The let-down when the reader reaches **murmillonem** is sudden and dramatic. On the *murmillo*, see **Horace 2.6.40–6.**

82–113. The rest of this section is given over to the story of **Eppia**, a senator's wife, who followed a school of gladiators (**ludum**) to Egypt.

82–4. Senatori = presumably the **Veiientus** mentioned in **line 113**, thought to be Fabricius Veiientus who achieved prominence under Domitian.

Pharon: Pharos was an island off the coast of Alexandria famous for its lighthouse.

Lagi: Lagus was the father of Ptolemy I of Egypt. The city is Alexandria.

Canopo = Canopus, an Egyptian town of proverbial decadence. See **1.26.**

85–7. These lines contain a previously unnoticed parody of Sappho 16.7–11 on Helen's leaving Menelaus for Paris: "Helen having left behind the best husband of all, went to Troy, sailing without any thought of her child or her family." **Immemor** directly parallels the Greek κωὐδὲ. . . ἐμνάσθη as does the recitation of family members left behind. Both Helen and Eppia sail east, leaving behind their legitimate husbands. But where Helen's case is cited by Sappho as an example of the overwhelming power of love and plays out against the epic context of the Trojan War, Eppia's story is one of sordid lust and the erotics of the arena. She loves **Sergius (line 112)** so long as he plies his trade. Where Helen leaves Menelaus for Paris, Eppia leaves the actor Paris (**Paridemque**), her former adulterous paramour and a favorite of Domitian's court, to follow the gladiatorial school.

Indulsit < *indulgeo, –ere*: "concede."

88–91. "Although she had led the life of a pampered maiden, she now held the sea in as much contempt as she had formerly held her good reputation."

Plumaque paterna = in the first instance, "her father's down mattress," a sign of wealth. However, if we remember the parallel with Helen, there is also a reminiscence of Leda and the Swan (see **line 63**).

Segmentatis . . . cunis = "a richly adorned cradle," referring to the coverlets.

Iactura = "loss."

Cathedras: see 1.65.

92–4. Eppia is pictured as an epic hero sailing out of Ostia through the Tyrrhenian and the Ionian seas. The Tyrrhenian stretches between Italy and Sardinia, north of Sicily.

94–7. We shift from the particular to the general. "Women only show courage in perversity."

98–100. "If a husband should order his wife to accompany him, she cannot even get on the boat, but if she's following a lover, she has a stronger stomach." **Sentina** = "bilge water."

Summus vertitur aer = "the top of the sky spins," i.e., she becomes dizzy.

100–2. "The one vomits on her husband, the other is at home with the sailors."

103–4. "Who has so inflamed Eppia's heart?" Understand *est*.

104–5. **Ludia** = "gladiator groupie."

105–9. "Tender Sergius is middle-aged and ugly as a stump." **Sergiolus** = ironic, affectionate diminutive.

Radere guttur: a short beard was worn before the age of forty.

Secto < *seco, –are secui sectum*: "cut," i.e. wounded in the arena.

Gibbus = "wart."

Malum = substantive.

Stillantis < *stillo, –are*: "to drip."

110–12. "All that mattered was that he was a gladiator." *Hyacinthos* = the name of a beautiful boy loved by Apollo.

111–12. These lines recapitulate **85–6.** Juvenal rounds off the exemplum with ring composition.

113. "Once he's retired, Sergius is no better than Veiientus." See **line 82. Rude** < *rudis, –is*: the wooden sword given gladiators on retirement.

114–35. What Eppia did on the private level, Messalina, the wife (40–8 CE) of the emperor Claudius did on the grand scale, when she would sneak out at night to work as a prostitute before coming home to her husband's bed, still unsatisfied. There is grotesque degradation in this scene [12]. The lower bodily stratum is featured prominently, and the heights of Roman society are brought low by their contact with it.

The dominant note throughout is that of a sterile, unproductive sexual obsession, The fact that Messalina's body had produced new life is acknowledged in the apostrophe to Britannicus (**line 124**). Yet that moment seems long past. Indeed, Britannicus is only addressed because his position as heir to the throne—which is underlined with **generose**—is undermined by his mother's behavior, which ultimately leads to Messalina's execution (see **10.329–36**), Claudius's marriage to Agrippina, the adoption of Nero, and the latter being named Claudius's heir. As a result of these events, Britannicus is removed from the line of succession, and his death at the hands of his step-brother is ensured. Nero could hardly afford to have a pretender to the throne in the imperial palace (Dio 61.34–5; Tacitus, *Annales* 11.12, 26, 29–32, 34–8; 12.1–3, 8–9; 13.14–17; Suetonius, *Divus Claudius* 36–9; *Nero* 33.2–3).

Messalina's body in this passage is portrayed as a sort of shock absorber (**line 126**). It is reductively anatomized in the image of the **rigidae . . . volvae** (**line 129**) which is pictured as a burning (**ardens**), autonomous entity that exists beyond the structures of human control. It has a mind of its own, representing a species of erotic hunger that knows no satisfaction. In **line 132**, the assonance of **lupanaris** ("whorehouse") with **pulvinar** ("divine or imperial pillow") identifies the imperial bed with the bordello.

114. quid . . . quid: introducing indirect questions dependent on **curas**.

115–19. "When she thought Claudius was asleep, she would sneak out with a maid to the house of ill repute."

118–17. These lines are generally switched to make the passage read more smoothly. **Et** is also a later addition. These changes are not strictly necessary (see Friedländer 1962). **Meretrix Augusta** is a great ironic juxtaposition.

Cucullos < *cucullus*, *–i*: "a hood" to conceal her identity.

Palatino: the imperial palace was located on the Palatine hill.

Tegetem < *teges*, *tegetis*: a mat that served as a bed for slaves and the poor, hence also prostitutes.

120–4. Galero < *galerum*, *–i*: "wig."

Centone < *cento*, *–tonis*: a "patchwork quilt" that serves as the door to the brothel.

Pappillis . . . auratis = "with gilded nipples."

Lyciscae = Greek for "Wolf-Girl." *Lupa* in Latin means "prostitute."

125. **Intrantis** = accusative plural.

126. The line is printed with brackets in most editions. I, however, follow Richlin (1986), "Although this line has only late manuscript support, it is surely good enough not to be bracketed. Note the emphasis given by the meter to the sense." The alternative reading of *ac resupina* for **continueque** is attractive.

127–32. "When it's quitting time, she doesn't want to go home." **Lenone**: see 1.1.55.

Tentigine < *tentigo, –tiginis*: "stiff," a "hard on."

133–4. Juvenal looks ahead to Messalina's successor, Agrippina, who is supposed to have poisoned both Claudius and Britannicus. **Hippomanes** = a membrane taken from the forehead of a newly born colt used in love potions.

Loquar = "should I mention?"

Privigno < *privignus, –i*: "stepson."

134–5. Agrippina shows that women commit sins far more serious than those of Messalina. **Coactae / imperio sexus** " driven by the commands of their sex."

Minimum = adverbial.

136–41. The satirical interlocutor reappears: "What about Cessenia? Her husband calls her chaste."

Bis quingena = "twice 500" or 1,000,000 sesterces, a dowry worth more than the senatorial census.

Tanti = genitive of price.

Macer: lovers are conventionally emaciated by their affliction.

Lampade < *lampas, –padis*: the proverbial "torch of love."

Libertas emitur: her freedom is bought and paid for.

Innuat atque / rescribat: flirtatious behavior described in detail by Ovid at *Amores* 1.4.

141. A wonderful *sententia* summing up the exemplum.

142–60. "What about the case of Bibula and Sertorius?" "Her beauty will soon fade." The topic shifts from female "perversity" to the impermanence of physical beauty.

144–7. "Once age sets in, his freedman will say 'pack your bags and leave.'" The once-smitten Sertorius does not even bother to deliver the news himself.

Emungeris < *emungo, –ere, –munxi, –munctum*: in the middle/passive, "to blow one's own nose."

149–52. "In the meantime, she is a virtual monarch, commanding her husband to compete with the neighbors in opulence." **Calet** = "she is aroused."

Ovem Canusiam: sheep from Canusia in the south of Italy bore the finest wool.

Ulmosque Falernas = "and Falernian elms." She wants not just wine, but whole vineyards. Elm trees were used to train the vines.

Pueros = "personal slaves."

Ergastula = "work houses" where slaves were sent for punishment. She wants not only the good slaves, but the bad ones too.

Domi = locative.

153–7. "The Saturnalia, an exceptional opportunity for extravagance, were celebrated as a public holiday from 17–19 December; and a fair called *Sigillaria* from the statuettes in clay (*sigilla*) which were a main article on sale there, went on for four days after 17 December. For the purpose of this fair, canvas booths (***casa candida***) were erected near the Saepta, in the Campus Martius; the effect of these booths was to cover up the walls of the *porticus Agrippae*, and perhaps other buildings. This *porticus* was adorned with frescoes representing the voyage of the Argonauts; consequently it was often called the *porticus Argonautarum* [. . .]. Jason would certainly be a prominent figure in the frescoes: he is called ***mercator*** sarcastically, because of the purpose of his voyage; the Argonautae are degraded to ***nautae***" (Duff 1970).

Crystallina = "rock crystal vases."

Murrina = "agate vases."

Adamas = "diamond."

Beronices = Greek genitive: the sister of Herod Agrippa II of Judea, she was the mistress of the emperor Titus (79–81 CE) before his accession to the throne.

157–60. The satirist indulges in a tangent as he describes the history of Bibula's new ring. **Barbarus . . . Agrippa** = Herod Agrippa.

Incestae: there were persistent rumors about relations between Agrippa and his sister.

Gestare: Housman's emendation for the repetitive *dedit hunc* is widely adopted. See Courtney (1980).

Mero pede = an outlandish circumlocution for "barefoot." Shoes were not worn on Jewish holy ground. See Courtney (1980) for a longer discussion.

161–83. "Is there not one woman worthy of marriage from the lot?" "No."

162–6. The argument self-deconstructs: "who could possibly bear a perfect wife?" **Sit . . . disponat** = concessive subjunctives.

Vetustos . . . avos = statues of consular ancestors.

Intactior: understand **sit**.

Sabina = ablative of comparison: the reference is to the rape of the Sabine women, when the newly kidnapped brides stepped between the lines of the Roman and Sabine armies lest their fathers and husbands slay one another.

Cui constant omnia = an accounting metaphor, "to whom everything is in balance."

166–9. "I prefer a charming hussy, to the imperious mother of the Gracchi [16–18]." **Venustinam** = a speaking name: "Charmer."

170–1. Cornelia's father was Scipio Africanus who defeated Hannibal and his ally Scyphax in the Second Punic War. **Migra** = "scram."

172–7. "Those claiming to be without fault are unbearable: look at Niobe." Niobe had fourteen children and in her pride claimed to outdo Latona who had two. But Latona's were Diana and Apollo who, when they heard the snub, killed Niobe's children with their arrows (**sagittas**).

172–4. The story is normally told from the perspective of Niobe. Juvenal gives us the view of her husband **Amphion**. **Paean** = a cult name for Apollo.

175–7. Amphion killed himself from grief leaving Niobe to carry out (**extulit**) the dead. **Scrofa . . . alba** = ablative of comparison: "the white sow." Juvenal refers to the sow with thirty piglets that served as an omen to Aeneas for the site of Alba Longa. It is a deflating comparison.

178–81. "Virtue is an intolerable vice when it's always thrown in your teeth." **Corrupta**: understand **femina**.

Aloes = Greek genitive. It, like **mellis**, is partitive. The aloe is proverbially bitter.

181–3. **Deditus** = "devoted."

Usque adeo = "so"

Effert = "extols."

Diem septenis . . . horis = "seven hours a day." The Roman day had twelve hours.

286–345. Juvenal returns to his opening theme, before launching into a new set of variations on feminine vice. "In the old days, poverty and hard work kept women chaste. Today they drink! And wine leads to all kinds of profanations!"

286–300. The good old days when life was hard.

286–90. **Vitiis contingi**: understand **castas . . . Latinas** as the accusative subject of the infinitive.

Parva . . . tecta is the first subject of **sinebant**. The others are **labor, somni, manus, Hannibal**, and **mariti**.

Vellere Tusco = ablative of cause: Etruria was known for its wool. The virtuous Roman wife, as tombstones attest, occupied herself with her wool-working.

Collina turre = the Colline gate, where Hannibal threatened Rome.

292–3. It is a truism of traditional Roman morality that peace leads to luxury and decadence, although war as a means of promoting feminine virtue is a *reductio ad absurdum*.

294–5. **Ex quo** = "ever since."

295–7. Luxury has brought in a flood of Greeks and their ways. See 3.58–125. **Sybaris** = a city in Magna Graecia of proverbial luxury.

Rhodos = wealthiest island of the eastern Mediterranean.

Miletos: a whole genre of erotic stories was known as Milesian tales. Note the spondaic fifth foot [44].

Tarentum: Juvenal is thinking of an incident at the beginning of the Pyrrhic war (281 BCE), when an ambassador from Rome was urinated on by a drunk at a festival of Dionysus, hence the city is **coronatum** ("garlanded") and **madidum** ("drunk" and/or "dripping with unguents") but also **petulans**.

298–300. Note the delicious oxymoron of **divitiae molles** as subject of **fregerunt**.

Venus ebria = "drunken lust." In early times, women at Rome were not allowed to drink. Observe how Juvenal carefully moves us from **madidumque Tarentum** to **divitiae molles** to **venus ebria** and thus returns to his main topic: the indictment of women. The careful rhetorical structure betrays an aesthetic aim beyond simple moral denunciation. *Satire* 6 is a *tour de force*.

301–45. A drunken woman knows no limits to her sacrilege or desires.

301–5. "Drunk women don't know their heads from their tails." **Inguinis**: see 1.40–1. As Courtney notes (1980), the implication is that a woman in such a condition would not know whether to kiss or fellate you.

Grandia . . . ostrea: any woman eating oysters in the middle of the night is up to no good.

Perfusa . . . unguenta = the subject of **spumant**. The perfumes foam with unmixed wine.

Concha = a bowl in the shape of a shell, normally used for perfumes.

Tectum is the subject of **ambulat**. She has "the spins" and is seeing double (**geminis . . . lucernis**).

306–8. This is a vexed passage. Many editions invert the order of **307** and **308** (Clausen 1956; Ferguson 1979; Dominick and Wehrle 1999), others preserve the manuscript order (Friedländer 1962; Labriolle and Villeneuve 1964; Duff 1970; Willis 1997; and Richlin 1986 with emendation); Courtney (1980) suspects that 307 is spurious and notes its textual attestation is shaky at best. The problem is the repetition of the name **Maura** and the general syntactic difficulty of the sentence. If we assume two sisters both named Maura, not an unusual practice in Rome where daughters took a feminized version of the father's *nomen*, then the passage as transmitted can be construed in the manner of Labriolle and Villeneuve 1964, "Come now and consider the grimace that Tullia makes when drinking in the air, and what Maura says, the sister of the famous Maura, when she passes by the ancient altar of Pudicitia." Of course, Maura is a slave name designating a girl of African descent and so her father would not have a true *nomen*. Nonetheless, given the practice as attested in free Roman families, there is no reason to consider it impossible among the slave population or their owners that two daughter would both be named for their fathers or country of origin.

Tullia: the *gens Tullia* was an ancient patrician family.

Notae . . . Maurae = a famed fellatrix at **10.223–4**, and hence the better known of the two.

309–13. The reason behind Tullia and Maura's grimace becomes apparent: the women hold drunken lesbian orgies and urinate (**micturiunt**) on the statue of the goddess. Note how this behavior recalls that of the crowd at Tarentum toward the Roman ambassador (**line 297**). **Longis siphonibus** = "long sprays"; Juvenal's knowledge of female anatomy is surprisingly limited.

Equitant = "they ride (one another)."

Moventur = "they reach orgasm" (Richlin 1986).

Calcas < *calco, –are*: "tread upon."

Luce reversa = "the next morning."

Magnos visurus amicos: on the way to the morning *salutatio*.

314–45. The passage concludes with another extended exemplum: the drunken debauchery that supposedly takes place at the female-only rites of the *Bona Dea*. They were held at the home of the *Pontifex Maximus* and presided over by his wife.

314–17. Maenades = the subject of all the plural verbs. The worshippers of the goddess are compared to Bacchants.

Cornu < *cornu, –us*: "horn, trumpet."

Attonitae = "in ecstasy."

Priapi = the ithyphallic god whose statues guarded gardens: genitive singular with **maenades**.

317–19. **Concubitus** = genitive singular.
Saltante = "pulsing."

320–3. "There, aristocratic women challenge (**provocat**) prostitutes in provocative behavior." **Lenonum ancillas** = periphrasis for "prostitutes."
Saufeia: an aristocratic name, see 9.117.
Pendentis . . . coxae = "swinging hips."
Medullinae = another aristocratic name.
Crisantis = "to shimmy." See Lucilius 9.340, *crisabit ut si frumentum clunibus vannat*, and compare Lucilius 7.280.

323. A wonderfully condensed and paradoxical *sententia*. Understand *est* with both clauses. **Inter dominas** = shared by the ladies, i.e., Saufeia and Medullina.
Virtus = "excellence," but in fact vice. **Virtus** is a masculine quality (derived from *vir*), here attributed to excellence in female vice and associated with aristocratic bloodline (**natalibus**). This is truly a world turned upside-down.

324–6. "These girls aren't play-acting. They could raise the dead." **Frigidus aevo / Laomedontiades** = "frigid old Priam."
Nestoris hirnea = "Nestor's busted balls." He was proverbially old.

327–9. "When they get all worked up, they call to let the men in." **Prurigo** = "an itch" you need to scratch.
Femina simplex = "woman on her own," i.e., both in her pure state and without a suitable partner. *Simplicitas*, normally a virtue, is here transformed into a synonym for lust.
Antro = "grotto."
Fas: normally used of religious sanction, here becomes synonymous with what is *nefas*, the admission of men to the rites of the *Bona Dea*.

329–34. "She's ready to take on all comers." **Adulter** = her normal paramour.
Cucullo: see 118.
Si nihil est = if he won't come.
Incurritur = "there is an assault on," both violent and sexual.
Spem servorum = both objective genitive, "what she hopes for from the slaves," and subjective genitive, "the hope possessed by the slaves," i.e., she will have used them up.
Conductus aquarius = "the hired water-carrier," a menial from outside the *domus*.
Mora nulla: understand *est*.

Quo minus = *quominus*.

Asello < *asellus*, *–i*: "a young ass," the ultimate degradation.

335–41. "Would that we could return to the good old days, before the transvestite guitar-player (**psaltria**) infiltrated the rites of the *Bona Dea*." Clodius Pulcher snuck into the rites dressed as a woman when they were held at the home of Julius Caesar (62 BCE). The rumor was that Clodius was having an affair with Caesar's wife, Pompeia. The episode led to their divorce and was made famous by Cicero in numerous attacks on Clodius [23].

Mauri atque Indi: i.e., the eastern and western extremes of the empire.

The basic structure of the relative clause is **psaltria penem . . . illuc . . . intulerit**.

Anticatones = a two-roll attack published by Caesar against Cato the younger, one of his most vocal opponents. See **Persius 3.44–51.**

339. Even a male with much smaller equipment knows to stay clear of the rites of the *Bona Dea*.

340–1. Pictures of males had to be covered. **Sexus** = genitive.

342–5. "In the good old days, no one would have dared do such a thing." To what period is Juvenal referring? His Golden Age, depicted at the beginning of the poem, is singularly unappealing and the late republic is the era of Clodius himself. Logical consistency is not the hallmark of either *indignatio* or its skillful portrayal [76]. **Simpuvium** and **catinum** = a "pouring bowl" and a "dish" used in religious rites.

Numae: see 1.12–18.

Vaticano . . . de monte patellas = "saucers from the Vatican hill," where cheap pottery was sold.

366–78. Some women prefer eunuchs.

366–8. There is no need for abortifacients. **Inbelles** = "unwarlike."

368–70. The best ones are not castrated until after puberty. **Pectine nigro** = "pubic hair."

371–3. "If you wait till the testicles are mature, only the barber loses." Such eunuchs do not grow a beard. **Bilibres** = "two pounders."

Damno = ablative of price.

Heliodorus = a surgeon.

374–6. "You can spot the eunuch made for his mistress's pleasure a mile away." **Custodem vitis et horti** = Priapus.

Provocat = "challenges."

376–8. "It's one thing to let a eunuch sleep with your mistress, quite another to let him sleep with your boy!" **Tondendum** = "in need of a haircut." Pretty slave boys had their locks cut after they had fully reached puberty, at which time it was believed they were past their erotic prime. The idea seems to be that such a well-endowed eunuch might be pleasing to the woman, but could injure the boy.

398–456. Women who act like men.

398–412. After a brief invective against women who love music [**cantet**] and musicians, Juvenal starts to inveigh against those who dare to present themselves as knowledgeable of current affairs, both personal and political, and thus as potential rivals in expertise to men.

398–401. **Coetus** = accusative plural: an outrageous sexual pun implies she has not only multiple conversational (**loqui**) but also multiple sexual partners. Of course, from the perspective of satirist, why else would she talk to men?

Paludatis ducibus = generals wearing their official cloaks (*paludamenta*). Although *paludamentum* is derived from the same root as *pallium*, "cloak," it looks and scans like the many adjectives derived from *palus*, *–udos*, "swamp," such as *paludosus*. One also cannot help but notice that **cumque paludatis ducibus** is in a chiastic relationship with **siccisque mamillis** in the next line. Thus, her dry breasts, because she has no children, are contrasted by an implicit *figura etymologica* with the general who is dressed for hard campaigning in the field and exposure to the elements. Wet and dry are thus inverted as markers of masculinity and femininity (see Miller 1998).

402–6. **Seres** = "Chinese."

Diripiatur = "torn apart," presumably when getting caught in the act. See **Horace 1.2.**

Modis quot = "in how many positions," another descending climax.

407–12. She has all the news on political and military developments overseas as well as natural disasters. **Instantem . . . cometen** = "the comet that is of great moment."

Regi Amenio Parthoque: Armenia was perpetually shifting between Roman and Parthian hegemony.

Quosdam facit = "some she just makes up." The asyndeton is harsh.

409–12. A list of the **rumores** she recounts (**narrat**). **Niphaten** = Greek accusative: a river in Armenia. For more, see Courtney (1980).

Nutare urbes, subsidere terras: presumably the earthquake that struck Antioch in 115 CE.

413–33. Worse is the hypermasculine woman who is aggressive to her neighbors, works out at the baths, and drinks too much.

413–15. **Loris**: see **Horace 1.10 [5]**.

Experrecta = "roused": this emendation, found in the scholia, was first proposed and best defended by Duff (1970). It has been adopted by Ferguson (1979) and Willis (1997). The text as transmitted, *exortata* or *exorata*, is universally printed with daggers when not emended.

415–18. **Latratibus** < *latratus, –us*: "barking."

Fustes = "cudgels." Note the clipped, military diction.

Illis = ablative of means, referring back to **fustes**.

418–23. "A terror to meet, she heads to the baths for a workout and a lower-body massage." **Occursu** < *occurro, –currere, –curri, –cursum*: "to run into, to oppose": supine.

Nocte = "nightfall or dusk." Romans bathed before dinner and dined between 2 and 3 pm. She, however, is excessive in everything she does.

Conchas = "bath tubs" here, see Friedländer (1962) and Courtney (1980).

Castra moveri: the metaphor is that of the general ordering his troops to decamp. She must have a substantial retinue.

Sudare: i.e., in the sauna amidst the hubbub of the clients and personnel (**magno . . . tumultu**). This is no retiring violet.

Massa = "weight"; she has been pumping iron. Normally, only men exercised before bathing.

Cristae = "clitoris" (Adams 1982: 98).

Aliptes = "masseur."

Summum dominae femur exclamare = transfer of epithet. The woman, and not her upper thigh, exclaims.

424–5. "Meanwhile, her guests wilt with hunger."

425–9. "She comes home red-faced (**rubicundula**) and drinks till she pukes."
Plena . . . urna = "with a full three gallons."

Sextarius = "a pint."

Orexim < *orexis, –is*: "hunger."

Redit: the subject is the wine, i.e., she throws up.

Loto < *lavo, –are, lavi, lautum* or *lotum*: "wash."

430–2. **Pelvis** = "basin."

Olet = "smells of."

Dolia = "a large wine jar."

Serpens: snakes in ancient lore were proverbially fond of wine. See Courtney (1980) for sources.

432–3. "It's all her husband can do to keep from throwing up himself." **Substringit** = "holds down."

434–56. In a typically Juvenalian anticlimax, the worst example of women who act like men are those who practice literary criticism.

434–7. **Discumbere** = "to recline" at the dinner table. We are to imagine a symposiastic discussion.

Periturae . . . Elissae: Dido's suicide at the end of the Book 4 of the *Aeneid.*

Comittit = "sets against each other."

Maronem: i.e., Publius Vergilius Maro.

Trutina = "scale."

438–440. "She silences everyone." **Causidicus**: see 1.30–9.

Praeco: see 1.99–101.

440–2. **Tintinnabula** = "bells."

442–3. "Juvenal refers to the custom of beating on pots and pans and blowing horns to frighten away an eclipse of the moon" (Richlin 1986).

444–7. "She respects no limits and should simply dress as a man." **Tenus** = a preposition, "down to." Men's tunics were belted-up to mid-calf. Women's extended to their feet.

Silvano: a god of the forest. He received sacrifice only from men,

Quadrante = "a penny," what men were charged at the baths. Women generally paid more.

448–51. "Women should not know too much, and what they do, they shouldn't understand." As usual, the kicker is in the end and is so absurd as to rob the speaker of credibility. While far from absolving Juvenal of misogyny, in many places this satire is as much a parody of Roman misogynist discourse as an example of it.

Dicendi genus: referring to the three recognized styles of speaking Attic, Asiatic, and mixed or Rhodian.

Curvum . . . enthymema = "a rounded-off enthymeme." An enthymeme is a truncated syllogism used as a rhetorical argument. This and the previous clause indicate a woman who has received formal rhetorical training.

Sed quaedam ex libris = "but certain things from books."

451–5. "I despise the woman who knows more than I." **Palaemonis** = Remmius Palaemon, a famed teacher of literarture and rhetoric (first century CE).

Antiquaria = "an enthusiast for archaic literature."

455–6. "She won't even allow her husband a grammar error."

Opicae: see 3.203–7.

474–507. A day in the life of an average woman: she governs her household like a tyrannical magistrate. Her pretensions are like her hair: piled high in front, it makes her look like Andromache, but from behind it reveals her to be a pygmy.

474–5. **Pretium curae** = "worthwhile."

Penitus = "through and through."

475–80. "If hubby's not in the mood, the whole household will pay." **Libraria** = the slave who weighed out the wool for the others to spin.

Ponunt . . . tunicas: for a whipping.

Cosmetae = the slaves charged with their mistress's toilette.

Liburnus = a slave from Dalmatia. They were favored as litter-bearers.

Poenas . . . pendere = "to pay the penalty."

Alieni: i.e., the husband.

Frangit ferulas = "breaks canes" by being beaten with them.

Flagello < *flagellum, –i*: "a whip of knotted cords."

Scutica = "a strap."

Tortoribus = "floggers," public slaves normally paid by the job. She pays them an annual salary.

481–5. "She has them beaten as she blithely goes about her business." **Obiter** = "meanwhile." Note how the enjambment [47] and repetition of **et caedit** in the same metrical sedes rhythmically enacts the repetitive beating.

Faciem linit = "puts on her make-up."

Pictae = "embroidered."

Longi . . . transversa diurni = a single papyrus in which the writing went straight across, rather than being divided into columns or sheets joined together, as was done in ancient books. Many official documents were written in the transverse style. There are two schools of thought concerning the content of the present document. Some (Duff 1970; Ferguson 1979) believe it refers to the *acta diurna*, a daily gazette instituted by Julius Caesar and referred to elsewhere by Juvenal. But the scholiast says it is an account book and Courtney (1980) argues that *diurnum* is nowhere else used as a singular substantive to stand for the *acta*. This view is persuasive.

Exi = the imperative. It is the object of **intonet** and modified by **horrendum**.

Cognitione = "an inquest," as if she were a magistrate. The term is technical.

486. "Sicilian tyrants show more mercy." **Praefectura** = "the governance."

Aula = "a palace," and by metonymy the seat of princely power. The fifth- and fourth-century BCE Greek tyrants who ruled Sicily compiled a remarkable record of cruelty. See **Persius 3.39–43.**

487–91. "If she has a date and is in a rush, her hairdresser comes in already stripped for her beating." **Constituit** = "has a date," see 3.12.

Solitoque decentius = "more becomingly than usual."

Isiacae . . . lenae = "of Isis the bawd." The temple of Isis was a popular place for assignations. See 9.22.

490. Note the ironic placement of **crinem** and **ipsa** to emphasize that **Psecas** fixes her mistress's hair after her own locks have been torn out.

491. **Umeros** = Greek accusative of respect. This line, with its emphasis on Psecas's naked shoulders and nipples, is simultaneously titillating and sadistic even as it condemns the mistress's cruelty in the service of her own transgressive liaison.

492–3. **Altior** = "too high."

Cincinnus = "curl."

Taurea = "bull whip."

Continuo = "immediately."

494–5. "Is it Psecas's fault you don't like your nose?"

495–6. "Another slave girl meanwhile curls her hair on the left side." **Volvit in orbem** = "rolls into a circle."

497–501. "Indeed there is a whole privy counsel to ensure that all matters of beauty are properly overseen." The analogy of the mistress of the house to a tyrant, begun with the **cognitio** (485) and continued with the discussion of her **praefectura** (486), is here extended with this parody of a governing cabinet. **Materna**: "one of her mother's servants, as some *amici principis* served more than one emperor" (Ferguson 1979).

Admotaque lanis: "now charged with measuring out the wool" for the other slaves to spin, she has retired her hairpin (**emerita . . . acu**).

Prima sententia: the retired hairdresser is the elder stateswoman of the group and called upon to give her opinion first, just as the *princeps senatus*.

Censebunt = a technical term used for giving opinions in the senate.

Tamquam famae discrimen agatur / aut animae = "as though it were a decision concerning her reputation or her life."

502–4. "Her curls are piled so high that from the front you'll see Andromache, but from the rear another." **Ordinibus** = "rows of curls."

Conpagibus < *conpages, –is*: "joints, seams." The hair was piled in rows of curls on top of their heads and held in place by a wire frame (Ferguson 1979). "Roman women in Juvenal's youth, as statuary attests, did wear elaborately piled-up hairstyles, high in front and low behind. The style continued in less extreme form at least through the reign of Trajan, when this poem was probably published; Trajan's wife Plotina looks on her coins as if a seam divides the jutting front of her head from the back" Richlin (1986).

504–7. "Tell us your counsel if she's shorter than a pygmy and has to stand on tip-toe to receive a kiss." **Cedo** has a short *e* and is a colloquial imperative (*ce* + *do*) meaning "give here, tell us."

Sortita est < *sortior, –iri, –titum*: "to have fall one's lot."

Cothurnis = the high, platform boots or "buskins" worn by tragic actors.

Erecta . . . planta = "on tiptoe."

610–26. "Women administer charms and potions that drive their husbands mad."

610–12. **Solea pulsare natis** = "to spank him with a slipper."

612–14. "On account of the drugs (**inde**), you play the fool and forget what you did." **Desipis** < *desipio, –ere* (*de* + *sapio*): "to act foolishly."

Caligo = "fog."

614–17. "This would be tolerable if the drugs did not make you as mad as Caligula." Most editions also print what are known as 614A–C. They are not widely attested, have been questioned since the time of Valla, and are generally printed in brackets. No modern editor accepts them as genuine.

Avunculus . . . Neronis = the emperor Caligula (37–41 CE). The periphrasis prepares us for the introduction of Agrippina in **line 620.** Nero's mother was Caligula's sister and Claudius's wife.

616. Another reference to the **hippomanes** discussed at **line 133. Caesonia** = the wife of Caligula.

Pulli < *pullis, –i*: "foal."

617. **Quod principis uxor**: understand *fecit*.

618–20. "Those dosed rage as if Juno had poisoned Jupiter." **Cuncta** = neuter plural.

Conpage: see **line 502.**

620–3. "Agrippina's poisonous mushroom for Claudius caused less harm." **Boletus** = "mushroom." Agrippina was supposed to have killed Claudius with a dish of mushrooms.

Tremulumque caput: Claudius suffered from a number of physical ailments whose symptoms were similar to Parkinson's and caused him to be viewed as a congenital idiot by his contemporaries, as Suetonius and Seneca testify, in spite of his considerable intelligence. The ancients were not generous to the disabled.

Descendere . . . in caelum: a brilliant oxymoron, in which Juvenal inverts the normal, vertical scale of values. Compare 1.147–9.

624–5. The proof that poison is less harmful than love charms: Agrippina's poison killed an idiot, but Caesonia's **potio** caused Caligula to decimate the ranks of the senators and equestrians. **Haec potio** contrasts with the earlier **boletus . . . ille**.

626. **Tanti . . . tanti . . . constat** = "costs so much."

Partus equae: see 616.

627–61. "They don't stop at poisoning their husbands but kill their children and stepchildren." With the description of this crime, the satire abruptly ends, with no attempt to synthesize the whole into a coherent indictment. Like all *saturae*, it is less an argument than a series of vignettes [11].

627–8. **Privignum**: see 133–4.

629–31. **Pupilli**: see 1.45–8.

Res = "fortune."

Livida materno . . . veneno = "Black with maternal poison," another wonderfully oxymoronic turn of phrase.

Adipata < *adipata, –orum*: a pastry made with lard or tallow.

632–3. **Papas** = a child's name for his *paedagogus*. Observe the alliteration.

634–7. A wonderful moment of generic self-reflexivity, "what is a satirist doing writing tragedy?" an acknowledgment of *Satire* 6 as a self-conscious literary creation, even as Juvenal claims he is simply reporting what he sees [10–11]. **Coturnum**: see 504–7.

Legemque: on the law of genre, see **Horace 2.1**.

Sophocleo . . . hiatu = with the voice of the great Athenian tragedian.

Bacchamur = "to rage in the manner of a Bacchant."

Montibus ignotum Rutulis caeloque Latino: such poems (**carmen**), and by implication such crimes, were unknown in primitive Italy, a recollection of the poem's opening invocation of the Golden Age. The Rutulians were the Italic people Aeneas's Trojans defeated to found Rome.

638–40. **Pontia**: a poisoner of her own children, mentioned by Martial. The scholiast claims she was Petronius's daughter.

Aconita: neuter plural antecedent of **quae deprensa**. See **1.158–9**

641. Understand *necavisti*.

643–4. "I am recounting nothing contrary to what the tragedians say about Medea and Procne." **Colchide** = the woman from Colchis, i.e., Medea. She killed her children to punish Jason for leaving her for a Corinthian princess.

Torva = "fierce, savage."

Procne: killed her son Itys, after she discovered that her husband Tereus had raped her sister Philomela and cut her tongue out.

644–6. "At least, they didn't do it for money." See **629**.

646–50. "There is less cause for amazement (**admiratio**) that these tragic heroines were driven over the edge by anger." **Minor . . . summis . . . monstris**: another oxymoronic juxtaposition.

Nocentes modifies **hunc sexum**. The sense here trumps the grammar, since the members of the female sex are by nature plural.

Iecur: see **Horace 1.9.66** and **Persius 1.25.**

Ut saxa: the simile emphasizes the uncontrollable rage of yesterday's heroines as opposed to the calculated greed of today's harridans.

Latus = the side of the mountain.

652–4. **Alcestim**: Alcestis was the paragon of wifely devotion. When her husband, Admetus, was fated to die, she took his place (but was later restored to life by Hercules). When today's wives, however, see her story played on the tragic stage, they are merely inspired to trade their husband's life for that of their favorite puppy (**catellae**).

655–6. "Husband killers today roam the street." **Belides** = the granddaughters of Belus: i.e., the Danaids, forty-nine of whom killed their husbands.

Eriphylae: Eriphyla convinced her husband to join the Seven Against Thebes in return for a gold necklace. He lost his life in the campaign.

Clytemestram: Clytemestra, the daughter of Zeus and Leda. Her mortal father was Tyndareus. She slew Agamemnon on his return from Troy.

657–61. "But where Clytemnestra did her work openly with an axe, her imitators use poison." **Refert** = "it matters, makes a difference." The *e* is long.

Bipennem < *bipennis*, *–is*: "two-headed battle axe."

Insulsam et fatuam = "stupid and boorish," unlike the means used today.

Tenui = "slender," as opposed to the massive axe, but also "elegant," a term of praise in Callimachean poetics. Today's poisoners are sophisticated artists as opposed to the boorish epic figures of yesteryear [**38–9**].

Pulmone rubetae: see 1.69–72.

660–1. "Nonetheless, even our latter-day Clytemnestras must sometimes use the sword (**ferro**), since our husbands, like king Mithridates, take precautions against poison." **Atrides** = "the son of Atreus," i.e., Agamemnon.

Pontica . . . medicamina: Mithridates VI of Pontus (120–63 BCE) immunized himself to poison by consuming small quantities. He was thrice defeated by Roman armies (**ter victi**).

9

If *Satire* 6 is on women, *Satire* 9 focuses on masculine sexual degradation. As in 6, questions of gender and sexuality are inseparable from those of class. *Satire* 9 offers a scathing look at aristocratic sexual practices from the perspective of a service provider. It features vivid imagery, and its concern with the lower bodily stratum recalls **Persius** 4 [12].

In *Satire* 9, normative social and sexual expectations are first undermined and then inverted again. This double inversion is a common rhetorical strategy in Juvenal (Miller 2001). One of its main effects is to reveal the arbitrary nature of Roman ideological norms, even as it stigmatizes deviations from them. This satire is as much a form of ironic self-reflection as a call for moral or political amelioration [33].

Juvenal tells the gigolo, Naevolus, the only solution to his and his patron's plight is to live rightly (**vivendum recte, line 118**). Yet not only does the satirist's advice fall on deaf ears, it is far from clear what it could mean to someone in Naevolus's position. Roman aristocratic culture placed very little premium on pulling yourself up by your boot-straps. Working for a living was simply beyond the pale for anyone with pretensions to being a gentleman (Courtney 1980: 425–6). How then *does* one live rightly when subjection and degradation relative to one's superiors are the tools of advancement and yet also disqualify one from the very status that is sought?

Satire 9, then, consists of an elaborately structured and interdependent web of ideological contradictions. First, Naevolus's patron, Virro, is in the socially dominant position, yet he is an effeminate. Not only does he expect his *cliens* to penetrate him, rendering the *patronus* a submissive *cinaedus*, and hence within the Roman scale of values the dominated party (Foucault 1986; Richlin 1992; Parker 1997), but his *cliens* also has to father his children because he is impotent. These facts, however, are far from putting Naevolus in a position of *de facto* dominance relative to his *patronus*. Instead, he is forced to offer him gifts to maintain his position within the household. This represents a reversal of normal patron–client relations in which largesse, symbolized by the *sportula*, is provided by the economically and socially dominant *patronus* (1.95–126; Winkler 1983: 112).

Second, Naevolus's roles are doubly inverted as well. Not only is he a socially dependent sexual dominant, but he is also possessed of outsized economic ambitions. He seeks not self-sufficiency but a household of skilled craftsmen, as well as a small estate, in return for his own inestimable skills (Fredricks in Ramage *et al.* 1974: 155). He desires the life of an equestrian gentleman in return for services that are by nature slavish, inasmuch as he puts his body at the disposal of another (Walters 1997: 39–40).

The satire is written in dialogue form [77] allowing both levels of the poem's argument to unfold freely. Naevolus's indictments of his patron's greed and perversity—common themes in Juvenal—also reveal his own venality and lack of moral self-consciousness. The unflattering depiction is all the more persuasive because it is the product of Naevolus's own words as he is egged on by his satiric interlocutor. Patrons and clients are, in this complex little masterpiece, both satirized and satirizing [32].

1–24. The satirist sets the scene. "Why so grim Naevolus? You used to cut an elegant figure."

1–2. **Marsya**: see **Horace 1.6.119–21.**

3–4. "Why does your face look like that of Ravola when he was caught rubbing the wet crotch (**inguina**) of Rhodope with his beard?" The name **Ravola** means "hoarse," presumably a consequence of cunnilingus. All forms of oral gratification were considered demeaning to the party performing them. For a man to perform oral sex on a woman was doubly demeaning (Parker 1997). Juvenal wastes no time in establishing the tone of the satire and in associating sexual and social hierarchies.

Rhodopes = Greek genitive, a prostitute's name.

5. In some editions, this line is printed in brackets. There is, however, no reason to believe it is an interpolation. As the scholiast notes, it seems to be an aside to the effect that a slave caught in a similar act would receive a cuff (**colaphum**).

Lambenti < *lambeo, –ere*: "to lick."

Crustula < *crustulum, –i*: "a cookie."

6–8. We move from sexual to financial corruption. **Crepereius Pollio** = a notorious spendthrift whose credit is so bad he can't find anyone to loan him money at three times the normal interest rate of 12%.

9–11. "Once, content with little, you were a witty dinner companion." **Vernam equitem** = an oxymoron. A *verna*, in its most basic sense, is a slave born in his master's house, although metaphorically the word was sometimes extended to mean simply "native born." An *eques* was a member of the second-ranking order in Roman society, just behind the senators. A *verna eques* is therefore someone who conflates two social categories. This, as was observed in the introductory note, is the essence of Naevolus. Thus Martial in 1.84 tells the story of Quirinalis who, when he wanted to have sons, *suas ancillas futuit* and so populated his estate with *vernas equites*. The more immediate point here is that Naevolus in the past was a witty *scurra* in demand on the dinner party circuit (see **Horace 1.4.86–9** and **2.8.20–4**).

Salibus < *sal, salis*: "salt, wit."

Pomeria = the sacred boundary round the city of Rome.

12–15. "But now you are unkempt." **Siccae** = "Not pomaded" (Courtney 1980).

Bruttia . . . calidi . . . fascia visci = "a band of hot pitch from Bruttium," used as a depilatory. Bruttium was filled with pine forests.

Fruticante < *frutico, –are*: "to become bushy," a grand word for a low subject. The fact that Naevolus in his prime would depilate his shins is the first clear sign of his status as a sexual professional. See **Persius 4.33–42.**

16–17. "Do you have the quartan fever?" See **Persius 3.88–93. Macies** = "leanness."

Domestica in this context = "chronic."

18–20. Juvenal paraphrases Lucilius 26.62, *animo qui aegrotat, videmus corpore hunc signum dare.* **Deprendas** = potential subjunctive, addressed to a generic "you," not Naevolus.

21. **Propositum** = "purpose."

22–6. "You used to be quite the lady's man and quite the man's lady." The temples were popular sites for assignations. Note how Juvenal interweaves the traditionally feminine cults with figures of effeminate masculinity, thus underlining the bisexuality that is a central feature of this poem and the point of gender contradiction around which its competing social and ideological values turn. On these cults, see **6.487–90** and Ovid *Ars Amatoria* 1.75–88. **Ganymedem**: Ganymede was so beautiful that Zeus took him to be his cup-bearer. He represents the pederastic ideal. His statue was part of the temple of Peace erected by Vespasian at the end of the Jewish War.

Advectae secreta Palatia matris = the Great Mother or Cybele. Her cult was brought from Phrygia in 204 BCE. Roman citizens were forbidden to join her castrated priests, the *Galli*. Her temple was on the Palatine and her public worship was relatively restrained. Private celebrations of her rites were more orgiastic and involved elements of the mystery religions. They were particularly attractive to women (Wiseman 1985: 200–6).

Aufidio = Aufidius Chius, a noted jurist and adulterer from the time of Domitian.

Inclinare = "to bend over" for anal penetration (Adams 1982: 192).

27–90. Naevolus responds with a tirade against the meanness of his patron.

28–31. "Occasionally we receive a cheap cloak and some second rate silver." **Pingues . . . lacernas**: "thick" or "greasy cloaks" (Ferguson 1979). The *lacerna* was worn over the *toga* and hence was its protector (*munimen*). Gallic fabric was coarsely woven and of poor quality.

Pectine = *pecten, –inis*: "comb, a weaver's comb."

32–3. "We are ruled by our fates, which are found in our pants." **Sinus** = the folds of the toga.

33–7. An elaborate periphrasis for, "if you can't perform, Virro no longer cares for you." **Si tibi sidera cessant**: if, as **lines 32–3** state, our fate is found in those parts that the folds of our togas hide, then for the stars (a figure of fate) not to be in our favor can only mean that we are impotent since as the next lines make clear the tool itself is phenomenal (**mensura incognita**).

Nervi = "penis."

Spumanti . . . labello: from fellation. See Catullus 80.

Virro = Naevolus's patron and a noted miser, the subject of *Satire* 5. He is otherwise unknown.

Blandae . . . tabellae = "love letters."

αὐτὸς γὰρ ἐφέλκεται ἄνδρα κίναιδος = a parody of the Homeric ἐφέλκεται ἄνδρα σίδηρος, "steel draws the man," a phrase that underlines the deep attraction of violence. Naevolus, however, says "the *cinaedus* draws the man" (*Odyssey* 16.294, 19.13). A *cinaedus* or "fanny shaker" is a man that desires to be penetrated and hence dominated by another man. Yet in this passage, he controls the other's fate (note how *sidera* recalls the missing Homeric σίδηρος [*sideros*] just after the discussion of **fatum**). Observe also how the *cinaedus* and the ἄνδρα (*vir*) are here implicitly contrasted as if they did not share a common gender. The middle/passive form of the Greek verb draws attention to the inversion of normative subject/object relations.

38. A **mollis avarus** is a contradiction in terms. An effeminate in Roman sexual ideology was by definition one who lacked self-control. Profligacy, not avarice, was associated with *mollitia* (Edwards 1993: 175).

40. Cevet: "Latin possessed two technical terms for types of sexual motion (in both cases that of the passive partner) *criso* and *ceveo*. *Criso* indicated the motions of the female in intercourse [. . .] *Ceveo* was used of the corresponding movements of the male pathic" (Adams 1982: 136).

40–2. "Do the math, Virro, you're getting a bargain." **Tabula** = "abacus."
Sestertia quinque = "5,000 sesterces," what Naevolus has received.

43–6. This passage contains images of eating, excrement, and sexuality in a context which is rich with metaphors of the earth and agriculture, yet is completely sterile. Food (**cenae**) produces excrement that, far from representing a potential source of renewed fertility, serves only as an obstacle to a sexual activity that brings neither pleasure nor fruit to the speaker. Thus Ferguson (1979) observes that the "agricultural metaphor" of ploughing "is common of sex . . . but in agriculture . . . the plough looks forward to harvest." **Pronum** = "inclined forward, easy."

Legitimum = "of proper size" (Courtney 1980).

Foderit < *fodio, –ere, fodi, fossum*: "to dig up, plough through."

46–7. "You, Virro, thought of yourself as a sexy young Ganymede (as if I should pay you)." **Dignum cyatho caeloque** = "worthy of being a cupbearer in heaven," hendiadys. See **line 22.**

48–9. A parenthetical aside directed at those of Virro's ilk. **Adseculae** < *adsecula, –ae*: "follower, servant," masculine.

Indulgebitis = "will show kindness to," with both **adseculae** and **cultori**.

Morbo: i.e., their "sick practices." This is not a reference to homosexuality per se, but to Virro's cinaedic desires. See Parker (1997) and Walters (1997).

Dare = "to give something in return for," here.

50–3. "But you have to send him gifts on every women's holiday!" **Viridem umbellam**: hardly traditional masculine fashion in Rome. The second person addressee here is generic.

Sucina = scented balls of amber popular with women.

Cathedra: see **1.63–8.**

53. Femineis . . . kalendis = March 1, the Matronalia. This is a golden line.

54–5. "Tell me my pet, for whom are you saving your storied wealth?" The addressee is once more Virro. **Passer** was used as a term of endearment. The sparrow was Venus's bird and had strong erotic connotations. See Sappho 1 and Catullus 2 and 3.

Apula < *Apulus, –a, –um* = "Apulian."

Milvos = "kites."

Lassas < *lasso, –are*: "exhaust."

56–60. "Your vines are fertile but you give nothing to your client's exhausted loins." **Trifolinus** = a region near Naples known for its wine.

Suspectumque iugum Cumis = "the ridge that overhangs Cumae."

Gaurus identified with Monte Barbaro, an extinct volcano and hence **inanis**.

Linit = "smears, daubs."

Victuro = future participle of both *vivo* and *vinco*. The wine will "live," and hence become an aged vintage, and it will "conquer" both its competitors and, perhaps, its consumers.

Dolia: see 6.430–2.

59–60. In punctuating these lines, I follow Courtney (1980; 1984), Labriolle and Villeneuve (1964), and Friedländer (1962). **Erat**: "The indicative in such cases, where English would say 'would have been', is regular" (Courtney 1980).

60–2. "Do you prefer to leave your young slave to your friend, the eunuch priest of Cybele?" The sequence of thought is difficult. Who is the priest of Cybele and why would he receive this legacy? He must serve as an image of the kind of depravity that would ensue if the already depraved patron did not make a bequest to his equally depraved client. There is also a crude joke: why should Virro leave his property to a priest lacking the very instrument whereby Naevolus earns his keep, and which would be necessary to enjoy the boy properly? The slave and his mother are, in turn, synecdoche for the property on which they live. I, with Courtney (1980) and Willis (1997), accept Housman's conjecture **melius nunc** for the manuscripts' nonsensical *meliusne hic*.

Casulis = diminutive of *casa*: the plural tells in favor of Courtney's (1980) interpretation, "toy houses."

Catello: see 6.652–4.

Cymbala pulsantis: a common attribute of a priest of Cybele.

63–5. The patron responds that Naevolus does not observe the proprieties. The fiction underlying patron–client relations is that they were spontaneous friendships founded on mutual good offices, not commodified relations of labor for hire, which Romans saw as little different from slavery (Bowditch 2001: 16–17). Patrons provided "gifts" for clients, and Naevolus, by having the temerity to ask, calls into question the fiction on which the institution rests. **Pensio** = "rent."

Acies = "keenness, vision," and in this context "eye." If Polyphemus had had more than one eye, Ulysses would have never escaped. The epic comparison is highly incongruous for the context and makes Naevolus appear as absurd a character as his patron is mean. Having only one slave certainly placed Naevolus several steps down the social ladder, but hardly at the bottom.

66–7. "I have to buy another, because this one just won't do, and then I'll have to feed two!" Naevolus and his patron are an unlovely pair.

67–9. Scapulis = "the shoulders," which need to be covered.
Cicadas = metonymy for "spring."

70–2. "But you fail to recognize the costs if I had left your wife a virgin." The *lex Iulia* (6.38–40) specified economic and social penalties for Romans of senatorial and equestrian status who did not marry and produce heirs. Virro needs to reward Naevolus for saving him from the social and financial disgrace of being unable to consummate his marriage. **Ut** = concessive.
Cetera = the shared object of both **dissimules** and **mittas**.

73–4. Ista = accusative of respect.
Modis: see 6.402–6. Virro is a voyeur.
Pollicitus: understand *sis*.

74–8. "As the creaking of your own bed testifies, while you listened outside, I saved your marriage." **Fugientem**: was she fleeing Virro or Naevolus? The grammar is ambiguous.
Rapui = "seized," but also "raped" (Adams 1982: 175).
Tabulas = "the marriage contract." She had asked for a divorce.
Migrabat: Highet's (1952) emendation of the vulgate *signabat* is widely adopted.
Te plorante foris: Virro ironically recalls the figure of the elegiac *exclusus amator*.

79–80. "Adultery saves marriages." **Dirimi** < *dirimo, –ere, –emi, –emptum*: "to part, separate, sunder."

81–3. "There's no escaping it. You are only a father by my good offices."

84–6. Libris actorum = *acta diurna*. See 6.481–5.

87–8. Legatum omne capis: the *lex Iulia* forbade the childless from receiving more than half of any legacy left them, the rest (**caducum**) went to another named in the will who happened to be a parent.

89–90. "You will gain additional privileges if I bring the family up to the full number, three." The *lex Papia Poppaea* (9 CE) granted special privileges to senatorial and equestrian households that produced at least three children.

90–1. The satirist replies, "what does he say in response?"

92–101. "To him I am a completely disposable sexual beast of burden." The ass was notorious for its lust.

93–5. "Please keep these complaints a secret." **Pumice levis** = "depilated."

96–7. The irony of Naevolus's complaint completely escapes him.

97–9. "He would not hesitate to kill me if his secrets were revealed." **Ferrum** = "sword."
Fuste = "cudgel."
Candelam adponere valvis: i.e., "to burn my house down."

99–100. **Annona** = "price."

101. **Curia Martis** = the Areopagus, an institution of Athenian political and judicial life whose constitutional function changed over time, but whose deliberations were secret.

102–23. The satirist replies: "A rich man has no secrets. The only real solution is living rightly."

102. **O Corydon, Corydon**: a direct allusion to Vergil, *Eclogue* 2.69, *O Corydon, Corydon, quae te dementia cepit.* The refined, unrequited homoeroticism of Vergil's pastoral contrasts markedly with the sordid reality of Naevolus's life.

103. **Ut** = concessive.

104–10. "No matter the precautions you take, by cock's crow the whole neighborhood will know."

106. **E medio fac eant omnes** = "make everyone withdraw from your midst."
Recumbat: see 3.8 and 6.434.

107. **Galli . . . secundi**: the cock was thought to crow three times.

108. **Caupo**: see **Horace 1.5.1–6.**

109. **Libarius** = "confectioner."
Archimagiri = "chefs," the only example of this Greek word in Latin.

110. **Carptores** = "carvers" at table.

110–12. **Baltea** = "belts or straps," here used to beat the slaves.

112–13. "Drunks will inquire about you at street corners (**compita**)." **Inebriet aurem**: a vivid metaphor.

114–15. **Quidquid** = *quod* and refers to the request made at **lines 92–4**.

115–17. "They'd rather betray your secret than content themselves with drinking only as much as the infamous Saufeia." **Falerni**: see **1.10.20–30.**

Pro populo faciens = "performing a sacrifice for the people," which would make her the wife of a consul or the *praetor urbanus*. As **6.320–3**, where we first meet **Saufeia**, shows, this is a reference to the rites of the *Bona Dea*.

118–19. See the introductory note. This advice goes for Naevolus as well as Virro. The OCT's daggers around **tunc est** are needless, as Friedländer shows (1962).

120–3. These lines are a mere repetition of what has come before and, written in a prosaic style, are unlikely to be Juvenal's. They are unknown to the scholiast and generally printed in brackets.

124–9. Naevolus thanks the satirist for his advice but says it is of little practical value. "What am I to do when age has robbed me of my attractiveness?" The invocation of the *carpe diem* motif from amatory poetry is deeply ironic. Moreover, as Juvenal's description of Naevolus in **1–26** indicates, it may already be too late. **Velox flosculus** = "the swift flower of youth."

130–3. "Fear not," the satirist responds, "as long as Rome stands, there will be need for your services." **Carpentis** < *carpentum, –i*: "a two-wheeled carriage," favored by women.

Qui digito scalpunt uno caput: a gesture considered effeminate.

134. **Erucis**: see **Horace 2.8.51**, an aphrodisiac.

135–50. Naevolus: "Homilies are fine for the fortunate, but I must earn my bread. I don't ask for much, just the necessary luxuries."

135–6. **Clotho et Lachesis** = "two of the Fates."

137–40. "I pray to my Hearth Gods that my retirement will be secure." **Tegete**: see **6.117–18.**

Baculo < *baculum, –i*: "beggar's staff."

140–6. Naevolus's list of necessities is extravagant. He expects an income (**fenus**) just below the equestrian census from his property, silver plate, litter-bearers to take him to the circus, an engraver and a painter. This is far more than is necessary to meet the needs of the **venter (line 136)**. It would certainly seem quite extravagant for one who earned his living with his **inguine (line 136)** and hence was considered little different from a slave (Ste Croix 1981: 198; Joshel 1992: 67–8, 152). Ferguson's notion (1979) that Naevolus hoped to use the slaves to become a small businessman and "go straight" is endearingly naïve.

Viginti milia: the expected income off the equestrian census of 400,000 sesterces was 24,000 per annum at the accustomed 6% annual rate. It must be remembered that in spite of their being slightly less well off than the senatorial class, the equestrians were anything but middle class. They represented the second order of the aristocratic élite in Roman society and were in the top 1% of the population (Ste Croix 1981: 41–2; Joshel 1992: 71–2).

Puri = "plain, unembossed."

Fabricius: C. Fabricius Luscinus, censor in 275 BCE, removed P Cornelius Rufinus from the senate for possessing 10 lbs of silver plate. On **notet**, see **Horace 1.4.1–5.**

Moesorum: a Balkan tribe favored as litter-bearers.

Locatum: Courtney's arguments for Heinrich's conjecture are persuasive (1980).

Curvus caelator = "a stooped engraver," from bending over his work.

Sufficiunt haec: the bucolic diaeresis highlights this pretence to modesty [51].

147–50. "When will I be at least moderately poor?" *Paupertas* does not designate poverty, but not being wealthy. Nonetheless, Naevolus wants far more than that.

Nec . . . saltem = "nor even."

149–50. Fortuna, like Odysseus fleeing the song of the Sirens, stuffs wax (**ceras**) in her ears when Naevolus prays. Sicily (**Siculos**) was the accepted location of the Sirens.

10

A classic example of Juvenal's later style [78], this poem was the model for Johnson's "The Vanity of Human Wishes." The argument is simple: men pray for power, eloquence, military success, longevity, and good looks, but none of these brings happiness. Its power lies in its vividly sketched vignettes of Sejanus, Cicero, Hannibal, Priam, and others. It ends with the now commonplace formula that all we should pray for is **mens sana in corpore sano (line 356)**.

This satire seems to promise philosophical repose. The world is to be laughed at with pity, not raked with the lash. As such, the poem is filled with the chestnuts of ancient moral philosophy. The good sense of these truisms has guaranteed the poem a large and receptive audience through the ages, where the misogyny of poems like 6 and the obscenity of 9 have at times led to their neglect.

Yet before we settle into smug self-satisfaction, it should be noted that the vignettes offer more than enough material to feed the sadistic pleasure associated with satire's lacerating attacks (see the introductory note to **Horace 1.2**). Few will forget the image of Sejanus's dead body being dragged by the hook, nor the scathing descriptions of impotent old age, and aristocratic nymphomaniacs. The joys of vicariously participating in the grotesque degradation of others have not been banished, but provided a more philosophical frame [33, 78].

1–53. Juvenal announces a program of Democritean satire that laughs rather than weeps at the follies of men.

1–4. Few are able to recognize the truly good. **Gadibus** = *Gades*, modern Cadiz, a settlement beyond the straits of Gibraltar.

5–6. Dextro pede: "auspiciously," or as we still say, "on the right foot."

8–14. "The very things we wish for—money, power, and eloquence—do us harm." **Toga** = metonymy for political power.

Torrens dicendi copia: an exemplification of the **facundia** in question.

Viribus is taken with both **confisus** and **periit**.

Ille = Milo of Croton a sixth-century BCE athlete who, in a demonstration of strength pulled apart an oak with his bare hands causing them to be trapped inside. Wolves subsequently devoured him.

Ballaena = "whale."

15–18. "Great houses arouse imperial envy." The examples all come from the conspiracy of Piso against Nero (65 CE). **Longinum** = *Longini domum*. C. Cassius Longinus was a leading legal authority and former consul. He was exiled to Sardinia, but recalled by Vespasian.

Senecae = the philosopher and tutor of Nero. His wealth was legendary. His nephew, the poet Lucan, was involved in the conspiracy. Both were forced to commit suicide.

Lateranorum: Plautius Lateranus, another conspirator, he owned a magnificent home on the *Mons Caelius* which later became the site for the basilica of St John Lateran. He was executed.

"The change of tense from **clausit** to **obsidet** gives a picture. The soldiers have closed Seneca's house, and are now proceeding to beset Lateranus" (Pearson and Strong 1892).

Cenacula = "garret."

19–22. "Even modest (**pauca**) wealth leads to fear." **Argenti vascula puri** = a direct quotation of 9.141.

Contum = "a pike."

Vacuus = "empty-handed" and "carefree." Note the alliterative pattern: *c . . . v . . . c . . . v*.

23–5. "Indeed everyone prays for riches."

25–7. "No poison is drunk from simple earthenware." **Aconita**: see 1.158–9 and 6.638–40.

Setinum: understand *vinum*. The wine from Setia was considered fine.

Ardebit: "a beautifully chosen word: 'glows', especially suitable to red wine, but also of the burning, consuming effect of poison" (Ferguson 1979).

28–30. This wonderful epigram, which introduces the programmatic portion of the introduction, is almost a direct quotation of Seneca's *De Ira* 2.10. There it becomes clear that the two *auctores* are Democritus and Heraclitus respectively. The rhetorical structure of Juvenal's sentence is elaborate. **Alter** assumes **auctor** and **sapientibus** refers specifically to "philosophers." The adverbial clause, **quotiens a limine moverat unum / protuleratque pedem**, goes with **ridebat** and **flebat**, connecting the two main clauses by asyndeton.

Democritus of Abdera, the grandfather of Epicureanism, was an atomistic philosopher of the fifth and fourth centuries BCE.

Heraclitus was the Pre-Socratic philosopher (circa 542–480 BCE) who said the world was a flux and was structured by a tension between opposites (hence **contrarius**).

31. Facilis: understand *est*.

Rigidi . . . cachinni = a striking oxymoron, "a stern cackle."

32. We have to laugh; there are not enough tears in the world.

33–5. "Democritus laughed, though his world was less absurd than ours." **Praetextae, trabeae, fasces, lectica, tribunal** = respectively, the purple-fringed togas worn by magistrates, equestrian ceremonial dress, the symbols of official power, the litters of the wealthy, and the platform on which curule chairs were set: all signs of ambition.

36–42. Juvenal describes the procession that preceded the games at the circus, led by a praetor or consul in a chariot. He was costumed as a triumphing general in the tunic and gold-embroidered (**pictae**) toga taken from the temple of Jupiter Capitolinus. **Sarrana** = "Tyrian," hence "purple."

Aulaea = "curtains," hyperbole for the toga's vast folds.

Coronae = a gem-encrusted crown of gold oak leaves held above a triumphing general's head, and hence above the head of the magistrate presiding over the games, by a public slave. It was too heavy to wear (**cervix non sufficit ulla**).

Sibi . . . ne placeat: another purpose of the slave in the chariot was to remind the triumphing general that he was a man, and hence not actually able to wear such a crown.

43–6. "But that's only the half of it!" **Da nunc** = "consider in addition."

Volucrem = the eagle on the ivory scepter held by the triumphing general.

Cornicines = "trumpeters."

44–6. The procession of Roman citizens (**Quirites**) in their freshly laundered togas (**niveos**) is transformed into the ritualized exchange of services (**officia**) that constituted the essence of the patron-client relationship (*amicitia*). **Praecedentia** refers to the *anteambulationes* or the "forerunners" who cleared the way.

Quos: antecedent = **Quirites**.

Sportula: see **1.95–126**.

Defossa < *defodio, –ere, –fodi, –fossum*: "to dig, to bury" and hence "conceal."

Loculos = "cash-boxes."

47–50. "Then too he found no shortage of fools to laugh at." **Invenit** = perfect. Its subject is **Democritus**.

Occursus < *occursus, –us*: "meeting."

Et = also

Vervecum < *vervex, –vervecis*: "dolt," see **3.293–6**.

Crassoque sub aere nasci: Abdera, in spite of producing several notable intellectuals, had a reputation for giving birth to dolts, sometimes attributed to Boeotia's "thick" air.

51–3. "He laughed at the joys, cares, and tears of the common man and gave Fortuna the finger." **Mandaret laqueum** = "ordered a noose for."

54–5. This is the transitional couplet between the introduction and the satire's main body. **Lines 56–345** take up what is **perniciosa**, while only **346–66** concern what is **fas**. **Incerare** = "to smear with wax," from placing wax-tablet petitions on the knees (**genua**) of cult statues, a striking comic image to revitalize a commonplace.

56–113. "Do not pray for power. Remember the example of Sejanus."

56–8. "Power subjected to envy casts down the mighty." **Pagina** = a bronze tablet affixed to a statue-base listing offices held.

58–60. "The statues are pulled down and hauled away." **Restem** = "rope."

Bigarum = "a two-horse chariot." This was a triumphal statue. Many such statues of Sejanus existed. In the imperial period, only members of the royal household were allowed to celebrate triumphs, although the lesser *ovatio* was still granted to successful generals.

Inpacta < *impingo, –ere, –pegi, –pactum*: "strike."

Securis = "axe."

Caballis = a low word. See **Horace 1.6.56–60, 100–4** and **Juvenal 3.118.**

61–4. "Then all gather round to watch the head of the one-time beloved of the people melt in the flames of the forge." **Follibus atque caminis** = "bellows and forges."

Adoratum = "having received cult honors."

Seianus = L. Aelius Seianus, an equestrian who was made prefect of the Praetorian Guard (20 CE). He became Tiberius's proxy after the latter's retirement to Capri in 26. Sejanus engineered a series of prosecutions that eliminated his rivals. Tiberius denounced him in a letter to the senate in 31 when he had been made consul and was at the pinnacle of power. He was subsequently prosecuted and executed along with his wife, children, and adherents.

Urceoli, pelves, sartago, matellae = "pitchers, basins, a frying pan, chamber pots."

65–7. "Let there be a great celebration: Sejanus's body is dragged out on a hook." **Cretatumque** = "whitened with chalk"; only a pure white animal can be offered to Jupiter.

Unco < *uncus, –i*: "hook," especially that used by the executioner to drag the body of dead malefactors to the Tiber.

67–70. The fickle crowd turns on their darling. **Delator** = "informer." Sejanus made liberal use of paid informants.

71–2. Tiberius's letter, as recorded in Dio Cassius 58.9–10, was read aloud in the senate by Macro, Sejanus's successor as praetorian prefect. Sejanus was expecting fresh honors but, as the lengthy letter unfolded, his doom was sealed. **Nil plus interrogo**: it's dangerous to ask too many questions.

74–7. "The *populus Romanus* is completely fickle as to whom they give their allegiance." **Nortia** = Etruscan version of Fortuna. Sejanus, who was born at Volsinii in Etruria, kept a statue of Fortuna in his house.

Oppressa < *opprimo, –primere, –pressi, –pressum*: "to press down, crush, take by surprise."

Secura = "off-guard."

Augustum: i.e. proclaim him "emperor."

77–81. "But the people have long since (**ex quo**) ceased to sell their votes and today wish only for two things: bread and circuses." Juvenal, in a typical move, simultaneously criticizes republican electoral corruption (**vendimus**) and laments the loss of the people's role in electing magistrates. In 14 CE, Tiberius ended popular elections and gave the senate control over appointing officials on his recommendation. **Effudit curas** = "has thrown off its burden," the subject is *populus*.

Panem et circenses: one of Juvenal's most famous lines.

81–7. An overheard conversation in the crowd about coming executions.

82. **Fornacula** = ironic diminutive of *fornax*: "oven, furnace." The whole expression is colloquial and is the equivalent to "it's getting pretty hot."

82–3. **Bruttidius** = Bruttidius Niger, aedile 22 CE. There is a joke in calling him **pallidulus**. "Mr Black is a little pale."

84–5. **Victus ne poenas exigat Aiax**: a common theme of the rhetorical schools. Ajax competed with Odysseus for the arms of Achilles and lost. As a result, he tried to kill the Achaean leaders but, in a fit of madness, slew instead a flock of sheep. Ajax here stands for Tiberius who, in his rage at Sejanus for poorly defending his interests, the speaker fears, may target others. Bruttidius was in the habit of declaiming in the schools.

86. The subject of **iacet** = Sejanus.

87–8. Everyone joins in desecrating the body of the fallen prefect lest their watching slaves inform on them. In this world turned upside-down, masters fear their slaves.

90–4. "Would you really want to trade places with Sejanus?" **Salutari** = "to receive the morning *salutatio*."

Illi . . . illum = "this fellow . . . that fellow."

Angusta Caprearum in rupe = "the narrow rock of the Goats," the modern island of Capri, to which Tiberius retired. There is a joke in picturing the reclusive emperor as a shepherd on a small island surrounded by a flock of astrologers (**cum grege Chaldaeo**).

95. **Egregios equites** = the *equites illustres*, equestrians that possessed the senatorial census and were entitled to wear a broad purple fringe on their toga.

Castra domestica = the praetorian guards, the only troops billeted in the city. Sejanus brought them into a single barracks.

96–7. A direct quotation of Plato, *Gorgias* 466 B11–C1, where Polus asks who would not want the power of a tyrant.

99–102. "Who would prefer to put on his robe of state as opposed to being a minor official in small town?" **Qui trahitur**: see **ducitur unco, line 66.**
Praetextam: see **lines 33–5.**
Fidenarum Gabiorumque: see 6.55–9.

101–2. See **Persius 1.126–34. Pannosus** = "ragged."
Ulubris = Ulubrae, a town in Latium near the Pontine marshes.

103–7. Sejanus proves, "the bigger they are, the harder they fall." **Seianum** is the subject of **ignorasse** in indirect discourse, dependent on **fateris**.
Tabulata: see 3.199.
Praeceps = neuter substantive and **inmane** = predicate adjective with **esset**.

108–9. "History shows his fall is not unique." The case cited is the first Triumvirate: Crassus, Pompey, and Caesar. M. Licinius Crassus was one of the richest men in Rome. In 60 BCE, he joined with the two powerful military leaders, Caesar and Pompey, to form a *de facto* junta. When Crassus died in an unsuccessful expedition against the Parthians (53 BCE), the arrangement quickly devolved into a rivalry between the two generals leading to civil war and Caesar's dictatorship. **Crassos . . . Pompeios** = men like Crassus and Pompey.
Flagra = poetic plural for *flagrum*: "a whip or scourge" used on slaves.

110–11. "Such great men fall, because they rise to power on prayers offered to malign deities."

112–13. "Kings and tyrants don't die in their beds." **Generum Cereris** = an ironic name for Pluto, who kidnapped Persephone to be his bride.
Sicca morte = one without blood or poison.

114–32. People wish for eloquence as well as power, but this too brings a harvest of woe.

114–17. "Every school boy wishes for the fame and eloquence of Demosthenes and Cicero." Demosthenes was the greatest of the Athenian orators (384–322 BCE). His *Philippics*, delivered against Philip of Macedon, were the inspiration for Cicero's speeches by the same name delivered against Marc Antony. The latter cost Cicero his life in 43 BCE [23–4, 30]. Demosthenes ended his life by committing suicide after he was condemned to death. **Totis**

quinquatribus = ablative of time within which: the festival of Minerva, March 19–23, goddess of wisdom and hence patron of oratory. It was a school holiday.

Uno . . . asse: a regular contribution given to the treasury of the temple, collected by the teacher.

Parcam: the schoolboys worship Minerva on the cheap.

Custos: see Horace **1.6.81–2. Vernula** = diminutive of *verna*: "house-born."

Capsae = a cylindrical container for carrying books.

118–19. The image of the waves of the fountain of genius delivering both men to death is extraordinary.

120–1. Cicero's hands and head were cut off and nailed to the **rostra** in the Forum as a warning to anyone who would presume to speak against members of the second triumvirate (Antony, Octavian, and Lepidus).

Causidici . . . pusilli = "no-account pleader."

122–4. Juvenal quotes Cicero's most infamous line from his fatuous and self-glorifying *De Consulatu Suo*. If Cicero had been as bad an orator as he was a poet he would have had nothing to fear.

124–6. **Divina Philippica** = vocative.

Volveris a prima quae proxima = "which you will have unrolled right after the first," a mocking epic periphrasis for "second." The second *Philippic* was considered Cicero's best.

126–8. The focus shifts to Demosthenes. **Torrentem et . . . moderantem frena**: there is a change of metaphor, but the notion is clear. Demosthenes was a master of control.

Theatri = a common place of political assembly.

129–32. Demosthenes's father was the owner of a sword factory, but the orator's rivals portrayed him as the son of a blacksmith. **Massae** = "lump" of metal.

Fuligine < *fuligo, –inis*: "soot."

Lippus: see **Horace 1.5.27.31.**

Carbone < *carbo, –onis*: "charcoal."

Incude < *incus, –udis*: "anvil."

Luteo Volcano = "the grimy smoke" of the forge.

Ad rhetora: i.e. to the teacher of rhetoric.

133–87. Others wish for military glory.

133–7. "Many believe the trophies of war are of superhuman worth." **Exuviae** = "spoils."

Truncis . . . tropaeis: "the epithet refers to the simplest form of a trophy, erected on the field after a victory: this was the stump of a tree, stripped of the leaves and branches, and then covered with captured weapons and pieces of armour" (Duff 1970).

Lorica = "a cuirass."

Casside < *cassis, –idis*: "a metal helmet."

Buccula = "a cheek-piece."

Curtum temone iugum = "a yoke cut from a chariot pole."

Triremis = "a trireme, warship."

Aplustre = "the stern ornaments of a ship."

Arcu = "a triumphal arch."

137–41. "From this it can be seen that the thirst (**sitis**) for fame is greater than the thirst for virtue." **Induperator** = archaic for *imperator*.

Discriminis = "distinction."

141–2. A bitter epigram: this has been the central concern of ethics since Plato's *Republic*.

142–6. "The ruin of the country is traded for a few lines on a tombstone (**saxis cinerum custodibus**)." **Quae**: the antecedent = **saxis**.

Discutienda < *discutio, –ere, –cussi, –cussum*: "to strike asunder, shatter."

Sterilis . . . fici = the *caprificus* or "wild fig." It, like fame, is incapable of propagating itself. Its roots can shatter solid stone. See **Persius 1.25**.

147–8. "Put Hannibal on the scale: what do you get?" **Hannibalem** = the great Carthaginian general who crossed the Alps from Gaul in the second Punic War and led an assault on Rome itself. He was definitively defeated at the battle of Zama in 202 BCE by Scipio Africanus [53].

148–50. "He whom Africa itself could not contain." **Mauro . . . oceano** = the Atlantic.

Rursus ad = "back to"

Aliosque elephantos: i.e., not Indian.

151–2. In the process of consolidating Carthage's holdings in Spain, Hannibal first came into conflict with Rome.

153–4. Note the vivid present tense verbs. **Montem rumpit aceto**: Livy 21.37 tells how Hannibal removed boulders by heating them with fire and dousing them with vinegar. Modern experiments show this works (Ferguson 1979).

155–6. Hannibal wishes to plant his standard (**vexillum**) in the Subura, Rome's red light district. See **3.5. Acti** = partitive genitive.

157–8. The irony fairly drips from these lines. **Gaetula . . . belva** = epic periphrasis for "elephant."

Luscum: Hannibal lost an eye in crossing the Arno.

159–62. After the war, Hannibal was the object of intrigues by both the conservative faction in Carthage and the Romans. He fled to Ephesus, before winding up in the court of Prusias, king of Bithynia, where he committed suicide (circa 181 BCE) to avoid being handed over to the Romans. **Praeceps** = "immediately"; in fact Hannibal did not leave Carthage until 195 BCE.

Cliens = Hannibal becomes just another abused Roman client waiting to pay his patron the required morning *salutatio*.

Praetoria = "palace."

163–6. **Res humanas miscuit** = "disturbed the lives of all men."

Cannarum = locative of *Cannae*, the battle at which Hannibal, though vastly outnumbered, defeated the Roman consuls L. Aemilius Paullus and C. Terentius Varro (216 BCE).

Anulus = a ring with poison in it.

166–7. The ultimate in trivialization: Hannibal's decision to cross the Alps became a topic of *suasoriae* in the rhetorical schools.

168–72. Juvenal's next exhibit is Alexander the Great. **Pellaeo** = "from Pella," the Macedonian city of Alexander's birth.

Gyarae . . . Seripho = two small Aegean islands used as places of exile. See 1.73–6.

A figulis munitam . . . urbem = "the city built from bricks," Babylon, the place of Alexander's death.

173. **Quantula . . . corpuscula**: the double diminutive reinforces the sharply pointed epigram.

173–8. The final exhibit is Xerxes. A side target is Herodotus, the Greek historian in whose chronicle of the Persian Wars these stories are found. Plutarch disputed Herodotus's title, "the father of history," calling him instead "the father of lies." Nonetheless, both marvels referred to in this passage appear to have been real. **Athos** = a mountain standing on a promontory in the north Aegean. After a Persian fleet had wrecked there in 492 BCE, Xerxes cut a canal through the peninsula. Hence, the mountain is **velificatus**: "sailed."

Constratum . . . suppositumque . . . solidum mare: Xerxes bridged the

Hellespont with boats. Thus he made the mountain into the sea and the sea into land. **Constratum** < *consterno, –sternere, –stravi, –stratum*: "to cover by strewing," of a ship "to cover with decking," hence the neuter substantive can mean "flooring, deck," an appropriate image of the sea decked over with boats.

Rotis = the wheels of the chariots.

Epota = "drank up." Herodotus says only the largest rivers were not drained (7.21).

Prandente = "while lunching," a wonderful comic detail.

Sostratus is unidentified. The scholiast claims that his armpits (**alis**) are dripping with the strain of recitation. Others see the wings (**alis**) of inspiration as wet with wine (a common meaning of *madidus*, see **6.295–7**). We need not choose. The one represents the poet's aspiration, the other the sordid reality.

179–85. "Xerxes had the winds flogged, but he returned home in a single boat." **Salamine**: the naval battle of Salamis (480 BCE) was the decisive engagement in Xerxes's invasion of Greece. The Athenians routed the Persian fleet, ending the Persian threat to the mainland Greeks and establishing Athens as the dominant naval power in Greece.

Corum atque Eurum = the Northwest and Southeast winds. Herodotus records Xerxes ordering the flogging of the Hellespont. Here he whips the winds.

Flagellis = diminutive of **flagra**: see **line 109.**

Aeolio . . . carcere = Aeolus's prison: the cave in which the god of the winds kept them locked.

Ennosigaeum = "The Earthshaker," a Homeric epithet for Poseidon. When a storm destroyed Xerxes's first bridge across the Hellespont, he not only had it whipped, but also had manacles (**conpedibus**) thrown in.

183–4. A sarcastic, satirical aside. "To be sure (**sane**), it was rather kind, since he did not also think him worthy of branding." Herodotus records that he heard that Xerxes actually did brand the sea (7.35). **Servire deorum**: a fine ironic juxtaposition.

185–6. Una nave = a post-Herodotean hyperbole.

187. A final epigram summarizes the section.

188–288. Many pray for long life.

189. Recto voltu: the opposition with **pallidus** and a comparison with **recta facie** at **6.401** makes it clear that this phrase refers to when you are composed, as opposed to when you are pale (**pallidus**) with worry. In the first case, (i.e. when you are composed) you pray for longevity (among other things); in the second case (i.e. when you are pale with worry) longevity is the only thing for which you pray.

191–5. The humbling deformities of old age.

194. The exotic epic description cleverly delays the rhetorical anticlimax of the final line. **Thabraca** = a town on the coast of Numidia.
Saltus < *saltus*, *–us*: "forest."

195. Apes were considered proverbially ugly.

196–200. "While youth enjoys many distinctions, old age has but one face."

197. **Ille** is widely obelized or emended by recent editors (Clausen 1956; Ferguson 1979; Courtney 1980; Willis 1997), although among those of previous generations it was generally left unchanged (Pearson and Strong 1892; Friedländer 1962; Labriolle and Villeneuve 1964; Duff 1970). It is omitted in some of the earliest manuscripts. The vulgate is readable but awkward. Finding none of the emendations persuasive, I have left the daggers to indicate a disturbance in the tradition.

199. **Leve** = "smooth," the first *e* is long.
Infantia = a return to helplessness.

200. **Misero** = dative of agent.
Inermi = "toothless."

201–2. **Captatori**: see 6.38–40. Cossus is unknown.

203–6. Wine, food, and sex no longer bring joy. **Ramice** < *ramex*, *–icis*: "rupture."
Nervus: see 9.33–7.

209. **Adfectat** = "to strive after."

209–10. **Partis . . . alterius** = "another part," the ear as it turns out, but the periphrasis leads us to expect another sexual excursus.

210–12. **Eximius** = "distinguished." Seleucus is otherwise unknown.
Aurata . . . fulgere lacerna: "to shine in a golden cloak," elaborate costumes are regularly attested for musicians.

213–15. **Cornicines**: see 3.34–8.
Concentus = "harmony."

215–16. **Puer** = "slave."

Quot nuntiet horas: Slaves were assigned to watch sundials to ensure that their masters were on time.

217–26. "His bloodless body is never warmed except by fever and is wracked by a legion of diseases too numerous to name." **Promptius expediam** = "I would more quickly set out."

Oppia = otherwise unknown, she appears again in 322.

Themison = the name of a famous doctor from the Augustan period.

Basilus = unknown.

Socios = "business partners."

Hirrus = unknown.

Exorbeat = *ex-sorbeat*: "drank dry." See 6.307.

Inclinet: see 9.22–6.

Hamillus = unknown.

226. A repetition of 1.25, a fine anticlimax that takes us back to Juvenal's first published poem.

227–32. The humiliations of physical debility. **Coxa** = "hip."

Luscis: see **line 158.**

Conspectum = substantive.

Rictum = "open mouth."

Hiat = "gapes."

Tantum ceu = "just so much as."

Pullus = "chick".

Hirundinis < *hirundo, –inis*: "swallow."

Ieiuna = "hungry" because she is giving the food to her young.

232–6. Dementia, however, is the worst.

236–9. The senile man disinherits his kin in favor of a skilled call-girl. **Phialen** = the mistress.

Tantum artificis valet halitus oris = either "the breath of her skilled mouth was worth so much" or "the breath of her skilled mouth was so strong." Fellatio was presumed to cause bad breath. See 6.47–9.

Carcere = "cell."

Fornicis: see 3.156.

240–2. "Even if you keep your senses, you'll still bury your dear ones."

243–5. "You grow old in perpetual mourning for the ever renewed destruction (**clade**) of your house."

246–7. The first example is Nestor of Pylos. **A cornice secundae** = "second only to the crow," who was believed to live nine generations.

248–50. **Nimirum** = ironic intensifier, "certainly."

Saecula = "generations."

Dextra: ones and tens were counted on the left hand, hundreds and thousands on the right. Nestor was believed to have lived to one hundred.

250–5. "I pray that you pay attention, however, to what the consequences of that long life are." Nestor buried his son Antilochus at Troy. **Parumper** = "for a little while."

Stamina: "the spindle" upon which the thread of his life is wound.

Acris = "fierce."

Ardentem: on the funeral pyre.

256–7. Two quick examples: Peleus, the father of Achilles, and Laertes, the father of Odysseus. **Ithacum** = the Ithacan. Ithaca was the home of Odysseus.

Natantem: on his ten-year return voyage from Troy, Odysseus was on two occasions shipwrecked and forced to swim for it.

258–64. Having gone through the elderly fathers on the Greek side of the Trojan War, Juvenal turns his attention to the most famous father from the other side: Priam. **Venisset**: The protasis of the condition is delayed until **line 263.**

Assaraci = the son of Tros and brother of Priam's grandfather, Ilus.

Funus = "corpse."

Ut: Ferguson's note (1979) contains a salutary reminder, "In translation we have to choose between saying that *ut* introduces a clause defining *Iliadum lacrimas* and that *ut* means 'when' (the subjunctive being explained by the conditional), but to the Roman listener *ut* was *ut*, blending the senses we analyse as 'when', 'as', 'in order to', 'with the result that', etc. We can get around it by 'with Cassandra leading' or 'and Cassandra would have led.'"

Cassandra . . . Polyxena: Priam's daughters. Cassandra was priestess of Apollo. She survived her father but was taken as a slave to Mycenae with Agamemnon where she was slain by his wife, Clytemnestra. Polyxena was sacrificed on the grave of Achilles.

Palla = a long rectangular shawl worn over the head by Roman women. It reached the knees. The tearing of clothing is a common gesture of mourning.

Carinas: i.e., the fleet in which Paris sailed to Sparta to seduce Helen.

267–70. The death of Priam. Juvenal recounts in condensed form *Aeneid* 2.504–58. **Tiara**: a specifically Asian headdress. Note the sharp alliteration of the *t*'s in 267.

268. Vetulus bos: the absurdity of Priam's sacrifice is driven home, even as the line is brought up short. Compare *Aeneid* 5.481 for a similar line ending.

269. Cultris: see **Horace 1.9.72–4.**

270. Ab ingrato . . . aratro = ablative of agent, because feelings are attributed to the plough.

271–2. Priam's wife, Hecuba, outlived him, was taken captive by the Greeks, and ultimately was turned into a dog. **Utcumque** = "at any rate." Understand *est*.

273–5. Nostros = Romans.

Regem . . . Ponti = Mithridates VI, see **6.660–1.**

Croesum = proverbially rich king of Lydia (sixth century BCE).

Solonis = Solon (circa 640–560 BCE), the Athenian lawgiver and poet who, when asked by Croesus who was the luckiest man alive, replied Tellus, an Athenian who died in battle and whose two sons survived him. The probably fictitious story is told in Herodotus 1.28–34. It includes the notion that a man's life can only be judged once we know his death.

Spatia ultima = "the last lap." Seneca in *De Tranquilitate Animi* 11 uses Croesus to make the same argument.

276–82. Marius too outlived his triumphs. Gaius Marius (157–86 BCE) was a popular leader and general. Saving Italy from an invasion by German tribes (104–101 BCE), he held the consulship an unprecedented seven times. He was later ousted by Sulla and reactionary elements of the aristocracy. To escape capture he hid in the marshes at Minturnae (**Minturnarumque paludes**); he was caught, imprisoned, and condemned to death, but helped by his executioner to escape to Carthage where he lived for a time as a beggar, before rallying his troops and returning to Rome. Shortly after, his health failed. **Hinc** = "from too long a life."

Illo cive = ablative of comparison with **beatius**.

Circumducto captivorum agmine = the line of captives in a triumphal procession (**pompa**). See **lines 36–42.** Note the serpentine procession of large alliterative words, underlined by elisions.

There is hiatus [49, 51] between **pompa** and **animam**: the prosody imitates the general's last gasp.

Opimam = "glorious."

Teutonico: the Teutoni were one of the Germanic tribes over which he celebrated a triumph.

283–6. Pompey almost died of fever in Campania (50 BCE). Cicero and Plutarch record his recovery as the cause of great rejoicing, but if the fever had taken him he would not have died wretchedly in Egypt, where he fled after having lost the civil war to Caesar and was then assassinated, his headless body left to molder on the beach. See **lines 108–9.**

Multae urbes et publica vota: public prayers for recovery.

286–8. "In contrast, Catiline and his co-conspirators suffered no such mutilation (**cruciatu**)." **Lentulus** = P. Cornelius Lentulus Sura, consul 71 BCE. After being expelled from the senate by the *nota* of the censor, he became praetor and later joined Catiline's conspiracy. He was strangled in prison on the order of the consul, Cicero.

Cethegus = C. Cornelius Cethegus, senator and another conspirator. He met the same end.

Catilina = L. Sergius Catilina, dissolute aristocrat who, after being defeated for consul in 63 and 62 BCE, tried to overthrow the state. He was thwarted by Cicero and died fighting.

289–345. Many mothers pray for beauty for their children, but it only brings them sorrow.

289–91. Delicias = "an extravagance."

291–2. Corripias < *corripio, –ripere, –ripui, –reptum*: "seize, rebuke." There's humor in the *mater* addressing the satirist.

293–5. The examples of **Lucretia** and **Verginia** are alleged to illustrate the perils of excessive beauty. Sextus Tarquinius raped **Lucretia**, the archetypically chaste wife of Collatinus. She later committed suicide. The ensuing uproar led to the overthrow of the Tarquins and the establishment of the republic.

Verginia: the object of the lust of the *decemvir*, Appius Claudius, she was killed by her father to prevent her violation. According to the tale told in Livy (3.44–8), this led to the succession of the plebs in 449 BCE and the end of the regime of the *decemviri*.

Rutilae = unknown.

Gibbum = "hump."

Suam: understand *faciem*, accepting the reading of the lesser codices.

295–8. Handsome sons are no better.

298–306. "Their parents are bribed to become their panders, even if they are by nature chaste." **Licet . . . licet**: two different uses of the same verb. The first is the idiomatic "although," the second the impersonal verb with the dative.

Veteres . . . Sabinos = archetypes of traditional Italic virtue.

306–9. The tyrant in his citadel (**arce**) was a staple of the rhetorical schools. **Ephebum** = a Greek term for a young man.

There is no evidence that Nero castrated or raped free-born (**preatextatum**) boys. Slaves, however, as Horace points out in 1.2, were another matter. **Loripedem** = bandy-legged.

Strumosum = "scrofulous," i.e., afflicted with tuberculosis of the lymphatic glands and the resulting tumors.

Utero = "belly."

310–11. "Rejoice in the face of your own son for whom greater marks of distinction await": ironic.

311–14. **Mariti / irati**: the genitive is awkward and in some later versions of the manuscript tradition an intrusive gloss (*exigere*) has crept in, but none of the proposed emendations has won wide assent and the dominant transmission is both readable and metrical.

Martis: in the *Odyssey* (8.266–369) Homer tells the story of Ares (Mars) committing adultery with Aphrodite and being caught in a trap (**laqueos**) by Hephaestus.

314–17. The outraged husband demands vengeance beyond even what the law allows. See **Horace 1.2.41–6, 133. Mugilis** = "the mullet," a fish with backward pointing spines, inserted into the anus of adulterers by outraged husbands. See Catullus 15.

319–22. "Soon aristocratic nymphomaniacs will be paying him for sex." **Servilia** = a member of the aristocratic *gens Servilia*.

Fiet = *fiet adulter*.

Illius = Servilia.

Non amat: a striking usage. In Roman poetry of the first century BCE, *amo* always includes the notion of sex, hence Catullus in poem 72 must struggle to distinguish emotional commitment from lust (*amare*). Here, *amo* is distinguished from the purely sexual. See Adams (1982: 188).

Exuet omnem / corporis ornatum = "he will strip every jewel from her body."

Oppia: see 220.

Catulla: mentioned at 2.49, otherwise unknown.

323. **Illic** = **inguinibus**.

324. The return of the satiric interlocutor.

325. Hippolytus was the object of his stepmother, Phaedra's affections. She, like Stheneboea with Bellerophon, alleged rape when refused. In Hippolytus's case the result was death, in that of Bellerophon, banishment and attempted murder. **Grave propositum** = "serious intent."

326–8. **Haec** = Phaedra.

Repulsa = ablative of the noun *repulsa, –ae*, governed by **erubuit**.

Cressa: Phaedra was from Crete.

Excanduit < *excandesco, –descere, –dui*: "to be hot" with passion.

Se concussere = "worked themselves up."

328–9. An epigram worthy of *Satire* 6.

329–31. "Say what is the advice to be given to someone whom Caesar's wife is determined to marry." The case referred to, as becomes clear in 333, is that of Messalina (see 6.114–35), who in 48 CE publicly married C. Silius while the emperor Claudius was away. When it was revealed to Claudius, Silius, Messalina, and many others were executed. Would the outcome have been any better for Silius, however, if he had said "no"? Messalina's wrath was equally to be feared. Juvenal sets up the scene as a rhetorical *suasoria*, or a declamation exercise in which advice is given to a historical figure.

331–6. **Patriciae** here = *nobilis*, not patrician in the technical sense.

Rapitur: there is an ironic reversal of gender roles here: Silius is the one who is taken against his will.

Sedet = another role reversal; normally in a Roman wedding the bride is led (*deducta*) to the groom.

Flammeolo: the only instance in classical Latin of the diminutive form of *flammeum*: "bridal veil," so-called from its orange color.

Tyriusque palam genialis in hortis / sternitur: "the purple coverlet of the marriage bed is spread out openly in the gardens." Messalina will not only marry her paramour publicly, but she will consummate the marriage in the open. The gardens (**hortis**) are those of Lucullus, which Messalina owned and where she took refuge after having been exposed to Claudius. **Tyrius** = "imperial purple," so called because the dye was made from shellfish found near Tyre.

Ritu decies centena . . . antiquo: she comes bearing a traditional and quite rich dowry of 1,000,000 sesterces.

Signatoribus = "legal witnesses."

Auspex: "The **auspex** gave the sanction of heaven to the nuptials, taking the omens before the marriage and performing a sacrifice as part of the ceremony. On this occasion, as on others in private and public life under the Empire, divination was practiced by the inspection of entrails, not by the flight of birds [. . .]. Messalina was determined to have everything done in proper form (**legitime**)" (Duff 1970). Cicero, however, notes that by the late republic the *auspex* served mainly as a witness (*De Divinatione* 1.28).

337. **Tu** = Silius.

339–41. "Whether you accept or reject her proposal, you fate is sealed." **Ante lucernas** = "before the lighting of the lamps."

342. Note how this swift all dactylic line ironically underlines the fact that Claudius is the last to know. **Dedecus** = neuter.

342–4. **Imperio**: another gender inversion; only the emperor held true *imperium*, but this is Messalina's.

Tanti = genitive of value.

344–5. "Choose your poison."

346–66. Conclusion: what we should wish for.

346–9. Let the gods work their will, they know what is best.

350. A fine summary epigram.

350–3. "We are led by blind impulse in our desires for spouses and issue, but the gods know what sort of wives and children we shall have in the end."

354–6. "Nonetheless we must pray for something when we make sacrifice, let it be for a sound mind in a sound body." **Sacellis** = diminutive of *sacrum*: "chapels, shrines," the first of three diminutives, at once ironic and underlining the modesty of proper sacrifice and prayer. The sense is that while these rituals must be done, they ought not to be taken overly seriously nor become the cause of ostentatious display.

Exta = "entrails."

Tomacula = "sausages."

357–62. "Pray for a courageous soul, free from the torments of anger, desire, and greed." **Ponat** = "counts."

358–62. Note the way the alliteration of the first line and three successive lines rhyming in *-ores* bring the proper wish to a crescendo. **Herculis aerumnas** = the labors of Hercules. These were originally assigned to him by king Eurystheus but the Stoics interpreted them as services to mankind by the hero. They thus became the objects of potential emulation.

Pluma = "feather bed."

Sardanapalli = the Assyrian king, Assurbanipal, famed for his luxury.

363–4. The aim of imperial philosophy was self-possession and self-sufficiency through the practice of virtue.

365–6. "The goddess Fortuna is a purely human creation."

CRITICAL ANTHOLOGY

THE ROMAN GENRE OF SATIRE AND ITS BEGINNINGS

Michael Coffey

1 Satire as a Roman literary genre[1]

When in the later part of the third century B.C. the Romans experienced the overmastering influence of Greek literature, the Greeks had already developed and brought to perfection a wide range of poetic genres from heroic epic and tragedy to scurrilous epigram. The greatest achievements of the Greek city states, notably Athens and the cities of Ionia, were followed in the third century by those of the Hellenistic period of elegance and refinement in Ptolemaic Alexandria. The Romans, although already under Greek influence of many kinds from Sicily and the settlements on the Italian mainland, had developed no indigenous literary culture of their own apart from various rustic measures, and accepted the mature forms of the Greeks of the mainland and of Alexandria with enthusiasm, making them their own. From crude beginnings Latin writers, by a gradually improving process of creative imitation, developed and expanded the main forms, epic, tragedy, comedy and, later, elegy, in such a way that much of Roman literary history may be seen as an attempt to continue and to rival the Greek tradition. But there was one important exception. For the Greeks satire was not an independent literary form. This was a unique Roman invention.

Towards the end of the first century A.D. the professor of rhetoric, Quintilian, in his work on the education of an orator, *Institutio Oratoria*, makes a critical comparison and evaluation of Greek and Roman literature genre by genre. Having asserted parity of success for Greeks and Romans in elegy he continues: *satura quidem tota nostra est* (satire is entirely Roman).[2] At this point he is no longer comparing relative merits. His claim is based not merely on the positive achievement of Roman satire but also on the lack of a body of Greek literature to which it could properly be compared. He hints obliquely at the primitive early satire of Ennius, but regards Lucilius as the first major satirist. After evaluating Horace and Persius very briefly he praises certain contemporaries whom he does not mention by name. He was no doubt referring particularly to Turnus, a satirist of the age of Domitian, whose works are no longer extant. It is very unlikely that Juvenal published any satires until after the death of Quintilian. The rest of Quintilian's syllabus of satire is devoted to

Varro, who wrote in the alternative convention of a mixture of prose and verse the kind of satire that was usually known as Menippean.[3] Quintilian offers no value judgement on Varro's satires, perhaps discreetly, but praises the vast range of his scholarly antiquarian output. That he does not mention the two great examples of Menippean satire of the first century A.D. that have come down to modern times is not surprising: Seneca's *Apocolocyntosis* was a slight work by an author for whom he had an unusual antipathy and the *Satyricon* of Petronius, in form a mixture of the Menippean convention and the despised genre of the novel, contained paederastic and other erotic topics such as could not have been prescribed to the youthful aspirant to eloquence.[4]

Quintilian's list makes it clear that we have access to all the Roman satirists except Turnus. Though the remains of the satires of Ennius, Lucilius and Varro are sets of disjointed fragments, the works of Horace, in Quintilian's view the finest satirist of all, Persius and Juvenal, and the *Apocolocyntosis*, have been transmitted complete, and the cruelly mutilated remains of the *Satyricon* are substantial enough to allow the modern reader to appreciate the qualities of this hybrid composition. Juvenal was the last Roman satirist. It is thus possible to study the history of Roman satire as an evolving literary form and to assess with some confidence the individual qualities of most of its pre-eminent exponents.

In discussing literature by genres Quintilian conformed to a method that was fundamental to Greek and Roman thinking about literature. Hellenistic scholars, some of them accomplished poets, proposed a complex system of classification that formed the basis of later literary theory.[5] Associated with criticism by 'kinds' was the notion of propriety. To Aristotle's immediate successor, Theophrastus, decorum was one of the four categories under which style was to be considered; a papyrus fragment which probably belongs to his work on style prescribes that certain words are to be admitted and others rejected.[6] In a versified discussion of plays and principles the tragedian Accius considered the nature of the genres and the difference between one and another.[7] His critic Lucilius, as is clear from the testimony of Horace, concerned himself with propriety of style. Horace himself regarded acceptance of generic distinctions as a necessary condition of writing poetry, and in the nicest matters of expression his practice accorded with his theory.[8] In the first century A.D. Seneca recognized in theory (*Epp.* 8,8), and for the most part in practice, finely distinguished levels of style.[9] Martial, complaining that a fellow poet has copied all his activities, lists the genres in descending order of nobility (and size): epic, tragedy, lyric, satire, elegy and epigram.[10] The point of Martial's poem is a self-depreciating descent to the bathos of his own epigrammatic miniatures. The joke depends in part on the tacit acceptance of a hierarchy of genres. Modern stylistic analysis has confirmed that in practice also Latin poetry preserved such distinctions.[11]

Along with the belief in a series of clearly defined genres went two important corollaries: first the recognition of an archetypal master in each genre to whom his successors looked back with a proud loyalty that was tempered sometimes by overt criticism and almost always by some departures in practice in accordance with changes in circumstances or in the taste of the times, and secondly the acceptance of the notion of a *lex operis*, the rules of stylistic behaviour within the genre that could when necessary be modified by the dictates of inventive genius. For all his criticisms of Lucilius in Book 1, Horace saw him as the inventor of the genre by whose standard his own work was to be assessed, and in Book 2 claimed explicitly that he was writing satire in the manner of Lucilius. Persius and Juvenal both acknowledged the caustic criticisms of Lucilius as the original precedent for attacks on vice and also mentioned Horace as part of their heritage.[12] [. . .] That satire had its own law of procedure is implicit in Horace's discussion of his work in the fourth and tenth satires of Book 1: the word *lex* is used of satire when in the opening of the first satire of Book 2 Horace reveals that to some critics his satire seemed too harsh and pushed beyond the law; but characteristically he juggles with different uses of *lex*, the criminal and civil law as well as the law of the genre. In his sixth satire Juvenal, after an impassioned description of murderesses in high places, exclaims in an indignant rhetorical question:

> *Fingimus haec altum satura sumente coturnum*
> *scilicet, et finem egressi legemque priorum*
> *grande Sophocleo carmen bacchamur hiatu*
> *montibus ignotum Rutulis caeloque Latino?*
> *nos utinam vani.*
>
> (6,634–8)

> (Do you really think that I am resorting to fiction while my satire usurps the style of tragedy, violating the bounds and law ordained by my predecessors and writing frenzied high poetry in a tragic manner of a kind unknown to the hills of Rome and the sky of Latium? I wish that it was all groundless.)

Having answered his question[13] by the wish that he was inventing his own themes Juvenal gives examples of vicious modern practices that rival and outstrip the infamy of heroines of myth and tragic poetry. He was aware that his tradition imposed a certain level of style on him and that his apparent assumption of an alien style required a disclaimer. The tradition of a law of satire is alluded to in late antiquity by John the Lydian, a Byzantine writer of the age of Justinian, who states that while Horace did not go beyond the traditional manner, Turnus, Juvenal and Petronius in their savagery departed from and violated the law of satire.[14] Whatever the pedigree of this judgement it demonstrates the abiding belief that satire was an independent literary genre with its own laws of procedure.

The style held to be appropriate for the satirist was informal and close to the language of everyday speech, for the most part that of the educated. The high style was deemed inappropriate for satire except as parody; hence Juvenal's disclaimer quoted above. In the same way an excess of vulgarity of expression was avoided. Lucilius seems to have admitted words of the utmost obscenity but some of the more extreme verbal obscenities that are common in Martial do not occur in the later satirists. Horace allowed certain obscenities in some of his early satires and in the language of the slave Davus (*Sat.* 2,7) which do not occur in any of his later works. His abandonment of such words reflects his own maturing judgement and perhaps also contemporaries' views on verbal decorum. The obscenities of language found in satirists later than Horace were used for special shock effect and are not part of the staple of their language.[15] This lexical restriction confirms the hint in Martial that satire was considered to be a somewhat more exalted form of writing than epigram.

Complementary to the overall formal classification of Latin literature by genres is a method of classification by topics which may occur in a number of genres. The poet's refusal to laud the exploits of an important political contemporary is found in the satires of Lucilius and Horace, who chose instead to write satire, and in works by Virgil and elegiac writers. The invitation to a frugal and morally unexceptionable meal is a topic common to satire (Juvenal, *Sat.* 11), lyric and epigram.[16]

It is perhaps all the more necessary nowadays to insist on the importance of the formal classification by genres in ancient literature and the existence of a hierarchy of genres, for in modern times there has been a widespread blurring of distinctions to which writers and critics in former ages would have responded instinctively. Though some great writers and distinguished critics have recognized the importance of differentiated genres and conventional topics, there has been a levelling down of stylistic propriety so that the high style no longer exists in literature except for paratragic buffoonery.[17] The ancient writers of the greatest talent were always able to transcend their formal inheritance much though they respected it, so as to blend the traditional with their own originality. One satirist of great genius, Petronius, broke through the inherited patterns so as to create in the *Satyricon* a unique blend of the quite separate genres of satire and the novel. He had no successor.

It is necessary to eliminate from the study of the Roman genre of satire various writings that have some topics or attitudes in common with it but have their own separate history. Phaedrus, the author of fables in verse who lived in the time of Augustus and Tiberius, has been included among the Roman satirists in some modern discussions on the grounds that fable was a traditional element in satire and that in offering a mixture of amusement and sage counsel his aim was similar to that of the satirists.[18] But in antiquity writers of fable were not regarded as part of the traditions of satire, and in spite of certain instructive affinities between the technique of the satirists and the personal and political innuendoes that underlie the words of Phaedrus, a collections of short fables is far removed from satire in matter and manner.

Nor is there any justification for including Martial among the Roman satirists. Epigram belonged to a different literary tradition, and Martial himself distinguished between satire and his own epigrams. It is only to be expected that in ridiculing wickedness and inanity Martial shared some topics and even some phrases with his friend Juvenal. We may also eliminate the tradition of *iambi* even though Lucilius was given the epithet *iambicus* in imperial times.[19] By writing epodes at the same time as his satires Horace demonstrates his belief that the tradition of Archilochus, which Lucilius seems to have accepted as a source of inspiration for his own work, was something distinct from satire. Quintilian (10,1,96) discusses the iambic tradition separately as a form apart. Also to be eliminated is the miscellaneous corpus of abusive verse that ranged from archaic curses on tablets, scurrilous inscriptions and extended poems of malediction such as the *Ibis* of Ovid, to the verses described as *Fescennini* that were written by the military dictator Octavianus on a defenceless subject, Asinius Pollio.[20] The gambits of rhetoric influenced satire in diverse ways, but the process of *invectiva*, the discrediting and vilification of an opponent in court, was not in itself to be classed as satire.[21] Thus the tradition of Roman satire excludes much that is labelled satirical in a wider context.

It is also important that the tradition of Roman satire should be seen as something quite distinct from that of didactic poetry. Horace's literary epistles of Book 2 and the *Ars Poetica* are a poetic exposition of a quasi-didactic kind that has nothing in common with the *Lucilianus character* of his satires, written many years earlier, other than the hexameter. The didactic poems of Hesiod, Lucretius and Virgil were compositions inspired by the Muse and akin to high poetry. The satirical mode that is found in Lucretius' condemnatory depiction of superstition and sexual passion may owe something of its fervour to Hellenistic popular philosophy, but his impassioned poetry derives from the Greek tradition of Empedocles.[22]

The line of verse satire ended with Juvenal, and satire in a mixture of prose and verse with Petronius. There was no attempt to revive the genre in the later part of the fourth century A.D. at the time of the final creative outburst of pagan literature. The tradition of Roman satire was lost in the dark ages and remained so throughout mediaeval times. The reading of Juvenal by some scholarly men in twelfth-century France and occasional references to the masters of antiquity by mediaeval Latin satirists are no indication of a line of continuity, nor has Nigel Longchamp's *Speculum Stultorum* the authentic qualities of Roman satire, even though it may have an enjoyable variety of contents.[23] A garbled reference to Juvenal by Walter of Châtillon does not inspire confidence. The case for the continuity of the classical traditions of satire cannot be made good.[24]

The beginning of modern scholarship on Roman satire was Isaac Casaubon's fundamental study *De Satyrica Graecorum poesi et Romanorum Satira Libri Duo* (Paris, 1605) in which he devoted the first book to examining the evidence for

Greek satyr plays, which he was able to separate completely from Roman satire. An inability to separate these two distinct genres had caused confusion in the previous century. Casaubons's second book is a thoroughly documented study of the different aspects of Roman satura, the primitive stage and the Lucilian and Menippean traditions, to which the efforts of modern scholars have comparatively little to add.[25] The next scholarly work of importance on the satire and history of satire was John Dryden's *A Discourse Concerning Satire* (1693),[26] which owes much to Casaubon but disagrees with his preference for Persius to Juvenal or Horace. Dryden seems to have switched from an earlier higher estimation of Horace to preference later in life for the more highly charged vituperation of Juvenal. Though his Discourse is a classic of English literary criticism, it should be read with some caution.[27]

It may be of use at this point to refer to two definitions of formal literary satire, one from Roman antiquity and the other modern. The fourth-century grammarian Diomedes, using no doubt the pronouncements of predecessors, defined satire as

> *carmen apud Romanos, nunc quidem maledicum et ad carpenda hominum vitia archaeae comeodiae charactere compositum, quale scripserunt Lucilius et Horatius et Persius; sed olim carmen quod ex variis poematibus constabat satura voactur, quale scripserunt Pacuvius et Ennius.*[28]
>
> (a Roman verse form that has been in recent times abusive and composed to censure the vices of men in the manner of Old Greek Comedy, as was written by Lucilius, Horace and Persius: but formerly satire was the name given to a verse form made up of a variety of smaller pieces of poetry such as was written by Pacuvius and Ennius.)

The definition is valid in that it describes the essential quality of the Lucilian tradition (the omission of the name of Juvenal does not affect its basic soundness) and also the primitive stage of Roman satire, but defective in its omission of the Menippean tradition. A modern definition is taken from the *Encylopaedia Britannica*: 'Satire, in its literary aspect, may be defined as the expression in adequate terms of the sense of amusement or disgust excited by the ridiculous or unseemly, provided that humour is a distinctly recognizable element, and that the utterance is invested with literary form. Without humour, satire is invective; without literary form it is mere clownish jeering'.[29] This definition is acceptable for Roman satire, except that 'wit' should be added to humour' and 'variety of contents' added to 'literary form'. There are not good grounds for refusing to accept satire as one of the traditional literary kinds.[30] Ancient critics so viewed Roman satire, which throughout its long history retained a recognizable though pliant form. The blend of traditional elements and novelty of subject matter in a supple literary medium gave the satire of the Romans an enduring strength that would lead to satire of high distinction in European literature after the Renaissance.

2 Satura: the name and origin of a literary form

The meaning of the word *satura* and its use as a literary term were already a matter for speculation in late republican times. There has also been much discussion on the part (if any) that was played by drama and ritual in the development of the literary form, Roman *satura*.

1 Satura *and the ancient grammarians' tradition*

The spelling *satura* represents the original form of the word. The spelling *satyra* seems to have arisen early in the Christian era and is based on a postulated connection between the Roman literary form and Greek satyrs and satyr drama. *Satira* is in origin simply a variant on *satyra.* Had *satura* not been the original form it is difficult to see how it could have arisen from *satyra*, let alone from *satira*.[1]

All three syllables of the feminine noun *satura* have a short vowel. As there is no evidence for a Latin nominal termination in *–ura*, *satura* is a loan word from another language, or else, as is more likely, it is an inflexion of the adjective *satur* that has come to be used as a noun, a feminine singular with a feminine noun to be supplied. The noun in agreement with the adjective *satura* through familiar usage came to be omitted, a procedure which can be paralleled, for example, by the optional omission of *cena* with *adventicia* or *adventoria*, a supper to celebrate an arrival.[2]

The primary meaning of the adjective *satur* seems to be 'filled full of food', 'replete'. The first attested occurrence is in a hymn of the Arval brothers, the guardians of the fertility of the fields.[3] There is a degree of metaphor in some of Plautus' uses of the word: in one passage there is punning on the senses 'filled with food' and 'satisfied with the play as a substitute for food' and in another *satura* is applied ambiguously to Alcmena as having the appearance of one who is both replete with food and also pregnant.[4] The adjective also carries overtones of richness when used of a deep colour, a fertile landscape or an opulent style of oratory.[5] Further, anything that is filled may well be filled with a variety of contents, and although it is unclear to what extent such associations were uppermost in the adjective *satur*, the shift in meaning from full to richly variegated was slight. The semantic range of *satur* was therefore extensive, and when the feminine *satura* came to be used alone for noun + *satura*, its meaning will to some extent have depended upon that of the noun omitted.

An approach to the solution of this question is to be found in a passage of the grammarian Diomedes that is the most important discussion in antiquity of the meaning of the word *satura*:

> *satura autem dicta sive a Satyris, quod similiter in hoc carmine ridiculae res pudendaeque dicuntur, quae velut a Satyris proferuntur et fiunt: sive satura a lance quae referta variis multisque primitiis in sacro apud priscos dis inferebatur et a copia ac saturitate rei satura vocabatur; cuius generis lancium et Vergilius in georgicis meminit, cum hoc modo dicit,*
>
> *lancibus et pandis fumantia reddimus exta*
>
> *et*
>
> *lancesque et liba feremus:*
>
> *sive a quodam genere farciminis, quod multis rebus refertum saturam dicit Varro vocitatum. est autem hoc positum in secundo libro Plautinarum quaestionum, 'satura est uva passa et polenta et nuclei pini ex mulso consparsi. ad haec alii addunt et de malo punico grana'. alii autem dictam putant a lege satura, quae uno rogatu multa simul conprehendat, quod scilicet et satura carmine multa simul poemata conprehenduntur. cuius saturae legis Lucilius meminit in primo,*
>
> *per saturam aedilem factum qui legibus solvat,*
>
> *et Sallustius in Iugurtha, 'deinde quasi per saturam sententiis exquisitis in deditionem accipitur'.*[6]
>
> (*Satura* takes its name either from satyrs, because in this verse form comical and shameless things are said which are produced and made as if by satyrs; or from a full dish which was packed with a large number of varied first fruits and offered among primitive people to the gods in a religious ritual and called *satura* from the abundance and fullness of the material. Virgil too makes mention of this kind of dish in the *Georgics* when he says [2,194] 'we offer steaming giblets on curved dishes' and also [2,394] 'we shall bring dishes of sacrificial cakes'. It may also be derived from a certain kind of sausage which was filled with many ingredients and according to Varro called *satura*, and indeed there is the following definition in the second book of his 'Problems in Plautus': '*satura* is raisins, pearl barley, pine kernels covered with mead, to which some people add pomegranate seeds'. Others say it was called *satura* from a compendious law which includes many provisions in a single bill, on the argument that in the verse form *satura* many small poems are combined together. Lucilius mentions this compendious law in his first book [48 M]: 'who might absolve from the law an aedile elected by a compendious measure', and Sallust in *Jugurtha* [29,5]: 'then his surrender is accepted as if by a compendious law with precise provisions'.)

The *testimonia* of other Latin grammarians such as Isidore and Festus derive from either Diomedes or his source; with one exception none offers any independent evidence.[7] The piece of additional information given by a scholiast on Horace that the *lanx satura* was offered in the temple of Ceres is probably no more than a plausible inference.[8] Diomedes refers to Varro and to no other authority, and the usual attribution of the main lines of Diomedes to Varro may be accepted with confidence. The etymologies are characteristic of Varro, and it is more than likely that the learned literary historian, himself a satirist, assembled theories of the origins of satire that became standard doctrine.[9] There is nothing of substance in Diomedes' account that need be later than Varro. Only the quotations from Virgil and Sallust are almost certainly later additions; any grammarian from Verrius Flaccus to Diomedes himself could have inserted them. It is likely that Diomedes' testimony all derives from a single work of Varro. One piece of evidence we are told was found in the *Plautinae Quaestiones*; the rest probably came from the same work. If Varro discussed *satura* elsewhere, the likeliest places are the *de Compositione Saturarum* and the *de Poetis*, which may have included a section on satire in its discussion of Ennius.[10]

As Diomedes' source offers four explanations of the derivation and origin of *satura*, it is clear that by the end of the republic much was already speculation and guesswork. None the less in one or other of these theories there may be some approximation to the truth. The first explanation does not deserve credence, Diomedes offers the ribaldry and obscenity of the satyrs, presumably satyr drama, as parallel to the derision and bawdry of satire, which he concludes took its name from these tipsy and frolicsome creatures of Greek myth and drama.[11] On this view the earliest Roman satirist used a Greek loan word as title. But there are weighty objections. First, such a background of unbridled jocularity and boisterous lechery is unsuited to the quiet satires of Ennius as preserved, which, as will be seen, are influenced mainly by non-dramatic Hellenistic poetry. This theory presupposes the vituperative satire of Lucilius and his republican successors.[12] Secondly there is a linguistic difficulty. The Greek adjective meaning connected with satyrs' is σατυρικός; this becomes *satyricus* in Latin, as in the phrase *satyrica fabula* used by Diomedes.[13] The Greek for satyr play is either some expression with σατυρικός such as σατυρική ποίησις or σάτυροι (plural); the latter form appears in Latin in Horace's phrase *satyrorum scriptor*.[14] Ennius could not have derived *satura* (singular) or *saturae* (plural) from these words. Had he wished to base his title on satyrs and plays about them we would expect him to have made some use of the adjective *satyricus*, which occurs with sophisticated ambiguity in Petronius' *Satyricon libri.*

In Diomedes' second and third explanations *satura* takes its name from a cult offering to the gods or from a cook's recipe. For the first of these Diomedes specifies the exact point of the figurative language: *a copia et saturitate rei*; the words *variis multisque* suggest that the metaphor included variety as well as abundance, and it may be assumed that the culinary metaphor carried similar associations.

In deriving *satura* from *lanx satura*, Diomedes quotes no evidence for this phrase; other late grammarians who used the same authorities mention *lanx satura* but no citation can be adduced from any source. Diomedes may have intended to mean not a *lanx satura* but a type of *lanx* called a *satura* (i.e. a noun); he cites two passages of Virgil that illustrate the use of *lanx* without *satura* as the dish on which sacrificial offerings were placed,[15] but he does not say which gods received such offerings. His second citation from Virgil refers to an Italian sacrifice to Bacchus; the first quotation comes from a general description of sacrifices at which wine was offered to the gods. Ceres must be excluded from their number, because in her cult no sacrifice of wine was made.[16] Here there is an implicit discrepancy between Diomedes and the Pseudacron Scholia to Horace, where it is said the *lanx satura* was offered in the temple of Ceres. But it is unlikely that the Horace scholiast preserves the words of the religious antiquarian Varro, while Diomedes is vague and incorporates quotations which are incompatible with the original authority. Whether the filled *lanx* belonged to any particular cult we cannot tell. Ceres is associated with sacrifice of first fruits, and the offering of a *lanx* to Bacchus does not preclude its use in a Ceres cult.[17] But there were many other recipients of first fruits and produce, such as Pales and the Lares, not to mention Carna, whose ritual was obsolete by the end of the republic. It is thus impossible to add the overtones of a particular ritual to a metaphorical title derived from *lanx satura*.[18]

Diomedes' third suggestion is that *satura* takes its name from a kind of stuffing. The word *farcimen* can be used either of the stuffing, the filling of the sausage, or the thing that is stuffed, the sausage itself; perhaps this was true of *satura* also.[19] That *satura* does not occur in Varro's description of fat, short and long sausages does not prove that it was not a species of sausage, for the list need not be regarded as including every kind of a food that must in its nature indeed have had many varieties.[20] Diomedes gives a recipe for a dish that seems to be some kind of stuffing and not the thing stuffed, though this is a distinction that should not be pressed. Assuming *satura* here to be an adjective, it is uncertain what noun is to be supplied. *Lanx* is a possible supplement here too, for it is the ordinary word for a serving dish. Other suggestions include *patina* (pan) and *olla* (pot).[21] As applied to a form of literature the point of the metaphor is once again fullness and variety. It is difficult to plot the full associations of the metaphor with precision. The recipe does not correspond closely to anything in Apicius' collection for gourmets of imperial times. This includes a recipe for sausage stuffing which contains the nuts of edible pines and spelt-grits (*alica*) instead of pearl barley. Many other dishes in Apicius contain some of Varro's ingredients,[22] but what sets Varro's recipe apart from these elaborate contrivances is the inclusion of pearl barley. Barley (*hordeum*) is a rare ingredient in Apicius; *polenta* seems not to occur there at all. Barley is the traditional food of gladiators and barley meal was used to feed farm animals.[23] It seems likely that Varro's recipe is a form of a dish eaten in republican times by country folk. Such a culinary metaphor would be suited to the vigour of satire as well as its variety.

This explanation of the word *satura* seems to be alluded to by one of the satirists. Juvenal describes the variety of subject matter of satire as *nostri farrago libelli* (1,86), 'the mash of my book'. *Farrago* is always used of mixed fodder for cattle, never of food for men.[24] It is not quite certain how the whole phrase is to be construed. Though it is generally assumed that the meaning is 'the mixed meal of which my book consists', it is possible to take the genitive as objective: 'the mixed meal that goes to feed my book'; the book is thus conceived of as an animal to be fed.[25] Juvenal with a jaunty and debunking metaphor thus alludes disrespectfully to what must have been by his time a standard textbook theory of origins.

The theory of *satura* as by origin a food rather than an offering to the gods has found most favour in modern times.[26] In our present state of knowledge one or other of these theories is the likeliest explanation of the metaphorical use of *satura*. It is difficult to choose between the two and perhaps they are not mutually exclusive. Whichever of the two views is accepted, it is probable that *lanx* is the noun to be supplied. The analogy of *patina* suggests that *lanx* too could refer to the contents of the dish as well as the dish itself.[27] That a Roman word for dish was used proverbially of a miscellany is clear from a poem of Meleager which after listing a series of scabrous and variegated paederastic achievements concludes:

> εἰ γάρ σοι τάδε τερπνὰ πόροι θεός ὦ μάκαρ οἵαν
> ἀρτύσεις παίδων Ῥωμαϊκὴν λοπάδα.
> (*Anth. Pal.* 12,95,9–10 = GP 4406–7)

> (If heaven were to provide you with such delights, lucky man, what a Roman dish of boys you will be preparing.)

Λοπάς is an ordinary word for serving dish and is almost certainly a translation of *lanx*. The Roman metaphor was so widely known that it could be used at about the beginning of the first century B.C. as the climax to a Greek epigrammatic poem.[28]

It was such a proverbial usage that Ennius took over in devising the title *Saturae*, 'the miscellaneous dish', for his collection or collections of miscellaneous poems. In so doing he had at hand in the Hellenistic tradition Σωρός 'the heap' (of winnowed grain), the title that Posidippus gave to a collection of assorted poems composed by himself exclusively or in conjunction with other poets.[29] It seems probable that Posidippus' title or some title like it led Ennius to choose a similar word that had no previous literary associations. The existence of Greek collections entitled σύμμεικτα (miscellanies) may have influenced Ennius' desire to compile a collection of poems, but it was a title such as Σωρός that led him to choose for his title a concrete metaphor rather than an abstract description.[30] The establishment of a relationship on the one side between Demeter and the Σωρός and on the other between *lanx satura* and Ceres would favour a metaphor from a religious offering. But both these connections are highly problematical.[31] It may perhaps be preferable to regard the title *satura* as derived from the language of kitchen and dining-room, a heaped and filling country dish of diverse ingredients to describe and illustrate a rich and variegated but unpretentious literary form.[32]

Thus one or even two of the theories preserved by Diomedes show how *satura* came to be used as a literary term; Ennius seems to have been the first to use it in this way. It is true that *satura* is unique among the major Roman literary forms in having a title that is genuinely Italian and not a Greek loan word, but it was the example of picturesque and fanciful titles in Hellenistic poetry that led Ennius to choose a concrete Latin word. The analogy of Σωϱός suggests that Ennius referred to a collection of miscellaneous poems or a book as *satura* (sing.) and to the whole corpus of his satires as *saturae* (plural). The use of *satura* to denote a single poem, as in Quintilian's reference to Ennius' dialogue between Life and Death as taking place *in satura* (9,2,36), is probably a later development when technical terminology had hardened. But Ennius may not have been consistent in his use of singular and plural, and so it is unwise to insist on a fine distinction in terminology particularly at an early stage in the history of the genre.[33]

Diomedes' fourth suggestion, that the use of *satura* as a literary title derived from legal terminology, may be dismissed quickly. There is no evidence for the phrase *lex satura* except in the statements of grammarians; *lex per saturam* with the meaning of a law with compendious or mixed provisions is attested in the second half of the second century B.C.,[34] but it may be argued that the phrase *lex per saturam* does not exist and is only found in contexts where the phrase *per saturam* is adverbial ('in a disorderly manner') with some such verb as *ferre.*

By this time *per saturam* was a catch-phrase used of a tacked law, a piece of legal engineering that was formally forbidden in 98 B.C.[35] The phrase *per* (or in) *saturam* thus implied an agglomeration of disparate items. The linguistic and social background to the development of this phrase is uncertain, but *lex* (*per saturam*) clearly had nothing to do with the origins of satire.[36]

Some scholars, suspicious of the multiplicity of explanations offered by Diomedes, have looked elsewhere for an etymology and connected *satura* with an Etruscan word *satir* or *satre* that is said to mean 'speak' or 'declare'.[37] This theory is attractive, as the title would describe the conversation and discourse of book satire. But there are difficulties. The meaning of the Etruscan word is not entirely certain, and attempts to postulate an Etruscan substrate to a Latin word are usually not without hazard.[38] It is also unlikely that Ennius would have chosen an Etruscan rather than, as was customary, a Greek loan word for the title of a genre that contained so much Greek material in its subject matter and presentation.

2 *Livy and the so-called 'dramatic* satura*'*

The foregoing discussion rests on the assumption that there was no literary *satura* in Rome or Italy before Ennius. An important piece of ancient evidence, however, suggests the contrary and must now be examined in detail. Livy narrates that after various attempts to rid Rome of the plague had failed, stage shows were introduced for the first time in 364 B.C. as a means of averting divine anger:

> *Sine carmine ullo, sine imitandorum carminum actu ludiones ex Etruria acciti ad tibicinis modos saltantes haud indecoros motus more Tusco dabant. Imitari deinde eos iuventus, simul inconditis inter se iocularia fundentes versibus, coepere; nec absoni a voce motus erant. Accepta itaque res saepiusque usurpando excitata. Vernaculis artificibus, quia ister Tusco verbo ludio vocabatur, nomen histrionibus inditum; qui non, sicut ante, Fescennino versu similem incompositum temere ac rudem alternis iaciebant sed impletas modis saturas descripto iam ad tibicinem cantu motuque congruenti peragebant. Livius post aliquot annis, qui ab saturis ausus est primus argumento fabulam serere, idem scilicet – id quod omnes tum erant – suorum carminum actor, dicitur, cum saepius revocatus vocem obtudisset, venia petita puerum ad canendum ante tibicinem cum statuisset, canticum egisse aliquanto magis vigente motu quia nihil vocis usus impediebat. Inde ad manum cantari histrionibus coeptum diverbiaque tantum ipsorum voci relicta.*
>
> (Livy 7,2,4–10)

(Players were called in from Etruria who danced to the music of the pipes without any verses or miming that corresponded to verses and produced graceful movements in the Etruscan manner. Later Romans began to imitate them, at the same time exchanging jests in improvised verse, suiting the gestures to the words, and so the practice became a custom and developed through regular use. The name *histrio* was given to Roman professional performers, for in Etruscan a player was called *ister.*[39] These did, nor, as had been the former practice, engage in an exchange of disorganized and uncouth verse like Fescennines, but enacted fully musical 'revues' with what was by now a set vocal line with pipe accompaniment and appropriate miming.[40] The story goes that after some years Livius, who was the first to depart from the 'revues' and compose a dramatic plot, and, according to the general custom of the times, was the actor of his own pieces, cracked his voice as a result of too many encores and gained permission to place a slave in front of the piper to sing, while he enacted the lyrics with a greater vigour of movement as he was not hindered by having to use his voice. As a result the practice was instituted for the actors to have the lyrics sung near to them as accompaniment of their gestures and to reserve the dialogue alone for their own voices.)[41]

In the next and final stage of Livy's account the performance of plays was left to professional actors, while amateurs continued the old practice of banter in verse and were responsible for playing the so-called 'after-pieces', which are usually identified with Atellan comedy, a vulgar farce of Italian origins.[42]

Livy here offers an account of the development of drama in Rome in five chronological stages, of which a *satura* that is enacted dramatically is the third, preceded first by imported wordless dances with music and then by imitation of the dances accompanied by crude rustic verses in dialogue; it is succeeded by a drama with a proper plot, dialogue and *cantica*, that is finally developed by professionals into an art form while the amateurs developed the rough exchanges of dialogue into formal after-pieces.[43] The dramatic *satura* that was part of this development was described as a musical stage show without an organized plot but with lyrics written out in full and probably dancing, all being accompanied by the music of the pipes, and its organization and professionalism were to be contrasted with the earlier improvised work of the amateurs.

There is no other evidence for such a dramatic *satura* except a passage of Valerius Maximus which is modelled on Livy or his immediate source and is even more patriotic than Livy in that it makes the first stage a Roman activity before actors were imported from Etruria.[44]

Some modern scholars believe that there was some such stage show in the early history of Roman drama but that it was not called *satura*, whilst others hold that *satura* was its original name.[45] There is, however, much in Livy's account that invites disbelief. It is possible that there was a plague in 365–4 B.C., for such information may have been taken from the Pontifical Annals.[46] It is also possible that players were imported from Etruria, though the practice during the Punic Wars of sending to Etruria on occasions of crisis is not necessarily confirmation of procedure in the earlier part of the fourth century B.C. But there seems to have been no source that could have provided Livy or his authority with an authentic tradition about dramatic practices in Rome in the fourth century. Verses of the Fescennine kind were a very ancient form of folk poetry, for they were associated to some extent with religious ritual. To seek their development in an imitation of an exotic dance form is not even plausible.[47] Livy's fourth stage likewise is demonstrably erroneous. A reliable ancient tradition held that Livius Andronicus produced his first play in Rome in 240 B.C., and this date has been generally accepted by modern scholars.[48] Livy's unspecific *post aliquot annis* neither confirms nor contradicts this, but his vagueness and the length of the chronological stages of his account raise grave suspicions. It is sometimes urged against Livy's veracity that Livius Andronicus was a schoolmaster and not an actor, but there is strong independent evidence that in addition to grammatical and literary activities he was a performer who took part in his own plays.[49] But one of the fundamental facts of Latin literary history is that Livius Andronicus introduced translations of Greek plays; and that it was from these that Roman drama originated. The omission of this fact makes Livy's account of Livius Andronicus incredible, and the absence of any mention of Greek influence discredits the rest of the story.[50]

An explanation may be suggested for part of Livy's procedure. He sketches the development of both the *diverbia* (dialogue) and *cantica* (lyrics) of comedy. Just as his dubious second stage was necessary to explain the *diverbia* of comedy without referring to Greek plays, so also a Roman dramatic lyric without plot was a necessary hypothesis to explain the *cantica* of Roman plays. It thus seems very likely that Livy's chronological sequence is groundless speculation.[51]

It has long been believed that Livy's chapter owes much to the Peripatetic formulation of the development of Greek drama from its beginnings to its maturity. In this theory an art form developed gradually to a peak of excellence, then underwent a slow degeneration and corruption. Even though some of the verbal correspondences suggested between Livy and Peripatetic treatises are not convincing, the description of the stages of dramatic evolution with Livius Andronicus occupying a position analogous to that of Crates, the fifth-century Athenian comic poet, show plainly the ultimate source of the framework of Livy's hypothesis. Livy's Roman sources found in Peripatetic literary theory a method of work that could be applied to the reconstruction of the early stages of Roman drama.[52] Interest was fostered by Crates of Mallos, who broke a leg as a result of an attempt to explore the *Cloaca Maxima.* His visit, thus notoriously prolonged, was an important influence on the development of literary theory at Rome.[53]

The question still remains: why was the hypothetical plotless stage show given the name *satura* or *saturae?* Nothing in Roman drama corresponds to the Greek satyr play, which had an important place in the theory and also the practice of Hellenistic times.[54] It is possible that a Roman theorist finding no existing Roman dramatic form to correspond to a satyr play was able to postulate a primitive form of boisterous stage show and by a piece of linguistic opportunism give to it a similar sounding literary title.[55] Further plausibility would have been given to the hypothesis by the existence of men in the guise of satyrs on the occasion of the *Ludi Magni* in Rome, a feature of the ritual that was instanced as an example of the similarity of Roman customs to those of Greece.[56]

Livy's motive in including this tendentious account of dramatic origins was in part at least patriotic. This accords with his approach to the writing of history: just as the Etruscan domination in politics was to be minimized so Greek influences on dramatic institutions were to be discounted.[57] Patriotism may also be found in his hint (if such it be) that the literary form *satura*, well established by the time he composed his first decade, had an Italian origin; in the etymology of *satura* implied in *impletas modis* he showed that the name also was Italian. But Livy's account is not merely uncritically patriotic. He is also influenced throughout his work by the notion that Rome's political and social life had degenerated from an early integrity.[58] Livy's account of development of drama belongs to this pattern of thinking, in which his hypothetical dramatic *satura* is part of a pristine dramatic purity uncorrupted by actors' vanity or material extravagance.

There has been much speculation about the identity of Livy's source or sources; Varro is often considered the most likely immediate source.[59] Some general indications support this, for patriotism and a belief in human degeneracy are both marks of Varro's way of thinking. But it seems unlikely that Varro, the conscientious and critical literary historian, wrote an account of the development of Roman drama which could not be reconciled with the fact of Greek influence, so that even if some details in Livy may be deemed to coincide with the views of Varro the account as a whole is probably not to be attributed to him. The poet and grammarian Accius has been suggested as Livy's immediate source; another possible source, though this too is a conjecture, is the grammarian Aelius Stilo, who was the teacher of Varro, but no certain solution of this problem is possible.[60]

The play title *Satura* lends no support to the hypothesis of dramatic *satura.* It occurs as the title of one of Pomponius' Atellans. As shown earlier, *satura* can be used of a pregnant woman. That this is the meaning here is confirmed by another Atellan title, Novius' *Virgo praegnans*, and by other descriptive titles.

As Pomponius is known only as a writer of Atellans, *Satura* is unlikely to have been a generic designation of another literary form.[61] *Satura* is also a title of a work by Naevius. This is more problematical. One fragment is extant:

> *quianam Saturnium populum pepulisti?*
>
> (why have you defeated the people dedicated to Saturn, i.e. the Romans?)

The language is not comic: the metre may be Saturnian, and the subject matter seems to be historical and solemn. If it were assumed that the line was in a context of paratragic burlesque, the title could be taken as similar to those discussed above, but this is a speculation, and it is safer to admit that assuming this title to be correctly given we do not understand it.[62]

Some advocates of the dramatic *satura* have sought to trace its influence in extant literary *satura* in such allegedly dramatic scenes and dialogues as the later part of the third satire of Horace's second book. But this approach is illusory. If there had been a dramatic *satura* we would expect it to have influenced early satire, particularly that of Ennius; the extant remains do not show such an influence. Traces of dramatic *satura* have sometimes been found in scenes of revelry and dancing in Roman comedy, but modern knowledge of New Comedy and of the conditions of Hellenistic performances makes such a view untenable.[63]

3 *Drama and ritual*

Dissatisfaction with the traditional etymologies has also led to a postulated connection with Etruscan more complex than that already discussed [. . .] It has therefore been suggested that *saturno* was the name of a fertility god brought by the Etruscans from Asia Minor who appeared early in Rome with the name Saturu and that scenes of song and dance at his festival were given the name *satura* with *lanx satura* as a symbol of fruitfulness. Livy thus preserves the truth about dramatic importations from Etruria.[64] To this theory there are two main objections. First, apart from the general flimsiness of the linguistic evidence offered, it is a fact of language that the *a* in *Saturnus* is unequivocally long. Secondly, as the extent of Etruscan influence on the Roman stage is problematical, it is unwise to base an elaborate theory about *satura* on any such hypothetical dramatic connection.

Two more theories link dramatic *satura* to the cult of a god. According to the first *saturi* are demonic men, the followers of Dionysus and *satura*, an abstract noun meaning 'satiety', is the song of the satisfied men. As dramatic *satura* is based on a cult of Dionysus, it is thus the counterpart in Rome of Old Attic Comedy.[65] This ingenious hypothesis has considerable charm, but it is too speculative to win assent, and so it must he concluded that Dionysus has nothing to do with satire.

The second theory seeks parallels for *satura* in the banter that was part of certain Demeter cults in Greece and Sicily and in the κυκέων or mixed potion that had an important place in the religion of Demeter or Ceres.[66] *Satura*, it is argued, is abstract and means 'fullness'. Dramatic *satura* is thus the dance and song that belonged to a Ceres festival.[67] Once again the speculation is enterprising, but it has serious weaknesses. There is no evidence for rough jesting at any Roman ritual belonging to Ceres and, as stated earlier, the association of the *lanx* with Ceres seems nothing other than the guess of a grammarian who speculated where his predecessors and betters had failed to specify.

In conclusion it seems that all attempts to seek the origin of *satura* in jocularities attendant on the cults of Saturn, Dionysus or Ceres fail to convince and that theories deriving the word *satura* from Etruscan are at best not proven. Unless new literary or epigraphical material appears, it is reasonable to accept, possibly with reservations, Diomedes' explanation that *satura* took its name from a full dish offered in solemn ritual or from a stuffed sausage.

3 The Satires of Ennius[1]

Ennius, the author of Rome's first great national epic, was also the creator of Roman *satura.* He was the first Roman to gather into the same book verses of varied topic and metre, and for this miscellaneous collection he chose the name *Saturae.* In making such a collection he followed precedents from Alexandrian poetry and scholarship; in his choice of title he was original, for the word had never been used before of a species of literature, and was unique among Roman literary titles in that it was not a Greek loan-word.

The late Latin grammarian Diomedes, whose testimony goes back to republican times, states that at first *satura* was poetry compounded of various pieces of verse as with Ennius and his nephew Pacuvius, and that later it developed in the hands of Lucilius and his successors into the poetry of castigation.[2] Quintilian also seems to refer obliquely to a pre-Lucilian stage of *satura*.[3] Ennius is the only exponent of this kind of *satura* of whose works we have any knowledge; no doubt they were earlier than the *Saturae* of his nephew Pacuvius, of which nothing whatsoever is known.[4] It is clear from Diomedes that the tone and contents of the earliest *satura* contrasted fundamentally with the vituperation in the works of Lucilius and later satirists. Thus while there is some element of censoriousness in the extant fragments of Ennius' *satura*, the quality for which satire has been famous is relatively unimportant in the work of its first practitioner.

1 *The life of Ennius*

Quintus Ennius was born at the small town of Rudiae (modern Rugge), near Lecce in ancient Calabria, the heel of Italy, in 239 B.C.; this was two years after the end of the first Carthaginian war and at a time when there was an intensification of Roman influence in southern Italy.[5] He was of Messapian stock, descended from invaders from across the Adriatic and no doubt with more plausibility than truthfulness claimed as his ancestor King Messapus, who had settled in Italy.[6] It is likely that he received his education at the nearby Greek city of Tarentum, and presumably this took place before Hannibal arrived in southern Italy after Cannae (216 B.C.). He served as a soldier in Sardinia probably with Rome's Calabrian auxiliaries and during this period came to the notice of M. Porcius Cato, quaestor in Sicily in 204 B.C., who was said to have brought him back to Rome with him.[7] The reason for Cato's action has occasioned much speculation. It is unlikely that it was Ennius' military prowess that attracted the attention of Cato. However hostile Cato's attitude to Greek culture then and later, it seems likely that he brought Ennius to Rome in order to be instructed by him in the Greek language, for the story that he learned Greek late in life is improbable.[8] In Rome Ennius, like Livius Andronicus before him, taught Latin and Greek in addition to his dramatic and other literary activities, and for all his connections with great men of the state lived on the Aventine until the end of his life simply and without the appurtenances of wealth.[9] In 189 B.C. he was taken by the consul Fulvius Nobilior on his campaign in Aetolia as his personal poet[10] and five years later, according to the ancient tradition, received Roman citizenship through the son of Nobilior, the colonial commissioner for Potentia.[11] Ennius stated himself and Horace confirmed that he habitually composed poetry when inspired by strong drink. But this should not be taken too seriously, as the connection between the inspiration of wine and that of poetry was traditional.[12] However he died of gout in 169 B.C. at the age of seventy.[13]

Ennius' first language was probably Illyrian, but when later he speaks of having *tria corda* he means that he was master of three media of thought and expression, Greek, Oscan and Latin. Oscan at that time was a *lingua franca* of southern Italy, and Ennius' sister, as the name of her son Pacuvius shows, was married to an Oscan. Greek was the dominant language of education and culture in southern Italy, and the label *semigraecus* was as true of Ennius' intellectual orientation as of that of Livius Andronicus.[14] Tarentum was no doubt able to supply him with a knowledge of the classics of Greek literature, even though its importance as an intellectual centre seems to have been in decline by the later part of the third century B.C.[15] Though Tarentum was probably the source of Ennius' basic knowledge of Greek culture, it did not infect him with the local hostility to Rome, and from early manhood Ennius must have been an admirer of Roman influence and achievement.

When Ennius arrived in Rome, Livius Andronicus, by then a poet held in high esteem and honoured by the commission to write a cult hymn in a time of crisis in 207 B.C.. may already have been dead,[16] and Naevius the dramatist and chronicler of the first Punic war, after his imprisonment for attacking the Metelli, had left Rome, bequeathing the lesson that without the support of powerful families no poet dare be outspoken.[17] The comic poet Plautus was already producing plays in Rome; in his *Miles Gloriosus* (211) he seems to refer to the imprisonment of Naevius as a current event.

Soon after his arrival in Rome Ennius came under the patronage of Scipio Africanus, whose African campaign culminating in the decisive battle of Zama (202 B.C.) he lauded in a poem *Scipio* (*Varia* 1–14V) probably written shortly after the events. Ennius was highly esteemed by Africanus, and an anecdote preserved by Cicero shows easy familiarity between Ennius and Scipio Nasica, the cousin of Africanus. The tradition that Ennius' statue and even his remains were placed beside those of the Scipios, though unlikely, suggests at least that he was particularly associated with the family and never completely estranged from them.[18] In later years he seems to have owed both a commission and his citizenship to the Fulvii, political rivals of the Scipionic bloc. Fulvius Nobilior was criticized by Cato for having taken Ennius on his campaign in Aetolia. The apparently changed attitude of Cato towards his former client may be explained in various ways. The former soldier who taught Greek had become a purveyor of pernicious Greek culture, and Fulvius Nobilior was a political enemy, who indulged in the Greek practice of having a poet in his retinue to celebrate his success.[19] Ennius was also a friend of Servius Sulpicius Galba, who seems to have been associated with the political group of Fulvius Nobilior[20] Ennius from time to time served various of the chief men of the state, but he should not be regarded as a catspaw in the political struggles of rival family groups. Whether or not one accepts the opinion of the grammarian Aelius Stilo that the description in the *Annals* of the discreet political confidant is a self-portrait,[21] the stories of easy familiarity with various members of the aristocratic establishment suggest that Ennius was able to perform commissions without being bought exclusively by a single political interest.

Ennius was well equipped to be a poet both of the great deeds of men and affairs and also of the minutiae of their social intercourse. He had lived among people of widely differing societies and languages, and was expert in the classics of Greek literature. He knew military life both as a serving soldier and as the companion of a general in the field, and as the confidant of some of the most successful politicians of the age he was no doubt privy to important manoeuvres of statesmanship.

2 The writings of Ennius

Ennius' main work was the *Annals*, the epic chronicle of the development of Rome from the beginnings to his own times. This was the archetypal creation of early Roman poetry and without it later poetry would have been fundamentally different.[22] He was also famous for his tragedies on Greek themes, many of them tales of the valour and suffering of war.[23] Thus he was primarily an inspired poet in the grand manner, the disciple of the Muses of Greek literature, who in the proem to the *Annals* stated that the shade of Homer had passed into him through a Pythagorean transmigration of soul.[24] But he also wrote in less exalted genres of poetry. His comedies, of which almost nothing is known today, had no great reputation in antiquity. He also composed historical plays or *praetextae*, a variety of occasional poems, and the *saturae.*

In this multifarious output no consistent pattern of poetic activity and development can be traced. The fragments are too few to show any stylistic evolution. Criteria from metrical technique are inconclusive, as Ennius may have permitted certain variations between the procedure of the *Annals* and that of the minor works.[25] External indications for dating his works are few. He completed the tragedy *Thyestes* shortly before his death.[26] The political poems *Scipio* and *Ambracia* were presumably written shortly after the events they celebrated.[27] The dating of the *saturae* is problematical. Reference to Scipio (frg. 10–11) would suggest a relatively early date, probably though not certainly before his patron's death in 184 B.C. If, as seems likely, the reference to the Ligurian town of Luna comes not from the Annals but from the *Saturae* this is a slight indication for a late date, as Luna did not become a Roman colony until 177 B.C.[28] But there is no reason to suppose that all the miscellaneous poems that made up Ennius' *saturae* were composed at about the same time. His main work, the *Annals*, occupied him for many years and may well have been interrupted from time to time by occasional poems in a more relaxed manner.

Porphyrio states that Ennius wrote four books of *saturae* and there is no good reason to doubt his explicit statement.[29] A corrupt reference in some manuscripts of Donatus was emended by Stephanus into *e sexto satyrarum Ennii.* Even if this emendation were accepted, it would be reasonable to argue that the numeral had been corrupted at an early stage and that the error is more likely to have arisen in Donatus, who quoted merely in order to identify a source of Terence, than in Porphyrio, who states explicitly how many books of *saturae* Ennius wrote.[30]

Our knowledge of the contents of Ennius' *saturae* is scanty. Some thirty-one lines of verse are extant, most of them isolated lines quoted by writers from the Christian era for some lexical or grammatical oddity. There are in addition a prose paraphrase of one of the *saturae* and a few indirect references. Some fragments of Ennius and references are customarily assigned to the *saturae* not through the explicit attribution of the citing authority but on grounds of literary plausibility.[31] Frequently a Greek parallel provides the only means of showing the possible context of a fragment.

Some of the satires are devoted to or at least included the writer's comments on his own life and descriptions of social situations:

Enni poeta salve, qui mortalibus
versus propinas flammeos medullitus. (6f.)

(Good health to you, poet Ennius for passing on to mankind a deep draught of blazing verse.)

These lines from the third book of the *saturae* illustrate one of the greatest difficulties in the interpretation of all fragmentary texts: we do not know whether the words purport to be spoken by Ennius or by some speaker whom the poet reports. If the poet is the speaker here, he either preens himself or justifies himself in the manner of a writer of Old Comedy. But the words may be spoken by an admiring god in a dream or (more likely) an ebullient fellow poet at a symposium or even a gratified patron.[32]

Other fragments mention men's calumny and insensitivity to abuse, possibly in a political situation (8–9, 63). There is also praise of Scipio Africanus in the manner of his separate encomiastic poem entitled *Scipio* (10f.).

It is sometimes impossible to tell the difference between the description of a situation from real life and the retailing of a speech or scene from comedy: *malo hercle magno suo convivat sine modo* (1) (he is stuffing himself to the back teeth; let him damn well suffer for it): the language is that of comedy; the subject may be a greedy contemporary or a stage parasite.[33] The proverbial *dum quidquid, des celere* (2) (what you give, give quickly) may have a similar context. The language of drama is also found in a four-line fragment in which Ennius uses the word *frustra* and its cognate verb *frustrari* nine times (59–62). There is a similar *tour de force* of repetitiveness in a higher genre in the soldiers' chorus in his *Iphigenia.*[34] A complaint about people who get in the way recalls scenes in comedy of the *servus currens* finding his path obstructed.[35]

There are certain elements of philosophy and moralizing in the *saturae*:

contemplor
inde loci liquidas pilatasque aetheris oras (3f.)

(from there I gaze on the bright and compacted edges of the upper air)

The words in themselves may suggest the language of philosophical speculation, for the closest verbal parallel is part of an exposition of Stoic beliefs in Cicero.[36] It is also possible that in the *satura* the solemn words may be deceptive and need not imply a consistently serious poem. Another fragment comments on the resemblance between man and monkey 'ugliest of beasts' perhaps in order to show the difference between appearance and reality.[37]

Moralizing may be present in a *satura* by Ennius in which *Mors* and *Vita* are introduced in debate, but nothing is known of the substance of this work. Quintilian instances it as an illustration of personified abstracts.[38] There is no known example in Greek of personified Life and Death in conjunction, but antithetical pairs of personified abstracts are found debating in both drama and rhetorical prose. Epicharmus wrote some plays in which such a conflict was one of the most important elements: Land and Sea probably expounded in debate the benefits they give to mankind.[39] There is in Aristophanes' *Clouds* a debate of personified abstracts, the Just and Unjust Arguments. In a work by the fifth-century Sophist Prodicus the young Herakles is confronted by two women, Pleasure and Virtue, who propounded rhetorically the advantages of the ways of life represented by them.[40] In Latin Novius composed an Atellan play with the title *Mortis et Vitae Iudicium.*[41] What, if anything, Ennius owed to some such theme we do not know; as he adapted a work attributed to Epicharmus in one of his miscellaneous poems, there is slight support for the influence of Epicharmus here. If the debating abstracts in Epicharmus' plays are any guide to the contents of Ennius' *satura*, Life and Death disputed over the benefits they brought to men. How the debate was resolved we do not know: some character may have decided between the two, or perhaps as in the *Agon* of Aristophanes' *Clouds* one of the contestants withdrew defeated.

The Aesopic fable with its attractive codification of simple folk wisdom provided writers of many kinds with a framework for moralizing. A fragment of Ennius begins the fable of the man who tried to catch fish by piping to them. Herodotus had applied the same story politically to the Eastern Greeks who refused to dance to Cyrus' tune, but we have no evidence about Ennius' context.[42] There is also found in Ennius' *saturae* the fable of the crested lark that moves its young from the ripe cornfield only when the farmer, having sought help in vain from those who might have been expected to give it, decides to do the work himself. Gellius paraphrases Ennius' fable in prose and quotes verbatim the two verses that point the moral; it is also possible to reconstruct from his paraphrase some of the phrasing of Ennius' trochaic lines.[43] In the Aesopic verses the story is developed in two stages; in Ennius there are three, for help is sought in vain from kin as well as from friends and the tale is expanded like a children's story with careful description of the trepidation of the nestlings. This simple manner of narration is in the tradition of the Aesopic verse fable, but it is very different from the subtle contrivance of Callimachus' fable of the olive and laurel interrupted in their argument by the bramble bush. Ennius does not seem to have taken anything from elaborate Hellenistic poetry or from the sophisticated telling of fable such as is found in Plato.[44] It is more likely that he is reproducing an Aesopic fable transmitted orally or from a simple school collection. The convention of retailing in verse simple folk tales with a moral application is found as early as Archilochus.

We may have some other traces of Ennius' *saturae.* Style suggests that the reference to *Lunai portum* (quoted by Persius, *Sat.* 6,9) belongs to them and subject matter suggests the same for the description of a walk with Galba.[45]

Ennius also wrote a number of minor poems with individual descriptive titles, which some scholars wish to include among the *saturae.*[46] These works are of two types: occasional pieces and adaptations of Greek originals. *Scipio* and *Ambracia* are composed in a particular political context and are obviously original.[47] The rest, based for the most part on minor Greek works, seem to have been written as they took the poet's fancy or as copies came to hand, e.g. *Sota*, a poem of virulence in keeping with the reputation of Sotades, its scurrilous Alexandrian source; the fragments referring to fornication, excrement and possibly human discontent;[48] and *Hedyphagetica*, an adaption, probably not a close translation, of a didactic work on gourmandizing by Archestratus, a fourth-century Sicilian writer.[49] But there is a weighty objection to including these poems among Ennius' *saturae.* Ancient authorities refer to these miscellaneous works by their proper names, but it is unlikely that this would have happened had they been part of the *saturae.* Where *saturae* have individual descriptive titles as with Varro's Menippeans, grammarians almost always cite by title and not vaguely *in saturis.* Two methods of quotation are never used for the same author. Had Ennius' miscellaneous works been part of the *saturae*, they would have been cited not by individual title but by the designation *saturae* with or without a book number. It may therefore be concluded that the *saturae* and *varia* are different works.

To what extent Ennius knew earlier personal poetry such as that of Archilochus and Hipponax either directly or through Hellenistic intermediaries we cannot tell. As discussed in the previous chapter, Posidippus' *Soros* may well have provided a model for Ennius' metaphorical title, but Callimachus' *Iambi* must have been the most famous precedent for a collection of poems on a wide range of themes in a variety of metres. Ennius owed much to Callimachus, who helped inspire the solemn introduction to the *Annals* and offered weighty precedence for writing in many different genres. But while the example of Callimachus' *Iambi* may have helped to induce Ennius to compile his own collection of miscellaneous poems, there is no evidence and little likelihood that he adapted them in detail, for many of their subjects are recherché and their style so artificial and oblique as to have provided later Greek theorists with textbook examples of allegorical expression and irony.[50] As Greek readers required commentaries for these works, Ennius would not have been able to introduce them to a Roman public.[51] His themes were taken from his own personal experience as well as from a wide range of reading.

3 Transmission and significance

We have little certain knowledge of the extent of the circulation in antiquity or of the quality of the ancient transmission of Ennius' *saturae.* When the text of Ennius was emended soon after his death by the grammarian Octavius Lampadio it is likely that the *saturae* were not neglected.[52] Horace's friend, the civil servant and satirist Julius Florus, made a selection from them along with pieces from Lucilius and Varro either as a commonplace book for his own easy reference or as an anthology for contemporaries.[53] In the general neglect of archaic poetry in the first century A.D., it is likely that copies of the *saturae* became increasingly scarce. In the following century Fronto made a *de luxe* copy of Ennius' *Sota* for the emperor; this may suggest that good copies of the minor works were by then not numerous. Gellius in his unbounded enthusiasm for the old-fashioned, visited learned libraries and painstakingly verified readings in Ennius; he seems to have had a complete edition of the *saturae* before him.[54] After the literary vogue had waned they became, like other archaic poetry, linguistic source-books for grammarians. Nonius in the early fourth century A.D., though having access, as it seems, to a complete text, sometimes excerpted inaccurately from such writers as Gellius, but after this time references to the *saturae* become still rarer.[55] The magniloquent *Annals* failed to survive the dark ages; it is not surprising that the unspectacular *saturae* fared no better.

The place of Ennius' *saturae* in the history of Roman satire is somewhat uncertain. To Diomedes and also by implication to Quintilian the Ennian stage of *satura* was in some ways a false start, and it seems likely that it had a very limited influence on later satirists. Lucilius in his earliest works takes over variety of metre but there is little other demonstrable indebtedness. None the less Ennius was the creator of more than the name of literary *satura*. It is perhaps a paradox that this rough-hewn genius sought a precedent for a collection of miscellaneous personal poems in highly sophisticated works from a mature stage of Greek civilization. To what extent the enterprising talent was able to overmaster the deficiencies of a crude literary technique we cannot know.[56] But although his *saturae* were probably worthy of the respect of the historian of literature rather than of its critical reader, it is unlikely that they were untouched by the power of his vigorous personality.

Notes to chapter 1 (The genre)

1 The only serviceable general handbook on Roman satire is that of U. Knoche. *Die Römische Satire* (Göttingen, 1971[3]). The thorough rewriting of the second edition was unfortunately terminated by the author's death: the contents and pagination of the chapters on Lucilius to the end are the same as in the second edition and further bibliography has been added by the editor W. Ehlers. Of great value is the introduction to O. Weinreich's translations, *Römische Satiren* (Zürich and Stuttgart, 1962[2]), vii–civ, perhaps the best single essay on Roman satire. G. Highet, *The Anatomy of Satire* (Princeton, 1962), provides a wide-ranging study of fundamental principles. J.-P. Cèbe, *La caricature et la parodie dans le monde romain antique des origines à Juvénal* (Paris, 1966), is a catalogue of great thoroughness. D. Korzeniewski, *Die Römische Satire*, Wege d. Forschung 238 (Darmstadt, 1970), gathers a number of the most important articles on the subject from 1920. W. S. Anderson has provided useful bibliographies: for 1937–55, *C.W.* 50 (1956), 33–40; for 1955–62, *C.W.* 57 (1964), 293–301, 343–8; for 1962–8, *C.W.* 63 (1970), 181–94, 199, 217–22.

A succinct and reliable history of the period during which all the satirists except Ennius and Juvenal wrote is provided by H. H. Scullard, *From the Gracchi to Nero* (London, 1970[3]). R. Syme, *The Roman Revolution* (Oxford, 1939) is the fundamental historical study of the times of Horace's satires. The Cambridge Ancient History X, *The Augustan Empire 44* B.C.–A.D. *70* (Cambridge, 1934) and XI, *The Imperial Peace* A.D. *70–192* (Cambridge, 1936), though the chapter on Hadrian is undistinguished, are valuable surveys of the Principate. A. Garzetti, transl. J. R. Foster, *From Tiberius to the Antonines* (London, 1974), covers the whole of the relevant imperial period in detail, emperor by emperor.

For the background of social history see J. P. V. D. Balsdon, *Life and Leisure in Ancient Rome* (London, 1969). J. Carcopino, *Daily Life in Ancient Rome* (revised edn, Harmondsworth, 1956) is concerned with life in the early empire; it is entertaining but not wholly reliable. The second part of W. Kroll, *Die Kultur der ciceronischen Zeit* (Leipzig, 1933) is valuable; for the early empire the copious study by L. Friedlaender, transl. J. H. Freese and L. A. Magnus, *Roman Life and Manners*, 4 vols. (London, 1908–13), is unsurpassed in the plenitude of its material but is cumbersome in its arrangement. J. Marquardt–A. Mau, *Das Privatleben der Römer* (Leizig, 1886) is a work of wide range with a full literary and epigraphical documentation that is conveniently presented for easy reference.

2 Quint. 10,1,93. On the meaning of the words see (against W. Rennie, *C.R.* 36 (1922), 21) G. L. Hendrickson, *C.Ph.* 22 (1927), 60. On Quintilian's judgement see also C. A. Van Rooy, *Studies in Classical Satire and Related Literary Theory* (Leiden, 1965), 117–23.

3 There is an authoritative interpretation of the difficult sentence *alterum illud etiam prius saturae genus, sed non solo carminum varietate mixtum condidit Terentius Varro* (10,1,95) by M. Winterbottom, 'Problems in Quintilian', *B.I.C.S. Supp.* 25 (1970), 191: 'The other well-known type of satire – one that arose even before Lucilius (i.e. the Ennian satire of varied metre) – was exploited by Varro, but now with a variety given not merely by metrical changes (but by an admixture of prose to the verse).' See further D. A. Russell and M. Winterbottom (ed.), *Ancient Literary Criticism* (Oxford, 1972), 380–400.

4 Note Quintilian's censure of Afranius for introducing paederastic episodes into his *togatae* (10,1,100). On Quintilian's treatment of satire see Weinreich viii and on

Quintilian in general G. Kennedy, *Quintilian* (New York, 1969), esp. ch. 5: Quintilian as a critic (101–22).

5 See also Quint. 10,2,22. For Aristotle's broad classification see his *Poetics*, 1447a8 and 16, 1448b24–1449a6, and D. W. Lucas, *Aristotle, Poetics* (Oxford, 1968) on the passages. A. E. Harvey, *C.Q.* 5 (1955), 157–75, examines the subtle distinctions of Hellenistic theory with reference to the 'kinds' of lyric poetry. R. Pfeiffer, *History of Classical Scholarship* (Oxford, 1968), 203–7, traces the Hellenistic beginnings of canons of accepted authors; see also L. E. Rossi, *B.I.C.S.* 18 (1971), 69–94.

6 O. Regenbogen, 'Theophrastos von Eresos', *R.E. Supp.* 7, 1530; G. A. Kennedy, *H.S.C.Ph.* 62 (1957), 93–104; *P. Hibeh* 2,183 and discussion by E. G. Turner. On decorum see also M. Pohlenz, 'τὸ πρέπον', *N. G. Göttingen* (Berlin, 1933), 53.

7 Accius *Didasc.* frg. 13 (Morel) = *Gramm. Rom. Frg.* (Fun.) 27; Leo, *Gesch.* 386–91.

8 Horace discusses generic distinctions and propriety in *A.P.* 73ff.; note esp. 86–8 and 92. See C. O. Brink, *Horace on Poetry 2* (Cambridge, 1971), on the whole passage. On Roman criticism by kinds, on hierarchy of genres and the notion of decorum associated with it, D'Alton 398–426.

9 In the imagery of his tragedies there are occasional lapses from the high style (e.g. *solvendo non es* (you are bankrupt), *Oed.* 942, where Gronovius' emendation is almost certainly right). Pliny (*Epp.* 6,21,4) describes the dilettante activities of an insignificant writer who wrote in the manner of both Old and New Comedy, distinguishing carefully between the conventions of the one and the other.

10 Mart. 12,94. Contrast his orderly list there with his haphazard list at 3,20 and with that of Statius, *Silv.* 1,3,101–4.

11 See particularly the very important study of the hierarchy of genres in the choice of appropriate vocabulary by B. Axelson, *Unpoetische Wörter* (Lund, 1945).

12 Pers. 1,114–8; Juv. 1,19f. and 51.

13 It is assumed here with Housman, Duff and Knoche (among others) against Clausen and probably the ancient scholiast that 634–7 are a vehement rhetorical question and not an ironical statement. Juvenal uses *operum lex* (7,102) of the historian's literary conventions.

14 Johannes Lydus, *Mag.* I,41R. This passage obviously derives in part from Hor. *Sat.* 2,I,If. and Juv. 6,635; see also F. Leo, *Hermes* 24 (1889), 82 (= Leo, *Ausgew. kl. Schr.* I 297f.) and Marx, I xii.

15 Lucilius' level of verbal obscenity may be deduced from 1186M. *futuo*, Hor. Sat. 1,2,127: the verb is continuative present: 'While I am actually on the job'; *cunnus*, Hor. Sat. 1,2,36 and 70; 1,3,107. Neither word occurs in the later satirists, though both are common in Martial. *Fello* in the obscene sense is not found in any satirist but is common in Martial and the writers of graffiti at Pompeii; see also A. E. Housman, *Hermes* 66 (1931), 408 n. 2 (= *Class. Papers* III 1180 n. 3). *Penis*, which is an obscene word to Cicero (*Fam.* 9,22,2) occurs in Horace only in an epode (12,8); it occurs twice in the violent denunciation of Persius' fourth satire (4,35 and 48) and twice in Juvenal, the witty sneer at 6,337 and the shock tactics of the brutal question at 9,43 (cf. the revolting expression at 2,33). On the avoidance of obscene words see further Cic. *Off* I,128f., Quint. 8,3,39, and Kroll 111f.

16 Mart. 5,78, 10,48; Hor. *C.* 1,20 (see Nisbet and Hubbard, *A Commentary on Horace Odes Bk I*, 244ff.); see in general the important study by F. Cairns, *Generic Composition in Greek and Roman Poetry* (Edinburgh, 1972); note esp . p. 6. On the topic of the invitation to the frugal meal see ch. 7 n. 76.

17 W. H. Auden, in conversation with Richard Crossman on BBC television, 28 Jan. 1973, talked of 'Opera, the last refuge of the high style'. Graham Hough, *An Essay on Criticism* (London, 1966), 84, vindicates the value of a theory of kinds: 'the true and necessary principle that each literary species offers its own satisfaction, operates on its own level and has its own proper principle.'

18 J. Wight Duff, *Roman Satire* (Cambridge, 1937), 106–14; N. Terzaghi, *Per la storia della satira* (Turin, 19442), 99–154. On problems of dating see B. E. Perry, *Babrius and Phaedrus* (Loeb' Classical Library, 1965), intro. lxxix n. 1.

19 Apul. *Apol.* 10. The supremacy of the abusive force of *iambi* is mentioned by Porph. on Hor. C. 1,16,22–4. Note Catull. frg 3: *at non effugies meos iambos.*

20 On coarse army songs see e.g. Pliny *N.H.* 19,144; Schanz-Hosius I[4] 21f. On primitive rude verses see also Gell. 15,4,3 and Fraenkel 58; on Octavianus' Fescennines see Macr. *Sat.* 2,4,21. On Ovid's *Ibis* see A. E. Housman, *Journ. Phil.* 35 (1920), esp. 316–18 (= *Class. Papers* III 1040–2).

21 Cicero *Cael.* 6 makes a distinction between *accusatio* and *maledictio* (cf. Austin *a.l.*). To Quintilian (12,9,8) mud-slinging is not the mark of a first-class orator (see Austin on 12,9,9). On the tradition of *invectiva* see R. G. M. Nisbet (ed.), *Cicero in Pis.* (Oxford, 1961), 192–7.

22 E. J. Kenney, *Lucretius, De Rerum Natura Bk 3* (Cambridge, 1971), intro. 17ff., discusses the possible influence of diatribe. C. Murley, *T.A.Ph.A.* 70 (1939), 380–95, provides interesting parallels but his conclusion that Lucretius may have a place in the history of satire is misleading. For Lucretius' place in the poetic tradition of Empedocles see W. Kranz, *Philologus* 96 (1944), 68–107. On didactic poetry see Diomedes *G.L.K.* 1,482 and W. Kroll, *RE.*, *s.v.* 'Lehrgedicht', 12,2,1842–57.

23 F. J. E. Raby, *A History of Secular Latin Poetry in the Middle Ages* 11 (1957[2]), 45–54, discusses knowledge of Juvenal in twelfth-century France, but his description of *Speculum Stultorum* as 'a true satire in the Roman sense' (98) is misleading.

24 The thesis of a continuity is developed unconvincingly by C. Witke, *Latin Satire. The Structure of Persuasion* (Leiden, 1970); rev. Rudd, C. R. 23 (1973), 42–4. On the reference by Walter of Châtillon see Raby (n. 23 above), 197.

25 The French poet and critic Boileau Despréaux published together with his ninth satire in 1666 a short discourse on satire that was confined to the Lucilian tradition.

26 J. Dryden, 'A Discourse concerning the Original and Progress of Satire', Of *Dramatic Poesy and Other Critical Essays*, ed. G. Watson, vol. II (London, New York, 1962), 71–155.

27 See Rudd 258–73.

28 Diomedes *G.L.K.*. 1,485 (= *C.G.F.* (Kaibel) 55f.).

29 The author of this article on satire in the standard 11th edn. of the *Enc. Brit.* is Richard Garnett; the definition is rightly retained in the 1973 edn. of *Enc. Brit.*

30 This denial is a passing weakness in Matthew Hodgart's useful general study of the principles and practice of satire, *Satire* (London, 1969), 31; note by contrast his sound formulation of the principles of the classical tradition of formal satire (ch. 5 esp. 132). Hodgart also believes that good satire possesses 'no single fixed style; it works by comparisons and contrasts' (63). This view of the fluid style of satire is in part endorsed by Horace (*Sat.* 1,10,11–15), but the ancient satirist also recognized the limits beyond which he should not proceed.

Notes to chapter 2 (Origins)

1 The manuscript tradition of the satirists and grammarians is confused on the point of orthography, but the spelling *satura* is found in such good manuscripts as the Montepessulanus (P) of Juvenal. For a thorough discussion of the orthographical problem see F. Marx (ed.), *C. Lucilii Carminum Reliquiae* (Leipzig, 1904 and 1905), I ixf.; see also Leo's critical note in *C.G.F.* (Kaibel) 55 and G. A. Gerhard, *Philologus* 75 (1918), 247. See also the discussion by C. A. Van Rooy, *Studies in Classical Satire and Related Literary Theory* (Leiden, 1965), 155ff. (see also index, 223). Van Rooy's book, notwithstanding the reservations expressed in *C.R.* 16 (1966), 72ff., is a very useful contribution to many of the problems discussed in this chapter; see rev., by F. Robertson, *C.Ph.* 61 (1966), 214–16.

2 *adventicia* with *cena* Suet. *Vit.* 13,2, with the noun to be supplied Petr. 90,5; *adventoria* (*cena*) Mart. *Praef.* 12.

3 *Carm. Lat. Epigr.* I (Bü); cf. Schanz-Hosius 1^4 19.

4 Plaut. *Poen.* 6–8; *Am.* 667f.

5 Sen. *N.Q.* 1,5,12 (of purple dye); Pers. 1,71 (of *rus*, the countryside); Cic. *Orat.* 123 (*oratio*).

6 Diomedes I 485 *G.L.K.*

7 Isidore *Orig.* 5,16 and 8,7,7; Fest. 417 L (315 M); the presence of another quotation to illustrate *lex satura* at Festus 416 L (314 M) does not invalidate the point even though this passage of Festus draws on Verrius Flaccus, for it too derives from Varro; see Leo, *Gött. gel. Anz.* (1906), 859 (= *Ausgew. kl. Schr.* 1,245). The one independent comment of importance is that of Isidore (20,1,8): *satietas ex uno cibo dici potest, pro eo quod satis est; saturitas autem a satura nomen accepit, quod est vario alimentorum adparatu compositum.* Isidore explicitly makes the distinction between a 'satiety that is caused by one kind of food and taking its name from sufficiency and a repletion that takes its name from *satura*, that is something obtained from a varied provision of things to eat'. To Isidore *satura* contains the notion of the variegated and of a miscellany.

8 Pseudacron on *praef. in serm. lib.* I (= *test.* V d) Marx).

9 See C. O. Brink, 'Horace and Varro', *Entr. Fond. Hardt* 9 (1963), 193.

10 For Varro's discussion of Ennius in *de Poetis* see Gell. 17,21,42f.

11 Wine as the source of the satyrs' hilarity is emphasized by Pseudacron and Isid. *Orig.* 8,7,7.

12 This objection has been made by many scholars, e.g. Knoche 9.

13 Diomedes *G.L.K.* I 490.

14 Arist. *Poet.* 1449a22; cf. 1449a20; also τὸ σατυρικόν Xen. *Symp.* 4,19; for σάτυροι in the sense of 'a satyr play' see Ar. *Thesm.* 157, Hor. *AP.* 235 and Brink *a.l.* To this may be added Weinreich's point, xxiii, that actors of satyr plays are never called *saturi* in Latin but *ludiones* or *histriones*, noting the gloss *ludio:* σατυριστής (*C. Gl.L.* II 430,2).

15 *lanx* also in Isid. 8,7,7 (= Marx *testimonia* VII) and Pseudacron, loc. cit. (n. 8 above).

16 Plaut. *Aul.* 354f.

17 On offerings to Ceres see Ovid *Fast.* 2,520; Cato *Agr.* 134.

18 Offerings to Pales Ov. *Fast.* 4,743ff., on which see W. Warde Fowler, *The Roman Festivals* (London, 1899), 81 n. 5; first fruits of the kitchen garden to the Lares,

Calp. Sic. 2,64f.; bean meal with lard was offered to Carna at the time of the bean harvest (Macr. *Sat.* 1,12,33 and Warde Fowler, 130).

19 *Farcimen* as stuffing or sausage meat, Isid. *Orig.* 20,2,28, as a sausage Gell. 16,7,11.

20 Varro *L.L.* 5,111. On the species mentioned there see the lucid note by J. Collart, *Varron, de Lingua Latina Livre V* (Paris, 1954), *a.l.*

21 Knoche 10.

22 Apic. 2,5,3 for a sausage stuffing (= B. Flower and E. Rosenbaum, *Apicius. The Roman Cookery Book* (London, 1958), recipe 59). Pine kernels and honey in a white sauce served with goose (Apic. 6,5,5 = Fl. & Ros. 231); spelt–grits and pine kernels in a chicken stuffing (6,8,14 = Fl. & Ros. 253).

23 *hordeum* with shoulder of pork (Apicius 7,9,3 = Fl. & Ros. 295). On *polenta* as an item in the simple life Sen. *Epp.* 110,18; see Schol. Juv. 11,20 (*miscellanea*), Pliny *N.H.* 18,72, Prop. 4,8,25 on food for gladiators; barley as food for pigs, Varro, *R.R.* 2,4,6, and as food to fatten stallions, Col. 6,27,8 and K. D. White, *Roman Farming* (London, 1970), 292.

24 See e.g. Virgil *Georg.* 3,205, Varro *R.R.* 1,31,5, Pliny *N.H.* 18,142.

25 Compare Horace's metaphor *liber nutritus* (*Epp.* 1,20,1–5). As well as referring to literary history *farrago* is self-depreciatory an attitude sustained by the diminutive *libelli.*

26 E.g. Knoche 10, and Weinreich xi. One may compare the development of the word farce from Latin *farcire*, to stuff, by way of the mediaeval usage of the stuffing for a bird and also of an impromptu amplification of the text of the Mass and of a play (*farsa*) to the modern meaning of a dramatic work intended solely to excite ribald laughter.

27 For *patina* as a cake see Apic. 4,2. It may be noted in passing that Tertullian's list of miscellaneous and anthology works includes the title *Acci Patinam*, but nothing can be safely inferred from it.

28 On the poem of Meleager see Gow and Page, *The Greek Anthology, Hellenistic Epigrams* (Cambridge, 1965), on 4398–407. They refer to *A.P.* 12,44,3 (= 1813 G–P) for another example of λοπάς in the sense of the contents of the platter. Gow-Page, intro. xvi, assign the compilation of the 'Garland' of Meleager to the early part of the 1st C. B.C. Hirzel, *Der Dialog* I 440 n. 4 points to Meleager's knowledge of Latin and of Roman customs in the reference at *A.P.* 12,95,10 to *lanx satura.*

29 On Posidippus' σωρός see Schol. *Il.* 11,101 (a comment of Aristarchus), W. Peek, *R.E. s.v.* 'Poseidippos', 22,1 (1953), 431–9, and H. Lloyd-Jones, *J.R.S.* 83 (1963), 75–99.

30 On σύμμεικτα see αἰτίαι σύμμεικτοι of Democritus (*D.K.V.* 11,91,15), αἰτίαι with a diversity of subjects, σύμμικτα συμποτικά of Aristoxenus frg 124 Wehrli. Colourful Greek titles such as are listed by Pliny *N.H. Praef.* 24, e.g. κέρας 'Αμαλθείας, λειμών, should be used with caution as parallels for *satura.* For some at least of these were commonplace books of excerpts from other authors with or without annotation by the compiler. On the process of compilation see Cic. *Att.* 2,20,6 and Gell. *praef.* 2.

31 For a postulated connection between Demeter and the Σωρός see the argument of Lasserre, *Rh.M.* 102 (1959), 222ff., based on an allegorical interpretation of Theocr. 7,155.

32 The possible influence of the *Soros* on Ennius' *saturae*, as suggested by the author, *Röm. Sat.* 417, is favoured by J. H. Waszink, 'Ennius', *Entr. Fond. Hardt* 17 (1972), 105.

33 On *satura* and *saturae* see W. Kroll, *R.E. s.v. 'satura'* 2,2 (1921), 192–200.

34 A speech against Tiberius Gracchus by T. Annius Luscus in 133 B.C. (*O.R.F.* 106 = Festus p. 416 L), also C. Laelius Sapiens, *pro se ad populum*, after 145 B.C. (*ib.* p. 119f. = Festus p. 416 L = 314 M). See Marx on Lucil. 48, and Ullman, *C.Ph.* 8 (1913), 177ff.

35 By the *Lex Caecilia Didia* (Cic. *Dom.* 53): see Rotondi, *Leges Publicae P.R.* (Milan, 1912), 335.

36 Amm. Marc. 16,6,3; Lact. 1,21,13 includes no qualifying word: Pescennius Festus (late 2nd C. A.D.) is said to have written *libri historiarum per saturam* (= Marx, *test.* xxix).

37 The relevance to *satura* of E. Lattes' equation of *satir-* and 'speaking' (see Lattes, *Bull. Soc. Ling.* 30 (1930), 82ff.) was first pointed out by P. Meriggi, *Stud, Etrusc.* 11 (1937), 196f. and n. 177 and was amplified by B. Snell, *S.I.F.C.* 17 (1940), 215. On *sátena = dictus* see E. Vetter, *Glotta* 28 (1940), 157 and 217.

38 Salutary scepticism on too wide an acceptance of Etruscan loan words in Latin is expressed by O. J. L. Szemerényi, *Hermes* 103 (1975), 300ff.; see also A. D. Momigliano *J.R.S.* 53 (1963), 98. The Etruscan derivation of *satura* is considered as no more than a hypothesis by Walde-Hofmann, *Lateinisches etymologisches Wörterbuch* (19543), *s.v. satura*, but accepted without discussion by L. R. Palmer, *The Latin Language* (London, 1954), 48.

39 *Ister* is often accepted as one of the most certain Etruscan loan words in Latin, but Szemerényi, loc. cit. (n. 38), 314–16 considers it to be of Greek origin by way of Etruscan.

40 The phrase *impletas modis saturas* is probably a piece of etymologizing on the basis of *satura* meaning something filled full; compare the other etymologies in this passage: in addition to *histrio* from *ister, fabula* and *argumentum* from *fari* and *arguo*; see Quint. 5,10,9 and B. L. Ullman, *C.Ph.* 9 (1914), 7–8.

41 For the phrase *ad manum* see Liv. 9,19,6: *ad manum domi supplementum esset*; and Pliny *N.H.* 35,97: *ad manum intuenti*; cf. Ov. *Fast.* 3,536. The separation of voice and gesture is confirmed by Cic. *de Or.* 1,254 and *Leg.* 1,11.

42 On *exodia* see G. Duckworth, *The Nature of Roman Comedy* (Princeton, 1952), 6 and F. Skutsch, *R.E. s.v. exodia* 6,2 (1909), 1686–9; on Atellans see Duckworth, 10–13; and for *Atellanicum exodium* see e.g. Suet. *Tib.* 45.

43 On the stages of Livy's account see Leo, *Hermes* 39 (1904), 67ff. and Weinreich, *Hermes* 51 (1916), 392ff.

44 Val. Max. 2,4,4: *paulatim deinde ludicra ars ad saturarum modos perrepsit.* On this passage see Weinreich, loc. cit. (n. 43 above) 404–7.

45 For the first view see e.g. G. Duckworth, op. cit. (n. 42 above) 10. Ullman's advocacy of a dramatic *satura* is fully documented and also moderate: 'The present status of the satura question', *N. Carolina St. Class. Phil.* 17 (1920), 379–401 (= Korzeniewski 1–30). See also J. H. Waszink, *Entr. Fond. Hardt* 17 (1972), 108ff., who refers to H. D. Jocelyn, *The Tragedies of Ennius* (Cambridge, 1969), 13.

46 See Weinreich, loc. cit. (n. 43) 389. It is clear from Cato (frg 77P = Gell. 2,28,6) that such an occurrence as a plague would have been mentioned in the pontifical annals. Livy states (6,1,1–3) that the records for the years after the sack of Rome

by the Gauls (387 B.C.) were more reliable. According to Cicero, *de Or.* 2,52, these annals recorded *res omnes singulorum annorum*; the introduction of dances from Etruria may have been included. On the *annales* see J. E. A. Crake, *C.Ph.* 35 (1940), 375–86, and J. P. V. D. Balsdon, *C.Q.* 3 (1953), 158–64. On sending to Etruria see Liv. 27,37,6 and Tac. *Ann.* 14,21.

47 On Fescennines at a harvest festival, Hor. *Epp.* 2,1,139ff., at a wedding, Cat. 61,120 (and Fordyce, *a.l.*); see also Marx, *Rh.M.* 78 (1929), 398–426.

48 The date 240 B.C. is given by Atticus and, as a result of research in *antiquis commentariis*, by Cicero, *Brut.* 72, who also refers to it at *Tusc.* 1,3 and *Sen.* 50; it seems to have had the confirmation of Varro (Gell. 17,21,42f.; see H. Dahlmann, *Entr. Fond. Hardt* 9 (1963), 13; Accius gave 197 B.C. as the year of Livius' first production, a dating which makes nonsense of Latin literary historian and was rightly contradicted by Cic. *Brut.* 72; it has however been revived by H. B. Mattingly, *C.Q.* 7 (1957), 159–63.

49 See Festus 446 L (333 M): *is* (i.e. Livius) *et scribebat fabulas et agebat*; cf. E. Fraenkel, *R.E. Supplbd* 5 (1931) *s.v.* 'Livius', 601.

50 Suet. *Gramm.* 1: *nihil amplius quam Graecos interpretabantur* (i.e. Livius et Ennius); see also Diomedes *G.L.K.* I 489. The transmitted titles of Livius' tragedies are on Greek subjects; the comic title *Gladiolus* (frg 1R [3]) is based on New Comedy; cf. Menander 'Εγχειρίδιον' (136–141 Kö. [2]) and 128–30 Austin.

51 O. Jahn, *Hermes* 2 (1867), 225–51 believed that the apparent chronological sequence was a schematic construction. His view was amplified by Leo, *Hermes* 24 (1889), 67–84 (= *Ausgew. kl. Schr.* I 283–300), and by G. L. Hendrickson, *A.J.Ph.* 15 (1894), 1–30.

52 Hendrickson, *A.J.Ph.* 19 (1898), 309 argues that the form of Livy's description comes from the same source as the schematic words of the *tractatus Coislinianus*, a Peripatetic treatise of unknown authorship and date, on which see *C.G.F.* (Kaibel), 50–3 and D'Alton 361. On the close parallel between Arist. *Poet.* 1449b7ff. and Livy's words see Hendrickson, *A.J.Ph.* 15 (1894), 7ff. Similiarly *in artem paulatim verterat* suggests the way of thought of ὀψὲ ἀπεσεμνύνθη (*Poet.* 1449a20). For another example of an account of the growth and degeneracy of literature (and the other *arts*) see Vell. Pat. 1,16,3–1,17.

53 On Crates, who visited Rome *c.* 168 B.C., see Pfeiffer, *History of Classical Scholarship* (Oxford, 1968), 235–45; for his writings on comedy, 242. His literary influence is described by Suet. *Gramm.* 2.

54 There was a censorious element in the Hellenistic satyr play e.g. in the *Menedemus* of Lycophron (Athen. 2,55c). On the development of the satyr play in Hellenistic times see Gerhard, *Philologus* 75 (1918), 250–60.

55 Roman theory saw a connection between satyr drama and *Atellana*: Porphyrio on Hor. *A.P.* 221: *satyrica coeperunt scribere ut Pomponius Atalanten* etc.; Diomedes *G.L.K.* I 489, 32–490, 18. See also the Greek term σατυρικαὶ κωμῳδίαι for *Atellana*, Nicolaus of Damascus ap. Athen. 6,261C, and Leo, *Hermes* 49 (1914), 164 n. 1 and 169ff. (= *Ausgew. kl. Schr.* 1 252 n. 1 and 257ff.).

56 Dion. Hal. *Ant. Rom.* 7,71,1 also refers to Fabius Pictor. Boyance, *R.E.A.* 34 (1932), 11–25, sees the origin of a dramatic *satura* in such a dance of satyrs, a view which is refuted by Weinreich xxiii. It is none the less possible that some informal quasi-dramatic pieces were enacted in Rome in early times, but we have no knowledge of their name or nature.

57 On Livy's patriotism see *Praef.* and P. G. Walsh, *Livy* (Cambridge, 1961), 144f.; also Ogilvie, *Commentary on Livy Bks 1–5*, pp. 140ff. and 255.

58 For the feeling of Rome's moral degeneracy see Liv. *Praef.* and P. G. Walsh, op. cit. (n. 57 above) 67f.

59 E.g. Weinreich, *Hermes* 51 (1916), 410 regards Varro as a probable source. For Varro's patriotism see also C. O. Brink, 'Horace and Varro', *Entr. Fond. Hardt* 9 (1963), 182; for his belief in degeneracy see further his Menippeans *passim.*

60 To Cicero, *Brutus* 60, Varro is *diligentissimus investigator antiquitatis.* Leo, *Hermes* 24 (1889), 79 (= *Ausgew. kl. Schr.* I 295) believed Varro to be the source, but later, *Hermes* 39 (1904), 67, under the influence of Hendrickson, *A.J.Ph.* 19 (1898), 288, who argued for Accius as Livy's immediate source and Pergamene writers as the remoter source, modified his opinion and advocated an unknown source earlier than Varro. On Aelius Stilo see *Gramm. Rom. Fragm.* (Fun.), pp. 51–76 and Schanz-Hosius I 232ff.

61 Pomponius, *Satura*: Frassinetti, *Fabularum Atell. Fragmenta* (Turin, 1935), pp. 40f.; frg II is a description of a treacherous and truculent woman. See also Pomponius, *Dotata* (Fras. p. 11). On the meaning of *satura* in play titles see Ullman, *C.Ph.* 9 (1914), 22f. For other unseemly Atellan titles see Pomponius, *Prostibulum* (Fras. pp. 36–8); *Hirnea Pappi* (Fras. p. 14).

62 Naevius *in Satyra* (*frg. poet. Lat.* p. 28 Morel), quoted by Festus 306 L (237 M). For contrasting views of the line see Weinreich xviif. and E. Fraenkel, *R.E. Supplbd.* 6, *s.v.* 'Naevius', 640,46.

63 Older scholars such as Birt saw the influence of dramatic *satura* at Plaut. *Stichus* 68 3ff. But it may now be assumed on the evidence of Menander's *Dyskolos* that the dances in the *Stichus* were probably from the Greek original. Support for Livy's account is sometimes sought in Horace's description of the development of Roman drama (*Epp.* 2,1,139–60); see Ullman, *T.A.Ph.A.* 48 (1917), 111–32. But for a full analysis of the important differences between the two accounts see Leo, *Hermes* 39 (1904), 67ff. and also Rudd, *Phoenix* 14 (1960), 36–44. Plautus probably also drew on the knowledge of solo performances among Greek Τεχνῖται, see E. Fraenkel, *Elementi Plautini in Plauto* (Florence, 1960), 323, 349 and 439 n.; T. B. L. Webster, *Hellenistic Poetry and Art* (London, 1964), 267ff.

64 F. Muller, *Philologus* 78 (1923), 269ff. On the word *Saturnus* see Walde-Hofmann, (op. cit. n. 38) *s.v.* and for the Etruscan origin of *Saturnus* see K. Latte, *Römische Religionsgeschichte* (Munich, 1960), 137.

65 K. Kerényi, *Studi e materiali di storia delle religioni* 9 (1933), 129–56 (= Korzeniewski 83–111).

66 F. Altheim, *Satura tota nostra est, Epochen der römischen Geschichte* 11 (Frankfurt, 1935), 245–71; see also Altheim's later study, *Satura, Gesch. d. lat. Sprache* (Frankfurt, 1951), 346–65 (= Korzeniewski 112–36).

67 On the rituals of Ceres see H. Le Bonniec, *Le culte de Cérès à Rome* (Paris, 1958), and on the Horace scholiast see n. 8 above.

Notes to chapter 3 (Ennius)

1 The standard reference text for all of Ennius' works is that of J. Vahlen, *Ennianae Poesis Reliquiae* (Leipzig, 1928[3]); *saturae* and *varia* will be found on pp. 204–29.

Also useful is the edition by E. H. Warmington, vol. I of *Remains of Old Latin* (Loeb Classical Library, 1956), 382–447. On Ennius' satires in general see particularly the full and judicious discussion by Waszink, *Entr. Fond. Hardt* 17 (1972), 99–137, the chapter by Van Rooy, *Studies in Classical Satire and Related Literary Theory* (Leiden, 1965), 30–49, and U. Knoche, *Die Römischse Satire* (Göttingen, 1971[3]), 11–20.

2 Sec chapter 1, n. 28.

3 Quint. 10,1,93 and 95.

4 Pacuvius lived until *c.* 130 B.C. (see Schanz-Hosius I[4], 100).

5 On Rudiae see Strabo 6,3,3; Cic. *de Or.* 3,168; on Ennius and Calabria Hor. *C.* 4,8,20. On the year of his birth Gell. 17,21,43 (quoting Varro *de poetis*), Cic. *Brut.* 72, Schanz-Hosius I[4] 87. On the historical background Leo, *Gesch.* 154 and Scullard, *Hist. Rom. World 753–146 B.C.*, 124 and 159ff.

6 Serv. on *Aen.* 7,691; Sil. It. 12,393ff.; Suda *s.v.* '"Εννιος'; Leo, *Gesch.* 150ff.

7 On the Iapygian and Messapian allies of Rome see Polybius 2,24,11 and Walbank *a.l.*, and Leo, *Gesch.* 155. On Cato's quaestorship see Nepos, *Cato* 1,4 and Scullard 111 n. 4.

8 For Ennius' rank and a fictitious account of his prowess (Sil. It. I2,393ff.) see Leo 151 n. 1; and for a sceptical examination of the tradition concerning Ennius' army career and his meeting Cato see E. Badian, *Entr. Fond. Hardt* 17 (1972), 155–63.

9 Suet. *Gramm.* 1. Cic. *Sen.* 14. Leo, *Gesch.* 157 n. 2. The Aventine was the quarter for craftsmen and merchants (Badian 168).

10 Cic. *Tusc.* 1,3; Scullard 184; on Fulvius Nobilior's *imperium M.R.R.* I, 360 and 366.

11 Cic. *Brut.* 79; on the colonies see Scullard 167ff. However, Cicero's testimony that Nobilior's son was Ennius' benefactor has been discredited by Badian, op. cit. (n. 8) 183–8.

12 *Sat.* 64 V; Hoar. *Epp.* 1,19,7.

13 On the date of Ennius' death see Cic. *Brut.* 78 and Scullard 223 n. 2; on the cause Jerome on 1849 = 168 B.C. (Jerome gives 168 B.C. wrongly).

14 Gell. 17,17,1 on Ennius' *tria corda.* On Messapian influences see Leo 153 and F. Skutsch, *R.E. s.v.* 'Ennius' 2589, 68. See also O. Skutsch, *B.I.C.S.* 21 (1974), 75–80.

15 H. Thesleff, *Introduction to the Pythagorean writings of the Hellenistic period* (Abo, 1961), 97f., who stresses the increasing importance of Sicily.

16 Liv. 27,37,7. Cichorius, *Röm. Stud.* 7.

17 201 B.C. was probably the year of Naevius' death Cic. *Brut.* 60; E. Fraenkel, *R.E. Supplbd* 6 (1935) *s.v.* 'Naevius', 625. He had been exiled shortly after his release from prison for attacking the Metelli, whose political ally Scipio Africanus was also lampooned (Jerome on 1816 = 201 B.C., Gell. 3,3,15 and 7,8,5). On the circumstances of Naevius' imprisonment see Momigliano, *J.R.S.* 32 (1942), 120ff. and Scullard 254. If Scullard's view is tight, the means used by the Scipionic parry to silence Naevius were unscrupulous as well as drastic.

18 Cic. *Arch.* 22; *de Or.* 2,276 (on the identity of Nasica see Badian, op. cit. (n. 8 above) 170ff.; Livy 38,56,4).

19 Ps. Aur. Vict. *vir. ill.* 52,3. On the rivalry between the Fulvii and the Scipios see Scullard 141ff. On the poet in the retinue see Cic. *Tusc.* 3,3 and Leo, *Gesch.* 158.

20 Cic. *Ac.* 2,51. Galba was praetor in 187 B.C. (*M.R.R.* I 368); on his political affiliations see Scullard 143 n. 1.

21 *Ann.* 234–51 from Gell. 12,4,1; O. Skutsch, *C.Q.* 13 (1963), 94–6 (= *Studia Enniana* (London, 1968), 92–4) sees here a blend of literary precedent (*G.L.P.* 111) and personal experience. There are autobiographical references in *Ann.* e.g. 377.

22 F. Skutsch, *R.E.* 5,2602,51ff. On the *Annals* see O. Skutsch, *The Annals of Quintus Ennius* (London, 1953) = *Studia Enniana*, 1–17.

23 On the tragedies see Leo, *Gesch.* 1 87ff. and the edition by H. D. Jocelyn (Cambridge, 1969).

24 For Ennius as disciple of the Muses see Varro, *Men.* 356 (compare Posidippus, *P. Brit. Mus. Inv.* 589,10); for his dream see O. Skutsch, op. cit. (n. 22 above), 9f.

25 On this see O. Skutsch, *C.Q.* 42 (1948), 99 (= *Studia Enniana* 38f.).

26 Cic. *Brut.* 78. The tradition (Gell. 17,21,43) that he wrote the 12th book of the *Annals* when he was sixty-seven years old is rejected by F. Skutsch, *R.E.* 5,2608.

27 It has been argued that *Hedyphagetica* is later than 189 B.C.; see O. Skutsch, *C.Q.* 42 (1948), 99 (= *Studia Enniana*, 38f.).

28 On the founding of Luna see Liv. 41,13,4; Scullard, 167.

29 Porph. on Hor. *Sat.* 1,10,46.

30 Don. on Ter. *Phorm.* 339 (= *Sat.* 14–19V): *e sexto satyrarum Ennii* was conjectured by Stephanus on the basis of *de sexto salis. . . .* of *dett.* The Vatican manuscript reads *de cen*, which might suggest the beginning, of such a title as Laberius' *Centonarius*, but any conjectural restoration is problematical. Vahlen and Leo are sceptical about the inclusion of these lines in Ennius' *Saturae.*

31 E.g. frg. 65. 64 may safely be assigned to Ennius' literary procedure on external evidence (see n. 12 above) and to one of the *saturae* on the grounds that he would have been unlikely to assert in high poetry a necessary connection between drink and poetic composition.

32 See e.g. Cratinus' self-justification in Πυτίνη, 'The Bottle'. There is a full discussion of this fragment by Waszink, op. cit. (n. l above) 113–19.

33 In a fragment of dubious attestation (n. 30 above) a parasite exults in his brief and carefree eagerness for food (14–19). The parasite's apologia is found throughout the tradition of Greek comedy and also in Roman adaptation. For the parasite in Epicharmus see 349ff. *C.G.F.* (Kaibel) and Pickard-Cambridge rev. Webster, *Dithyramb, Tragedy and Comedy* (Oxford, 1962[2]), 273f., in New Comedy Webster, *Studies in Later Greek Comedy* (Manchester, 1970 2), 5f. and in Rome, Duckworth, *The Nature of Roman Comedy* (Princeton, 1952), 265ff.

34 *Scen.* 234–41, on which see O. Skutsch, *Rh.M.* 96 (1953), 193–201. There is a similar word play in Philemon *C.A.F.* (Kock) frg. 23. There is artifice in such verbal jingles but nothing in the variegated fragments that is firmly to be associated with the high style. There is likewise variety in the metrical forms used (cf. ch. 1, n. 28), for the fable of the lark the so-called *versus quadratus*, trochaic *septenarii*, such as were used in both drama and popular songs; cf. Gell. 2,29,20 and E. Fraenkel, *Hermes* 62 (1927), 357–70 (= *Kl. Beitr.* II 11–24). Other fragments are in hexameters, iambic metres and (59–62) Sotadeans; on 59–62, which cannot be the accentual Saturnian metre, as in Warmington (*R.O.L.* I, 393), see Vahlen ccxi.

35 *5.* On the *servus currens* see e.g. Plaut. *Curc.* 280ff. and *Men. Dysk.* 81ff.

36 Cic. *N.D.* 2,101; cf. Zeno, *S.V.F.* I 115. Similar words in Ennius' *Euhemerus* describe the man Jupiter gazing up at the sky (*var.* 100). Astronomical passages are common in the tragedies, e.g. *Iph.* 215–8, 242–4.

37 69; see Cic. *ND.* 1,97.

38 *Mortem ac Vitam, quas contendentes in satura tradit Ennius* (Quint. 9,2,36). M. L. West, *H.S.C.Ph.* 73 (1969), 120, offers as parallel a Sumerian debate between Winter and Spring.

39 The personification of Death alone is found in Eur. *Alc.* 28ff. and Ennius *scen.* 245. Epicharmus' titles include *Land and Sea* (23–32 Kaibel) and *Hope or Wealth* (34–40 Kaibel).

40 Ar. *Nub.* 889–1104 and Dover's commentary. Xen. *Mem.* 2,1,21–34 (= DKV II 313ff.); W. K. C. Guthrie, *A History of Greek Philosophy* III (Cambridge, 1969), 277f.

41 Novius frg 63 Frassinetti (= 63R^3) from Nonius 768 L.

42 *Sat.* 65; Hdt. 1,141.

43 *Sat.* 21–58 (Gell. 2,29,3ff.). Vahlen, ccxii, Ribbeck, *Rh.M.* 10 (1856), 290ff., Norden, *Agn. Th.* 379 n. 2.

44 Call. *Iamb.* 4. Contrast also Ennius' simplicity with the satirical reference in Callimachus' fable in *Iamb.* 2 based on Aesop 383 Halm (see *Dieg.*, an ancient commentary on Callimachus, 6,30f.). For Plato see e.g. *Phaedr.* 237B.

45 A. E. Housman, *C.R.* 48 (1934), 50f. (= *Coll. Papers* III, 1232–3); O. Skutsch, *C.Q.* 38 (1944), 85f. (= *Studia Enniana*, 25ff.). See Cic. *Acad.* 2,51 for Ennius' walk with Sulpicius Galba.

46 For a history and a refutation of the view that all the minor poems were included among the *saturae*, see Waszink, op. cit. (n. l above) 106f. The miscellaneous poems are grouped together by Vahlen under *varia*; see Warmington, *R.O.L.* 1,394ff.

47 That *Scip.* 8 is similar in language to *Sat.* 10f. is not good evidence for assuming that they belong to the same poem. The exact genre of *Scipio* and *Ambracia*, both of which contain more than one metrical form, is uncertain: F. Skutsch, *R.E.* 5, 2399, 20.

48 Sotades, notorious for his attack on the incestuous marriage of Ptolemy Philadelphus (Athen. 14,621A), wrote in various genres (Suda); Susemihl I 243ff. For the form of Ennius' title see F. Skutsch, *R.E.* 3, 2602, l.

49 Fragments of Archestratus are preserved by Athenaeus (3,92D; 7,300D; 3I8F; 320A). The possibly broken quotation by Apuleius, *Apol.* 39 suggests that Ennius adapted freely; see F. Skutsch *R.E.* 5, 2602, 30, and further E. Fraenkel, *Beobachtungen zu Aristophanes* (Rome, 1962), 123ff. on stylization in Ennius' translations. The comment by Apuleius that Ennius' discussion of fish could not be faulted by connoisseurs suggests that the subject was treated neither flippantly nor, as an attack on extravagance, censoriously.

50 On Call. and Ennius' *Annals* see O. Skutsch, op. cit. (n. 25 above) 8ff.; on Callimachus', πολυείδεια (multiplicity of forms) and criticisms of it *Iamb.* 13, where he refers to Ion of Chios as a precedent (*Dieg.* 9,32–8). The artificial style seems to belie the programmatic profession (frg 112,4ff.) of seeking a πεζὸν νομόν (mundane pasturage), and has with justification been called *eine dichterische Umgangssprache* by Page, *Entr. Fond. Hardt* 10 (1964), 249. *Iamb.* 4,13 was an example of disingenuous disclaimer (ἀστεϊσμός) according to Trypho περὶ τρόπων 24, *Rhet. Gr.* 3,206,15 Sp., and *Iamb.* 5 of ἀλληγορία (*Rhet. Gr.* 3,245,6 Sp.).

51 The Greek commentaries of the 1st C. A.D. were no doubt the successors of an older tradition of exegesis: see R. Pfeiffer, *Callimachus* II (Oxford, 1953), xxviii and cii and also Susemihl I 369f. The influence of Callimachus' *Iambi* on Ennius' *saturae* is overestimated by Deubner, *Rh.M.* 96 (1953), 289ff.

52 Gell. 18,5,11. On the whole process of the transmission and *Nachleben* of Ennius see Vahlen's full treatment, xxiv–cxxxi.

53 *saturarum scriptor, cuius sunt electae ex Ennio Lucilio Varrone saturae*: Porph. on Hor. *Epp.* 1,3,1; F. Skutsch, *R.E.* 5,2616,62.

54 See Sen. *Epp.* 58,5 for a characteristically unfavourable judgement; for enthusiasm, Fronto 4,2 (61N); Gell. 13,20,1; cf. 18,9,5; 18,5,11. Vahlen lxxxiiiff.

55 Vahlen lxxxix; W. M. Lindsay, *Nonius Marcellus' Dictionary of Republican Latin*, (Oxford, 1901), 5. On the ancient transmission of archaic Roman poetry see H. D. Jocelyn, *The Tragedies of Ennius*, 54ff.

56 Stylistic uncouthness is a matter of degree: to Ennius Naevius was a crude old-timer (Cic. *Brut.* 76).

ROMAN SATIRISTS AND LITERARY CRITICISM

W. S. Anderson

On April 9, 1778, Boswell dined with Samuel Johnson at the home of Sir Joshua Reynolds, in the august company of such people as Bishop Shipley, the painter Allan Ramsay, and Edward Gibbon. With Johnson present, it was inevitable that any dinner would develop into a symposium and that the conversation would range over the widest spaces. On this occasion, the diners began to discuss Horace. I now quote Boswell: "The Bishop said, it appeared from Horace's writings that he was a cheerful contented man. Johnson: 'We have no reason to believe that, my Lord. Are we to think Pope was happy, because he says so in his writings? We see in his writings what he wished the state of his mind to appear.'"

Johnson rightly drew a distinction between the poet's state of mind and the attitude which he chose to present in the first person in any particular personal poem. Moreover, he chose for analogy Alexander Pope, that misshapen genius, whose body would seem to be the archetype for that of the so-called twisted satirist imagined by the romantic mind, whose poems, however, run the gamut of attitudes from Horatian wit to Juvenalian indignation. This kind of distinction, which is reflected today in the critical terminology adopted by students of English literature especially, in the much-used word *persona*, has unfortunately not percolated down to many readers of classical literature. One of the most patient sufferers from our ignorance is Roman poetic satire. Too many, it seems to me, ignore the fact that Lucilius, Horace, Persius, and Juvenal were poets first and foremost.

From the first satires written by Lucilius, it was conventional for the *persona* to disclaim poetic ability, especially in contrast to the writers of epic and tragedy, and instead to place his emphasis on the down-to-earth, truthful qualities of his material. Let us see how these ideas were expressed in the works of Lucilius, Horace, Persius, and Juvenal, then how expert Latinists have dealt with them.

The voice cries out in Lucilius: "I utter spontaneously whatever comes into my head according to the promptings of my heart, according to the immediate occasion, whether it be my state of health, my passion or anger against my concubine, my partisan political feelings, or what have you. Secondly, I am no poet like Ennius. I dabble at verse for the entertainment of the uncritical. I prefer to call my products plays (*ludos*) or mere conversation-like prose (*sermonem*). I can write so freely that I dash off 200 verses an hour, indeed 200 verses after a good dinner."

A proper critic today might be on his guard against such claims; the average Latinist has not been. The latter seems to use the following reasoning. "These words are spoken by Lucilius and must be sincere confessions on his part. Now, since he denies to himself poetic ability, we may ignore all poetic considerations that would, of course, be relevant to a talented writer like Vergil, and instead we should concentrate our scholarship on what is after all more reliable factual material: namely, what the Satires of Lucilius tell us about his biography, the social practices and historical situation of his day." As a result of such reasoning much excellent matter has been deduced from the Satires, matter, however, that is peripheral to the purposes of the poet; and, on the other hand, many mistakes have been committed by those who pursue a biography of Lucilius in the behavior of the *persona*.

Thus, the scholarship on Lucilius is remarkably unbalanced. On the one hand, there are elaborate analyses of his political thought and his place in the party politics of the Second Century B.C. On the other, scholars have permitted the most uninformed generalizations on literary matters to escape their lips, as, for example, that Lucilius is prosaic in all but meter or that his poetry is formless. When they compound their error by making guesses about the poet from the words spoken by the *persona* in a specially designed dramatic context, they radically distort the true proportions of Lucilius's poetry. Lucilius is a libertine, says one eminent Italian, because his Satires talk so much about affairs with prostitutes. Lucilius exhibits the mentality of an old soldier, says another scholar, because he again and again discusses military matters. In the midst of this, nobody cares to grapple with the problem of the poetic purpose of satire. It does not seem to cross the mind of serious scholars that, had Lucilius desired merely to express the socio-political ideas that interest modern critics, then he would have done so quite frankly in prose. Instead of identifying the *persona* with Lucilius, we should be studying the processes by which this *persona* is effectively created and the novelty that the poet achieved in producing the first extensive personal verse in Latin literature. The question to ask is not: What can we learn about the biography of Lucilius? The question to ask is: What does this speaker, this *persona*, with his wild invective, his frank eroticism, his witty anecdotes, and his serious moral judgments, accomplish for the poem? It is no accident, therefore, that some recent studies in Germany and Italy have demonstrated that, far from being a clumsy versifier, Lucilius was a sophisticated poet, closer to the polished Alexandrians than many a contemporary writer.

When we proceed to Horace, we find him deploying the same conventional argument in the mouth of his *persona*. "I have a compulsion," says that character, "to speak out, to tell the truth with a smile (*ridentem dicere verum*), at least in the intimate company of my confidential friends. On the other hand, I lack the talent to produce genuine poetry, epic or tragedy, so I play at this (*haec ego ludo*)." If all things were equal, we should expect critics to treat Horace in the same cavalier fashion which has marked their handling of Lucilius. Fortunately, a number of new factors introduce differences that avert the worst errors of Lucilian analysis. In the first place, a good biography of Horace has come down to us from Suetonius and rendered otiose much biographical conjecture. Second, Horace's Satires survive complete, whereas Lucilius's poems are entirely fragmentary and so seem to encourage extravagant hypotheses and reconstructions. Finally, there are other quite different poems of the same poet, iambic vituperation, lyrics of the most diverse tones, and literary epistles, to warn us that Horace could don almost any mask at will, in order to show us, as Johnson long ago noted, the attitude which he chose to manifest. I do not think that anyone has actually said it, but the fact is, that Horace's *persona* as satirist acts a great deal older and more serious morally than his *persona* as lyric lover, drinker, and advocate of *carpe diem*; and yet the external evidence unanimously proves that he wrote and published the Satires ten or more years before the lyric Odes!

I should say, then, that Horace is the most adequately appreciated verse satirist of Rome. Not that a few critics do not pursue the old will-o-the-wisps. Did Horace really take that trip to Brundisium? Did he really have that conversation with the bore? On the whole, though, knowing that Horace boasts a great reputation in lyric, they somewhat mystifiedly accept the fact that his Satires are poetry and talk very learnedly of his superiority to Lucilius. If here and there an incautious word escapes them and they call the contents of Serm. 1.5 (the trip to Brundisium) a versified diary and make of Serm. 1.7 a rather unnecessary anecdote, they nevertheless will fight anyone who denies Horace's rank as a poet. Almost no one would follow that misbegotten Crocean, Durand, who recently argued that, because not only the Satires but the Odes were earthbound, devoid of soaring lyric sentiments, Horace must not be called a "poet" at all—no one, that is, except the distinguished Italian academy that awarded one of its most coveted prizes to Durand. But despite such absurdities in Horace's homeland, Horace can defend himself. His successors are in a far worse plight.

Persius, as we might expect, uses the same conventional argument in his Program Satire. The *persona* says: "Like Midas's barber, I am bursting with the truth about mankind and must speak out. However, I am no high-flown poet, but a half-boor (*semipaganus*) in matters of art; I produce pretty modest stuff, a great deal of nothing (*tam nil*), boiled down (*decoctius*) and direct rather than ornate." Our external controls on this disarming confession do not help us so much here. Six short Satires of Persius have survived and nothing else but fourteen apparently prefatory lines; in addition, a good biography was produced within a few generations of his death. However, unlike the *persona* of Horace's Satires, who is pleasing and constitutes a good model of sound moral thinking, the *persona* of Persius offends many and is so radically inconsistent with his programmatic disclaimer that critics find vast difficulties with these Satires.

There are many who eagerly agree with Persius that he is no poet and so pursue the usual factual material offered by any literature. Their favorite interest is the Stoic substance of Persius's discourse. By proving the self-evident, that Persius uses Stoic ideas, they believe that they have contributed immensely to the understanding of the Satires. Then, there are those who chase the red herring of political allusions. Persius wrote, they say, under the monstrous Nero; it is inevitable that he would make some references to the emperor. And they can find them everywhere! Almost any innocent remark, political or otherwise, made by the earnest *persona* can be twisted into a sneer against Nero. The climax of such maunderings—at least, I hope it is—is the recent hypothesis by one of Belgium's most eminent Classicists that Nero had Persius poisoned!

Italy celebrated this past year the anniversary of Persius's death, with a typical Italian *festa* in Persius's home town, Volterra. On this august occasion, various dignitaries assembled to do honor in their own academic way to the distinguished citizen of the town. Among the lectures delivered to commemorate the poet's passing was one that has since been twice printed, apparently because the speaker, the noted Latinist Paratore, did not wish the world to miss his brilliant thesis. He develops an interesting twist on the biographical fallacy. The authoritative biography tells of a session where Persius apparently recited some of his works and the young Lucan, when his turn to recite came around, burst out with rapturous words of praise. But, notes Paratore, Satire 1 opens with a sharp attack on the institution of public readings (*recitationes*). We must conclude from Satire 1, then, that Persius loathed such sessions and would *never* stoop to reading his Satires in public, and consequently it is necessary to emend the biography by removing the offending passage. Thus, the *persona* forces the facts about the poet to conform!

Meanwhile, the literary problems connected with Persius languish. If critics could grasp the fact that his Stoic ideas are so superficial as to be negligible and his political ideas non-existent, they might realize that Persius's main claim to glory is his fascinatingly labored manner of expressing these commonplaces through a specially contrived *persona*. With him more than any other satirist in poetry, the gap between the disavowal of poetic ability and the vast effort made to produce poetic moralization is patent. Therefore, the task of the critic—that ideal critic who has not appeared for Persius in 1900 years—remains to interpret those poetic methods first, knowing quite well that the disclaiming of talent forms a conventional and always ambiguous aspect of the *persona*, that the producer of poetic satire would not have essayed the genre without fundamentally poetic purposes.

The last victim of distorted criticism is a far greater poet than Persius, but one would hardly learn this from reading some of the latest discussions. In the conventional manner, Juvenal lets his *persona* make the same statements in Satire 1 as were made in the satires of his predecessors: "It is difficult not to write satire, for I cannot endure the many vicious scoundrels of this corrupt city. I admit that I have little talent, but my spontaneous indignation makes my verse, such as it is." Once again, the critics face these programmatic statements, identify them with the feelings of Juvenal, and try to decide whether this vaunted indignation is as sincere as the speaker makes it out to be. Those who, like Gilbert Highet in his *Juvenal the Satirist*, feel the sincerity of this anger then pursue the source of it. Highet argues this way: "Something very strange and violent must have happened in the first part of Juvenal's life to produce such powerful repercussions in the second [that is, the indignant Satires]. . . . Satirists are peculiarly sensitive, and their sensitivity means suffering. They have come into personal conflict with stupidity and injustice, and their satires are the direct result." Accordingly, Highet constructs an ingenious biography for Juvenal. Juvenal's indignation in the early Satires, he argues, resulted directly from his hatred of the villainous emperor Domitian, who had exiled him in or about A.D. 93 to Egypt.

It is not impossible that Juvenal was in fact exiled, but the evidence is ambiguous. Highet goes wrong in generalizing erroneously about the suffering of satirists—Lucilius, Horace, and Persius had no such impetus to write that we can discover—and then searching for some traumatic experience to motivate Juvenal's indignation. Similarly, when he comes to Satire 6, Highet feels compelled to explain its violent attack on women through an imaginary chain of sad circumstances, a fictional marriage of Juvenal with a proud, selfish, and intolerable Roman lady. Granted, the indignation of the *persona* strikes the reader as something new and powerful in Roman satire. However, it is no more original than Horace's smiling irony or Persius's intolerant Stoicism, and it can be successfully explained on a poetic level without resort to biographical conjecture. Merely that we lack any good biography of Juvenal does not mean that we should allow our imaginations free rein.

It must be said in behalf of Highet that he likes Juvenal and uses his biographical methods to give the Satires a sympathetic interpretation. Opposed to him are those who deny the sincerity of Juvenal, who insist on a sharp dichotomy between what Juvenal says and what he does. According to one of the most vigorously antagonistic critics, De Decker, there is in the Satires a poet occasionally, but more frequently an orator who undermines the work of the poet by his patently false methods for displaying indignation. Juvenal is, then, predominantly a *declamator*, a declaimer for the audience. With the help of misunderstood Crocean ideas, the Italian Marmorale has refurbished the dichotomy. Since in his view Juvenal lacks sincerity and emotional depth and, on the other hand, manipulates the literary *topoi* dexterously, Marmorale denies to him the rank of poet and instead christens him a "*letterato*," a professional writer, in the pejorative sense.

Light comes to the darkened minds of Classicists these days from their more sophisticated colleagues in English. In the past twenty or thirty years, English satire has become again a respectable field for scholarship, and some of the sharpest brains have concentrated their labors on Dryden, Pope, and Swift. Maynard Mack's delightful essay, "The Muse of Satire," starts from disagreement with Highet's biographical methods and proceeds to outline the conventional character of the *persona* in Pope. More recently, Alvin Kernan has discussed Jacobean satire in an important book, *The Cankered Muse*. Kernan has shown that the Jacobeans favored a violent *persona* like that of Juvenal, whereas the Augustans favored Horatian methods. Even more important, it seems to me, is Kernan's suggestion that, in the case of these violently indignant speakers, the poet has deliberately attributed to them objectionable and offensive ways, more or less as a warning to the audience to dissociate itself from their indignation. In other words, sometimes the *persona* created by the satiric poet is so distinct from the poet's biography that the two are opposites.

I suspect that Kernan's theories provide the solution to the critical dilemma over Juvenal: that Highet is right in a sense to argue for sincerity and Marmorale right in a sense to belabor the insincerity. If, following Kernan, we maintain a distinction between Juvenal and the speaker he creates for the Satires, then we can call the speaker genuinely indignant; but we must also add that Juvenal has so portrayed him that his prejudices and exaggerations are unacceptable, and for sound poetic reasons. The *persona* is indignant, but wrong, in many cases, as, for example, in his universal denunciation of women, even the most upright; reading or listening to such ranting, the Roman audience recognized the untruth and re-interpreted the described situations, stimulated by the Satires, more accurately.

We are possibly, therefore, at the beginning of a new era in studies of Roman satire, lagging as usual a generation behind the critics of English literature. We are discovering the conventions of the genre and seeing some of the implications of the critical doctrine that separates poet from personal speaker in the poem. When, therefore, the speaker in satire tries to distract us from the art of the poet and forces us to attend to his so-called "truth," we are less willing to be deceived than formerly. Nor shall we be perturbed to find that, after all, Roman satire is poetry.

THE PROGRAMMATIC SATIRE AND THE METHOD OF PERSIUS I

John Bramble

It was common practice for the Roman satirist to give an account of his genre, arraigning public vice, perhaps ridiculing the insufficiencies of the other literary forms, and informing the reader of the tone which he himself intended to adopt. The vehicle for this account was the programmatic satire. It is quite clear that Horace *Satires* II.1, Persius I, and Juvenal I are related compositions. Their shared features have been duly discussed in the secondary literature. Noting that a scholiast entitles Juvenal's first satire *cur satiras scribat*, also the corresponding formal characteristics of the three programmes, L. R. Shero concludes:[1] 'Each of the satires is constructed upon a traditional framework; and we may reasonably conclude that a satire of this type, ostensibly justifying the writing of satire by means of conventional devices and stock arguments, came to be looked upon as an indispensable feature of the satirist's stock-in-trade.' More recently, E. J. Kenney has detected the following 'pattern of apology':[2] 'First, a pronouncement, lofty to the point of bombast, of the satirist's high purpose and mission. Second, a warning by a friend or the poet's *alter ego* or the voice of prudence – call it what you will. Third, an appeal by the satirist to the great example of Lucilius. Fourth, a renewed warning. Fifth and last, evasion, retraction and equivocation.'[3] But similarities apart, there is a marked degree of divergence in procedure. It is this – innovation within convention – which will occupy my attention.

First, we notice that Persius' programme deals with the blight which has invaded contemporary literature; secondly, that this blight is indicative of moral deficiency. Through criticism of style, the satirist effects another, more serious criticism – of morals. By way of contrast, he emerges with his chosen genre, and his exclusive audience, as one of the last ethically irreproachable Romans, and as the last adherent of sanity and health in style. The major part of the satire is composed of a subtle commerce between style and morals, which engineers an impression of total corruption. Previous critics have noted the presence of a moral dimension alongside the literary-critical, but there has been no analysis of the exact nature of their interaction. We are correctly guided by the comment of, for example, G. C. Fiske, 'His main concern is after all rather with literature as a social phenomenon than with literature as an art', also, 'Persius is, as usual, more concerned than Horace with the social conditions which breed poetry of this type';[4] compare Shero, 'It is important to remember that Persius' attack upon the literary tendencies of his day, with which the greater part of the satire is occupied, is in reality an attack upon the prevailing moral corruption of which these tendencies are the efflorescence. The underlying moral debasement is suggested especially in vss. 15–21,[5] 30–35, 83–87, 103–106',[6] and W. H. Semple, 'It is this change in literature, originating in the common luxury of the age, that Persius regrets in his first satire.'[7] The position is clarified by Kenney, who notes the all-important link between the programme of Persius and Seneca's one hundred and fourteenth *Epistle*: 'The body of the satire between vv. 12 and 120 is taken up with a dissertation on literature and morals at Rome, much of which recalls the 114th *Epistle* of Seneca and which is founded on the same text, *talis hominibus fuit oratio qualis vita.*'[8] Style reflects life.

Like Persius, Seneca attributes decline in literature to the decadence of the times. After the preliminary formulation of the principle, we find that style follows the proclivities of society – *genus dicendi aliquando imitatur publicos mores* . . .; and can be proof of moral decay – *argumentum est luxuriae publicae orationis lascivia* (§2) – that is, it can operate as a symbol of decadence. Maecenas is singled out to illustrate the proposition, *non oratio eius aeque soluta est quam ipse discinctus?*, §4; *soluta* and *discinctus* could be interchanged. Man and style are identical. His literary affiliations are paralleled by the outward display of his personal life, *non tam insignita illius verba sunt quam cultus, quam comitatus, quam domus, quam uxor*, §4. A list of the stages in luxury's progress which have prepared for the downfall of Roman literature occurs at §9, the catalogue including *cultus corporum*, *supellectilis*, *ipsae domus*, *cenae*, symptoms of decline similar to those of Persius, who inveighs against physical appearance – *cultus corporum* – at 1.15 f., furniture – *supellectilis* – at 17 and 52–3, and banquets – *cenae* – at 30 ff. and 51 ff. Here, then, is a series of potential correlatives to the phenomenon of stylistic decay.

The history of the idea behind the Senecan *Epistle*, that literature is a guide to morals, is partly documented in the excursus at the end of this chapter. Adopting the concept, Persius in turn made morals mirror style, assisted in his dramatic development of the principle by the extensive possibilities inherent in the moralistic colour of literary-critical vocabulary. For rhetoricians and critics employed an idiom which was equally valid in matters of style and matters of morality: in particular, literary blemishes were chastised as if moral offences. Sometimes the analogy is only latent, or even inactive: witness Quint. VII. 3.56, *κακόζηλον, id est mala affectatio, per omne dicendi genus* peccat, *nam et* tumida *et* pusilla *et* praedulcia *et abundantia et arcessita et* exultantia *sub idem nomen cadunt*, where *peccat* is the only unequivocally moral element, even though the various stylistic faults might have been developed into concrete representations of vice. For instance, turgidity – *tumida* – need not have been so closely confined to style: parallel images from those vices which swell the human body – gluttony, perhaps, or gout – could have expanded its area of reference. Likewise, *pusilla* might have been accompanied by a depiction of mental weakness, *praedulcia* and *exultantia* by images of effeminacy and sexual excess. A similar catalogue of defects occurs at Quint. XII. 10.73:

> falluntur enim plurimum qui *vitiosum* et *corruptum* dicendi genus, quod aut verborum *licentia exultat* aut puerilibus sententiolis *lascivit* aut inanibus locis *bacchatur* aut casuris si leviter excutiantur flosculis nitet aut praecipitia pro sublimibus habet aut specie libertatis *insanit*, magis existimant populare et plausibile.

Again, the terminology has latent moral import, but is metaphorically weary, tied by a merely tenuous thread to its place of origin in life.

But properly handled, it had distinct potential. Many terms drawn from human moral existence were at the satirist's disposal: for example, besides those already seen in Quintilian, *effeminatus*, *ebrius*, *pinguis*, and *meretricius*. So when Persius turned to the shortcomings of contemporary literature, he was not only equipped with a principle which directly correlated life and style, but he also had at hand a vocabulary predisposed to disapprobation. If he had used it as it stood, the first satire would have contained a moral dimension anyway, an inevitable circumstance of the terms. But his focus would have been centred on literature, since nobody acquainted with the metaphors of the schools would have been led by mere recurrence to the awareness of moral corruption required by Persius as satirist. In effect, he would have remained a literary critic. But in order to justify his choice of genre, evidence of moral concern must coincide with treatment of literature, so earning the title of satirist, as well as literary critic.[9] His solution is to rejuvenate the stylistic metaphors, by taking them back to their place of genesis in life, so reversing the process which gave them birth. Actual effeminacy now corresponds to stylistic effeminacy; gluttony to turgidity; over-meticulous dress to fussy ornament in style; disease and distortion to disfigured composition. From the theoretical principle, *talis hominibus fuit oratio qualis vita*, and its ramifications in literary-critical terminology, Persius creates a class of images which refer simultaneously to life and letters. To these he adds several reminders of the now dishonoured past, and through the recurrent incidence of *auricula*, backed up by the repeated *euge* and *belle*, insinuates that Rome's ears are diseased and incapable of true judgement. My next chapter will be devoted to these various motifs and images, in an attempt to discover something of their history and background, before I go on to assess their function in the context of the first satire.

But first a few words on ancestry. It has been observed that the programmatic satire had its own conventions: can we find a Lucilian or Horatian precedent to the method of Persius – to the depiction of life and letters as interrelated entities? In the case of Lucilius exact conclusions are difficult. Ingredients of the later prescription can be discerned, in book twenty-six for instance, of which J. H. Waszink writes: 'His program . . . presents a discussion of the poet with a friend who, like Trebatius in Horace, tries to persuade him out of his purpose of writing satires, but who finally – again like Trebatius – capitulates before Lucilius' argument, viz., that the poet has not only the right but also the duty towards his fellow-citizens to attack and blame anything detrimental to Roman society.'"[10] Then there is book thirty, with its disclaimer of malicious intent. There are observations on the moral mission of satire, and on its style; but it is hard to say if there was anything which foreshadowed Persius' sustained identification between the two. Such evidence as remains is collected in the excursus.

There is something highly elusive in Horace's accounts of his genre – a lack of explicit comment, and a tendency to deceive the reader with ironic and elliptical half-truth: this is poetry, not methodical literary theory.[11] But amidst the subtleties and evasions two salient elements emerge – treatment of the satirist's moral mission to society, and of matters appertaining to style. However we find no prolonged correspondence or parallelism, owing, no doubt, to the special nature of Horace's concerns. Unlike Persius, he is not motivated to criticise literature which is downright corrupt: consequently there is no question of relating literary decadence to the prevalent morality. His stylistic pre-occupation is with the manner of satire and the position of Lucilius. The *fautores Lucili*,[12] ignorant of true Callimachean ideals, must be defeated, in a battle fought with their own metaphors. By calling Lucilius' verse careless and muddy, Horace worsts his opponents in the terms of their own professions.[13] But Lucilius the *inventor* must survive for reinterpretation in the work of his only legitimate successor. Absorbed in this precarious task, Horace never had occasion to correlate style with the vices and follies which, as moralist, he felt moved to expose. But even though Lucilius' morals had to be preserved intact, he might have cast aspersions, pertinent to their peculiar stylistic aberrations, on the characters of his own literary opponents: for example, Crispinus and Fannius, *Sat.* I. 4.14 f., 21–2, might have been indicted as criminals, to give a double edge to his criticisms. Likewise, the epithets *turgidus* and *pulcher*, used respectively of the bloated epicist Furius and the precious Hermogenes at *Sat.* I. 10.17 and 36, might have become full-scale evocations of gluttony and effeminacy. But as they stand, they are only the merest insinuation of the possibility that there may be some flaw in their characters. There is just conceivably a moral note at *Sat.* I. 10.60–1, *amet scripsisse ducentos / ante cibum versus, totidem cenatus*, where Horace directs attention to the dinner perhaps in order to condemn Lucilius' prolixity by association with the insensitive process of eating. In this case we would have an instance of the alimentary metaphor. But Lucilius composes before eating as well as after; and at *Sat.* II. 1.73–4 his food is the modestly respectable vegetable, which would hardly lead to an 'undigested' style. Of course there is the possibility that these times of day were particularly suitable for literary composition, in which case *cibus* would not in itself be especially significant. Apart from one occasion when he seems to be voicing moral objections to the epic – and these objections are rather playful[14] – the only time we see any kind of liaison between *vita* and *oratio* is during his treatment of the style appropriate to the satirist's βίος, or *persona.* And here he is very allusive: *Sat.* I. 4.13 f., *haec ego mecum / compressis agito labris; ubi quid datur oti, / illudo chartis*, implies that his virtuous self-questioning leaves a desirable mark on his style; again, II. 1.73–4, *nugari cum illo et discincti ludere, donec / decoqueretur holus, soliti* (if indeed the allusion is to composition), perhaps suggests that the virtues of vegetarianism are carried over into style. Finally, at II. 6.1 ff., the satirist's modest Callimachean professions are matched by similarly modest social and economic ambitions: *modus agri non ita magnus.*[15]

The method of Persius is distinctive, independent of anything in the literary-critical or programmatic satires of Horace. The types of metaphor deployed were not original creations; literary theory explains their pedigree. But what does appear to be original is the way in which he consistently accommodated these metaphors to moralistic ends.

Excursus

Literature as a revelation of life

M. Puelma Piwonka, *Lucilius und Kallimachos*,[16] and M. H. Abrams, *The Mirror and the Lamp*,[17] have discussed ancient and modern manifestations of the fundamental concept behind Seneca's one hundred and fourteenth letter and Persius' first satire. Plato presents us with a version of the idea that literature reflects life at *Rep.* III. 11, 400 d: τί δ' ὁ τρόπος τῆς λέξεως καὶ ὁ λόγος; οὐ τῷ τῆς ψυχῆς ἤθει ἕπεται; Taken over by New Comedy – Menander, fr. 143 K, ἀνδρὸς χαρακτὴρ ἐκ λόγου γνωρίζεται, and Terence, *Heaut.* 384, *nam mihi quale ingenium haberes fuit indicio oratio*: pointers to some form of characterisation through style, albeit at a typical level – the concept is transmitted to Cicero, who writes of the Gracchan orator Q. Aelius Tubero, *Brut.* 117, *sed ut vita sic oratione durus incultus horridus*, expressing the analogy in more formulaic form at *T.D.* V. 47, *qualis . . . ipse homo esset talem esse eius orationem*, and recoursing to the personal level at *Rep.* II. I, of the elder Cato, *orationi vita admodum congruens.* Other biographical instances of the idea appear at, e.g., Plut. *Dem. et Cic.* 1 ἔστι δέ τις καὶ τοῦ ἤθους ἐν τοῖς λόγοις ἑκατέρου δίοψις, and *Cat. Mai.* 7, τοιαύτην δέ τινα φαίνεται καὶ ὁ λόγος τοῦ ανδρὸς ἰδέαν ἔχειν, while Juv. IV. 82 employs it in a sinister fashion: *cuius erant mores qualis facundia.*

Returning to the theorists we find Demetrius *de Eloc.* 114, and several Senecan variations on the subject: *Ep.* XL. 6, *quid de eorum animo iudicet quorum oratio perturbata et immissa est nec potest reprimi;* XL. 2, *pronuntiatio sicut vita debet esse composita*; LXXV. 4, *haec sit propositi nostri summa: quod sentimus loquamur, quod loquimur sentiamus: concordet sermo cum vita*; CVII. 12, *sic vivamus sic loquamur*; CXV. 2, *cuiuscumque orationem videris sollicitam et politam, scito animum quoque non minus esse pusillis occupatam.* A close parallel to the wording of the hundred and fourteenth letter – *talis hominibus fuit oratio qualis vita* – is found at Aristides *Or.* 45, vol. II. 133 Dind., οἷος ὁ τρόπος τοιοῦτον εἶναι τὸν λόγον, a later instance of the formula advanced at Quint. XI. 1.30, *profert enim mores oratio et animi secreta detegit. nec sine causa Graeci prodiderunt, ut vivat, quemque etiam dicere.*[18] From the written or spoken word we can come to large conclusions about character. Exterior mirrors interior. Similarly, clothes can signify a mental state,[19] as the face reveals thoughts.[20]

But in the defence of epigram or elegy, literature ceases to reflect life: e.g. Cat. XVI. 5–6, Ov. *Tr.* II. 353–60, Mart. I. 4.8,[21] Plin. *Ep.* VII. 9 (cf. Mart. VIII, *praef.*), Apul. *Apol.* 11, Auson. *Eidyll.* 360 f. The poet's reputation stands intact, his compositions dissociated from personal life, and therefore no evidence against him. Strato's disclaimer of sincerity, *Anth. Pal.* XII. 258, warns future generations against finding autobiography in his poetry. Allied to this convention is Callim. *Aet. praef.* 21 *ff.*,

> καὶ γὰρ ὅτε πρώτιστον ἐμοῖς ἐπὶ δέλτον ἔθηκα
> γούνασιν, Ἀπόλλων εἶπεν ὅ μοι Λύκιος
> '. . .] ἀοιδέ, τὸ μὲν θύος ὅττι πάχιστον
> θρέψαι, τὴ]ν Μοῦσαν δ'ὠγαθὲ λεπταλέην.'

Implied here, and in its Latin counterparts, Virg. *Ecl.* VI. 1–5 (*pingues . . . oves, / deductum . . . carmen*), and Hor. *Sat.* II. 6.14–15 (*pingue pecus domino facias et cetera praeter / ingenium*), is a denial of the principle of reflection: letters and life must be kept far apart. Literary style is one thing, *modus vivendi* quite another. Callimachus' humorous rejection of the rule of correspondence indicates its commonplace status: Virgilian and Horatian reminiscence show that it had become nationalised – and a little banal.

In Lucilius, mainly in the first satire, we catch an occasional glimpse of what seem to be correlations between literature and life: e.g. 84–5 M, *quam lepide lexis conpostae ut tesserulae omnes / arte pavimento atque emblemate vermiculato*, where pedantic style is associated with a complicated mosaic.[22] Similarly, at 15–16, '*porro "clinopodas" "lychnos" – que ut diximus semnos / anti "pedes lecti" atque "lucernas"*', the pretensions of a ponderous style are criticised not only by the formal ridicule of the Graecisms, but also perhaps by the luxurious connotations of *clinopodas lychnosque.* The demand for simple *Latinitas* may contain another demand – for directness in our ethical outlook. Other possible examples of parallelism are 12, *praetextae ac tunicae Lydorum opus sordidulum omne*; 13, *psilae atque amphitaphi villis ingentibus molles*; and 17, *chirodyti aurati, ricae, toracia, mitrae*, where allusion to luxuriant oriental dress and appurtenances may extend to criticism of Asianic bombast.

Notes

1 'The Satirist's Apologia', *Univ. Wisconsin Stud. Lang. Lit.* XV (1922), 148 ff., esp. 163.
2 *PCPhS* ns VIII (1962), 36.
3 Cf. W. S. Anderson, quoted below.
4 'Lucilius, the *Ars Poetica* of Horace, and Persius', *HSCPh* XXIV (1913), 19–20.
5 The 'debasement' extends past line 21.
6 *Op. cit.* p. 159 n. 13, apparently appended as an afterthought. At least, it contradicts his option (p. 148) for a predominantly literary-critical theme: 'The greater part of Persius' satire is devoted to discussion of literary ideals and to detailed literary criticism; and Juvenal's satire is mainly a succession of vivid sketches of contemporary follies.' The antithesis is misleading.
7 *The Bulletin of the John Rylands Library* XLIV (1961–2), 163; cf. G. L. Hendrickson, *CPh* XXIII (1928), 99–112, observing that vice explains incompetence of taste.
8 *Op. cit.* p. 36. Contrast W. C. Korfmacher, *CJ* XXVIII (1932–3), 276 ff., and A. Cartault, *RPh* ns XLV (1921), 66 ff., who wrongly interpret the poem only as a criticism of literature.
9 It must be admitted that in the Roman context 'satire' and 'satirist' do not invariably have predominantly moral connotations. *Satura* included many types of composition (including literary-critical pieces), but its most pronounced tendency was towards the moral: hence I allow myself the antithesis 'literary critic' and 'satirist', though the two are in some ways complementary.
10 *Mnem.* ser. 4, vol. XIII (1960), 30.
11 For full bibliography, *v.* C. O. Brink, *Horace on Poetry, Prolegomena to the Literary Epistles* (Cambridge 1963), and *The 'Ars Poetica'* (1971).
12 *V.* Suet. *Gramm.* 2 and 14.
13 On this type of water imagery, *v.* Wimmel pp. 222 ff., probably commonplace by the time of, e.g., Sen. *Contr.* IV *praef.* 11, *multa erant quae reprehenderes, multa quae suspiceres, cum torrentis modo magnus quidem, sed turbidus flueret.*
14 *V. Sat.* II. 1.7 ff., Trebatius' recommended cures for Horace's sleeplessness. A swim, or a bottle of wine, will produce deep sleep: if he must write, why not compose epic? Ideas of mental sluggishness (*somno . . . alto*) and drunkenness (*irriguum . . . mero . . . corpus*: cf. *irriguo . . . somno* at Pers. V. 56, meaning 'drunken sleep'. Lucr. IV. 907 and Virg. *Aen.* III. 511, sometimes adduced, are not to the point) are related to epic. The association of the three adds up to a Callimachean objection to the unwieldy higher genre. Horace's sleeplessness could be interpreted as a literary virtue: cf. Callimachus' tribute to the 'slender' Aratus at *Epigr.* XXIX. 4, Ἀρήτου σύμβολον ἀγρυπνίης. Deep sleep could result from the *pingue ingenium* of the uninitiated; and 'wine-drinking' is the pursuit of the careless. Trebatius is implicitly disqualified by his vulgar character from recognising Callimachean *bona carmina*, his crassness having led him to recommend epic, the genre of the *turgidi*, the moral status of which suffers by association with wine-drinking and sleep.
15 Cf. Virgil's incorporation of stylistic professions into the situations of his *Eclogues*: *v.* W. V. Clausen, 'Callimachus and Roman Poetry', *GRBS* V (1964), 194–5, on

the oblique assertion of Callimachean aims at *Ecl.* I. 2 and VI. 8 with the adjective *tenuis*, to which add X. 70–I, where *gracilis* transforms the weaving of the basket into a symbol for 'slender' composition (Serv. *ad loc.*, 'allegoricos . . . tenuissimo stilo'; cf. T. E. V. Pearce, *CQ* ns XX (1970), 336 on the rarity of *gracilis* as a critical term), so creating ring composition with *tenuis avena* of l. 2.

16 Frankfurt 1947, pp. 28 ff., 'Die Einheit der Kriterien fur die Formen des Sprach- und Lebensstils'.

17 Oxford 1953, ch. ix, 'Literature as a revelation of personality'.

18 Some of the above are cited by Summers on Sen. *Ep.* CXLV. 1. I thank Dr A. J. Woodman for the references to Plutarch.

19 Cf. Quint. VIII *pr.* 20.

20 V. R. G. M. Nisbet on Cic. *in Pisonem* I. 20, *voltus denique totus, qui sermo quidam tacitus mentis est*, with references.

21 But Mart. VII. 84 is a counter-example: epigram reflects life, like a picture.

22 A symbol of luxury: cf. *pavimentum tesselatum* in Fabianus *ap.* Sen. *Contr.* II. 1.12, and *lacunaria pavimentorum* at Sen. *Ep.* CXIV. 9; perhaps also Hor. *Carm.* II. 14.27, and Cic. *Phil.* II. 41, *natabant pavimenta, madebant parietes.*

INVECTIVE AGAINST WOMEN IN ROMAN SATIRE

Amy Richlin

> *Nescis . . . quantum saturam matronae formident.*
> Fulgentius, *Mythologiarum*

Discussion of the nature of invective against women in Roman satire begins here from two axioms: that Western published literature has largely been written by and for the benefit of men; and that (perhaps, therefore) much of Western literature concerns tensions between levels in social hierarchies. Satire is a genre intrinsically concerned with power; the satirist writes against those who oppress him or those whom he feels he ought to be able to oppress, depicting himself worsted by plutocrat, general, or noble, or sneering at out-groups (foreigners, "pathic" homosexuals, women, freedmen, and so on). By expressing his hostility, the satirist asserts his own power, and makes himself and his like-minded audience feel better. At the same time, the performance of the satire reinforces the desired social norms. For Roman satire, as for the satire of many other cultures, the satirist himself is a "normal" male.

Satire often attacks by means of a stereotype, and it is too often assumed that such stereotypes constitute exaggerated but basically realistic versions of their prototypes.[1] This assumption directs attention toward the chimerical figures of the victims of satire and away from the one set of people for whom the stereotypes constitute evidence – the "normal" males themselves. For any stereotype surely must encode a statement about the writer's and audience's feelings about the real people satirized; invective against women can best be understood as the concrete manifestation of a societal notion of women. The hugely exaggerated and emphasized features in the stereotype tell us nothing (directly) about Roman women, but plenty about the fears and preoccupations of Roman society with regard to women, as enunciated by male satirists.

The body of ancient literature that contains invective against women, or comic stereotypes of women, is enormous; in Latin, a list of only the most notable sources would include the comedies of Plautus and Terence, some of Catullus, Horace *Epod.* 8 and 12 and *S.* 1.2, Ovid *Ars Amatoria*, Petronius *Satyricon*, the *carmina Priapea*, Martial, Juvenal 6, and Apuleius *Metamorphoses*, especially Book 9. The purpose of the present study is only to bring forward the most striking and idiosyncratic features of Roman invective against women, and so no chronological examination of the sources will be made. It is enough to note here that their picture of women is entirely consistent, and shares many features with the Greek comic stereotype of women. But while a great number of the particulars of the Roman stereotype are traditional[2] and conventional,[3] the prominent and large space allotted to misogynistic invective in Latin literature and the freedom and variety of the use of stock motifs suggest that the material is not just there *pro forma.* In addition, misogynistic invective is the same at all levels, from graffiti to formal verse satire. If a genre of literature can be viewed as anthropological artifact, the nature of Roman invective against women has clear implications for the function of Roman satire within Roman society.[4]

To begin with, the Roman satiric stereotype of women can be broken down into three gross categories: young women (attractive), young women (repulsive), and old women (repulsive). This definition depends entirely on sexual and physical qualities. Social status – married, unmarried, or divorced; slave, freed, or freeborn; prostitute or not – often plays a part, but the frequent lack of specification of such status is only too well-known a problem.[5] Status is clearly only an incidental feature.

Satire depicts some women as attractive, some as repulsive. In all cases the poet, a male narrator, defines what attracts and what repels. Attractive women – young wives and mistresses – are typified as promiscuous[6] and drunken,[7] sometimes as jealous[8] or mercenary.[9] This stereotype reflects the same concerns evinced by the Roman laws on marriage, divorce, and adultery, especially the early law, which placed wine-bibbing on a level with adultery as cause for divorce.[10] The obsession with adulterous behavior in wives can easily be understood in an ancestor-worshiping society; the reasons for the assimilation of adultery with drunkenness are less obvious.[11] Though drunkenness is occasionally connected with promiscuity (Juv. 6.300–345), it can stand alone to typify misbehavior by a woman – she makes a spectacle of herself at a dinner party (Juv. 6.425–33). The early sources indicate that the husband and agnates wished to prevent (or detect) secret drinking. The situation must stem from the structure of the early Roman household, in which the husband would often be away from the house and the wife would be left in control of it; ideal behavior is manifested by Lucretia, who spins late into the night with her maids while her misbehaving counterparts spend the evening drinking and carousing (*in convivio luxuque*, Livy 1.57.9), like men. Both sets of women are available for discovery; a wife's behavior then is always potentially a source of help or detriment to her husband's *dignitas.* The attractive woman must be safely incorporated into her husband's persona.

Repulsive women populate the pages of satire: why? The poet and audience must be taking pleasure in examining them and proclaiming their disgust. One whole class of such women differ from the attractive ones only in their physical form; they are would-be wives and mistresses, promiscuous and drunken like the rest, but depicted by the writer as so hideously ugly that he must refuse them when they pursue him.[12] The other class of repulsive women are old; their age and decrepitude are enormously exaggerated, they too like to drink, and, though they often offer the narrator money or a large dowry to marry or service them, he usually resists, with loathing.[13] The interest of Roman satire in graphic descriptions of this repulsive stereotype seems much more difficult to understand than the interest in the attractive stereotype; the reasons for it may perhaps be sought in the peculiar features of Roman invective against women.

The fantastic age of the old women attacked in Roman invective is conventionally expressed by a list of hyperbolic comparisons with heroes and heroines of Greek mythology. Some examples:[14]

quae forsan potuisset esse nutrix
Tithoni Priamique Nestorisque,
illis ni pueris anus fuisset

who perhaps could have been the nurse
of Tithonus, Priam, and Nestor,
if she hadn't been an old woman when they were boys

(*Pr.* 57.3–5)

Pyrrhae filia, Nestoris noverca,
quam vidit Niobe puella canam,
Laertes aviam senex vocavit,
nutricem Priamus, socrum Thyestes

Daughter of Pyrrha, stepmother of Nestor,
a woman whom Niobe as a girl saw white-haired,
Laertes as an old man called his grandmother,
Priam his nurse, Thyestes his mother-in-law

(Mart. 10.67.1–4)

istud . . . belle
non mater facit Hectoris, sed uxor.

This . . . thing
not Hector's mother does becomingly, but his wife.

(Mart. 10.90.5–6)

The lists share a basic structural characteristic: they define the women in terms of family relationships. Not only are these old women coevals of the proverbially elderly, they are part of the family, and they are not wives. They are daughter, stepmother, grandmother (also in Mart. 3.93.22, contrasted with wife), mother-in-law, sister (*Pr.* 12.2), wetnurse, even mother (specifically contrasted with wife, Mart. 10.90, 11.23.14). At *Pr.* 57.7–8 and Mart. 10.90.3 (cf. 8.79), the old woman is also specifically denied to be a girl, *puella.* The point of this definition of the old woman is that in each case she remains extremely eager for sexual intercourse, often directly rejected as a partner by the narrator, and in the crudest terms: *ne desim sibi, me rogat, fututor*, "she begs me that I not desert her as her fucker" (*Pr.* 57.6, cf. 12.5–7); *vis futui gratis, cum sis deformis anusque*, "you want to be fucked for free, when you're ugly and an old woman!" (Mart. 7.75.1). The woman in Mart. 10.90 is reproached for depilating her crotch, and told this activity is proper to wives, not mothers. Thus in each case old women are marked off from sexual union with men (wifehood) by a demonstration of disgust at sexuality in old women, and the statement is clearly made that sexuality is attractive only in young women (wives).

As the fantastic age and non-marital family status of old women bars them from intercourse, so the bestial ugliness of all repulsive women in satire stigmatizes intercourse with them as disgusting (though not inconceivable). Animal invective is unusual in Latin[15] by far the most extreme examples apply to women.[16] At its mildest such invective compares old women to crows, proverbially long-lived;[17] the woman who persists in depilating her crotch is told not "to pluck the beard of a dead lion" (Mart. 10.90.10).

The invective becomes more specific when it deals with a woman's physical flaws, either part by part or focusing on a single part. The most notable examples of the part-by-part technique[18] are Horace's *Epodes* 8 and 12: in 8, the woman is described as old (1–2), black-toothed and wrinkle-browed (3–4), with flabby stomach and misshapen, swollen legs (9–10), with an anus like that of a cow with diarrhea (5–6) and breasts like a mare's teats (7–8); in 12, she is "fit for black elephants" (1), and smells like an octopus or a goat (5), bedaubed with cosmetics made from crocodile dung (11). Martial (3.93) compares a woman with grasshoppers, ants, spider-webs, crocodiles, frogs, gnats, owls, goats, and ducks. When a poet focuses on a single part, it is generally the woman's genitalia: often depicted as filthy and loose (compared with the buttocks of the statue of a horse, the gullet of a pelican, and a salt fishpond, Mart. 11.21.1, 10, 11, with other, non-bestial comparisons; described as crawling with worms, *Pr.* 46.10); sometimes too bony (Mart. 3.93.13, 11.100.4); sometimes white-haired (Mart. 2.34.3, 9.37.7); too noisy (Mart. 7.18).

Some generalizations can be made about the referents chosen. Many of the animal referents are outlandish, and have unusual shapes and sizes as well - (elephant, octopus, crocodile, pelican); insects are even further removed from humanity. The descriptions often allude to diseases, smell, and/or fecal matter, and relate the woman to one of an animal's orifices, especially mouth or anus (cf. Cat. 97.7–8, where the mouth of a male victim is compared with the vagina of a urinating she-mule). At the same time the idea of decay is also often present (*putidam*, *putres*, Hor. *Epod.* 8.1, 7; *putida*, *Pr.* 57.2; *putidula*, Mart. 4.20.4), so that the worms of *Pr.* 46.10 are surely those of decomposition, despite the fact that the woman is addressed as *puella* (*Pr.* 46.1). Old women themselves are repeatedly addressed as corpses, from the imagined funeral of Horace *Epod.* 8 to direct equation (*caries vetusque bustum*, "decay and old tomb," *Pr.* 57.1; *mortua, non vetula*, "a dead woman, not an old one," Mart. 3.32.2); one woman is imagined as lusting in her grave (Mart. 10.67). What is more startling, the genitals themselves are treated as the women's relics or tombs (*inter avos . . . tuos*, "among your ancestors," Mart. 9.37.8; *busti cineres*, "the ashes of your funeral pyre," Mart. 10.90.2), and Martial concocts an elaborately grotesque funeral/wedding, ending with the line *intrare in istum sola fax potest cunnum*, "only a funeral torch can get into that cunt of yours" (3.93.27). It might be postulated that the disgust attributed specifically to the female genitalia, as an outlandish, foul-smelling, possibly diseased or decayed, and bestial orifice, is generalized in satire to the woman as a whole, and especially when the narrator wishes to reject her sexuality.

In fact old women evoke the most intense expressions of fear and disgust, along with a sense that they constitute a sort of uncanny other. The role of old women in ancient literature includes a range separate from the role of mother – old nurse and adviser, madam, witch; and the sphere of activity of the witches/nurses/advisers in Latin literature is primarily sexual and perverse. Like the aged nurses of tragedy and epic who lead Phaedra and Myrrha astray, Dipsas in Ovid's *Amores* (1.8), the *lena* of Tibullus 1.5, and Acanthis in Propertius 4.5 serve as the companion of the poet's mistress and advise her to be promiscuous. Their function is to remove the attractive young woman from the poet's exclusive control and to pervert the sexual behavior of the mistress; the old woman's role easily combines that of witch and madam (cf. Mart. 9.29.9–10). Witches also have the ability to charm a beloved (Vergil *Aeneid* 4.478–521; Hor. *Epod.* 5.81–82). But their charms include abortifacients (Juv. 6.595–597; cf. Ovid *Am.* 2.14.27–8) and poisons (Juv. 6.610–617), so that they pervert the traditional female functions of procreation and feeding and make them deadly.

Moreover, witches can directly threaten male characters. Horace's awful Canidia tortures a little boy (*Epod* 5). The witches in Hor. *S.* 1.8 perform fearsome magic rites near the statue of Priapus, plucking poisonous herbs with which to control people's feelings; he frightens them away by farting, and undercuts their importance by revealing them as old women with false teeth and hair (46–50). The crones at the end of the *Satyricon* (134–138) try to bring Encolpius back to sexual potency with an eye to their own satisfaction, finally inserting in his rectum a leather phallus anointed with a mixture of oil, pepper, and nettleseed. And the witches of Apuleius' *Metamorphoses* embody wrongful knowledge: Meroc, who urinates on the narrator and causes the horrible death of the man who tries to desert her, the narrator's friend Socrates (*M.* 1.11–19); the anonymous witches who cut off Thelyphron's nose (*M.* 2.30);[19] and, paramount, Lucius' dangerous hostess, whose arts provide the means whereby his mistress turns him into an ass (*M.* 3.24–26). Old women in these cases represent a side of female behavior that maliciously threatens males with cuckoldry, sterility, usurpation, rape, or death, all of which activities any male would presumably wish to discourage, and all of which weaken the assumption of male control over women.

The same sort of threat appears to emanate from female genitalia.[20] As has been shown, the genitals form a major vehicle for invective based on animal metaphors, and disgust for them reaches the point of a perception of them as decayed or dead. It should be noted that nowhere in Latin is there a favorable direct portrayal of female genitalia;[21] they are described only as part of repulsive women.

The outstanding example of such a description forms part of the Priapic poem from the *Virgilian Appendix*, listed in the Oxford text (151–53) as *Priapeum "Quid Hoc Novi Est?"* (83 Bücheler). The poet threatens his recalcitrant penis: instead of lovely boys (21–23) and girls (24–25), the penis will be forced to enter the horrible vagina of a very old woman (26–37):

bidens amica Romuli senis memor
paratur, inter atra cuius inguina
latet iacente pantice abditus specus
vagaque pelle tectus annuo gelu
araneosus obsidet forem situs.
tibi haec paratur, ut tuum ter aut quarter
voret profunda fossa lubricum caput.
licebit aeger, angue lentior, cubes,
tereris usque donec, a, miser, miser
triplexque quadruplexque compleas specum.
superbia ista proderit nihil, simul
vagum sonante merseris luto caput.

A two-toothed mistress who remembers old Romulus
is ready, amidst whose dark loins
lies a cave hidden by a flaccid paunch,
and, covered by skin wandering in year-long cold,
cobwebbed filth obstructs the door.
She's ready for you, so that three or four times
this deep ditch can devour your slimy head.
Although you'll lie there weak, slower than a snake,
you'll be ground repeatedly until – o wretch, wretch,
you fill that cave three times and four times over.
This pride of yours will get you nowhere, as soon as
your errant head is plunged in her noisy muck.

In this poem the threat embodied by the vagina is abundantly clear. It is to be feared by the personified phallus; it is foisted off onto a repulsive person, the aged woman, while the attractive boy and girl in 21–25 tempt the reader with only external parts of their bodies. The vagina is sinister (*latet, abditus*, 28) and physically dangerous; a cave or deep ditch (*specus*, 28, 35; *profunda fossa*, 32), it will devour and grind the phallus (*voret*, 32; *tereris*, 34) for which the author expresses pity (*a*, *miser*, *miser*, 34). It is filthy; hidden by the belly (*iacente pantice*, 28) and covered by folds of skin (*vagaque pelle tectus*, 29), it collects dirt over the years (*araneosus . . . situs*, 30). It is also intrinsically foul – cold (*annuo gelu*, 29) and mucky (*sonante . . . luto*, 37).

Latin is weak in metaphorical obscenities,[22] and the presence of any consistent sexual analogy is worthy of notice. As has been seen, female genitalia are compared in Latin with foul, wet, enclosed spaces and with the enclosure of the tomb, the perception which accords well with that of *"Quid Hoc Novi Est"*; other terms for the female genitalia include *fossa*, "ditch" (*Pr.* 46.9, 78.6; cf. Juv. 2.10); *barathrum*, "abyss" (Mart. 3.81.1); *recessus*, "inner parts" (Mart. 7.35.7). This negative view places the writers of invective in an ambivalent position. They can discover the genitalia, exposing what really lies inside the shell of a woman, as does this Pompeiian graffitist, who wrote on a doorway (*CIL* 4.1516):

hic ego nu<nc> <f>utuii formosa fo<r>ma puella
laudata a multis set lutus intus eerat

Here I now fucked a gril beatiful to see,
prased by many, but she wass muck inside.

But this implies personal experience; the narrator has touched the foul substance. Alternatively, he can define female genitalia out of the realm of the sexual, as does Martial (10.90.7–8):

erras si tibi cunnus hic videtur,
ad quem mentula pertinere desit.

You are wrong if this seems to you to be a cunt,
to which a prick has ceased to pertain.

Cunnus then = *id ad quod mentula pertinet*; but no more specific positive description exists in Latin. The heterosexual satirist must then experience what he despises in order to expose it, or reject it without explaining what he would prefer.

Roman humorists thus use two stances when writing invective against repulsive women: rejection, in which the male narrator refuses to have anything to do with the woman beyond describing her; and revelation, in which the male narrator describes the loathsome features of a woman with whom he has had intercourse. The first stance seems logical, separating the narrator from the foul qualities he enumerates. The premise is that the woman begs the narrator to have intercourse with her, and he tells her to go away; for example, *Pr.* 12, in which the god spends the first six lines on the great age of the woman, 7–9 describing her prayer that the god's *mentula* not desert her, and the last six lines speaking his command to her. He tells her to remove her genitalia from his presence: *tolle . . . procul et iube latere*, "take it far away and order it to hide . . ." (12. 10).[23] But the disgust and desire for separation evinced by such a stance are somewhat undercut by the narrator's attention to detail, for the reader is obviously meant to be fascinated as well as repelled; the moralistic speaker of Mart. 10.90 uses some of the crudest obscenities in Latin.

And so in Horace *Epod.* 12, as in other poems,[24] the narrator specifically describes himself as in bed with the woman he loathes. This imagined coupling has great force, repeatedly and graphically exposing the reader to smell, sound, and feeling, as well as to sight. The writer commonly rejects the woman not only verbally but physically, boasting that she cannot arouse him; whereas normally impotence is cause for shame and chagrin (e.g., Ovid *Am.* 3.7), here it is a sign of the woman's failure. Appropriately, it is the writer's genitalia which reject such women on his behalf.[25] Yet the writer is somehow sexually involved with the woman; in *"Quid Hoc Novi Est,"* the act of being ground up paradoxically (and, in the poem, regrettably) causes the penis to grow (33–35).

Like the women whom the writer does not touch, these women beg, offer gifts (Hor. *Epod.* 12.2), and even promise large amounts of money. The ludicrous monster in Hor. *Epod.* 12 reverses the norms of elegy, comparing herself with the beast of prey and her lover with the fleeing lamb or kid (12.25–26). She has the alarming strength of a wild animal; so, too, the writers attribute strength to the offers of money, which can be persuasive.[26] Thus this theme is tied with that of *captatio* of wealthy old women by impecunious suitors (e.g., Juv. 1.37–44).

The revelatory descriptions, then, aim at exposing and vitiating female attempts to control a sexual situation in a male way. Where the woman offers money (as male lovers in epigram often do), the narrator wants to make it clear that the money itself is the only attraction – the woman is worthless in herself, and the narrator is doing her a favor even to touch her. Where the woman offers only herself, the narrator again wants to make it clear that the initiative rests with him: he decides whether the woman should be rated as human or bestial, and without his arousal there is no intercourse. The underlying message here is not one of fear but of assertion. In the social situation of love-making, the male retains control by his right to choose how he will perceive the female.

Conclusions

The nature of Roman invective against women leads to three generalizations. First, at the most elemental level, invective against women flows from the wellspring of satire, fear of the other: in this case, female genitalia and old women other than wives and mothers. Fear produces mockery, which disguises the fear as contempt (fear plus power), adds the further disguise of humor, stratifies the situation (the satirist has the better of his victim), and establishes an otherwise unattainable control over the feared object. The practice of depilation by Roman women demonstrates their cooperation with the male anxiety expressed in invective.[27] The female genitalia, which apparently swallow up the male, and the anomalous old woman (too old to be a wife, yet not a mother), once stereotyped and castigated no longer have as much power over the male. They are re-created to conform with the satirist's fantasies: thus he controls them. For the issue is not primarily one of sex, but of power – or it is sexual only insofar as sex can be used to implement and signify power. The reduction of women, first separated into "attractive" and "repulsive," to stereotypes viewed part by part enables the satirist to view women as intrinsically vile, both morally and physically. (And surely, when the elegists invert this relationship between normative male and flawed woman, the change is only superficial; the relationship remains preoccupied with power, the woman viewed part by part is controlled by the viewer, dominance pairs off with submission, and the inversion serves mainly to titillate poet and reader.)[28]

The more specific significance of the female genitalia can be seen by comparison with invective against male homosexuals. The beautiful boy is the male equivalent of the attractive woman, and the anal area of such boys is often described and praised, unlike the genital area of attractive women.[29] Adult "pathic" homosexuals are the male equivalent of old and/or repulsive women, and the anal orifice of such men is often attacked in terms similar to those used of repulsive female genitalia.[30] Only very rarely are male genitalia described as disgusting (an old man's penis. Catullus 25.3; Mart. 11.46). It is clear that an orifice which is penetrated by the penis, or which submits to the penis, becomes disgusting when the one who submits is one who is normally barred by age from such submission. Being penetrated always signifies submission; but where it is proper, in Roman culture, for young women and boys to submit to adult males, it is not proper for old women and adult males to do so. Hence their orifices are perceived as improbably over-used and stained; hence it is the word *puella*, "young girl," which is very commonly used to mean "mistress" or "prostitute." But why is there no praise for the genitalia of the young woman? The answer seems to be that, in fact, there is only a *cunnus* when the *mentula* does *not* pertain to it (when the woman is old); the *cunnus* of the mistress, wife, and mother simply does not exist. *Cunnus* in relation to a sexually attractive woman signifies an undescribed but inferior orifice (Mart. 11.43.11–12); the contaminator of the cunnilinctor (common in graffiti; cf. Mart. 12.59); or, by pejorative synecdoche, the woman herself (Mart. 6.45.1; cf. Hor. *S.* 1.2, 69–71, *Pr.* 68.9–10). In short the negative perception of the female genitalia precludes their specific association with attractive women – just as breasts are seldom explicitly mentioned except in derogatory contexts.[31] Conversely, the anal and genital orifices conveniently represent people deemed inappropriate as sexual partners – old women and adult males.

Finally, the fear of female genitalia *per se*, along with the use of them as pejorative sign, falls into alignment with the social function of Roman invective against women.[32] As invective demonstrates the intrinsic vileness of the female, as it bars certain women from sexual acceptability, so it shows publicly what the correct place of women is. The rare attacks on lesbians predictably focus on a woman's pre-emption of a male role in intercourse.[33] The stereotypes, both attractive and unattractive, present women with a finite and predetermined set of options: the attractive stereotypes, along with those in moralistic literature, give women a set of aspirations (though satire makes it clear that men expect even attractive women to be seriously flawed – frivolous and oversexed – and so these flaws are incorporated into the stereotype "attractive"); the repulsive stereotypes give women a set of boundaries, warning them that certain types of women can expect only mockery and revulsion for manifestations of sexuality, even for existence. Women exposed to invective must acknowledge that the acceptable married woman produces legitimate children and limits her sexual activity to her young married life; public performance of invective, from graffiti to formal verse satire, serves as a societal endorsement by the whole audience of the norms outlined therein. Hence the use of bizarre animals in invective against women; inappropriate behavior removes women from humanity.[34] Such an extreme sanction would seem to be needed by a society that married off most women, at an extremely young age, and demanded marital fidelity of them, while men married later and usually had access to prostitutes and slaves of either sex.[35]

More specifically, invective against women (today quite similar to the Roman) demonstrates the place of women with respect to literature; the female is subject matter, the narrative voice is male. A woman who wishes to write satire can only malign herself and her kind, since satire by nature and tradition consists partly in the maligning of women; and so we have the comedienne – the dumb blonde, the strident shrew, the fat woman, and the hag. If the women's movement has abandoned this sense of humor, no wonder.

Lehigh University

Notes

1 For example, on male "pathic" homesexuals, Gilbert Highet, *Juvenal the Satirist* (New York 1961) 59–64, 117–127; on women, Ulrich Knoche, *Roman Satire*,

tr. Edwin S. Ramage (Bloomington, Indiana 1975) 148; R. P. Bond, "Anti-feminism in Juvenal and Cato," in *Studies in Latin Literature and Roman History* (I), ed. Carl Deroux (Brussels 1979) 418–447.

2 Sources collected by Victor Grassmann, *Die erotischen Epoden des Horaz* (Munich 1966) = *Zetemata* 39, 12–22, 23–34; Vinzenz Buchheit, *Studien zum Corpus Priapeorum* (Munich 1962) = *Zetemata* 28, 88–89.

3 Some parallels collected by Ilona Opelt, *Die lateinischen Schimpfwörter und verwandte sprachliche Erscheinungen* (Heidelberg 1965) 26–28; cf. also Amy Richlin, *Sexual Terms and Themes in Roman Satire and Related Genres* (diss. Yale 1978) 206–216. 229–232, 233–246, 255–268; and J. N. Adams, *The Latin Sexual Vocabulary* (Baltimore 1982) 80–109.

4 This technique is now being well applied in anthropology, usually for material in oral circulation; most helpful for the study of Rome is the work of Gary H. Gossen on the Chamulas of southern Mexico, who share many cultural characteristics with the Romans. Especially pertinent here: *Chamulas in the World of the Sun* (Cambridge, Mass. 1974) 97–109; "Verbal Dueling in Chamula," in *Speech Play*, ed. Barbara Kirshenblatt-Gimblett (Philadelphia 1976). For an examination of the social significance of the denigration of the female body, the best source remains Philip E. Slater, *The Glory of Hera* (Boston 1968) 23–99, 410–439; many of the marital patterns described by Slater apply to the Romans as well, cf. Keith Hopkins, "The Age of Roman Girls at Marriage," *Population Studies* 18 (1964–5) 309–327. See also Elizabeth V. Spelman, "Woman as Body: Ancient and Contemporary Views," *Feminist Studies* 8 (1982) 109–131.

5 Viz. the discussions of the status of women in erotic poetry: e.g., Saara Lilja, *The Roman Elegists' Attitude to Women* (Helsinki 1965) 35–42; Gordon Williams, *Tradition and Originality in Roman Poetry* (Oxford 1968) 526–542.

6 Lucilius 680 Marx, 781 Marx; Catullus 11, 37, 58, 59, 67, 76, 111; Hor. *S.* 1.2.77–108; *Pr.* 26; Petron. *Sat.* 16.2–26.6 (Quartilla), 109.2–3 (Tryphaena), 126.5–7 (Circe); Mart. 2.31, 4.12, 6.45, 7.30, 8.53; Juv. 6.100–114, 115–132, 300–334, *O.* 31–34, 548, 567; 10.220. This was a serious topic in moralistic poetry (e.g., Hor. *C.* 3.6.21–32); the strongest form of this theme holds that even the chastest of women is promiscuous at heart, the best example being the tale of the Widow of Ephesus (Petron. *Sat.* 110.6–112.8).

7 Juvenal 6.300–351, 425–433; Mart. 12.65.

8 Esp. in comedy, as for instance the jealous wife in Plautus' *Menaechmi*; cf. Habinnas' wife (Petron. *Sat.* 67) and the hypocritically jealous wife at Juv. 6.279.

9 Cat. 110; Hor. *S.* 1.2.47–53, 2.5.70–72; Mart. 3.54, 9.2, 9.32, 10.29. 11.50; Juv. 4.20–21, 7.74–75.

10 Esp. the elder Cato in Gellius, *Noctes Atticae* 10.23.4; also Dion. Hal. 2.25.6, Val. Max. 6.3.9, Pliny *HN* 14.89–90; some discussion in Sarah B. Pomeroy, *Goddesses, Whores, Wives, and Slaves* (New York 1975) 153–154.

11 See Alan Watson, *Rome of the XII Tables* (Princeton 1975) 31–38, for discussion (not conclusive) 1; Sarah B. Pomeroy, "The Relationship of the Married Woman to Her Blood Relatives in Rome," *Anc Soc* 7 (1976) 215–27.

12 *Pr.* 32, 46; Mart. 11.97; cf. Mart. 11.23 (rejection of would-be wife and description of the indignities she must suffer if the poet should take her).

13 Lucilius 282–283 Marx, 1065–1066 Marx, and ?302, 766–767 on drunkenness;

Ovid *Am.* 1.8.3–4, 114 (drunkenness); Hor. *Epod.* 8, 12; *Pr.* 12, 57; *Virgilian Appendix "Quid Hoc Novi Est?"* Oxford 151–153; Mart. 1.19, 2.33, 3.32, 3.93, 4.20, 7.75, 8.79, 9.29, 9.37, 10.39, 10.67, 10.90, 11.21, 11.29, and cf. 3.72.

14 Cf. also *Pr.* 12; Mart. 3.32, 3.93, 9.29, 10.39; *"Quid Hoc Novi Est?"* 26.

15 For the use of animal invective in rhetoric, cf. R. G. M. Nisbet, *M. Tulli Ciceronis in L. Calpurnium Pisonem Oratio* (Oxford 1961) 195.

16 A few graphic animal comparisons used of men in Catullus: 25.1–4, 69.5–10, 97.5–8.

17 Pliny *HN* 7.153; e.g., *Pr.* 57.1, Mart. 10.67.5.

18 Cf. *Pr.* 32. 46; Mart. 3.53, 3.93, 9.37.

19 Mutilation by cutting off ears and nose is cited as a punishment for adulterers (Mart. 2.83, 3.85; Vergil *A.* 6.494–497) and in other circumstances where the shaming of the victim was a desideratum (Tac. *Ann.* 12.14).

20 The most important general study here is Karen Horney. "The Dread of Woman," *IntJPsych* 13 (1932) 348–360; I see now Carol R. Ember, "Men's Fear of Sex with Women: A Cross-Culture Study," *Sex Roles* 4 (1978) 657–78. On the general significance for Greek culture of fear and disgust for the female genitalia, see Slater, *op. cit.* 12–23; he outlines the association of pubic hair with overpowering sexuality in women, although his conclusions are disputed by Martin Kilmer, "Genital Phobia and Depilation," *JHS* 72 (1982) 104–12. Cf. Martial's comments on depilation, and the Priapic allusion to worms in the vagina, 46.10.

21 The closest example is perhaps the Pompeiian graffito *CIL* 4.1830: *futuitur cunnus <pil>ossu<s> multo melius <qu>am glaber / . . . con<ti>net va<p>orem* . . .; or the highly metaphoric treatment at Apul. *M.* 2.7.

22 Compare in general the vast store of sexual metaphor in Aristophanes collected by Jeffrey Henderson, *The Maculate Muse* (New Haven 1975); those for female genitalia there range from very positive to very negative, and the metaphors from holes and hollows are not particularly negative (# 150–158).

23 Cf. Mart. 3.32, 3.93, 7.75, 10.67, 10.90, 11.97.

24 Cf. *"Quid Hoc Novi Est?"*; *Pr.* 32; Mart. 11.21, 11.29.

25 Hor. *Epod.* 8.18–20, 12.14–15 (here the poet lets the woman prove his potency by complaining of his prowess with another woman); and esp. Mart. 9.37, where the *mentula* "sees" the old woman.

26 *Pr.* 57.8; Mart. 11.29 (cf. 7.75, 9.37).

27 Mart. 3.74, 10.90, 12.32.21–22.

28 *Contra* Judith P. Hallett, "The Role of Women in Roman Elegy: Counter-cultural Feminism," *Arethusa* 6 (1973) 103–124, with subsequent discussion in *Arethusa* 6, 267–269, 7 (1974) 211–219; she sees in elegy a sincere ideological counter to traditional Roman attitudes towards women. Cf. Mart. 9.37, where the poet virtually dismembers the woman by enumerating her false parts: hair, teeth, complexion, even eyebrows – then lets his *mentula* reject her. The parts listed are not much different from those praised by an elegist. For the technique of part-by-part praise in the Renaissance, see Nancy J. Vickers, "Diana Described: Scattered Woman and Scattered Rhyme," *Critical Inquiry* 8 (1981) 265–279.

29 See Amy Richlin, *The Garden of Priapus: Sexuality and Aggression in Roman Humor* (New Haven 1983), chapter 2.

30 Cat. 97; the anus is *laxus*, *Pr.* 17.3; *tritus,* Mart. 2.51.2; and called *fossa*, Juv. 2.10.

Cf. also Mart. 6.37. Pathic homosexuals were proverbially afflicted by anal warts or piles; the slang term was *ficus* "fig" or *marisca* "cheap fig" (Mart. 1.65, 4.52. 6.49.8–11, 7.71, 12.33; *Pr.* 41.4, 50.2; Juv. 2.13), and Martial once uses *marisca* to mean a woman's anus as compared with the preferable anus of a boy (12.96). Luciius draws an analogy between befoulment by women and by boys: *hoec inbubinat, at contra te inbulbitat <ille>* (1186 Marx), "she rags on you, but then again he be-merdes you"; cf. *Pr.* 68.8, ?69.4; Mart. 9.69.1. 11.88. 13.26; Juv. 9.43–44.

31 Hor. *Epod.* 8.7; Mart. 2.52, 3.53.3, 3.72.3, 3.93.5, 14.66, 14.149.

32 Cf. Horney (above, n. 20) 360.

33 Mart. 1.90, ?7.35, 7.67, 7.70. "Bassa" is the name of the woman attacked in 1.90; another Bassa (4.4) is the victim of a long invective list attacking her foul smell, including several animal similes resembling those in 11.21.

34 See Edmund Leach, "Anthropological Aspects of Language: Animal Categories and Verbal Abuse," in *New Directions in the Study of Language*, ed. Eric H. Lenneberg (Cambridge, Mass. 1964) 23–63, esp. 60–61.

35 See Hopkins (above, n. 4).

THE MASKS OF SATIRE

Susanna Morton Braund

Satire as drama

To view satire as a kind of drama is perhaps the most illuminating approach available. There is some basis for this in the ancient evidence about the origins of satire. We have seen in the Introduction that there may be a link between *satura* and satyrs and that Livy's account of the history of Roman drama included a stage-show called *satura.* [. . .] Moreover, the satirists themselves connect their work with Greek Old Comedy. But whether or not such links are accepted, the analogy between satire and drama invites thoughts of performance. These are poems written not to be read silently but to be performed in front of an audience. The view of satire as drama reminds us that the authors of satire are using dramatic forms, primarily the monologue and the dialogue. [. . .] This use of the forms of drama distinguishes satire from epic (whose hexameter metre it borrows), in which the predominant form is third person narrative. [. . .] Satire, then, combines the forms of drama with the metre of epic. It is a hybrid form.

To view satire as a kind of drama, as a performance, helps us resist seeing satire as autobiography. This type of interpretation, which was prominent earlier this century, is the result of a post-Romantic view of poetry as the expression of emotions straight from the heart. The fact that satire often uses the first person presentation doubtless seemed to support such a view. It is now generally accepted that this kind of post-Romantic interpretation is inappropriate to any kind of Roman poetry, even love poetry. Roman poetry is the product of a highly educated elite and an arena in which the intellect as much as the emotions are exercised. To ask if the expressions of the passions of anger or pity or love are what we would call 'genuine' is not a question the Romans would have framed or even, perhaps, understood. For the Romans, the most important ideas were those of plausibility (*fides*) and appropriateness (*decorum*): how *convincing* a display of anger or pity or love is this? This throws the emphasis onto the quality of the performance. That is why it is helpful to see satire as a type of drama. And that is why I distinguish between the authors of satire and the 'satirists' they create in their poems: these dramatic characters who perform upon the satiric stage are not to be confused with the writers of satire.

Masks and satire

To see satire as a type of drama leads easily to the idea that the writers of satire use various masks or *personae* in their poems. Many types of theatrical performance in Greco-Roman antiquity used masks (*personae*) which served as an instant kind of characterisation. This was especially so where there were stock characters with stock masks. For example, in 'New Comedy' written in Athens by Menander and others in the fourth century BC and imitated in Rome by Plautus and Terence in the early second century BC, the irritable old father and his son, the love-lorn young man, the domineering old wife and the scheming slave are some of the stock characters. And in the native Italian form of drama called the Atellan farce stock characters included the fool and the glutton. Rather like the dramatic poets, the writers of Roman satire are creating roles, even if those roles are complex and ambiguous and, at times, shifting. And this view of the voices of Roman satire as a series of *personae* would not have been alien or difficult for the original Roman audiences. It seems that the Romans thought of life, perhaps more than we do, in terms of roles performed and the variety of *personae* adopted in differing circumstances.

A very explicit statement of this outlook is found in Cicero's theory in *On Duties* (*De officiis*) 1 concerning the four *personae* available to each individual. The first *persona* is the universal one of the human self, of being a human as opposed to an animal; the second *persona* is that of the individual with particular skills and capacities, for example, strength, attractiveness, wit and shrewdness. The third *persona* is that which arises from circumstances, for example, high and low birth, wealth and poverty, and the fourth is the *persona* which consists of our individual choice of role in life. Cicero explains that this might be a decision to specialise in philosophy or law or oratory, to follow in your father's footsteps or deliberately to take a different course. These ideas drawn from Cicero's philosophical analysis of the individual's place in society suggest how readily the Romans thought in terms of *persona* – the image presented to society. And although we do not so readily conceive of ourselves as playing out roles, we might usefully compare the function of 'image-makers' in affecting the popular perception of public figures such as politicians and members of the Royal family, of sporting heroes and film-stars.

The use of the mask to create an image (*persona*) and the emphasis upon plausibility and appropriateness and performance is by no means confined to Roman satire but is part of a much wider phenomenon. It pervaded all aspects of the public life of the Roman elite. Nowhere is this more visible than in the rhetorical education of the young Roman. This education was designed to equip the sons of the elite for life in a highly competitive socio-political milieu in which the chief means of attaining superiority was skill in public speaking. Skill in public speaking centred upon being convincing: acting out the appropriate role in the most effective way possible. For the Romans, drama and rhetoric were mutually interdependent.

Drama and rhetoric

The basic education of young Roman boys from wealthy families was in Latin and Greek language. Then, at about the age of eleven, boys went to the *grammaticus*, the teacher of literature, for lessons in reading and the interpretation of texts. We can get some idea of the syllabus – or at least the ideal syllabus – from Quintilian, a professor who was writing at the end of the first century AD. He laid down the texts that he thought should form the programme of studies for school-boys in his twelve-book *The Training of an Orator* (*Institutio Oratoria*), for example, 1.8.5–6:

> That, then, is an excellent procedure, to begin by reading Homer and Virgil, although for the full appreciation of their merits the intellect needs to be more firmly developed: but there is plenty of time for that, because the boy will read them more than once. In the meantime let his mind rise with the sublimity of heroic poetry, take its inspiration from the greatness of its theme and be filled with the highest feelings. The reading of tragedy is also useful, and lyric poets nurture the mind, so long as there is a careful selection of not only the authors but also the passages from their works which are to be read. For the Greek lyric poets are often risqué and even in Horace there are passages which I should be unwilling to explain to a class.

Not exactly a Roman National Curriculum, but perhaps the nearest thing! Literature was studied not for its own sake but to develop skill in public speaking. And the most privileged boys, between the ages of fifteen and eighteen usually, proceeded to a teacher who specialised in this type of training – the teacher of rhetoric, the *rhetor*.

The education in rhetoric was modelled on the Greek system in which public speaking was divided into three types of oratory: judicial oratory, deliberative oratory and epideictic oratory. Judicial oratory, also called forensic oratory, consisted of speeches of prosecution and defence in cases being heard in the courts. (The word 'forensic' actually derives from the Roman practice of having its law-courts meet in the forum.) Deliberative oratory involved making speeches advising or urging or rejecting a proposed course of action in the Senate, for example, or any other body making such decisions. And epideictic oratory, that is 'display' oratory, consisted chiefly of speeches of praise (also called panegyrical and encomiastic speeches) about a god or an individual or a city or about a public building such as a temple. The opposite to panegyric is invective, where the 'display' speech attacks an individual or place.

The training in all three kinds of public speaking was done through a combination of exercises and the study of specimen speeches. Students had to compose practice cases on specific or general themes. The earliest Roman handbook which survives, the *Rhetorica ad Herennium*, which dates from around

80 BC, shows the set topics which were thought likely to crop up in senatorial debates and in the law-courts. But our fullest source is the writings of the Elder Seneca of the first half of the first century AD. Seneca's works are memoirs of famous rhetorical teachers and famous orators of his time. This body of Roman declamation, i.e. public speaking, is divided into *Suasoriae* (persuasions) and *Controversiae* (disputes).

Suasoriae consist of advice given to famous characters from history or legend on the proper course of action they should take. For example, 'Agamemnon deliberates whether to sacrifice Iphigeneia, for Calchas says that otherwise sailing is impossible' (Seneca *Suas.* 3); 'Alexander the Great, warned of danger by an augur, deliberates whether to enter Babylon' (*Suas.* 4); 'Cicero deliberates whether to beg Antony's pardon' (*Suas.* 5); 'Antony promises to spare Cicero's life if he burns his writings: Cicero deliberates whether to do so' (*Suas.* 7). In giving this advice, the orator would often appeal to concepts such as honour (*honestum*), right (*fas*), fairness (*aequum*), advantage (*utile*), obligation (*necessarium*), duty (*pium*) and so on.

In a *controversia*, the speakers argued on opposite sides of a legal or quasi-legal case: competition was, therefore, a central feature of this kind of declamation. Plausibility was important, but so was innovation. These two demands pulled in opposite directions at times, as can be seen from a couple of examples. First, in the case of the prostitute priestess (Seneca *Contr.* 1.2), a virgin who had been captured by pirates and sold into prostitution but later returned to her family seeks a priesthood. The dilemma is deepened by the story: she appealed to her clients for assistance but when one client refused, a struggle followed in which she killed the man; she was, however, acquitted of his murder. The *controversia* consists of arguments as to whether or not the woman is eligible for priestly office, given the legal requirement that a priestess be chaste and pure. Another example is Sen. *Contr.* 1.5, 'The man who raped two girls'. The law cited here is as follows: 'A girl who has been raped may choose either marriage to her ravisher without a dowry or his death.' The situation posed is this: 'On a single night, a man raped two girls. One demands his death, the other marriage.' The *controversia* consists of the arguments for and against the different outcomes. It is a matter of some debate how close such cases were to real-life legal cases. The general suspicion is that the emphasis on originality resulted in a lurid and grotesque flavour which seems to resemble the obsessions of our tabloid newspapers today.

Personae, persuasion and power

The Roman education system, then, was directed towards public speaking. The training in words was paramount: the emphasis was upon anything and everything that might impress and persuade: clever arguments, paradox, point (*sententia*), vivid description (*enargeia*), the arousal of emotions. And this training gave the speaker the means of adopting different *personae* on different occasions, depending on the circumstances, and of doing so convincingly. The young aristocrat needed this skill to succeed, because Roman public and political life centred upon public speaking. Power was in the word. And because this training was shared by the members of the elite, they were in a position to recognise and appreciate the use of precisely this skill by others both in declamation and in other spheres of expression, such as poetry.

Rhetoric and satire: Cicero and Juvenal

An example which brings together rhetorical theory and the practice of Roman satire will show how this works. Cicero provides a list of the topics which an orator can use to arouse indignation or pity from his audience in the conclusion (*peroratio*) of his speech *On Invention* (*De inventione*) 1.100–9. His extensive list of fifteen topics which can fire the audience's indignation (1.100–5) shows a striking similarity to the kinds of things Juvenal's angry speaker says. It would be possible to draw examples from throughout Satires 1–6 but the point is perhaps made most effectively by focusing upon one extended passage. The closing passage of *Satire* 6 (627–61) is in effect the peroration to Juvenal's angry satires and it is particularly rich in these marks of indignation. The message here is that women are capable of the worst crimes. This general message corresponds to the following topics in Cicero's list:

> 2. Passionate demonstration of the parties affected by the act which is being denounced: all people or superiors or peers or inferiors.
>
> 7. Demonstration that the deed was foul, cruel, wicked, tyrannical.

The passage starts with a warning addressed to wards and to children about their stepmothers and mothers:

> Why, now it is lawful to murder a stepson.
> I'm warning orphans as well: if you own a sizeable fortune,
> watch out for your lives; don't trust anything served at table.
> Those blackening cakes are highly spiced with a mother's poison.
> Let somebody else be the first to munch what she who bore you
>   offers you;
> get your nervous tutor to test the drinks.
>
> (*Sat.* 6.628–33)

This corresponds to topic no. 11 in Cicero:

> 11. Demonstration that the crime was committed by a person who least of all should have committed it and who might have been expected to prevent it happening.

The vivid picture created by the details of 631–3 is typical of the graphic descriptions which abound in Juvenal and which put into practice Cicero's advice to the orator:

> 10. Enumeration of the attendant circumstances to make the crime as vivid as possible.

The speaker proceeds to appeal to the Roman state:

> You think this is fiction? That my satire has donned theatrical boots,
> that going beyond the bounds and law of earlier writers
> I am raving in Sophocles' gaping style a lofty song
> of things unknown to Rutulian hills and Latin skies?
> (634–7)

This connects with Cicero's first piece of advice to the orator, that indignation may be aroused by:

> 1. Consideration of the great concern shown by the relevant authority – the gods, ancestors, rulers, states, Senate, authors of laws – about the matter under discussion.

The next lines make it clear that the woman's murder of her children was premeditated:

> Would it were all a dream. But Pontia cries 'It was me!
> I confess; I got some aconite and administered it to my children.
> The murder was detected and is known to all; but I am the culprit!'
> Two, do you say, at a single meal, you venomous viper,
> two at a sitting? 'Yes, and seven, had there been seven!'
> (638–42)

This exactly puts into practice item 6 on Cicero's list:

> 6. Indication that the act was premeditated.

By calling her a 'venomous viper' (641) the speaker places the murderess on a bestial level, fulfilling another element of Cicero's advice:

> 8. Demonstration that the deed is unique and unknown even among savages, barbarians and wild beasts, typically acts of cruelty committed against parents or children or acts of injustice towards people who cannot defend themselves.

The remainder of the poem introduces a comparison between the horrific heroines of Greek tragedy and modern women which is designed to show how much worse modern women are:

> Let us believe what tragedy says concerning Procne
> and the cruel woman of Colchis; I won't dispute it. They too
> dared to commit some monstrous crimes in their generation –
> but not for the sake of cash. Extreme atrocities tend
> to cause less shock when fury incites the female to outrage,
> and when, with their hearts inflamed by madness, they are carried down
> like boulders wrenched from a mountain ridge as the ground collapses
> and the vertical face falls in from beneath the hanging cliff-top.
> I cannot abide the woman who assesses the profit, and coolly
> commits a hideous crime. They watch Alcestis enduring
> death for her man, but if they were offered a similar choice
> they would gladly let their husband die to preserve a lapdog.
> Every morning you meet Eriphyles in dozens, and also
> daughters of Danaus; every street has a Clytemnestra.
> Whereas, however, Tyndareus' daughter wielded an oafish
> and awkward two-headed axe which needed both her hands,
> now the job is done with the tiny lung of a toad –
> though it may need steel if your son of Atreus is now immune,
> as the thrice-defeated monarch was, through Pontic drugs.
>
> (643–61)

This is an excellent case of Cicero's ninth recommendation:

> 9. Comparison of the deed with other crimes to enhance the horror.

And, finally, it is clear that the speaker expects his audience's sympathy throughout, just as the orator trying to simulate and provoke indignation does, according to Cicero:

> 14. Request to the audience to identify with the speaker.

The convergence of rhetorical theory and practice in this passage – and throughout Juvenal's satires – would have been appreciated by his audience who had received the same grounding as the poet. When De Decker entitled his important monograph of 1913 *Juvenalis declamans*, he drew attention to a crucial aspect of Juvenal's approach to satire. This was augmented by Scott's 1927 study of the grand style in Juvenal: anger, after all, is a big emotion and needs an expansive form of expression.

Both scholars understood well the close relationship between Roman poetry and the rhetorical education of the Roman élite. (Modern reservations surrounding the word 'rhetoric' are completely inappropriate in a Roman context. In our society it is possible to say of a politician's speech, 'it's just rhetoric', as a way of dismissing that speech without engaging with it, probably because we feel distanced from the entire process of politics. The élite Romans with whom we are concerned here, by contrast, were constantly engaged in politics.) Juvenal, like his élite audience, was trained to be a showman: to create whatever *persona* is required for the context and to make it a convincing creation. And this does not apply to Juvenal alone. The same applies to whatever *persona* is selected: the mask of anger, the mask of mockery or the mask of irony. In every case, the poems of Roman satire are best understood as performances and as miniature dramas.

THE BODILY GROTESQUE IN ROMAN SATIRE: IMAGES OF STERILITY[1]

Paul Allen Miller

> The joyful, open, festive laugh. The closed, purely negative satirical laugh. This is not a laughing laugh. The Gogolian laugh is joyful.[2]

It is virtually impossible today to write about the body, the grotesque, or the comic without encountering the work of Mikhail Bakhtin. Since the publication of *Rabelais and His World*, Bakhtin's concepts of "carnival" and "grotesque realism" have become major players in all such discussions.[3] One of the unfortunate side effects of this phenomenon has been that more often than not the historical and generic specificity of Bakhtin's argument has been lost in the rush to hail the triumph of the lower bodily stratum, the celebration of fertility, and the subversion of authority wherever images of the grotesque are to be seen.[4] This cavalier appropriation of his concept of carnival has, in turn, made it easy to discredit Bakhtin's analyses by simply pointing out examples of the grotesque to which carnival exuberance seems foreign, if not antithetical.[5] One such case is Roman satire.[6] This paper, however, will demonstrate the essential correctness of the Bakhtinian position in regard to Latin satire by returning from the vague, widely disseminated image of carnival gaiety that has been attributed to Bakhtin to the specificity of his text in which he argues that satire, though often rich in grotesque imagery, is essentially bereft of the idea of its regenerative force. Consequently, the festive laughter of carnival and the negative laughter of satire are always, as in our epigraph, strictly distinguished.

More importantly, Bakhtin, in the chapter entitled "Rabelais in the History of Laughter" makes a sharp distinction between satire and the carnivalesque, and between the classical body and the grotesque. For him, satire, far from representing the revivifying gaiety of carnival festivity, exemplifies a one-sided negativity whose predominant thematic structure is one of stasis rather than growth.[7] Any form of grotesque degradation that does not include a strong restorative element within it represents not the fulfilment of carnival but its loss. Writing about the grotesque ritual of crowning the king of fools and the consequent uncrowning of normative authority that he saw at the heart of carnival gaiety, Bakhtin notes:

> This ritual determined a special decrowning type of structure for artistic images and whole works, one in which the decrowning was essentially ambivalent and two-leveled. If carnivalistic ambivalence should happen to be extinguished in these images of decrowning, they degenerated into a purely negative exposé of a moral or socio-political sort, they became single-leveled, lost their artistic character, and were transformed into naked journalism.[8]

This genre of the "purely negative exposé" represents for Bakhtin the world of satire. And while we may find the artistic evaluation of such works as "naked journalism"[9] less than satisfying, this statement clearly demonstrates the impossibility of simply assimilating Bakhtin's concept of satire to the carnivalesque. The presence of the grotesque is simply not a sufficient ground on which to determine that a given work belongs to the tradition of carnival.

In addition, the classical body, i.e., the ideal body of high classical sculpture and art, for Bakhtin is one which is sealed and finished. It does not leak. The grotesque body, however, is one whose orifices are open to the world. It spills over well-defined bounds. It is budding and feculent.[10] If Bakhtin's basic distinction between carnival and satire is accurate, then, we would not expect the grotesque bodies of Roman satire to produce images of carnival fecundity. Instead they would be negative creations—icons of sterility, degradation, and ultimately death.

This paper will argue that such a characterization of Roman satire is essentially correct and will examine six representative passages in this light, two from each of the major surviving Roman satirists: Juvenal 9.43–46, where the bisexual gigolo[11] Naevolus negatively compares servicing his master's cinaedic desires to the labor of a common slave ploughing his master's field; Juvenal 6.116–35, in which the empress Messalina is shown moonlighting at a whorehouse; Persius 1.15–25, where bad (i.e., effeminized) poetry is represented as invading bodies whose orifices are open and liquid, penetrating the loins, tickling the innards, and feeding the ears; Persius 4.33–41, in which Alcibiades depilating his genitals is compared to a farmer weeding his field; Horace's wet dream on the journey to Brundisium, *Satires* 1.5.82–85, a passage in which the poet's comic, frustrated sexuality is implicitly juxtaposed with the serious political work of Maecenas, Antony, and Augustus; and Horace 2.8.42–56 in which the presentation of the pregnant lamprey at the climax of the *Cena Nasidieni* leads to the collapse of a dust-filled canopy hanging over the table. In each of these cases, the bodies in question appear as open, leaking vessels, and in each of these cases images of farming, food, or banqueting appear in close proximity, and in each case sexuality is present. Yet this intermixing of grotesque bodies, food, and sex does not lead to increase or growth, but rather to sterility, decline, and/or fruitless frustration.[12]

The truth of this understanding can perhaps best be seen by directly comparing the first scene from Juvenal to one in Rabelais, the birth of Gargantua. The birth of Gargantua is remarkable on a number of levels. The setting is a feast at Mardi Gras during which Gargantua's mother consumes "sixteen quarters, two bushels, and six pecks" of poorly-washed tripe, as a result of which she has a monstrous attack of diarrhea that causes her to go into labor. "O belle matiere fecale que doivoit boursoufler en elle" [Oh what fine fecal matter to swell up inside her!].[13] The miraculous birth itself occurs as a result of a softening of the right intestine and the astringent which was applied as a remedy:

> Dont une horde vieigle de la compaignie, laquelle avoit la reputation d'estre grande medicine . . . luy fesit un restrinctif si horrible que tous ses larrys tant feurent oppilez et reserrez que à grande pene, avecques les dentz, vous les eussiez eslargiz, qui est chose bien horrible à penser . . .
>
> At this point a dirty old hag of the company who had the reputation of being a good she-doctor . . . made her an astringent so horrible that all her sphincter muscles were stopped and constricted. Indeed you could hardly have relaxed them with your teeth which is a most horrible thought . . .[14]

The medicine has a similarly constricting effect on Gargamelle's womb, causing the young giant to be born from his mother's ear (in a parody of Mary's conception of Jesus through hearing the word of the Holy Spirit). This scene's saturation with images of feasting, excrement, death, and new life is in many ways typical of Bakhtin's understanding of grotesque realism. In it, the womb and the bowels, sexuality and shit, birth and death are here tied up into one "grotesque knot" of carnivalesque vitality.[15]

Juvenal's view of the grotesque is very different. It is not fertile and revivifying, but sterile. The passage from *Satire* 9 at which I want to look has many of the same elements found in the birth of Gargantua. It contains images of eating, excrement, and sexuality in a context rich with metaphors of the earth and agriculture (9.43–46):

> an facile et pronum est agere intra viscera penem
> legitimum atque illic hesternae occurrere cenae?
> seruus erit minus ille miser qui foderit agrum quam dominum.[16]
>
> Do you think it's nice and easy to thrust a proper-sized penis
> into a person's guts, encountering yesterday's dinner?

> The slave who ploughs a field has a lighter task than the one who ploughs its owner.[17]

Although we have in this scene the same essential set of elements as in the birth of Gargantua, the accent placed on them is very different.[18] Everything here leads to nothing. Food does not produce new life, only excrement that, far from representing a potential source of renewed fertility, functions only as an obstacle to a sexual activity that brings neither pleasure nor fruit to the speaker. Thus Ferguson observes that the "agricultural metaphor" of ploughing "is common of sex . . . but in agriculture . . . the plough looks forward to harvest."[19] In this scene, however, there is nothing positive, or even profitable, about the activity since Naevolus' rhetorical question occurs in the course of a conversation about his difficulty in receiving proper remuneration for the services he renders. This sexual act is sterile not only in the literal sense, because it cannot produce offspring, but also metaphorically because it is without rewards, either monetary or emotional. Time in this poem is not pregnant with the future but held static in the sterility of the present.[20] The grotesque in Juvenal's satire, as Winkler notes, does not revitalize but represents "ambivalence, alienation, the crossing of established boundaries and aggression,"[21] all of which are treated as negative values.

Roman satire, thus, like Roman sexual norms generally, does not exalt the fluid and the open, but the solid, the closed, the literally impenetrable. In the Roman world, as Catharine Edwards argues:

> Virtue is noble, dry and hard . . . found in public places, pursuing the public good, winning public renown. Pleasure, on the other hand, is wet, soft (*mollis*, *enervis*) and characteristic of slaves . . . The ultimate fate of pleasure is not fame, but disgrace and death . . . virtue is presented as masculine, pleasure as feminine.[22]

Unsurprisingly, Roman satire, like Roman society in general, also exalts the hard, the dry, and the masculine and degrades the soft, the liquid, and the feminine.[23] It is a phallic form that specifically eschews the relativizing and revitalizing dialectic of the carnivalesque in which top and bottom, life and death, inside and outside constantly metamorphose into one another.

True to this concept of the genre, *Satire* 6 features a misogynistic narrator who directs his ire against women and marriage. In the process, there are numerous descriptions of feminine behavior and sexuality, representing them as simultaneously grotesque and sterile. The open sexual body of the woman here does not give birth to new life as in the case of Gargantua's mother but to a kind of wasting lust that saps the generative powers of both the family and the state. A prime example can be found in the description of the empress Messalina slipping out to a whorehouse as Claudius slept (6.120–32):[24]

sed nigrum flavo crinem abscondente galero
intravit calidum veteri centone lupanar
et cellam vacuam atque suam; tunc nuda papillis
prostitit auratis titulum mentita Lyciscae
ostenditque tuum, generose Britannice, ventrem.
excepit blanda intrantis atque aera poposcit.
[continueque iacens cunctorum absorbuit ictus.][25]
mox lenone suas iam demittente puellas
tristis abit, et quod potuit tamen ultima cellam
clausit, adhuc ardens rigidae tentigine volvae,
et lassata viris necdum satiata recessit,
obscurisque genis turpis fumoque lucernae
foeda lupanaris tulit ad pulvinar odorem.

But with her black hair hidden beneath a blonde wig,
she entered the steamy bordello with its old quilt
and took up her empty cell. Then naked with gilded nipples
she hawked her wares beneath the lying name plate, "Coyote,"
and displayed the belly that was your home, noble Britannicus.
She blithely received everyone, demanding cash from all comers.
(Lying down, one after another, she absorbed the thrusts of all.)
Then, when the pimp sent his girls home, she left sadly,
though she stayed as long as she could and was the last
to close her cell, still afire with the lust of her erect clitoris,
and exhausted from, but not yet sated with, men, she went home,
and filthy, her cheeks black from the smoke of the shameless lamp,
she bore the odor of the bordello to the imperial pillow.[26]

No doubt there is grotesque degradation in this scene. The sexualized, lower bodily stratum is featured prominently, and the heights of Roman society are brought low by their contact with it.[27] But degradation is only half the story of carnival. The other half is revitalization.[28] The fact that Messalina's body had produced new life is explicitly acknowledged in the apostrophe to Britannicus. Yet that moment seems long past. Indeed, Britannicus is only addressed because his position as heir to the throne—which is underlined with *generose*—is being undermined by his mother's behavior, behavior that ultimately leads to (or at least provides the rationalization for) Messalina's execution, Claudius' marriage to Agrippina, the adoption of Nero, and the latter being named Claudius' heir. As a result of these events, Britannicus is removed from the line of succession and, thus, his death at the hands of his stepbrother is ensured, since Nero could hardly afford to have a pretender to the throne alive in the imperial palace (Dio 61.34–35; Tacitus, *Annales* 11.12, 26, 29–32, 34–38; 12.1–3, 8–9; 13.14–17; Suetonius, *Divus Claudius* 36–39; *Nero* 33.2–3). Sexuality in this satire doesn't lead to new life but death.

Nor does the erotic lead to happiness or pleasure in *Satire* 6. As with the case of Naevolus, sexuality is reduced to its least idealized, most materialized manifestations, providing neither joy (Messalina is exhausted but not satisfied) nor gain. The open sexual body is reduced to a mechanism, a sort of shock absorber that receives the thrusts of phallic sexuality in a repetition compulsion that has neither erotic nor reproductive rhyme nor reason. It is reductively anatomized in the image of the *rigida volva*, which is pictured as a burning (*ardens*), autonomous entity that exists beyond the structures of human control and certainly outside of any festive community. Indeed, it has a mind of its own, representing a species of erotic hunger that knows no satisfaction. Its voracity is limited neither by Messalina's extraordinary efforts to feed it nor by the social laws that forbid it. By the same token, Messalina is here pictured as having an unsatisfiable erection (a kind of female satyriasis) and is therefore implicitly gendered as male. As such her sexual relations, on the ideological level, become every bit as homoerotic, and hence unregenerative, as those between Naevolus and his master in *Satire* 9. Finally, in the last line *lupanar*'s (whorehouse) assonance with *pulvinar* (divine or imperial pillow) identifies the imperial bed with that of the bordello. Again we have degradation without redemption. For this identification signifies neither the sexual regeneration of the imperial household nor a positive release of libidinal energy.

The same terms, seen in the two scenes from Juvenal, are found again in the same essential relation in Persius: food that does not revivify; sex that does not satisfy; and grotesque degradation that does not edify. Our first example comes from Persius 1. In it, we move from the literal buggering of Naevolus to figurative sodomy. The penetrating party here is not a degraded gigolo, but a degraded and effeminized poetry that lacks the rough solidity that Persius and Roman ideology prizes. This kind of poetry, as Maria Wyke has recently pointed out with special reference to this passage, is most traditionally embodied within the Roman universe of genres by the soft verse of elegy, which stands in opposition to the phallic and hypermasculine form of satire.[29] By the same token, the penetrated party is not the literal empress, but Rome's cultural elite attending a recitation in the capital. The imagistic context of this poetic pedication is important. It is filled with liquidity, trembling, and food (1.15–25):[30]

scilicet haec populo pexusque togaque recenti
et natalicia tandem cum sardonyche albus
sede leges celsa, liquido cum plasmate guttur
mobile conlueris, patranti fractus ocello.
tunc neque more probo videas nec voce serena
ingentis trepidare Titos, cum carmina lumbum
intrant et tremulo scalpuntur ubi intima versu.
tun, vetule, auriculis alienis colligis escas,

> articulis quibus et dicas cute perditus "ohe"?
> "quo didicisse, nisi hoc fermentum et quae semel intus
> innata est rupto iecore exierit caprificus?"

> Truly you will read these things from a lofty chair to the public, your hair slicked back, wearing your new toga, and pale then with your birthday sardonyx, when you will have lubricated your quavering gullet with a fluid modulation, effeminate[31] with your lusting eye. Then you may see huge Tituses all aquiver in a manner unseemly and their voices unsettled, while poems penetrate their loins, and their secret parts are tickled by feathery verse. You old reprobate, do you gather delicacies for others' ears that would cause you, all eaten up with gout and dropsy, to cry, "Stop, that's enough"? "But why have such learning, if this ferment and this wild fig tree, when it has grown inside, might not burst forth from my ruptured liver"?

The shifting images that characterize this scene offer a fascinating tour of the Roman satirical grotesque in all its sexual and alimentary dimensions. We begin with the dandified poet whose pallor is a sign of excessive sexual passion.[32] The emphasis on the throat, its moisture and rippling quality, put the reader in mind of the reciter's affected speech and prepare the audience for the combined images of perversion and *gourmandise* yet to come.[33] The throat is not only the site of poetic articulation and potential gluttony but also of the passive sexuality implicit in the poet's demeanor. This reading is strengthened by the description of the poet as both effeminate and possessed of a lusting, indeed "orgasmic" eye, whose quivering adds yet another level of fluidity that threatens to undermine the dry, solid virtues of the masculinist, Roman norm.[34] The poetry itself becomes the instrument by which the audience is sodomized, unmanning even the most burly of old-time Romans, as these huge Tituses are pictured as being metonymically penetrated by the poet's throat (i.e., his quavering organ of poetic articulation). This creates a bizarre image of oral/genital, or more probably oral/anal, contact in which both parties are passive—since the action moves from one open orifice to the other—a kind of impossible sexual monstrosity in Roman ideology's normative zero-sum game.[35] This last image in turn is metamorphosed into an evocation of poetry as a kind of food for the ears in which the image of penetration is transformed into one of passive consumption, but with the emphasis once again on the use of an inappropriate orifice.[36] This is not the revivifying food of the Rabelaisian feast, nor does it recall the birth of Gargantua through Gargamelle's ear. These poetic *mignardises* are the refined delicacies of decay. They are associated with dropsy and gout, the diseases of decadence and impotence, rather than with fuel for new life.[37] Thus the grotesque marriage of food and sexuality in Persius' satire brings forth, not a new generation of laughing giants, but sterility, decline, and ultimately death. It is not so much a feast for the ears as a plague. The final image of fermentation and sterility that we see in the wild fig, which by definition bears no fruit (Pliny *NH* 15.79, Juvenal 10.45),[38] bursting forth from the frustrated poet's guts sums up the sterile perversity of the poetic exercise. At the same time, the phallic thrust of the fig tree[39] from the poet's liver, the seat of lust,[40] implies a destructive and empty eroticism more reminiscent of Messalina's moonlight excursions than Gargamelle's tripe-induced labor.

This intermingling of sexual and gastronomic imagery stands out even more sharply in our second passage, taken from the conclusion of Persius 4. Here the young Alcibiades, whose political aspirations have at the beginning of this satire been deflated by Socrates' biting irony, is pictured sunning himself naked when a stranger, in language grotesque and obscene, suddenly compares the young man's efforts at depilation to those of a man unsuccessfully weeding his garden (4.33–41):[41]

> at si unctus cesses et figas in cute solem,
> est prope te ignotus cubito qui tangat et acre
> despuat: "hi mores! penemque arcanaque lumbi
> runcantem populo marcentis pandere vulvas.
> tum, cum maxillis balanatum gausape pectas,
> inguinibus quare detonsus gurgulio extat?
> quinque palaestritae licet haec plantaria vellant
> elixasque nates labefactent forcipe adunca,
> non tamen ista filix ullo mansuescit aratro."

> But if all oiled up you should be relaxing and fixing the rays of the sun in your skin, there is a stranger nearby who touches you with his elbow and bitterly spits out, "What morals! To show the people both how you weed round your cock and the hidden part of your groin, your shriveled hollows.[42] But when you comb the balsamed wool on your chops, why does a shaven little whistle stand out from your groin. Though five official oilers and depilators should pluck those seedlings and shake your boiled buttocks with hooked tweezers, nonetheless that hedge would not be tamed by any plow."

The passage starts on a tone of effeminate luxury as the well-oiled Alcibiades is pictured sunning himself in the nude. The use of the verb *figo* for the rays of the sun, however, introduces a sharper tone, giving us a first, veiled image of penetration. The exclamation *Hi mores* in 35 reminds the reader of Cicero's famous, *O tempora, o mores!* at the beginning of the first Catilinarian,[43] a reminiscence whose resonance is reinforced by Alcibiades' political ambitions, discussed at the satire's beginning. With the very next word, *penem*, the satirical process of grotesque degradation begins, illustrating for the reader not only how far this work is from a discussion of affairs of state, but also, to the

Stoic audience for whom Persius was consciously writing, how far a satire of Alcibiades in the age of Nero was removed from the moral condemnation of Catiline in the time of Cicero. The irony is only heightened by a comparison of the inconsequential nature of the former to the genuine drama of the latter. The stakes for the republic in Persius' day could not have been lower. The battle has already been lost. The young, dissolute aristocrat is no longer threatening to overturn the republic, but has become emperor in the person of Nero.

This implicit contrast between present decadence and past vigor is continued throughout the passage by a series of allusions to the poetry of Cicero's contemporary, Catullus (cf. *c.* 49). Thus in the very next line the interlocutor accuses Alcibiades of displaying his depilated private parts to the general public. The verb he chooses, *pando*, is used in almost the exact same context in Catullus 6, where the poet demands that Flavius display his *latera ecfututa*. The word *pando* is not widely used by most authors and is found nowhere else in Latin literature in an explicitly sexual context.[44] Thus Persius' usage is striking and the sentence *penemque arcana lumbi / . . . marcentis pandere vulvas* can be fruitfully read as an allusion to its lone literary predecessor, *latera ecfututa pandas*. Yet, while the contexts of the two passages are similar in their graphic sexuality and imagery, the upshot of Catullus' call for Flavius to display his debauched loins is not merely shame and degradation but also the invocation of genuine carnival renewal. Flavius is said to be enjoying a hot, if rather *déclassé*, affair, and Catullus proposes to call both him and his *febriculosum scortum* to the heavens with his verse, revealing that which Flavius had hoped would remain hidden, but immortalizing his erotic adventures at the same time. The tone is playful and teasing. It is far different in the case of Persius. The result of Alcibiades' public display of his private parts will be shame alone.

A second Catullan allusion can be seen in line 41. The plough that the interlocutor claims will not be able to tame the brush that grows round Alcibiades' anus (*non . . . ullo mansuescit <u>aratro</u>*) reminds the attentive reader of Catullus' evocation of Lesbia at the end of poem 11. Here her voracious, phallic sexuality is compared to the traditionally masculine image of the plough, and Catullus himself is portrayed as the effeminized flower that is her victim (*flos . . . tactus <u>aratro</u> est*).[45] In both Persius and Catullus the central point of the image is the inversion of expected gender relations; neither Catullus nor Alcibiades should be ploughed. But whereas the image in Catullus is pathetic, since he is portrayed as the victim of Lesbia's brutality, in Persius, Alcibiades is portrayed as merely perverse. Moreover, while Lesbia's sexuality in 11 is seen as too robust, it is not inherently different from that of Flavius' *febriculosum scortum* in poem 6, which like poem 11 forms part of the opening sequence of the Catullan *libellus*. Vigorous female sexuality, however, only had its place within the Roman imaginary among the *scorta* Flavius frequented. Thus Lesbia's sexual passion is not irredeemable per se, but inappropriate for one of her social station and for the kind of relationship Catullus assumed to exist between them. It is this knowledge of wasted potential that gives the Catullus and Lesbia story its pathos, its sense of lost joy, of love betrayed. It is why Lesbia's sexuality continues to haunt him long after he has ceased to esteem her (*c*. 72). Alcibiades on the other hand is not only inherently perverse in his pursuit of his cinaedic desires, but those desires will also remain unfulfilled. Depilate as he might, no plough will ever penetrate that bracken. He can never be either Catullus or Lesbia.

The tissue of republican literary allusions that Persius deploys here shows that on every level Alcibiades is an absurd and degraded figure. He not only lacks the stature of a statesman such as Cicero, but even of a villain like Catiline. His *déclassé* erotic adventures lack both the carnivalesque potential for redemption of Flavius and his *scortum* in Catullus 6 and the tragic irony of Lesbia's phallic voracity in poem 11. Indeed, they appear to lack the prospect of pleasure at all. These references to the literary past, therefore, create a subtle counterpoint that reinforces the univocal condemnation of the object of grotesque degradation in Persius' satires, a process continued in the agricultural metaphors that run throughout the passage. Beginning with *runcans* ["weeding"] in line 36, continuing with *plantaria* ["seedlings" or "hair"] in line 39, and finishing with *filix* ["hedge"] and *aratrum* ["plough"] in line 41, Alcibiades' groin is consistently allegorized as a field of weeds.[46] Yet this profusion of vegetative growth gives no hint of a future harvest to be enjoyed. The closest the reader comes to a feast here is the boiling (*elixus*)[47] of Alcibiades' buttocks, preparatory to the failed attempt at depilation. This too, however, like all the others, is to be a fruitless sexual endeavor.[48]

Our last pair of examples is the least grotesque, Horatian decorum knowing greater restraint than is found in either Juvenal or Persius. In the first passage, Horace, on his way to Brundisium with Maecenas, who is to attend an important meeting of the representatives of Augustus and Mark Antony, has stopped at a villa.[49] The evening's entertainment features two lower-class yokels whose comic buffoonery is laughed more at than with. The next day Horace and company continue their journey to Apulia where they take shelter from the burning Scirocco at a tavern whose promise of hospitality proves illusory. Not only does the kitchen smoke and the chimney catch fire, but that evening the poet is stood up by a girl who had promised to come to his bed. As a consequence of his frustration, he has a wet dream and soils himself. The passage stands out as the sole description of a nocturnal emission in ancient literature, outside of a technical philosophical or medical context.[50] The scene features the open, liquid body, but directs the force of that image back on the satirist himself:

> hic ego mendacem stultissimus usque puellam
> ad mediam noctem exspecto: somnus tamen aufert
> intentum Veneri; tum immundo somnia visu
> nocturnam vestem maculant ventremque supinum

> Here in bed I wait like an idiot till midnight for that tease of a girl: sleep however carries me off, still intent on sex; then dreams stain my nightshirt and my up-turned belly with obscene fantasies.
>
> (1.5.82–85)

This passage can be seen as an example of that gentle, if somewhat grotesque, self-mockery that is the trademark of Horatian satire. Yet, though Horace's self-parody makes his work more ironic and consequently less one-sided and less negative than that of his successors, his use of the grotesque is very similar. In Bakhtinian terms, one might say that while Horatian satire is more dialogic than that of Juvenal and Persius,[51] since it more explicitly dramatizes the undermining of the speaker's authority, it is no more carnivalesque. For not only is the conjunction of food and sexuality, implied by the metonymic link between the one night's feasting and the next night's wet dream and bespattered belly, every bit as sterile as that seen in Juvenal and Persius, it is also less subversive than that of his successors. Horace's little comedy is always kept at a safe distance from the authoritative discourse represented by Maecenas and Augustus.[52] Indeed, Horace's journey ends at Brundisium but the actual treaty was reached at Tarentum, outside his presence. Horace thus keeps a strict *cordon sanitaire* between the eruptions of his body and of the satiric grotesque and the centers of power and patronage to which he was then trying to gain access.[53] Such a strategy of containment necessarily limits the power of the grotesque in Horatian satire. For Bakhtin, however, carnivalesque renewal requires the subversion of the existing hierarchies of power. The double movement of uncrowning and recrowning must both be given their full scope for the laughter of the carnival to be truly present. By marginalizing his own misadventures, while subtly juxtaposing the small joys of private life with the unnamed anxieties of the public man, Horace carefully leaves the structures of power and their ruling ideology firmly in place.[54] The liquidity and crossing of borders that the grotesque implies is not only fruitless in this case but also strictly contained.

Our final passage comes appropriately enough from a failed feast, the *Cena Nasidieni* of *Satires* 2.8. As the concluding satire of the second volume it offers a final commentary on the theme of the proper feast that runs throughout the book. The central problem of the text as a whole is how to avoid excess and, hence, that crossing of boundaries that constitutes the grotesque.[55] Thus in 2.2, a peasant that Horace recalls from his boyhood, Ofellus, extols the virtues of a simple diet. In 2.4, Catius, with a fervor normally reserved for the arcane secrets of the mysteries or the hidden truths of philosophy, recalls the extravagant recipes of an unnamed gourmet, whom Deena Berg has identified as Nasidienus.[56] The implicit contrast between the gourmets, Catius/ Nasidienus, and the simple farmer, Ofellus, is then rendered explicit by 2.6's fable of the City Mouse and the Country Mouse, a tale told in the context of Horace's own modest contentment as he spends a night of quiet conviviality with friends at his Sabine farm.[57] This monologic installation of his own practice as the model to be imitated is, however, overturned in 2.7 when the slave Davus notes Horace's inability to follow his own counsels of moderation whenever a dinner invitation from Maecenas arrives. This uncrowning of Horace leads us to 2.8 in which the satirist asks the comic poet Fundanius to recount the tale of a dinner party the latter attended with Maecenas. Poem 2.8, thus, offers a set of final reflections on the theme of proper conviviality without imposing a sense of monological closure, since Horace himself remains tangential to the narrative framed by Fundanius' comedy.[58]

In that comedy, Nasidienus is seen as a pretentious host who aspires to being part of Maecenas' circle but whose very eagerness condemns him as irredeemably vulgar. Yet whereas the braggart host's exclusion is definitively signaled when his guests abruptly depart, leaving the meat course untasted, Horace in a typically dialogic and distancing gesture does not directly participate in that condemnation.[59] The climax of this comic meal that leads to the guests' departure is a dish of pregnant lamprey, surrounded by shrimp "swimming" in a peppery sauce, all presented in the *trompe l'oeil* fashion dear to Roman gourmets (2.8.42–44):[60]

> adfertur squillas inter murena natantis
> in patina porrecta. sub hoc erus: "haec gravida" inquit
> "capta est, deterior post partum carne futura."
>
> Then a lamprey is brought in, stretched out on a platter between swimming shrimp. At this the master of revels said, "this fish was caught pregnant; the flesh would be of poorer quality after having given birth."

The feast, of course, is the site of the carnivalesque par excellence. Gargamelle gives birth during the celebration of Mardi Gras. But the *Cena Nasidieni* is a feast gone awry. Whatever mirth arises in it is directed against the host rather than toward a celebration of conviviality, the open body, and excess that leads to carnival's cycle of degradation and renewal. The grotesque at this feast is not in the service of renewed vitality, but rather reminds the reader that transgression leads to failure and humiliation. Where Bakhtin notes that the pregnant body is one of the privileged sites of grotesque realism, representing as it does the erasure of the boundaries between bodies and the consequent potential generation of new life,[61] the pregnant lamprey is sterile and perverse.[62] It will never give birth but has been frozen in this state for the purposes of consumption. The grotesquerie is then compounded by it being presented as if it were alive with shrimp swimming about. As Arrowsmith famously remarked of Petronius' Trimalchio, Nasidienus "does not know what might be called the mortal modalities . . . By eating he proposes to forget death, to 'seize the day' and to live; he passionately desires life, but with every mouthful he takes, he tastes death."[63] The conjunction of the feast and sexuality in this scene gives rise not to regeneration but to a kind of death-in-life, symbolically evoked by the *trompe l'oeil* presentation of the pregnant lamprey.

The grotesque degradation implicit in this scene, however, goes well beyond the perverse image of pregnancy aborted by a feast. Indeed the question arises, with what is the lamprey pregnant? The answer to Horace's audience might well be less obvious than it seems to us. For, as a number of Horace's Renaissance commentators note, as well as more recently Lejay, lampreys were widely believed in the ancient world to mate with vipers. Thus Nasidienus' *pièce de résistance* was not simply grotesque but, to a Roman audience, potentially dangerous.[64] Moreover, as Prudentius notes (*Hamartigenia* 581–607), the female viper was thought to conceive through a bizarre form of oral intercourse during which the head of the male was bitten off. Her offspring, in turn, were born by gnawing their way through the mother's entrails, thus killing her. The lamprey, therefore, whose womb is filled with baby vipers, not only fuses the images of fertility and sterility, but its consumption demands that fusion for it can only be eaten while still pregnant, since, were it to carry its venomous brood to term, it would be consumed by its offspring and its flesh would be inedible. This fusion of birth and death in the image of the pregnant lamprey, which serves as the emblem of the overzealous gourmet's violation of boundaries, marks the turning point in the satire's narrative and signals the beginning of the denouement that will leave its host abandoned and the final course untasted. Immediately after the lamprey is brought in, the master of ceremonies engages in a long and pompous disquisition on the sauce in which it is swimming. At this moment, the tapestry overhanging the diners collapses, covering the tables and guests with "as much dust as the north wind blows from the Campanian fields" (2.8.56). Thus, as Kirk Freudenburg notes, "In the annihilation of the fish course, death injects itself into Nasidienus's dinner party in its most unthreatening, comic form."[65] But, as we have seen, death in a less comic form was implicit in the image of the pregnant lamprey all along, and in point of fact, the party never recovers from this disaster. For Nasidienus and his aspirations of admission to Maecenas' charmed circle, it is the beginning of the end.

As in our first example from Juvenal, this last passage from Horace has all the same elements as those found in the birth of Gargantua, only, as was the case with Juvenal, the accent is different. Pregnancy, feasting, agriculture, and death all appear. Yet the pregnancy does not produce joyful, new life, but is abortive and signifies a perverse commingling of species that conjures death. The feast in the *Cena Nasidieni* is not the site of communal celebration and new life, but is left uneaten, with its host ridiculed and abandoned. The fields are not fertile. They merely blow dust. Death is not celebrated as part of the cycle of existence but functions merely as a sterile end. What separates this passage from those of Juvenal and Persius is the satirist's bemused distance from the invective moment. For, as we have noted, in poem 2.7, the poet has conceded the compromised nature of his own position in the book's ongoing debate on the nature of the proper feast. Thus in 2.8, while the grotesque degradation that appears in Fundanius' account of the *Cena Nasidieni* may be absolute, the poet's relation to that degradation is left ambiguous. In Horace's last satires, it seems, the grotesque is deployed within a more thoroughly dialogized frame than is found in either of the other satirists or in his own earlier work, but the signification of the grotesque within that framework is unchanged.

In sum, these six passages (and more could be added) indicate that Roman satire, through its deployment of the grotesque, privileges by negation the closed, the solid, and the finished over the open, the fluid, and the boundless. As such, it is located firmly within the mainstream of traditional Roman morality which, as defined by Catharine Edwards, privileges the dry, the hard, and the masculine over the fluid, the soft, and the feminine.[66] This understanding of satire allows one final point to be made. If the preceding analysis is correct, Roman satire can be described in psychoanalytic terms as a discourse of the phallus that defines itself in opposition to those very features of the grotesque that make its humor work, features that it ultimately labels as, if not feminine, then at least effeminized. It rejects that model of unbounded desire, of wetness, transgression, and leakage, that Anne Carson has demonstrated was attributed to women in the ancient world.[67] This is substantially the same model that Irigaray has embraced under the rubric of "fluid mechanics" as an antidote to the oppressive certainties of a masculinist logic that privileges the bounded entity over the open and grotesque, as Micaela Janan has recently made clear.[68] Satire in this view is a vehicle for that same phallic and aggressive ideology first described by Amy Richlin in *The Garden of Priapus*.[69] Its humor does not seek to open up the world to change and the other, as does the Rabelaisian grotesque, but to affirm the rigidities of present and past by always picturing the violation of boundaries as leading to death and sterility—and that's no carnival.

Yet satire is also obsessed with the very images of food, sexuality, and the grotesque that are associated with that same potential for regeneration that the satirical vision appears to lack. How are we to understand this continued presence of the rejected other? On the one hand, the satirist's pose as the scold of decadence and the maintainer of boundaries requires that such a partition between same and other, masculine and feminine, and good and evil be strictly enforced. This is the essence of the ideology of the bounded form. On the other, the binary logic of the partition itself creates a kind of structural desire for the excluded, without which the boundary, and hence the satirist, could not exist. The logic of exclusion is thus always, ultimately, self-undermining, and it is through the unsustainability of the satirical stance, through the very vitality of the vile bodies it denigrates, that carnival's hope (however muted) of resurrection reasserts itself as the unacknowledged, and indeed forbidden, ground of the satirical grotesque.

Notes

1 My thanks to Susanna Braund, Martha Malamud, and *Arethusa*'s anonymous referees for their many helpful suggestions. A special debt of gratitude is owed to Barbara Gold who first saw these ideas many years ago in the ill-formed and overfed work of an equally grotesque M.A. student. All remaining deformities are, of course, stubbornly my own.

2 Bakhtin 1986.135. I want to thank Susan I. Stein for bringing this passage to my attention.

3 For a survey of recent work on the grotesque, see Robertson 1996.1–14 and 119–24.

4 On this phenomenon and its pernicious effects, see Emerson 1993.128–32; Rubino 1993.141–43; Eagleton 1989; Stallybrass and White 1986.13–15, 30–35, 72–75; and Jacobs 1991.74, 80. On the attempt to identify carnival and the grotesque, and then generalize from Bakhtin's conclusions to genres and periods beyond those which he specifies, see Platter 1993 and forthcoming. For an example of this simple identification of the grotesque with the carnivalesque, see Andreas 1984. 62–66.

5 Carnival has become the focus of controversy within Bakhtin scholarship. The debate, more often than not, has political overtones. In general, those scholars who place the most emphasis on carnival represent leftist or neo-Marxist readings of Bakhtin, while those involved in the current drive to devalue carnival's place within the Bakhtin canon are avowedly conservative critics. Only by treating the concept with historical and generic precision will it be possible to move the debate beyond a rather sterile ideological interchange. See Morson and Emerson 1990. 3–4, 11, 67, 77, 92–96, 102, 104, 106–19, 124–25, 161–62, 433–52, 479 nn. 6–7; Emerson 1994; Shepherd 1993.xvi–xxi; Gardiner 1992.2–6, 9–22, 107, 138, 197 nn. 3–4 and 8, 215–16 n. 11; Holquist 1990.8, 34–35, 157–58; Frow 1986.64–68, 97–99, 133–39, 158–59; Todorov 1984.11. Stallybrass and White record Tony Bennet's claim that "Bakhtin's study of Rabelais should hold an exemplary place in materialist cultural criticism" (1986.7). See also the exchange of letters between Hirschkop and Shepherd on the one hand and Morson on the other in *PMLA* 1994.116–18. For a general discussion of the multiple readings of Bakhtin currently in circulation, see Miller and Platter 1993a.117–20.

6 See Gowers 1993.30–31 on Bakhtin's view of the grotesque as being "too rosy" to account fully for its use in Roman satire; a similar critique is found in Richlin 1983.70–72. For an analagous view from the perspective of Greek literature, see Rössler 1986.

7 Bakhtin 1968.28–29, 37–39, 81, 114, 211; Gardiner 1992.47; 207 n. 20. This is a distinction that eludes Byrd in his otherwise excellent article on Freudian influences on Bakhtin's theory of laughter (1987).

8 Bakhtin 1984.126.

9 It recalls the naive, mimetic vision of the genre found in the work of critics like Highet 1962.3; Duff 1936.6; Gérard 1976.iv–ix, 35–38. In Bakhtin's case, however, he is talking more about a rhetorical and generic stance rather than the actual representation of reality. Journalism, in its pretense to present "just the facts," is necessarily a monologic genre.

10 Bakhtin 1968.23–34; Rebhorn 1993; Gowers 1993.128.

11 This is not to say that Naevolus is a common prostitute. As Braund 1988.130–77 points out, he is a *cliens* with equestrian pretensions, who "chooses to make his living sexually" (p. 155).

12 Admittedly these six cases do not prove that the grotesque in Roman satire always and everywhere functions in exactly this fashion. To make that case would require a much longer article that would soon grow tedious from the necessary repetition an exhaustive study implies. It is sufficient to note that many more examples could be added to the list proffered here and that evidence for the satirical grotesque as a celebration of the powers of regeneration is far harder to come by. For a similar reading to the one offered here of more passages from Juvenal, see Miller forthcoming. On Persius, see note 47.

13 The translation of Rabelais is from Cohen 1981.48; the passage itself can be found at Rabelais 1962.38. The spelling and accentuation reflect sixteenth-century practice.

14 Cohen 1981.52; Rabelais 1962.48–49.

15 Bakhtin 1968.163. For a fuller treatment of this passage and a defense of Bakhtin's reading of Rabelais, see Miller forthcoming.

16 The texts of Juvenal and Persius are both taken from Clausen's OCT (1959).

17 Translation by Rudd 1992.

18 On the importance of "accent" in Bakhtin, see *inter alia*, Bakhtin 1981.276–77, 282, 288–94.

19 Ferguson 1979 ad loc.

20 Anderson 1960.260.

21 Winkler 1991.24.

22 Edwards 1993.174.

23 Edwards 1993.63–64, 192–94; Richlin 1984; Kennedy 1993.31–33.

24 Braund 1992a.76, 82.

25 This much debated line is printed with brackets by Clausen 1959, accepted without comment by Ferguson 1979, bracketed by Friedlaender 1962, Knoche 1950, and Rudd 1992 (who prints it only in his notes), and dropped by Green 1974 and Labriolle and Villeneuve 1967 (orig. 1921). A good summary of the arguments on both sides can be found in Courtney 1980, who notes that it could have been deleted for reasons of prudery. Courtney advances the variant reading *ac resupina* as a remedy for the problematic *continue*, which is accepted by Rudd 1992. In the absence of compelling evidence for deletion, the line should be retained. The emendation to *ac resupina* is attractive.

26 All translations are mine unless otherwise specified.

27 See Richlin 1995.205: "In Roman thought, the use of makeup seems primarily to be connected with the idea that the female body is something that needs to be fixed. This idea appears to underlie both the real use of makeup by real women . . . and the references to makeup in the works of male authors . . . Disgust with the lower parts of the female body—what Bakhtin calls the 'material lower bodily stratum'—is generalized to the whole body, dealt with palpably on the face . . ."

28 Bakhtin 1984.125–27, 164.

29 Wyke 1995.119–20, 126.

30 Morford 1984.36.

31 The translation of *fractus* as "effeminate" may not be immediately obvious. The

poem as a whole is about effeminacy and in this passage the notion of being "broken" clearly means something like "powerless" or "impotent." Quintilian, in a passage on corrupting music, uses *fractus* as a gloss on the adjective *effeminatus* (1.10.31). See the *OLD*; Conington 1874; Bramble 1974.76–77; Jenkinson's translation, 1980; and Edwards 1993.81–82 on the Elder Seneca.

32 Bramble 1974.72–75.

33 Morford 1984.36.

34 Bramble 1974.76–77; Barr 1987 ad loc.; Gowers 1993.183. On *patro*, cf. Porphyrion on Horace *Satires* 1.5.84, a passage to be discussed later.

35 Bramble 1974.78–79; Barr 1987 ad loc.

36 On 22's *auriculis* as a pun on *auri-culis*, see Bramble 1974.95.

37 Gowers 1993.182–85; Barr 1987 ad loc; Connington 1874 ad loc.; Bramble 1974. 84–85, 87.

38 Bramble 1974.93

39 "The connotations of the *caprificus* must be derived from the *membrum virile*," Bramble 1974.93, although Adams 1982.113–24 notes that the *ficus* itself generally represents the site of anal penetration. Thus a thrusting fig is an oxymoron analogous to the oral/anal penetration discussed above. The *caprificus* is of course the wild fig.

40 Bramble 1974.90–91.

41 Morford 1984.52. There is disagreement on whether the character addressed at the end of the satire is Alcibiades or not. See for example Connor 1987.58–59.

42 *Vulvas* is difficult. *OLD* lists this passage under its second definition, "the female sexual organ," as the sole example of its use for a male homosexual. The plural is likewise difficult to explain except as a poeticism inapt for the plain speaking context and metrically unnecessary. Nonetheless the theme of effeminacy is a constant throughout Persius and this image merely takes it to its logical conclusion. Likewise, the manuscript tradition is unanimous. Thus I follow Bo 1967 and Forcellini et al. 1965 in understanding for *vulva*, "per similitudinem dicitur etiam de podice viri qui muliebria patitur." See Juvenal's use of the same term in 6.129 examined above. There he employs terms normally used for describing male sexuality, *tentigo* and *rigidus*, to portray Messalina's overly aggressive sexuality, just as Persius here uses terms normally reserved for women to describe Alcibiades' effeminized sexuality. See Adams 1982.103–04. I owe the translation "hollows" to my colleague, David H. J. Larmour.

43 Cf. Martial 9.70. On the Catullan context of Martial's recollection of the first Catalinarian, see Swann 1994.18–19.

44 The word is used only twice more in Catullus, once in Horace, three times in Caesar, four times in Plautus, once in Terence, and three times in Petronius—all in neutral contexts. It is never found in Sallust, Tibullus, or Cicero's letters and *rhetorica*, but oddly enough six times in his poetry and once in the *Pro Sestio*. Persius uses it only this once. Ovid is quite fond of the word, using it twenty-three times, but thirteen are set phrases about hair and the rest are equally innocuous. Likewise it is found thirty times in Vergil and frequently in Livy, but always in strictly neutral contexts.

45 Persius' line is in fact polyphonous, echoing, as Barr 1987 ad loc. notes, Vergil *G*. 2.239 and Horace *S*. 1.3.37 as well.

46 As Richlin 1995.187–88 observes, woman's *forma*, in its *inculta* state, is also com-

pared to "sterile soil" and "toothed brambles" in the opening lines of Ovid's *Medicamina Faciei*. Persius may have had this passage in mind.

47 See Bo 1967, and Barr 1987. Gower 1994 has an excellent discussion of the themes of precocious and hence luxurious growth, failed harvest, and boiling, reduction, fermentation and rot in both Persius' satires and contemporary depictions of Nero. Her analysis demonstrates that our reading of the present passage can be extended throughout the corpus of Persius. See also Malamud 1996.39.

48 Connor 1987.61.

49 Rudd 1982.54; on Horace's decorum, see Gowers 1993.126.

50 Heuzé 1988.119.

51 This is not to say that Persius' satire necessarily presents us with a single coherent point of view. Indeed, part of the difficulty, and part of the point, of Persius' satire is to challenge the reader to (re)construct the poem's speaker and in the process to (re)examine his/her own self-construction. See Henderson 1993.

52 Gold 1987.134–35

53 Fedeli 1992.49; Braund 1992b.19.

54 On the difference between Persius and Horace, see Gowers 1994.132, "Persius' satires are a special case, since satire is writing that, in theory, cannot exist without contemporary reference. And in this area comes the oddest Neronian 'fulfilment' of all: instead of Horace's neutral compromise, which, most unsatirically, propped up the Augustan regime, we have Persius' muzzled underground bark . . ."

55 Gowers 1993.7, 121–22; O'Connor 1990.23; Berg 1996.142.

56 Berg 1996.148–49.

57 Berg 1996.147–48.

58 Caston 1997.236–42.

59 Braund 1992b.24–25; Baker 1988.226–27.

60 Gowers 1993.156–57, 172; Benedetto 1981.48; Caston 1977.244.

61 Bakhtin 1968.21–27; 1984.164.

62 O'Connor 1990.27. Gowers 1993.173 sees an allusion to legacy hunting.

63 Arrowsmith 1966.308. See also p. 309, "In the field of sexual appetite, satiety, indulgence to the point of debility, appears as impotence. As constipation stands to food, so impotence stands to sexuality; both are products of *luxuria* in a society which has forgotten its cultural modalities and which cannot recover life . . ."

64 See Lejay 1966; Lambinus 1577; Cruquius 1597; Bond 1670, citing Oppian (*Halieutica* 1.554–79), Athenaeus (7.312e, in turn citing Nicander *Theriaca* 822–24), and Pliny the Elder (*NH* 9.23).

65 Freudenburg 1993.234; Benedetto 1981.48–49.

66 Edwards 1993.175.

67 Carson 1990.133–45, 153–60.

68 Irigaray 1977; Janan 1994. On Irigaray and feminism's compatability with Bakhtin, see Herndl 1991.10–11; Schwab 1991.57–62; Nell 1995; and Nell forthcoming.

69 Richlin 1983.57–80.

Bibliography

Adams, J. N. 1982. *The Latin Sexual Vocabulary*. Baltimore.

Anderson, W. S. 1960. "Imagery in the Satires of Horace and Juvenal," *AJP* 81.225–60.

Andreas, James R. 1984. "The Rhetoric of Chaucerian Comedy: The Aristotelian Legacy," *The Comparatist* 8.56–66.

Arrowsmith, William. 1966. "Luxury and Death in the Satyricon," *Arion* 5.304–31.

Baker, Robert J. 1988. "Maecenas and Horace *Satires* 2.8," *CJ* 83.212–32.

Bakhtin, M. M. 1968. *Rabelais and His World* (trans. by Hélène Iswolsky). Cambridge, Mass.

—— 1981. "Discourse in the Novel," in *The Dialogic Imagination* (trans. by Caryl Emerson and Michael Holquist, ed. Michael Holquist), 259–422. Austin.

—— 1984. *Problems of Dostoevsky's Poetics* (ed. and trans. Caryl Emerson). Minneapolis.

—— 1986. "Notes Made in 1970–71," *Speech Genres and Other Late Essays* (trans. by Vern W. McGee, eds. Caryl Emerson and Michael Holquist), 132–58. Austin.

Barr, William. 1987. *The Satires of Persius* (trans. by Guy Lee). Liverpool.

Barta, Peter I., Paul Allen Miller, Chuck Platter, and David Shepherd (eds.) Forthcoming. *Carnivalizing Difference: Bakhtin and the Other*. Chur.

Bauer, Dale M. and S. Jaret McKinstry, (eds.) 1991. *Feminism, Bakhtin, and the Dialogic*. Albany.

Benedetto, Andrea di. 1981. "Le satire orazione II,8 e II,1: Epilogo e prologo 'luciliano' di un libro 'non luciliano'?" *Vichiana* 10.44–61.

Berg, Deena. 1996. "The Mystery Gourmet of Horace's *Satires* 2," *CJ* 91.141–52.

Bo, Dominicus. 1967. *Auli Persii Flacci Lexicon*. Hildesheim.

Bond, Johannis. 1670. *Horatius Flaccus cum commentariis selectissimis variorum & scholis integris*. Rotterdam.

Bramble, J. C. 1974. *Persius and the Programmatic Satire: A Study in Form and Image*. Cambridge.

Braund, S. H. 1988. *Beyond Anger: A Study of Juvenal's Third Book of Satires*. Cambridge.

—— 1992a. "Juvenal Misogynist or Misogamist?" *JRS* 82.71–86.

—— 1992b. *Roman Verse Satire* (Greece and Rome: New Surveys in the Classics 23). Oxford.

Byrd, Charles. 1987. "Freud's Influence on Bakhtin: Traces of Psychoanalytic Theory in *Rabelais and His World*," *Germano-Slavic Review* 5.223–30.

Carson, Anne. 1990. "Putting Her in Her Place: Woman, Dirt, and Desire," in *Before Sexuality: The Construction of Erotic Experience in the Ancient Greek World* (eds. David M. Halperin, John J. Winkler, and Froma Zeitlin), 135–69. Princeton.

Caston, Ruth Rothaus. 1997. "The Fall of the Curtain (Horace *S*. 2.8)," *TAPA 127*. 233–56.

Clausen, W. V. (ed.) 1959. *A Persi Flacci et D. Iuni Iuvenalis Saturae*. Oxford.

Cohen, J. M. (trans.) 1981. *Rabelais: Gargantua and Pantagruel*. New York.

Conington, John (trans. and ed.) 1874. *The Satires of A. Persius Flaccus*. Oxford.

Connor, Peter. 1987. "The Satires of Persius: A Stretch of the Imagination," *Ramus* 16.55–77.

Courtney, E. 1980. *A Commentary on the Satires of Juvenal*. London.

Cruquius, Iacobus. 1597. *Q. Horatius Flaccus: cum commentariis veteris et Iacobi Cruquii Messenii, Literarum apud Brugenses Professoris*. Lugdunum Batavorum.

Duff, J. Wright. 1936. *Roman Satire: Its Outlook on Social Life*, (Sather Classical Lectures, vol. 12). Berkeley.
Eagleton, Terry. 1989. "Bakhtin, Schopenhauer, Kundera," in *Bakhtin and Cultural Theory* (eds. Ken Hirschkop and David Shepherd), 178–88. Manchester.
Edwards, Catharine. 1993. *The Politics of Immorality in Ancient Rome*. Cambridge.
Emerson, Caryl. 1993. "Irreverent Bakhtin and the Imperturbable Classics," in Miller and Platter, 1993b.123–37.
—— 1994. "Getting Bakhtin Right and Left," rev. of *The Dialogics of Critique: M. M. Bakhtin and the Theory of Ideology* by Michael Gardiner, London 1992, in *Comparative Literature* 46.288–303.
Fedeli, Paolo. 1992. "In viaggio con Orazio da Roma a Brindisi," *Aufidus* 17.37–54.
Ferguson, John. 1979. *Juvenal: The Satires*. New York.
Forcellini, Aegidius, Josephus Furlanetto, Franciscus Corradini, and Josephus Perin, (eds.) 1965. *Lexicon Totius Latinitatis*. Padua.
Freudenburg, Kirk. 1993. *The Walking Muse: Horace on the Theory of Satire*. Princeton.
Friedlaender, Ludwig. 1962. *D. Junii Juvenalis Saturarum Libri V*. Amsterdam. Original = Leipzig 1895.
Frow, John. 1986. *Marxism and Literary History*. Cambridge, Mass.
Gardiner, Michael. 1992. *The Dialogics of Critique: M. M. Bakhtin and the Theory of Ideology*. London.
Gérard, J. 1976. *Juvénal et la réalité contemporaine*. Paris.
Gold, Barbara K. 1987. *Literary Patronage in Greece and Rome*. Chapel Hill.
Gowers, Emily. 1993. *The Loaded Table: Representations of Food in Roman Literature*. Oxford.
—— 1994. "Persius and the Decoction of Nero," in *Reflections of Nero: Culture, History, and Representation* (eds. Jas Elsner and Jamie Masters). Chapel Hill.
Green, Peter (trans.) 1974. *Juvenal: The Sixteen Satires*. London.
Henderson, John. 1993. "Persius' Didactic Satire: The Pupil as Teacher," *Ramus* 22.123–48.
Herndl, Diane Price. 1991. "The Dilemmas of a Feminine Dialogic," in Bauer and McKinstry 1991.7–24.
Heuzé, Phillipe. 1988. "En repartant pour Brindes," in *Présence d'Horace* (ed. R. Chevallier). Tours.
Highet, Gilbert. 1962. *The Anatomy of Satire*. Princeton.
Hirschkop, Ken and David Shepherd. 1994. "Bakhtin and the Politics of Criticism," *PMLA* 109.116–17.
Holquist, Michael. 1990. *Dialogism: Bakhtin and His World*. London.
Irigaray, Luce. 1977. "La 'méchanique' de fluides," in *Ce sexe qui n'en est pas un*, 103–16, Paris.
Jacobs, Deborah. 1991. "Critical Imperialism and Renaissance Drama: The Case of *The Roaring Girl*," in Bauer and McKinstry, 1991.73–84.
Janan, Micaela. 1994. "Beyond Good and Evil: Tarpeia and Philosophy in the Feminine," Presentation at APA.
Jenkinson, J. R. (trans.) 1980. *Persius: The Satires*. Warminster.
Kennedy, Duncan. 1993. *The Arts of Love*. Cambridge.
Knoche, Ulrich (ed.) 1950. *D. Iunius Juvenalis: Saturae*. Munich.

Labriolle, Pierre de and François Villeneuve. 1967. *Juvénal: Satires*. Paris. Original = 1921.

Lambinus, Dionysius. 1577. *Dionysii Lambini Monstroliensis Regii Professoris in Q. Horatium Flaccum ex Fide atque auctoritate complurimum librorum manuscriptorum a se emendatum, & aliquoties recognitum, & cum diversis exemplaribus antiquis comparatum, multisque locis purgatum*. Frankfurt am Main.

Lejay, Paul. 1966. *Oeuvres d'Horace: Satires*. Hildesheim. Original = Paris, 1911.

Malamud, Martha. 1996. "Out of Circulation: An Essay on Exchange in Persius' Satires," *Ramus* 25.29–64

Miller, Paul Allen. Forthcoming. "The Otherness of History in Rabelais' Carnival and Juvenal's Satire, or Why Bakhtin Got it Right the First Time," in Barta, Miller, Platter, and Shepherd. forthcoming.

—— and Charles Platter 1993a. "Introduction," in Miller and Platter 1993b.117–20.

—— and Charles Platter (eds.) 1993b. *Bakhtin and Ancient Studies: Dialogues and Dialogics*, *Arethusa* 26.2.

Morford, Mark. 1984. *Persius*. Boston.

Morson, Gary Saul. 1994. "Reply," *PMLA* 109.117–18.

—— and Caryl Emerson. 1990. *Mikhail Bakhtin: The Creation of a Prosaics*. Evanston.

Nell, Sharon. 1995. "At 'Play with [an] Unruly Woman': Official Culture and the Carnivalesque in *Salammbô*," *Synthesis* 1.101–18.

—— Forthcoming. "The Last Laugh: Carnivalizing the Feminine in Piron's 'La Puce'" in Barta, Miller, Platter and Shepherd, forthcoming.

O'Connor, Joseph F. 1990. "Horace's *Cena Nasidieni* and Poetry's Feast," *CJ* 86.23–34.

Oxford Latin Dictionary. 1968–82. Oxford.

Platter, Charles. 1993. "The Uninvited Guest: Aristophanes in Bakhtin's 'History of Laughter,'" in Miller and Platter, 1993b.201–16.

—— Forthcoming. "Novelistic Discourse in Aristophanes' *Acharnians*," in Barta, Miller, Platter and Shepherd, forthcoming.

Rabelais, François. 1962. *Oeuvres complètes* (ed. Pierre Jourda), vol. 1. Paris.

Rebhorn, Wayne A. 1993. "Baldesar Castiglione, Thomas Wilson, and the Courtly Body of Renaissance Rhetoric," *Rhetorica* 11.241–74.

Richlin, Amy. 1983. *The Garden of Priapus: Sexuality and Aggression in Roman Humor*. New Haven.

—— 1984. "Invective Against Women in Roman Satire," *Arethusa* 17.67–80.

—— 1995. "Making Up a Woman: The Face of Roman Gender," in *Off with Her Head! The Denial of Women's Identity in Myth, Religion, and Culture* (eds. Howard Eilberg-Schwartz and Wendy Doniger), 183–213. Berkeley.

Robertson, Alton Kim. 1996. *The Grotesque Interface: Deformity, Debasement, Dissolution*. Frankfurt am Main.

Rössler, Wolfgang. 1986. "Michail Bachtin und die Karnevalskultur im antiken Griechenland," *QUCC* 23.25–44.

Rubino, Carl. 1993. "Opening Up the Classical Past: Bakhtin, Aristotle, Literature, Life," in Miller and Platter, 1993b.141–58.

Rudd, Niall. 1982. *Juvenal: The Satires*. Oxford.

—— 1982. *The Satires of Horace*. Berkeley. Original = 1966.

Schwab, Gail M. 1991. "Irigarayan Dialogism: Play and Power Play," in Bauer and McKinstry 1991. 57–72.

Shepherd, David. 1993. "Introduction: (Mis)Representing Bakhtin," in *Bakhtin, Carnival and Other Subjects: Selected Papers from the Fifth International Bakhtin Conference, University of Manchester, July 1991* (ed. David Shepherd), xiii–xxxii. Amsterdam.

Stallybrass, Peter and Allon White. 1986. *The Politics and Poetics of Transgression*. Ithaca.

Swann, Bruce W. 1994. *Martial's Catullus: The Reception of an Epigrammatic Rival*. Hildesheim.

Todorov, Tzvetan. 1984. *Mikhail Bakhtin: The Dialogical Principle* (trans. by Wlad Godzich). Minneapolis.

Winkler, Martin M. 1991. "Satire and the Grotesque in Juvenal, Arcimboldo and Goya," *Antike und Abendland* 37.22–42.

Wyke, Maria. 1995. "Taking the Woman's Part: Engendering Roman Love Elegy," in *Roman Literature and Ideology: Ramus Essays for J. P. Sullivan* (ed. A. J. Boyle), 110–28. Bendigo.

INDEX